Gender Remade

Citizenship, Suffrage, and Public Power in the New Northwest, 1879–1912

Gender Remade explores a little-known experiment in gender equality in Washington Territory in the 1870s and 1880s. Building on path-breaking innovations in marital and civil equality, lawmakers extended a long list of political rights and obligations to both men and women, including the right to serve on juries and hold public office. As the territory moved toward statehood, however, jury duty and constitutional co-sovereignty proved to be particularly controversial; in the end, "modernization" and national integration brought disastrous losses for women until 1910, when political rights were partially restored. Losses to women's sovereignty were profound and enduring – a finding that points not to rights and powers, but to constitutionalism and the power of social practice as Americans struggled to establish gender equality. *Gender Remade* is a significant contribution to the understudied legal history of the American West, especially the role that legal culture played in making the passage from territory to statehood.

Sandra F. VanBurkleo is Associate Professor of History at Wayne State University.

Cambridge Historical Studies in American Law and Society

Series Editor

Christopher Tomlins, *University of California, Berkeley*

Previously published in the series:

Reuel Schiller, *Forging Rivals: Race, Class, Law, and the Collapse of Postwar Liberalism*

Ely Aaronson, *From Slave Abuse to Hate Crime: The Criminalization of Racial Violence in American History*

Stuart Chinn, *Recalibrating Reform: The Limits of Political Change*

Ajay K. Mehrotra, *Making the Modern American Fiscal State*

Yvonne Pitts, *Family, Law, and Inheritance in America: A Social and Legal History of Nineteenth-Century Kentucky*

David M. Rabban, *Law's History*

Kunal M. Parker, *Common Law, History, and Democracy in America, 1790–1900*

Steven Wilf, *Law's Imagined Republic*

James D. Schmidt, *Industrial Violence and the Legal Origins of Child Labor*

Rebecca M. McLennan, *The Crisis of Imprisonment: Protest, Politics, and the Making of the American Penal State, 1776–1941*

Tony A. Freyer, *Antitrust and Global Capitalism, 1930–2004*

Davison Douglas, *Jim Crow Moves North*

Andrew Wender Cohen, *The Racketeer's Progress*

Michael Willrich, *City of Courts: Socializing Justice in Progressive Era Chicago*

Barbara Young Welke, *Recasting American Liberty: Gender, Law and the Railroad Revolution, 1865–1920*

Michael Vorenberg, *Final Freedom: The Civil War, the Abolition of Slavery, and the Thirteenth Amendment*

Robert J. Steinfeld, *Coercion, Contract, and Free Labor in Nineteenth Century America*

David M. Rabban, *Free Speech in Its Forgotten Years*

Jenny Wahl, *The Bondsman's Burden: An Economic Analysis of the Common Law of Southern Slavery*

Michael Grossberg, *A Judgment for Solomon: The d'Hauteville Case and Legal Experience in the Antebellum South*

Gender Remade

Citizenship, Suffrage, and Public Power in the New Northwest, 1879–1912

SANDRA F. VANBURKLEO

Wayne State University

CAMBRIDGE
UNIVERSITY PRESS

CAMBRIDGE
UNIVERSITY PRESS

32 Avenue of the Americas, New York, NY 10013-2473, USA

Cambridge University Press is part of the University of Cambridge.

It furthers the University's mission by disseminating knowledge in the pursuit of
education, learning, and research at the highest international levels of excellence.

www.cambridge.org
Information on this title: www.cambridge.org/9781107098022

First published 2015

Printed in the United States of America

A catalog record for this publication is available from the British Library.

Library of Congress Cataloging in Publication Data
VanBurkleo, Sandra F., 1944– author.
Gender remade : Citizenship, Suffrage, and Public Power in the New Northwest, 1879–1912 /
Sandra F. VanBurkleo.
    pages   cm. – (Cambridge historical studies in American law and society)
Includes bibliographical references and index.
ISBN 978-1-107-09802-2 (hardback)
    1. Women – Legal status, laws, etc. – Washington (State) – History.   2. Sex discrimination
against women – Law and legislation – Washington (State) – History.   3. Equality before
the law – Washington (State) – History.   I. Title.
KFW91.W6V36   2016
342.79708′78–dc23   2015024727

ISBN 978-1-107-09802-2 Hardback

Dedicated to past and present graduate advisees
at Wayne State University
whose words and ideas remake the world

Contents

Illustrations

Acknowledgments

Books and articles never belong entirely to the authors named on title pages. *Gender Remade* would have languished for years more, had it not been for gifts, large and small, and a number of timely interventions. At Wayne State University, colleagues and students pushed me constantly not only to refine arguments, but also to finish the bloody thing sometime before retirement. In Detroit, I am indebted in disparate ways to Denver Brunsman (now at George Washington University), Elaine Clark, Liz Faue, Liette Gidlow, Chris Johnson (for an amazing eleventh-hour reading), Marc Kruman, Janine Lanza, Betsy Lublin, Joan Mahoney, Karen Marrero, Brad Roth, Bruce Russell, Larry Scaff (for early talk about Weber and "disenchantment"), Stanley Shapiro, David Silverman (also at George Washington), Anca Vlasopolos, and Frank Wu. Five of these long-suffering scholars have jumped ship since I first put fingers to keyboard. Brunsman bravely slogged through half-baked pages, even after leaving Detroit. Charlie Hyde provided convivial luncheons. Gidlow forced deeper thought about Progressivism. I extend particular thanks to Janine Lanza, who introduced me to practice theory, offered smart readings, kept a back-up copy in case of disaster, and generally did what friends do, even from Paris.

Students' contributions have been invaluable. Graduate students Dave Collins, Amy Holtman French, Adam Geffen, Eric Haddon, Andrew Hall, Nick Kyser, Robert Olender, Yvonne Pitts, Jim Schwartz, Bonnie Speck, and Karen Turlay provided conversation and tenacious research assistance at important junctures, despite Neolithic microform readers and ridiculous wages. Nina Perez skillfully compiled the index. I am grateful to these and other students for enduring so much talk about the New Northwest and for helping me to resolve worrisome points of interpretation. Our administrative services officer, Gayle McCreedy, managed a long train of interventions with great skill. Periodic financial and practical support also advanced the work. I particularly note a sabbatical leave as well as varieties of aid extended by the

Graduate School and Office for Research, department head Marc Kruman, and the Humanities Center. Together, the College of Liberal Arts and Sciences; the Department of History; and the Gender, Sexuality, and Women's Studies Program subsidized illustrations.

Beyond Detroit, colleagues offered hospitality, advice, fortification (particularly in 2001–2002), and kicks in the backside. At the outset, Don Nieman and the late Christine Compston encouraged me to write a book rather than a long article. Chris also provided a guest room and other amenities in Bellingham, Washington. In Seattle, Suzanne Lebsock (then at the University of Washington) organized a luncheon at the faculty club so that I might talk with graduate students, suggested the book's title ("Gender Remade"), and encouraged me to hire an advisee, Karla Kelling, who skillfully read several newspapers that I'd been forced to abandon.

In various ways, I am also indebted to Robby Baker, Gordon Bakken, Sally Gordon, Tom Green, Dirk Hartog, Linda Kerber, Maeva Marcus, the late Peggy Pascoe, Harry Scheiber, Philippa Strum, and Mel Urofsky (who invited me to share the Washington story with members of the Supreme Court Historical Society). The late Kermit Hall – surely the most accomplished member of what Chuck McCurdy once called the Minnesota Mafia – was simply there, providing encouragement, advice, a sounding board, bibliographic suggestions, and the rare impish grin. The loss is incalculable. I am particularly grateful to Linda (who once called early findings "delicious") for keeping faith when I was adrift, and to the generous but unsparing Peggy, who said from her commentator's podium at an American Society for Legal History session, "Surely you don't mean to say that Washington's women achieved equality with a civil rights bill? What about the sex right?" Such comments were, shall we say, riveting. Philippa Strum arranged a one-term respite at the Woodrow Wilson Center. Colleagues at the Ohio Legal History Colloquium, convened periodically at the Ohio State Law School, provided sage comments; I especially thank Les Benedict for sharing ideas about hybridization and the extent to which all American jurisdictions are hybridized. Participants in an Oakland University–WSU colloquium offered criticism just as I had begun to frame arguments. Sally Gordon intervened heroically, more than once. As series editor, Chris Tomlins guided an exhausted author to harbor and offered indispensable counsel. Referees improved the work; Cambridge University Press personnel, beginning but not ending with Debbie Gershenowitz and Dana Bricken, helped me transform an unwieldy manuscript into a book.

Some debts can be settled only by writing good books. Decades later, I recall the many times and ways in which Paul L. Murphy pushed his graduate advisees away from undue fascination with black-letter law toward constitutional politics, law's moral deposits, and, most of all, law's many faces, only one of which takes a woman's form in New York harbor. When I last walked and talked with him at a conference in Houston, he claimed to be thrilled that I had moved once again in directions unlike his own – and then he was gone. But memory keeps us alive, much as books do – as Paul said in 1996, "Your books will outlive you by at least a century" – and so I name him again. In addition, my best buddy, Julie C. Larson, makes it possible to persist, despite all manner of trouble, by sensing what I need ("Should I get on a plane?") and when she should prod ("When are you going to retire?").

Even harder to thank are the scholars whose work informs what I've done here. Often, a book or article shoves what we're doing in a fresh direction, yet these amazing gifts – often from strangers – appear as a kind of residue in footnotes. Years ago, Peter Goodrich's mind-bending scholarship led me to consider how public memory entombs and refashions ancient practices. Dirk Hartog forced many of us to think about constitutionalism's many layers and expressions; Chris Tomlins remade the concept of legalities and provided fresh ways to think about what happens in unfamiliar places. Carole Pateman's *Sexual Contract* shattered my understanding of liberalism. A chapter in Calvin Trillin's *Killings* – an exploration of customary Appalachian responses to certain homicides – haunts me to this day. Like Oliver Wendell Holmes, I have not abandoned legal science altogether, but I have been exposed to the great outdoors more fully than in my youth.

Archivists and librarians contributed decisively with their professionalism, friendship, and deep knowledge of holdings. The now-retired David Hastings and his staff at the Olympia (main) branch of the Washington State Archive pushed the project into overdrive when it was little more than a possibility; David also opened doors at other archives and cheerfully lent support by mail and phone, long after my final visit. Most recently, Lupita Lopez speedily supplied information, a missing photocopy, and case-file photos. Capable helpers also emerged at the Bellingham, Ellensburg, Belleville, Cheney, and Grays Harbor branches of the State Archive. Sympathetic archivists at the Ellensburg branch tolerated the photocopying and bulk mailing of case files to an extent never before witnessed on the premises. One staffer noted laconically that should Mount Hood bury collections beneath tons of lava, he would simply refer visitors to the archive's Michigan branch. Personnel at University of Washington Special Collections and Microfilm Division, Western Washington University's Center for Pacific Northwest Studies, the Washington State Historical Society, Washington State University Special Collections Division at Pullman, the photographic experts at the Whatcom County Historical Society in Bellingham (especially Jeffrey Jewell), the Library of Congress Manuscripts Division, Wayne State University Libraries, and University of Michigan Libraries, all aided the cause substantially. Robert Ellis of the National Archive found the case file for *Bloomer* v. *Todd* – a feat that I had not accomplished on site. Edward Nolan of the Washington State Historical Society unsuccessfully searched for images of two elusive women; Ashley Mead heroically intervened in other ways. I also thank librarian Jean Fisher of the Northwest Room, Tacoma Public Library, for unstinting efforts in pursuit of Zerelda N. McCoy, Henrietta Somerville, and others. Photographic experts at the University of Washington, Special Collections, and at Washington State University, Special Collections, responded swiftly to last-minute pleas for help. To this day, nobody can find an image of the indispensable McCoy. Larry Cebula, Jeff Creighton, Anna Harbine, and Frank Oesterheld of Eastern Washington University (Cheney) and the Northwest Museum (Spokane) searched for images of May Arkwright Hutton and George Turner, assessed the value of unprocessed manuscripts, and provided an image of Turner. The marvelous staff at the Center for Pacific Northwest Studies at Western Washington University unearthed photographs as well as priceless judicial proceedings, wherein I found hard evidence that female jurors indeed had shut down courtrooms in two counties for the better part of a year.

Let me underscore the importance of these unsung professionals. Much of what appears in footnotes would never have emerged from boxes without their suggestions and elbow grease. Time and again, staffers greeted my questions and quite burdensome requests (*"How* many copies?") with smiles, gladdened by the knowledge that I was using their collections. Nobody frowned – well, one staffer in Olympia *did* frown when I forgot to wash my hands. Without helpers thinking about what might lurk in old crates, case papers and jury rolls might have remained as clerks of court had left them a century ago. One hardy soul in Special Collections at Washington State in Pullman, Washington, responded to an appalling request ("I can tell you who wrote it and when, but I can't tell you the collection name") by finding the missing document, and hence the citation, in two days flat. The Secretary of State and special-collections departments of Washington's universities and museums should be applauded roundly. I should add that genealogists eagerly offered assistance. I especially thank Spokane's Charles Hansen, who helped me confirm that Nevada Bloomer existed (the name was too good to be true) and that she was indeed married to a saloon owner (also too good to be true).

And finally this: Before the book existed – indeed, when I still thought of the Washington story as a brief diversion from an "important" book about freedom of speech – my partner, Edward Martin Wise, who died without permission in October 2000, stumbled on the odd fact of female grand jurors in Gilded-Age Washington in an old case book on statutory titling, which led me to read territorial reports from cover to cover. He then said, "That's too interesting to pass up. Why not go there for Thanksgiving break and see what's going on?" I think of him as the book's godfather, which partly explains why it took me so long to finish: I have been slow to learn that finishing is not synonymous with abandonment or forgetting. But, because I dedicated another book to his memory, I offer this one to my graduate advisees at Wayne State University. I also fulsomely thank my new partner, Larry Hart, for providing "flattes" (fake lattes), endless puns, and proofreading. Only Larry and a few others know how often I have been distracted or sequestered with knitting needles. I also thank my two brilliant lawyers, Stuart Sherman and David Brockman, and my CPA, Gayle Infeld, for saving my sanity in mid-book.

It goes without saying that I accept full responsibility for mistakes and thick-headedness. State historians may well find naiveté or carpet-bagging: I'm a Midwesterner, after all, presuming to explain developments in a place with huge conifers, mountains that resemble the teeth of carnivorous animals, and a body of water considerably larger than any of the Great Lakes. Because colleagues cannot foresee what will be made of their offerings, they should be held blameless – unless I win prizes, in which case they should accompany me to the podium.

Periodical abbreviations

BBR	*Bellingham Bay Reveille*
BH	*Bellingham Herald*
CC	*Columbia Chronicle*
CP	*Chicago Post*
CT	*Chicago Tribune*
LAT	*Los Angeles Times*
LCB	*Lewis County Bee*
LE	*Leavenworth Echo*
LJ	*Labor Journal*
NN	*New Northwest* [Portland]
NYT	*New York Times*
OR	*Oregonian* (or) *Daily Oregonian* [Portland]
PH	*Pullman Herald*
PSWA	*Puget Sound Weekly Argus*
PSWC	*Puget Sound Weekly Courier*
SJI	*San Juan Islander*
SDPI, SPI	*Seattle Daily Post-Intelligencer* (or) *Seattle Post-Intelligencer*
SFC	*Spokane Falls Chronicle*
SFR, SR	*Spokane Falls Review* (or) *Spokane [Daily] Review*
SP	*Seattle Press* (or) *Seattle Daily Press*
SPT	*Seattle Press-Times*
SS	*Seattle Star*
ST, SDT	*Seattle Times* (or) *Seattle Daily Times*
TDL, TDT	*Tacoma Daily Ledger* (or) *Tacoma Daily Tribune*
TT	*Tacoma Times*
WJ	*Woman's Journal*
WP	*Washington Post* (Washington, DC)
WR	*Whatcom Reveille*

WS   *Washington Standard*
WWS   *Walla Walla Statesman*
WWU   *Walla Walla Union*

[Titles cited fewer than three times have not been abbreviated. Before 1890, newspapers were irregularly paginated and titled; I give page numbers where they were available and ignore title variations such as Daily or Weekly, when variations appear erratically].

REPOSITORIES AND ABBREVIATIONS

Newspapers published in Washington Territory and State are widely available in microform and in digital formats, as at the Washington State Library and Historical Society, both in Tacoma; the University of Washington Library in Seattle; Central Washington University, Ellensburg; or Washington State University, Pullman. For that reason, I omit repository names unless I used originals or clippings. The *Woman's Journal* is available on microfilm at Hatcher Graduate Library, University of Michigan. The Washington Historical Society offers a useful online newspaper collection. New York, District of Columbia, California, and Illinois titles can be found in historical-newspaper digital collections. I do not use the term "sic" to indicate spellings or usages unlike our own.

The Washington State Archives' holdings are scattered across the state. Records of the territorial courts, early state supreme court, and attorney general's office are now stored largely in Olympia at the main branch; other judicial records are housed at other branches. Archivists provide expert advice about the archival network and its digitized finding aids. I use these abbreviations:

PNC   Center for Studies of the Pacific Northwest (Western Washington University)
PSRA   Puget Sound Regional Archives, Bellingham
UWSC   University of Washington Special Collections (Seattle)
WSA-Belle   Washington State Archives, Belleville
WSA-C   Washington State Archives, Cheney
WSA-E   Washington State Archives, Ellensburg
WSA-GH   Washington State Archives, Grays Harbor
WSA-O   Washington State Archives, Olympia (main branch)
WSHS   Washington State Historical Society
WSU-SC   Washington State University Special Collections (Pullman)

I

"We are kings and queens"
Introduction

Our national ideal is the nation of kings, a royal people, every man of us a king, every woman of us a queen. Now a king has his ... proprietary rights ... , not for his selfish pleasure but for the good of society. His days ... are spent for the general welfare.

– Justice Roger Sherman Greene (1886)

Every man here was born of a woman and man, and every woman here was born of a man and a woman, and we inherit equally from each. ... [W]e are each ... co-heirs, we are kings and queens – not kings with a queen-consort walking behind, but fellow sovereigns – Williams and Marys, Ferdinands and Isabellas!

– Mary Johnston (1912)[1]

Some years ago, I stumbled across a little-known decision of the Washington Supreme Court in the 1912 case of *Henrietta Somerville* v. *State of Washington*.[2] With her husband, Somerville owned and managed a paper-box factory in Seattle, where Henrietta employed and directly supervised a large number of mostly self-supporting women. With the encouragement of employees, she had filed suit in King County contending, as had male bakers in *Lochner* v. *New York* (1905), that women ought to be able to strike up their own bargains, particularly when the job and workplace were safe and pleasant. At issue was a maximum-hour law that state legislators had adopted a year earlier – the same kind of protective legislation that had been affirmed in the U.S. Supreme Court's better-known *Muller* v. *Oregon* ruling in 1908.[3]

---

[1] Mary Johnston, "Address," December 1912, in Marjorie Spruill Wheeler, *Votes for Women: The Woman Suffrage Movement* (Knoxville, TN, 1995), p. 160. Johnston was a novelist and suffragist. See also "Judge Greene's Charge, Seattle, August 30," in *SDPI*, August 31, 1886.
[2] *State of Washington* v. *Henrietta Somerville*, 67 Wash Rpts 638 (1912).
[3] *Lochner* v. *New York*, 198 U.S. 45 (1905); *Muller* v. *Oregon*, 208 U.S. 412 (1908).

In Washington, as elsewhere, an augmented state presence in the workplace formed part of a stereotypically Progressive drive to secure the health and welfare of consumers and workers in an age of rapid industrial and urban growth – particularly underage, non-unionized, endangered, or non-voting workers. In coastal cities, women's groups and laborites zealously pursued hour limitations for municipal workers engaged in physically taxing labor, but also for children and women employed by private firms. In *Muller*, the justices approved limitations on workdays for the women employed at Kurt Muller's laundry essentially by permitting an exception in the case of women to the general ban, rooted in Fourteenth-Amendment jurisprudence, on legislative interference with the terms of employment. As with legislation elsewhere, Washington's statute required "mechanized firms" not engaged in seasonal work to send women home after eight hours – a reform that effectively ruled out the possibility that men and women might realize economic parity.[4] But many self-providing women (aided by an odd mixture of social feminists, unions, and entrepreneurs) argued that liberty of contract attached as readily to women as to men. Why not rely on *Lochner* and kindred decisions in which courts had affirmed workers' right to sign contracts and assume workplace risk without public superintendence, especially in non-hazardous settings?

Ordinarily, *Somerville* might have elicited little more than a passing glance. Well before 1908, states routinely enacted sex- and age-specific hour laws; after 1908, and notwithstanding the occasional victory for *laissez-faireism*, federal courts generally followed the rules set out in *Muller* and *Lochner*. Nor was the idea of an hour ceiling foreign to Washingtonians: Into the 1880s, labor organizations, several political societies, and even some businesses had either advocated or adopted a daily limit on work for municipal employees, workers in hazardous industries, and young workers, albeit with provision for overtime pay, often as part of the so-called eight-hour movement. In 1883, one reformer urged the imposition of ten-hour workdays on farms to encourage young boys to continue in agriculture.[5] Because the facts and legal issues in *Muller* and *Somerville* seemed to be analogous and women's inadequacies a matter of what the court called "common knowledge," the box maker lost. Somerville's lawyers had presented ample evidence of factual differences between the two cases, which the state conceded. But, in the end, speaking for a unanimous bench and appropriating portions of *Muller*, Justice Herman Crow pronounced the law a reasonable exception to the rule against state intervention; Washington's interest in protecting vulnerable classes, notably children and other "minors," amply justified regulation. When Somerville's counsel

---

[4] Session Laws, State of Washington, Ch. 37, 1911, Act to Regulate the Hours of Work in Canneries and Other Mechanical Firms, p. 131.

[5] See, e.g., "Victoria Carpenters," *TDL*, March 19, 1884 (a new union of public workers seeking nine-hour days). For a firm's decision to adopt a ten-hour rule for men, see "Ten Hour Movement," *SDPI*, November 12, 1886 ("8 of the ten mills" ran ten hours to pre-empt unions and "the red flag"). See also "Ten Hours a Day's Work on Farms," *WWU*, September 21, 1883.

demanded and got a re-hearing – the women, they insisted, were men's political and civil equals and fully capable of assuming workplace risk – they lost again. In the Court's estimation, the *Muller* precedent, while not a perfect fit, bore at least a family resemblance.

Somerville's fascination, then, lies not with state imposition of sex-specific hours legislation, but rather with the court's juvenalization of *enfranchised, propertied* employees. Washington's women had been granted civil, marital, and political equality after 1879; and, while the suffrage had been lost in 1889, women had been re-enfranchised by constitutional amendment in 1910. In what sense were fully enfranchised, propertied adults legal "minors," incapable of assumptions of workplace risk? Even more intriguing, constructions of female laborers in *Somerville* were largely unchanged from those deployed in 1902, when women had not yet been readmitted to polling places. In *State v. A. G. Buchanan*, the court had affirmed the constitutionality of Washington's 1901 maximum-hours law, the 1911 statute's antecedent, which forbade companies from employing women for more than ten hours a day.[6]

Had women's enfranchisement and agency within marital estates made no difference? *Somerville* jarred badly against federal judges' willingness to distinguish between enfranchised and non-enfranchised citizens when evaluating the merits of state protection. If ballots were citizens' main weapon against tyrannical or custodial government, as courts regularly claimed, how did limitations happen? And what about economic agency? Some years before *Muller*, counsel for Buchanan had demanded an explanation for legislative meddling with propertied adults; in *Muller*, justices to some extent had permitted state protection of adult women because they lacked constitutional standing sufficient to defend their interests at the polls. Some years later, when federal justices invalidated a sex-specific minimum-wage law in *Adkins v. Children's Hospital*, they pointed (if somewhat disingenuously) to the new Nineteenth Amendment as proof that female worker-citizens were capable of self-defense.[7]

The opinions rendered in *Somerville* and, in slightly different ways, in *Buchanan* thus engage modern readers because of the apparent ease with which justices demoted a large segment of the electorate to a bizarre semi-sovereignty. To be sure, wage-earning women throughout the nation had been subjected to hours limitations, and justices' job was to apply relevant doctrine to cases at bar. But Washington's bench had witnessed, and often participated in, a protracted struggle for sex equality immediately before statehood; the women in *Somerville* and *Muller* were not similarly situated.[8] In *Muller* and *Adkins*, actual or prospective enfranchisement arose as a fact that

---

[6] *State of Washington v. Buchanan*, 29 Wash Rpts 602 (1902). See also Chapter 6.

[7] *Adkins v. Children's Hospital*, 261 U.S. Rpts 525 (1923).

[8] In this book, sex refers to biological differences; gender refers to the social process[es] by which sex is transmitted or translated into social practice.

could alter outcomes. In territorial Washington, women had claimed co-equality and co-sovereignty within marriage, owned businesses and farms, claimed custody of children at divorce, amassed considerable experience as voters in general elections, had served as jurors, and begun to occupy elective offices. In 1912, women could vote as a matter of constitutional right. Kurt Muller's employees could not claim analogous investitures as members of the constituent power. Yet, despite women's political and economic agency, Justice Crow failed to chart a new course by distinguishing the case from *Muller*.

CONTINGENCIES

As with every story worth telling, this one begins with the land and its people. Nowadays, Americans think of the well-populated Seattle-Tacoma metropolis as a cultural and economic magnet. But, in the 1870s, would-be settlers conceived of Washington Territory as remote and empty – a blank cultural slate somewhere to the north of better-known settlements like Portland and San Francisco. As white homesteading advanced, isolation and disorganization powerfully challenged prevailing views of self-rule in republics. What would the community tolerate as citizens began to push the boundaries of civic possibility? What exactly would the rules of the game look like, and who would decide?

Originally part of Oregon Territory, Washington became a separate entity on March 2, 1853, with Congressional adoption of an organic act.[9] Within the geographically complex territory – a patchwork of forests, rugged and heavily glaciated mountains, lush farmland, seacoast, and high tundra – information and people moved slowly, particularly before railroaders breached the Cascades, regularizing and hastening the mails. Few elements of western life mattered more than the fact of partial or postponed rail lines and financial controversies related to railroaders. In 1889, six years after the driving of a golden spike in Montana and coincident with statehood, the Northern Pacific Railroad arrived in Tacoma. Before then, Seattle and Tacoma were outposts along a rail spur leading north from Portland. Spokane Falls and coastal towns communicated sporadically and seasonally. As Susan B. Anthony learned when her train stalled for days behind a broken plow, mountain roadways disrupted the movement of goods and people.[10]

Development included a number of seemingly disparate pieces. Telegrams, ground travel, and ocean-going vessels were expensive and (in the case of the telegraph) maddeningly cryptic – all of which not only limited public information but also drove up consumer prices. Imported nails and tableware

---

[9] An Act to Establish the Territorial Government of Washington, Statutes at Large, 32nd Congress, 2nd Session, Ch. XC, pp. 172–9, approved March 2, 1853.
[10] "Completion of the Northern Pacific Railroad," *SDPI*, September 9, 1883. On the breaking of a plow, see Susan B. Anthony Diary, January 5, 1872, in Ann Gordon, ed., *Selected Papers of Susan B. Anthony and Elizabeth Cady Stanton*, Vol. 2 (New Brunswick, NJ, 2000), p. 267.

cost more than citizens could afford. Newspaper editors regularly solicited capital investment on behalf of Washington's growing towns, where residents clamored for work and a wider range of commodities – among them, vegetables, books, bread, machinery, matches, dairy products, clothing, and potable beer. As a Seattle writer put it in an 1882 plea for industrial investment, "Railroads will bring people into the country, but if there is nothing for them to do they will go away again."[11]

As in other relatively healthy borderlands, demographic changes shaped development. Between 1880 and 1890 alone, the territory's population grew by about 375 percent, from 75,116 (well beyond the 60,000 required for statehood) to slightly more than 357,000. Urbanization also proceeded apace, from an official zero percent in 1880 to 28.5 percent at statehood. In 1890, Seattle claimed 42,837 residents; Tacoma had 36,066; and Spokane Falls, barely a village in 1880, boasted 19,922. The number of women stubbornly remained stuck between 37 and 38 percent of the total population in 1870, 1880, and 1890; most of them were white.[12] Before 1900, moreover, black populations were modest and largely male. Black residents in Seattle grew from near zero in the late 1850s to 406 in 1900, when populations began to expand and to include a greater number of skilled workers. In 1880, census workers reported about 14,800 Indians; a decade later, the number rose to 20,375, then dropped in 1900 and 1910 to slightly more than 19,000.[13]

Mining or lumbering outposts, when not beset by walkouts and mercenaries, suffered from the kinds of social disarray that afflict heavily male societies without decent roads, jails, families, and religious societies. Roughneck workforces and drunkenness proliferated. Miners and sawyers witnessed hundreds of injuries and deaths each year; employers ignored fines and other, unenforced sanctions.[14] Seacoast residents struggled against underemployment, gambling rings, prostitution, and dank saloons. Chinese settlers – probably no more at any time than 1 percent of urban populations – provided inexpensive labor in occupations that white men eschewed, but also triggered violence. The Chinese Exclusion Act, after all, did not address settled Asian communities. In

---

[11] "Factories Needed," *SDPI*, August 24, 1882.

[12] Thomas W. Riddle, *The Old Radicalism: John R. Rogers and the Populist Movement in Washington* (New York, 1991), esp. pp. 74–6; United States Census, 1870, 1880, 1890. Undercounting is likely with Chinese and Indians, transient miners or lumbermen, fisherman, and waterfront roughnecks.

[13] Quintard Taylor, *The Forging of a Black Community: Seattle's Central District from 1870 through the Civil Rights Era* (Seattle, WA, 1994), p. ix; U.S. Census, 1880, Indian Census by State and Territory. See also Carlos Arnaldo Schwantes, *The Pacific Northwest: An Interpretive History* (Lincoln, NE, 1996, rev. ed.), p. 229. It is unclear whether the 1880 number (from the census) includes the 6,239 Indians that Schwantes reports as Indians not living on reservations. These numbers are unreliable, given the poor quality of territorial censuses. See also "Population of the Territory," *WS*, October 21, 1887. Numbers for Kanakas, half-breeds, blacks, mulattoes, and the Chinese appear separately, and, with whites added (137,800), do not total 144,009; 59,328 were said to be female.

[14] Washington State, *Annual Report of the Labor Department* (Olympia, WA, 1904), p. 13.

the mid-1880s, when Washington probably contained no more than 2,575 Asians, anti-Chinese rioting in Seattle and Tacoma stained the territory's reputation and fueled skepticism in Congress and elsewhere about its readiness for statehood.[15]

Social and political organization came slowly. The Women's Christian Temperance Union, the Knights of Labor, the People's Party, and other instruments of civic mobilization languished until the early 1880s. In 1882, a journalist could say accurately that "party lines have not been closely drawn . . . , and voters have been influenced by their friendships or enmities." The Democratic and Republican parties were major forces by the late 1880s, but even at mid-decade, organizations touting the words "people" or "independent" attracted many voters. The Knights peaked in about 1886, though influence persisted.[16] Republicanism finally emerged as the dominant party into the 1920s; the occasional Democratic victory often reflected sympathy with Populism and a diffuse anti-monopolism.

Within party circles, moreover, wealth production and statehood trumped almost everything. In 1878, just as delegates concluded work on a proposed state constitution, Democrats and Republicans held pre-election conventions, responding in unison to concerns about labor unrest in mining and lumbering, the Chinese question, Indian-white tensions, and chronic delays in railroad completion. Neither party addressed suffrage. Both denounced attempts to pit labor against capital, demanded an end to Indian reservations and "evil" Chinese migrants, and castigated railroaders' flagrant abuse of the public trust.[17]

While gradual formalization also characterized women's societies, informal mobilization of women and their male allies often turned political or legal tides. Women periodically massed in courtrooms and legislative hallways in support of female lawyers, women accused of crime by all-male juries, and men prepared to defend women's interests. The women's club movement finally crystallized in the mid-1880s, coincident with territorial adoption of equal suffrage; in Tacoma, women met to discuss "great questions" affecting "society and the world."[18] Mixed-sex reformism similarly achieved critical mass only by 1883–85. Men and women alike opposed endemic drunkenness; firm links between women and anti-saloonism had not yet crystallized. In 1883, only in part to attract female voters, the Republican physician-governor William Newell condemned the pandemic use of a substance "with no redeeming or compensating influences for good" and pledged support for temperance legislation.[19]

---

[15] For rare praise of the Chinese, see "A Chinese Junk Village," *PSWC*, October 6, 1882.

[16] "The Election," *PSWC*, November 10, 1882.

[17] "Democratic Platform," *SDPI*, September 11, 1878; "Republican Platform," ibid., October 25, 1878.

[18] "Tacoma Woman's Club," *TDL*, March 20, 1884.

[19] Address of Governor William Newell (1883), in Charles M. Gates, ed., *Messages of the Governors of the Territory of Washington to the Legislative Assembly, 1854–1889* (Seattle, WA, 1940), pp. 242–3. Speeches were widely circulated; e.g., "Governor's Message," *SDPI*, October 4, 1883.

Nevertheless, by the late 1880s, isolation and disorganization yielded with speed and finality to many of the sweeping transformations associated with the nineteenth century. In the east and Midwest, finance capitalism, industrialization, urbanization, galloping state paternalism, and a mass democracy all had emerged in modern dress well before the twentieth century. Gilded-Age Americans witnessed the re-nationalization of political parties and partisan realignment by 1896, global marketing, advances in transportation and communication, agrarian radicalism, unionism, and glimmerings of Progressive reform. In places like Kentucky or Michigan, balanced sex ratios and economic self-sufficiency appeared before the Civil War; decades before Seattle and Tacoma opened post offices, the transportation revolution had lowered production costs and altered perceptions of time and space. In the New Northwest, settlers labored to cut roads through mountains with brute force, attract workers, and supply midwives, doctors, and seamstresses with sewing needles; elsewhere, Americans erected sprawling factories, worried about frontier *closings*, and mounted a World's Fair to celebrate technological prowess.

Washingtonians thus witnessed the convergence of multiple developmental processes that other regions had been able to absorb gradually. As a result, the territory's economy and society were fractured, imperfectly modern, and inherently unstable. Allison Parker and Stephanie Cole point to "key moments in American history when the state was being defined and redefined"; Benedict Anderson once identified a tangled "skein of journeys" that state- and nation-building entail.[20] However characterized, Washington's pre-statehood circumstances generated social strain and numerous examples of carts before horses. Rapid population growth, first-generation farming, and helplessness in the face of avalanches, fires, and earthquakes co-existed with industrialization, labor unrest, and trans-Pacific as well as regional commerce. In November, 1883, journalists decried the loss by fire of a new brewery, malthouse, and county building in Seattle; the city had modern fire equipment but lacked water, the "first essential," and adequate water pressure.[21] Six years later, a wave of fires in several mostly wooden cities revealed an appalling lack of attention to public safety in frantic building campaigns. Rude lumbering camps bore scant resemblance to elegant hotels and opera houses, yet they were only a few miles apart.

Into the 1880s, as capitalists elsewhere orchestrated merger movements, bubbles, and union-busting on an unprecedented scale, Washingtonians labored to construct factories and canneries, the main engines of a modernizing society. In 1879, a Seattle editor boasted that the number of people employed in western factories had tripled since 1870. Average income

---

[20] Allison Parker and Stephanie Cole, eds., *Women and the Unstable State in Nineteenth-Century America* (College Station, TX, 2000), p. ix; Benedict Anderson, *Imagined Communities* (Brooklyn, NY, 2006), p. 115.

[21] Editorial, *WS*, November 16, 1883.

for a laborer was $913, as compared to $787 in New England; annual savings in Washington and New England were $117 and $231, respectively. This supposedly gave "indisputable evidence of the adaptation of the West" for industry. Yet, at the same moment, settlers complained of Indian raids and sought help with land clearance. Crooks mingled with and sometimes dogged upstanding citizens: In December, 1879, a lawyer with a thriving city practice offered land for sale, sternly admonishing "land grabbers" to stay away.[22]

Isolation encouraged legal hybridization – that is, the intermingling and merger of common-law rules of practice, continental doctrines (particularly in domestic-relations and property law), and evolving social and gender practices – some inherited, others a response to new circumstances. By the late 1870s, these accumulated legalities had softened, complicated, or replaced doctrines prevailing in older communities; as Pierre Bourdieu reminds us, with time and popular acquiescence, a people's "history becomes nature."[23] The republic's *ancien regime* – including surviving elements of the law of coverture, itself substantially weakened and hybridized over the course of the century – no longer mirrored the self-constructions of Washingtonians accustomed to mutuality, if only to survive in ramshackle hamlets and camps where the only certainty was perpetual uncertainty.

It is here, not in Progressive America, that we encounter the underpinnings of Hattie Somerville's lawsuit and her attorneys' oddly futile defense. Settlers first organized campaigns for sex equality, aided occasionally by prominent suffragists from Oregon and elsewhere, in 1871–73. Territorial legislators refused to universalize the suffrage, but augmented married women's economic freedom steadily until, in 1879, they abruptly passed a comprehensive, sex-neutral community-property statute and remarkable civil-rights law. By 1880, women claimed autonomy in the marketplace and within marriage, including equal rights to custody of children, with the important exception of husbands' exclusive right to sexual services and their ability to act alone as administrators in many community-related transactions. Lawmakers had granted women and men co-equal investiture in property – associations that Americans had long associated with constitutional sovereignty. Experiences of freedom broadened: In 1883, largely in response to the unanswerable fact of co-sovereignty, assemblymen enfranchised loyal adult white women. Ancillary rights and duties traditionally bundled with the ballot attached automatically to new voters, no less than they had attached to white men without property at the moment of their investiture in Jacksonian

---

[22] "Western Manufactures," *SDPI*, November 22, 1879; untitled advertisement, ibid., December 27, 1880 (for land sale).

[23] Pierre Bourdieu, *Outline of a Theory of Practice* (Cambridge, UK, 1977, 2005 ed.), p. 78. As used here, the term "legalities" refers to a contingent bundle of informal and formal rules of conduct that members of a community take to be binding and limiting. See also Christopher Tomlins and Bruce Mann, eds., *The Many Legalities of Colonial America* (Chapel Hill, NC, 2000), esp. pp. 1–24, 272–92.

America, or to black men during Reconstruction, when nobody yet realized how thoroughly new federal amendments would be ransacked. Among them were the jury-service obligation as well as rights to hold public office, claim a nationality, and practice law. In Washington, clerks selected jurors from tax censuses or poll books; co-tenancy of marital estates qualified women for jury duty whether they had voted or not. To sit on petit juries, women had to be resident, tax-paying citizens; legislators added a "householder" requirement for grand juries.[24] Again west of the Cascades, courtrooms boasted large numbers of female jurors and bailiffs. By about 1885, it was newsworthy but not horrifying for women to hold minor public offices. Excluded were military service, roadwork obligations, and wives' right to claim separate nationalities and domiciles. But Washingtonians could not imagine, much less abide, women in militias; mixed-sex juries and county commissions were sufficiently heart-stopping.

Only by 1886–88 did Washingtonians confront the extent to which their legalities departed from practices elsewhere; amid social unrest on all sides, women who had voted and complied with hand-delivered calls to jury duty stood accused of gender betrayal. Critics increasingly complained that they behaved in polling places, and even more certainly in courtrooms, as sexualized, subjective *women* rather than as objective, representative *citizens*. Because they had invaded masculine citadels *as women*, they sabotaged neighborhood justice, subjected private knowledge to public scrutiny, and imperiled statehood. Opponents seized on women's ambivalence about (and periodic denunciations of) jury service, dalliances with "cranks," and participation in anti-vice campaigns to condemn equal suffrage. These disputes, in turn, triggered pitched warfare. Boundaries around a white male electorate hardened, as did cultural and psychological barriers around courthouses. Women (and men unable to perform white manhood) stood accused of destabilizing the polity, discouraging investment, and delaying or sabotaging statehood.

By 1888–89, women had been driven from sites of public judgment. Resurgent common-law doctrines and related social practices, the latter functioning as a customary constitution, had prevailed. No longer did co-equality and co-sovereignty protect women from charges of sex-driven incapacity, subjectivity, and weak-mindedness. Washington achieved statehood with a white-male electorate. A few women practiced law; many others farmed or owned businesses and jointly occupied marital estates. Only in 1910, after years of decorous lobbying and parading, did legislators re-institute universal suffrage by constitutional amendment.[25] By then, however, women's

---

[24] E.g., An Act in Relation to Qualification of Grand and Petit Jurors, Laws of Washington Territory, 1862, Section 1, p. 33. Clerks of court selected grand jurors from county lists of "all qualified electors and householders" and petit jurors from county lists of "all qualified electors."

[25] For a brief discussion, see Rebecca Edwards, "Pioneers at the Polls," in Jean Baker, ed., *Votes for Women: The Struggle for Suffrage Revisited* (New York, 2002), esp. pp. 98–9.

equal membership in the constituent power had been compromised, common-law rules of practice had reappeared in domestic-relations litigation, and the traditional bundle of rights and obligations associated with political equality had unraveled. In 1911, women were relieved automatically of jury duty "by reason of sex" unless they asked to serve – an exemption that many women welcomed. In effect, Washingtonians had constitutionalized the home vote.

The fully constituted, wholly self-governing citizen who survived these trials was manly and white, but, within important limits, willing to share space with well-deported, capable women, whose sovereignty in a formal legal sense had been partitioned, in keeping with social theory. Such men typically did not object to woman suffrage; only women could defend home interests. They did intend, however, to prevent "gender chaos" and to control courtrooms, statehouses, and the terms of labor contracts; in Kevin Murphy's words, they were "red bloods," not "mollycoddles." By 1912, women claimed civil rights, custodial rights, an eroded but still robust claim to marital equality, and the right to vote. But the clouding of women's equal title to constitutional sovereignty – a cloud affirmed by judicial decision – placed access to citizens' obligations out of reach for much of the twentieth century.[26]

PROBLEMATICS

How and why, as Washingtonians moved from the tumultuous 1880s to 1912, did hierarchical, gender-laden views of citizenship supplant egalitarian views and practices? Did uneasy women object to the equality principle itself or to specific experiences during the performance of obligations? To what extent had the statehood ritual and economic modernization shaped these judgments? More broadly, what do these developments tell us about the nature of resistance to equal suffrage and the decision in most jurisdictions to disallow mixed jury service or permit it only on request? What can New Northwestern conversations and choices reveal about Americans' evolving conceptions of citizenship and ongoing eastern resistance to equal suffrage? And why do the losses of legal and constitutional ground that women experienced in Gilded-Age Washington so closely resemble the trajectories that Cornelia Dayton and Laura Edwards identified, respectively, in early Connecticut and in the antebellum south?[27]

Responses form a chapter not only in accounts of the Northwest's developing legal-cultural fabric, but also in understandings of public life

---

[26] Kevin Murphy, *Political Manhood: Red Bloods, Mollycoddles, and the Politics of Progressive Era Reform* (New York, 2010). For gender chaos, see Carol Pateman, *The Disorder of Women: Democracy, Feminism, and Political Theory* (Stanford, CA, 1990), and Lori Ginsburg's use of the concept, "Pernicious Heresies ... ," in Parker and Cole, *Women and the Unstable State in Nineteenth-Century America*, op cit., pp. 139–61.

[27] *Women Before the Bar: Gender, Law, and Society in Connecticut, 1639–1789* (Chapel Hill, NC, 1995); Laura F. Edwards, *The People and Their Peace: Legal Culture and the Transformation of Inequality in the Post-Revolutionary South* (Chapel Hill, NC, 2010).

before World War I. Most obviously, *Gender Remade* provides a detailed account of Washington's slide from formal sex neutrality toward the sex-specific inequalities embraced in *Somerville*. But, more experimentally, it aims to pry open the doors and windows of constitutional history: The findings of historians of gender typically find their way into the master narrative only when they affect federal developments – the long career of ERA, the decision against "sex" in the Fourteenth Amendment, or the abolition of polygamy. Nor have the new western and environmental histories appreciably altered frames of reference. Idaho, Oregon, or Washington still seem foreign and separate – places with local histories that join the national saga abstractly, as when developments illustrate "slavery and the territories" or "economic nationalism," or when federal judicial decisions drown out volatile, site-specific understandings of constructs like sovereignty, federalism, dependency, protectionism, or fundamental law. Yet nineteenth-century eyes and ears were trained much more closely to the ground than our own; to view westerners as clients of a continental, totalizing constitutional culture before 1918 is to misunderstand and homogenize the categories within which much – perhaps most – of the citizenry made sense of their world.

On the other hand, while historians of women have attended to important parts of the western story, including the enfranchisement of women, accounts usually emphasize ballots and women's political agency in securing the vote – i.e., the politics of suffragism. Examinations of women's self-actualization have transformed male-centric accounts, within which the state inscribed freedom on passive women, into woman-centered or universalized accounts. But the fact that jury service and office holding traditionally accompanied the suffrage often escapes notice, as does the possibility that jury service might have been more controversial than balloting. As a result, the plight of the female juror – her appearance in 1884 and catastrophic disappearance during the passage to statehood in 1888–89 – has yet to be closely examined.

Gender Remade shows that territorial battles to secure universal suffrage and equal civil or marital rights were far more complex than scholars have been able to see, given preoccupations with federalization of the suffrage and then with the supposedly decisive suffrage-temperance connection. In Washington, the furor over mixed-sex juries antedated and then developed alongside mixed-sex, anti-vice campaigns. The spectacle of women sitting in jury boxes initially persuaded opponents of suffrage to think of political *equality* (that is, universal investiture with political rights and obligations) as a degenerate, unwelcome, and harmful departure from customary practice. Many citizens believed, too, that a weighty load of obligations in addition to those borne at home fostered *inequality* and *injustice*. Finally, critics condemned outrageous, quasi-pornographic anteroom exposures of women's bodies and bodily or maternal functions ordinarily sequestered at home; by comparison, talk about the bodies of female voters had been formulaic ("unsexed") and mild. As controversy and social violence mounted, strange bedfellows gathered to reconsider and eliminate the taproot – that is, egalitarian suffrage and domestic relations law, and beneath those constellations, the bedrock question of whether citizenship ought to be predicated on perfect equality. All citizens occupied houses but perhaps did not require the same number of rooms. In short order and despite fierce protest, officials introduced new legalities and a gender hierarchy taken to be compatible with "national manhood"[28] and with practices in other states – the seats, notwithstanding the Civil War, of citizenship and domestic practices.

The lack of scholarly interest in the jury-service obligation is puzzling. There ought to be more to read than a handful of articles and books, scattered paragraphs, and a chapter in Linda Kerber's landmark *No Constitutional Right to be Ladies*. Indeed, if the question is how Americans conceived of political equality in particular locations, female lawyers' pioneering accounts of how men and women interacted in mixed-sex courtrooms remain the most useful in print. Joanna Grossman and Gretchen Ritter constructively disagree about the relationship between suffrage and jury duty, mobilizing impressive evidence to say, on Grossman's side, that jury duty was linked to political freedom – a position that this book supports – and on the other side, that jury duty has been a civil rather than political right. But scholarship does not explain why men continued to command jury boxes after 1920, except to suggest that men always reserved sites of power for themselves, sought to preserve female delicacy, or took women to be suited by nature to domesticity, as if past behavior and chivalry offer sufficient explanations.[29] Historians of labor and Progressivism describe Seattle's post-statehood tumult but largely omit the jury crisis as well as the deeply gendered statehood battle. Indeed, classic studies of citizenship and the suffrage typically omit jury service altogether or give it passing notice. But Americans, and the English before them, had long associated voting rights with commensurate obligations, which together encouraged (as modern scholarship shows) such admirable traits as empathy and altruism. Surely Susan B. Anthony thought that enfranchisement imposed obligations – as in 1867, when she told hostile New Yorkers that suffrage led directly to the seating of all citizens "indiscriminately ... upon juries."[30]

How, then, did Americans decide to sever political obligations from ballots in the case of sex? With the exception of the right to a nationality, we simply do not know, beyond the commentary surrounding leading twentieth-century

---

[28] Dana D. Nelson, *National Manhood: Capitalist Citizenship and the Imagined Fraternity of White Men* (Durham, NC, 1998).

[29] Johanna Grossman, "Women's Jury Service: Right of Citizenship or Privilege of Difference?" *Stanford Law Review*, Vol. 46 (1993–94), pp. 1115–60, as at p. 1137 (" ... in Washington, as elsewhere, the all-male jury tradition continued"); Gretchen Ritter, "Jury Service and Women's Citizenship before and after the Nineteenth Amendment," *Law and History Review*, Vol. 20, No. 3 (Autumn 2002), pp. 479–515, locating jury duty within the tradition of representative government.

[30] "Hearing before the Committee on Suffrage, New York Constitutional Convention, in Albany," June 27, 1867, in Ann Gordon, ed., *The Selected Papers of Elizabeth Cady Stanton and Susan B. Anthony, Vol. II: Against an Aristocracy of Sex, 1866–1873* (New Brunswick, NJ, 1997), p. 75.

judicial cases. Exclusion of women continued into the modern civil rights era: Only in 1975, when a rapist in Louisiana contended that an all-male jury did not represent a fair cross-section of the population, did the U.S. Supreme Court finally declare that men and women had an equal obligation to sit on juries as well as equal opportunity as individuals to seek exemption. Sweeping, gender-based relief from citizenship obligations was unconstitutional. But the Court in *Taylor* v. *Louisiana* located women's right to occupy jury boxes, not in the Nineteenth Amendment, but in the Fourteenth; only later did justices re-associate jury duty with the right to vote, thus underscoring the mystery of the divorce of political rights from duties in the first place.[31]

A better understanding of how women came to be shut out of courthouses requires the excavation of layers of culture. Constitutional historians have been slow to embrace the problem of how ordinary citizens have lived or understood organic law, and have treated legal equality and sovereignty as more or less fixed constellations of rights and powers, handed over to particular groups at intervals in the march toward 1920 and then the 1960s. Equally problematic has been a tendency, in the absence of war or riot, to assume the framing power and universal application of formal legal instruments. When citizens have been denied citizenship rights, the presumption often has been, not that membership in the constituent power was just as contingent on culture formation as any other legal fiction, but that impediments to equality have been aberrational and fleeting – as with the Ku Klux Klan's interference with black voting, or the U.S. Supreme Court's denial of Susan B. Anthony's right to cast ballots in federal elections. But the maldistribution of public goods, if not 'natural,' has been naturalized in America, as elsewhere; the idea that men and women might occupy the same sovereign ground was profoundly radical and discontinuous into modern times. More has been at issue, in other words, than the multiplication of rights or the razing of temporary, mechanical barriers to equality.

Fortunately, the center of gravity is shifting, away from introverted studies of public law's formal structure and framing power toward an appreciation of interactions between disparate legalities and of the ways in which citizens internalize and experience constitutionalism. Increasingly, the goal has been to limn "the way of life and thought that we construct, negotiate, institutionalize, and finally (after it is all settled) end up calling 'reality.'"[32] But thorny questions about translation and transmission persist: How exactly

---

[31] Kerber, *No Constitutional Right to be Ladies*, pp. 124–220, esp. pp. 110–11. For affirmation of old rules, see *Hoyt* v. *Florida*, 368 U.S. 57 (1961); for reversal, *Taylor* v. *Louisiana*, 419 U.S. 522 (1975). For one brief notice of this odd disassociation, see Akhil Reed Amar, *America's Unwritten Constitution: The Precedents and Principles We Live By* (New York, 2012), pp. 287–8.

[32] Jerome Bruner, quoted in Clifford Geertz, *Available Light: Anthropological Reflections on Philosophical Topics* (Princeton, NJ, 2000), p. 192. See also Robert Baker, *The Rescue of Joshua Glover* (Athens, OH, 2006), pp. 179, 188, on public dialogue and law's failure to achieve social peace.

do ideas about rights, sovereignty, and legitimacy find their way into practice? Under what conditions do embedded social practices yield to or defeat innovative legalities? Challenges often are methodological: How might scholars capture what Robert Baker calls the "dialogue" between people and governments about the merits of particular rules or practices? How and when have constitutional precepts influenced behavior? Participants don't always explain themselves. Occasionally, social practices dictate silence, as with talk about rape or women's bodily functions. Governmental archives threaten to overwhelm informal testimony. Yet day-to-day talk imparts social meaning to otherwise disembodied, purely forensic constructs; in public and private conversations – not to mention poems, cartoons, and nasty letters to the editor – we can see more clearly how boundaries come to be erected or razed around individuals and groups. Equally important, we can begin to assess where constitutional idealism begins to fray or buckle in contests with industrial capitalism, nationalism, and other powerful forces.[33]

Where might we look for evidence of constitutional practice in a social sense? In Washington, public-policy statements form one part of an evidentiary universe. Law's stories, deposited in hundreds of case files and newspapers, provide another, humanizing window into citizens' habits of mind and legal fluency. For all of their pomp and circumstance, justices propose boundaries that mean little without popular acquiescence, however grudging, much as embedded social practices depend for life on social utility and agreement. Gilded-Age Americans, moreover, expressed their citizenship in multifarious ways far beyond the polls: Literate citizens wrote revealing letters and mailed them to editors or politicians. They often functioned as third parties to civil or criminal disputes, affirming membership in the constituent power through writing, reading, or gathering in power-laden spaces. Public prints (Washington boasted at least a hundred before statehood) were another primary site of legal-cultural reformation. Newspapers also preserved information about governmental activities lost in natural disasters, as with urban fires in 1889. The sheer quantity of talk was exhilarating. It could also be overwhelming. In crisis times especially, as these chapters readily attest, Washingtonians generated astonishing volumes of speech, reasoning together as if in a community-wide trial or colloquium.[34]

Regional differences figure large in this story and in other, untold or half-told stories. Although westerners have been largely absent in the constitutional scholar's master narrative, they have always been there – not passively or abstractly, but as agents shaping their own society and influencing other Americans. Indeed, as we will see, Washington's territorial disasters probably reinforced a wall of anti-suffragism erected at the Mississippi River. The West

---

[33] On the centrality of western newspapers, see Patricia Nelson Limerick, "Making the Most of Words," in William Cronon et al., eds., *Under an Open Sky: Rethinking America's Western Past* (New York, 1992), esp. pp. 178–80.

[34] For a list of more than a hundred prints, see "Washington State Press," *SPT*, June 2, 1893.

and Midwest have been more than shapeless borderlands to citizens who thought of themselves as dynamic parts of national life, and sometimes as loyal adults denied their birthright; as if to illustrate the point, Washington's male leadership finally refused to be treated as marginalized dependents – i.e., as wives or children – within a national household. This would not entirely surprise historian Richard Slotkin, who finds an overbearing brotherhood of industrial "commanders" in the place once occupied by the likes of George Custer. But Slotkin and others miss interplay between the restoration of male headship in government and the territory's close brush with male–female co-sovereignty.[35]

Local contingencies cannot be overestimated. In Washington, isolation and rude circumstances initially fostered introversion and a keen sense of the *sui generis* quality of self-created spaces, which served as crucibles for experimentation. Washington's growing citizenry included a number of individuals whose conceptions of citizenship, sovereignty, equality, and constitutionalism itself had been shaped by personal experiences of civil war. Yet, while Washingtonians inhabited post-war discourses alongside other Americans, other influences shared and often dominated the stage. After 1870, citizens at some remove from national developments were preoccupied with construction as well as Reconstruction. The night-terrors that lumberjacks experienced in the territory's dense forests had to do, not with the terms of black emancipation or presidential patronage, but with the possibility of lopping off arms and legs. Thus, the historians' received categories ("Reconstruction," "The Gilded Age") are at least temporarily inapt and unhelpful. Only in the early 1880s did the emancipatory possibilities embedded in Civil War amendments and Radical Republican idealism finally gain traction beyond a handful of nationally affiliated reformers, only to collide head-on with several other forces of equal or greater influence.

FROM NEAR-EQUALITY TO DEPENDENCE

It would be tempting to conclude, given the tsunami-like arrival of industrial capitalism and its critics, that Progressivism caused or shaped the *Somerville* opinion and its social context – as if the label explains itself and subsumes everything around it. That, however, would be a mistake. The word "progressive" and its derivatives appear regularly in public prints and elsewhere. But meanings shifted over space and time. Only with the appearance of industrial squalor and exploitation, Theodore Roosevelt's party, and a wave of urban reformism in Washington's coastal cities do we find capitalization of the term and meaningful shifts in habits of mind. When they finally appeared, moreover, Fourteenth-Amendment arguments in judicial

---

[35] Richard Slotkin, *The Fatal Environment: The Myth of the Frontier in the Age of Industrialization, 1800–1890* (Norman, OK, 1998), esp. Ch. 20.

footnotes, or the term "progressive" (or "Progressive") to indicate paternal government, referred to strategic choices from within the languages available to lawyers or reformers. Those choices were not immediately apparent or available. Only when new stockpiles of forensic weaponry, law reports, and Thomas Cooley's *Constitutional Limitations* had made their way to law offices in remote territories; when jurists had absorbed the post–Civil War outpouring of new ideas; and when Washingtonians had moved decisively toward economic and political integration could they be wielded effectively against, say, prohibitionist attempts to deprive saloon owners of property rights or legislative regulation of wages and hours. To make matters more complex, a taste for state paternalism settled over the landscape unevenly and sprang from different sources: Seattle (the location often taken to be synonymous with "Progressive" Washington) was not Spokane Falls, nor did it resemble vice-ridden Tacoma or renegade towns like Walla Walla and Bellingham.

Not surprisingly, law-minded Washingtonians determined to maximize wealth production and restore or reconfigure paternal control of public life reverted to the time-honored language of coverture, reinforced by contemporary flirtations with biological determinism. The law of coverture had been a formative influence in shaping social practices carried into the territory after 1853 – practices that changed slowly and that could function as an informal, pre-emptive constitution. By 1889–90, women and men no longer occupied quite the same rung on the civic ladder. Yet this powerful revival is curiously absent in accounts of resistance to sex equality. Elements of coverture typically appear in scholarship as old chestnuts, falling by the wayside one by one in the march toward modernity. After 1888, however, doctrines and practices long implicated in women's incapacitation resurged, weakening claims to co-sovereignty beyond marital estates, where formal authority as self-governors came to be severed from the political realm – that is, partitioned and domesticated – even as the right to cast a vote on behalf of home was constitutionalized.

Modifications of citizens' formal relationships to public power supported broader goals. When combined with hyper-nationalism (expressed as statehood fever) and industrialization, they dramatically supported campaigns for statehood and installations of an entrepreneurial fraternity at the head of the public table. This is not to say that autonomous market forces – or, for that matter, autonomous rules of law – single-handedly shaped public culture, or to deny human agency in mapping social norms and boundaries. Rather, it is to say that a fragile experiment in self-rule, undertaken at a late stage in national development and against the grain of customary practices, could not withstand the imperatives of political and industrial integration. Neither Progressivism nor the common law *per se* inspired Washingtonians to eliminate mixed-sex practices and re-masculinize citadels of public power; rather, change expressed the deeply ironic "modern" – the seeming need, as officials sued for statehood and flexed economic muscle, to abandon political experimentation, embrace state paternalism, and produce wealth. Law makers set about regulating markets (including the labor market) and nipping at the heels of equal-rights legislation when it competed with common-law norms, not to be villainous, but to merge with other Americans and embed modern views of women's class interests in public policy. To be modern was to escape primitivism, vassalage, and emasculation, but also to experience what Max Weber called "disenchantment" – in this case, the collapse of sanctified republican constitutionalism in contests with markets, social science, and *real politic*.[36]

In all of this, the interventions of brave or ruthless individuals mattered more than usually. One or two such agents can leave deep imprints on small-scale societies, particularly when settlers lack long-term experience with the place itself. In Washington, Abigail Duniway, Zerelda McCoy, May Arkwright Hutton, and a number of other women's-rights activists repeatedly altered the course of territorial development. Associate Justice George Turner masterminded campaigns to deprive women of political equality; his chief opponent, Chief Justice Roger Sherman Greene, had set the stage for gender chaos more or less single-handedly. Greene's developing ideas about the co-sovereignty of human beings (i.e., "kingliness" and "queenliness") combined with a countervailing faith in women as *sui generis* repositories of virtue, particularly when seated on juries, both aided and crippled the sex's prospects well into the new century.

INEQUALITY AND DISENCHANTMENT

In the end, *Gender Remade* is about ancillary rights, especially mixed-sex service on grand and petit juries, the constitutional sovereignty that compelled women to serve, and decisions against egalitarian practices. In modern America, jury service typically calls to mind, not the polity, but a criminal-justice system divorced from politics; for the most part, we have lost nineteenth-century understandings of the jury as an integral component of representative government. Women's struggle to participate in (or gain exemption from) systems of public judgment thus seems apart from and secondary to the battle for suffrage. But Greene and others conceived of jurors' votes as "judicial ballots" analogous to electoral ballots,[37] and members of juries as community delegates no less important than legislators – indeed, as exemplars of what J. R. Pole has called the citizens' "moral agency."[38] Certainly scholars nowadays think mainly of ballots when they encounter terms like "universal suffrage" or "political freedom." Elements of the bundle of

---

[36] For the original Weberian idea, see H. H. Gerth and C. Wright Mills, eds., *From Max Weber, Essays in Sociology* (New York, 1958), p. 350 and passim.

[37] Roger S. Greene, "Charge to the Grand Jury . . . ," *NN*, September 1, 1884 (widely reprinted).

[38] J. R. Pole, *Contract and Consent: Representation and the Jury in Anglo-American Legal History* (Charlottesville, VA, 2010), pp. 96–7. (The jury's "moral agency" and distance from interest-group politics distinguishes it from other representative institutions; impartiality depended on mobilizing a "substantial admixture of relevant elements," not by exclusion.)

political rights and obligations no longer seem to be inseparable, perhaps because lawmakers no longer conceive of them as aspects of a single constitutional problem. Alexander Keyssar – arguably the nation's leading historian of the suffrage – has nothing to say about juries. Given virtual eradication in modern times of the idea that jurors render decisions analogous to those reached at the polls or in legislatures, it is easy enough to ignore talk about the corruption of neighborhood-based panels, the jury's relationship to self-rule, the grand jury's role in civic education and public peace, or the need to empanel juries as representative of society as, say, town meetings or elections. Washingtonians knew better. As Governor Eugene Semple put it in 1887, the grand jury was "a popular body, . . . always fresh from the people, and on account of the method of its selection and its . . . changing constituents, . . . the most difficult body to control that is known to the law."[39]

Why, then, did Washingtonians dispense with mixed juries, and how was that development linked to Justice Crow's decision to characterize fully enfranchised, propertied women as wards? Again, Benedict Anderson provides part of the answer: In his view, the whole point of losing oneself in the nation is to join an entity that both transcends and affirms individual interests; in the process, citizens can remake the past and justify the sacrifice of whatever stands in the way – as with the suspension of a woman's right to vote in advance of national practice, which not coincidentally ended women's service on juries.[40] The uproar surrounding jury service – related as suffrage never had been to women's bodies and strangers' access to private knowledge – had shattered social peace. In Washington, jury service and the threat of mixed-sex office holding, not suffrage *per se*, had been an insult to social practice, or, as one Washingtonian put it, the community's "fundamental constitution." Lawmakers therefore severed old links between suffrage and the traditional bundle of ancillary rights and obligations. If mixed-sex juries could not function as credible repositories of local morality and as interpreters of fact, and especially if many women preferred not to serve, then they had to be excluded, less because they were not "householders" in a legal sense (though lawyers made exactly that case) than because they disrupted and fouled masculine culture. At the polls, women might plausibly cast the 'home vote' while representing property; as jurors, they could never hope to impersonate men or fully embody the citizenry.

Historian Peggy Cooper Davis once said that "cultures become richer and evolve in directions of social equity and human freedom when they attend to their neglected stories – to those people, ideas, and events that its members were once somehow predisposed to neglect."[41] Into the twentieth century, many

---

[39] Governor Eugene Semple to the Eleventh Biennial Session of the Legislative Assembly, October 9, 1887, in Gates, ed., *Messages of the Governors of the Territory of Washington*, p. 270.

[40] Anderson, *Imagined Communities*, p. 144 and passim.

[41] Peggy Cooper Davis, *Neglected Stories: The Constitution and Family Values* (New York, 1997), p. 251.

Washingtonians forgot or disowned the radically democratic elements of their own narrative; instead, many – perhaps a large majority – reimagined the territorial era as a primitive dress rehearsal for a better integrated, more grown-up, less magical world. Strangeness, including the terrors (or thrills) of sex equality, had been eclipsed by a less frightening but modern conformity. Women were re-admitted to spaces beyond home on the state's terms; community property, the foundation of political equality, was squeezed to the breaking point; and lawmakers inserted a custodial state between "minors" and employers.

It was perhaps heartening that, in 1911, the Washington Supreme Court ruled in a case involving an elderly woman that neither "eccentricity in the matter of dress" nor her activities as an "ardent woman suffragist" proved mental incapacity.[42] But women's sovereignty had been compromised, and, with it, the possibility of demanding roughly equal access to citizens' rights and obligations. Between 1898 and 1912, suffragists rarely spoke of ancillary rights; suffrage was the main political duty for which women contended and home the realm for which they spoke. When finally granted access to the ballot box, women moved into the new century as the disabled, adult minors described in *Buchanan* and again in *Somerville*. No longer did Washingtonians 'speak' at the polls as equally authoritative members of the sovereignty. Neither scholars nor activists have been wrong to think that rights mattered: The ability to make a binding contract empowered more than one wife in dealing with neighbors, bankers, and conniving children. It was no small thing for a woman to be able to demand the arrest of an inveterate drunk or protest commitment to an asylum. Nor was it chimeric for suffragists to believe that casting a ballot alongside men gradually delegitimized atavistic social practices, including economic dependency. But in Washington and as Elizabeth Cady Stanton saw clearly, erosions of sovereign authority facilitated the loss of rights, especially ancillary political rights and obligations. Without sovereignty, grants of right were little more than promissory notes or leaseholds, to be renewed or revoked at the pleasure of the fully sovereign. Once "woman citizens" had lost standing as constitutional equals, subsequent multiplications of rights could only fall short. For men and women alike, the loss was enduring and catastrophic.

Throughout, I have tried to heed Mary Beard's warnings about portrayals of women as passive slates upon which the liberal state periodically inscribes rights and privileges. Social historians rightly complain about the way in which historians of public life have constructed formal governments as gigantic engines responsible for every advance in civil-rights history. But, as Sara Evans noted some time ago, it is no answer to ignore state power, as if women lived entirely beyond the bounds of legal discourses or had never dined at

---

[42] *Mrs. O. I. Converse* v. *W. A. Mix*, 63 Wash Rpts 318 (1911), 318, 322.

cultural tables.[43] In Washington, I should add, both sexes defied stereotypes: Men often shared the reformist stage. Women participated in government, sharing responsibility for the fruits of state action. Many women, no less certainly than men, were seduced by law's promises, only to find themselves, as Hattie Somerville's workers soon learned, robbed of property in rights or differently constrained. This mixture of valor and dishonor gives pause – as when a woman, Nevada Bloomer, conspired to smash equal suffrage, or when a Democrat, Governor Eugene Semple, sacrificed business and political prospects to oppose Bloomer's well-placed supporters.

The book progresses chronologically. Early chapters sketch the emergence of a rights regime rooted in sex-neutral agency with property theoretically capable of vesting men and women with near-equality. They also track the emergence of instability, resistance, and political mobilization as women moved into citadels of public power. Chapter 4 explores gender chaos, violence, the humiliation of would-be female jurors, and the resurgence of social practices, functioning as a customary constitution, as courtroom integration continued. Chapter 5 explores pitched battles between the territory's political departments over citizens' obligations; a related struggle between territorial citizens and Congress over the terms of statehood; and the elimination of both woman suffrage and mixed-sex jury service in two decisions of the territorial supreme court. Final chapters describe statehood settlements, re-articulations of gender and racial hierarchies, revisions of community-property law, and women's re-enfranchisement without co-sovereignty or the jury obligation. Washingtonians had renounced parts of their own past and remade gender; as of 1912, with memories of egalitarianism steadily dimming, the citizenry inhabited (in sociologist Robert Bellah's words) "the description of a place and not ... the place itself."[44]

---

[43] Sara M. Evans, "Women's History and Political Theory: Toward a Feminist Approach to Public Life," in Nancy Hewitt and Suzanne Lebsock, eds., *Visible Women: New Essays on American Activism* (Champaign-Urbana, IL, 1993), pp. 119–39.

[44] Robert N. Bellah, "American Civil Religion in the 1970s," *Anglican Theological Review* (July 1973), p. 9, quoting Wallace Stevens. The late Kermit Hall generously shared this article with me.

2

"She does not go into utter slavery"

Toward equality and co-sovereignty

> She retains, in the eyes of the law, a personality of her own. She does not, in marrying, barter her very self away. She does not go into utter slavery. She is still recognized as having a personal interest of her own, both in her skilled faculties and in her body. . . . She has, as distinct from her husband, the rights of 'life, liberty and the pursuit of happiness,' rights inalienable even by nuptial bargain.
>
> – Associate Justice Roger Sherman Greene (1877)[1]

When Washington Territory entered the union as a constitutional dependency in March, 1853, its laws and social practices closely resembled those of older common-law jurisdictions. Into the 1860s and early 1870s, statute books continued to reflect the presence of lawyers trained in eastern or Midwestern law offices, where the common law held sway and, with the notable exception of New York, where continental rules of practice had substantial influence. But the territory did not long remain a dutiful apprentice to legal convention. Into the 1870s, as Washingtonians moved to regularize and systematize legislation, as judicial decisions multiplied, and as populations expanded and diversified, territorial legal culture on both sides of the Cascade Mountains gradually, if unevenly, absorbed many of the formal rules of practice prevailing in California, Texas, and other community-property jurisdictions.[2] At the same time, gender and other inherited social practices absorbed and began to reflect the experiences and beliefs of citizens living in rough-hewn, lightly populated communities far removed from homelands.

Once in motion, hybridization steadily advanced, as did citizens' fluency in neighborhood legalities. By 1880–81, when legislators commissioned a new law code, civilian-inspired notions of community property and co-tenancy of

[1] *Mary Phelps and John S. Phelps v. S. S. City of Panama*, 1 Wash Terr Rpts 518 (July 1877).
[2] On practices in Texas and California, see Ray August, "The Spread of Community-Property Law to the Far West," *Western Legal History*, Vol. 3, No. 1 (Winter/Spring 1990), pp. 36–66, esp. pp. 58–60.

marital estates suffused the territory's domestic-relations and property law, largely replacing common-law doctrines of coverture. The interdependency and mutuality borne of circumstances reinforced these choices. No longer would married women cede title to their own labor, their ability to secure custody of children after divorce, or (with some exceptions) their ability to deal in marital property within and beyond marriage. At issue were not only women's civil and political rights, but also, and more fundamentally, their authority as co-sovereign householders to make law, manage marital property, expect state recognition and support of rights, and enter public spaces alongside men. No longer would officials deal with women vicariously, through husbands or fathers. Nor could legislators easily deny political rights to similarly situated, adult citizens solely on the ground of sex difference when they possessed a roughly equal list of civil rights and equal membership in the constituent power. Common-law doctrines and the social practices developed in concert with them did not vanish altogether and indeed proved to be powerful enough ultimately to defeat proposals for sex neutrality in courtrooms. But, as the 1870s advanced, women plucky enough to migrate to Washington could expect minimally to hold property, or to marry and to find within marriage a propertied foundation for claims of co-sovereignty. At the same time, albeit with important exceptions, legal reasoning and public conversations manifested egalitarian habits of mind strikingly at odds with inherited social practices. It was plausible, in other words, for a justice to say in 1877 that a married woman, no less than her husband, possessed a separate, inalienable interest in her own body and its productions.

THE CASE OF MARY PHELPS, A MARRIED WOMAN

In 1877 – the year that federal troops formally withdrew from the south and the nadir of a cruel economic downturn – Associate Justice Roger Sherman Greene of the Supreme Court of Washington Territory rendered an opinion in the case of a married woman, Mary Phelps, joined in the suit by her husband, John Phelps, both of Missouri. They had sued the owner of an ocean-going vessel in admiralty for damages some months after Mary, who had been travelling alone, had tumbled headlong into an open hatch while the boat lay in port near Seattle. Nobody contested the facts. As the ship's counsel put it,

All was hurry, bustle and confusion. The cabin waiters were busy clearing off the dinner tables. . . . In this state of things, Mrs. Phelps passed . . . to her stateroom, and during the short space of time she was in it, the hatch was opened. The first officer with a lantern in his hand started down in a hurry to close the port-hole. Before the officer had reached the middle deck, and while he was on the ladder descending, Mrs. Phelps came out of her stateroom, fell in, and landed in utter darkness in the bottom of the ship. No warning was given ... and no guard was on duty.[3]

Profoundly injured in the mishap and in pain, Mary Phelps expected to be disabled for the rest of her life. Attorneys for the ship's owner conceded the severity of her injuries. In Greene's words, "Her system received a severe shock. She was hurt much internally .... She broke her right arm ... and sustained ... a compound comminuted fracture of the right elbow joint, the shattered bones ... protruding through her dress." She was raised to the deck with a block and tackle; at trial, her "elbow joint could not be moved." Instead, the owners argued that Missouri law rather than Washington-territorial law governed the case, that Mary had contributed to her injuries by negligently entering a dark hallway, and that Philip might sue to collect damages for his wife's physical injury but not for pain or for Mary's care, "loss of her time," or "reduction of her power to earn money." Husbands assumed custody of wives: "The libellants are married. The injured party is the wife. The losses are the husband's." Had Mary been self-supporting, she might have garnered a substantial award. But she was John's wife. If he could collect at all, given jurisdictional uncertainty and custodial duties, the recovery would be modest.[4]

Even as Americans moderated or eliminated many old rules of practice, such arguments were still plausible. During the last half of the nineteenth century, the law of coverture had been eroded but not entirely purged from law codes, much as the law governing industrial accidents, nuisance, and negligence had been unsettled but not yet revolutionized or made gender neutral in response to technological change. Lawyers and judges sometimes fanned the flames of tradition, particularly when remaining elements of husbandly headship seemed to be imperiled, but also when expediency dictated a resort to old law, including, as here, Joel Bishops' canonical works on domestic-relations law. Only four years earlier, the U.S. Supreme Court had declared in the case of *Myra Bradwell* v. *U.S.* that the fact of femininity, combined with time-honored legal fictions (such as married women's contractual incapacities), barred even a well-qualified female attorney from practicing law in Illinois. Appellate courts in Wisconsin and elsewhere took much the same position, albeit in the face of a rising tide of criticism. Men still lawfully monopolized voting booths, juries, and public offices. Economic equality continued to elude salaried women. And, while courts increasingly discouraged actions of trespass when wives or daughters were assaulted, husbands still claimed property rights in women's sexual and domestic services. When a woman entered a marital indenture, she promised political allegiance, physical submission, and economic

---

[3] *Mary Phelps and John S. Phelps* v. *S. S. City of Panama*, 1 Wash Terr Rpts 518 (July 1877), 520–4. The court ignored the jurisdictional argument. Two years later, Chief Justice Lewis confronted a challenge to evidence introduced in the original suit and further challenges to admiralty jurisdiction in territorial courts. Justices agreed that the organic act contained "whatever jurisdiction we have"; *Phelps* v. *Steamship Panama*, 1 Wash Terr 615 (1879), 615.

[4] *Phelps* v. *City of Panama*, 525–7.

assistance – a form of subjection originating in medieval theories of unitary, male sovereignty (i.e., *petit* kingship) within households. Put differently, in the absence of statutory change and notwithstanding an amount of blinking in courtrooms and living rooms, a wife's body and its productions still could be described as part of a man's domain, a site of lawful exploitation, encumbered with mutual but unequal rights and duties. Husbands still could be construed – albeit less and less persuasively – as masters entrusted with an indentured woman's well-being. Men spoke for households at voting booths; constables deferred to husbands' right to punish household dependents. In many jurisdictions, a woman's right to her own earnings had not yet been established by statute. If the proceeds from the ruination of Mary Phelps' bones and internal organs belonged to John, and if she could expect to passively endure a lifetime of pain and dependency, married women had gained little from fifty years of reform.

These were problems, not simply of power in a political sense, but of constitutional authority – that is, a person's publicly acknowledged capacity to legitimize acts of state power, to be self-ruling, and to expect governmental protection of one's person and property. And, because the law of marriage formed part of culture, the same social practices affected unmarried people. The idea that Phelps commanded her own body and its productions cut to the heart of coverture's main engines. Where the control of property had been relinquished or divided, men's ability to justify exclusive management of marital property softened appreciably; as a co-tenant of marital property, a woman might be more or less indistinguishable from her husband. Her *status* as a wife, however, competed with claims to sovereignty and personal security; the elimination of incidents of coverture did not in itself liberate married women, given the common-law view of marriage as a social institution, a species of contract apart from ordinary agreements, in which the state was deeply implicated.

In his *Phelps* opinion, as elsewhere, Roger Greene wore both principle and sentiment on his sleeve. The main issue ostensibly was the jurisdictional question, which he resolved quickly; his real interest lay elsewhere: The rest of the long opinion bristled with annoyance at the ship owner's counsel for asserting unreconstructed doctrines by which women lost custody of earnings (including monetary damages) and their own bodies at the moment of marriage, depending upon men for physical and economic security. While a wife's relationship both to her husband and to society were changed by marriage, he wrote, "yet she retains, in the eyes of the law, a personality of her own. She does not, in marrying, barter her very self away. She does not go into utter slavery. She is still recognized as having a personal interest of her own, both in her skilled faculties and in her body . . . . She has, as distinct from her husband, the rights of 'life, liberty and the pursuit of happiness,' rights inalienable even by nuptial bargain." Surely American law protected a wife "as an individual, in the enjoyment of such inherent rights," if not in her possession of every imaginable right. Greene could not resist taking a swipe at rules of practice that assumed a husband would cherish his wife "as his own flesh." This was governance "by presumptuous chivalry," sheltering the "very oppression it thought safe to ignore." Had not the owners contracted with Mary for passage? Had not the carrier's liability for her safe passage also begun? Surely the owners' negligence in failing to warn an aging woman of an open hatch had been "gross."[5] Most important, while Mary Phelps had contracted for passage on the *City of Panama* as an individual, she had gathered less for serious harm than might an unmarried woman. In fact, the *Panama's* owners had appealed in part to reduce the 5,000 dollars' damages that the district court had awarded.

Because the Phelps case raised questions about the extent of damages, Greene offered an alternative theory of a woman's relationship to family, her self-sovereignty, her property in rights, and the monetary value of losses of such property. He ruled that the award, far from being too generous, was much too small. This was not a question of "what worth one's life or one's limb might be to somebody else, but of what it is *to one's self.*" Any comparison between the amount of damages "to wife and heirs, on the loss of husband or protector ... is beside this case. Nor can we follow those judges who hold, that loss or diminution of ability to earn a livelihood should be left out of account, in the case of injury to a married woman. Because a husband is able to provide for her to-day, does not insure her against the death or disability of her husband tomorrow." Greene did not favor damages to meet future losses. But he did regard a wife's physical ability to support herself as "a *separate estate and inalienable possession,* which, indeed, she may never need to draw upon; but is, nevertheless, hers, ready for any exigency." Greene estimated Mary's loss of capacity to be "two thirds of what she previously possessed." The accident had caused permanent hardship and disfigurement. But the greatest injury was pain. Because physical suffering was "intense and excruciating," he tripled the award: "Against her inconvenience and disfigurement we place 2,000 dollars. Reckoning [her lifespan] at about thirteen years, and the yearly value of her mere physical ability *to earn her own livelihood by the labor of her hands* at five hundred dollars, we give her ... three thousand dollars" for a total of 15,000 dollars.[6]

[5] *Phelps v. City of Panama*, 518–21, 532–6. Emphasis added. Briefs do not resolve the question of whether the ship's owner made retrograde arguments solely to evade responsibility. See Mary Phelps and John Phelps v. S. S. City of Panama, Case File No. 286, WSA-O. Greene may have been influenced by developments in Oregon; see arguments about the "more rational and enlightened maxims of the civil law" as compared to the law of coverture, and the irrationality of chivalric "fictions"; *Rugh* v. *Ottenheimer*, 6 Oregon Rpts 231 (1877), 235. Seattle's main paper discussed an Oregon law permitting wives to collect and be sued for damages; "Rights of Married Women," *SDPI*, November 18, 1878. In 1888, Oregon judges decided that "progress" mandated elimination of disabilities and "recognition of [wives'] individuality"; Inara K. Scott, "A Window for Change: Conflicting Ideologies and Legal Reforms in Late Nineteenth-Century Oregon," *Willamette Law Review*, Vol. 37 (2001), pp. 449–50.

[6] *Phelps* v. *City of Panama*, 532–6 and passim.

TERRITORIAL CHIEF JUSTICE
ROGER S. GREENE
1880   —   1887

FIGURE 2.1. Chief Justice Roger Sherman Greene (1840–1930), c. 1895–97, was a warrior for co-equality on juries and at the ballot box for women and other disempowered groups. Photographer: George N. Moore. From University of Washington Libraries, Special Collections, Seattle, WA, AR-96-A-249. Used by permission.

In an age marked by widespread judicial interest in conserving traditional marriage, a federally appointed judge had announced that a wife's body belonged to her alone – that her physical well-being formed part of a valuable "separate estate," and that central elements of coverture were unjust and disingenuous, disregarding nature's law and misrepresenting men's nature. A married woman, no less than any other citizen, was self-sovereign, not as a matter of legislative grant, but as a birthright. Neither judges nor legislators dared to meddle with a man's inalienable right to be secure in his person and to expect state assistance in the project. On what ground, Greene asked, might a woman expect anything less? Did not governments exist to facilitate the pursuit of life, liberty, and happiness for everyone?

In Roger Greene, Mary Phelps had found a sympathetic mediator. The son of a Baptist minister in New England and former resident of Missouri and Illinois, Greene had earned undergraduate and law degrees from Dartmouth in 1859 and 1862. He had served on the Union side during the Civil War, initially as captain of a company of black volunteers, then as judge advocate. Severe wounds forced him to resign his captaincy and move to Chicago, where he practiced law with United States attorney Perkin Bass. By the mid-1870s, he was a Baptist and Radical Republican, disgusted with his party's waning interest in the expansion of citizenship rights to women and black men. In 1870, President Ulysses Grant offered Greene a post on the Washington Supreme Court; Rutherford Hayes appointed him Chief Justice in 1879, just as legislators began to dismantle gender hierarchies. He supported an array of causes – e.g., temperance, the Loyal League, the People's Party, and the Knights of Labor – all unabashedly partisan. By his own testimony, moreover, he was the author of sections of the 1881 civil code that placed spouses "on the same level as regards their individual and relative rights."[7]

In short, well before rendering his *Phelps* decision and for decades afterward, Greene steadily advanced his vision of a self-perfecting republic governed by a mixed-sex popular sovereign, often by siding with unpopular groups and enlisting small armies of women – in his view, society's moral compass and a completing factor in public life. These commitments followed him into retirement, when he took on problems related to industrial and urban growth, juvenile poverty in Seattle, animal abuse, black rights, and seaman indigence. To say the least, Greene's activism generated mixed reviews. After his promotion to Chief Justice, admirers called him the "great" judge, the embodiment of justice, and a pillar of the bar; opponents dismissed him as a partisan "crank," at best a loose cannon, possibly a lunatic.[8]

The radically egalitarian idea that wives governed their own bodies and thus merited damages as individuals departed significantly from doctrines prevailing elsewhere. To be sure, Greene's brethren were bound by the territorial organic

[7] Roger Greene to Clarence Bagley, April 4, 1916, Clarence Bagley Papers, UWSC, Box I-31.
[8] Upon leaving the territorial bench, Greene entered law practice in Seattle with John McGraw, state governor after 1892, and others; see McGraw death notice in 22 *Green Bag 496* (1910) and Struve Collection, Box 77, Roger Greene file, UWSC. He struggled with poor health; e.g., Greene to Clarence Bagley, March 19, 1926, Clarence Bagley Papers, R. S. Greene File, UWSC. See also RSG to Bagley, on his inability to "read writing or print" or even "read what I am writing," ibid., February 15, 1926. There is no published account of Greene's life; unofficial writings are scarce. See the poorly documented manuscript history of the Territorial Supreme Court, Charles Beardsley Collection, Ch. 29, "Roger S. Greene: The Great Chief Justice," WSA-O, and Riddle, *The Old Radicalism*, 76. See also Barbara Babcock, "Women Defenders in the West," *Nevada Law Review*, Vol. 1 (2001), pp. 2–3. Impolite terms recur; e.g., WS, August 27, 1886 ("that crank").

act and periodic Congressional adjustments of territorial rights and powers. But Washington Territory, with other territories, occupied an ambiguous constitutional space: While the organic act possessed some of the attributes of state constitutions, in formal terms it was a federal statute and territorial courts were not clearly *federal* courts authorized to interpret federal texts. Such uncertainties were both liberating and perplexing. Unlike many other territories, moreover, Washington rubbed elbows with old Spanish colonies that had enshrined the notion of co-tenancy within marriage. As in Kansas, Montana, and the Dakotas, citizens did not vigorously resist female participation in community affairs, in part because women, in Washington as in other borderland societies, were essential to economic and social development. It made little sense to lock up women's capital in trusts or other passive sites. Settlers also viewed women of European ancestry, beginning with the so-called Mercer movement of the 1860s, as a civilizing force. But all women were prized – hence, the willingness of male settlers to accept the derisive term "squaw man" as a price to be paid for common-law or indigenous unions with Indian women.

Over time, new social imperatives fostered women's autonomy as well as greater stringency with irresponsible men. In 1861, for instance, justices of the Territorial Supreme Court ruled that costs paid to a wife of poor reputation whose husband had abandoned her might include anything, including items "beyond the bounds of the statute."[9] Women not only taught in rude schoolhouses but also helped to build and furnish them. They labored over gory benches in fisheries and canneries, baled hay, wielded hatchets, ran smokehouses, sold eggs and butter, cooked for lumberjacks, made clothing, delivered babies, managed shops, and tended livestock. It was usual for a woman to "sling her rifle over her shoulder and go after game, ... bring it down with a keen eye and a steady hand," butcher it, and cook it over a wood-burning stove.[10] Skewed sex ratios led publicists to call regularly for female migrants; without them, the territory lacked not only families but also women's capital and specialized knowledge of cooking, cheese making, spinning and weaving, gardening, nursing, baking, and primary education.

Given associations among property, social contribution, and full membership in the constituent power, a female presence in public life was likely, if not inevitable. At an early moment, both men and women surmounted cultural barriers: Daniel Richardson Bigelow, a prominent legislator and champion (with his wife, Ann Bigelow) of temperance and

---

[9] E.g., "Questions and Answers," *WS*, March 6, 1885 ("Do you practice under the code system? Yes; our code is based upon those of California, Ohio and New York"). Commentators worried about the impact of innovation on migration; this writer urged lawyers not to imagine that the territory's mixed system was "out of the world" or "under dominion of the king of the Cannibal Isles." See *J. K. Thorndike* v. *Elvira Thorndike*, 1 Wash Terr Rpts 175 (1861), 175–6; for briefs, Thorndike v. Thorndike, Case File No. 31, 1861, WSA-O.

[10] "Women of the West," *Belford's Magazine*, repr. in *WP*, November 4, 1888, p. 10.

equal suffrage, urged the legislative council in 1854 to expand the electorate because democratic theory required it. "I believe," he said, feeling his way along an unmarked path, "that those half breeds who have adopted the habits of civilization, pay taxes, etc., should have the right of suffrage. ... I can hardly see why all who are governed by law should not have a voice in making it." A man lacked the right to "restrain his fellow man in any of his natural liberties or to deprive him of his property without his consent"; on the same "democratic ground, ... women's right to vote is easier ridiculed than answered by sound argument."[11]

Also in 1854, Arthur Armstrong Denny, a celebrated co-founder of Seattle, unsuccessfully asked members of the first assembly to adopt equal suffrage: The organic act mandated a male electorate for the first election but left subsequent decisions about voter and office-holder qualifications to legislators:

[E]very white male inhabitant above the age of twenty-one years, who shall have been a resident of said Territory at the time of the passage of this act, and shall possess the qualifications hereinafter prescribed, shall be entitled to vote at the first election, and shall be eligible to any office within the said Territory; but the qualifications of voters and of holding office at all subsequent elections shall be ... prescribed by the Legislative Assembly, Provided, That the right of suffrage and of holding office shall be exercised only by citizens of the United States above the age of twenty-one years, and those above that age who shall have declared on oath their intention to become such.[12]

In 1867, assemblymen purged Confederate sympathizers from the electorate and enfranchised "all white American citizens above the age of twenty-one." Sex neutrality was accidental, but lawmaker Edward Eldridge quickly seized the moment.[13] So did suffragist Mary Olney Brown, who had witnessed women's attempts as early as 1867–68 to vote in local elections and written letters to prominent women encouraging them to vote at the next election. Neighborhood practices prevailed. She had been "looked upon as a fanatic"; the law seemed to be "in advance of the people." Even when some Republicans decided that lawmakers indeed had enfranchised white adults with "civilized" habits, women stayed home; said Olney, they lacked the "courage to go to the polls in defiance of custom."[14]

Undaunted by social practice, Brown announced in 1869, just as women began to vote in Wyoming, that she would join her husband on Election Day.

---

[11] Daniel Bigelow, 1854, quoted in Shanna Stevenson, "Daniel R. Bigelow: Early Washington Territory's Venerable Pioneer Lawyer and Statesman," *Columbia* (Winter 1993–94), pp. 31–2.

[12] An Act to Establish the Territorial Government of Washington, Statutes at Large, 32nd Congress, Session II, Ch. XC, Section 5, Qualifications of Voters, p. 174. On Denny, see Agnes Peterson, "Arthur Armstrong Denny: A Bibliography," *Washington Historical Quarterly*, Vol. 13 (July 1922), p. 209.

[13] See Charles K. Wiggins, "John P. Hoyt and Women's Suffrage," *Washington State Bar News*, Vol. 43, No. 1 (January 1989), p. 17.

[14] Mary Olney Brown, "Account of Attempts to Vote in Washington Territory," in Susan B. Anthony et al., eds., *History of Woman Suffrage*, Vol. III (Salem, NH, repr. 1985), pp. 780–1.

Conservative neighbors raised a "hue and cry" about a wife and mother determined to wade into "the filthy pool of politics." But, she reasoned, even if the law had not been intended for women's benefit, it was time to take advantage of it. Some "gentlemen" at her door tried to dissuade her; hecklers assailed her husband's manhood. Brown held fast. When election officials denied her a ballot, she delivered a lecture redolent of Radical-Republican constitutionalism and white privilege to a captive audience of voters: "I am a 'person,' declared by the fourteenth amendment to be a citizen, and ... I am a native-born citizen of the same race and color of these gentlemen by whom I am surrounded" – Indian men were lawfully voting – "and whose votes you do not hesitate to receive"; even without the territorial statute, the amendment had enfranchised women.[15]

Election judges turned Brown away. By mid-1870, however, tides began to turn. In the air was talk not only about suffrage but also about the formalization of a community-property regime akin to Oregon's and California's. Brown later contended that, on the suffrage front – if not on the rapidly mutating domestic-relations scene, about which she was silent – many Washingtonians had examined the law and decided that women had a right to vote. In May 1870, she published an appeal urging women to seize the moment. On the appointed day, a respected woman organized a picnic; a number of female revelers "handed in their ballots as if they had always been accustomed to voting, and everything passed off pleasantly."[16] But legislators were skittish. While the organic act empowered legislators to fashion an electorate after the initial organizational election, the neighborhood's customary constitution militated against equal suffrage. Moreover, if the Civil War amendments excluded women – and, by the mid-1870s, federal judges were reading them stringently – legislators would be advancing women's rights beyond federal guidelines.[17]

Suffragists persisted, wielding many of the tenets of republican constitutionalism to which Americans had turned since the 1780s, buttressed by the emancipatory readings of constitutional texts then prevailing within national reform circles. In 1871, Susan B. Anthony visited Washington while traveling with Oregon suffragist Abigail Duniway and others to secure equal suffrage beyond Wyoming. She addressed citizens in public squares and schools; in the territory's first woman suffrage convention; and, by invitation, in a joint session of the Washington Assembly. Anthony congratulated legislators for bravery; this was the first time in American history that a woman had addressed lawmakers in session. She wasted no time: As citizens and persons, women surely could vote "under the guarantees of the 14th and 15th Amendments." She was less interested in the word "male" than in the

---

[15] Ibid.   [16] Brown, Account, *HWS*, Vol. III, pp. 784–6.
[17] See *Minor* v. *Happersett*, 88 U.S. 162(1874) and *Bradwell* v. *Illinois*, 83 U.S. 130 (1873).

seemingly revolutionary language of the Fourteenth. In her view, as in Brown's, republican governments existed to secure property, including property in rights, to every member of the constituent power, male or female.[18]

But Anthony went further, as Roger Greene would do in *Phelps*, invoking self-sovereignty and a citizen's right to law: "The right of self-protection has been conceded from the earliest ages of antiquity. . . . The theory of our Government is embodied in the Declaration of Independence which declares that 'all men are created equal; . . . endowed by their Creator with certain inalienable rights; . . . 'that to secure these rights, Governments were Instituted. . . , deriving their just powers from the consent of the governed.'" Paramount was an obligation to resist tyranny. Thomas Jefferson had declared, after all, that, whenever government became "'destructive of these ends, it is the right of the people to alter or abolish it, and institute a new government.'" How could this be done peaceably without equal suffrage? The disenfranchised did not experience freedom, and servitude violated the Thirteenth Amendment. Once women overcame "the restraint imposed by popular sentiment" and voted, they would see that political autonomy unlocked doors "to knowledge, to equal wages, to honor, to prosperity." She also predicted a large migration of women to the territory.[19]

In November, 1871, Anthony addressed a convention in Olympia, called to encourage "concert of action" among women voters, teach parliamentary procedures, and discuss the duties of public officers so that women might be ready, even at the "sacrifice of personal feeling," for civic duties. Eventually, if not at once, women would vote and hold public office. Organizers included Mary Olney Brown, Ann Bigelow, and fourteen others. The association resolved, first, to secure women's "equality in the enjoyment of every right, moral, social and political," chief among them "her privilege to representation in a Government" that taxed her property and punished infractions of law. Second, members sought judicial recognition of civil equality for women, whether married or not.[20]

For many traditionalists, nightmares about a runaway train filled with wild-eyed women had been realized. On one side, the editor of Olympia's most influential newspaper had been won over by Anthony's graceful and forceful arguments: While suffrage might be inessential for women "surrounded by all the luxuries of wealth," it might be as "essential as the life blood to those who labor early and late for their daily bread." Who could oppose right and justice? Citizens might honestly differ about the social merits of impartiality, but in the end, it was

[18] Susan B. Anthony, "'Women Already Voters': Speech to the Territorial Legislature of Washington," in Gordon, ed., *Selected Papers of Susan B. Anthony and Elizabeth Cady Stanton*, Vol. III (October 19, 1871), pp. 456–7, or Papers of Elizabeth Cady Stanton and Susan B. Anthony, Microfilm Ed., Reel 15, pp. 793–4.

[19] "Legislative," *WS*, October 21, 1871. See also Anthony, "Women Already Voters." Washington legislators, however, did not regularly tout women's rights as a magnet for settlement.

[20] "Founding Convention of the Woman Suffrage Association and Grand Lodge of Good Templars, November 8–9, Resolutions," and "Woman Suffrage Convention," *NN*, October 27, 1871, and November 17, 1871.

simply "a question of right." On the other side, and especially in counties east of the Cascades, reformers stood accused of ingratitude, ignorance, and degeneracy. In eastern Walla Walla, a reporter pronounced Anthony's schoolhouse lecture "scattering." One of her strong points, he gathered, was that wives did not enjoy their "full share of the financial income of the partnership." Did not half of all married women fail to contribute "by their earnings to the funds of the concern?" Did they not "simply manage the household, control the servants, and entertain company," while the man paid bills? God had created man with "knotted muscles and prominent cords"; women's anatomy suited her for "dolls and needlework."[21] In Seattle, journalist Beriah Brown pronounced Anthony less a reformer than a "Revolutionist" aiming to smash the family and the "legitimacy of offspring, recognizing no religion but self-worship." Suffragism would "let loose upon society a pestilential brood"; the scheme was "coarse, sensual and agrarian, the worst phase of French infidelity and communism." Eastern wags sometimes agreed: In 1883, the *Christian Index* noted that Washington was about to universalize the vote and urged every emancipated woman to "betake herself to the Territory. We can spare her here."[22]

Cooler heads gradually prevailed. On October 14, 1871, Daniel Bigelow had introduced a toe-in-the-water bill that would have allowed women to vote on their own enfranchisement. It failed.[23] In its place, however, legislators adopted a school law permitting any citizen to run and vote for school offices (legal voters included tax-paying, twenty-one-year-old inhabitants in residence for three months). Then, instead of amending or repealing the vague 1867 law, the Assembly provided in late 1871 that, with the exception of school elections, women would not vote until Congress acted. Despite the organic act's seeming grant of legislative power to shape the electorate, lawmakers lacked an authoritative reading of the act. Even if they had correctly inferred legislative power after the *first* round of elections, which classes might then be included? Were women "householders" if they lived with men? Did the phrase "administration of elections" refer to procedures, voter classes, or both? And what about obligations? Here, the organic act was silent.[24] But juries were

---

[21] "Woman Suffrage," WS, October 1, 1871; unidentified clipping, "Walla Walla, Washington Terr, September 23, 1871," in Papers of Susan B. Anthony and Elizabeth Cady Stanton, Microfilm Edition, Reel 15, p. 754.

[22] "Miss Anthony's Lectures," *Territorial Dispatch & Alaska Times* (Seattle), November 6, 1871; "Glimpses and Glances," *Christian Index*, December 13, 1883.

[23] Washington Territorial Assembly, Journal of the House of Representatives, October 1871, Speech of the Hon. D. R. Bigelow, on Female Suffrage..., October 14, 1871, WSA-O; and Stella Pearce, "Suffrage in the Pacific Northwest: Old Oregon and Washington," *Washington Historical Quarterly* (1912), pp. 106–14. See also T. A. Larson, "The Woman Suffrage Movement in Washington," *Pacific Northwest Quarterly*, Vol. 67 (April 1976), pp. 780–8.

[24] Act to Establish a Common School System..., Acts of the Territorial Assembly of Washington, 1871, pp. 15, 27; An Act Relating to Elections, Acts of the Territorial Assembly of Washington, 1871, p. 36. The organic act was reprinted in Acts of the Territory of Washington, 1879, pp. 291–306.

powder kegs. During the same tour, Anthony visited California to support Laura Fair, convicted by male jurors of murdering her lover. No sooner had Anthony criticized masculine juries than listeners morphed into a "furious mob." Anthony cancelled her tour and fled to Yosemite to recover: "Never in all my experience have I been under such fire."[25]

"A SEPARATE ESTATE AND INALIENABLE POSSESSION"

For the moment, direct representation in government as co-sovereigns had eluded Washington's women. In 1875, two years after the defeat of yet another Eldridge juggernaut, a bill sponsored by Elwood Evans also failed, but by a vote of eleven to fifteen. Untested federal amendments threatened variously to liberate or blacklist women, and assemblymen lacked confidence in the organic act as a foundation for egalitarian reform. Help came instead from the inter-related realms of contract, property, and domestic-relations law. As a launching pad for property-based imputations of constitutional equality, these changes proved to be far sturdier than national instruments, particularly as federal courts began to rein in Radical-Republican idealism. In effect, Washingtonians carved out a legal space remarkably free, at least for the moment, of federal constraints.

Since the 1840s, Elizabeth Cady Stanton's followers had pointed to relations between economic independence within marriage and self-sovereignty; neither Stanton nor any of the female lawyers practicing in western territories would have been surprised to learn that co-equality within households and in the marketplace could neutralize or weaken the doctrine of marital unity, a primary underpinning of the law of coverture. Who could deny ballots to co-sovereigns? As Stanton put it in 1854, "The right to property will, of necessity, compel us in due time to the exercise of our right to the elective franchise, and then naturally follows the right to hold office."[26] Some years later, she pointed to recognition of women's property rights as an indispensable precondition for "the radical reconstruction of the marriage relation," beginning with the contract itself, which then could be viewed as a civil convenience struck up between co-equals, entirely dependent on mutuality. Without co-equality, married women would never be able to claim co-headship with men – a singularly powerful foundation for enfranchisement.[27]

[25] For the Fair incident, see Babcock, "Women Defenders in the West," pp. 7–8. On appeal, another all-male jury reversed the conviction. See also Carole Haber, *The Trials of Laura Fair: Sex, Murder, and Insanity in the Victorian West* (Chapel Hill, NC, 2013).

[26] "Address to the New York Legislature," 1854, in Beth M. Waggenspack, *The Search for Self-Sovereignty: The Oratory of Elizabeth Cady Stanton* (Westport, CT, 1989), p. 103.

[27] Stanton addressed the related topics of marital estates, the marital contract, and divorce many times; but see "Address of Elizabeth Cady Stanton on the Divorce Bill [in New York Senate]," 1861, Vol. I, in Gordon, *Papers of Elizabeth Cady Stanton and Susan B. Anthony*, Vol. 1, pp. 405–8; and for "radical reconstruction," ECS to Isabella Beecher Hooker, May 24, 1869, ibid., Vol. II, pp. 244–6.

In 1871, lawmakers erected two milestones: Even as legislators expressly ruled out female participation in general elections, they authorized an election to secure permission to convene a pre-statehood constitutional convention.[28] In addition, they passed a community-property statute defining the rights of married people. Now, spouses individually retained property brought into the marriage with its proceeds "as though no marriage existed"; thereafter, assets acquired by the joint or individual labors of the pair, along with earnings, redounded to the community, unless kept apart in separate estates. But the sketchily drafted law, likely a poor imitation of Oregon's older statute, betrayed inexperience with statutory construction and civilian practices. The law provided that property owned at marriage would be separate property; yet a wife could still buy land "for her own benefit" with no apparent limitation on the source of funds. Wives but not husbands could retain earnings from separate property when "necessary," as when men failed to provide support. Section 23 abolished dower.[29]

Revisions followed. As of November, 1873, spouses retained property owned before marriage as well as assets later amassed by gift or inheritance, with all resulting income, as separate property; partners could dispose of assets as they chose. All other property acquired by either person became community property. Legislators addressed spousal agency: As provided in common-law states, husbands retained the management and control of the woman's separate property during marriage. But "no alienation, sale or conveyance of the real property of the wife, or any part thereof, or any right, title, or interest therein, and no contract for the alienation, sale or conveyance of the same . . . and no lien or encumbrance" would be valid unless undertaken in writing by husband and wife, acknowledged by her. Nor could he sell her separate property to settle his own debts without written permission.[30]

Over the next six years, emendation continued; by 1881, revisions and fresh thinking coalesced in a new law code. A husband could not sell or otherwise dispose of real property unless the wife joined with him. He possessed "absolute power of disposition" only over a couple's personal property, and, even there, the law exempted property described in separate estates, pre-marital agreements, or wills. In keeping with previous legislation and practices elsewhere, lawmakers again disallowed curtesy and dower but

[28] Act to Submit to the Voters of Washington Territory . . . a Proposition for Calling a Convention to Frame a State Constitution . . . , Acts of the Territorial Assembly of Washington, 1871, p. 98.
[29] Act Defining the Rights of Persons and Property as Affected by Marriage, Acts of the Territorial Assembly of Washington, 1871, pp. 67, 70, 73. For the Oregon law, see An Act Relating to the Rights of Married Women, 1872, Laws of Oregon, Section 1. See also Inara K. Scott, "A Window for Change: Conflicting Ideologies and Legal Reforms in Late Nineteenth-Century Oregon," *Willamette Law Review*, Vol. 37 (2001), pp. 449–50. On the legality of the abolition of dower, see *Hamilton* v. *Hirsch and Hayden*, 2 Wash Terr Rpts 223 (July 1884), discussed below.
[30] An Act Defining the Rights of Husband and Wife, Acts of the Territorial Assembly of Washington, 1873, pp. 450–4.

made a woman's wealth and earnings separate property, if kept apart from joint accounts. Finally, nothing prevented reassignment of managerial responsibilities to women by mutual agreement, and either partner could request a trustee if a spouse mismanaged or squandered community holdings.[31]

On the all-important question of unitary household command, the common-law presumption of male headship and a husband's indivisible sovereignty (or *petit* kingship) within families had largely disappeared; in its place was the civilian-inspired, organic concept of co-tenancy or co-headship – i.e., ownership of and title to the entire estate jointly and severally. Who could contest the sovereignty of women (or contend for disabilities of sex) if spouses were equally vested? Propertied citizens formed part of a popular sovereign unless disqualified for cause; at least in theory, every otherwise qualified married woman authorized exercises of governmental power, as did men, and claimed a right to representation.

Nevertheless, and notwithstanding criticism of the law of coverture – one writer called it the source of women's "bondage"[32] – both patriarchy and judicial paternalism remained in significant residue. To hedge women against the machinations of dishonest men, for instance, legislators made special provision for the security of women's separate property (i.e., the portion reserved for her own use, in trust or otherwise, after marriage, distinguishable from joint tenancy within the marital estate). As in older jurisdictions, legislators invited wives to record separate property with county courts. And men did retain ordinary administrative powers over wives' separate real property during marriage. This was to rearticulate the old idea that, while women retained title to inherited land, men were presumptive administrators in transactions short of sale, supposedly to eliminate uncertainty, prevent waste, and preserve property for heirs. Nor did lawmakers eliminate men's right to dictate women's domicile.[33]

With economic depression lifting and boosterism well afoot, relations between the sexes further mutated, beginning with constitutional convention delegates' contributions to women's political and civil emancipation. In autumn of 1878, fifteen delegates met at Walla Walla to draft a document for submission with a statehood petition. Washington would have been the first state to approach Congress with a mixed-sex electorate, should the document provide for it; at virtually the same moment, the hotly contested Sixteenth Amendment again lay on Congressional tables. Eldridge, Duniway, and a

---

[31] An Act Relating to and Defining the Property Rights of Husband and Wife, Laws of Washington Territory, 1879–80, pp. 77–81; or An Act to Establish and Protect the Rights of Married Women, Papers of Governor Elisha Ferry, Legislation, 1879, Box K-1–5 (the original act), WSA-O.

[32] E.g., "The Bondage of English Women," repr. *PSWC*, October 6, 1882.

[33] An Act Relating to and Defining the Property Rights of Husband and Wife, Laws of Washington Territory, 1879–80, p. 81.

number of other, local activists lobbied hard for a constitution with impartial suffrage; they also submitted a petition of 581 citizens for a "true Republican Constitution" that guaranteed to all citizens the elective franchise. More remarkable, one delegate urged a provision, informed in part by California's draft constitution, ensuring that no person in the state could be "denied the right to pursue any lawful occupation, calling, or profession, on account of Sex, nor shall such right be in any manner abridged on account of Sex."[34]

Courage was perhaps contagious. On the eighth day, participants considered another resolution to constitutionalize the 1873 community-property statutes. Lawyer Benjamin Franklin Dennison argued that the new framework should spare married women the disabilities of coverture and "plainly define their rights to make and enforce contracts relating to their separate property and personal rights." Surely all property brought into marriage or acquired afterward by gift, devise, or descent would be separate property; all else gathered during marriage by either partner would be common property. Others urged extra-constitutional delineation of the rights of married people, including equal rights to custody and in children's labor. Finally, delegates sought to keep wives' separate property away from husbands' debtors, the entirety to be managed by her as if she were unmarried.[35]

At the same time, delegates drew a bright line between civil and political equality. Section 1 of Article IV provided that every man over the age of twenty-one and a resident was an elector; that any twelve persons within the electorate constituted a trial jury; and that grand juries consisted of seven persons, both voters and householders, any five of whom could indict. In the end, conventioneers promised only to put woman suffrage on the ballot in a ratification election as a separate article. School offices and suffrage were extended to both sexes. A last-ditch measure (printed later under "miscellaneous") allowed legislators, in the event voters rejected equal suffrage during ratification, to either hold a new election or adopt equal-suffrage legislation.[36] Male voters accepted the constitution but rejected political equality by a margin of almost 3 to 1, in part because anti-suffragists yoked it to a poison-pill prohibition article ("It shall be lawful for the electors of any county, municipal corporation or precinct . . . to prohibit by a majority vote the sale or disposal of spirituous liquors in less quantities than one gallon except for medicinal or mechanical purposes"). The governor's post-convention

---

[34] See Constitution of Washington Territory, Article V, Section 24. See also Proceedings of the 1878 Convention (Walla Walla), Papers of the Secretary of State, State Constitution, Box 96-A-63, pp. 35–7, 50–4, 80–1, and passim, WSA-O. California adopted a state constitution in 1879, publ. 1880; Article I, section 21, provided that no "special privileges or immunities shall ever be granted which may not be altered, revoked, or repealed by the Legislature, nor shall any citizen, or class of citizens, be granted privileges or immunities which, upon the same terms, shall not be granted to all citizens"; The Constitution . . . , Statutes of California (1880), p. xxiv.

[35] Proceedings of the 1878 Convention (Walla Walla), pp. 50–4, 80–1, WSA-O. [36] Ibid.

message briefly laid out both proposals; mostly, though, he urged railroad completion to energize "productive industry."[37]

Then, in October, 1879, and without much fanfare, legislators moved dramatically to secure an egalitarian society. According to eye-witnesses, a suffrage bill failed in the Council (or upper house) after passage by two-thirds in the lower house.[38] But it failed by only two votes. In November, legislators considered a bill (the fate of which is unclear) by which adults whether married or not might be able to adopt children. More important, they amended the 1873 community-property act to further "establish and protect the rights of married women"; despite disagreements about phraseology and rumblings about back-door suffragism, modifications found their way into the 1881 law code. Now, men and women managed marital estates in almost every respect as tenants in severalty. Most amazing of all, with the exception of the polity, lawmakers established an equal-rights regime, in the process reserving the right to institute equal suffrage: "All laws which impose or recognize civil disabilities upon a wife, which are not imposed or recognized as existing as to the husband, are hereby abolished, [p]rovided, That this shall not confer the right to vote or hold office upon the wife, except as is otherwise provided by law; and for any unjust usurpation of her natural or property rights, she shall have the same right to appeal, in her own individual name, to the courts of law or equity for redress and protection that the husband has." In a shift from 1871 policies by which women claimed custody of children only if men were unavailable, lawmakers mandated joint custody and ceded men's rights in children's labor: The "rights and the responsibilities of the parents . . . shall be equal, and the mother shall be as fully entitled to the custody, control and earnings of the children as the father; and in case of the father's death, the mother shall come into as . . . complete control of the children" as a father did when the mother died.[39]

Taken together, these acts also aided single women and widows; if married women relieved of common-law disabilities might bargain with men for equal wages, so might their unattached sisters, particularly as formal changes began to seep into legal culture. It was one thing to exercise privileges by virtue of a legislative grant, and quite another to claim them as a consequence of co-equal,

---

[37] Brown, Account, in Anthony, *History of Woman Suffrage*, Vol. III, p. 786. See also "Governor's Message," *SDPI*, October 9, 1979. (Article 1 read, "No person, who is otherwise a qualified elector, shall be denied the right, on account of sex, to vote or hold office . . . .")

[38] Abigail Duniway, "Letter from Olympia, From the *Oregonian*," *NN*, October 18, 1883.

[39] "The adoption of children," *SDPI*, November 4, 1879. The document in question was House Bill No. 80, An Act to Authorize the adoption of children. See also An Act to Establish and Protect the Rights of Married Women, Laws of Washington Territory, 1879–80, p. 151, and "The adoption of children," *SPDI*, November 4, 1879. For the 1871 law, see Laws of Washington Territory, Chapter 32, 1871, p. 89. In November, 1883, lawmakers strengthened penalties for insobriety and allowed any family member to lodge a complaint against a drunk; wives could maintain suits in their own names and retain damages as separate property; An Act to Amend Chapter CXIII of the Code of Washington, Entitled, "To Declare Certain Persons Habitual Drunkards . . . ;" Laws of Washington Territory, 1883, pp. 32–3.

propertied agency and investiture. To escape dependency of any kind was to move closer to full membership in the constituent power. In November, 1879, an editor in remote LaConner cast aspersions only partly in jest on the status and authority of dependent classes in the territory: It would be appropriate and just if legislators disenfranchised paupers and criminals of every description. "It is not always a man's own fault that he is dependent upon charity, but it does show that he is deficient in some of the qualities that should distinguish the sovereign citizens of a republic."[40]

THE CASE OF RICHARD HOLYOKE, A MARRIED MAN

To what extent were Washingtonians naturalizing egalitarianism? Prominent citizens certainly urged women to exercise initiative, as when Olympia's Clarence Bagley urged young women to "stay upon the farm and cultivate it to their own growth and good, and to that of the whole world. In this way may women show their independence, their ability to stand alone."[41] Law's stories provide additional evidence of citizens' fluency in community legalities. During the August, 1879, term, for example, just as Washingtonians enacted an innovative equal-rights regime, Roger Greene's Third District Court in Seattle heard an appeal in the well-publicized case of *Wilterwood* v. *Stafford*, which further illustrated citizens' ability, for better or worse, to manipulate legal rules. A married woman had pled coverture in order to escape contract performance while living apart from her husband. Greene described the plight of wives when subject to the full weight of coverture and noted recent alterations in the law of domestic relations. Then, with visible annoyance, he ruled that, if a woman dealt in property and lived separately, she could be sued. "Taking the abilities of an independent residence and maintenance, she must take also its disabilities. If she can sue, it is because she can contract; and if she can contract, she can be sued."[42]

Another decision vividly revealed spousal familiarity with legal constructs that could be manipulated to advantage. In 1882, Greene's colleagues, after a year of evidence gathering beyond lower-court documents, heard arguments in *Richard Holyoke* v. *D. B. Jackson*. In 1881, Holyoke had been sued for breach of contract and fraud in a land sale; Jackson allegedly had falsely claimed title and a right to sell, then failed to convey the deed. The facts were not disputed: In April, 1880, Jackson had run into Holyoke – a land speculator and sawmill supervisor – in Port Gamble, where Holyoke had stopped on a trip to Olympia. Jackson had been eyeing one of the Holyokes' town lots in Seattle for some time and offered to buy it for 3,000 dollars. Holyoke accepted. But, according to Jackson, he said that he could not sign over the deed because "his wife [was] not

---

[40] [Allen Weir], "The Suffrage Question," *PSWA* [LaConner], November 20, 1879.
[41] Clarence Bagley, "The Wives of Farmers," *PSWC*, December 8, 1882. Bagley was a scholar and pro-suffrage moderate.
[42] "District Court Decision," *SDPI*, August 27, 1879.

with him." Jackson paid 200 dollars' earnest money; Holyoke promised to talk to his wife and return within ten days so that Jackson might receive the deed and pay the balance.[43]

Subsequent events are murky. Richard supposedly returned home, only to learn that his wife refused to sell. Under community-property rules, he could not alienate real property that formed part of the marital estate without his wife's voluntary, written agreement. Richard later described an exchange that fairly bristled with self-possession: "Well – she said very pointedly, she would not sign it unless she was compelled to, She said, I will go to Seattle and see a lawyer and if I am compelled to sign it I will but not unless – I came to Seattle with her." There, as Richard put it, they visited lawyers, "I agreeing to sell and my wif[e] refusing to sign." Attorneys told her that "she could not be compelled to sign the deed unless she wished to, [s]he said she would not – was not willing, and would not sign the deed." Richard was willing to sign over the deed, but counsel told him that "it would only complicate matters, unless my wife was willing to sign with me, I better not do it." Holyoke returned to Port Gamble. While his wife waited at the wharf, he found Jackson and witnesses, flaunted a money pouch, and tried to return the deposit with interest. An irate Jackson rejected the offer and filed suit.[44]

Richard Holyoke's motives perhaps were impure. As a Seattle real-estate agent testified, April of 1880 had been a "lively time in property"; a real-estate boom had been afoot even as Holyoke and Jackson completed their business. Although the lot was worth $3,000 or $3,500 on April 17, its value probably soared within days of their agreement. A long-time resident of Front Street confirmed the fact of a boom. Most damningly, land agent August Mackintosh recalled that, on April 17, one lot already had been worth $4,000 or $4,500, and that a "considerable rise" in property values appeared, lasting for a week. Experts agreed that, by about April 25, the Holyoke lot was worth as much as 5,000 dollars. Counsel for Jackson spent days establishing the lot's value, arguing inaccurately that married men could sell land alone. Holyoke's lawyers stood on the plain words of the statute, which specified written spousal agreement. They also moved to strike virtually all of the damaging testimony. But the evidence stood, powerfully suggesting that the pair had conspired to escape a badly timed bargain.[45]

What happened in Seabeck? Perhaps Richard had told the truth: He had been hoist on his own petard. Or perhaps the Holyokes learned that their property had doubled in value and conspired to avoid conveyance. Richard may have

---

[43] Richard Holyoke v. D. V. Jackson, Transcript of District Court proceedings, July term 1882, testimony of D. V. Jackson, Case File No. 331, WSA, pp. 50–1. The first name of Holyoke's "wife" nowhere appears. See social notices, *SDPI*, November 4, 1882: "Richard Holyoke, superintendent of the Seabeck sawmill, is at present in this city."

[44] Richard Holyoke v. D. V. Jackson, Case File No. 331, p. 191.

[45] Ibid., District Court proceedings, July term 1882, testimony of Henry L. Lester, M. R. Maddocks, and Angus Mackintosh, pp. 55–8, 61–3.

wanted to let the bubble expand, or Mrs. Holyoke may have distrusted her husband's penchant for speculation. In any case, the pair could and did rely on detailed knowledge of a married-woman's authority within the marital estate: The wife owned land in severalty; Richard's lawful management ended when he attempted to transfer title without her agreement. Moreover, the proceedings, whether feigned or not, required Richard to endure humiliation for unmanliness in exchanges with Jackson, lawyers, and witnesses. Throughout the trial, he insisted that he was still willing to sell but that his wife was not. In court, lawyers circled around unmanly deportment, trying to shame him into recantation or capitulation. On one occasion, Holyoke confessed that, when he had told one of Jackson's lawyers that his "wife would not sign, he said well I guess she will, I said she would not – I told him my wife was down board on the steamer he could go down and see her, he did not wish to." His wife shared the pants, or so he admitted under oath.[46]

When Holyoke lost, his attorneys filed an appeal in June, 1882, contending that Richard had been powerless to consummate the sale, given the wife's power to bar the performance of a real-estate contract undertaken by the husband alone, and the territory's obligation to defend co-tenancy. Jackson's counsel argued fraud and Jackson's vested right in the contract, given earnest-money acceptance. On July 22, 1882, Roger Greene relieved Richard Holyoke of responsibility for damages upon repayment of earnest money with interest. Given the justice's participation in the framing of community-property legislation, he no doubt welcomed an opportunity to interpret his handiwork. The bulk of his opinion in *Holyoke* v. *Jackson*, which enjoyed a long career in Washington jurisprudence, painstakingly explored relevant sections of the new law code. If the question was whether a husband, without his wife's agreement, might contract to sell community property, the answer was a resounding no. As of 1879, spouses were "a compound creature of the statute, called a community." Sometimes, that creature was inaccurately deemed a "species of partnership." But, within the estate, the "proprietary interest of husband and wife are equal, and those interests do not seem to be united merely, but unified; not mixed or blent, but identified." In land dealings, "husband and wife are, by the law of 1879, joint trustees for their mutual benefit in the community. . . . [N]either can act without the other." To be sure, management could be vested in either or both by mutual consent, but neither claimed greater proprietary rights than the other; while legislators in 1873 had vested administrative powers in men, the 1879 law laid them "upon husband and wife together" – a departure from the common-law and a long stride toward co-headship.[47]

Egalitarian norms, including women's equal right to work, surfaced often. A resident of an anti-suffrage county, to give an example, while disgusted with

---

[46] Ibid., District Court proceedings, jury instructions, p. 66.

[47] Ibid., District Court proceedings, Brief for the Defendant and Plaintiff in Error, Brief for the Defendant and Original Opinion, p. 4; *Richard Holyoke* v. *D. B. Jackson*, 3 Wash Terr Rpts 235 (July 1882), 238–9, 241. Where texts differ, I use the published report.

"female ranters," averred that employers always had "room for women, as for men, and *she is as much entitled to it*, when by a proper preparation she is fitted for filling the place."[48] Public prints conveyed information about rules of the game. Witness this 1882 letter from rural Cheney (almost certainly written by attorney Lelia Robinson) conveying legal minutia: If a woman with either real or personal property married, she retained control of it, same as a man does"; but all property acquired after marriage became "community property, belonging as much to the wife as to the husband." If a man died first, his wife retained control of the entire property, "the same as the husband does now," without further ado. If he could no longer work, she could support him with her money. If a husband died with property and the wife had none beyond community property amassed after marriage, she could assume title to all of his property without paying a lawyer, "as she must ... do now, simply because she is a woman." In some respects, the mother's legal personality still carried no weight; she had been "foolish enough to be born a *female* instead of a *male*." But the idea of woman's inferiority to man was losing ground; intelligent men were "taking up the matter of equal rights in earnest. ... [W]hat I want," she added, paraphrasing a well-known, pro-suffrage slogan, "is equal rights with man in every respect. I do not want any more, and will not be satisfied with any less."[49]

Increasingly, seaboard activists contended that equal suffrage, far from damaging the case for statehood, actually advanced it. To make the point, they circulated letters from Wyoming Governor John W. Hoyt, a convert to the cause after some years' experience with mixed-sex politics. As he told Susan B. Anthony, a woman "goes from her home to the polls with a sense of duty performed, standing on her own footing and speaking for herself. ... The discussion of public questions between man and wife tends to mutual respect. ... The husband is proud of the woman, as a fellow citizen, who is his wife."[50] But opposition was stiff – beginning with members of Congress who failed to see, as Mary Olney Brown put it, that a territory should be denied statehood, not for democratization, but for proposing a "class constitution, thus depriving half the citizens of their constitutional rights."[51] Moreover, well beyond 1883, Spokane-area conservatives virtually ignored the question of political equality. Eastern Washington was a world apart from Puget Sound – a thinly settled land of hard-scrabble ranching and "rough-looking men" driving logs down the Yakima River, some of whom were "on a bender." These were occupations to

---

[48] "Woman as a Bread-Winner," *WWU*, December 23, 1882. Emphasis added.

[49] "L.M.M.," pseud., "Property Rights, Cheney, February 13, 1882," *NN*, February 23, 1882.

[50] Governor John W. Hoyt, *National Citizen and Ballot Box*, May 20, 1881, Elizabeth Cady Stanton and Susan B. Anthony Papers, Microfilm Edition, Reel 21, Frame 1006. See also "Woman Suffrage in Wyoming," *SDPI*, November 25, 1882, and "Advantages of Woman Suffrage, From the Boomerang," *SDPI*, February 1, 1883 ("Woman suffrage [rests on] equity, ... confirmed by experience").

[51] Mary Olney Brown, "From an Old Worker, Olympia, May 11, 1882," *NN*, May 18, 1882.

which "no weak manhood need aspire." When Spokane Falls journalists gave play to women's rights, they invariably had in mind wealth production: In mid-1882, one writer grudgingly conceded that equal suffrage might result in better wages for underpaid shop and cottage workers.[52]

Everywhere, women won praise for economic savvy. In 1878, Seattle residents learned of a woman in Colfax who had opened a hotel in advance of settlement to support nine children and provide a public service. The now-valuable hotel was in itself a "strong argument" in favor of an equal-suffrage state constitution. When an anti-suffragist from Falls City predicted that female voters would no longer take care of their children, A. H. Page of Seattle tied politics to economy. She had come west to "find her liege lord, and owner, keeping house alone" and had "set things to right." But, she said, "I am a woman, and I have talked with hundreds of my fellow sisters." Many had never "had a care for themselves. . . . But let them lose a husband and father of a large flock of little ones . . . and where does she find herself? Her property put under administration, a guardian appointed for her babies." She urged public and private democracy: In a school a hundred miles away, a man and woman were teachers. The man instructed fewer than thirty pupils, the woman more than fifty; yet he received for his services "nearly double that of the woman. . . . Think you if women had a vote these things would be so?"[53]

"OUR OWN SALVATION IS IN PADDLING OUR OWN CANOES"

As civil equality gained adherents, its political analogue seemed less exotic. On October 26, on the heels of passage of an anti-quackery statute, legislators confronted a bill "to allow women to vote and exercise the rights to which they are naturally entitled." The measure failed by two votes, as in 1879. But Abigail Duniway suspected that another "good bill" might be in the offing. Opponents insisted, as usual, that only a crazed handful sought the franchise. But impatience mounted. "Really wanted? Just as if this thing had not been petitioned for . . . by thousands of women . . . , session after session." Two years earlier, a petition signed by 730 citizens, mostly women, asked for equal rights; the memorial had been "laughed over . . . and remarks made about it of such an insulting nature" that women finally gave up in disgust. This statute, however, seemed to Duniway to be superior to antecedents; its sponsors, possessed of a "more liberal spirit," did not "narrow [their] views down to the thickness of a hair."[54]

---

[52] "Into Eastern Washington by Rail," *SDPI*, August 22, 1882. See also, e.g., "Washington" (on Mormonism), February 25, 1882; "Our Farmers and Gardeners," August 2, 1881; "A Great Change" (on railroads), June 9, 1881; "Difficulty with Indians," March 31, 1881; editorial, April 28, 1881 (on railroads); "Dairying," June 20, 1881; all *SFC*. Dozens more could be cited. For suffrage and wages, see "What Female Suffrage Will Do," *SFC*, July 11, 1882.

[53] "What a Woman Can Do," *SDPI*, October 8, 1878; anonymous letter, ibid., October 18, 1878; A. H. Page, "The Woman Suffrage Question," ibid., October 23, 1878.

[54] "Reporter," pseud., "Washington Legislature," *OR*, October 29, 1881. Damage in original.

FIGURE 2.2. Abigail Scott Duniway (1834–1915) of Portland, OR, owner-editor of the influential *New Northwest*, tirelessly organized women for suffrage throughout the region; n.d. From the collections of the Oregon Historical Society, Salem, Oregon. Image 78930. Used by permission.

In the end, constitutional principle – including popular sovereignty and bars against takings of property in rights – won the day, as when the old-guard suffragist Sarah Hughes insisted in 1880 that, in her name, Elizabeth Cady Stanton "<u>demand</u> that the government <u>restore</u> to me that which it has <u>unlawfully</u> and <u>unjustly</u> deprived me of. Either by a sixteenth amendment or an act of Congress declaring all free and equal without regard to sex."[55] On

---

[55] Sarah H. Hughes (Slaughter, W. T.) to Elizabeth Cady Stanton, May 6, 1880, National Woman Suffrage Association Collection, in Papers of Elizabeth Cady Stanton and Susan B. Anthony, Microfilm Edition, Reel 5, pp. 507–8. Emphasis in the original. The Declaratory Act idea was a feature of the so-called New Departure.

November 1, 1881, a gathering of suffrage supporters in Columbia resolved to pursue equal rights with "fresh courage" on the "plain principles of justice that underlie a government that ought to be, but is not, of the people and by the people." The opposition would have to find a better reason than "because" for abrogating liberty and justice. A day later, Duniway addressed perhaps 100 women in the assembly lobby. The group loudly called for attorney William H. White of Seattle, who "in a few eloquent and telling remarks upheld the cause of woman suffrage on the simple grounds of justice and right." Duniway realized that she inhabited a free space in which citizens might conjure up freedom; there was "no constitution with inhibitions descended from Paleozoic times, to be amended."[56]

Weeks later, Duniway's "good bill" appeared. Sponsors had tied the right to vote directly to investitures in property, including marital estates on which men and women jointly paid taxes. Equally important, they had decided that woman suffrage fell within the spirit, if not the letter, of the organic act. Mr. Smith of Whitman introduced House Bill 103 to "confer the right of suffrage on certain tax-payers"; the object of the bill was to allow citizens at least twenty-one years of age who paid taxes on property valued at $500 or more to vote, "providing that they shall not be debarred on account of sex." A motion to postpone indefinitely was lost – whereupon lawmakers adopted the bill, 13 to 11. It failed in Council, but only nine of twelve members voted.[57]

As earlier, continuance partly reflected concern about another statehood petition in Congress. A territorial delegation had submitted the fruits of the Walla Walla convention in mid-December, 1881; surely radical electoral policies would sabotage the project. At virtually the same moment, though, William Lloyd Garrison – one of several peripatetic reformers to visit Washington periodically – urged a large audience in Olympia to provide for equal suffrage now and save trouble; it was difficult to "eradicate a wrong once crystalized in organic law," given "how absurdly binding bad precedents are."[58] Roger Greene, however, enraged many of his countrymen with unilateral appeals to Congress. The nephew of New York's Republican Senator Elbridge Gerry Lapham, Greene was a primary force behind Lapham's presentation in 1881 and again in May, 1882, of petitions from "sundry citizens" of Washington Territory, including "the officers of that Territory, the associate justices of the supreme court, the secretary of the Territory," and businessmen, praying that in case of the admission of Washington and other territories, Senators would drop the word "male" from the suffrage clauses of state constitutions. Less than a month later, a memorial

---

[56] "Notes from Olympia," *OR*, November 9, 1881; untitled, ibid., November 5, 1881; "Washington Legislature," ibid., November 3, 1881.
[57] "Washington Legislature," *OR*, November 18, 1881.
[58] "Woman Suffrage, Speech by William Lloyd Garrison ...," *OR*, October 22, 1881 (speech was in Portland; he described a stop in Olympia and synopsized his presentation).

appeared conveying the Sixteenth Amendment. Not surprisingly, Washington's petition was tabled.[59]

Congressional inaction encouraged local suffragists to build on a growing body of equal-rights legislation. Civil equality and co-sovereignty within marriage offered unimpeachable grounds for enfranchisement; as Duniway and others had predicted, the suffrage bill, once revived, was in such a shape that lawmakers could "hardly fail to vote for it." Governor Newell was known to support the cause. Luminaries apparently had taken the question under advisement after the new law code appeared in 1881, concluding (in the words of an ex-councilman) that "the ballot justly belongs to woman."[60] A last-minute attempt to fob off the decision on voters in a future election – Duniway called it "political 'bush-whacking'" – failed miserably. On November 15, 1883, council members approved election-law amendments, 14 to 7.[61] Key forces behind this dazzling move apparently were Mary Olney Brown, other local women, the omnipresent Duniway, and progressive legislators; only Spokane Falls and its environs withheld support. The WCTU's Frances Willard had galvanized Seattle audiences in June, 1883, with pro-suffrage talk and a lecture about the evils of drink; Olympians hoped that politicized temperance workers would be an "aid in shaping legislation." Others (including Duniway) feared exactly that result: During an October, 1884, Democratic rally in Tacoma, an assembly candidate warned that, while he supported citizens' independence, women should avoid societies that would "prejudice their cause."[62]

---

[59] See Delegate Brent introducing a bill "To provide for the formation and admission into the Union of the State of Washington"; Congressional Record, House, Vol. 13, 47th Congress, 1st session, 1881, Part I, December 19, 1881, p. 207, and Part 2, March 9, 1882, p. 1755. Representatives repeatedly offered resolutions in support of a federal woman-suffrage amendment; ibid., December 19, 1881, May 22, and June 5, 1882, pp. 207, 1755, 4144, 4508, 5859. On June 5, 1882, the Committee on Woman Suffrage read (favorable) majority and (unfavorable) minority reports; ibid., May 22, 1882, p. 4144.

[60] "Reporter" (not Abigail Duniway), "Territorial Matters," *OR*, November 16, 1881; "Significant Changes of Opinion," *NN*, October 25, 1883.

[61] "A Subterfuge Bill," *NN*, November 1, 1883. See also *SDPI* ("New Suffrage Bill"), November 17, 1883, reporting attempted derailment, which enraged suffragists. An "elated" Duniway attended; "The Territorial Capital," *SDPI*, November 17, 1883. Californians learned swiftly; "The Pacific Coast, Woman Suffrage Assured in Washington Territory," *LAT*, November 17, 1883. On bush-whacking, see Duniway, "The Woman Suffrage Bill," *OR*, November 1, 1883. See An Act to Amend Section 3,050, Ch. 238 of the Code of Washington, Acts of the Territorial Assembly, November 28, 1883. Printed in advance of adoption in *WS*, November 23, 1883, and elsewhere; papers often reprinted elections laws; e.g., *WS*, April 23, 1886, or "The Woman Suffrage Bill," *WR*, November 30, 1883.

[62] Journalists tracked Duniway; e.g., *WS*, October 20, 1882. See also "Miss Willard's Reception," *WS*, June 22, 1883. Beginning in mid-1883, the WCTU sponsored Friday-night meetings in Seattle. See "The Democrats. Reasons Why Their Ticket Should Be Elected," *TDL*, October 28, 1884. Statements could be threatening: "It is now the duty of every woman in the Territory to exercise the duty which has been imposed upon her. Whether they vote or not, they will be held responsible equally with the men for the administration of public affairs"; "Woman Suffrage,"

Duniway's *New Northwest* reported "great excitement" in Olympia, gave the lion's share of credit to its editor, and dismissed local suffragists as "stay-at-home constituents" unwilling to lobby and otherwise get their skirts dirty.[63] Bostonians had the news within hours and New Yorkers the next day. In mid-November, 1883, coastal residents mounted a ratification jubilee. Accompanied by street fairs, dinner parties, the "booming of guns," and the "ringing of bells," Washington's council and assembly had eliminated all mention of sex from election laws. Legislators also had defeated high-license legislation, unpopular with both saloon patrons and many suffragists who preferred "local option" to extremism and who associated state control of private choices with tyranny. Newspapers exploded, as with "WOMAN EMANCIPATED. ... Triumph of the Most Important Measure Ever Acted upon by the Legislature." Boats and trains carried visitors from great distances.[64] Olympians joked that woman suffrage would "lead to increased sales of white shirts." A huge gala, held in Olympia's Columbia Hall on November 19, continued into the night; "Mrs. Hale," elected to a county school-commissioner seat, thanked those who had "stricken the shackles from her limbs." Speakers touted popular rule. The venerable Judge Orange Jacobs noted that the world had not ended after all; Washingtonians had affirmed that, when republics were founded on the virtue and intelligence of the people, the "fabric would be strong."[65]

Emancipation had been rooted in the equality principle, to be sure, but also in social fact: In formal terms, who could deny ballots to intelligent, propertied members of the sovereignty or ignore the fact of women's day-to-day contributions to territorial wealth and population growth? As a lower-court

WR, December 7, 1883. For the Republican side, see "Reasons Why King County Republicans Should Vote for Voorhees," *SDPI*, October 30, 1884.

[63] "A[bigail] S[cott] D[uniway]," "Washington's Legislature – The Woman Suffrage Bill Passes the House by a Two-Thirds Vote, To the Readers ...," and Duniway, "Letter from Olympia," *NN*, October 18, 1883. Washington suffragists had decided to step back. In the November 1, 1883, issue of *NN*, Duniway again decried local suffragists' passivity ("babes in the cause"); see "A Subterfuge Bill ...," ibid. The House decision was nearly bi-partisan; *NN*, November 1, 1883.

[64] "Washington's Women," *WJ*, December 8, 1883, and "Woman Suffrage Conceded, Olympia, WT, Oct. 18," *NYT*, October 19, 1883. On a pro-suffrage petition from 175 women, see "Washington Legislature," *WWU*, November 1, 1883, part of a tidal wave of petitions. See A[bigail] S[cott] D[uniway], "From Olympia," *NN*, November 15, 1883, and "Woman Suffrage in Washington Territory," *LAT*, October 19, 1883, p. 1. For party affiliations, see *WWS*, "The Next Legislature," September 29, 1883 (council had 4 Democrats and 8 Republicans, the House 11 Democrats and 13 Republicans). On high license, see "The Territorial Capital," *SDPI*, November 22, 1883, and "Yesterday a city councilman ...," *TDL*, April 4, 1884 (high license reduces tax revenues). For "WOMAN ...," see "Our Territory to the Front ...," *WS*, November 16, 1883; "Washington's Women," *NN*, November 22, 1883. For "boats and trains" and cannons, see "From the Capital," *SDPI*, November 21, 1883. See also "The Woman Suffrage Bill Passes the House," *WWS*, October 27, 1883, a tiny notice in an anti-suffrage print.

[65] "The Jubilee," *WS*, November 23, 1883. In the same vein, see "Woman Suffrage Passed," November 22, 1883, *PSWA* [Port Townsend], noting passage, predicting that none of the promised "evils" would occur, and noting that "old fogys" had lost.

judge explained in May, 1884, "You can frame no argument against woman's right to the ballot that would not equally affect man's right to the same great privilege." Noting a shift from bar rooms to public halls, a farmer thought that republicans had "nothing to fear from the ballot placed in the hands of the intelligent women of the Nation, but rather from the corrupting influences of ... ignorant male voters." He urged "equal and exact justice to all, special privileges to none. Let woman have a hand in making the laws by which she must be governed. Taxation without representation brought about the rebellion."[66]

Lawmakers wisely anticipated future attempts to interpret terms such as "citizen," "person," "he," and "his" literally. As of November, 1883, all American citizens older than twenty-one years and "all American half-breeds over that age, who have adopted the habits of the whites," as well as loyal aliens, were entitled to hold office or vote. Lawmakers added two more provisions. First, they retroactively neutralized male-centric statutes: "Wherever the word 'his' occurs ..., it shall be construed to mean 'his or her,' as the case may be." Second, they purged masculine nouns from sections of the 1881 code governing jury selection. Appropriate officers would identify "all persons qualified to serve in their county" as *petit* and grand jurors, selecting forty-eight persons qualified to serve as the former and forty-eight other persons for the latter in courts of each district. The law freed counties to use the census, poll lists, or other sources to determine eligibility. Election laws that conflicted in any way were rescinded.[67] Final votes did not follow party lines: In Council, three Democrats and four Republicans had supported sex-blind suffrage, with three Republicans and two Democrats opposed. In the House, seven members on each side supported the legislation, with a Democrat from Thurston County breaking the tie. Opposed were five Republicans and two Democrats.[68]

Still, territorial leaders stopped short of a complete sweep of common-law rules. In the wake of general elections, Benjamin Dennison – a second judicial district judge, a mainstay at the Walla Walla convention, and a long-time champion of sex neutrality – offered a reading of territorial policies, noting, among other points, that alien women whose fathers had been naturalized or who had married citizens could vote without further ado; lacking such

---

[66] "Here's Our Position," *WR*, November 30, 1883; editorial, ibid., July 18, 1884; "Woman Suffrage," ibid., August 22, 1884.

[67] An Act to Amend Section 3050, Chapter 238 of the Code of Washington; An Act to Amend Section 2080, of Chapter CLII of the Code of Washington Territory, Relating to Grand and Petit Jurors; Laws of Washington Territory, 1883–84, pp. 33–35, 39. News soon reached other locations. See, e.g., "Woman Suffrage Assured in Washington Territory," *LAT*, November 17, 1883, p. 1, and "Woman Suffrage in Washington Territory," ibid., October 19, 1883, reporting House passage by a vote of 14 to 7. Confusion remained. When legislators failed to alter an 1881 school law, prevailing laws both extended and limited the franchise in school elections; one specified only men, the other both sexes. This was an error, not malice. See "Voters at School Elections," *SDPI*, September 23, 1884.

[68] "A Deliberate Falsehood," *WS*, October 24, 1884. A Republican paper in Chehalis later claimed that R. C. Kerr of Port Townsend broke the tie; "A Letter," *LCB*, October 29, 1886.

connections, non-citizens had to declare an intention to become citizens six months before an election. Unmarried, alien women were effectively dissuaded from emigration. Even post-victory celebrations were subtly marked by many century's experience with coverture: Invitations to husbands included unnamed wives; separate invitations were issued by full name to "unmarried ladies and gentlemen."[69] Other unsightly blemishes appeared in the law code and judicial reports. Beyond making rules by which women *could* be assigned managerial responsibilities if marital partners preferred (or if circumstances dictated), and *could* be granted power to sell property held in trust by legislative permission, lawmakers retained the common-law rule that, short of selling or willing joint property or inherited real estate and without written agreements to the contrary, men could undertake ordinary transactions alone. Husbands still claimed an exclusive, common-law right to domestic and sexual services. And, in *Maynard* v. *Valentine* (1880), a ruling remembered largely for its affirmation of the legality of past legislative divorces, justices had received the common-law view of domicile.[70]

More positively, experiences of equal standing emboldened women who might otherwise have remained silent. In November, 1883, for instance, a lawyer forwarded a petition to Duniway begging citizens interested in securing equal rights for women to take up the cause of Mrs. William O. Green, an aging widow from Walla Walla who faced confiscation of much of her land. Officials in Walla Walla, knowing that she lacked authority to sell land held in trust, had declared part of it to be within town boundaries; when she died, title would be lost. Her only recourse was a petition. The document bore the signatures of a hundred Walla Walla men and women. Wrote Duniway, while women had cause to complain of any law that handicapped a mother or widow, leaving them unable to liberate capital or sell land, they could rejoice at the "sense of justice everywhere observable among gentlemen." Surely legislators saw the injustice of doctrines that denied widows the management and control of assets merely because they had married before 1879.[71]

---

[69] "Following is an opinion ...," *PSWC*, December 11, 1883. The Cable Act of 1922 partly addressed this problem; see Candice Bredbenner, *A Nationality of Her Own: Women, Marriage, and the Law of Citizenship* (Berkeley, CA, 1998). See also "In Honor of the Legislative Assembly," *PSWC*, November 27, 1883. The rules were laid out before elections; e.g., "Women Who Are Entitled to Vote and Hold Office," *SDPI*, September 30, 1884.

[70] *Lydia A. Maynard* v. *Thomas B. Valentine*, 2 Wash Terr Rpts 3 (1880). An inheritance depended upon the legality of legislative divorce. For briefs, see Lydia Maynard v. Thomas Valentine, Case File No. 319 (1880), WSA-O. See also the notice of appeal to U.S. Supreme Court, "The Supreme Court," *SDPI*, September 28, 1884. On Hoyt's ruling that marriage was a "status," not a "contract," and thus off-limits to the contracts clause, see "A recent decision ...," *TDL*, March 29, 1885. Men sometimes complained of excessive democracy; e.g., "The women of Washington ...," *WR*, December 26, 1884 ("the laws give her ... nearly all" of a man's property, leaving nothing for previous wives or children).

[71] A[bigail] S[cott] D[uniway], "From Olympia," *NN*, November 15, 1883. The outcome of Green's case has not been discovered.

In the first week of November, 1883 – well before Council passage of the bill on November 15 and its enactment four days later – women attended school elections in large numbers; female voters apparently secured a tax increase for schools, despite the "dirty little slurs" of "pot-house politicians."[72] Suffragists assured citizens that occasional, mixed-sex balloting would be decorous. A Spokane editor boasted that the territory, "so young in years, must be accredited in history with taking the lead of century-old states in performing an act of such transcendent wisdom and justice" – and one that required no more public notoriety than "attending a concert."[73] Those who had warned of social revolution were disappointed: One Seattle pundit observed, only a few days after the 1883 mixed-sex elections, that "household, social, business and political affairs" would go on as usual. Women were "already quite well protected in their property rights by our laws. ... The wifely and motherly women will neglect none of their home duties by going once or twice a year to the primaries or the polls."[74]

Evidence of energy and heroism piled up: In Whatcom County, voters had to travel ten or fifteen miles to cast ballots in 1884 elections, often on foot; suffragists pleaded with officials to set up small precincts so that women could vote easily without long absences from home. In Seattle and Tacoma, women registered in significant numbers in advance of the elections of May, 1885. On March 21, 1884, women constituted 83 of 522 registrants in Tacoma (about 15 percent); on April 5, the number grew modestly (in Tacoma's First Ward, 14 out of the 18 citizens registering were women; in the Second Ward, 18 of 76; and in the third, 20 of 101). One city clerk offered to make house calls if "at any time seven ladies get together and want to be registered."[75] In Walla Walla, women attended a school election, in spite of the city's embarrassing failure to revise election ordinances.[76] In September, 1884, on the eve of school elections, Seattle journalists noted that statutes both included and excluded women; an 1881 law had not been revised. More important, male estate management erased women whenever tax assessors failed to list wives separately, which effectively limited school elections to single women and

---

[72] [Abigail Duniway?], "Woman Suffrage," *OR*, November 6, 1883.

[73] "An Important Event," *SFC*, November 22, 1883, repr. in *OR*, November 27, 1883. Governor Hoyt of Wisconsin had urged Newell to support woman suffrage; "In a letter to Gov. Newell," *PSWC*, December 11, 1883. Newell did so just before the election.

[74] "Equal Before the Law," *PSWC*, November 20, 1883.

[75] Editorial, *WR*, July 18, 1884; "City Registration," *TDL*, March 21, 1884; and "City Registrations," ibid., April 5, 1884. City clerks (like clerks of court) seemed to use "Miss" and "Mrs." when women registered; errors will be in the direction of undercounting, since other registrants were cited only with initials and surname. On March 22, 1884, *TDL* noted another 12 women out of 66; on March 29, 15 out of 102; on April 2, 1884, 12 out of 30. Numbers likely are not anomalous. See also "The May Election," *TDL*, March 26, 1884.

[76] E.g., "Who Can Vote?" *WWU*, July 9, 1883. In Walla Walla, neglect perhaps had to do with excitement about the arrival of the NPR; see, e.g., "Realizing a Dream," *WWU*, September 18, 1883, on the eve of the election, and "Hasty Legislation," *WWS*, December 8, 1883.

wives with separate property. Women attended the polls anyway. Election judges in at least one jurisdiction even suggested that spouses did not pay taxes jointly. "A person 'liable to pay' taxes," they wrote inaccurately, "is one who holds property in his or her name and whose name appears, or is liable to appear, upon the assessor's list of persons owning assessable property. A married woman, not having separate property, and whose name does not appear on the assessor's list, is not ... in law 'liable to pay any tax' even though she, with her husband may have community property, for which the husband is assessed and upon which he pays taxes. This has ... been the rule heretofore. If so, it has not been changed by the legislation." As late as October, 1884, officials still listed women as dependents and barred them from primaries. In Colfax, Kate P. Wolfard reported that, while "voting our school tax recently, no lady was permitted to vote unless she had real property, taxed and deeded in her own name."

As women have been free but a little while, comparatively few are tax-payers except in the name of their husbands, and many of us were kept from voting on this account. There was considerable discussion ..., some contending that women should and others that they should not vote. ... Just before our primary meetings ..., parties sent word to several ladies that ... [their votes] would not be taken at the primaries. This deterred many from going. Verily, 'man's rights dies hard.'

When women stayed away from polls, tongue-lashings ensued; one woman asked non-voting neighbors why they preferred old-style "disabilities."[77]

Observers knew that if women developed a taste for politics, governance would be altered beyond recognition, particularly if contributions won praise. As an Olympian noted in summer of 1884, women could double the size of the electorate. He warned, too, that nobody could predict how women would vote, least of all their husbands. "The women of this Territory have now, so far as their civil and political rights are concerned, been placed upon a full equality with men. Many women who ... were accustomed to suborn their ideas in politics to those of their husbands for the reason that none of the public responsibilities of citizenship rested upon their shoulders, will begin to see the matter in a different light." They would "study and think." A Democratic editor found it "surprising how unanimously the people favor woman suffrage. Has the principle changed or have the people progressed?"[78]

Poll watchers continued to track female voters. At least sixty-two women voted in Olympia city elections in early 1884; a Seattle reporter sighted twelve women proudly lined up to vote some months later as well as ninety-nine

---

[77] Editorial, "Voters at School Elections," *SDPI*, September 23, 1884. Confusion seems to have been resolved; by 1885, e.g., papers underscored the phrase "male and female" before school elections; "Who Can Vote Today," ibid., November 7, 1885. See also Kate Wolfard, "From Whitman County, Colfax," *NN*, October 9, 1884. For "disabilities," see "D," "Don't Want to Vote," *WS*, October 17, 1884.

[78] "The Vote for 1884," *WS*, August 22, 1884; "Reward the Faithful," ibid., October 31, 1884.

women in three of Olympia's wards. Pro-suffrage journalists, probably in response to rumors of lower-class women unsexing themselves for pay, depicted elections as harmless events. The *Walla Walla Union* spotted a "great number of ladies ..., all representative women – wives of our leading citizens – whom anyone would be proud to call mother. Yes, these ladies voted ... and their fair names have not suffered in consequence."[79] Skeptics supposedly had been overcome by the "spirit of justice," a desire to "put his own or his neighbor's wife right before the law." Women had appeared "singly, in pairs, and in numbers, and selected their tickets and voted as intelligently, and certainly more quietly, than men ordinarily do." Even the dubious *Walla Walla Union* conceded that the sexes were now co-sovereigns, standing on the "ground of equality, with mutual respect. ... *It is the service which kings and queens render to each other*, not that which courtiers give to their sovereigns."[80]

After general elections in early November, 1884 – the first real test of women's engagement with partisan politics – observers noted unprecedented turnout: "Never before since the neighboring mountain peaks were molehills" had Olympians seen "so large a vote." In Olympia, every "wife, sister, mother and sweetheart who can get to the polls has already gone and deposited the exponent of her delivery from thraldom." Often, entire families walked from the "nearer rural districts" to the courthouse. Days later, in a plea for statehood, the same paper estimated the electorate at 42,000, of which 10,000–11,000 were women. In remote areas, however, numbers dropped: In January, 1885, for instance, a Whatcom statehood booster counted 8,308 women among 43,842 voters.[81]

Ironically, while biological determinism rarely appeared in the suffrage camp, the most vocal advocate of both equal rights and women's *sui generis* capacity for social purification was Roger Sherman Greene, as of September, 1883, not only the territory's chief justice but also president of a major temperance society. In his call to convention, Greene invited female voters and jurors to help him prosecute a "deadly feud between the bottle and the ballot." But, for the most part, arguments rooted in men's and women's

[79] "Local Notes," *WS*, January 18, 1884 (ninety-nine women voting, eleven in Olympia's first ward, fifty-one in the second, and thirty-seven in the third). See also editorial, "Voters at School Elections," *SDPI*, September 23, 1884. For good election reportage, see "School Election," *WWU*, November 5, 1883, repr. *NN*, November 15, 1883. Olympians were also reported in "School Election," *PSWC*, November 6, 1883; see also editorial, *Daily Chronicle* [Dayton, WA], November 10, 1883.

[80] "Strong Suffrage Testimony," reprinted from Olympia Courier, *SDPI*, November 9, 1883; "Stand on a Proud Equality," *WWU*, November 6, 1883. Emphasis added.

[81] "The Election in Olympia," *TDL*, November 5, 1884. In the same vein, see "Kalama Happenings," ibid., November 11, 1884. In Kalama, near Oregon, Sarah Johnson was "the first woman to vote ..., and probably the first in the territory." See also "No Reason for Refusal," *TDL*, October 29, 1884. On the sex ratio and marital prospects, see "Husband Hunting Ground," *WS*, June 18, 1886. See also "Let Us Reason Together," *WR*, January 16, 1885.

separate natures emanated from anti-suffragists and anti-vice activists.[82] Racial
slurs appeared in both camps: Oppositionists, for instance, warned that
mindless legislators might be "letting Chinamen and Indians vote next."
Cartoonists depicted suffragists as allies of degenerate Asians, Indians
("treacherous, indolent, worthless savages"), petty crooks, and other bad
seed. On the reform side, a German-born legislator compared whites' elevated
views of women to those of the "soulless" Chinese whose women were "slaves"
and of Indians whose "squaws" were "beasts of burden."[83]

Within pro-suffrage circles, however, activists typically occupied the time-
honored ground of republican constitutionalism, particularly the equality
doctrines associated with Civil War. On October 17, 1883, to give one example
among many, during final debates in the House, self-described male suffragists
beat back tirades against the ruination of home with logic and law. Who could
prove that women did not want to vote? If some men chose not to vote, should
they be disfranchised? There had to be "liberty for all – government by all and for
all." One lawmaker wanted "all men to take a heartfelt interest in our government,
and what is right for men is right for women." Neighborhoods and marriages
would benefit from "the dissemination of liberty, justice and equal rights."[84]

Skeptics and pragmatists sometimes chose to hide in watch: They saw no way
around republican theory, sensed how winds were blowing, respected women's
contributions, or valued social peace. A few examples suffice: A Walla Walla
reporter, noting some "ladies listening in the lobby," thought that a House
member had said what women wanted to hear: "Why should you disfranchise a
woman because she lives with a man; is she not as essential to the maintenance of
the nation as he?"[85] Cynicism, resignation, and hostility were not absent. Just
before adoption of a new election law, the Republican *Courier* announced support

[82] Roger S. Greene, "Call to Convention," *SDPI*, September 19, 1883, also published in "Woman's
     Column, Temperance Convention," *WR*, September 18, 1883. For outsiders, see untitled
     editorial, *WJ*, May 17, 1884 (on public housekeeping); Abigail Duniway, "For the Good She
     Can Do," *NN*, November 15, 1883 (women had a duty to "give representation to the home,"
     support laws that "affect home," and protect children). As an example of the recessive mother-
     hood discourse, see "Equal before the law," *PSWC*, November 20, 1883. ("Most of the training
     that fits men to become good citizens is given them by their mothers, and it seems very absurd
     that an intelligent mother . . . should not be as capable of casting a vote as intelligently as her son
     who has just been released from her authority.")
[83] Editorial, *Seattle Herald*, October 18, 1883; repr. *NN*, October 25, 1883; editorial, *SPI*,
     November 23, 1879. From time to time, Washingtonians received information about and
     exhibited interest in black rights, including judicial rulings, as when editors publicized a mass
     meeting organized by Frederick Douglass and Robert Ingersoll to protest the Civil Rights Cases;
     "Editorial Notes," *NN*, October 25, 1883. For the "genial German" legislator, see
     "Representative Besserer's Address at . . . Ratification," *NN*, December 6, 1883. See also "A
     New Amendment," *SDPI*, December 8, 1883.
[84] "Letter from Olympia," *NN*, October 25, 1883. For similar comments, see reprint from New
     Northwest, "Letter from Olympia," *WJ*, November 10, 1883.
[85] "Legislative Correspondence," *WWS*, October 20, 1883. See also "Woman Suffrage a Fact,"
     ibid., November 24, 1883.

for it in order to expand representation, do "justice to one-half [of] our citizens, and break away from the conservatism, prejudice and pride that have so long barred the way." But editors added this: "To those who vote for it out of selfish considerations, based upon the hope of future aid and support, we say your expectations are well founded." Still others hoped mainly for a restoration of harmony. One Council member allowed that American devotion to liberty of conscience and political equality mandated equality; women had proven themselves to be worthy partners. But he issued a warning: Officials never should be made to regret "making you before the law what you have been in other departments of life – man's equal." After adoption, a Dayton writer claimed that, while his friends did not support "all the doctrines advanced by some Woman Suffragists; yet we are not afraid that the ballot will be abused in the hands of woman. ... Let women vote, if they want to, under the same restrictions as men." In Seattle, a resigned citizen simply invited women to vote "like little men."[86]

Not surprisingly, condemnation and outright intimidation of women came most reliably from eastern counties. In Pomeroy, a newspaper office invited women to send their names on a postal card to his office so that he could determine whether women "desire to have the right of suffrage extended to them." He then would publish the names, which would "aid the cause, if the women really wish to vote." Silence would indicate a lack of interest.[87] A sore loser noted that, if women labored with the same zeal at home, they would be better off. Orin Belknap of Spokane set aside the question of the "instinctive aversion, common to American manhood, to all movements of this kind" and focused on facts – the "mental unfitness of women for the *privileges* of the suffrage" and the "physical inability of women for the duties entailed by the ballot." Obligations loomed large. Women could not judge with "cold, judicious impartiality" and made poor soldiers. He did not find political equality in the Bible.[88]

Coincidentally or not, critiques of American Indian dependency merged briefly with equal-suffrage discourse. Suggestions of a retrograde, federal paternalism appeared as early as 1879, when journalists began to characterize Indians as "dependents" who should be encouraged to "claim no annuities whatever from the Government," but rather be "entirely dependent on their own efforts for sustenance."[89] In November, 1883, assemblymen submitted a

---

[86] Editorial, *Olympia Courier*, October 12, 1883, reprinted in *PSWC*, October 16, 1883 under the heading "It is quietly whispered ...." See also *Dayton State Journal*, October 20, 1883; reprinted in *NN*, November 1, 1883, and "Notes," *SDPI*, October 31, 1883. See also Councilman's Speech, "Reforms and Reformers," *NN*, November 29, 1883.

[87] "Suffrage Test," *Washington Independent*, December 6, 1883. If we are to believe the editor, women told him ten months later that they feared their property would be "alienated" if they voted; he assured them that it would not be. "The ladies need have no fear ...," ibid., October 16, 1884.

[88] "Woman Suffrage," *WWS*, November 24, 1883; Orin Belknap, "The Woman Suffrage Law," *WWS*, December 8, 1883. Emphasis added.

[89] "Indians as Citizens," *SDPI*, May 15, 1879. A Whatcom County resident observed in 1885 that, when a treaty with the Lummis had lapsed in 1879 – a pact that permitted land sales only to other

petition – four years before the Dawes Severalty Act, and just as women had escaped dependency – for the abolition of territorial Indian reservations and wardship. Legislators pressed the equality principle with indirect nods to women – i.e., the perpetuation of race distinctions that marked Indians as "inferiors and dependent," whether as "wards of the Government or prisoners upon ... reservations." It was time to secure "uniformity of rights as men and women." They demanded an end to race distinctions and treatment of Indians as "other men are treated with the same right to enjoy property, the same right to pursue happiness." Indians should not enjoy "rights to acquire or hold land superior to or different from the American citizen."[90]

****

No sooner had suffrage been universalized than it began to complicate struggles for statehood. Washingtonians spoke incessantly after 1878–79 about the Northwest's brilliant economic future and the need to make rough-and-tumble cities and towns more attractive to immigrants. In one man's fairly typical words, the best hopes of the people lay in "the public domain," by which he meant the expansion of home industry. Even Roger Greene, in an 1882 grand jury charge, foresaw a "day of great material prosperity ... dawning upon Puget Sound. Our business interests and population have this season received an unprecedented impulse."[91]

Economic development, in turn, required political integration – and both objectives collided with electoral radicalism. In November, 1883, assemblymen passed an act enabling Washington to gain admission to the union; but, as a Seattle writer put it, because by the act's provisions women would have been accidentally disfranchised in the new state, the bill had been hotly debated. Another writer tied women to statehood, not as equals but as co-civilizers: "Just as woman excels man in refinement and virtue, will the administration of public affairs be placed on a higher plane." Equality generated good press. "The eyes of the nation are upon us. Many will come to our shores to breath[e] the pure air of political freedom. Our advance to statehood has been aided by a long stride." Prominent Democrat Thomas Burke did not doubt that the quest for equality

---

Indians – he had expected immediate sale of the best lands to whites so that unmanly, dependent Indian men would leave; "The Lummi Indians," *WR*, March 27, 1885.

[90] "Memorial praying the abolition of Indian reservations," Congressional Record, House, 48th Congress, 1st Session, Vol. 15, part 1, November 28, 1883 and January 30, 1884, p. 753. See also "Work or Starve," *WWU*, September 25, 1883, urging the elimination of the "red wards of the Nation" and adherence to uniform rules. For the Dawes Act, see "An Act to Provide for the Allotment of Lands in Severalty to Indians on the Various Reservations," Statutes at Large, 49th Congress, February 8, 1887. In 1884, another writer decided that Congress would be "doing the Indians themselves a valuable service by making it necessary for them to work" and putting lands "in the hands of white men who would put it to some good use"; "Puyallup Indian Reservation," *TDL*, April 1, 1884.

[91] "Judge Greene's Charge [of October 9]," *SDPI*, October 10, 1882.

figured large in the public imagination. But, in his words, the question of statehood transcended all others; voters should support whichever candidates could deliver an acceptable state constitution, with or without equality. In December, 1883, Seattle editors embraced a letter from LaConner advising Delegate Thomas Brent to stop proposing a new convention. Washingtonians sought immediate integration. The Walla Walla constitution enjoyed popular support; it was "wise and conservative .... If we attempt to improve upon it ... the change may be so radical and unsatisfactory that the people would refuse to ratify it." In the District of Columbia, journalists warned that a territory "already knocking at the door of the Union ... should not come to Congress in a Gainsboro hat, hoop-skirts and high-heeled gaiters."[92]

As with Indian dependence, so with the status of the territory. Said Brent on the eve of women's enfranchisement, "Our wealth, our population ... give us the right to choose our own rulers and to make our own laws. ... [W]e are over one hundred thousand strong, yet we exist in a sort of colonial vassalage. No choice, either directly or indirectly, as to who shall be our rulers. We have no representation in the councils of the nation."[93] National integration thus secured and affirmed a robust citizenship. Still, in 1882–83, statehood boosters purveyed an ill-sorted brew of machismo, anti-colonialism, liberal constitutionalism, and social science. One exemplar yearned for an escape from "that colonial condition" which deprived westerners of the "inalienable right of managing our domestic affairs in our own way." Revolutionary fathers had died to secure the right of self-government; only a "degenerate man" would stand down.[94]

---

[92] "State Admission," *SDPI*, December 12, 1883; "True to their Nature," *WP*, December 19, 1883, p. 2; "Admission," *WR*, December 12, 1884, and "Woman Suffrage," ibid., November 14, 1884 (suggesting a woman-only vote to see if women really meant to persist).

[93] [Thomas H. Brent], "The Right Hand of Fellowship," *SDPI*, August 15, 1882. A Republican, Brent served as Washington's at-large delegate to Congress from March, 1879, to March, 1885. He was succeeded by Democrat Charles Voorhees who served until 1889. For "grandeur," see untitled half-page article, *SDPI*, August 27, 1882. On the public domain, see ibid., September 19, 1878; for "wind," see "Railroads and Gas," ibid., October 22, 1878; for immigration and Seattle, "Room for Immigrants," ibid., May 16, 1879. See also "Extension of American Commerce," ibid., November 5, 1878. The Republican Party platform of October, 1878, had no suffrage plank; "Republican Platform," ibid., October 25, 1878.

[94] "The Constitution," *SDPI*, October 22, 1878. In the same vein, see "New Northwest," SPI, August 20, 1882.

3

"Equal rights with man in every respect"

Practicing mixed-sex democracy

> To Paddy, John Bull, or Hans,
>   There is never need to say,
> "Make very good use of your franchise,
>   Or else we will take it away."
>
> But as you are only women,
>   With instincts and reasons low,
> Just see that you vote correctly,
>   Or back to your place you go. . . .
>
> – "Luelling" (1883)[1]

By autumn of 1883, Washingtonians had fashioned a formidable equal-rights regime rooted in civil equality and co-headship within marriage – an achievement seemingly supported by neighborhood legalities, including the organic act. The successful implementation of equal suffrage in early 1884 further bolstered claims (as speakers explained at a suffrage gala) that woman was now man's equal, able to "kill the votes of bad men with their own" and enforce "equal representation for equality." Only the churlish few promised surveillance – perhaps because they, with thoughtful observers on all sides, recognized the quicksand on which suffragism rested. Scholarly lawyers like Roger Greene feared that territorial legislation backed largely by boilerplate clauses in a federal statute (the organic act) lacked the legal-cultural authority of constitutional guarantees. In addition, only a few noticed that property *in* rights exercised for long periods with Congressional acquiescence might be off-limits to takings of the kind intimated in "Luelling's" bad poetry and openly threatened elsewhere: "If you use it well, we will leave it in your hands; if not, and you abuse it, when we frame our State Constitution we'll leave you out."[2]

---

[1] "Luelling," pseud., "To the Women of Washington," *NN*, December 6, 1883.
[2] Legislative News, *SDPI*, November 21, 1883.

Throughout American history, ballots had formed part of a bundle of rights and obligations. On the face of it, the organic act presented no impediment to women's exercise of the entire bundle. Both sexes surely had access to office holding. Beyond Section 5, in which Congress had extended the "right of suffrage and of holding office" to those "citizens of the United States" that the Assembly might enfranchise, Section 4 mandated election by qualified "voters" to the assembly: At its first session and thereafter, the Council had consisted of nine members "having the qualifications of voters"; the House had eighteen with the same credentials as Council members.[3]

Still, while there was little reason to doubt that equality vested everyone with non-military, ancillary rights and obligations, volleys were exchanged early on. In January, 1884, a no-holds-barred writer calling himself "El Toro" claimed that, given unequal burdens, women could not be voters. They were a privileged class exempt from the enforcement of laws, eager to vote but unwilling to serve with men as policemen or soldiers. Since they lacked experience with and knowledge of public affairs and were undeniably not men, their judgments would be "partial" at best. A rejoinder soon appeared: "Juno" assailed "El Toro" for libeling all women and reminded him that, by his own measure, only a few courageous men should vote. Suffrage was neither a question of "sentiment nor expediency, but one of justice"; it was a "*right*," not a "*privilege*," bestowed not on a class but on individuals.[4]

Well and good. But the gauntlet had been thrown down – and in the same year, it was thrown down more forcibly in courtroom struggles that pitted supporters of household democracy against the keeper of a Tacoma brothel, a gambler, and a hunter who had used dogs illegally. The battle would be fought, not on the terrain of ballots alone, but on the relatively unmapped ground of citizens' obligations, especially jury duty. When social practices collided with new possibilities and expectations, the result was euphoria, gender chaos, and unprecedented fright.

"DABBLING IN THE POLITICAL POOL"

In 1883, most politically active women expected to be invested with a weighty bundle of ancillary duties, shorn of those associated with brute force, and without the right to claim nationalities different from those of husbands. Suffrage leaders waxed eloquent: In November, 1883, Lucy Stone predicted that Washington's new equal-suffrage statutes would be hailed as "the most important success ever gained" – and not only for the electorate.[5]

---

[3] An Act to Establish the Territorial Government of Washington, Statutes at Large, 32nd Congress, Session II, Ch. XC, § 4 and 5, "Legislative Assembly," "Council," and "Representatives," pp. 173–4.
[4] "El Toro," "Suffrage Again," January 10, 1884, and "Juno," "Woman Suffrage," January 24, 1884, both in SFC.
[5] L. S., "Suffrage Successes," WJ, November 24, 1883.

Nothing prevented well-regarded women from seeking public offices.[6] Giddy letters to newspaper editors probably terrified the faint-hearted. One woman, after urging women to vote, added that she hoped capable women might "hybridize .... Now is our time, let us select a woman, and ... elect her as Delegate to Congress. What need we care for any of the political parties that do not care for us? Our own salvation is in paddling our own canoes." Because conventions had become odious, she proposed that women skip them, the better to avoid "bickerings and embitterments." Instead, they should name a candidate for territorial delegate, paving the way to "Washington city and the future glory of womanhood." Meanwhile, Republicans in Colfax nominated Mrs. James, Mrs. Beach, and Mrs. Trimble to be the territory's first female convention delegates. Dr. Ella Whipple and others attended the same event as delegates from Seattle. Was Pandora's box ajar? The very idea that women, and married women at that, might strike off on their own plainly alarmed the *Standard*'s editor, who saw "no reason why they should organize themselves into a separate party on the ground of sex, nor do we imagine that they will ever do so." But the possibility had arisen.[7]

In Washington, as elsewhere, ambitious women had waited more or less patiently for admission to the bar. Lelia Robinson had migrated from Massachusetts to Cheney and then to Seattle, hoping to benefit from women's advanced standing. In October, 1884, after some effort, attorney Mary Leonard – a French woman who had moved from Portland to Seattle with the advent of equal suffrage – became the first female lawyer to pass the Washington territorial bar.[8] Robinson no doubt spoke in 1883 for all of her comrades: "It is not reasonable that I should throw aside my mental endowments and devote myself to some handicraft. It is too illogical and severe a doctrine, and I cannot accept it." Robinson despised irrationality: "That men lawyers are jealous or afraid to compete with women is too absurd an idea to consider. That women would unduly influence juries by smiles and tears is almost as untenable." It was "right

---

[6] An Act to Establish the Territorial Government of Washington [the organic act], Statutes at Large, 32nd Congress, Sess. II, Ch. XC, § 4, "Legislative Assembly," "Council," and "Representatives," pp. 173–4.

[7] Mary Sartoris, "A Women's Party," *WS*, August 22, 1884. See also "Western. Proceedings of the Republican Territorial Convention," *TDL*, September 5, 1884.

[8] For Leonard's bar passage, see "Another Female Lawyer," *SDPI*, October 24, 1884. Born in France, Leonard had been acquitted of murdering her husband in 1878, then moved to Oregon and to Seattle in 1883. In 1885, the Oregon Supreme Court ruled that, while attorneys ordinarily could be admitted to practice with a certificate of admission from another state, "liberality" did not extend to women. Justices pointed to the Lelia Robinson decision in Massachusetts, ruling that Leonard, "being a woman," did not qualify. Once the assembly "adopts an enabling act, empowering the courts to admit women ..., or confers upon that sex other rights," they could "exercise the power granted"; "Supreme Court of Oregon," 17 *Chicago Legal News* 256 (1884–85). See also "Female Lawyer," *TDL*, October 25, 1884. Leonard's examining committee, C. H Hanford, Thomas Burke and E. P. Ferry, admitted her on October 24, 1884. The same paper described Robinson as a "refined and intellectual" resident of Cheney who chose to "live where women have equal rights with men"; "Miss Robinson," ibid., May 13, 1884.

and proper that women who ... can properly prepare themselves, should be allowed to choose the law as a vocation, and that persons ... should be enabled to engage one."[9]

After 1879, moreover, well before legislators had embraced equal suffrage, journalists reported mounting interest among women in local office holding. Women had been serving without incident as school officials since at least 1877–79, mainly in rural areas. Social conservatives sometimes argued that women's allegiances after marriage conflicted with political or economic pursuits: "As a rule," wrote a reporter, "... celibacy and [an] active occupation for woman must go together."[10] But a significant number of married and single women appeared early and often as office seekers; when hostility or confusion appeared, they exhibited great forbearance. In November, 1879, Seattle reporters announced the nomination of Mrs. A. H. Stuart to an immigration commission. A scant year later, after Cowlitz County Republicans nominated Mrs. A. B. Huntington for school superintendent, they reversed course, citing "an impression prevailing that a woman was not eligible to the office"; when they learned that territorial law allowed it, she was re-nominated. Huntington was well educated with business and teaching experience; sex did not disqualify her. At virtually the same time, an annoyed correspondent from Slaughter (Kitsap) County reported that voters of both sexes had elected two school-board directors – one of them female – and a clerk. Controversy ensued. Women had been "in full attendance, determined to no longer submit to that tyrannic rule of taxation without representation, and brought out Mrs. Dr. M. O. B. as candidate for ... School Director." She had prevailed by two votes. But one of the county's "ex-Solons" detected a flaw; in a new election, she lost. "Law is deep and mysterious," she said, " ... But is it not a little irregular for judges to revoke their own action, and call a new election?" In 1883, a writer urged Seattle's mixed-sex electorate to choose an "elevated, cultivated gentleman" as territorial superintendent – a man who commanded several disciplines and might inspire boys to "manly" ambition – instead of a "mere school teacher" with a "brow-beating" personality.[11]

By September, 1882, each party seemed to be honoring suffragism, or so a number of public prints concluded, by including women on partisan slates. Republicans in Garfield County nominated Mrs. F. G. Morrison for School Superintendent; Walla-Walla Democrats named Miss Tina Johnson for a similar post. Other examples appeared. In Tacoma's Pierce County, "Mrs. Greer" won an

---

[9] "Women Lawyers," *Washington Independent* [Pomeroy], March 8, 1883.

[10] "Woman's Enfranchisement," OR, October 22, 1881. On office holding in Wyoming, see "Women in Wyoming," PSWA, November 29, 1883: "All the leading ... citizens favor women suffrage. Many do not favor women holding office, but everyone ... regards their voting as a matter of justice."

[11] "Olympia," SDPI, November 13, 1879; "Woman's Rights," ibid., November 5, 1878. The outcome is uncertain. See also "We'Uns," "Slaughter and its School Election," SDPI, November 13, 1879; "The Territorial Superintendent," SDPI, November 1, 1883.

uncontested election for superintendent in November, 1882. A Republican convention in Yakima City unanimously chose Mrs. Ella M. Stair as its candidate for Superintendent of Public Instruction. A Yakima wag extended good wishes from her friends who *"cannot vote for her."* On the eve of 1882 elections, pro-suffrage writers supported Mrs. P. C. Hale's bid on the People's Party ticket for superintendent. A dedicated and qualified widow, she was said to be the choice of "nine-tenths of the men and women of the county," in part because she could "devote herself wholly to ... service."[12]

Equality-minded Washingtonians registered disgust when anti-suffragists ran for office. Such women supposedly sought the "emoluments of offices that would never have been open to them but for the work of the suffragists." When running for school-board seats, they distinguished between the notoriety of the ballot box and service to schools. On one hand, as scholarship shows, education could be seen as an extension of home life; on the other hand, given requirements that office holders be eligible to vote, legality was unclear. Critics noted financial motivation, as when a Portland writer chastised Mrs. A. Bush of Pacific County who had strongly opposed equal suffrage, believing that "a woman's place was at home and that she should not mix in politics." She now was a county school superintendent and "regularly draws her pay. Whether or not she still thinks women should not 'dabble in the political pool,' we do not know." Tina Thompson, a Democratic nominee for superintendent, also opposed mixed suffrage. How could she run for such a post without suffering the contamination that she once said was "inseparable from political office-holding"? How could Mrs. Dahlgren serve the public without the ability to influence policy? Criticism continued into 1884. "No non-voting class is politically educated," wrote "T. W. H."; even self-disenfranchised public officials operated at a great disadvantage.[13]

Women sometimes joked about political ambitions: Suffragist Betsy Baker announced that she hoped for statehood so that she could be "the first governess ... and thus vie with Queen Victoria." But, more often and more seriously, social and economic contributions amply justified office holding as well as the suffrage. In late 1884, criticism of Mrs. Florence Chick (a Republican nominee for superintendent and a woman's-rights activist) for daring to run for office provoked disagreement from Seattle businessman David T. Denny: "A great many object because, they say, 'a woman cannot perform the service.' ... I beg leave to differ." He recalled women on "rough mountainous roads on

[12] Untitled editorial excerpting the Olympia Standard, *NN*, October 19, 1882. See also Hale's comments at the ratification celebrations in 1883, warning listeners that "not much could be expected of her," since she was only twenty-one years old; "The Jubilee," *WS*, November 23, 1883; "There are three lady candidates...," *NN*, October 21, 1882 (Hale ran again alongside a woman put forth by the People's Party who previously had "elevated her nose" at the idea of women's rights).

[13] Editorial, "Two Women Who Oppose," *NN*, October 12, 1882; "T. W. H.," "Officials without Votes," *WJ*, March 15, 1884.

horseback" with "children in their arms" who "did all the housework," and yet they could not serve as county school superintendent? Equality involved more than ballots. "Why all this talk about equal rights, if we do not give the women anything more than the privilege to vote?" This "hollow mockery" was "not honorable for the lords of creation."[14] Another citizen argued that elective offices were "as naturally her sphere of work as ... the smaller domain of home," and not just in schools. Where *credentials* were equal, voters should favor the woman.[15] Yet another held that, were it not for bad roads and hooliganism, he would support any woman for any office. Politicians gave "fat turkeys" to men and "buzzards" to women. In the present case, he feared for a woman's safety. But he did not object to female office holding. A third correspondent quoted a local dignitary who had said that woman, "like man, reaches her highest position and truest destiny" when she became an "intelligent *factor in the world's work.*"[16]

Whether with turkeys or buzzards in hand, thirteen women became school superintendents in the autumn elections of 1884. One man insisted that men had lost to women, and vice versa. Reporters crammed pages with news of female inroads. In caucuses and primaries, Republicans nominated Dr. Ella Whipple of Vancouver for County School Superintendent. Twenty-nine women voted in a Yakima City primary; there, a woman served as secretary and two more became convention delegates. East Vancouver sent four married women to the convention; Washougal sent two. Mrs. Kate C. Eckler served as the Dayton member of the Republican Central Committee; four women's names appeared on the Republican primary ticket at Olympia and one succeeded. At Tumwater, partisans chose two female delegates. The Republican Central Committee of King County included Mrs. Florence Phillips, Mrs. Mary Thomas, Mrs. Florence Chick, and four men; Mrs. A. J. Frost represented Lake View at the Pierce County convention. "That women want a part in the politics of the day is continually more apparent," wrote a journalist a month later. In one precinct, an "extraordinary innovation" emerged with two women's nomination for Justice of the Peace and Constable. "It may not be more than two years before

---

[14] [Elizabeth] Betsy Baker, "The Votes of Eight Ladies," *SDPI*, November 12, 1884. See also D. T. Denny, letters to the editor, "The School Superintendent," ibid., October 30, 1884. If this was David Thomas Denny Sr., he was a financier, politician, and founder of Seattle in the 1850s; if not, it was his well-regarded son, David Thomas Denny, Jr. "Mrs. Chick" was almost certainly Mrs. Florence [Mrs. George H.] Chick, an officer of the King County WERA; see signatures, "To the Women Voters of King County," *SDPI*, October 31, 1884. See also "Republican Ticket," ibid., September 27, 1884. She was "overwhelmingly defeated" by Democrat O. S. Jones; "The Vote of King County," ibid., November 8, 1884; and "Women in the Washington Election," *NN*, November 20, 1884, reporting as well that an eight-six-year-old woman voted.

[15] Eastern On Looker, "The School Superintendent Question," *SDPI*, November 1, 1884.

[16] E. S. I[noraman?], "The School Superintendent," *SDPI*, November 1, 1884, who argued that Republicans put a woman on the ticket "to secure woman voters," and editorial, ibid. Emphasis added.

we have women seeking election to Congress." Two married women in Seattle, Mrs. J. Anderson and Mrs. Eliza A. Forbes, became justices of the peace; Mrs. Mary Dunbar lost, but with 40 percent of the vote.[17]

Still, when ambitious women threatened to move beyond lower echelons, they met substantial resistance or surprise. In summer, 1884, Tacoma Republicans refused to permit women to sit as delegates or to participate in primaries; they had not passed an unnamed test. Only after protests, and with a "fair number of women in the galleries," did two women actually sit on the convention floor. In 1885, two years after enfranchisement, Tacomans were astonished when two women, Mrs. Cleaves and Mrs. Balcom, won seats on the Belleville city council, the first women elected to policy-making positions.[18] Wrote a disgusted Duniway, "The Republican convention of Pierce County gave women no recognition," except to cast thirteen votes for activist Zerelda Nichols McCoy – a resident of Tacoma, former official on the Puyallup Indian reservation, and candidate for the Assembly – who demanded that no one be nominated unless sympathetic to woman suffrage. In the end, the "male element" declined to recognize women, ignored McCoy's candidacy, and failed to nominate a woman for school superintendent.[19]

In September, Duniway urged Democrats to fill the vacuum created by faint-hearted Republicans. "Ladies" from Seattle even presented a gavel to the convention chair. Yet Democratic delegates officially said nothing about suffrage and ancillary rights until final publication of the platform. Delegates advanced only one woman's name (Miss Condon), and then without her knowledge, as a candidate for superintendent – she later declined – and devoted the lion's share of the platform to railroad-land forfeitures, the Chinese, and gross-earnings taxes. One plank endorsed the anti-suffrage national platform, while another took a swipe at prohibitionist attempts to eliminate public and private drinking – a position that Grover Cleveland was said to have endorsed ("In a free country the curtailment of the absolute right of the individual should only be such as is essential to the ... social order of the community").[20]

[17] "Female School Superintendents," *SDPI*, December 13, 1884; "Female J.P.s," ibid., November 9, 1884; "Women in Politics," ibid., August 26, 1884; "Washington Women in Politics," *NN*, September 4, 1884. Two years later, the People's Party boasted five female delegates; "People's Party County Convention," *SDPI*, August 29, 1886.

[18] "Territorial Brevities," repr. *WR*, *TDL*, February 11, 1885; "Editorial, "Dissatisfaction," *SDPI*, September 3, 1884. Much of the convention's time was consumed with railroad land forfeitures. See also "The First Day of the Republican Territorial Convention," *SDPI*, September 5, 1884.

[19] "Washington Women in Politics," *NN*, September 4, 1884, quoting the *TDL* at some length. For grudging anti-suffrage admissions that women did take an interest in partisan politics, see "A Sample Specimen," *SR*, May 18, 1885. On McCoy, see below.

[20] On railroad forfeitures, see, e.g., "How Can They Do It?" *SDPI*, October 29, 1884. See also "The Democracy of King County, in Convention ...," *SDPI*, September 7, 1884. For Condon, see "Declines the Nomination," ibid., September 9, 1884. See also the warning about Democratic plans for repeal; "Women who appreciate ...," ibid., September 16, 1886.

Still, black-letter law and citizens' experiences of mutuality imposed limits on partisan resistance, if not to office holding, then surely to its foundation in suffrage. The moderate Democrat and U.S. Attorney, William H. White, cited equal access to property and membership in the constituent power as roadblocks to disenfranchisement. "Single women in this Territory have the same untrammeled right to acquire and hold property as single men," he began, moving in steps from civil to constitutional equality and every sovereign citizen's right to direct representation:

... Since 1869, dower, the indi[cator] of woman's former servitude, has been abolished, and all property acquired after marriage ... belongs equally to the husband and wife. ... Now, in a free government no one can safely enjoy property unless they have a voice in the enactment of laws .... The means to carry on the government is realized from the taxation of property. To say to the women owners of property that they shall have no voice in its preservation, in its taxation, is to repudiate a principle dear to every American– that is, that taxation without representation is tyranny. Again, if persons are to be governed by law, they naturally demand to be consulted when the law is made. To be governed ... by rulers in whose selection they have no choice is simply the exercise of power without right, and is tyranny.[21]

"THERE IS A NEW ELEMENT TO BE DEALT WITH – A 'NEW CITIZEN'"

What about the jury-service obligation? Less than a year after election-law revision, Democrats meeting at Walla Walla disclosed their platform at the eleventh hour; it included a plank endorsing equal suffrage but eliminated compulsory jury duty for women. If propertied women could not be barred from an obligation long associated with full citizenship, surely they ought not to be forced: "We are in favor of so amending the law as *to relieve women from compulsory jury duty within this Territory*, and with this amendment we heartily endorse the present law extending the right of suffrage to women, and declare that the elective franchise should not be denied to any citizen on account of sex."[22] In mid-September, Duniway praised Democrats' positive step forward but reminded them that citizenship entailed duties as well as "rights and powers." Territorial women suffered "little annoyance from jury service"; testimony abounded that juries were "valuable aids in enforcing the statutes." Why not register jurors and voters simultaneously? Women who preferred not to sit on juries could avoid politics altogether; those who were ready to fulfill "to the letter their demands for equal rights" would cheerfully register.[23] Break-away factions also addressed the question of what political

[21] "The Democracy of King County, in Convention Assembled ...," *SDPI*, September 7, 1884.
[22] Voorhees, "The Democracy of Washington ...," *SDPI*, September 11, 1884. Emphasis added. See also "Proceedings of the Territorial Democratic Convention [September 10]," *TDL*, September 11, 1884. See also comparison of platforms, "Democratic and Republican Principles," *SPI*, October 1, 1884, where the Democrats' anti-jury-duty plank re-appears.
[23] "Jury Service for Women," *NN*, September 18, 1884.

equality entailed: King County's new Independent Republicans, unhappy with Democratic policies toward monopolists and with suffrage compromises, published a platform defending the equal, inherent rights of both men and women. In mid-September, however, Pierce County Independents declared, "We believe that all citizens, of either sex, who are tax payers, should be allowed the right of suffrage, *but we demand that all female citizens should be relieved by law from jury duty.*"[24]

Meanwhile, journalists dogged female jurors; by comparison, the tracking of office holders had been slight. In Tacoma, at least eleven married women had been summoned for grand-jury service; fourteen female names appeared on the *petit*-jury list, a dozen of them married. Editors encouraged debate of the jury-duty question. On one side, activists claimed that Tacoma's female jurors amply proved women's interest in public life: They not only turned out to the polls, but they also showed "a surprising fortitude in accepting the disagreeable task of serving on juries." None resorted to "subterfuges to escape," as men did, but accepted "martyrdom in a spirit all the more commendable from the great distaste they must naturally feel." A Cincinnatian predicted that Washington's success with jury integration invited imitation from coast to coast and a better class of jurors everywhere. First District Judge Samuel Wingard applauded the prospect of reliable women: "I would much rather have a good woman on the jury, than the average ... scrubby juryman."[25]

In August, 1884, a Seattle newcomer (probably Lelia Robinson) described the situation in great detail. She had visited Roger Greene's courtroom prepared to criticize the "imposition of jury duty on women," but changed her mind after observing a *petit* jury with equal numbers of men and women. The latter embodied feminine decorum and sophistication; there were two bailiffs in attendance, "husband and wife." Court personnel had never seen such an "intelligent, honest and reliable jury." Indeed, a grand jury composed of six women and eleven men had been so effective that "gambling and prostitution received a tremendous check" and liquor sales had plummeted. Women were intrepid. One grand juror, the wife of an ex-judge, had been in the midst of laundry when the sheriff arrived. "Why, how can I do it?" she asked. Comparisons to military service appeared here, as elsewhere:

The sheriff admitted that he didn't know. ... [T]he little woman rose to the emergency and as Putnam of Revolutionary fame left his plow in the furrow and rallied to the field of

---

[24] "Another Convention, the Independents, Not Satisfied with the Action of the Democrats ...," *SDPI*, September 9, 1884, repr. *NN*, untitled, September 18, 1884. See also H. K. Moore, Jacob Ralph, E. G. Bacon, "Platform of Pierce County Independents [meeting of September 16, Tacoma]," *SDPI*, September 19, 1884. Emphasis added. See also "The Independents," *TDL*, September 17, 1884.

[25] "Jury List," *TDL*, May 27, 1884 (Roger Greene's circuit); two untitled editorials, ibid., May 25, 1884; "About Jurors," ibid., June 24, 1884; "Judge Wingard of the first district ...," ibid., May 9, 1884. See also a Baptist minister, [Rev.] D. J. Pierce, "Woman Suffrage," *SDPI*, October 23, 1883 (about Wyoming success with mixed juries).

battle, so did she have her clothes in the suds, and within an hour's time she had found a neighbor's daughter ... to take care of her house, had changed her dress, and was the first juror to arrive in the Court room, much to the surprise of her husband, who was there on behalf of his clients, and who did not know that his wife had been summoned.[26]

Others agreed. Orange Jacobs submitted an enthusiastic report from Whatcom: "The world is moving! Eight women are on the grand jury just organized."[27] But close-to-the-ground journalistic surveillance and the naming of names cannot have pleased everyone. On Christmas Day, 1883, Seattle newspaper subscribers learned that the "first women on any legal jury in the Territory of Washington, or on the Pacific coast," had been seated in the District Court for Skagit County – "Mrs. Bradley, Mrs. Anderson and Mrs. Calhoun." Confusion ensued: All three had been willing to serve, though Calhoun ultimately did not, apparently because she was foreign-born. Nobody knew that her husband's citizenship sufficed. The sheer novelty of the empanelment had created "an intense sensation" – whether good or bad is unclear – in the small town.[28]

On the question of voting *per se*, activists easily (and often accurately) characterized anti-suffrage outbursts as departures from a general rule of acceptance. But negative responses to mixed-sex juries and to the general problem of women's relationship to the long list of traditional obligations were far from aberrational. To reduce voter turnout, opponents contended that women were susceptible to jury duty only if they actually voted; suffragists made clear that jury duty could happen to anyone. "Do not be deceived by them," wrote Mrs. C. P. Minkler in April, 1884. "We are legal voters whether we vote or not, therefore it makes no difference in that respect."[29]

From time to time, suffragists also told women that they could be excused for cause. But was it true? The law code did not list child care or laundry or pregnancy as ground for exemption. What about charges of intellectual inadequacy, domestic neglect, and gender transgression? And how could women possibly fulfill traditionally male obligations? The list had not expanded to accommodate women's patriotic contributions. "Some say it will not do for her to sit in the jury room," wrote a male defender. "Very well, let her not do so if she so elects. How few male voters ever act as jurors. The writer has

---

[26] Trimontaine, "Women and the Suffrage," *SDPI*, August 27, 1884. The name refers to the three hills on which Boston originally was built. A number of sentences resemble Lelia Robinson's later essay, "Women Jurors" in *Chicago Legal Times* (see below). Roger Greene admitted her to the bar in Seattle in 1884. See also praise for women's deportment in King County courtrooms; "Women as Jurors," *Washington Independent* (Pomeroy), December 11, 1884.

[27] O[range] Jacobs, "Women Acting as Grand Jurors," *NN*, January 17, 1884.

[28] "The Grand Jury of the District Court for Skagit County ...," *PSWC* [Port Townsend], December 25, 1883. The *PSWC* reported on December 27 that she should have been empaneled. Tracking of female jurors continued well into 1886; e.g., "District Court Proceedings," *WS*, June 11, 1886 (noting "two lady jurors" in a criminal trial).

[29] Mrs. C. P. Minkler, "To the Ladies of Montesano," *WS*, April 4, 1884.

been a voter for nearly twenty years and has never yet been called to act as a juror. 'Woman cannot fight' . . . . Very true, and nine-tenths of the needless . . . wars of history would never have been fought" with women in charge. Suffragists circulated bits of praise from anti-suffrage sources, as when Prosecuting Attorney McFadden, a known skeptic, witnessed mixed-sex juries at Chehalis and concluded that a woman juror was superior to a man and "more anxious to do her duty." But court personnel apparently had in mind de- or re-gendering a masculine space: Much foul language had been purged, for instance, in order to persuade her that she was "in her own home" and not in a setting reminiscent of a Masonic temple.[30]

Citizens took sides. In June, 1884, controversy swirled around a former assemblyman, P. B. Johnson, now an editor in Walla Walla, who apparently had been ambivalent at best about woman suffrage a year earlier. Deeper study of the situation led him to say that mixed suffrage was misguided, largely because jury duty was "exceedingly disagreeable and irksome" to women themselves. Duniway quickly secured testimony from eleven *petit* jurors in Tacoma, all married women: "We, the undersigned, jurors of the last term . . . for Pierce County . . . wish to contradict the statement . . . . We found our duties neither irksome nor disagreeable . . . . Some of us could have been excused for the best of reasons, had we sought such privilege. The jury was fourteen hours in deliberation on one case, and twenty-four hours on another; and there were more complaints from the men than from the women." Her comrades had served cheerfully and would "do so again."[31]

Jury sequestration, though, invited embarrassment or trauma. Physical mingling involved unwelcome jostling or disclosures of private information ordinarily secreted at home. A brief, womanly presence at the polls, even in a pub or other manly space, seemed comparatively safe. References recur to childbirth, babies, pregnancy, "sickness" (a polite reference to menstruation or maternal nausea), and other incidents of women's sexuality, particularly those brought to light when jurors were cloistered "to sift the evidence, hearken to the charge . . . and discuss what the verdict shall be." But, equally, men preferred not to reveal their proclivities and shortcomings – as if women might be ignorant of them. The "sickening scandals, gross indecencies and nasty pruriencies," while presented as vulgarities that only men could bear, included not only evidence of rape, incest, and wife beating but also spittoons, clouds of tobacco smoke, and bawdy jokes. Concerns were not allayed when legislators in 1886 adopted a mini-Comstock law aimed at purveyors of lewd literature and other indecencies, and made juries the "sole and exclusive judges as to whether or not the matter circulated is obscene or indecent."[32]

---

[30] "Strong Suffrage Testimony," *SDPI*, November 9, 1883, repr. "The School Election," *PSWC*, November 6, 1883; "Woman as Jurors," *NN*, February 28, 1884.

[31] "Results of Deeper Study," *NN*, July 3, 1884.

[32] See, e.g., a reference to making "sickness" a sex-specific excuse for exemption, "Washington Legislature," *NN*, December 10, 1885. Ladies rarely spoke of menstruation, morning sickness,

Many Washingtonians recoiled at the prospect of strangers gawking at bare-breasted mothers feeding babies, or wives developing friendships with men in isolated chambers, sometimes overnight, that could disrupt or taint women's relationships (to use Roger Greene's phrase at Port Townsend) with "husband, fathers, sons." Nor could non-wage-earning, non-professional women gain exemption for domestic work or physical distress as automatically as could men for their business concerns; speaking of "sickness," particularly if strange men forced a woman to indicate what kind of sickness, could be humiliating or disabling (in the sense of reinforcing the idea of disabilities of sex). In 1886, the *New Northwest* disgustedly reprinted a series of letters condemning jury duty for women: Not only were women forced to stop nursing babies for want of private space, but, if juries failed to reach a verdict, wives would be "locked up in the jury-room, like any other jury, over night." The strong odor of rape or kidnapping permeated many of these warnings. Men did not want to come home and discover that the sheriff had absconded with wives and daughters for jury service or any other purpose. The extraordinarily violent tropes associated with women on juries serve as a rough indicator of citizens' sense of actual or imminent violation of gender practices. Why else would citizens "rise as a unit," arguing that jury duty was the "one thing that will destroy the modesty of woman, ruin her virtue, and *wreck her home*"?[33] Thus, in Whatcom County, court personnel carved out spaces that might accommodate women and their special needs; journalists made things worse by naming names: "On the suggestion of His Honor, Judge Greene, eight [women] had been duly summoned on the grand jury – thus equally dividing with the ladies that blessed privilege of unearthing and investigating the criminal conduct of evil doers. The following were sworn in as grand jurors ... : LADIES, Mrs. M. H. Mayhew, Mrs. Will D. Jenkins, Mrs. J. G. Powell, Mrs. R. E. McPherson, Mrs. R. Merriam, Mrs. E. A. Vernon, Mrs. E. C. Pentland, Mrs. L. M. Durkee," followed by the names of eight men, none of them married to empaneled women. The group retired to "cozy quarters over the city drug store" which had been vacated "out of courtesy to the female portion of the jury." Greene personally provided reading material and hymn books, as of to elevate and sanctify the scene.[34]

Washingtonians were not alone. Across the nation, harsh language betrayed an attenuated sense of gender transgression. Certain secrets were off limits to strange men. Most notoriously, in 1879, Justice Ryan of the Wisconsin Supreme Court said in his ruling against attorney Lavinia Goodell's right to practice law that the physical intrusion of female bodies in courtrooms not only offended nature but was "treason against it"; unfit for women's contemplation

and hot flashes; to hear them mentioned even indirectly indicates strong concern. See also "The Circulation of Obscene Matter," *SR*, April 1, 1886.
[33] "A Texas Scribbler Answered," *NN*, November 18, 1886; "Jury Service for Women," ibid., December 18, 1884.
[34] "District Court Items," *WR*, January 11, 1884; "Local Matters," *True Tone*, October 31, 1885.

("unclean") were issues tied directly to women's bodies – e.g., "sodomy, incest, rape, seduction, fornication, adultery, pregnancy, bastardy, legitimacy, prostitution, lascivious cohabitation, abortion, infanticide," and so on. Consider as well the well-known ditty about female jurors in Wisconsin courtrooms. A little-told preface to the poem ("Nice little baby, don't get in a fury, "Cause mama's gone to sit upon the jury"), reprinted in Tacoma, involved a nursing mother called against her will to jury duty, whose "infantile responsibility" awoke and "began to make things lively" until he was fed in open court.[35]

Activists wielded autobiography to inform and persuade. In response to a fierce essay about "joyless" female jury service in the west, Winnie F. Thomas of Seattle's WERA and WCTU chapters asked why anyone would expect jurors of either sex to be joyful. She had never been an advocate of suffrage and thus was "unprepared for the duties before me in the use of the privilege given in the franchise." Her first activity had been jury duty, and "though it seemed the most objectionable as well as the most important as a test of woman's power," she did it anyway. "The results ... exceeded general expectation, the women as a rule being interested and edified .... [W]omen in the jury box are called upon to exercise many powers outside of the sphere hitherto marked out for them. ... Never having been in Utah or Wyoming, I do not know how much joy was experienced there, but should imagine very little in the right to ... share the responsibilities of straightening out the tangled up mess of public affairs. ... It is impossible to tell ... how much of woman's sense of justice has not only been ignored, but scorned."[36]

Two female jurors' story, however, illustrated the rough handling of women and the problem of forced intimacy. In November, 1884, Almira Kidd and Nellie Wood had served as jurors in Seattle, where minorities were "not allowed to exist," in a smuggling case involving the "Lone Fisherman." The women alleged that bullying had begun at once in a staircase encounter with a man who warned that he would "hang the jury" and that they could do nothing. An unhappy juror, Mrs. Ludlow, advised them to do as the men did. When Kidd insisted that she would judge for herself, another juror, Mr. Jones, declared that she had no right to an opinion until the judge had delivered his charge. "This act of thinking for oneself," she wrote, "was the occasion of threats of being reported, punished, complained of." As tempers flared, Ludlow declared that the burden was too weighty for women; she hoped it would be the last time they would be used as jurors. Kidd and Wood refused to convict on the ground that prosecutors had not made their case; after supper, Ludlow slept on two anteroom chairs in plain view of strangers. By morning, someone had written

[35] Justice Ryan in Lavinia Goodell's case, quoted in VanBurkleo, *Belonging to the World*, op cit., p. 163; "Female Jurors," *TDL*, November 2, 1884.
[36] "Woman Suffrage in the West," reprinting a hostile *NYT* article, with response from an "ex-juror" [W. P. Thomas], *SDPI*, front page, September 16, 1884. Thomas was the president of the Western WCTU. See her elaboration on the topic, below.

over their seats, "We are tired of the women." When Ludlow accused them of harming the women's-rights cause, they lost patience. "What has woman's rights to do with it?" asked Wood. "We are here to decide whether this man is guilty or not." An acquittal ensued, whereupon Jones wagged his finger at Wood: "You ought to be ashamed of yourself to hold out against ten of us." He threatened retaliation; according to Kidd and Wood, threats later bore fruit in the form of peremptory challenges in Greene's Seattle courtroom. "It was a plain open challenge ... and cast a reflection on our right of opinion and judgment as jurors."[37]

Children – the ultimate middle-class symbols of innocence – sometimes sat with their mothers in jury boxes or witness stands and could be manipulated by lawyers. In 1887, Lelia Robinson retrospectively described a trial for assault and a vicious stabbing. The main prosecutorial witness was a woman; the jury included six women, some married; the accused was a young widow "from one of the back mining-districts." The witness was "vile and ugly," whereas the prisoner was "beautiful and seemed entirely honest and good." The unattractive woman, a neighbor of the accused, supposedly resented her appeal to a particular man. One of the jurors had been summoned hastily and so had brought her small boy to court, where he watched the proceeding at the end of the jury box from a rocking-chair provided by the sheriff. The accused had brought her daughter; the pretty child ran about inside the bar making friends with lawyers and officers of court, "looking longingly up at the kind-faced judge [Greene], but not quite daring to mount the steps of the bench, and then returning to her ... mother, to fall asleep on her breast." The jury convicted her. But Robinson, keenly aware of the destabilizing role that children and neighborhood lore had played, was not certain that justice would prevail until Greene read the verdict.[38]

Small wonder, then, that women registered extreme discomfort or that public officers sometimes tried to sabotage mixed-sex jury service, given a general failure to democratize households or to prevent the quasi-pornographic reception of privacies. In May, 1884, the Superintendent of Public Instruction in Salem, Oregon, composed a report after a long stay in Seattle about the city's response to equal suffrage in which he assumed the conveyance of a bundle of rights – that is, the "right of suffrage and the ... imposition of the responsible duties springing therefrom." But, in Washington, officials were openly tampering with jury rolls, if only to aid frightened or angry women. A letter included in Powell's report suggests that the King County sheriff chose only those who he knew to be "representative women"; they understood "what was expected of them" and did it unflinchingly. While

[37] Almira Kidd and Nellie Wood, "Coercion of Jurors," *SDPI*, November 11, 1884. See early notice of the two women's holdout, "Failed to Agree," ibid., November 7, 1884. Reprinted as "Women on the Jury," *WP*, December 19, 1884, p. 7. See *U.S.* v. *Lone Fisherman*, 3 Wash Terr Rpts 316 (1887).

[38] Lelia Robinson, "Women Jurors," *Chicago Legal Times*, Vol. 1, No. 29–31 (1887).

praising the improvement of anterooms and trial outcomes, Powell noted that women had, "in many instances, shrunk from the performance of jury duty, just as might have [been] expected," though they had not refused to serve.[39]

As tensions grew, women's-rights activists mobilized: At least seventy-five of them gathered at Seattle's King County Courthouse in September, 1884, to found the Woman's Equal Rights Association [WERA], plan another meeting, and extend an invitation to other women. In light of the rising tide of anti-jury sentiment, members feared a softening of legislative support for suffrage itself. In September, 1884, more than a dozen prominent women attended a rally and steamboat ride, which ended with a storm and mud bath for everyone. But, before disaster struck, Mrs. Orange Jacobs and Mrs. Amos Hurst demanded a fair trial of equal suffrage and the return only of pro-suffrage men.[40] When Abigail Duniway again visited the territory on election eve in October, 1884, she addressed the jury-service quandary: Women wanted to be "free to use our power both at the polls and in the jury room." Would women be altered by long stays in anterooms? One Oregonian traveler had expressed fear that his juror wife might mingle promiscuously with eleven men. Said Duniway unhelpfully, "You have been away from home a long time; how do you know but that eleven dozen men may have been there. I think you had better go home." She worried about attempts to bar women from juries basically for inviting promiscuous speculation. "A woman who conducts herself properly can travel all over this land without fear of being molested. ...."

The same holds good in the jury room, and there is no more danger of one woman sitting on a jury with eleven men that there is of one man sitting on a jury with eleven women. ... This talk of relieving you of jury duty is dangerous. It is the entering wedge to your disfranchisement, and if you send Legislators who will vote to take away your right to sit on a jury, what is to hinder them from relieving you of your ballot.

In convention, Democrats had laughed about "the jury taffy they had extended to the women in their platform"; they had been surprised to see many women "refuse taffy."[41]

Into 1884, Duniway repeatedly addressed undercurrents of anxiety. Jury duty was "a great bugbear to some opponents of woman suffrage," she noted. "To hear the talk of gossiping men, one would imagine that all the time of all women will be used in jury service as soon as women are enfranchised; yet ... a

---

[39] L. J. Powell, "Woman Suffrage in Washington," *NN*, May 9, 1884. This is probably Prof. L. J. Powell, who died in Seattle in 1887 after a career in both Washington and Oregon.

[40] "Woman's Equal Rights Association," *SDPI*, September 12, 1884; "Republican Rally at Houghton," ibid., September 28, 1884.

[41] "Mrs. Duniway," *SDPI*, October 31, 1884. See also the excerpt from *NN*, credited to Duniway but significantly rewritten, "Writing of the political situation ... " (" ... the Democrats have tendered women a bit of taffy in shape of a plank that offers to excuse them from 'compulsory' jury duty. Wise women refuse to accept this proffered amnesty, considering it a reflection on their patriotism to ask them to shirk the duties of citizenship while enjoying its honors"), *WWU*, November 1, 1884, editorial page.

man serves on a jury but once in a score of years. ... Occasionally it might be inconvenient for a woman to serve, just as it is occasionally inconvenient for a man to do so; but certainly no one would propose the disfranchisement of men on that ground." Granting that it might be "the fearful thing which some people imagine, it would be as easy to exempt women because of their duties in the home as to exempt a class of men." But she opposed exemption, though word choices suggest a degree of concern about women with multiple burdens: "Competent and *unencumbered* women should serve." She then made a bad situation worse by suggesting that jurors, having served an apprenticeship in jury boxes, could move into public offices and help frame territorial law.[42]

Increasingly, the issue for critics of equality was whether suffragism would founder on the shoals of ancillary rights. In Walla Walla, a female voter asked an editor to solicit letters from women about jury service. Since enfranchisement meant more than "permission to vote," it was perhaps time to learn whether women were "butterflies or slaves ... [and] silence now would be cowardly if not criminal."[43] In August, 1884, on the eve of a Republican convention, Seattle commentators identified two questions animating local politics – whether railroaders would receive unearned land grants, and whether voters would tolerate "interference with the law conferring the ballot upon woman in this territory," less because of balloting than because of their presence on juries. Would Republicans stand firm, in keeping with the "wishes of voters"? As a WERA speaker observed on the eve of 1884 general elections, while confusion reigned on the question of the "political doings" of women, they wielded enormous influence.[44]

Unease sometimes spawned paranoia. In 1884, a widely circulated magazine warned that, once women decided to combine and form majorities, they would "absolutely control legislation"[45] and trial outcomes. Great consternation emerged about the composition of *petit* juries in Justice John Hoyt's district court – the county that would generate the all-important Rosencrantz case: A *petit*-jury list for the Pierce County Court was said to be composed entirely of women. In autumn, the male element was exhausted; some women were added by the judge to create panels. In preparing the venire, the clerk was forced to rely on a supplementary list composed wholly of women, to which the court resorted when men were unavailable. There seemed to be "some doubt of the legality" or efficacy of the procedure. Writers speculated that women's presence in the wings may have encouraged men to excuse themselves, leaving litigants

---

[42] "Women as Jurors," *NN*, February 28, 1884; "Women Vote at Seattle," ibid., July 17, 1884. Emphasis added.

[43] "One of the Enfranchised," "A Woman's Question," *WWU*, November 1, 1884.

[44] Editorial, *SDPI*, August 21, 1884; "The Ladies' Meeting," *SDPI*, October 18, 1884. See also "An Appeal to the Women Voters of King County," ibid., October 26, 1884, printing a resolution, asking women to support a slate of Republicans and Independents who were "squarely" behind equality.

[45] "Women Voters," *The Saturday Review*, Vol. 57, May 31, 1884, p. 698.

entirely at the mercy of inexperienced jurors.[46] But destabilizing, discriminatory practices worked both ways. In November, 1885, an angry would-be juror suggested that courts were retreating from the use of women on panels and pointed disapprovingly to female opposition. "Here, in our corner of the globe," she noted sharply, "there is a new Administration. New, because there is a new element to be dealt with – a 'new citizen.' ... Our County Commissioners seem to have forgotten the new citizen. Therefore, she rises [to ask] ... 'Why?' We allude to the drawing of the jury for the coming term of Court, to be held in Thurston County. We accepted the duty of the jury as a privilege as well as a citizen's duty. We served ... faithfully, and according to the verdict of the Court, well; and now ask why we are excluded from the present empanel? Is it because some have declined? Or is it a political trick to have its weight at the coming Legislature?"[47]

In March, 1884, a particularly nasty attack on mixed-sex juries appeared in Whatcom County. To some extent, concern reflected local reliance on saloon taxes. But, in the main, critics dragged men over the coals for refusing to govern or to protect women from mortification. "M.D.C." claimed to be unable to see "what honor comes in neglecting her home duties to sit hour after hour on jury and be obliged to listen to such vile slander ... as to call the blush of shame to the brow of a modest man. It is the greatest disgrace that could fall upon us. Are not the gentlemen of to-day just as capable of running the affairs of county and state as in the past?" With others, "M.D.C." also lambasted invasions of women's privacy. Jury duty was "the greatest piece of imposition I ever heard of, for ladies who would prefer to live their old life in the heart of their family and leave the affairs of county and state to the opposite sex, can have no voice in the matter, but must be ... actually dragged by officers of the law to the courtroom, *no matter what their condition may be*, and there must be forced to tell why they were not in readiness." If women "*say they were sick*, that wont do, for the old blear-eyed, bloated-faced judge without one spark of manhood ... will ask you how long you have been sick, and a thousand and one questions ... , just because you are a woman." It was scandalous that women would be "studying up points of the law, attending law-suits and sitting jury and stumping the county." "Mrs. Dickenson" agreed, condemning "women's rights being forced upon us." It would take a strong argument "to persuade women that it is their duty to sit on juries." They could vote and engage in charitable works instead.[48]

---

[46] Correspondence page, *WS*, April 24, 1885; repr. "The Pierce County Jury, From the Tacoma News," *NN*, May 14, 1885. For Rosencrantz, see below. The all-woman jury cannot be found in Thurston County records. See also "The Duty of Jurors," *SDPI*, April 15, 1885, about a "mother of two" supposedly incapable of objectivity on an unspecified jury when another mother was in the dock.

[47] "A Woman's Query," *WS*, June 5, 1885.

[48] "Go Slow," *WR*, January 11, 1884; M.D.C., "Against Woman Suffrage," ibid., March 7, 1884, front page, emphasis added; Mrs. Dickenson, "Woman Suffrage. A Reply to M.D.C.," ibid., September 19, 1884, front page.

Opponents laid bare women's sense of double burden and embarrassment. In January, 1885, for instance, Justice Samuel Wingard supposedly told the *Walla Walla Union* that, in his experiences of mixed-sex juries at Dayton, women made "as good jurors as the average juryman," but could not serve without neglecting home duties that they alone could perform. At Dayton, he added, some women had to be excused for ill health, and others were "made sick by being compelled to stay out all night with a lot of obstinate men and women." Wingard conceived of homemaking as a *bona fide* occupation: Women should be excused from jury duty "as are preachers, doctors, lawyers, firemen, millers, postmasters and others."[49] A. R. Smith was far less accommodating: "Women did not ask for suffrage. It has been forced upon them, and I think it is an outrage that ladies should be 'raked over' on the question of being qualified or whether it is her place." The problem of obligations loomed large. "How many lies and disreputable charges are brought against men running for office? How will it be when women take an active part against a woman candidate? ... Had the women the privilege to refuse to act on juries or do other duties forced on her by the suffrage bill, then she might welcome the doctrine .... When the time comes to collect poll and road tax, the poor man will have to labor six days to work out his tax unless his wife puts on the pants .... Of course women want roads, but will they make them?"[50]

More and more, it was necessary to show that political rituals were respectable and to hold politicians' feet to the fire. Into 1885, Duniway portrayed elections as community fetes in which men walked "side by side and arm in arm with their wives" to cast ballots. On the eve of the 1884 elections, the WERA stepped up its educational and voter-registration drives. On October 11, 1884, at a mixed-sex meeting at the Tacoma YMCA, the WERA formed a committee to canvass the city and remind every woman of the "pressing necessity" of voting at the next election. Another committee, composed of Lister, Munroe and McCoy, would select a "thoroughly woman's rights man" to run for Council. Meanwhile, activists published letters to party leaders demanding a public airing of their positions on suffrage. McCoy and Mrs. Frances Barlow, for example, as WERA officers, averred that government had violated its principles in depriving "one-half of the nation of any voice" and asked Democrats if they agreed. A similar letter, addressed to George W. Byrd of Pierce County and C. W. Young in Kitsap County, both Republican nominees for council and assembly, bore the signatures of ten WERA members (including Lister, Barlow, and McCoy), and asked them to pledge support for equality.[51] At month's end, the WERA

---

[49] "Judge Wingard ...," *WWU*, January 24, 1885, editorial page.
[50] A. R. Smith, "Both Sides of Woman Suffrage," *WR*, August 22, 1884, front page.
[51] R. R. R., "From One of the New Voters," *NN*, November 20, 1884; "Equal Rights Association," *TDL*, October 12, 1884; "Some Leading Questions," ibid., October 2, 1884; "Many Women Voters," ibid., September 14, 1884; and "Are They For Woman Suffrage?" ibid., September 18, 1884.

urged women to support Judge Orange Jacobs, four other Republicans, and one Democrat for Council. While women ought to be free to make their own choices, it was vital to support unflinchingly pro-suffrage men.[52]

Certainly jury duty seemed to jeopardize the broader cause of political equality. In October, 1884, in a pre-election "last call," Duniway warned of a plot to eliminate woman suffrage, largely because conspirators feared "the power of women in the jury-box." Success would be a blow to territorial women and to "the civilized world."[53] At a WERA-sponsored event in Seattle, Orange Jacobs, William H. White, and Duniway addressed the dangers that stalked women, chief among them, "the proposition to relieve women from 'compulsory' jury duty, against which the wisest of the new voters are exclaiming . . . with the zeal that proves them truly worthy of all the rights of citizenship." A few weeks later, Duniway again confronted Democratic promises of jury-duty exemption: Some women, perhaps many, might welcome a change – though not poor women; one woman had said that she had served ten days as a juror and had earned thirty dollars – "the first money she had ever earned in her life 'doing nothing.' The secret was out." Much of the opposition to mixed-sex panels came from men seeking easy cash; a law that relieved women from "compulsory duty at the wash-tub or mop-stick" might be more beneficial. Mercifully, voters returned a pro-suffrage majority to the Assembly: Surely the election had allayed fears about women's lack of interest in voting. But turnout occurred in spite of widespread confusion about jury duty and politicians' disinterest in finding alternative, legitimate ways for women to serve their communities.[54]

"THAT HE, WITH HER AND NOT APART FROM HER, MAY RULE"

Before 1883, Justice Roger Greene had taken a conventional view of jurors. In 1882, he did suggest, a bit unusually, that a juror's vote might be analogous to that of a legislator. But, in the main, he simply advised jurors to exercise good sense in determining fact and in expressing the neighborhood's moral sense. A year later, he said again that, beyond fact-finding, a grand jury's special duty lay in "discouraging vice and promoting virtue."[55] In October, 1883, however, complacency vanished. Greene eagerly welcomed a Pierce County grand jury

---

[52] "An Appeal to the Women Voters of King County," *SDPI*, October 26, 1884; "To the Women Voters of King County," ibid., October 31, 1884 ("The aggressive work has been done for us, and done by men," so women should vote for them); "More Independent Women," *NN*, October 23, 1884. WERA members planned to distribute their own ballots.

[53] "The Last Call," *NN*, October 30, 1884, front page.

[54] A[bigail] S. D[uniway], "Editorial Correspondence," *NN*, November 6, 1884, front page. See also reports of high turnout among women at November 4 election; "Woman Suffrage a Success," ibid., November 6, 1884; Duniway, "Editorial Correspondence," ibid., November 13, 1884, front page, emphasis added; "The Election in Washington," ibid., November 13, 1884.

[55] Roger Greene, "Charge to the Grand Jury, District Court . . . ," *PSWA*, September 8, 1882.

composed of six men and six women and immediately began to exploit both the jury as an institution and women's special attributes as community exponents. He had presided over seven mixed-sex *petit* juries and had concluded that mothers ought to be able to migrate from private to public life without impediment: The administration of justice at home had long been regarded as woman's work; men supposed her to be a reliable counterbalance to domestic evils. Why not elsewhere? "[T]his educatory and judicial process has been freely allotted woman as within the proper province for her." Yet, by a "strange inconsistency and perversity," she had been denied the privilege of participation in public life – for "assuming the place of such an *educator and judge*" – and refused "any direct voice in what shall be done." In his reading of the Bible, this was wrong: "Equally to woman as to man was given the primitive right and duty to subdue and rule the earth." Why not use women's brains and moral sense? *"Let the one who can be of most use, be used for the state."* Woman merited inclusion on the same basis as man, "for all that she is worth." Gender ascriptions were limiting and enriching. No human being had "so profound a knowledge of human nature as the observant matron who has reared a family, and no one is more competent to deal intelligently ... with most cases." Women's lives differed from men's; this fact diminished *"her serviceableness in some cases and in some respects"* but added *"at least as much in others."*[56]

As 1884 advanced, Roger Greene came to function as a lightning rod for citizens who feared social derangement. As early as December, 1883, Olympians accused him during a trial for perjury of delivering purely technical rulings that destroyed public faith in law. Then the same editors, who by 1883–84 sought a Democrat to take Greene's place, shifted gears, away from charges of cold-blooded technicality toward allegations of hot-blooded emotionalism and religious zealotry. Part and parcel of this shift was the suggestion that women in jury boxes were proving to be pliant, weak-minded acolytes, susceptible to the judge's charisma. He provided ammunition. In a remarkable grand jury charge in January, 1880, for example, he had said this: "Good citizenship is faith and hope in Him. ... Responsibility of the gravest sort rests upon you and me"; if citizens lacked understanding, they could give over the mystery to a judge conversant with God. "I am, gentlemen, a religious man." For a growing number of observers, Greene was an egomaniacal polygamist. His behavior was "anything but the actions of a sane man"; the new voters "so lately entrusted with a voice in support of law, *a rule which lies at the foundation of the social fabric*, should

---

[56] Greene, "Charge to the Grand Jury, Opening of the District Court," *SDPI*, October 9, 1883. See also "Women as Jurors," reprinting Portland and Chicago papers, *NN*, February 4, 1885; a Chicago reporter had been in Greene's courtroom and learned that "peculiarities ... of both sexes would be brought to bear on all cases, woman's intuition coupled with man's logical faculties would ... lead to correct and just conclusions." See also "Charge to the Jury," *TDL*, May 20, 1884. Emphasis added.

reflect upon this matter before they implicitly entrust a man whose official recognition of their rights has been attended by acts ... of very doubtful propriety. The *people* have had enough of Judge Greene."[57] To some extent, Greene's pastoral tone reflected not only his Seattle lay ministry, but also the belief, as laid out in 1878, that "ministers of the law" had been called to control and educate citizens behaving like a "lot of school boys without a master." Critics were unrelenting. In early 1885, the *Standard* assailed a brilliant "madman" who could be "thrown off his balance mentally ... by his surroundings and the advice of those who worship in the same sanctuary." The same writers chastised women for squandering hard-won power on a "fanatical Judge" devoted to the "Connecticut Blue laws."[58]

Did women's presence in jury boxes flout natural law? Roger Greene thought not; indeed, he began a campaign to tear down walls and weaken restrictive oppositions – as with nature and social assignment, private and public realms, women and virtue. In 1884, he tried to associate purity with both sexes. This was a risky undertaking: More was at issue than women's purity or modesty. Purity spoke to contamination and modesty to cloaks of secrecy around bodies or private knowledge. Greene saw that the issue was gender transgression and insults to social practice when women metamorphosed into law-givers. Yet, should walls actually fall, men would resist feminization. Women, Greene argued, were no more liable to corruption than men; both sexes ought to embody morality. Here, he had to deal with social practice and women's self-constitution: Port Townsend women worried about "the delicacy and modesty which are an honor and ornament to your sex. But in a few hours, by an *easily gained familiarity, you will lose all embarrassment,* ... and ... discover that in the properly regulated court or grand jury there is nothing to shock the modesty ... of the most innocent or refined. The law loves modesty and purity in man as well as woman. It recognizes no such distinction between man's modesty and woman's as would impute a sacredness to the one not belonging to the other. ... But it does regard purity of heart as being that qualification which ... fortifies ... a man or woman against pollution."[59]

---

[57] "Cause and Effect," *WS*, November 9, 1883; "District Court," *SDPI*, January 27, 1880; "Judge Greene," *WS*, November 26, 1884. Emphasis added.

[58] "An Independent Judiciary," *SDPI*, November 23, 1878; editorial, "Judicial Qualifications," *WS*, January 2, 1885. See "Laudable Ambition of a Judge," suggesting that he might be better suited to work as a barber, where he could ask everyone, "[D]o you love Jesus?" ibid., June 5, 1885. See also "A Lesson of the Hour," *WS*, July 17, 1885. For a typical "law and order" plea, see "The Appeal of a Woman to the Women of Seattle," *SDPI*, July 10, 1885 (advocating female support of the "law and order" slate).

[59] "Judge Greene and Women Jurors, August Term, 1884, Port Townsend," 17 *Chicago Legal News* 29 (1884–85). See also "Instructive to the New Voters. Chief Justice Greene's Charge to the Grand Jury of Port Townsend, W.T.," *NN*, September 11, 1884, repr. "Judge Greene and Women Jurors," 17 *Chicago Legal News* 29 (1884). Myra Bradwell explained that this was "such an unusual proceeding" that she gave a "liberal extract."

In the air, then, were serious concerns about the possible loss of equality through its association with zealotry and a cruel publicity. A Seattle correspondent urged female voters and jurors to ignore controversy and to embrace jury duty, "the badge of sovereignty," at all cost.[60] Greene himself saw danger in the very idea that vested rights should be tossed aside for cowardice. "The women suffrage and jury question is regarded largely by the great mass of the people as being experimental," wrote a Puget Sound observer. He had asked Greene for his opinion on the success of new legislation: "Said he, 'I can say that my expectations ... of women ... were very high, and that the results are coming fully up to those expectations.'" Men who benefitted from questionable practices "naturally shrink from having their doings judicially investigated by pure minded persons"; there was "bitter opposition to women serving as jurors; and ... many of our best women shrink from jury duty as one would shrink from a cold shower, but yet in nearly every instance ... they have expressed satisfaction at having performed [their] duty. We need them to purify and elevate the machinery of justice."[61]

Like Duniway, Greene knew that fundamental rights belonged in constitutions, not in law codes or statutes. But territories lacked autonomous constitutions. He therefore urged Seattle women to ignore implied threats of rescission; statehood would bring constitutional standing. In the meantime, women shared with men "the privilege of government" and attendant responsibilities. In his words, it was regrettable that "right stands evidenced by only statutory and not constitutional or organic law, for it is ... liable to be misconceived. Because it is statutory, one is apt to think it as ... a thing of sufferance." Female jurors were bound to feel "embarrassed and restrained." But the sexes stood precisely alike as to powers of self-rule, equally the beneficiaries of statutes. If women's rights were weakly founded, so were men's. Greene then interrogated the wall between private and public realms. Equality reflected "the enlightened proposition ... that such franchises are naturally and inherently, and should be constitutionally, her right. In fact, our legislation of last fall was a return to first principles. ... We are just escaping from feudalism. That monstrous offspring of brute force ... was a system of castles and fences ... to shut in power and shut out liberty, and shut up women." Republicans did not believe in "crowding the men out"; but they did believe that, "regardless of sex, all upon ... whose possession of rights, the laws are to operate – all, who are liable to be accused of ... breach of the laws – all on whose labor or property contribution is to be levied ... should be free to participate in saying what those laws shall be." For purposes of civil government, legislators gave "magisterial power ... to the male sex over the

[60] E. B. Ingraham, "A Word to Women," *SDPI*, July 5, 1885.
[61] "How It Works," *PSWA*, March 13, 1884, quoting a letter from Greene. The "cold shower" metaphor recurs; see, e.g., "The ladies of the Temperance Union," *TDL*, March 26, 1884. ("Some shrink from voting because they fear they will be liable to be called to jury service. ... [M]any shrink from voting, as Judge Greene says, as from taking a cold shower bath.")

female," but no such power "inheres naturally in the relation of the sexes, or in the relation of marriage," which was "naturally of partnership and love." Civil and marital equality thus compelled the razing of the public-private wall: "As husband to wife in the home, so to the great extent is man to woman in the state." It was man's duty to "assert for woman the partner's place with him, that he with her and not apart from her, may rule."[62]

The men and women assembled in Greene's courtrooms understood their notoriety. Foreman L. B. Andrews noted that deliberations had been harmonious: "[N]o objection can be made ... to the association of the male and female sex."[63] For good or ill, the jury charges and proceedings that editors publicized in the mid-1880s often originated in Greene's courtroom, in part because the judge personally conveyed his writing to editorial offices. Into 1885, moreover, Greene stoked the fires. In June, to offer one example, the chief justice composed and read an annual report to members of the Puget Sound Baptist Association. "We have girdle of truth, breastplate of righteousness, foot armor of peace, shield of faith and helmet of salvation that we may in security stand to wield offensively the sword of the spirit, which is the word of God." Baptists ought to resist all intemperance, whether in the use of alcohol or otherwise, in public or at home. "We are against the lust for it, and against the practice of it. We are against secret indulgence and against open display." By February, 1886, he had chosen sides in a doctrinal dispute between factions of Tacoma's First Baptist Church, personally baptizing members of a schismatic group. Reverend B. S. MacLafferty excommunicated all of them and told Greene to "Stay at Home."[64]

Still, experiences of jury service could be life-changing. In June, 1886, Seattle's Winnie Thomas, who was one of the first to record lawyerly resistance to mixed-sex jurors, elaborated on her coming-of-age. Before the King County sheriff delivered a summons, she claimed to have been perfectly satisfied with her life; she decided to vote in support of social reform. While she was still "chicken-like, just breaking my shell," she awoke to find herself a "full-fledged citizen," but was "somewhat astonished, altogether mystified at what I should do."

'Why, sir,' she told the sheriff, 'I am not fit to serve on the jury.'
'Why, madam, what reason have you to offer?'

[62] Front page, "Charge of Judge Greene to the Grand Jury [in Seattle]," *SDPI*, October 7, 1884. See also Duniway on one of Greene's criminal trials; "Women on a Petit Jury," *NN*, January 24, 1884. Women had stood tall against "croakers" and immorality.

[63] Foreman L. B. Andrews, "Report of the Grand Jury [October 18]," *SDPI*, October 19, 1884. Occasionally, newspapers published jury payments; see names of six women paid for *petit*-jury service, "District Court Proceedings," ibid., November 26, 1884; see also "District Court Proceedings," ibid., December 16, 1884, which suggests that women were serving the same number of days overall as men on both petit and grand juries.

[64] "Puget Sound Association," *SDPI*, June 28, 1885; "Baptist Church War," *TDL*, February 28, 1886. See also Greene's signature as a member of the organizing committee, "Baptist Convention for the North Pacific Coast," *SDPI*, November (3?), 1885.

'Why,' I replied, 'I am not capable; you want some one who can keep track of both sides of a case and then have judgment and determination.'

'Have you no other excuse? If not, you must allow me to be the judge;' and he very politely bowed himself out, leaving me in such a state of bewilderment as I never before experienced. My trembling knees ... telegraphed the purport of his message, but I concluded that my case was a hopeless one.[65]

Thomas decided to "go to Judge Greene: he would let me off." After listening, Greene "smiled and said that it was out of his power to excuse me, and if it were in his power he would not let me off, for I was the right person to be there." The day arrived; Thomas went to her doom. The fact that lawyers had objected to women on the grand jury the previous day increased anxiety. When a gambling case came up, she was called but then "objected to. Truly, what next? I simply stepped out of that jury-box and tried to find a corner. I did not know whether to feel slighted or complimented. I was sure of only one thing, I was not wanted on that case. But I soon had some company: one, two, more ladies were called off, and as they left what a smile passed over the faces of the lawyers! But more ladies were in the Jury-box. So they gave that up."[66] Thomas served a five-week term, experienced cloistering, and gathered compliments. One man contended that a "'real nice woman' would not sit on the jury," she wrote. "He made himself very conspicuous in his efforts to 'let them have enough of it.' But somebody else got enough of him ..., and he was excused." She also noted changes in the courthouse. "Tobacco-smoke, cigars, and spittoons disappeared"; knitting needles and other feminine paraphernalia replaced them.[67]

Roger Greene was fast becoming a liability. In April, 1885, he won praise for bringing a Snohomish-Indian man accused of murder to justice. But, a month later, a Whatcom County journalist charged him with irrationally demanding that purveyors of liquor prove good moral character in advance of licensing – a bar that few could meet.[68] He also became the target of a smear campaign, spearheaded by the bankrupted *Seattle Chronicle* and *Star*, to force his resignation. Greene had appointed a receiver to oversee the paper's bankruptcy and had removed the editor. The judge supposedly had "set up a little kingdom of his own in the Third District," the better to "control the consciences" of the people. Enemies rose to defend him; one lawyer who disliked Greene stoutly defended his abilities. In early 1885, the Young Men's

---

[65] "Women in the Jury-Box. Experience of Mrs. W[innie] F. Thomas of Washington Territory," *Chicago Daily Tribune*, June 29, 1886, p. 9; repr. as "A Female Juror: A Woman Relates Her Experience on a Washington Territory Jury," *Tacoma News*, August 6, 1886, but without attribution.

[66] "Women in the Jury-Box," op cit.

[67] Ibid. See also "A Seattle Lecturer," *SDPI*, December 11, 1886. Thomas later testified as to her experience before WCTU conventioneers in Minneapolis.

[68] "We are glad ...," *WR*, April 3, 1885 (*Territory* v. *Meigs*); "Last week ...," ibid., May 22, 1885.

Independent Political Club rebuked enemies of the judge and urged law-abiding citizens to cease interference with the judiciary.[69] Greene denied wrongdoing but indicated that he would not serve another term. In a "card" to newspapers, he noted the duty of citizens to lodge grievances but also the citizens' right of self-defense. Throughout, the main issue may well have been mixed-sex juries, which the same editor had described as the "first great show" of feminine power in which women drove out a "small army" of miscreants as members of "hermaphrodite juries."[70]

In a sense, Greene's "small army" indeed was hermaphroditic. Greene aimed to construct spouses as co-equal sovereigns occupying both realms jointly and severally, though with slightly different responsibilities, as if the whole were a marital estate. He had said as much in Mary Phelps' case, and he would do so again in several critical tests of mixed-sex juries. "Man," he told Port Townsend grand jurors in 1884, "... represents the farm, the shop, the office, and the battle field; woman the home. ... *Home is the germ and trunk of the State. Of childhood and home, woman is the competent representative,* and apart from her there is no fitting one." A "free man or a free woman is to be the real king or queen of the State"; the man or woman lacking a "simple and decisive voice" in the judicial business of government was "a subject and more or less a serf. ... If woman should have any influence in the capitol, she should have the counterpart influence in the court house." He warned women of a "determined movement afoot" to send them home; they should "make a record ... like what your sisters who have served on juries heretofore have already made." He also denounced unconstitutional confiscations of property in rights: To disenfranchise people who were "already free" was to "impose upon them the most dishonoring penalty that can be visited upon a criminal."[71]

---

[69] "Misrepresentation Reproved," *SDPI*, December [15], 1884; "Endorsement of Judge Greene," ibid., January 23, 1885; "Judge Greene," ibid., June 18, 1885. For outrage, see "An Indignant Mother's Protest," ibid., May 24, 1885. See also "Good Moral Character," ibid., May 10, 1885. For Chronicle controversy, see "Misrepresentation Reproved," ibid., December 17, 1884; "The Court and the Editor," ibid., May 23, 1885; and for a "long job," ibid., April 20, 1885. See also "Observer," "The Chronicle and Judge Greene," ibid., May 16, 1885, defending Greene's integrity. For "little kingdom," see "Judge Greene's Censorship," *WS*, April 24, 1885. See also "An Order of Court," ibid., April 18, 1885.

[70] "Card from Judge Greene," repr. SDPI, *NN*, May 7, 1885; "Displeased with Results," in part from Seattle Mirror, *NN*, October 2, 1884. Similarly, see "Ulterior Motives that ... Shape the Ends of Justice," *WS*, October 1, 1886. See also "Our Judiciary," *WS*, March 5, 1886; untitled, repr. undated article from WWS, in *WS*, August 8, 1886; and "He Made a Mistake," *WR*, January 16, 1885. But see "Mr. Justice Greene's Charge ...," *True Tone*, November 14, 1885, noting that he had been "dragged into a ... muddle" and dismissed as a "crank," but had proved to be an "honest and upright law-giver."

[71] Judge Roger Greene, Grand Jury Charge, Port Townsend, WA, August, 1884, in Stanton et al., *History of Woman Suffrage*, Vol. 4 (1902). Also printed in 17 *Chicago Legal News* 30 (1884–85). See also "Charge ...," *NN*, September 11, 1884. Emphasis added. Greene's ideas, in turn, generated talk about jury reform to eliminate panels staffed with women and "idlers": "The Jury System," repr. *WWU*, *WR*, February 1, 1884; "Grand Juries," *TDL*, January 4, 1885.

Greene thus contributed to competing schools of thought. On one hand, liberal lawmakers like the chief justice added bricks to the edifice of civil, marital, and political equality; indeed, in 1885, assemblymen expanded an 1877 statute that permitted spouses to testify against or on behalf of one another in criminal trials; now, they spoke as individuals in all disputes, civil and criminal. On the other hand, citizens who valorized essential, ineradicable gender distinctions (again including Greene, albeit as "separate but equal" distinctions of great value to government) characterized the fiction of equality as an insult to both nature and social practice. Casting a ballot was one thing; overnight, close deliberations in anterooms were quite another. "Betsy Blake," for one, urged Washingtonians in late 1884 to stop imposing identical political burdens on men and women beyond the polls. Did the citizenry really want a female Congressional delegate? Blake asked politically active women to "reflect a moment." Should they "as a minority, to gratify an ambition, impose upon a majority by forcing upon them all the duties of citizenship, including jury duty so dreaded and evaded by many?" Could a mother burdened at home give undivided attention to evidence?"[72]

In Port Townsend, staff writers expressed concern in early 1884 about the involuntary nature of women's jury service; they had noticed that, unlike male voters who could escape for causes listed in the law code, women without businesses or professions typically could not. Why not exempt the entire class? Failing that, why not use female jurors only when disputes involved women, the better to ensure sensitive readings of fact and avoid humiliating encounters? "The woman suffrage question is being practically tested at this term of our local district court by ladies serving as grand jurors," wrote the editor. At first, he had supported equality: "Considerable comment is being made of the fact of unsavory criminal cases coming before this jury, and it is argued by some that the jury box is an improper place for a lady to be." He had not seen that it "detracts from the womanly character of the ladies in question." Should a "poor, chaste girl" be cross-examined in court before a body composed only of men? He had seen no reason to exclude women from jury service, especially when other women were implicated. But, on reflection, he had changed his mind: While he deplored "the old, threadbare argument" about women's incapacity or the suggestion that they became "she-men," he now opposed compulsory service. The "plain inference" was that women serving on the grand jury had "lowered themselves so much that no man need respect them." At issue were women's reputations and something akin to a reign of terror. "We do not believe that ladies should be dragged into court to serve on juries against their will, or where such service would discommode them in the affairs of home; neither do we [want to] abuse those who ... so serve."[73]

[72] "What Our Lawmakers Are Doing," *SDPI*, December 23, 1885; "Betsy Blake," "Woman Suffrage," *WS*, September 5, 1884.
[73] "The woman suffrage question...," *PSWA*, March 6, 1884; "Women's Rights," ibid., March 13, 1884.

Clerks of court virtually everywhere memorialized strangeness, self-consciously listing female juries at the head of jury lists with "Mrs." or "Miss" in front of surnames, followed by men's initials and surnames (e.g., R. J. Smith); others wrote out women's first names but not men's. Women knew that they stood on foreign soil and that new obligations compounded their already heavy burdens. Why did equality create inequality? What if exemptions never materialized? In February, 1884, Mrs. E. A. Woodruff addressed delegates at a suffrage convention: "The cry often goes up, that if we are allowed to vote, we shall have to work the roads, serve in the army, hang men, and ... do many other disagreeable duties." In Congress, a Texan had warned that women would have to "work the roads and make rails"; he proposed saving them with disfranchisement. She replied, "Do you yourself work the roads? ... A great many able-bodied men, we know, hired substitutes to represent them in our late war. Were they disfranchised ... ? All men are not required to serve in the army." Women would even pay a poll tax to secure "equal wages for equal work." Her advice: "Take your place on the road, then, and let the man of the house stay at home and keep house, where he thinks the women have an easy time."[74]

But the path forward was murky and, especially in the hinterland, public information was lacking or inaccurate. Anti-suffragists did their best to terrify ordinary women and ridicule sympathetic men. "A common error," wrote a journalist on the eve of general elections in 1884, "is in the assumption that ladies who refrain from voting will escape liability to jury service." Not so. In many counties, jurors were drawn from the census, not from poll books. Should all women "refrain from voting they would all still be liable to jury duty .... Hence, let all the ladies vote with impunity. There are only two ways for your wife to escape the summons ... namely, have her play sick and send in a doctor's certificate ... or run her out of the territory .... [G]o complacently about your business and let your wife get experience of the jury room"; perhaps her report would "furnish information which may enable you to vote wisely."[75]

THE CASE OF MOLLIE ROSENCRANTZ, KEEPER OF A BAWDY HOUSE

As anti-jury-duty sentiment expanded, women's-rights activists learned that an "organized and persistent effort, backed by money and influence," would be made at the next legislature to repeal equal suffrage.[76] Duniway agreed: Given the uproar over jury duty and a growing sense of social instability, shrill anti-vice campaigns might be the final straw, particularly if women alienated saloon patrons. "Threats have been made," she said. Men feared "the power of women in the jury-box ... and at the polls." Women should support the friends of woman suffrage without regard to party. The situation worsened. Two weeks

[74] Mrs. E. A. Woodruff, Washington, "A Woman Voter's Address," *NN*, February 21, 1884.
[75] "Women Jurors," *TDL*, October 19, 1884. Mrs. C. P. Minkler, "To the Ladies of Montesano," *WS*, April 4, 1884.
[76] "To the Women Voters of King County," *SDPI*, October 31, 1884, signed by WERA officers.

before Christmas in 1885, Duniway issued another warning coupled with recrimination. While the "experimental stage" of reform had been satisfactory, many women had not shown the sense of public duty befitting the "great privilege" of suffrage; too few had "risen grandly to the occasion," disproving those who would arraign their capacities by "intelligent suffrages" and "conscientious discharges of jury duty." She urged anti-vice crusaders to "make haste slowly."[77]

Meanwhile, implementation of mixed-sex juries varied over the landscape. In coastal counties, women appeared at an early moment and persisted; east of the mountains, participation was virtually non-existent. As Puget Sound-area women became adept at the political process, however, and particularly as activists began to link female jury service to anti-vice crusades, participation increased. Reformers had worked feverishly during so-called Law and Order campaigns in mid-1884 to cart sympathetic men and women to the polls. In these plans, mixed grand juries played a critical role: According to a King County report, tides began to turn when a "celebrated grand jury on which women sat" had cleaned out "lawless lava-bed dives." Vice peddlers had "kept up a continual howl against Woman Suffrage" to prevent law enforcement; female grand jurors had been "insulted," resolving to mobilize more women.[78]

Near Puget Sound, women's presence in courthouses steadily expanded. In Pierce County, where WERA activists were mobilizing women for public duties and where a rising tide of opposition reflected a notoriously vice-ridden economy and city council, the nature and number of treasury warrants changed dramatically. In summer of 1881, the county had reimbursed only one woman for service as a witness; all jurors and bailiffs had been male. In 1882, women accepted public money for "medicine," "care of pauper," "nursing pauper," or witnessing. In 1883, however, minor office-holders appeared: Mrs. C. J. S. Greers collected fees as superintendent of schools in November; Lidda (perhaps Lidia) St. Clair secured payment as School Board Examiner and Gunine Grainger received two dollars for service on an unnamed "jury," suggesting a half-day's wait or witnessing.[79] Thereafter, women's

---

[77] [Duniway], "The Last Call," *NN*, October 30, 1884, front page; [Duniway], "A Warning," *NN*, December 10, 1885. Physical remains vary: In some counties, nothing survived courthouse fires of 1889, or fragments survive in adjacent records. The poor record has obscured female participation; but occasional jury lists in newspaper (especially in eastern Washington) strongly suggest that, where little or nothing survives, women were absent.

[78] "First Defeat of the Gambling and Liquor Fraternity," from Seattle Mirror, *NN*, July 24, 1884.

[79] In 1884, jurors received three dollars a day. See Pierce County Records of the Treasury, Record of Warrants Issued, PSRA-Bellevue, pp. 244–362. This clerk did not maintain a uniform style when dealing with women, particularly after 1884; he listed Mrs. F. Barlow as Frances Barlow, for instance. Clerks of court typically used Mrs. (with initials) to describe a married woman, Mrs. (with woman's first name) for widows, and first-last names for unmarried women. But this clerk did not, so we cannot easily know whether the five women named last were married. The two Listers, however, figured in the Rosencrantz and Walker cases (see Ch. 4). In Olympia's

names multiplied. On May 24, 1884, the district-court clerk in Tacoma listed eighteen grand jurors, six of them married women (Mrs. J. E. Steel, Mrs. E. Monroe, Mrs. M. F. Galligher, Mrs. F[rances] Barlow, Mrs. E[lizabeth] Lister, and Mrs. E. J. Ross). Lister's name appeared next to that of her husband, David; the Listers, Barlow, Monroe, and perhaps others were WERA activists. Warrants again issued on June 10 to twenty-five *petit* jurors, including Sarah Place, Mrs. S. C. Fay, Estelle B. Mann, Mrs. S. B. Gitchell, and Mrs. A. J. Westover. In November, "clerks" Kate A. Seitze and Alice M. House received eighteen dollars each. A month later, two male *petit* jurors and seventeen (and, separately, another twenty) male grand jurors received payment, as did Barlow, Julie McFarland, Teresa Argersinger, Monroe, and May J. Patrick.[80]

Indications of resistance from within the King County bar appeared in spring of 1884, during a district-court trial of a woman named L. E. Hall; information appeared initially as reprints of *Chicago Review* interviews of King County jurors. "[C]ertain sections of law were read by Mr. Haynes and referred to by Mr. Burke and Mr. McNaught [counsel for the accused] in an effort to disqualify the women," one juror had said, "on the ground that we were not citizens, nor even persons, according to the construction of the law." Roger Greene allowed them to sit but warned that the question would have to be tried before the nation's highest court. Until that court decided that they were not citizens or persons, Greene "seems to consider that we are, and will give us the benefit of the doubt.... Yours for equality before the law."[81] As if nothing untoward was afoot, the Territorial Supreme Court in July, 1884, affirmed the constitutionality of the "somewhat radical" legislation of 1869 and 1871 (as Justice Samuel Wingard put it) that had abolished dower and curtesy on the ground that only an expectancy had been destroyed, not a vested right.[82]

But trouble clearly lay ahead. Initially without much fanfare, territorial judges confronted two madams, both residents of Tacoma. The arrests and municipal trials emerged from the work of the intrepid Zerelda Nichols McCoy, then Vice President of the National Woman Suffrage Association in Tacoma

Thurston County, a surviving grand-jury list for 1884 showed one unmarried woman (Lucy Hackshaw) seated on a panel of thirteen; ten more women, all married, awaited empanelment with two dozen men. In rural Mason County, another stray grand-jury list dated May 9, 1884, included only men. See Grand Jury List for 1884, Records of the Auditor's Office, Thurston County, and List of Grand Jurors selected by the County Commissioners of Mason County on the 6th May 1884, Auditor's Office, both WSA-O.

[80] Pierce County, Records of the Treasury, Warrants Issued [bound volume], PSRA, pp. 362–404.

[81] L. E. Hall, "From a Woman Juror," Seattle, April 27, 1884, *NN*, May 1, 1884.

[82] *Lovica Hamilton v. Leopold Hirsch and James Hayden*, 2 Wash Terr Rpts 223 (July 1884), esp. p. 227. For detail, see discussion in Chapter 2. See also Case File No. 373, Lovica Hamilton *v.* Leopold Hirsch and James R. Hayden, WSA-O. The attorneys arguing against "radical" legislation included George Turner, just before he joined the Supreme Court; on the other side was William Murray, later for the defense in *Bloomer* v. *Todd*. Dower had been recognized in Washington in 1862 and eliminated in 1871; *Emily A. Ebey* v. *Ebey and Beam*, 1 Wash Terr Rpts 185 (1862). Abolition of dower and curtesy followed expansions of married women's economic agency over many decades.

(NWSA) and secretary of WERA. In 1884–85, the city's reputation for sleaze grew almost daily. Sex slavers prowled the streets; liquor flowed freely. McCoy claimed that she personally had turned in proprietors of two houses of ill repute – one run by Mollie Rosencrantz, the other by Annie Walker – to city constables; one reporter credited a next-door neighbor with witnessing Rosencrantz' activities and also alerting police, after which several men visited and berated him with "insulting language." The "first haul" was made at Walker's establishment; the city marshal arrested her with "two of her girls" who paid ten-dollar fines. After another raid at a gambling house, the marshal nabbed Rosencranz, Lina Langry, and Hazel, three employees of the Star lodging house, and Maud Raymond, from another establishment, who also paid ten dollars each with costs.[83]

Finally, on warrants sworn out by McCoy, the two madams were detained. Walker's trial was postponed; Rosencrantz got an immediate hearing. The police court's Judge Campbell had promised McCoy a bench trial; instead, she learned that Rosencrantz would be treated to a full jury trial. According to McCoy, the marshal ignored requests for female jurors and summoned only men. Six jurors heard testimony from Zerelda's husband, army surgeon Dr. James McCoy; Zerelda herself; and reformer Virginia Darborow. The room was too small for the crowd. Evidence abounded that Rosencrantz was the keeper of a brothel and the girls her employees; she claimed to own a respectable boarding house, and jurors agreed. In Walker's case, the defense did not call witnesses and only two jurors indicated an interest in testimony. Having been told by a council member that the city would not pay costs, Campbell dismissed the suit. Said McCoy, a jury of "'good and true' men" decided that Rosencrantz kept a reputable lodge, "resorted to by many so-called respectable men, married and single." The city council threatened to charge complainants with costs. In high dudgeon, McCoy invited women to tour the boarding house so that they could "pattern their homes to this model" and keep sons and husbands at home. McCoy's lawyer applied for indictment and re-trial in Pierce County district court.[84]

---

[83] "The Disrobed Truth," *TDL*, March 14, 1885; "Tacoma has not yet …," ibid., April 16, 1885; "Houses of Prostitution," ibid., May 28, 1884 (in all, the city treasury got 120 dollars and court officers another 36 dollars); "Police Work," ibid., November 22, 1884. Much of this intelligence appeared long after the Rosencrantz appeal.

[84] "The Police Court," *TDL*, December 12, 1884; "Police News," ibid., December 14, 1884. Information appeared in a long essay, Zerelda N. McCoy, "Open Letter to the People of Tacoma," *SDPI*, December 19, 1884, p. 2. The same article appeared in *WR*, "Somewhat Suggestive," January 23, 1885; the editor described McCoy as a "worthy but homely" woman whose "good work" had gone "too far." After May, 1885, city elections, McCoy blasted Republicans for closing ranks against women delegates in convention, adding this: The "machine was set to work and a straight ticket ground out, the nominee for Marshal having been a member of the jury which last December pronounced a house of ill-fame a respectable lodging house"; Zerelda N. McCoy, "From the Terminal City," *NN*, May 7, 1885.

In May, 1884, the grand jury that had included the two Listers and Barlow indicted Rosencrantz for keeping a house of ill fame, whereupon her attorneys formally objected to the presence of five married women on the panel. The statute required householder status; surely only married men were householders. A scant month after the United States Senate's Woman Suffrage Committee had reported favorably on a resolution to submit the Sixteenth Amendment to states,[85] these salacious trials were no longer about brothels, but rather about equality's roots in co-sovereignty. Rosencrantz challenged not only the legality of the indictment, but also the validity of laws governing elections, community property, and civil equality. The organic law, after all, did not say that lawmakers could expand the pool of candidates for grand and *petit* juries – only that they could regulate the electorate. Did that power extend to the calling of mixed-sex grand juries? Did co-headship of households divide the *petit* king's sovereign authority in half such that Elizabeth Lister could serve on juries? Did these practices violate the intentions of the framers of the organic act?[86]

In a May, 1884, circuit-court session, Roger Greene delivered a white paper in *Rosencrantz* v. *Territory of Washington*. On appeal, he would be in recusal. His opinion had to lay out the fruits of extensive legal research for the benefit of less scholarly brethren on the Supreme Court; he also had to outflank attorneys in the Haines law firm in Seattle, who had feigned the case with McCoy's unwitting help. "None but householders can be grand jurors, under our statute," he began. "It is contended that married women living with their husbands are not householders. That they were not at common law, and were not in this Territory, prior to the passage of [the community-property section of the law code] is doubtless true. But have not the provisions of that chapter wrought a change in the law?" The term householder meant "one who manages and controls a household, not as agent, but as principal. Such a manager ... might at common law be either a woman or a man. But at common law, a wife living with her husband was deemed always his agent .... She was under civil disability, which prevented her from acting, or being recognized, as partner and principal, with him ..., and which prevented her from being regarded as acting otherwise than as under duress in his presence."[87]

Step by step, Greene showed that spouses were "coequal principals and agents of each other"; both were "householders, if either is." In the management of a woman's separate property, the woman individually assumed the character of householder as if unmarried and maintaining her own household. It was even possible for her to be "the absolute proprietor and manager of the homestead ... ,

[85] Congressional developments on woman suffrage were always widely reported, even in remote towns; see, e.g., "Women's Suffrage," *Northwest Enterprise* [Anacortes], April 12, 1884.
[86] *Mollie Rosencrantz* v. *Territory of Washington*, 2 Wash Terr Rpts 267 (July 1884), 271–2. For case file, See also Mollie Rosencrantz v. Territory of Washington, Case File No. 387, WSA-O.
[87] "Law and Order," *OR*, April 23, 1885, name misspelled ("Zarelda"); "Women as Jurors," *WS*, May 30, 1884, and "Women's Rights," *TDL*, May 24, 1884, both printing the opinion. Emphasis added.

so as to be the regulator . . . of all, including her husband." Recasting parts of his *Phelps* and *Holyoke* rulings, he addressed the bedrock fact of sovereignty: "I conceive the true intent of our statute to be, to put every wife into that position . . . which a wife ought to occupy, . . . sharing not theoretically, nor sentimentally, nor by his bare sufferance, but practically *by command of the commonwealth, his cares, his responsibilities, his authority and his rule.*"[88]

Lauded by one Tacoman as a "subtle and powerful logician, and a jurist of profound erudition,"[89] Greene saw clearly that, while the forces behind the *Rosencrantz* appeal aimed narrowly at juries, the main target was co-equality. Once the case moved to Olympia on appeal, the parties made no secret of their laser-like focus on the legal-constitutional foundations of mixed juries. Did legislators really mean to divide the sovereign head of household, thereby setting the territory at odds with practices in older jurisdictions? Said the madam's lawyers, the jury statute adopted in 1883 clearly violated the command (enshrined in the code of 1881) that, in the absence of positive law to the contrary, Washington follow the common law, which regarded the husband and wife as one person. Because the framers of the organic act had common-law rules in mind, subsequent legislation must be construed strictly. The 1881 code had restricted electors to men and grand jurors to householders: Were not the five women "residing with their husbands, and maintained by them"? Defense attorney J. C. Haines pointed to Mrs. F. Barlow, Mrs. Elizabeth Munroe, Mrs. E. J. Rossand, and Mrs. Jeanette Fuller; the jury foreman, David Lister, was married to Elizabeth Lister. If she lived with David "as his wife," he was "the head of the family, and the only householder therein"; when they both served, their home was represented twice.[90]

On the other side, the organic law seemed to authorize legislators to alter the composition of the electorate, to distribute civil rights, and to shape the law of domestic relations. Surely spouses, as co-owners of the marital estate, were co-sovereigns and thus were equally qualified for voting, jury service, dealings in property, and office holding. The 1879 civil-rights law had abolished sex-specific disabilities with respect to marital property, with the exception of minor managerial rights. Was not the capacity to deal in property a foundation for claims of sovereignty? Minimally, Americans aimed to represent all property at the polls; just as clearly, the 1883 election law extended the ballot to all citizens, into which category women surely fell. If these linkages held, there would be scant ground to deny women access to public offices such as voter, juror, lawyer, or bailiff.

[88] Ibid. Emphasis added.
[89] "Women as 'Householders,'" *TDL*, May 25, 1884, editorial page.
[90] For briefs and preliminary arguments, see Rosencrantz v. Territory of Washington, Case File No. 387, Records of the Supreme Court of the Territory of Washington, WSA-O. Lelia Robinson was on the brief, though on the madam's side; she later explained that, while her sentiments ran otherwise, a lawyer could not always pick clients; see Letter to the Equity Club, 1887, in Drachman, *Women Lawyers*, op cit. She likely had no choice as an employee of J. C. Haines, counsel for Rosencrantz.

The state attorney worked his way along a poorly marked road: Legislators had "full power and competent authority" to make laws governing elections, judicial procedure, and the meaning of householder. The assembly had not said that a householder was the sole head of a family, only that "every householder, being the head of a family," enjoyed certain prerogatives as a co-householder (which was not the same as half of a householder), one of whom might be designated an administrative head for convenience. A person was a householder, he continued, leaning on Greene's district-court opinion but also departing from it, who could " reasonably be said to be in charge, and having devolved upon him or her the duty of ... supporting a family; as a general rule the husband, no doubt, is the householder; but too often these burdens and duties are cast upon the wife, and in such case she is the householder ... entitled to whatever privileges belong to a 'head of a house.'" Greene had not said that administrative power inscribed men ordinarily with householder status and woman only occasionally. But, in either case, status depended on agency with property. "The general tendency of legislation in this territory," he noted, "has been to abolish all distinction between the civil and property rights of men and women, and in those respects the whole system of the common law has been swept away, and in its stead a system of laws has been adopted which," although imperfect, surely could be construed to "secure to married women all that was clearly intended to be secured to them."[91]

Did women's civil and marital rights lead inexorably to voting and jury service? The editor of the cautiously pro-suffrage (and Democratic) *Washington Standard*, writing in autumn of 1883 amid frenzied talk about woman suffrage in city elections, thought that litigants had raised exactly that question. At trial, jurors assigned prison terms, transferred property, and imposed fines. What if women spoke illegitimately – i.e., lacked the sovereign authority and knowledge of the neighborhood required to pass judgment?[92] Other observers condemned radical departures from coverture. In October, 1884, a Whatcom writer tied the Supreme Court's July decisions on dower rights to *Rosencrantz:* Surely lawmakers could undo Greene's opinion and then restore a widow's rights in her husband's lands by re-enacting the dower law of 1869.[93]

Rosencrantz v. *Territory* swiftly found its way to the Territorial Supreme Court. There, Associate Justice John Philo Hoyt lent fulsome support to women's co-sovereign right as householders to sit on juries. An Ohioan by birth, Hoyt had served in the Union Army and practiced law in Michigan from 1868 to 1878, where he served with distinction in the assembly. Seeking a warmer climate, he secured an appointment as Secretary of Arizona Territory, served as governor in 1877, and a year later moved to Idaho, supposedly to complete Governor Brayman's term after a scandal. When Brayman retained his

[91] *Rosencrantz* v. *Territory of Washington*, 2 Wash Terr Rpts 267 (July 1884), 271–2.
[92] "The Right to Vote in the City," WS, September 14, 1883, after a city election.
[93] "Important Decisions," WR, October 10, 1884.

office, President Arthur appointed Hoyt to the Washington bench in 1879. For his entire career, Hoyt had been a moderate, reform-minded Republican and temperance supporter.[94]

In 1884, Hoyt willingly joined Greene in good causes, but he was not a zealot. The "only important question," he declared in *Rosencrantz*, was whether enfranchised spouses could be grand jurors without reference to marital status. Hoyt did not doubt that obligations attached to voters. The 1881 code made "all electors and householders" potential grand jurors; married women were both and so could be seated alongside men. At common law, he admitted, a wife had not been a householder; coverture eliminated her right to be heard as to the disposition of property or custody of children, and likely made her ineligible to speak for the neighborhood. But this harsh rule had been eliminated. The right of the wife to participate in propertied affairs had been "more and more recognized by the laws of nearly all of the States and Territories"; the "radical legislation" of 1879 had replaced coverture with a relation characterized by "absolute equality." Among the act's radical elements were its allocation of sovereignty to both partners, who had vested rights in the marital community and, once exercised, in the suffrage.[95]

Because others found it impossible to divide the sovereignty of a household head without smashing it – in theories of kingship, either the lord was whole, or there was no lord at all – Hoyt explained how it could be done: "[I]t is said, that if they are thus equal, then neither of them is the head of the family, and therefore not the keeper of a house, as each is only a half of a housekeeper. This, however, does not follow, as each of them has the absolute right to control the family and household in the absence of the other, and each has all the responsibilities and rights growing out of such control." At common law, the *baron* (or *petit* king) had "sole control, and was therefore properly ... held as the head of the family; by our statute the two together, and acting jointly, have like sole control, and are, therefore, jointly the head of the family." A wife had "exactly the same measure of control over the children ... as her husband, with the same right to ... their earnings, and the same voice in ... the family government."[96]

Rosencrantz's finding of "absolute equality before the law" did not please everyone.[97] Roger Greene certainly supported the principle: As he immodestly

---

94 See John Philo Hoyt Biographical Collection, WSA-O, and Charles K. Wiggins, "John P. Hoyt and Women's Suffrage," www.appeal-law.com/constitution/hoyt/html, 1988. Hoyt has been confused with Governor Hoyt of Wisconsin, in office when that territory adopted equal suffrage in 1869.

95 *Rosencrantz v. Territory*, 272–3. Greene was in recusal. After service in the state constitutional convention, Hoyt gained election to the Washington Supreme Court, where he sat until 1897, the last two years as chief justice. With other Republicans, he was swept out of office in 1896, became a law professor, and later served as a referee in federal bankruptcy court in Seattle.

96 *Rosencrantz v. Territory*, 274–7.

97 "Married Women, Decision of the Supreme Court of Washington Territory. Absolute Equality before the Law," *TDL*, October 22, 1884, publishing the opinion, with which Justice Wingard concurred.

put it in 1916, "Suffrage for women was agitated and promoted and secured mainly by the women. But my wife and I favored it, and of all the men in the territory I probably was ... by reason of my office ... its most influential and effective promoter."[98] More concerning was Associate Justice George Turner's fierce dissent. Even as May Arkwright Hutton – a suffragist and fearless champion of workers' rights – began to push for equality in eastern Washington, opponents had been gathering around Turner, a resident of Spokane Falls and an avowed enemy of household democracy. A native of Missouri and by 1896 a so-called Silver Republican, Turner had served with Union forces as a telegraph operator and commenced law practice in Mobile, Alabama. When he arrived in Washington, journalists hailed him as an "energetic and efficient officer," a good lawyer, and a "fine specimen of Caucasian manhood; about six feet in height, straight as an arrow, and not over thirty-five years of age."[99]

From the moment of his appointment to the Washington bench, however, Turner crossed swords with Hoyt and Greene. Attorney Lelia Robinson, who viewed Roger Greene as "one of the best of living men" and who had worked with Turner, noted politely in 1887 that he was "a southern man ... appointed by President Arthur," and, on the question of male–female equality, possessed of views "contrary to that of the majority of the bench."[100] In his *Rosencrantz* dissent, Turner denied that women were "competent under the law, as grand or petit jurors," or that wives living with their husbands were householders. He dared not contend that territorial laws as written had not introduced civil equality; instead, he distinguished between rights, obligations, and sovereign command, and strictly construed Congressional delegations of power to lawmakers. Throughout, he also expressed misgivings about legal rules (in the words of a journalist) "entirely at variance with American manhood."[101]

Turner's opening salvo was protectionist: "I cannot say ... that I wish to see them perform the duties of jurors. The liability to perform jury duty is an obligation, not a right. In the case of woman, it is not necessary that she should accept the obligation to secure or maintain her rights. If it were, I should stifle ... the repugnance that I feel at seeing her exposed to influences

[98] Roger Sherman Greene to Clarence Bagley, April 4, 1916, Clarence Bagley Papers, UWSC, Box I-31. In 1884, the AWSA sought a letter from Greene to read in convention; "Female Suffragists," *TDL*, November 20, 1884, p. 1.

[99] Claudius Johnson, "George Turner, A Character from Plutarch," *Washington Law Review and State Bar Journal* (November, 1943), pp. 167, 173, 176, who also called him "modest and unassuming." See also Johnson, "George Turner, Part I" and "Part II," *Pacific Northwest Quarterly*, Vol. 3 (1943), pp. 243–69, and Vol. 4 (1943), 367–92. Turner sat on the Washington Territorial Supreme Court from 1884–88, led statehood convocations, and after years in law practice, served in the U.S. Senate in 1897 for a term. On his pro-silver, anti-bank positions, see "Judge Turner's Views," *The Dawn* (a Populist print), January 9, 1897; he ended his career as a fusionist Democrat.

[100] For Robinson, see "Women Jurors," *Chicago Legal Times*, Vol. 1, No. 32 (1887), 25, 32.

[101] *Rosencrantz* v. *Territory*, 267–68.; "An Antediluvian View," *WS*, November 2, 1883.

FIGURE 3.1. After statehood, the territorial Supreme Court's Associate Justice George Turner (1850–1932) served briefly in the United States Senate; n.d. From the collections of the Northwest Museum of Arts and Culture, Spokane, WA. Used by permission.

which ... [must] shock and blunt those fine sensibilities ... the protection of which ... is her most sacred right." Conceding that women exercised civil rights and the ballot lawfully, he trained big guns on territorial corruptions of Anglo-American law. The task was formidable. Unmarried women and widows dealt in property and clearly were co-sovereigns within marital estates, and American lawmakers had been chipping away at the law of coverture since at least the 1840s. Turner also admitted that, if "one woman is competent as a juror, all women having the same qualifications are competent. If women may try one case, they may try all cases." But because that choice was uncongenial, he argued that laws governing the "important incidents of a jury trial," unlike the right to vote, were by "express constitutional provision, what they were at the common law" in 1853 – that is, male. Only Congressional amendment could alter immutable meanings embedded in the organic act at the moment of its adoption.[102]

In this exercise, Turner had to prove that Washingtonians had ignored the limits of legislative power under the organic act and ignored Congress' presumption that territories would install the law of coverture. In the 1850s, he wrote, when a husband was living with his family, he was "in contemplation of law the head, and the only head, of the family." Surely the term householder bore no relationship to a "holding of property" – that is, to civil rights – but referred solely to the "head, master, or person who has the charge of, and provides for a family." Had lawmakers presumed to situate "civil and property rights of husband and wife on an equal footing" so that they were "equal as to rights and obligations in the household, and therefore ... both of them ... heads of the family, and both of them householders"? If so, they had shattered all governance within the marital estate, which existed apart from a citizen's right to buy a house or wagon. The logical conclusion would be, in republican Washington as in King George III's England, "not that the law had created two heads of the family, but that it has deposed from the position of superiority what was formerly the one head, and that now there is no head. ... *The idea of a double head in nature or in government is that of a monstrosity.*"[103]

In what sense was marital co-headship hermaphroditic? English theories of kingship portrayed monarchical sovereignty as indivisible; the unitary head of household embodied "the idea of legal supremacy" or household command. A man, as head of the family at common law, had "the right to be obeyed by all the family, including the wife." For good measure, Turner gestured toward the socio-biological essentialism that had undergirded Fourteenth-Amendment rulings since the 1870s, including *Bradwell v. Illinois.*[104] *Plessy v. Ferguson* Without embracing the "separate but equal" trope, he noted ineradicable differences in the sex's "mental and physical constitution": Man-made law "would not make white black, nor can it provide the female

---

[102] *Rosencrantz* v. *Territory*, 272–3. Turner characterized the organic act as a quasi-constitution – i.e., as an instrument with greater force than most statutes. Greene, by contrast, valorized the acts of the assembly if they comported with federal constitutional principles. In 1870, he even held that local authorities could alter the terms of officials elected solely under territorial law; *D. W. C. Davidson* v. *Isaac Carson*, 1 Wash Terr Rpts 207 (1870), 307–8. See also *E. A. Nickels* v. *Frank Griffin*, 1 Wash Terr Rpts 374 (1872), 378–9. Understandings of organic acts merit further study.

[103] *Rosencrantz* v. *Territory*, ibid., emphasis added.

[104] E.g., *Myra Bradwell* v. *State of Illinois*, 83 U.S. Rpts 130 (1872). See also *Plessy* v. *Ferguson*, 163 U.S. Rpts 537 (1896), as at 551–2: Legislation was "powerless to eradicate racial instincts or to abolish distinctions based upon physical differences, and the attempt to do so can only result in accentuating the difficulties of the present situation. If the civil and political rights of both races be equal, one cannot be inferior to the other civilly or politically. If one race be inferior to the other socially, the Constitution of the United States cannot put them upon the same plane."

form with bone and sinew equal in strength to that with which nature had provided man." Failing to heed nature or its emanation, the law of coverture, assemblymen sought to "wip[e] out in every respect the supremacy of the husband" and "put the wife upon a plane with him in the matter of rights and obligations." One of the incidents of juries had been their masculinity; changes in women's civil standing did not alter a necessary reliance on male judgment. Women had domestic obligations and did not require seats on juries to defend interests. Mollie Rosencrantz had been denied her right to law – i.e., to be indicted by men. Finally, Turner attacked the law's construction: The organic act specified that a statute could not "embrace two objects"; legislators could not 'find' jury service by implication in an election law. The seating of women on juries required a separate statute.[105]

For the moment, the dissent was published and filed. But nobody imagined that they had seen the last of George Turner or the mixed-sex jury question. Indeed, within weeks of *Rosencrantz* and only a few months before Grover Cleveland abruptly relieved Justice Samuel Wingard of his judicial post,[106] Greene and Wingard turned back several other challenges to mixed grand juries. One appeal involved Annie Walker – the second madam that Zerelda McCoy had turned over to police – indicted by the same panel challenged in *Rosencrantz*. Walker's counsel contended, after Turner, that the 1881 law code had provided for "indictment by a common law Grand Jury, which was a jury of men"; that jury service was a duty, not a right, and therefore beyond the scope of election law; and that both the federal constitution and the organic act recognized "householder" to mean the "master who provides for it," as if women no longer occupied marital estates jointly.[107] Prosecutor Charles Bradshaw, struggling to defend sloppy statutes, argued that the Code of 1881 was irrelevant, given the assembly's full power to alter the composition of electorates; that women were electors and thus amply qualified for *petit* and grand jury service; and that both sexes were householders, in the sense that they jointly inhabited marital estates. He declared that jury service was both a right and a duty, and simply asserted the assembly's power to modify juries with alterations of the electorate.[108]

---

[105] *Rosencrantz* v. *Territory of Washington*, 274–5, emphasis added. In 1912, a California scholar noted that jurists still were divided as to whether English, masculine understandings of juries forever controlled law practice; Percy L. Edwards, "Constitutional Obligations and Woman's Citizenship," 75 *Central Law Journal* 244 (1912), esp. 245–7.

[106] Grover Cleveland's justice department appointed William G. Langford to replace Samuel Wingard, who sued for wages to 1887, the end of his four-year term, lost, and lost again on appeal to the U.S. Supreme Court; *Wingard* v. *U.S.*, 141 U.S. 201 (1891).

[107] *Annie Walker* v. *Territory of Washington*, 2 Wash Terr 286 (1884); and Annie Walker v. Territory of Washington, Case File No. 388, Plaintiff's Brief and Defendant's Brief, WSA-O. Details of Annie Walker's bawdy life in San Francisco and Tacoma emerged at her death, when her son claimed a large estate; "Annie Walker's Career," *TDL*, August 1, 1889.

[108] Ibid.

Similarly, in *George Schilling* v. *Territory*, the grand jury that found a true bill against a gambler had included four married women, Louisa Denny, Lucinda Jacobs, Caroline Maddocks, and Emma Wood; in *Charles Hayes* v. *Territory*, Mrs. A. R. Elliott and Mrs. Agnes W. Prather had participated in the indictment of hunters who had illegally used dogs. In *Hayes*, nobody contested the presence of the unmarried Lucy Hackshaw; given statutory language, her claim to householder status was sound. In each case, Greene and Wingard simply pointed to *Rosencrantz.*[109] In *Hayes*, however, the Chief Justice could not resist sarcasm in response to Turner's insistence that women living with husbands could not be jurors: "This Court, circling through its four phases like the moon, has already once, when differently constituted, ... thrown its light upon that question. What it then saw it sees now." Since Turner had taken an excursion into history, Greene outdid him: The qualification for jury duty in 1787 had been "the ancient phrase, 'Liber et legalis homo.' ... [T]he jury must be free, lawful, and of the human race. This definition was rigid as far as freedom and humanity were concerned, but elastic as to lawfulness. Custom and statute prescribed the lawfulness. For a jury to try one sort of an issue, males were not Liber et legalis homines, and females were; for a jury to try another sort, both men and women were; for the trial of ... ordinary issues, males only were competent." All depended on law and custom, which changed with society; lawmakers could modify the qualifications of jurors by statute, so long as they did not flout Congressional rules or seat jurors "who are under duress of servitude, or who are monkeys or angels."[110]

Confusion was not restricted to territorial courtrooms. After publication of Congressional debates in December, 1884, Washingtonians saw that their statehood petitions, the Sixteenth Amendment, and territorial legalities were joined at the hip. Consider the sharp exchange between Senators Lapham, Hoar, and Conger. All were old-line Republicans schooled in civil-war politics. Hoar had presented a memorial of the Pennsylvania Woman's Suffrage Association protesting the admission of Dakota with a male electorate. He noted that, under ordinary conditions, the petition would simply lie on the table. But these were extraordinary times. While he shared women's abhorrence for manhood suffrage, he thought it unwise for "the persons who entertain that opinion to insist upon having Congress in its present state of opinion impose its views," since a majority of both Houses would likely deny admission to Washington Territory and Wyoming when they submitted petitions with equal-suffrage constitutions. Dakota alone

---

[109] See Walker v. Territory, Case File No. 388; *George Schilling* v. *Territory of Washington* and *Walker* v. *Territory*, 2 Wash Terr Rpts 286 (July 1884); and *Charles Hayes, et al.* v. *Territory of Washington*, 2 Wash Terr Rpts 286 (July 1884), also Case File No. 391; all case files at WSA-O. Hays' indictment had occurred in Hoyt's courtroom; *Territory* v. *Charles Hays et al.*, File 2287, Thurston County District Court, indictment in case file, WSA-O. The correct spelling is "Hays." See previous discussion of Thurston County jurors in 1884.

[110] *Hayes* v. *Territory*, 288–9, and Turner's brief concurrence, 290.

would gain admission. When he asked colleagues to table the motion, Conger moved to associate Dakota, Washington, and Wyoming. Fearing a loss all around, Hoar urged the tabling of Sixteenth Amendment petitions and admission of Dakota with a male electorate, as requested. Later, lawmakers could revise election laws and constitutions as they saw fit. Then, Washington moved to center stage:

MR. CONGER. Will the Senator allow me to make one remark? The Territory of Washington, to which this relates . . .
MR. HOAR. The memorial relates to Dakota.
MR. CONGER. I thought the Senator's remarks applied to Washington Territory. The Territory of Washington in its laws already provides for female suffrage.
MR. HOAR. If the Senator will pardon me, this is a protest against the admission of Dakota containing a clause in the constitution adverse to female suffrage. The remark which I made was that I thought the friends of female suffrage . . . would not be wise in making Congress to impose its opinion upon that question on new Territories which knock at the door, because if that were done Congress would be more likely to reject Washington and Wyoming on that account. . . .
MR. CONGER. . . . [M]y remark was that Washington Territory by a vote of its own people having granted woman suffrage, any existing condition there ought not to prejudice Senators here against the admission of Washington Territory as a State. . . .
MR. HOAR. I do not believe it would, and I do not want to establish that principle by voting against Dakota myself on the other ground.
MR. LAPHAM. . . . The Committee on Woman Suffrage considered the question [of a suffrage amendment] while the Dakota bill was pending . . . and we concluded that it would be unwise to . . . ingraft that provision upon the proposed bill for . . . admission. . . .
MR. HOAR. I think the example of Washington Territory and of Wyoming will soon be very potent on Dakota.[111]

Similarly, in Washington, suffrage discourse seeped into statehood talk. As admissions bills moved through Congress, Tacomans railed against disabilities: "Washington territory, with one nonvoting delegate, is of no consequence in a log-rolling congress . . . . [W]ith two senators and a representative she would not be despised. . . . We want to roll logs with the rest of the crowd. . . . Very few true American citizens . . . want to pass their lives in political bondage." There followed a telling enumeration: 41,842 persons were said to have voted in the 1884 general elections, from which the "woman vote" of 8,368 was subtracted, leaving a more relevant "male vote" of 33,474. Calculations of the electorate used the latter number.[112] Delegate Brent, a non-voting member of the House, confessed that he felt like a "self-respecting woman does when disfranchised

---

[111] Congressional Record, Senate, 48th Congress, Vol. 16, Part 1, December 18, 1884, p. 325.
[112] "Western Washington. A Brief History and Account of its Resources," *TDL*, January 1, 1886. For similar information in public debates, see Congressional Record, Senate, 49th Congress, 1st session, March 30, 1886, p. 2911. Also see "Population Enough for a State," repr. *WWU*, *SDPI*, November 23, 1884, where women also appear as voters who distort real numbers.

because she is 'only a female.'" He was "only a delegate,"[113] akin to a wife. Territorial lawmakers memorialized Congress in terms eerily reminiscent of resolutions adopted by suffrage conventions: "Earnestly, this people pray that Congress will remove their political disabilities" so that they might enjoy "the constitutional guarantee of a government republican in form, where the government derives all its just powers from the consent of the governed." Washingtonians did not elect their own officers; they were denied representation in Congress. Virtual representation enforced "a dependence as humiliating as that so terribly denounced" by Thomas Jefferson against Great Britain. Much as Gilded-Age suffragists had demanded Congressional adoption of a declaratory act restoring rights unlawfully confiscated, so assemblymen prayed that *"disabilities ... be removed and we be restored to those rights which belong to American birthright and citizenship."*[114] On April 8, Daniel Voorhees endorsed statehood for Washington, reminding colleagues that a "sense of dependence weighs down and embarrasses the people of a Territory. ... There is a looking toward the seat of government ... inconsistent with any self-reliant ... community."[115]

****

In November, 1884, Washington Territory experienced another election cycle; reporters continued to track women's appearances at the polls and in courthouses.[116] Turner's critics were brutal. On New Year's Eve, 1884, for instance, the *Waltsburg Times* compared his ruling against female jurors to Roger Taney's decision in *Dred Scott* – i.e., that a freedman had "no rights that a white man is bound to respect." This would not be the last time Dred Scott's case would be analogized to a Washington ruling. Perhaps the judge next would decide that, while "women have a right to sit as jurors, they cannot vote." What if he had ruled that men could not be jurors? Women merited "every right of the franchise enjoyed by men."[117]

Women did not miss apparent divisions among Republicans on the question of women's political standing. Hoyt, Greene, and Turner, after all, claimed to be Republicans; a rapidly mutating Republican Party still could accommodate all three, although less and less satisfactorily in Greene's case. And, for many women, suffrage and its attendant duties were not their main or only concerns.

---

[113] "A Delegate's Humiliation," *NN*, February 28, 1884.
[114] Congressional Record, House of Representatives, 48th Congress, Vol. 15, Part 1, January 30, 1884, pp. 752–3. Widely reprinted; see "Mr. Caton's Memorial," *WS*, November 23, 1883, and *WWS*, November 24, 1883. Emphasis added.
[115] Congressional Record, Senate, 49th Congress, 1st session, Vol. 17, Part 3, March 26–30, January 8, 1886, p. 3253.
[116] E.g., "Mere Mention," *WS*, November 7, 1884 (turnout of 312 women at Olympia).
[117] "After a 'Learned Judge,'" repr. Waltsburg Times, *NN*, December 31, 1884. A year later, an editor in Pomeroy mysteriously inserted a partially plagiarized version; "Poking Up Judge Turner," *Washington Independent*, December 17, 1885.

As early as late October, 1884, a citizen writing from tiny Eagle Harbor could say, on one hand, that many of her friends had been moved to tears (and to the Republican side) by Mrs. Thomas' equal-rights lectures, but, on the other hand, that many of them planned to hold their noses and vote Democratic in order to secure what the party's platform averred – equal access to the polls, early statehood, acquiescence to railroaders' demands until lines were completed, and the elimination of jury duty for women. Public discussions of citizens' rights and obligations could resume, once Washington made the passage to statehood.[118]

In Tacoma, women's uneasy relationship with jury boxes came clear even as Rosencrantz moved through the courts. The number of women appearing for service on Tacoma juries expanded slowly and in erratic bursts. In 1884, two women earned grand jury fees (Mary A. Meath and Elizabeth Spinning) with fourteen men; in February, 1885, only a female school-board examiner received a Pierce County treasury warrant, although on May 11, two married women and twenty-three men received jury fees. Then, between June 1 and June 8, 1885, the county paid a dozen women, many of them WERA activists, for *petit*-jury service. One of them was Zerelda McCoy, followed by brief notice of another comrade-in-arms (Mrs. J. E. Clendenin). The WERA's foot soldiers were beating bushes for their judicial allies.[119]

Nevertheless, Pierce County women steadily vanished. Social practice did not support repeated courtroom incursions; an atmosphere of gendered transgression was almost palpable. In April, 1885, the *Standard* revealed something of a brouhaha: "The *petit* jury list of the Pierce county Court ... is composed entirely of women. ... [A]t the November term the 'male' element was exhausted, some women being added by the judge in making up juries. In preparing the venire for the present term the Clerk was confined to a supplementary list composed wholly of women. There seems to be some doubt of the legality of juries."[120] In July and August, 1885, juries and bailiffs were male. On December 1, sixteen men and two married women appeared as grand jurors (Mrs. Jane Galli[gh]er and Mrs. J. W. Bowers); on December 9 and

---

[118] C. Rank, "Politics in a Country Precinct," *SDPI*, October 30, 1884. Thomas' lectures were said to have succeeded because she avoided Susan B. Anthony's tone. The Democratic governor Eugene Semple's election in 1886 was attributed widely to women's impatience with men on every side of the suffrage question. On crossing the aisle, see "The Price of Admission," *SR*, October 17, 1886, ed. page.

[119] Pierce County, Records of the Treasury, Record of Warrants Issued, PSRA-Bellevue, pp. 404–22. Several women were WERA members. Perhaps the group moved en masse. One historian noted in 1927 that twelve women (including McCoy) served on the same *petit* jury in 1884 (allegedly the first all-female jury in the territory); I read the journal to say that twelve women were in the pool with twelve men. See W. P. Bonney, *History of Pierce County, Washington*, Vol. II ([Tacoma?], 1927), p. 916. My thanks to Jean Fisher for this citation. No image of Zerelda N[ichols] McCoy can be found, despite an extensive search; after 1889, she vanished from public life, though she published poetry.

[120] Untitled, *WS*, April 24, 1885.

10, two male jurors and Elizabeth Smith (probably unmarried) received payment. Thereafter, Belle Mann regularly served as one of three bailiffs; clerical treatment of women's names indicates that only single women served on grand juries, with married women relegated to *petit* juries. In February and March, 1886, the county paid three female and sixteen male *petit* jurors. In April, Mrs. E. J. Clendemin, Mrs. L. L. Brown, Mrs. L. M. Kelley, and Mrs. Jane Bowlin served in criminal trials. Only in July did another woman appear (Maggie Farr), unmarried and noted separately following payments to twenty-one men; Clara Connick and Mrs. Fanny Berry served as grand jurors on a panel of sixteen. In September, two grand jurors (Parilla Elder and Mary Frost, both single), two *petit* jurors (Mrs. L. B. Getchell and Mrs. M. B. Potwin), and the ubiquitous Belle Mann appeared. On November 12, the county paid three female and twenty-five male election clerks. Women last served on March 15, 1887, when four wives received payment as *petit* jurors. Thereafter, Pierce County seated only men. The WERA's David Lister, the grand-jury foreman in *Rosencrantz* whose manhood and headship had been so fiercely challenged, surfaced again on a grand jury in autumn, 1888, but without the courageous Elizabeth Lister, who had served alongside her husband a scant two years earlier.[121]

---

[121] Pierce County Records of the Treasury, Record of Warrants Issued, PSRA, pp. 404–639. See Lister's signature as foreman, Rosencrantz v. Territory, Indictment and True Bill, Case File No. 387, WSA-O. Without apparent exception, the Pierce County clerk used first names for single women, "Mrs." for married women, and two initials ("S. B. Jones") for men. But certainty would require extensive work in precinct-level census records; without it, a modest undercounting of women is possible.

4

"A compound creature of the statute"

Jury duty and social disintegration

> In two words I can tell you who govern this community. The juries. ... A jury speaks not for itself, but for the commonwealth. It speaks as to the facts representatively, just as the judiciary speaks as to the law. Its utterances are the property of the public.
>
> – Chief Justice Roger Sherman Greene, 1885[1]

In 1884–85, confusion reigned. On one side, and despite poor health, Roger Greene continued to fend off attempts to erode women's co-sovereignty; oppositionists had in mind reintroducing common-law rules of practice in civil disputes. In early 1887, for example, Greene derailed a husband's attempt to lease community land without his wife's participation, calling it a contravention of policy. Defendants' attorneys had rested their case on a statute of Henry VIII, characterizing their client as a "remainderman"; Greene conceded that in England, under medieval law, such arguments had carried weight. But in Gilded-Age Washington, where "the condition of things is widely different," husbands and wives sold real estate together.[2] Throughout the territory, an atmosphere of possibility and mutuality led women to explore new modes of dress and to speak publically of forbidden subjects – among them, women's physical vulnerability, as when a woman disagreed with a lecturer who proposed a return to Biblical grounds for divorce: "Adultery is bad," she wrote under her own name, but far worse to "beat and kick and starve a wife," and a "million times worse to blind and disfigure wives with vitriol; yet ... you would refuse divorce to a woman."[3]

---

[1] "Trial of Daniel Hughes, Text of the Charge of Judge Greene to the Trial Jury," *SDPI*, November 3, 1885. Emphasis added.

[2] *Daniel Hoover* v. *David J. Chambers*, 3 Wash Terr Rpts 26 (January 1887), 31.

[3] Mary L. Smilax, "Divorce," *SDPI*, August 29, 1884. Personal security continued to be the least discussed aspect of women's supposed equality.

On the other side, after swords had crossed in *Rosencrantz*, and with statehood seemingly within reach for the first time in a decade, tables began to tip against mixed-sex practices and, in less obvious ways, against co-sovereignty. Perceptions of danger and social derangement consumed public energy. To make matters worse, self-serving railroaders dug in their heels at public expense. A bill pending in Congress demanded that railroaders forfeit lands or accept taxation; it was unclear whether the NPR and other roads ever intended to contribute to the commonweal or even finish the rail network. As Washington's Delegate Brent put it, every public burden had been lifted from the shoulders of the NPR and "put upon the weak and overburdened shoulders of the settler."[4]

Danger and social instability metastasized. Washingtonians fretted about Chinese invaders, vice peddlers, communists and unionists, unmanly Indians, prohibitionists, Mormons, and ambitious women. As Seattle's main newspaper concluded, "Politics in Washington Territory are in an unstable, almost ... volcanic state."[5] Female jury service still rankled; nursing mothers, babies, and small children sat beside men, sometimes sequestered with strangers, ridiculed, or threatened. Juries permitted neighbors to express outrage, restore public order, and rearticulate standards of conduct. But women allied with Roger Greene threatened to eliminate companionable games and whiskey. Lawyers increasingly disrupted courtrooms whenever women served as jurors; women sat under duress or vanished altogether. Shrill anti-vice campaigns confirmed suspicions about women's sex-laden inadequacies as exponents of community values. Many citizens yearned for the recent past when saloons had purveyed inexpensive, masculine pleasures; when men had monopolized public judgment; and when women kept house or earned supplementary income. Indeed, a common denominator seemed to be the collapse of recognized gender ascriptions – in the flesh, as with women in courtrooms, or metaphorically, as when unmanly Asians and "communists" displaced or emasculated white householders. Threads in the social fabric, once relatively distinct, formed a skein of tangled relationships; as Renisa Mawani observed in British-Columbian race relations, "contradictory entanglements" emerged that soon implicated women's bodies, labor, and bad impersonations of men. Amidst galloping economic modernization, in other words, every road seemed to lead to the woman problem, which in turn led Washingtonians to reconsider hierarchies of gender and race.[6]

Social practices had been pushed hard with impartial voting, but women with ballots still could be women, conceptualized as the home vote or as representatives of property. Not so with jurors, who embodied masculine

---

[4] Congressional Record, House, 49th Congress, 1st Session, Vol. 17, Part 7, July 26, 1886, pp. 7562–3, 7566.
[5] "The Duty of the [Republican] Convention," *SDPI*, August 28, 1886.
[6] Renisa Mawani, *Colonial Proximities: Crossracial Encounters and Juridical Truths in British Columbia, 1871–1921* (Vancouver: University of British Columbia Press, 2009), p. 205.

steadiness and fairness. With riots in the streets and uncertain justice in courts, social conventions resurged. Where did sovereignty lie? Said a Tacoman, mob law "engendered a spirit of resistance to all law. ... In assuming the authority that rightly appertains only to the sovereign power, to society, the mob strikes a blow at the very root of representative government." Perhaps with the restoration of unitary, masculine command, citizens would be spared grotesque encounters in courthouses; women would work mostly at home, with productive forays into wage labor. The Chinese would be purged, Indians could adapt to white civilization, and Washington would become a state.[7]

Did sex equality jeopardize statehood? On December 8, 1885, Indiana's Daniel Voorhees – the father of Washington delegate Charles Voorhees – introduced bills in the Senate to annex a portion of the Territory of Idaho to Washington Territory and to "provide for the ... admission into the Union of the State of Washington." Senator Blair at the request of the National Woman's Suffrage Association introduced a joint resolution in support of the Sixteenth Amendment.[8] In January, 1886, territorial legislators responded to *Rosencrantz* and other pressures: An amended election law conferred suffrage on "American citizens, *male and female*," as well as "American half-breeds, *male and female* ... and all other inhabitants, *male and female*" who intended to become citizens.[9] Ominously, however, South Dakota's governor had vetoed a similar bill on the ground that it threatened statehood and, in 1887, Wyoming abolished equal suffrage on the same ground, though with firm promises of restoration, once territorial men had approved a state constitution.[10]

"FREE GOVERNMENT CAN ONLY BE ASSURED WHEN THE CONDITION EXISTS"

In the mid-1880s, Washingtonians might be forgiven for thinking that their developing society and the broader nation were flying apart. Communication and transportation steadily improved, and participation in both regional and Pacific markets expanded. But instability accompanied integration, often in areas of life that seemed at first blush to have nothing to do with gender

---

[7] Editorial, "Is Mob Law Justifiable?" *TDL*, April 4, 1884. Emphasis added. For talk about Indian "civilization," see, e.g., "The Composition of an Indian Boy," *SDPI*, August 29, 1884 (lauding white education); "The Same as White People," ibid., February 19, 1886, applauding Indians' "progress[s] towards civilization"; or, for the idea that Indians must amass property or perish, "Indians as Citizens," ibid., August 2, 1887.

[8] Congressional Record, Senate, 49th Congress, 1st session, December 9, 1885, pp. 123, 137.

[9] An Act to Amend Section 3050, of Ch. 238 of the Code of Washington Territory..., Acts of the Territory of Washington, 1885–86, pp. 113–14. Emphasis added.

[10] "Suffrage in the Territories," *NN*, April 15, 1886; Honorable John W. Kingman, "Woman Suffrage in Wyoming," 1876, Schlesinger Women's Studies Mss., Reel 35, Series 1-E, No. 23; Constitution of Wyoming, 1889, Article No. VI, § 1 and 2. For speculations on suffrage and statehood, see, e.g., "A Stupid Jest," *TDL*, April 10, 1886 (rumors were a "mean pretext").

equality. Workplace violence swept the nation; on one day alone in March, 1886, more than a dozen strikes, slowdowns, or walkouts filled newspapers.[11] As early as 1883, a woman's club founder claimed to be exhausted by "all this agitation." Did civil war between labor and capital lie ahead?[12] In June, 1886, attention turned to business stagnation, a decline in commercial revenue, the "want of profitable employment to an estimated population of two million American workingmen," and a prevailing fear of bankruptcy. In Chehalis, Editor J. T. Forrest warned that the "dark and threatening" political horizon would "soon break forth in all its fury." Only in times of popular unrest did "communistic ideas" germinate; communities would have to "bring together all classes of the people in support of the law" and harmonize differences.[13]

Relations steadily deteriorated between employers and workers. In 1883–84, Horatio Alger-style tales of fantastic luck had multiplied: Young men with little capital and ample energy supposedly prospered where "value is put into the virgin soil by first occupancy"; so many avenues had opened to make money that a sober, earnest man could hardly fail. Walla Walla reporters said simply, "New England is ruled by capital and the West by labor." But, as the economy grew sluggish, the tone changed. Earlier, a hopeful writer styling himself "Rustler" had observed, "We have no strikes . . . . But it is the newness of the country . . . that have prevented them, as is generally the case in all new countries. The elements of the difficulty are here." Now, labor and capital were at loggerheads. "What have we but force? When all law is set aside, then if labor must dictate (which God forbid), we have but a Commune, who will set aside all laws!" As early as spring, 1884, newspapermen began to warn off settlers looking for wages: The times were quiet; the territory offered "small inducements" to men who wanted to work for others.[14] By April, 1886, Olympians openly talked about open revolt. Strikes meant war – "not a war between organized States . . ., but between organized factions . . ., which ranges neighbor against neighbor, and draws lines of battle in city streets." An interviewer asked Judah Benjamin, the Confederacy's ex-secretary, whether there would be more hostilities, and if so, what kind. "It may arise between the East and West," he had replied, "between the territories of the manufacturers and those of the agriculturists." In fifty years, states with

---

[11] "Story of a Strike," *TDL*, March 7, 1886, and on the same page, "Other Strikes . . . Engineers' Strike . . . Street Car Strikers . . . " and more ("Rioting Strikers," "Anarchists Sowing Seeds of Sedition," "Chicago Dynamiters," "Bombs and Revolvers"). For examples given, see *TDL*, March 5, April 23, 25, May 2, 5–6, 8–9. *TDL* and *WS* were pro-union.

[12] Clara Sylvester, "Letter from Olympia," *NN*, March 1, 1886.

[13] "Financial Schemes," *TDL*, June 22, 1886; editorial, *LCB* (Chehalis, WT), July 14, 1886; "The Prevailing Topic," *WS*, February 26, 1886. See also "How They Should Be Dealt With," *SDPI*, July 27, 1886, about socialist/anarchist plots.

[14] "Come West, Young Man," *WR*, November 2, 1883; "Our Hope for Statehood," *WWS*, February 24, 1883; "Rustler," "Labor and Capital," *PSWA*, December 1, 1882; "Labor and Capital," *PSWA*, December 1, 1882; "Home-Makers Wanted," *TDL*, April 5, 1884. See also "Could Not Stand the Press," *TDL*, March 14, 1884.

turbulent populations would be unable to govern certain "elements."[15] Seattle writers contended that Populists and unionists were pitted against manly independence – i.e., "every employer who is determined to run his own business; ... every man who seeks to accumulate anything; ... every man who seeks to protect his own property from fire and pillage."[16]

Under better circumstances, social strain might have been manageable; as it was, actual and prospective violence triggered backlash in defense of beleaguered white men and their attributes or practices. Poets celebrated masculine self-rule: "We be workingmen, we!/ Ours be shoulders Labor worn,/ Still, though sometimes overborne,– /Still, though toil be paid with scorn,/ Independent, we!"[17] The *Seattle Daily Times* blasted political radicals as "emasculated libertines." Anarchists and socialists (as with Indian men) liked to "loaf, drink beer, smoke and steal"; their wives labored to pay rent. Still others pointed to idiotic conflations of communism with manliness. "Why," asked a defender of the Knights of Labor, "is every attempt at a solution of the labor question by urging that justice be done to all men alike, met with protests against ... the communistic tendency of such attempts?" He further accused "true communists" of sloth, irrationality or duplicity, and seduction. Traditionally, spears of this kind had been hurled at transgressive women who, like witches, "work only with their tongues"; here, they castigated "dishonest ranters who want a general and equal distribution of all property" without a day's work. The professional communist believed that a man deserved less than a fair return on labor; surely these "loud-mouthed ranters" and idlers were less than "manly." Union men valued fairness; they demanded only that the laborer earn his wages and that they might belong to the worker himself, thereby honoring "the *equality of all men*" and the "rights of each man."[18]

Women armed with ballots and the prospect of equal wages in manufactories and canneries both enriched and complicated the workplace. Readers of the widely circulated, anti-suffrage *Oregonian* learned as early as 1882 that fragile women deserved low wages: "Never in the history of the world had woman so little occasion to bewail her lot as to-day."[19] Reporters lavished praise on young

[15] "Terence V. Powderly," *WS*, April 9, 1886; "Judah P. Benjamin, The Secretary of the Ex-Confederacy ...," *TDL*, April 2, 1884, front page.

[16] "Those who have been most zealous ...," *True Tone*, March 27, 1886, front page. Editors also raged about the loss of a factory because of strikes and riots.

[17] "Song of the Workingman," *True Tone*, May 1, 1886, by James A. Martling, author of *Poems of Home and Country* (1885). Other verses condemned "communes," "anarchists," and "agrarians."

[18] "Labor Food," *SDT*, June 21, 1886; "Anarchists at Home," *SDT*, June 8, 1886; "Not Communism," *TDL*, February 13, 1886, p. 2; "The Ten Hour Movement," *SDPI*, November 23, 1886.

[19] "Women's Work and Wages," repr. Springfield Republican, *OR*, August 16, 1882, front page. But, less often, readers encountered the view that manual labor was bad for women ("Occupations and women," *OR*, August 27, 1881) or that women who sought "special considerations" had "only themselves to blame" for poor wages; "Woman of Tomorrow," *SDPI*, December 10, 1886.

women who were "extending rapidly their usefulness, daily becoming more self-helpful ..., turning accomplishments to practical account and branching out into fields of industry hitherto filled by men or totally unfilled." Work made women "more intelligent," not less womanly or charming. At least one dared to say that women should settle over Protestant parishes, as when Tacoma's May C. Jones preached to acclaim in two Baptist churches. Civil equality encouraged self-defending speech. "It is not an uncommon thing for a woman to have to worry her husband for ten cents for car fare ...," said a critic of unpaid housework. Sharing the fruit of his labor with his partner in "the domestic firm never occurred to him. He was quite willing to trust her to keep the honor of his home and name ... but a doubt as to her business incapacity never crossed his mind."[20]

Should women produce wealth or stay home? Before 1887, women's ability to generate and manage wealth usually won praise – even though women's presence on the labor scene, combined with civil equality, destabilized men's claim to a "family wage."[21] Contrary voices lurked on the sidelines. One observer insisted that housewives were the "sole anchorages of the republic," a main line of defense as "alien" visionaries jeopardized ten million men with families. In the year of women's enfranchisement, an undercurrent of worry appeared about the new woman worker – her tendency to accept low wages, though not as low as the Chinese; her political weakness in relations with employers and government; and, given ongoing shortages of women, a loss of skilled housekeepers as they migrated into better-paid work."[22] But, into 1885, women's defenders predominated. The Knights of Labor, for example, championed "equal pay for equal work ... for both sexes," an eight-hour workday for everyone, and industrial cooperatives. Pro-union prints celebrated the Knights' position: "If the pay of men is inadequate to support a family," wrote Olympians, "how much less is the stipend doled out to the many thousands of women in the larger cities who are compelled to support themselves, and sometimes helpless children, on one-fourth the wages of her brother man?" Small wonder that the Knights' position troubled wage-earning men, exemplified perhaps by writers in eastern Washington who warned repeatedly that the Knights and their ilk would "bring the final disaster on labor" by luring women into the labor force and arraying angry men against employers.[23]

[20] "Young Men and Women," *SDPI*, November 15, 1883; "A Woman Minister," *NN*, February 11, 1886; "Domestic Unhappiness," *WR*, June 5, 1885.
[21] "A Wife and Home," *PSWA*, December 9, 1886. The family wage has been widely remarked; e.g., Alice Kessler Harris, *Out to Work* (New York, 2003), p. 321.
[22] E.g., "Household," *WS*, May 18, 1883. Counterexamples abound – as with Kathleen, "Woman Workers," *Northwest Enterprise*, November 17, 1883, describing in immense detail the professional and clerical opportunities for women in Washington, DC, and elsewhere.
[23] "Preamble and Declaration of Principles of the Knights of Labor," *WR*, April 17, 1885; "The Labor Movement," *SFR*, November 17, 1886. "The Knights of Labor ...," *WS*, December 31, 1886. The Knights supported woman suffrage and expressed guarded sympathy for temperance crusaders.

Pressures on women increased with persistent economic stagnation. Householders sometimes foraged for food. Rhapsodic depictions of men's chances yielded to the fact of an unevenly developed economy. Would-be immigrants learned that, in eastern counties, extractive enterprises did not generate "the productive wealth that builds up towns and cities, or at least the kind that most greatly benefits the trading and wage-receiving classes. It is a kind of wealth which stands in pools and does not spread out over the whole country."[24] Yet lumbering, mining, and herding supported large numbers of underemployed men. Boosters repeatedly urged women to abandon lucrative factory work, given a "serious glut," and respond to calls for domestic help.[25]

But women and men alike resisted such advice. "Now that woman is enfranchised ...," wrote a self-described male friend, "women's work has a new importance to us." Tangles emerged: A female worker would carry her interests, at home *or beyond*, into the polling place to defend herself and perhaps to resolve the "war" over the merits of liquor and saloons, which were destroying otherwise productive "armies of men." Girls and women could revel in autonomy, no longer in a rush to marry. Women's skills would become lucrative occupations – among them, cake baking.[26] In 1885, Seattle's leading paper offered the Reverend T. W. Talmage's essays against unequal wages. The "curse of our American society" was that girls were taught "to get somebody to take care of them"; the question ought to be how to "take care of themselves." A resident of rural Pomeroy agreed: Nothing mattered more than girls' education so that they might earn their own living.[27] Accounts multiplied of women's and girls' economic promise and the health benefits of work; in 1885, a frail Iowa teacher won praise for outperforming young men on a farm, running heavy equipment and lifting bales. While her employer thought that she now would make a fine wife, he hoped that she would strike out on her own.

[24] "Encourage Manufactures," *WWS*, July 16, 1883. In the same vein, see "Washington Territory," *Walla Walla Weekly Statesman*, May 19, 1883, describing opportunities for able-bodied men, listing work that only men ordinarily undertook (mining, lumbering, etc.). See also "A Word to Young Men," *WWS*, December 20, 1883, advising young men not to expect easy money and a life of leisure.

[25] "Western Washington," *PSWC*, March 11, 1884; editorial, *WS*, February 26, 1886; see also "Laboring Women," ibid., May 7, 1886, on the "surprising" extent to which women in the east had moved into "the branches of occupation" usually regarded as masculine. Nobody mentioned "family wage," but the meaning was clear: Women dragged down men's ability to support a family with his own earnings.

[26] "Woman's Work," *WS*, January 6, 1884; "Women and Home," and "New Business for Women," repr. Albany Journal, *PSWC*, January 22, 1884. In the same vein, see "Business Women," *SDPI*, September 10, 1884, urging parents to train girls in business so that they could find their own way.

[27] E.g., Rev. T. W. Talmage, "Women Should Have Equal Compensation With Men," *SDPI*, July 13, 1885; also Talmage, "A Woman Has a Right to do Any Thing She Can Do Well," ibid., June 28, 1885, and Talmage, "Women Must Work," ibid., June 26, 1885. Thomas DeWitt Talmage was a free-thinking Presbyterian. See also "Poor Girls," *Washington Independent* [Pomeroy], March 1, 1883.

Said a Whatcom journalist, women did not receive equal pay for the same work, as law provided. The trouble lay in the fact that "girls are not taught (as boys are) that they must rely upon their own exertions for their support. . . . They do not properly prepare themselves for a successful competition with men in the different pursuits of business life." A Spokane correspondent was glad to learn that women were investing 'pin money' in mining claims. This was "women's rights in the right direction."[28]

Women's economic contributions and civil standing also entered statehood debates in the United States Senate. On February 5, 1885, for instance, just as Senator Cameron of Pennsylvania proposed a national suffrage resolution, Senator Hoar addressed relationships between political and civil standing. He pointed to Washington, where women had exercised "brains as well as hearts" and transacted their own affairs; new avenues of self-support had been found, and the "doors of our colleges have ceased to creak their dismay." Twelve states had extended limited suffrage; three territories admitted adult citizens to the ballot-box. On what ground did "manly" family heads monopolize government? One-seventh of the nation's bread-winners were women, many of them poor and defenseless. A woman who owned "railroad or manufacturing or mining stock may vote unquestioned . . ., but if she transfers her property into real estate she loses all voice in its control." In Washington, Hoar added, as if one topic implied the other, "out of a total vote of 40,000, 12,000 ballots were cast by women." Their place was not "solely at home any more than that the farmer should never leave his farm, the mechanic his shop, the teacher his desk." If women paid taxes, managed estates, and produced wealth, they should vote; he could find no "abstract justification" for women's exclusion and the enfranchisement of men similarly situated.[29]

"IT IS ALWAYS TRUE ECONOMY . . . FOR A HOUSEHOLD TO DO ITS OWN WORK"

"Aliens" further complicated a sense of political danger and social derangement – all of which affected not just members of suspect classes, but also immigrant or indigenous women perceived to be right-minded and loyal. The Church of Latter-Day Saints, for instance, profoundly threatened Gentile social practices. As Mormonism expanded beyond Utah into Western Washington and elsewhere, journalists routinely condemned polygamy as a

[28] "That Western Girl," WS, October 16, 1885; "Give the Girls a Chance," WR, February 1, 1884; [Mom n Pop?], "Editor Review," SFR, March 13, 1886. See also "A Woman Captain," TDL, March 16, 1884, contending that whatever a man could do, women could duplicate, if muscle was not required.
[29] Congressional Record, Senate, 48th Congress, 2nd session, February 6, 1885, pp. 1324–5. See also "In a letter to the women . . .," WR, October 30, 1885 (Greene telling Minneapolis suffragists that 12,142 women in 41,842 voted in an 1884 election, numbers that an anti-suffragist called "preposterous").

"foul iniquity."[30] But Washingtonians could not have foreseen that their peculiar legalities would intersect with talk about equal suffrage in polygamous Utah, threatening to taint Washington by association. By 1886, the general question of democratization in Washington, Wyoming, and elsewhere came to be linked rhetorically to the Edmunds Act and its elimination of woman suffrage in Utah. When George Hoar rose to defend political equality and oppose the bill on January 5, 1886, he moved first to strike out sections prohibiting equal suffrage. While he despised polygamy, he could not support the disfranchisement of Utah's women. Why not? Because some of them were monogamous, and because, by all accounts, equal suffrage had succeeded in Wyoming and Washington: To deprive women who were not plural wives of a right already granted was to treat them as criminals. When Edmunds scoffed, Hoar rejoined that the ballot "once conferred was as much a vested right as any right of property," whether in Utah or Washington.[31]

Only a few Mormons lived east of the Cascades. But polygamy smacked of degeneracy: What could be worse than a collection of wives voting as one man dictated? At the same time, the church's practices illustrated federal neglect of territories. Why did Congress ignore an "unnatural," atavistic patriarchy? A Port Townsend reporter compared Mormonism to analogous Indian barbarisms, noting dismissively that Snohomish reservation Indians were not married "after the style of the pale face," but moved from one woman to another, a hideous merger – as with Mormonism – of religion with "animal lust." One writer characterized the federal Indian commissioner as a "crank" because he had tried to force Indian men to "confine their copper-colored affections to one tawny maiden." Best to leave them to their "legion squaws"; these were men only in the most primitive sense.[32]

Still, these insults paled as compared to the hatred visited on Asian men and their supposedly degenerate women. The Chinese empire's supposed designs for the Northwest and, eventually, for North America intersected with conversations about economic development, the labor force, family stability, threats to white

[30] Untitled editorial, *LCB*, October 9, 1885. Anti-Mormon squibs appeared every several days; but see, e.g., "The Mormon Situation," *SDPI*, November 6, 1885; on women held in thrall, "Mormon Mummery," *WWU*, September 18, 1883. Congressional debates also appeared; e.g., Senator Edmunds on the disfranchisement of Gentile as well as plural wives; untitled article on Congressional proceedings, *NN*, January 7, 1886. For a rare, positive view of a Mormon's second marriage, see "A Mormon Courtship," *TDL*, March 19, 1884.

[31] "Congressional," *Tacoma Daily News*, January 6, 1886, p. 1. The link between women's right to vote and polygamous "enslavement" appeared regularly; e.g., "Ingersoll on Black," reprinting selections from a debate between Robert Ingersoll and a polygamist; *OR*, October 29, 1881. A defender of human rights, Hoar also opposed Chinese exclusion. See also "A Vested Right," on Judge Jeremiah Black's assurance that suffrage was a "vested right," in Utah and elsewhere, *NN*, August 26, 1886.

[32] "Through the system...," *WWS*, July 28, 1883; "Polygamy Must Go," *PSWA*, March 4, 1886; "The Mormon Problem," *TDL*, February 22, 1885; "Won't Give up his Squaws," *WR*, October 12, 1883; "More Squaws, Less Whisky," ibid., October 19, 1883.

manhood and womanhood, public-health hazards, and statehood. Witness a Tacoma editor's hyperbolic alarm about invasions of "leprous, prosperity-sucking, progress-blasting Asiatics" who "befoul our thoroughfares, degrade the city, repel immigration, drive out our people, break up our homes, take employment from our country men, corrupt the morals of our youth, establish opium joints, buy or steal the babe of poverty or shame, and taint with their brothels the lives of our young men."[33] The Chinese undersold whites in the labor market; the empire soon would dispatch "millions" of entrepreneurs as well as yet more laborers who would "wrest from our own youth and manhood the labor they need."[34] Even Greene concluded that the Chinese, while meriting state protection as subjects of treaties, illustrated a racial difference "absolutely irreducible and irreconcilable."[35] But violence helped no-one. In October, 1885, he warned a mixed-sex grand jury that, while the Chinese presence was "an evil," any attempt to drive them out lawlessly was "suicidal." He reserved special disdain for "persons who are among us but not of us ... labor imposters, too lazy to work," who fomented anti-Asian unrest for their own purposes.[36]

Perhaps Chinese men were not men at all. Supposed experts saw beskirted men not simply as an economic threat, but as a sub-human, effeminate challenge to white men's virility and headship. "The American home and family," wrote a patriot, "is the inherent strength of the Union"; so long as "native self respect [and] pride of household and name exist, so long will our institutions be impregnable." A Chinese man did not seek to command a nuclear family. A white man knew that "the most cherished objects of his heart are being attacked"; even the "sturdiest manhood" would lose self-respect. Another partisan of white labor noted Asians' "dull and animalized visage" and taste for repetition, so devoid of the "aspirations, the high humanity" of normal men.[37]

---

[33] "Chinese Invasion of Tacoma," *TDL*, February 19, 1885. For anti-Chinese activities in Idaho, California, and elsewhere, see Carlos Arnaldo Schwantes, *The Pacific Northwest: An Interpretive History* (Lincoln, NE, 1996, rev. ed.), as at pp. 153–60. In 1887, after the final anti-Chinese riot in Seattle, 200 Japanese arrived to work in canneries and logging projects; thereafter, Japanese communities grew rapidly, joining residual Chinese and black populations in Seattle's "international district"; p. 158.

[34] Editorial, *TDL*, November 11, 1885. [35] "Irreducible Differences," *TDL*, October 27, 1885.

[36] E.g., "Judge Greene in Opening ...," *LCB*, June 26, 1885. Greene's charges appeared even in rural hamlets. See, e.g., partial publication of the charge in Pomeroy, months later; "From a Legal Standpoint, Judge Green[s]'s Powerful Charge to the Seattle Grand Jury," *Washington Independent*, October 15, 1885.

[37] "The Chinese Evil," *SDPI*, December 8, 1885; editorial, ibid., November 6, 1885; "The Chinese and the China Question ...," *WS*, July 30, 1886 and August 6, 1886 (parts of an essay series); and "The Prevailing Topics," ibid., February 26, 1886. See also "The China Question," *WS*, September 24, 1886. In the same vein, see talk about unmanly drudges, the lack of individualism, and paganism in, e.g., "The Chinese Must Go," *TDL*, September 23, 1885 and September 30, 1885 (same heading) or "Church and Chinese," ibid., November 18, 1885. The Ledger's language was so libelous that a reader protested; E. Meeker, "More of Mr. Meeker's Views," ibid., October 19, 1885.

As with talk about Mormons and Indians, allegations of Asian distortions of gender stood in sharp relief to North American practices. In 1883, an editor had argued that virtually all Chinese women in North America had been prostituted and every Chinese male "unmanned."[38] The Chinese, dependent on the Six Companies, supposedly passed the contagion of dependency to white men by underselling them in the labor market. Rural Washingtonians occasionally lynched Chinese men for assumed sexual crimes, as with the rumored rape of a small white girl in 1883. But allusions to work figured just as prominently: If slave masters had been feminized by sloth and luxury, Chinese men reveled in women's work – although the emperor surely was idle and in that sense emasculated. Did a territory that enfranchised certain classes of aliens mean to admit "squads of ... yellow-visaged knights of the wash-tub" to residency and naturalization? White workers perhaps should take over Chinese laundries and carts, however lowly the work might be, and pass anti-Chinese labor laws.[39]

Why not use white women in the place of unsafe Asians? In 1885, a Whatcom resident noted that Chinese men frequently put women out of work: "They super[s]ede the girls, not only in the kitchen but in the woolen mills and shoe factories. In every other country but this, starvation finds its antidote at the washtub"; on the Pacific coast, "the heathen chokes off competition of white laundresses." To be sure, white men also lost place: In 1884, Tacomans formed a "brotherhood" to rout Chinese labor for the benefit of "mechanics, laborers, and other hardworking men."[40] But women's work more closely resembled the jobs at issue; indeed, four years later, Governor Eugene Semple characterized Chinese men as workers interchangeable with but inferior to white women: "The Chinese continue to be the house servants in ... towns. As washermen, they are nearly universal. ... There has been a general belief that white women could not be found who would do these tasks, after the employment had been degraded by ... the Chinese." But in Tacoma, where the Chinese had been ejected, "*young women* have readily taken their places." At hand was a "docile race of servitors" held in thrall by tyrants, uninterested in earning the amount required to support "a self-respecting American man of family." Better to hire local women.[41]

Physical traits, raiment, and disinterest in self-sovereignty provided clear evidence of gender confusion. Chinese men had a fondness for skirts, braids (the "plaits in Confucius' pigtail"), silks, and "vividly colored drapes and fine embroideries." They lacked body hair. Like women, they defined themselves

---

[38] "Four Chinese Women," *TDL*, March 25, 1886.
[39] "Must the American Go?" *TDL*, February 28, 1885; "A Shocking Rape," *WWS*, October 6, 1883; "Chinese in Snohomish County," *SDPI*, October 7, 1885. See also suggested laws to ban Chinese laundries or launderers; "American Citizens to Be Favored," ibid., December 4, 1885.
[40] "Chinese Curse," *WR*, May 22, 1885; "Labor Organization," *TDL*, March 15, 1884.
[41] Message of the Governor of Washington Territory to the Legislative Assembly ..., Olympia, 1888, Eugene Semple Papers, Box 14, Folder 13, Ephemera, UWSC.

relationally, as members of extended families or cogs in an empire rather than as individuals. Every Chinese male was "registered," his location tracked by Asian overseers. Relations between the Emperor and his subjects reflected the "most absolute form of a centralized government" and barbaric patriarchy. Wrote one journalist, at once fascinated and repelled by the fact of a faceless, headless political family, "No man stands supported and alone among the Chinese." An 1885 diatribe against Chinese men ("Do white men rule here?") accused them of usurping woman's place throughout America. Women no longer moved west; "the coolie came, and all avenue for female employment was cut off." In effect, each Chinese man took the place of "an American home."[42]

China's pseudo-men thus joined the lengthening list of undesirables bent on displacing white women and emasculating white men. Perhaps the Chinese would ally with the secretive Knights of Labor and communism. Whatever might happen, an angry Tacoman concluded that Northwesterners need not include the Chinese in a "brotherhood of man" or imagine that a "fatherhood of God" extended to them. Even if God intended a fraternity, its members need not "all live in the same home.... [W]e have other brothers, at home ... needing our assistance." Correspondents even urged the use of convict labor in the place of the Chinese if profits accrued to the territory and not to prison contractors.[43]

In October, 1885, one of several anti-Chinese Congresses met in Seattle and resolved to eliminate Chinese "slave labor." The group vowed to avoid violence, but the tone was ominous: Speakers worried aloud about the danger of mobs in a time of unemployment.[44] As if to fulfill the prophecy, whites attacked Chinese laborers at Squak (or Squaw) Valley some thirty-five miles from Seattle. A number of working-class whites, Indian Curley, and Indian Johnny were arrested for rioting and conspiracy; Daniel Hughes was detained for murder. Governor Squires called up the Home Guard.[45] The crisis deepened.

---

[42] "The Prevailing Topics," *WS*, February 26, 1886; "The Chinese Invasion," *Dayton Chronicle*, October 9, 1883. On fealty, see "The Chinese and the China Question," *WS*, August 13, 1886, front page; "Chinese Exclude Women," *WR*, October 23, 1885; "Must the White Man Go?" ibid., September 4, 1885. For "plaits," see "The Chinese," *WWU*, October 16, 1883.

[43] Ibid. Also see "Convict Labor," *TDL*, December 12, 1885. It is unclear whether this plan aimed to replace only public workers. In fin de siècle California, convict labor was used in municipal projects; Lawrence Friedman and Robert Percival, *The Roots of Justice: Crime and Punishment in Alameda County, California, 1870–1910* (Chapel Hill, NC, 1981), p. 302. Washingtonians also thought that prison contractors sabotaged white men; e.g., "Convict Labor," *TDL*, December 12, 1885.

[44] "The Anti-China Congress," *WS*, October 2, 1885. For additional information about anti-Chinese agitation, see "The Chinese Problem," *SDPI*, October 7, 1885. In an anti-Chinese meeting of November 18, 1885, citizens insisted that they had done a great service peaceably; "Anti-Chinese Meeting," ibid., November 8, 1885.

[45] "The Governor's Report," *WS*, October 23, 1885. See also "The Troops Are Here," *SDPI*, November 8, 1885. The valley's name was printed "Quak." For the two named Indians, see Territory v. Paul Bayne et al., October 1885, Case File No. 4624, King County, PSRA. Rumsey and Hughes were indicted separately for killing a "Chinaman, Mock Goat"; charges against six others were dropped.

On October 17, a federal grand jury in Seattle indicted Chinese agents who had smuggled workers from Canada. Asians, they decided, were "neither of our religion, our race, nor our civilization." No country prospered with alien labor: "This nation is but a great household, and it is always true economy, where possible, for a household to do its own work." Roger Greene did not dispute the general critique. Notwithstanding his ongoing defense of the Chinese as rights-bearing human beings – grand juries had been convened in Pierce and King Counties to hear evidence in cases involving anti-Chinese violence as early as 1883 – he had no trouble criticizing the "cheapness of Chinese labor"; Chinese "alienage," which prevented population growth; the "export of the earnings of the Chinese"; "race and class irritation"; and "insecurity to property and life." In the end, judge and jury agreed that smugglers were not businessmen and so could be removed.[46]

But, as Greene considered the plight of the Chinese, his mind turned again to questions of individual sovereignty in republics. On November 1, 1885, he thanked the men and two women of a territorial grand jury for returning indictments against members of anti-Chinese mobs; later, they would consider evidence of murder in the case of Daniel Hughes. As with Mary Phelps, so with the Chinese. Was it not manifestly unlawful "to deprive a man of his life by force or fright"? Any force aiming to deprive any human being of happiness was unlawful; America welcomed all visitors, whether "English, German, or Ottoman." Moreover, while he did not believe that all workingmen set out to murder Asians, many had behaved violently and damaged the social fabric.[47]

The chief justice then embroidered on evolving theories of human rights and the role of mixed-sex juries. Republics, he thought, depended for sound representations of sovereign authority on assemblies and juries working in tandem. As early as 1880, he had analogized "judicial ballots" to the electoral variety and then associated both with citizens' affirmations of neighborhood values. Throughout 1884, as here, he regularly acknowledged that mixed-sex panels lay beyond the bounds of social practice, but insisted on their necessity, particularly in times of unrest. Women, far from destabilizing juries, made them more representative and reliable. "In this country, what may be termed the judicial ballot, on all principal questions of fact . . . can be cast by a juror only. It is the unappealable expression of the judgment of the people . . . and is of the most searching and positive import for the enforcement of law and the maintenance of good morals and peace." Woman was entitled to "share with

---

[46] "What a Seattle Grand Jury Thinks," *TDL*, October 18, 1885; and "Report of the Grand Jury," *SDPI*, October 20, 1885. See also "District Court Proceeding," *SDPI*, October 17, 1885; [Roger Greene's Charge to Grand Jury], *LCB*, October 9, 1885. See also "Smuggled Chinamen," *TDL*, October 4, 1884.

[47] "The Grand Jury's Work," *SDPI*, November 12, 1885. See also "The Chinese Must Go – Lawfully," ibid., September 24, 1885, for proceedings of a special meeting about the Chinese "menace to workingmen," and more information about the same Anti-Chinese congress, September 29, 1885, ibid.

man all liberalizing ... exercises of mind and heart." She had a right to "meet and confer with other men and women on a broad, sympathetic human basis, *outside the cramping walls of set and etiquette, and at some sacrifice of taste and habit.*"[48] Social practices, however powerful, would have to bend and mutate, particularly when they no longer advanced social goals. In republics, sovereign citizens sought consensus within an ever-expanding body representing every social class and, most important, an equitable distribution of rights: "All rights in society are related to and complementary of the rights of others. Government is for all men indiscriminately . . . . It cannot give to one class more rights than to others without abridging the rights of those others . . . . It cannot allow one class to define what rights another class shall have without deserting its governmental trust, and delivering over the latter class to irredeemable tyranny."[49]

Amid disastrous anti-Chinese rioting in Tacoma and Seattle, and parallel attacks on mixed-sex juries, Greene again convened a grand jury to evaluate evidence in the case of Daniel Hughes. At the same time, legislators had begun to formulate anti-Chinese measures; well-regarded lawyers and businessmen condemned the "hordes of Chinese" determined to "gobble up" the country.[50] Now, Greene explicitly characterized juries as the embodiment of the wills of sovereign citizens. In crisis time, it mattered more than usually that the sovereign coalesce to secure social peace: "The finality of the trial jury's finding ... makes it second in importance to ... no functionary. ... Reverence for the law ..., respect for the courts, security in property and liberty and life, all depend at last upon what the juries say."

... If ever free institutions fail us, it will be when honor and patriotism ... no longer appear in the verdicts of our juries. *In two words I can tell you who govern this community. The juries. In one word I can tell you who will scramble into anarchy any English speaking nation that falls into decay: Juries.* A good verdict is the collective expression of the considerate individual judgment of each person on the jury. No member has a right to shirk his or her personal responsibility for the soundness of the result. ... *A jury speaks not for itself, but for the commonwealth. It speaks as to the facts representatively, just as the judiciary speaks as to the law. Its utterances are the property of the public.*[51]

Shortly afterward, with Greene increasingly under siege for defending the Chinese as if they were fully human, he presided over the indictment and trial of perpetrators of xenophobic attacks on Chinese workers. The men had rushed

---

[48] Roger Sherman Greene, grand jury charge, in "District Court," *SDPI*, January 27, 1880; see also Greene, "Charge to the Grand Jury," *NN*, September 1, 1884. Widely reprinted. In 1885, he linked judicial ballots to representative government; see above.

[49] "Rights and Duties of Citizenship, ... Chief Justice Greene," *WWU*, November 21, 1885.

[50] D[avid] T. Denny, "A Few Questions from a Citizen [Seattle]," *SDPI*, September 30, 1885.

[51] "Trial of Daniel Hughes, the Text of the Charge of Judge Greene to the Trial Jury," *SDPI*, November 13, 1885. Emphasis added. Greene did have sympathizers, if not on the question of universal human rights, at least on the question of due process; e.g., L[uke] McRedmond, "The Chinese Question," *SDPI*, December 4, 1885.

into a Chinese labor camp and, at gunpoint after dark, forced them out into the snow and marched them for many miles before scattering. One reporter was aghast. The Chinese were "leprous curses," but this was cowardice: "If ... men have not got manhood and nerve enough to do their work in the day time they ought to be driven out ... with the Chinese."[52]

In January, 1886, the Assembly demanded federal enforcement of the 1882 Chinese Exclusion Act, military expulsion of Chinese nationals already settled, and stiffened penalties for smugglers. Some legislators suggested that riots and the murder of a police commissioner had been little more than an attempt to protect white labor. Surely competition between whites of both sexes and Asians portended the "destruction of white labor and the consequent overthrow of ... our republic, to the maintenance and stability of which white labor is so important a factor." Petitioners applauded Seattle's male grand jurors ("farmers, manufacturers, and businessmen") who had stood firm against the Chinese, ignoring female hold-outs.[53] In a comparatively mild critique of Greene's repeated reminders that Chinese residents were protected by treaty, Luke McRedmond – an Irish immigrant and prominent Democrat – bade Greene to consider the plight of local men. The Declaration of Independence bestowed on citizens "the majesty of manhood"; the Chinese were neither "human" nor manly. In late 1883, Asian men's weak gender ascriptions allegedly had resulted in the marriage of a Chinese man with "plaits" to another man cross-dressed for the occasion. In a serialized, front-page essay about "the China Question," editors frankly aimed to "[p]repare the leaven for a vigorous popular uprising, by lawful methods, ... whenever the question shall assume a political form." New York's James A. Whitney supposedly had got it right: The Chinese infestation, which affected wage labor as well as Washington's statehood prospects, was the most vital question of the day, surpassing woman suffrage and all else.[54]

In February, 1886, after yet more confrontations between Chinese laborers and whites in coastal cities, Governor Watson Squires declared martial law, and Washingtonians began to shoehorn the Chinese problem into a widening critique of industrial abuse. Citizens mobbed Loyal League meetings, where

---

[52] "Forcing the Chinese Out," *LCB*, January 22, 1886.

[53] "Notes" and "Territorial Legislature," *TDL*, January 12, 1886, p. 1. See also "Anti-Chinese Legislation," *TDL*, January 28, 1886; editorials, *SDPI*, January 23 and 28, 1886. The legislation stalled. Perhaps lawmakers knew that Greene and others took them to be unconstitutional; but see "An Open Letter," *SDPI*, January 27, 1886, signed by two dozen men, including lawyers, who insisted that legislators could prevent unfair competition. Finally, see "An Experiment Suggested," *TDL*, January 26, 1886, p. 2 (Chinese vegetable peddler had been arrested in Seattle to test the legality of an ordinance licensing "hucksters and peddlers"; Greene rejected the appeal).

[54] L[uke] McRedmond, "The Chinese Question," *SDPI*, December 4, 1885; "A Heathen Chine[s]e," *WWU*, November 29, 1883. The "plaited" man supposedly had not noticed the substitution. See also "The China Question," *WS*, September 24, 1886, editorial page.

men and women explored ways to squelch anti-American influences.[55] Eugene
Semple, an entrepreneur and Democratic aspirant for the statehouse,
condemned the martial-law decision as a betrayal of the government's duty of
"defending, protecting and advancing ... personal freedom." Loyal-League
alarm intensified when a mixed-sex, Pierce County grand jury found no
evidence of socialistic cabals in mob activities.[56] Greene confided in his uncle,
U.S. Senator William M. Evarts, that in Seattle, "deadly purposes and plotting"
lurked beneath the surface. He feared "civil war on a small but terrible and ...
expanding scale" with international implications; violence affected both the
"coast and nation." Greene had few doubts that rioters had deliberately killed a
police commissioner.[57]

On February 8, 1886, coincident with Squires' martial-law declaration,
Greene had personally intervened amid rioting in Seattle, ordering the Sheriff
to bring the Chinese to his courtroom with the militia's help. There, he asked
individuals whether they wished to stay or leave; some were placed on a
steamship.[58] The chief justice, who supported Squires' home-guard decision,
also had ordered the arrest of mob leaders on charges of murder, conspiracy,
assault, and rioting.[59] One observer mourned "blood in the streets." When
Greene refused to prosecute Judge Thomas Burke and others who had helped to
put down mobs on the ground that they were officers of the court, critics
accused him of favoritism and "fanaticism."[60] In June, 1886, a territorial

---

[55] Editorial, *TDL*, February 10, 1886. See also "Poverty," ibid., February 16, 1886 the "needy
millions" in London and elsewhere would "rise in their might").

[56] Speech draft, Vancouver, W.T., March 8, 1886, Eugene Semple Papers, UWSC, Box 14, Folder
12. On March 11, Semple told "General King" in Seattle that that the upcoming election would
be decided on the martial law question, and that he was going to deliberately inundate
Republican papers with his views on the question. See also Resolutions at Vancouver, W.T., in
1886, opposed to the governor's decision to institute martial law; Semple Papers, Box 14, folder
2. By June, 1887, he was prepared to use force to put down riots; see ES to Mayor of Seattle, and
ES to sheriff of Pacific County, June 13, 1887, Semple Papers, Box 1, Folders 3 and 4,
Correspondence Outgoing.

[57] Roger S. Greene to Hon. William M. Evarts, February 12, 1886, Thomas Mercer Papers,
University of Washington Special Collections, University Archives, Access. No. 4817–001,
File V.

[58] Editorial, November 6, 1885; "The Chinese and the China Question ...," July 30, 1886 and
August 6, 1886 (an essay series in five installments); "The Prevailing Topic," February 26, 1886;
all in *WS*. The Knights of Labor denied accusations of alliance with the Chinese; e.g., "To the
Public," ibid., February 19, 1886. For Greene's intervention, see "The Uprising at Seattle," ibid.,
February 12, 1886.

[59] "The Uprising at Seattle," *WS*, February 12, 1886, p. 2; "The Chinese," *SDPI*, February 10,
1886; "The Chinese, An Attempt to Expel Them Met by an Organization of Citizens," and "The
Duty of Citizens," ibid. Squires' mobilization of "citizen soldiers" was widely reported; e.g.,
"Citizen Soldiers and People," *True Tone* (Seattle), February 13, 1886; "An Interesting State of
Affairs at Seattle," *SR*, February 9, 1886; "At Seattle," ibid., February 10, 1886.

[60] Editorial, *TDL*, February 10, 1886, p. 3; for "unusual powers," see editorial, *WS*, December 18.
1885. For blood in the streets, see "Martial Law," *SDPI*, February 10, 1886. See also "Judge
Greene's Fanaticism," *TDL*, October 7, 1885 (on defense of the Chinese as subjects of federal
treaties). See also "The China Question," *WS*, September 13, 1886.

grand jury haplessly admonished citizens to uphold the law: The Chinese were in Washington legally; the same men and women, sitting as a federal grand jury, condemned "communists" who had instigated anti-Chinese agitation along the seacoast.[61]

What if Congress should decide that a territory incapable of maintaining public order should wait for statehood? Had mixed-sex juries aided or impeded restorations of peace? Why had women held out against male majorities? If the jury was an effective bulwark against disorder, why had rioting continued after swift indictments and verdicts? Why had the governor been forced to call up the guard? Even the pro-suffrage Senator Dolph noted anxiously that Washington's "insurrection" drove home the citizenry's obligation to ensure "the maintenance and enforcement of law ..., whether socially, in the jury-box, or when called upon to quell actual disturbance of the peace."[62]

In August, 1886, the Western Washington Republican Party gathered to settle nominations and write a platform. A likely candidate for territorial delegate to Congress was Roger Greene, described by his nominators as a man "aloof from politics," someone who could harmonize party factions and who garnered "universal respect."[63] His nomination did not survive the convention. But Republicans approved a platform that directly addressed the behavior of the territory's chief magistrates: "We believe that the present law in regard to the qualification of votes, male and female, should be retained" and that "coolies" should be removed. In keeping with Greene's printed jury charges, they condemned the people's attempts to "correct the evils of which they complain by riotous outbreaks and defiance of the National authority" and praised Greene and Squire for reasserting "the authority of the law."[64]

As 1886 advanced, Greene's radical-republican speculations became longer, more detached from the cases at hand, and more disorganized. How, he wondered, might legislative dominance within republics coexist with self-rule? Always, the lynchpin was the mixed-sex jury, an institution infused with the whole people's sovereignty, created to ensure fealty to their law. As householders governed families, he decided, so citizens controlled republican institutions, including juries. Again, Greene took dead aim at the wall between public and private realms. In August, in an uncommonly long address to a mixed panel in Seattle district court charged with deciding the fate of anti-Chinese rioters, Greene spread his ruminations over the record and personally delivered copies to newspapers. The chief justice had contemplated "almost every form of government realized or projected"; the American form was "the finest in the world, and excepting the disfranchisement of women, the freest possible under the present conditions of the race. If there is any oppression or

---

[61] "Grand Jury Report," *SDPI*, June 5, 1886; "Report of the United States Grand Jury," ibid., June 6, 1886.

[62] Congressional Record, Senate, 49th Congress, 1st Session, March 31, 1886, p. 2956.

[63] "The Republican Candidate," *SDPI*, August 24, 1886.

[64] "Republican Convention in Seattle" and "Republican Convention," *SDPI*, August 29, 1886.

tyranny among us, it is not due to our form of political government. ... Our people are beyond dispute sovereign." There was "no deprivation of liberty, no encroachment upon liberty which the people are not able ... to correct upon an appeal made to them."[65] Enter a phalanx of sovereign, front-line jurors: Men and women together ruled both families and the state. "If one means by freedom, an unrestrained power to do as he pleases, he has in mind something utterly hostile to the true American idea. The free man of his imagination is the ... despot of history." Rather, the American idea of freedom was "that exalted conception of individual kingliness which Christianity has diffused throughout the enlightened peoples of the world. Our national ideal is the nation of kings, a royal people, every man of us a king, every woman of us a queen."

Now a king has his station ..., not for his selfish pleasure but for the good of society. His days ... are spent for the general welfare. ... Every citizen should be free to ... work out all the true kingliness that is in him .... Scope for enjoyment of his freedom must be ... kept open to him. To this end, he has his personal and property rights most jealously guaranteed. For who can be kingly, who has not control of his own person and has no property he can justly call his own?

On the basis of this idea, the freedom of each citizen consists with the freedom of every other .... But the other sort of freedom is consistent with nothing but ... endless private war .... [I]t is of the utmost concern for the peace and authority of society that the sovereign people maintain their authority.

... A mother gives a command to her boy. He perhaps, is inclined to disobey, and says to himself, 'Mother says I must, but need I really? She says she will punish if I disobey; but will she do what she says?' He proceeds to test the matter, and unless the mother ... compels obedience ... the tables are turned, and ... he is ruling her.

Something analogous happens when the people say a thing to their legislature and fail to do it in their courts. ... Even an improvident law ... must be enforced. Such a law is a bad thing, ... but want of loyalty to the sovereignty of the people is worse, and so long as that law remains unrepealed, there is no wise course but to insist that as an utterance of the people it shall receive the respect due to the people themselves. It is of paramount importance ... that the authority of the people be maintained. *The only normal, quiet and steady way of maintain it is by the action of the juries ..., setting an example of subordination to law and compelling others to the like subordination.*

Mixed-sex juries thus embodied and affirmed the sovereign command of the people, conceptualized as a household. As children obeyed mothers, so citizens observed legislation. Those who countermanded jurors' lawfully promulgated decisions – even when statutes awaited correction – sabotaged the 'kingly' and 'queenly' principle at the heart of republics: "Every indictment you legally find will be a ... *stroke for the maintenance of the authority of the whole body of the people as sovereign.*"[66]

[65] "Judge Greene's Charge [Seattle]," *SDPI*, August 30, 1886.
[66] "Judge Greene's Charge [Seattle]," *SDPI*, August 30, 1886, repr. August 31. Emphasis added. See also Senator Dolph's partial agreement: At the heart of republican government was "the jury-box"; Congressional Record, Senate, 49th Congress, 1st Session, March 31, 1886, p. 2956.

Unrest continued into 1886. Fear caused writers to forgo punctuation: "There are rumors in the air – vague and indefinite whisperings – which unreliable and perhaps meaningless as they are should not be allowed to pass unnoticed.... These rumors are all of the turmoil in the near future – the whispers are all of unquiet and unrest." Was there still an American people?[67] When Democrats met in Tacoma to draft a platform, they ignored women's rights and tried to pass a resolution (ultimately tabled) asking President Cleveland to remove Squire and Greene for "violating their oaths of office by imposing and enforcing martial law during the recent clashes with the Chinese."[68]

Where did self-supporting women fit in contests between white and Chinese men? Tacomans repeatedly noted in 1885 that Asians ought to be excluded from the labor market because they were willing to live on almost nothing, competed disastrously with white male labor, and "rendered it almost impossible for white girls and women to obtain employment." Once Asians had been purged, women could take their places at slightly better pay and white men's wages would rise commensurately.[69] White women thus superseded Asians but effectively supported white men's higher wages. Hence, the steam laundry at the Tacoma Hotel took on experienced laundresses from California and fired all but a few Asians, who would undertake the meanest work, which, in turn, white men refused to do.[70] Months later, the People's Party encouraged women to seize control of shop floors not only as an avenue to independence, but also to crowd out Chinese workers, elevate wages for native-born men who could move upward, and advance economic growth. In March, 1886, Tacoma's mayor urged the Ladies' Cooperative Union to create a segregated, "pure" workplace for women until Chinese contaminants could be removed; thereafter, female workers would return to facilities managed by men.[71]

Discourses sometimes converged in individuals; when liquor seeped into the mixture, stress was insupportable. Consider this outburst in summer of 1886 from a female voter, prohibitionist, member of Seattle's Loyal League, and critic of pro-Chinese jury decisions: Why were the rights of the Chinese more important than the rights of citizens to be free of the ravages of drunken mobs? "We women, whose husbands and sons tramped the streets through

---

[67] "Seattle Alarmists," *TDL*, May 8, 1886.
[68] "Voorhees Renominated, The Democracy Retains Its Old Leader," with party platform; *SDPI*, August 19, 1886. On tabling, see "That Resolution," *WS*, September 3, 1886. For another rendition of the censuring text, see "Squire and Greene," ibid., August 20, 1886.
[69] "The Chinese Must Go," *TDL*, September 23, 1885; in the same vein, "Under Which King, Benzonian?" ibid., October 4, 1885 (the "coolie" had to go if competing with white women).
[70] "The Chinese Must Go," *TDL*, March 31, 1885. Editors noted that the hotel possessed the "latest improved" equipment; women would not be overworked.
[71] "Women's Co-Operative Union," *TDL*, March 14, 1886, p. 6. The outcome is unknown. Rarely, observers urged the hiring of Chinese workers, in one case instead of blacks; "Chinese vs. Black Labor," *SPI*, September 12, 1882. See also "Women's Co-Operative Union," *TDL*, March 14, 1886, p. 6.

mud and rain those memorable days and nights of last February, to maintain the dignity of the law, we, too, remember ... the victory of lawlessness last July."

The whooping, ... the carousing, the speech-making and the jeers of that summer night have not yet faded from our memories. ... Many nights we wondered why the dignity of the law to protect the Chinese must be preserved at so much greater hazard than that of the law to ... save our boys from ruin. The loyal men and women may by a clear majority ask for immunity from the saloon curse that is daily dragging our business men, our bright boys and husbands ... down, down, down through financial wreck, through physical ruin, through social ostracism ... to despair and death. ... We women who cast out our loved ones our all, to stand between a hissing, howling mob and a motley mass of ignoble, icon worshipping Chinese, that the dignity of the law might be preserved.

Officials had told her that if prohibition carried, it could not be enforced, to which she said, "Shame."[72]

"HEAVEN'S OWN FAIRY STORY"

As "A Loyal Woman's" distress makes clear, battles over free-flowing alcohol made a fraught scene much worse. Not only was drunkenness endemic, but organized anti-saloonism, despite significant male participation, increasingly carried a feminine inflection, alongside hung juries, "law and order" campaigning, and workplace confusion. A Spokane writer described gender derangement: "Women become unwomanly, ministers forget those teachings that were prescribed by the meek and lowly Jesus, and display hatred, venom and malice, and the common man is blinded to the right and privileges of others."[73] Both sides adopted the violent tropes of war and emasculation. A temperance worker declared, "Vice is the ax which lays vigorous manhood in the dust. There are women who think it not unwomanly to wish to dull the edge of that weapon. Ballots are not mere soft pieces of paper; they have grit and backbone. ... Hurl them at the ax and see if it is not blunted."[74] Ambrose French Grow of Winslow, Washington, urged women to "slay" the saloon power with the "ballot in one hand and the other uplifted toward heaven."[75] A minister in Olympia announced that the "Rum Power must be smitten and ground to powder" and that God for that very purpose had given woman the ballot. One anonymous Spokane writer implicated manhood: Bad enough that

---

[72] "A Loyal Woman," "What Is Loyalty?" *SDPI*, June 24, 1886. For a similar plea, see another woman's plea: unsigned letter to the editor, *LCB*, June 18, 1886.

[73] "It is conceded ...," *SR*, February 9, 1886, editorial page.

[74] "Excelsis," "Woman and the Ballot," *SDPI*, July 10, 1885. See also the piece published in 1883 after legalization of suffrage alleging that new voters had been led astray by a man's "liberal" religion at the expense of a better candidate; "The Town Election," *WS*, January 18, 1884.

[75] A. F. Grow, "A Temperance Sermon," *SDPI*, April 16, 1885. Ambrose French Grow (1825–1909) wrote "Reminiscences of Galen," serialized in *The Clyde Times* (1908); see www.wayne .nygenweb.net/galen/oldgalenreminiscences.html.

purifiers assailed "the constitutional rights of the citizen"; they even wanted to close high-class pubs so that, when a man wanted a drink, he could "take it like a man" and not have to sneak into a dive and "get drunk on mean goods."[76]

Lawmakers regularly confronted a range of proposals – among them, Sunday closing, enhanced penalties for domestic violence and public inebriation, local option, high license, and the closing of all saloons. Of these, the first two were the least controversial. In late 1884, a mostly male petition drive, supported by a modest number of women, persuaded the Seattle city council to enforce Sunday closing in the face of opposition from pub owners.[77] Local option mandated precinct-level elections in which voters selected "dry" or "wet"; voters could shutter saloons for a year, with owners granted only a few days to close doors. Local-option proponents increasingly stood accused not only of unconstitutional takings of saloon property, but also of illegally depriving customers of the right to consume freely. Wets increasingly trained fire on the WCTU, the Prohibitionist Party, and fanatics like Roger Greene. In Walla Walla, for instance, community leaders not only dished out meanness (an 1882 petition was said to be the work of "3,000 male women"), but also rejected temperance speakers – as when commissioners permitted the NPR's Henry Villard to speak at a courthouse but denied the same venue to Frances Willard on the ground that the building could only be used for county and public or political meetings. When dozens of men petitioned for reconsideration – the event was as political as Villard's – they failed.[78]

As a local-option bill moved through the Assembly in late 1885, the association between local- option and women tightened. WCTU members, other women, and sympathetic men began to fill galleries and a lobby behind the bar, a restraint on the Council's main floor. The hall thus became a quasi-courtroom and observers active parties in a social drama.[79] On December 20, 1885, when lawmakers first confronted the bill, tensions ran high; by January 5, 1886, the act approached a third reading and final Council vote: "[T]wo rows of the chairs outside the bar were occupied by fair and enthusiastic temperance workers who smiled and smiled as one after the other of the members ... filed into position." Judge Dennison averred that, if passed, the measure would sound "the death knell of the liquor traffic in this territory." Members agreed to postpone.[80]

---

[76] "License vs. Prohibition," *SR*, June 1, 1886.

[77] E.g., "The Sunday Law Sustained," *SDPI*, October 23, 1884. Men outnumbered women by a huge margin.

[78] "The Woman Cause," *WWS*, November 18, 1882; "Should Be Changed," *WWU*, July 17, 1883.

[79] See Victor Turner, *Dramas, Fields, and Metaphors: Symbolic Action in Human Society* (Ithaca, NY, 1974), esp. pp. 23–59, on social or civic drama.

[80] "At the Capitol," *TDL*, December 20, 1885. In preparation for the vote, journalists had laid out the religious and marital associations of each member of the Assembly. They found that, of thirty-six, only three were unmarried. Twenty-five had "no religion, claiming to be liberal or free-thinkers." See also "Territorial Legislature," *TDL*, January 6, 1886.

The next day, a mixed-sex crowd burgeoned. Doorkeepers acted as ushers to "a continuous stream of men and women, until every seat in the lobby was filled and an overflow of privileged people crowded within the bar, and as the last bill was disposed of there was a general turning toward the clock. . . . 'The time for the special order has arrived,' said the speaker, and there was a rustle . . ., a leaning forward in expectancy. Silence followed," and then Lewis, the father of the local option measure, rose to introduce it. A critic rejoined: The "liquor traffic could not be expected to die without a severe struggle"; his fatal amendment was rejected. After another pause, the speaker announced that the bill was ready for its final reading. Said Lewis, 'The question is not upon the passage of the bill – there is no doubt about that . . . but shall it pass unanimously?'" He argued, not that local option would purify society, but that the law symbolized home rule. Government was "founded upon local option. We decide our school matters . . . by local option." The lobby rang with applause. Dennison pronounced it a "woman's bill" and asked for unanimity; the audience gave "joyful approval."[81]

As adopted, the bill not only prohibited the sale of intoxicants whenever a majority of the legal voters of any precinct so chose, but also affirmed equal suffrage ("in construing this act, . . . [n]ouns and pronouns of the masculine gender include the feminine gender"). In the event of loss, saloonists got a longer time to settle their affairs. The WCTU's Frances Willard told Carrie White of the western Washington union that "repeated victories in your noble territory read like heaven's own fairy story."[82]

Between adoption and signing, citizens (notably but not only businessmen) pelted legislators and the governor with petitions. Notwithstanding the participation of a good many men, women alone encountered slings and arrows. Sometimes, opponents castigated the law for its anti-republican and anti-majoritarian origins. Several hundred citizens of Tacoma, described as "the heaviest taxpayers, real estate owners, merchants and bankers," inveighed against bills written in secret that expressed the arbitrary will of cranks like Roger Greene and his growing harem of Law-and-Order women. Republican precepts shared space with gender anxiety and disdain for the ubiquitous chief justice: Laws, they argued, should express the "deliberate will of the majority . . ., and should be such as are demanded for the whole people as a body politic. . . . This law is invidious in its character." A minority had excited "malignant and bad feeling"; such a law created ill will, promoted

---

[81] "Territorial Legislature," *TDL*, January 8, 1886. Emphasis added.

[82] "Acts of the Last Assembly," *WS*, March 18, 1886; An Act to prohibit the sale of intoxicating liquors in the several election precincts of Washington Territory . . ., Laws of Washington Territory, 1885–86 (February 1886), called the "local option law," published widely; e.g., *WS*, March 12, 1886, p. 1. See also "Local. Greeting from Miss Willard," *TDL*, March 4, 1886. Legislative journals published in newspapers do not carry information about the jury-service bill; but this may well have been the opening salvo leading to the 1888 law. Also printed as "Moral Legislation," *NN*, February 18, 1886.

discord, and restricted a "man's right to trade and traffic." Law should never reflect the "arbitrary will of a few enthusiastic moralists and fanatical reformers." Into 1887, allusions to Greene's influence on subjective women persisted – as when anti-suffragists argued that women ought to make decisions without the aid of "fawning sycophants" who (in the words of another writer) caused women to "unite spiritual with temporal interests." Judge Thomas Burke, usually a Greene ally, warned of a "confiscation" of lawful liquor licenses by "preachers ... of high morality" influenced by fraught women whose "eyes run over with sympathetic tears and kindness of heart."[83]

After adoption, and just as anti-Chinese violence reached fever pitch, temperance workers set about arranging precinct elections for June, 1886.[84] Willard's followers knew full well that success had played into the hand of those who would deprive women of both ballots and seats on juries. Said Willard, legislators had defeated an "attempt to 'relieve' women of jury duty" on the ground that they could not make dispassionate judgments. Heedless, she plunged on: "Who that reads this record can say, that 'politics' and 'law' are not, potentially at least, the most practically religious domains that ... power can enter?"[85] Also heedlessly, the WCTU officially adopted planks supporting the law conferring suffrage on women and stood firm against repeal or modification. Leaders also suggested that there be multiple elections and grants of sufficient time for "persons engaged in the liquor traffic, to withdraw their capital and dispose of their property, without material loss or damage." But it was probably too late; the war on saloons had been firmly tied to women's political personalities and deranged "judicial ballots."[86]

Backlash was swift. In Garfield County, a town council passed a high-license ordinance doubling the license fee (from $100 to $200) but also barring women from all saloons. Journalists implied a degree of unmanning: When a legislator could be seduced by "honeyed words" and "baskets of flowers" (WCTU supporters had carried such baskets into legislative chambers after passage of local option), he was a "very cheap man."[87] Occasionally, reporters mocked other men: Perhaps the time had come, said one, when the "sovereignty and dignity of man ... should be carefully guarded, protected and salted down for the benefit of the rising generation. ... What will become of the sovereignty of exalted man if the mothers and wives of this Nation are allowed to openly and

---

[83] "Local Option," *TDL*, January 22, 1886. On local option and takings, see "An Unwise Measure," *TDL*, January 15, 1886, and "Local Option," *TDL*, January 24, 1886 (Judge Burke accusing Greene of takings). Information circulated about opinions in other jurisdictions; e.g., "Judge McCay of the United States Circuit Court for Georgia ...," *True Tone* [Seattle], April 24, 1886 (prohibition destroyed proprietary rights "without compensation," violating the Fourteenth Amendment).

[84] "The Local Option Law," *TDL*, January 19, 1886.

[85] "Local. Greeting from Miss Willard," *TDL*, March 4, 1886.

[86] "The Platform," "The Declaration of Principles Adopted by the Prohibition Territorial Convention," *SDPI*, September 10, 1886.

[87] "We have no doubt ...," *TDL*, January 30, 1886, editorial page.

defiantly desecrate the sacred precincts of a saloon with their hymns?" How grand to be "born into this world a noble male sovereign!"[88]

In short, hostilities directed at women in courtrooms had been compounded. Fearing such a result even without the jury controversy, Susan B. Anthony had discouraged alliances with temperance until women commanded electoral majorities; as she told Washington's Elizabeth Boynton Harbert, temperance could only "<u>divide</u> our ranks."[89] The *Standard* pronounced such fears "fully verified." Why flout basic constitutional precepts? "The founders ... wisely guarded against a union of creed with those principles which guaranteed freedom to the people." Everyone should reject sectarian attempts to limit freedom. "This feeling of distrust does not originate with the vender of intoxicating liquors ... but from men and women of sobriety.[90]

The rift between suffragism and temperance widened. On one hand, towns in fact were infested with vice; men squandered pay on gaming, liquor, and red-light districts. The *Lewis County Bee* repeatedly denounced Duniway's "washy harangues"; she lived in another state but dared to ridicule Narcissa White. In mid-1886, *True Tone* castigated Duniway for urging women to stay away from local-option elections: "After laboring ... for twenty-five years, to secure for women the ballot, she now advises the women to stay away from the polls" when they finally could assail "the worst enemy that ever invaded the household." On the other hand, Orange Jacobs likely was relieved when, in June, 1886, Seattle and Tacoma voters flocked to elections and defeated prohibition by large majorities.[91] Women apparently had not voted as a bloc. The election also spoke to women's growing political acumen. WCTU members and their opponents busily escorted friends to the polls, hired carriages, and distributed ballots; in major cities, the vote was the largest ever seen. This was not a test of the strength of the temperance movement, one reporter added, but a measure of the city's "attachment to the election process."[92] Shortly afterward, George Turner antagonized many of his friends by ruling local option a valid exercise of the assembly's police powers, reversing a circuit ruling by Justice

---

[88] "Female Prohibition," *Washington Independent* [Pomeroy], November 19, 1886.

[89] Susan B. Anthony to Elizabeth Boynton Harbert, December 9, 1883, in Ann D. Gordon, ed., *Selected Papers of Elizabeth Cady Stanton and Susan B. Anthony: When Clowns Make Laws for Queens*, Vol. IV (New Brunswick, NJ, 1997), p. 306.

[90] "A Natural Result," *WS*, July 2, 1886; untitled editorial, *WS*, October 8, 1886. See also Duniway's wish that Washingtonians could jettison prohibitionism and return to temperance; "A Negative Suffragist Speaks," *NN*, January 6, 1887. In April, 1886, editors reprinted a piece supposedly written by Abigail Duniway advising women to wait until they are voters so they could drive out all of the saloon owners; untitled, *TDL*, April 6, 1886.

[91] E.g., "Consistency," *LCB* (Chehalis, W.T.), July 14, 1886; "The Clarke County Register says ...," *True Tone*, April 17, 1886; "By Large Majorities," *TDL*, March 4, 1886. See detail in "'License' or 'No License,'" *NN*, July 1, 1886 (prohibition was defeated along the western coast and in larger towns but had succeeded in a number of rural towns and villages – e.g., Colfax, Dayton, Chehalis, Prescott, Pomeroy, Payallup, La Conner, Snohomish).

[92] "Prohibition Defeated, the Majority in Seattle over a Thousand," *SDPI*, June 29, 1886; and "The Election," ibid., June 30, 1886.

William Langford, who had deemed the act an unconstitutional delegation of legislative power "to a body of the people [voters] not authorized ... to exercise the function of legislators."[93]

"A JURY SPEAKS ... AS TO THE FACTS REPRESENTATIVELY"

By 1886, then, women's reputation and standing as both electors and community representatives had frayed. Proposals had been appearing since 1883 to purify the electorate. In ways that smacked of southern treatment of blacks, such proposals did not directly implicate sex; rather, they urged loyalty, residency, or property thresholds. If married-women's names did not appear in good form on tax rolls, fewer of them would vote. In 1883, a few months before adoption of an equal-suffrage bill, the anti-suffrage *Walla Walla Union*, without explaining the "broad proposition that the right of suffrage is too free everywhere," proposed limiting the city vote to men who had paid taxes on real or personal property for the previous year.[94] Once equal suffrage had been adopted, proposals multiplied. Olympians suggested election-law emendation to require evidence of taxes actually paid, ruling out proof only of marital-estate co-tenancy – a practice about which women had complained during the 1884 primaries. "The ideas which have prevailed on unrestricted suffrage, under ... all circumstances," noted a writer in 1883, "are rapidly adjusting themselves to common sense.... [Experience has] dispelled the illusion that citizenship carried with it unlimited political privileges which may ... very arbitrarily affect the inherent rights of others."[95] At issue was the bundle of rights that voters might exercise ("unlimited political privileges"). His idea survived until it seemed to threaten working-class men. In the midst of an anti-Chinese meeting in 1885, a speaker abruptly decried the idea that lawmakers might deprive workingmen of their political rights by introducing a property-tax qualification.[96]

Hundreds of women were self-disenfranchising. Non-voting sometimes evinced a lack of support for temperance or law-and-order campaigns. One woman said that she had no interest in general politics (men's "personal duty"); others stayed home on the mistaken ground that engagement led directly to jury

[93] "Judge Turner Decides the Local Option Law Valid," *SDPI*, November 18, 1886. See also "Another Decision," *WS*, November 26, 1886, and, in his home town, "Judge Turner's Decision," *SFR*, November 5, 1886. For Langford, see reprint of *WWU* article in *LCB*, September 14, 1886, or "The Local Option Case, Syllabus of the Decision Rendered by Judge Langford," September 10, 1886, *WS*, front page. For Duniway's comments, see "Didn't She Tell You So?" *NN*, September 9, 1886. Complaints about anti-vice ordinances persisted for years; e.g., "Saloon Men Protest," *TDL*, October 21, 1888.

[94] "Avoid Danger," *WWU*, July 10, 1883, p. 2.

[95] "The Right to Vote in the City," *WS*, September 14, 1883, following a city election. He also had in mind eliminating ne'er-do-wells. On the same points, see "City Charter and other Legislation," *WWU*, October 27, 1883, p. 1.

[96] P. P. Good Speech, "Anti-Chinese," *SDPI*, December 6, 1885.

duty. Brave or light-hearted accounts of women's experiences in public still circulated; but it was difficult indeed to mobilize women for voting, electioneering, and jury duty with anti-suffragists hurling insults and former supporters in full retreat. In October, 1886, a Pomeroy suffragist fairly exploded: "Let every woman ... who is a qualified elector, go to the polls at the coming election. Let your voice be heard and your influence felt. ... If you fail to exercise the right of suffrage, such failure will furnish the strongest possible reason for depriving you of it. Nay, more. If you voluntarily fold your hands ..., you ought to be disfranchised." The ballot had been given, not as a "keepsake, but ... as a weapon."[97]

As the community became more circumspect, supporters began to jump ship, as in 1885 when Olympia's main print – long the "most steadfast champion of the rights of womanhood" – chastised women for rank stupidity and disobedience during their probationary period. They had been cautioned against "allowing passion or prejudice to control their actions in the convention or at the polls"; they had failed to "discharge intelligently ... the highest duties of American citizenship." If women could violate an implied contract, so could lawmakers. "The arguments used, the assurances given ... that women would bring to bear the same discretion as her brother man in the exercise of this right, obtained for the measure a respectable vote .... It was urged upon the broad ground ... that all good citizens should have the right to participate in the privileges and duties of a government." Because rights claims had been "unanswerable," equal suffrage had ensued. But women, apparently incapable of objectivity, had been struck by "the recoil of a weight whose momentum was acquired from their own misdirected strength."[98]

Women persisted and often succeeded, as when Mrs. Hinds of Port Townsend became City Assessor, the only woman ever appointed to a municipal office in that town. But Hinds worked with numbers behind closed doors. In contrast, jurors experienced bullying, smoking, off-color stories, the face-to-faceness of criminal trials, jostling, and personal interrogation. Suffragists struck back, sometimes with lectures, more often by flooding newspaper offices with articles and letters, to say that difficulties were not of women's making. But letters were not apt to turn the tide. According to Mrs. S. M. Wall, for instance, women prized their "newly acquired liberties," not to mention income, even though "every conceivable 'bluff'" was afoot to "make their duties as jurors odious." How did she know? She had worked hard for her three dollars a day.

The panel was in one case composed very largely of women; and one man, the foreman of the jury, hung them night and day, while he and others befogged the room with tobacco

---

[97] "Rachel," "Woman's Experience with her First Vote," *SDPI*, November 20, 1886; "Citizen," "Duty of Voters," ibid., July 17, 1886; "Go to the Polls," *Washington Independent*, October 28, 1886.
[98] "A Lesson of the House," *WS*, July 17, 1885.

smoke and often made contemptuous remarks.... [such as], "We'll make 'em sick 'o the business," "We'll give 'em enough 'o jury service."... But the laugh was turned against [him] when one of the ladies having been made ill by tobacco smoke, he [succumbed] to the same intolerable nuisance and get excused himself, thereby losing the point he had hoped to make – that women were unable to endure the fatigue of jury service.... But the triumph came when each woman, having faithfully discharged her duty as juror, was herself discharged, bearing in her hands the glittering prize of three dollars per day, and, going ... home, found that the domestic machinery had run smoothly .... It was better than a trip to San Francisco. It saved the expense of a journey, gave me needed respite from the long monotony of home duties, enabled me to be an instrument of good, and netted me quite a convenient sum in the bargain.[99]

Although evidence is scanty, those convenient sums no doubt empowered women of modest means. In January, 1887, Mrs. G. A. Weed of Seattle acknowledged that the "most effective bugbear" wielded by anti-suffragists had been jury duty. But women sometimes found it lucrative as well as a "delightful relief from labor and a refreshing treat mentally." A seamstress said that "she never had imagined before how easy a man's work was nor how well it was paid."[100] In 1889, as a response to the decision to eliminate equal suffrage, a Washingtonian calling herself "M. R." described past jury service in one of Greene's courtrooms just after mixed-sex juries had appeared. While registering amusement at the incompetence of Irishmen and unread lawyers, she also noted the thrill of economic freedom and personal reconstitution. "At the end of the court week," she wrote, "we found ourselves possessed of twenty-one magnificent dollars, and much valuable experience; and then we were of such importance in our own eyes! Mab inscribed herself in my album as a United States Juror .... Perhaps we had afterward some added feelings of our own dignity, and a sense of responsibility to the community." She bought a gold pen so that she could horrify friends with letters about jury duty.[101]

For his part, Roger Greene was dismayed by co-equality's apparent fragility. In June, 1885, Republican Senator George Hoar of Massachusetts, a staunch supporter of equal suffrage, had asked Greene to send him an evaluation of territorial experiences with "ambisexual suffrage," or perhaps Greene volunteered. Hoar read the result at a meeting of the New England Woman Suffrage Association and then sent it to the *Woman's Journal*. For twelve terms, Greene said, he had held court with mixed-sex juries. He took it to be "a fact beyond dispute that no other twelve terms so salutary for restraints of crime have ever been held in this Territory." For fifteen years, he had yearned to feel

---

[99] "From the Port Townsend Argus," *NN*, August 26, 1886; "Editorial Correspondence," ibid., May 14, 1885, front page.

[100] Mrs. G. A. Weed, "Woman Suffrage: Comprehensive Letter ... from a Washington Territory Woman Who Did Not Advocate Its Adoption," *NN*, January 6, 1887.

[101] M. R., "On a Jury in Washington Territory," *Overland Monthly*, Vol. 13, No. 73 (January 1889), pp. 41–6, esp. 46.

"underneath and around me ... this upbuoying might of the people." In the beginning, women had been ignorant of the importance of political involvement and so had opposed it. Now, opponents included the "immoral element," a "smaller element, the high-toned class" which reveled in fashion, and a small but respectable element governed by notions of man's superiority that lay "curled up upon itself, altogether like a chick in an egg-shell that ought to hatch, but doesn't." Mixed-sex judgment was as "necessary to a well-ordered State as to a well-ordered household."[102]

Notwithstanding this ringing endorsement, women and the natural-rights arguments deployed after 1879 had been caught in a snare rooted in social practice, which resisted gender transgressions, and socio-medical theory, which justified social hierarchies and essentialism. Backlash had been brewing since late 1883, when anti-suffrage forces first signaled alarm at the number of women interested in jury duty. Roughly coincident with the Democrats' recommendation of an end to compulsory jury duty for women, opposition to suffrage itself had deepened. By 1886, Democrats in Chehalis were said to be opposed to equality and nearly all of the party's nominees had declared themselves opposed. One candidate, when asked to state a position, "choked under the effort" and finally said he favored woman suffrage but did not think they should be required to sit on juries.[103]

Did the right to vote *have* to convey ancillary rights and obligations? If not, how would Americans justify sex-specific exemptions, given prohibitions against class legislation and the jury's association for much of American history with political equality? Neither Duniway nor Susan B. Anthony had patience with the idea that voting could be a stand-alone privilege, or that male juries satisfied the constitutional requirement of trial by peers. "An esteemed contemporary is worried because hereafter in Washington Territory women will serve on juries," said Duniway in 1884. Nothing but a "good and sufficient excuse will excuse them"; there could be "no place where women are more needed than in courts and on juries." On the one side, critics of the jury system had long worried about a "wholesale business in the indictment line" populated by idiots and ne'er-do-wells – to which list they had appended women as social turmoil increased. On the other side, allies of Duniway and Greene championed an expanded representation of the popular sovereign on juries in order to fortify the republic – a position that ultimately supplied arms to the enemy.[104]

---

[102] Roger S. Greene, "An Emphatic Endorsement," *NN*, June 25, 1885; printed also as "Judge Greene on Women," *WR*, January 16, 1885
[103] "Female Suffrage," *LCB* (Chehalis, WT), October 19, 1886.
[104] "Women Acting as Grand Jurors," *NN*, January 17, 1884. See also Duniway, "Washington as a Teacher," *NN*, December 11, 1884 (men, not women, rendered juries farcical). Most notoriously, when Susan B. Anthony stood trial in 1873 for the federal crime of being a woman while casting a ballot in a presidential election, attorney Henry Selden contended that women formed part of the sovereignty and thus deserved an equal presence on juries.

Even Republicans began to reconsider women's suitability for public work, beginning in late winter, 1885, when interest in election-law revisal resurged. On January 7, 1886, a member described only as an "orthodox" Republican introduced House Bill 156. Two days later, just as the Local Option Act succeeded, House Bill 159 appeared with a different sponsor. As referred to committee, it provided that women ordinarily would be excused from jury duty "without giving reasons." Nowhere did sponsors explain why women, unlike men, did not have to give reasons.[105]

As early as 1884, newspaper correspondents in Washington and elsewhere took note, for better or worse, of the cultural shock that accompanied female jury service. Writing from Ainsworth, Washington, for the *Chicago Tribune*, one special correspondent reported that, on the ballot question, many predictions had fallen by the way: Married women simply did not vote as their husbands commanded, especially in cities. But jury service was problematic: Women had not considered the weight of the entire bundle of political duties or their own unsuitability. "Apparently the advocates of female suffrage had not looked forward to this disagreeable accessory of the franchise. Voting was easy enough, but jury-duty speedily became a terror to them."

In most counties the Sheriffs put the names of women into the jury-box; ... where they neglected to do so, the Judges had the error rectified. The women had voted; now they must take their chances with the men, and not shirk the burdens of citizenship. The conspicuous women advocates of the new suffrage law urged heroism upon the victims of the panel, but most of them plead to be excluded.... Two of the Territorial Judges were quite lenient ..., but the third, Judge Green, insisted on the women serving unless they had the strongest reasons.... In one county where ... no names of women had been drawn he set aside the entire panel, had the names of female citizens put into a box ... and required the Sheriff to draw every alternate name from that box.

The inadequacy of mixed juries was said to be painfully apparent in criminal trials, and more apparent in grand-jury rooms. Women were saturated with and disabled by sex. They brought children; they were pregnant; they fainted in airless chambers. They showed the "usual feminine tendency to jump to conclusions and trust to intuition rather than evidence." Lawyers distrusted this "new element in the jury-room" because they applied "higher moral law without regard to any part of the statutes save the penalty clauses." Female jurors, in sum, were "incapable of weighing evidence without prejudice."[106]

Courtrooms increasingly witnessed disruption on an unprecedented scale, even after John Hoyt supposedly had resolved the question of wives' "householder" status. Not surprisingly, both the number of female jurors and the scale of disruption grew wherever Roger Greene presided, if only because he

[105] See "The Legislature," *SDPI*, November [5?], 1885, and "At the Capitol," *TDL*, December 20, 1885, p. 1; for Bill 156, see "Territorial Legislature," ibid., January 10, 1886, p. 4, and for Bill 159, ibid., January 12, 1886, p. 4. The proposed bill appeared in newspapers; see, e.g., *LCB*, June 25, 1886. The "orthodox Republican" was said to be William Teft (not Taft).

[106] "Woman Suffrage," by "E.V.S.," *Chicago Daily Tribune*, August 17, 1884, p. 9.

forced the constabulary to gather women. Courtroom personnel often struggled to find women sufficient to staff panels. In January, 1885, for instance, the district court sitting in Whatcom County selected and actually seated six women as grand jurors and seven as *petit* jurors for the year, but the list of seconds was painfully thin. In May, the same court published an official list that included five married women among fifty additional, potential grand jurors; the parallel listing for *petit* jurors, also fifty names long, contained only three women. Perhaps women could not be found, or perhaps the sheriff barely looked. It remained for a judge to issue repeated, time-consuming venires; each new call occupied a day in cities, more in the hinterland. Small wonder that judges sometimes let the sheriff's men (or residents hiding in their homes) have their way.[107] On the coast especially, women arrived, mingled with men for a few years, and (with the exception of a small army of determined WERA activists) gradually disappeared until 1911, more than two decades after statehood and a year after women's re-enfranchisement.

After several uneventful terms, Roger Greene's courtrooms suddenly exploded, beginning in Seattle. Women arrived in April term, 1884; Greene easily appointed a crier and two bailiffs, Margaret Mallory and Charles Mallory, who were almost certainly married. Nor did anyone object when, in *Mary M. Anderson v. Louis Anderson*, the judge and a mixed-sex *petit* jury assigned custody of children to Mary.[108] But Greene's formal call for a grand jury was another matter. The sheriffs (aided by federal marshals, as it turned out) for King and Kitsap Counties produced fifteen men. Five were excused for cause, whereupon the judge intervened. Were women unavailable? Resistance of some kind clearly was afoot. "It appearing to the Court," wrote the clerk in formulaic language, "that there are not enough Grand Jurors present it is ordered by the Court that a special Venire issue to the Sheriff of King County for seven persons to serve as Grand Jurors," returnable at 2:00 on the same day.

In late afternoon, Greene seated sixteen grand jurors from a list that included fifteen men, five of whom again were excused for cause, and at least six women – Louisa De[nny?], Laura E. Hall, Lucinda D. Jacobs, Caroline Maddocks, Margaret J. Pontius, and Emma W. Wood. The usual opportunity arose for challenges to jury members – whereupon lawyers for seven litigants rose *en masse* to challenge female jurors on the ground that five of them were "women and not citizens of the United States" and thus not qualified to sit as grand jurors. Greene disallowed the challenges – all of the women, he said, were either native-born or naturalized – whereupon attorneys charged that four married women (Denny, Jacobs, Maddocks, and Wood) were not householders and therefore not qualified, which challenge the Court also overruled. After granting

---

[107] "Jurors for January Term," *WR*, January 2, 1885; "GRAND JURORS" and "PETIT JURORS," ibid., May 15, 1885. The jury rolls from Whatcom County have not survived, so it is impossible to learn whether these women were ever empaneled.

[108] King County Government, Judicial Administration, Territorial District Court Journal, Vol. H, [April 13?], 1884, p. 257, PSRA.

a half-dozen motions for exceptions, Greene waived further challenges. At the same term, a number of women, married and single, served without incident as *petit* jurors on the court's territorial side in criminal trials – e.g., in the Schilling case on April 18, which was appealed to the Supreme Court because of the mixed-sex grand jury, not the trial jury. Into May, married and single women's presence on *petit* juries was commonplace; lists of payments issued on May 8 indicate that almost all of them served more than one day, particularly in or near Seattle. Three more mixed-sex trials occurred in the same month.[109]

By October 6, 1884, when court opened in Seattle, the situation had deteriorated. First on the docket was one of several petitions to withdraw a challenge to the grand jury (*Territory* v. *A. Baker*) from a previous term. Sarah Malson agreed to serve alongside three men as bailiff; as usual, Roger Greene summoned a grand jury, which came to include six men and at least five King County women – Susan Maddocks, Agnes Danst, Johanna Boyd, Agnes Coleman, and Mattie Keys. Without official explanation, however, Kitsap County had returned only men. Maddocks and Keys were "excused for good and valid reasons." Suddenly, Greene commanded the sheriff to procure eighteen additional jurors; when the court reconvened a day later, the new group included activist Winnie Thomas and five other women (Mary Scott, Cornelia Jenner, Julia Hawley, Agnew Coleman, and Johanna Boyd). Ex-governor Elisha P. Ferry objected on the grounds that the jury did not require reconstitution and that none of the women had been selected properly – that is, by the county commissioners of King or Kitsap.[110] After Greene granted an exception, the jury withdrew to deliberate. Meanwhile, between October 8 and 11, women again sat as *petit* jurors without incident. In the case of *Territory* v. *Johnny and Paddy*, Loretta Denny served as jury foreman on a panel with four other women. A payment list confirms that most women sat for more than a day. For one panel, Mrs. C. M. Clayton had been tapped as a talesman, suggesting that women waited with men in the wings on the off-chance of

[109] King County Government, Judicial Administration, Territorial District Court Journals, April 14, 1884, Vol. H, PSRA, pp. 245–8, PSRA. For payments, see Vol. H, p. 456. For criminal trials, including Schiller, see pp. 302, 298, 305. The fifteen men initially called included Thomas H[o] skins, Patrick Hayes, D. H. Hawley, F. Jacobus, John San[jotino?], Moses Morris, J. E. McDonald, J. R. Miller, J. W. Ma[rple?], D. T. Wheeler, A. T. Neely, Amos Bun[gert?], Thomas Moran, John P. Freberg, and James H. Murray. Clerks employed different styles; this clerk recorded women uniformly by their first name but without marital status. Other clerks listed women at the head of lists, or used Miss and Mrs., indicating a degree of self-consciousness or strangeness. Among the criminal cases with mixed-sex juries in April Term, 1884, were *Territory* v. *Frank Wright and Henry Seymore* (2 women), *Territory* v. *August Reimers* (4), *Territory* v. *Sam and Lee* (2), *Territory* v. *Prichard and Lester* (3), *Territory* v. *Doran* (2), and *Territory* v. *Celestine* (2), ibid., Vol. H, pp. 298, 305, 322, 335, 345–7, 434–7, and passim. In November term, a few entirely masculine panels appeared, as with *Territory* v. *Ah Ling and Ah Ging*, ibid., Vol. H, p. 322. In King and Pierce Counties, women tended to serve more days when they lived in the host town, which speaks volumes to the burden of distance.

[110] King County Government, Judicial Administration, Territorial District Court, Territorial District Court Journals, 1852–89, Vol. I, PSRA, esp. p. 112. For juror payments, see p. 443.

money or an opportunity to experience jury duty; each grand juror except Maddocks and Keys received pay for multiple days.[111]

In April, 1885, tensions abated. Laura Hall and four men served as bailiffs, and the grand jury initially boasted two women. Greene issued a call for nine additional jurors and secured two more women (Elizabeth Foss and Margaret Oakley). Sarah Gross was excused from *petit*-jury service for cause; the court met productively and adjourned.[112] But the storm had been delayed. In October, for purposes of indictment, bedlam effectively shut down Greene's courtroom for weeks. On October 5, Mrs. Kate Reagan had signed on as bailiff with a few men. The grand jury as summoned included at least three women – Annie Jones, A. E. Horton, and J. C. DeMott, all from King County; again, no women appeared from Kitsap. Annie Jones' departure for cause alongside two men was unacceptable to Greene: He sent for five additional persons; Martha Fulton, Hannah Allen, Sarah Russell, Harriet Herndon, and R. Hopkins (sex unknown) appeared the next day.[113]

In the end, the grand jury included Horton, DeMott, Fulton, Allen, Russell, Herndon, and several others. But two lawyers rose at once to challenge a jury with a female majority in language fast becoming formulaic. A. E. Horton, J. C. DeMott, and four others stood accused of being women or females; three more were said to be married women, "each residing with her husband, and therefore none of them is a householder." Insisting that wives and husbands both were householders, Greene overruled the challenge but permitted appeal. Meanwhile, mixed-sex *petit* juries continued to decide cases without apparent strife.[114] In Seattle, whatever women's marital status, lawyers seemed to trust women to evaluate facts but not to say whether a citizen was blameworthy enough to go to trial.

On May 3, 1886, Greene was ill; jurors and staff awaited a judge until 10:00 PM, when John Hoyt called the court to order.[115] At hand were anti-Chinese agitators, many of them members of the Knights of Labor. Again, a group of five

---

[111] Ibid., Vol. I, pp. 132–57, 175–223, 398–9, 441–3. Talesmen were citizens hired to fill seats when venires failed to produce enough jurors.

[112] Vol. J, pp. 32–47, esp. 41, and passim. On April, 23, 1886, however, only one woman (Winifred Green) was paid alongside almost sixty men; on March 12, 1887, four women received payment on a similarly long list; King County Government, Judicial Administration, Territorial District Court Journals, Vol. M, PSRA, pp. 368–9, 465–6.

[113] Given this clerk's erratic journal style, Hopkins likely was male, but I cannot guarantee it; he occasionally listed women with two initials, though far less often than with men. I have determined the sex of some litigants by comparing journals with jury payment lists.

[114] Journal K, pp. 29–37, 64–7, and passim, esp. p. 32.

[115] For a report of Greene's failing health and serious "eye problems," see "Judge Turner to Hold Court," *SDT*, May 21, 1886. This new print got the judge's name wrong (Hoyt). For the mixed-sex jury's names, see "Grand and Petit Jurors," ibid., May 8, 1886; publication was routine. It is perhaps telling that, when Judge Orange Jacobs agreed to pick up mail for the ailing Greene, he had to deal with "sacksfull"; untitled, ibid., June 24, 1886, inside page. See also ibid., June 23, 1886; the judge was resting on Vancouver Island for the summer.

bailiffs included Mrs. Kate A. Reagan. In response to the grand-jury summons, at least four married women had appeared – Mrs. S. Packard, Mrs. Amelia Biondi, Mrs. Martha Gerrish, and Mrs. L. V. Ward. An extraordinary uproar ensued. Journalists later charged court officials and Roger Greene with jury-packing. Supposedly, a venire had been quashed, eliminating two well-regarded women (Mrs. Stadelman and Mrs. Allen) and replacing them with two local toughs who could be counted on to defend workingmen.[116] Challenges flew around the courtroom; United States and territorial grand juries were empaneled and re-empaneled. On June 1, 1886, for instance, lawyers argued, "1st, the jurors, Mrs. Amelia Biondi and Mrs. S. V. Ward, are married women living with their husbands and are therefore incompetent,"

2nd, The Juror Mrs. Martha Gerrish is a woman and is therefore incompetent, 3rd, the juror E. B. Mastic, James L. Smith, Mrs. Martha Gerrish, Andrew Weymouth, all are residents of the County of Jefferson and are therefore incompetent ..., 4th, the jurors George B. Walker, Al C. Kimbal, Mrs. L. V. Ward, Isaac Denny, Olof Polson, W. H Fore[st], E. H. Baxter, James Bush, Stephen Churey and B. F. Loveland ... were summoned by ... a deputy Marshal and not by the marshal.

Greene, who had abandoned his sickbed, overruled complaints so that the panel might convene.[117]

Confusion reigned for the rest of the term. Lawyers objected to both females and married women; they objected as well to the legality of the proceedings, notably circumventions of procedure to procure women and the apparent dragooning of out-of-district jurors. As the *Seattle Daily Times* later explained, challengers argued, first, that the panel had been drawn "from all counties of the third judicial district instead of the counties of King and Kitsap"; second, that jurors had been "selected and summoned in large part by a deputy marshal" – the *Whatcom Reveille* called him a "boy deputy" – and, third, that the grand jury was "not summoned to appear at any regular or legal term of the court." Finally, attorneys alleged that some jurors were women and some married women. When the grand jury reconvened, clerks listed more women than earlier (Mary A. Atkins, Mrs. M. J. Carman, Mary L. Livesley, Mary L. Packard, Mary L. Partridge, Jennie G. Sanders, and fourteen men). Again, *petit* jurors escaped challenge. Onlookers heard testimony in a myriad of trials with at least a dozen women assessing the facts and delivering remarkably old-fashioned verdicts – as in *William Perry* v. *Belle Perry*, where jurors punished a wife for "deserting her husband without his consent."[118]

[116] For accusations of packing, names, and "boy deputy," see "Packing Juries," *WR*, May [7], 1886, front page.

[117] King County Government, Judicial Administration, Territorial District Court Journals, Vol. L, PSRA, pp. 130–44, 233–4, 311, and passim, PSRA. The payment listing for the term confirms the presence of at least seven female grand jurors, perhaps a few more (clerical styles changed). For payments, see Vol. L, p. 434 (all served for nineteen days) and Vol. M, p. 38 (also more than two weeks each).

[118] Ibid. For newspaper details, see "District Court," *SDT*, June 1, 1886.

The new term opened early in August, 1886, with Roger Greene and the United States attorney, William H. White, in attendance. Kate Reagan appeared as one of the bailiffs, but only one woman, Mary Griswold, responded to the grand-jury venire. Nobody challenged her presence. Finally, after additional jurors were summoned at great cost in time, five women were empaneled, though the clerk failed to record any of their names in the journal.[119] Women continued to serve in large numbers on *petit* juries, if sometimes by themselves; in a conspiracy case involving one anti-Chinese vigilante and an accused socialist, Greene addressed his remarks to "Lady and Gentlemen."[120] If scanty evidence can be trusted, women increasingly banded together, and, in Seattle, court officers seem to have extended unusual courtesies. A women sent a newspaper notice to women in King County in October, 1886, asking them to support Mr. McGraw for sheriff because he was a "woman's suffrage man" and had welcomed women "at the court house door with his genial smile, which did much to reassure us. All that could be done for our comfort and convenience was done, and he has ever made our duty at the court house as easy and pleasant as could possibly be." At least two women entered together ("us"); they had to be "reassured."[121]

On December 4, 1886, three additional female grand jurors appeared. In 1886, however, justice was effectively suspended: Almost every case was continued without explanation – as with the Perry Bayne case, continued from February 1886 to June 1886, and then into the February, 1887, term, where it finally resumed with a male *petit* jury. By early 1887, women were gone, including Kate Reagan. When court resumed in February, 1887, with Greene on the bench for the last time, personnel remarked on the absence of women. What's more, the same three women served on every criminal panel during the term (Julia Greene again, with Rebecca Lanning and Netti Minick). All resided in Seattle; they did not have to travel to and from the courthouse for hours or days.[122]

On March 12, 1887, in his Seattle courtroom, Roger Sherman Greene swore in his replacement, Richard Jones, who in turn approved a motion to admit Greene to practice in territorial courts. Eben Smith, president of the King County Bar Association, read a memorial later published in regional newspapers: After a tenure of seventeen years, members of the bar "united in testifying our high appreciation of the eminent Christian Virtue, unflagging

---

[119] "District Court Proceedings," *SDPI*, August 31, 1886. The women were Amanda Atwood, Julia A. Green, Mary Griswold, Fannie R. Smith, and Mary K. Thorndike. The journalist also confirmed that Kate Reagan served as a bailiff.

[120] "The Charge to the Jury," *SDPI*, November 16, 1886.

[121] J. H. H., "A Card to the Women of King County," *SDPI*, October 28, 1886.

[122] King County Government, Judicial Administration, Territorial District Court, Journal L, PSRA, pp. 311–16, 368–9, 434, 471–7; Journal M, pp. 36–8, 134–5, and passim. For all-male lists, see Vol. M, as at p. 135. The final payment list emanating from Greene's tenure shows a number of female *petit* jurors, two of them with thirty-one days' pay; see Vol. M, p. 182.

industry, uniform patience, profound and varied learning, sincere anxiety to do justice, and absolute independence [of this] ... upright Magistrate."[123]

Chief Justice Jones wasted no time. On March 13, he managed a clean sweep of jury boxes. New venires issued for grand and *petit* juries, all of which returned men. Bailiffs were male. Jones did not issue additional venires, even though grand juries did not include citizens of Kitsap County, only King. The only woman in attendance was Bertha Piper, a journal clerk; the aptly named, new clerk of court was William Ledgerwood. In subsequent terms, venires still used the word "persons," but men answered. The number of men excused for cause also increased; in his three remaining terms, Jones hired more talesmen than in all of the years from 1884 to 1887.[124]

In Jefferson County at Port Townsend, women's presence also generated significant tumult. In March, 1884, with Roger Greene again presiding, women were summoned from poll books, were not empaneled, but were paid for waiting. Port Townsend women apparently formed part of a secondary jury pool; a list appears at each term of women and a handful of men excused from service after a day's wait. Greene retained the same female foreman for the entire term, and no doubt to the displeasure of the clerk, issued numerous venires to secure a handful of women. We may never know why Greene could not mobilize women for service; scarcity or resistance imposed heavy burdens on Mary Brown, who sat alone on *petit* juries with men for the entire term.[125]

By autumn of 1884, the chief justice repeatedly did battle with the sheriff, the public, or both; when officers returned only men, Greene demanded fresh efforts. But opposition finally achieved critical mass on February 23, 1885, before the grand jury could deliver a true bill in the Port Townsend hearing of evidence in the case of Charles O'Green, accused of first-degree murder with a shotgun. To say the least, Hoyt's *Rosencrantz* ruling had not settled the question. The grand jury included at least five women – Harriet Phillips, Mabel Marting, Martha Webber, Maggie Luke, and Mary Simons. When asked if they objected to the panel, counsel challenged "certain women members" who were "not house holders, nor qualified grand jurors." Greene overruled the objection as usual and allowed an exception. The next day,

---

[123] King County Government, Judicial Administration, Territorial District Court, Journal M, PSRA, pp. 374–5. For "most remarkably impressive" and the memorial spread over the record, see "The Old and New Chief Justice," *SDPI*, March 13, 1887. See also reprint in part, "To the Retiring Judge," *WR*, March 18, 1887. Memorials reveal that Greene had been admitted to the Supreme Court of New York's bar on January 16, 1866.

[124] For Jones' commission, see King County Government, Judicial Administration, Territorial District Court, Vol. M, PSRA, pp. 372–3. For Greene's admission to practice and a testimonial, see ibid., pp. 374–80. The sweep begins at pp. 375–6, continuing into Journal N, pp. 1–117. Charles Munday was the new U.S. attorney. See, e.g., pp. 202–3, 522–3, and passim, for examples of male juries and names of new clerks. Masculinized sessions continued through 1888–89; Vol. O features an explosion of talesmen and excuses "for cause." See also Vol. L, pp. 36–8, 134–5, 368–9; Vol. M, p. 390 and passim.

[125] District Court Journal, Jefferson County, Vol. H, PSRA, as at pp. 82–3, 84–5, and passim.

jurors brought in a true bill; on February 24, a *petit* jury convicted O'Green of second-degree murder. But women were disappearing: The O'Green *petit* jury contained only the unmarried Sarah E. Pixley; a married woman, Mrs. A. M. Davis, had been eliminated during the plaintiff's peremptory challenges. Two days later, Pixley sat again on a jury that convicted William Black of the federal crime of supplying liquor to an Indian; Theresa Jordan and Sarah Waterman were excused without explanation, and Mrs. Davis fell to the defendant's peremptory challenges.[126]

By mid-August, 1885, challenges were more robust. Charles Armstrong and other scoundrels stood before a grand jury that included five married women, Mrs. Lillie Lukey, Mrs. Galia Pettygrove, Mrs. C. W. Calhoun, Mrs. J. Engle, and Mrs. L. Blowers. Counsel immediately challenged the legality of the first four on the ground that they were "married Women living with their husbands, and neither one has any separate house hold, and no house save and except the community house belonging to herself and husband, and no household save the children of herself and her said husband, and it further appearing that Mrs. L. Blowers is a married woman whose husband is living." It is likely, given courtroom exchanges, that Mrs. Blowers was informally separated. Attorneys thus objected to the "five persons last above named because they are not men, and of Mrs. Lukey, Mrs. Pettygrove, Mrs. Calhoun, and Mrs. Engle, because they are not householders." So, while married women could be challenged on the ground that they were not householders, as the case of Mrs. Blowers makes clear – she lived alone – any female grand juror was fair game by reason of sex. Greene overruled objections; there is no indication of an appeal.[127]

Throughout 1885, King and Jefferson County women appeared and were paid for service, singly or two and three at a time. But continuances multiplied in Seattle, Tacoma, and Port Townsend. Beyond courtrooms, to make it worse, men and boys rioted in the streets. By October, 1885, courtroom discipline had eroded, as evidenced by clerical confusion. Clerks apparently had assumed that women would be excused – but then they served, requiring erasures of the phrase "excused by reason of sex." Throughout the March, 1886, term, Jefferson-County lawyers overwhelmingly chose male jurors. Only two women were paid for *petit*-jury service (Nellie Purvis and Mrs. Anna Norton); in October, moreover, Purvis was empaneled, removed, and re-empaneled.[128] By early 1887, female jurors entered Port Townsend courtrooms typically in the company of other family members, as if under siege. In March, 1887, the list of

---

[126] Final Record, 1877–89, Third District Court [Port Townsend], Jefferson County Clerk, Acc. No. 85-3-216, February 23–27, 1885, PSRA. Mrs. Davis probably was not a widow; this clerk used women's first names when they were not currently married.

[127] Final Record, 1877–89, Third District Court [Port Townsend], Jefferson County Clerk, Acc. No. 85-3-216, February 23–27, 1885, PSRA. See also Territorial Court Records, Jefferson County, Acc. No. 86-2-179, PSRA, Vol. 42, Jury Lists, for names and confirmation of payment.

[128] District Court Journal, Jefferson County, Vol. H, Port Townsend, PSRA, as at pp. 82–3, 84–95, and passim.

petit jurors sitting in the assault trial of Charles Spere included no women. On March 30, Anne B[eauden]hower and Maxine P[eyson] were both excused; reasons were not disclosed. The jury that convicted Charles Summers for burglary was entirely male.[129] Also in spring term, 1887, Mrs. W. Ward sat on a grand jury, accompanied by her husband, Frederick; she served only a day, whereas Frederick continued his tenure. At the same term, two other women served a day each and were excused. Days later, "Mrs. Virginia" was empaneled with her husband and possibly with her daughter. In November, May Mann was the only woman summoned, though she was paid for several days' service. As in Seattle, the arrival of Richard Jones abruptly altered practice. In the October, 1887, session, all grand and *petit* jurors were male, even after Greene twice issued special venires. Payroll records show a male population of jurors, bailiffs, and other courtroom staff, excepting only a female journal clerk.[130]

Washingtonians sometimes learned of the composition of grand juries from newspapers; in Belleville's Whatcom County, where judicial records barely survive, these brief notices permit a glimpse of courtroom realities. On May 14, 1886, for instance, the *Whatcom Reveille* published an astonishing list of forty-eight grand jurors selected for the year, twenty of whom were married women or widows ("Mrs."). The *petit*-jury lists similarly included roughly half of each sex (twenty out of forty-eight, one of whom, "Julia," was likely unmarried); while the number who actually sat on panels is unknown, Greene's hand (and the efforts of Bellingham suffragists) can be discerned in the gender balance.[131]

John Hoyt's Second District Court sessions in Olympia first listed women as potential jurors on June 13, 1884, in the wake of his *Rosencrantz* ruling. Between June 13 and June 24, women sat as *petit* jurors on six criminal trials, one of which was dismissed; on four of the remaining five, three or four women appeared with eight or nine men. But, while men's names varied, women's names recurred: Mary Shelton, Amelia Philbey, and Maggie O'Conner, for example, served together on four panels, and [E]dna Roberts served on two. The case of *Territory* v. *Maurer*, the only trial for homicide, concluded on June 17, 1884, with an all-male jury. In December, 1884, after Hoyt instructed the sheriffs of Thurston and Mason Counties to procure a mixed grand jury, women again appeared. Ellen Work, Florence E. Drake, and Jesse Ferguson served with fifteen men, without apparent courtroom disturbance; at the same term, Hoyt presided over nine criminal trials, with women seated on five panels. But jurors' names recur, not among men, but among female members (Mary Ballard served twice, Emily Bunson and Hepsibah Brown three times). In

---

[129] Final Record, 1877–89, Third District Court [Port Townsend], Jefferson County Clerk, Acc. No. 85-3-216, February 23–27, 1885, PSRA.

[130] District Court Journal, Jefferson County, Vol. H, PSRA, as at pp. 82–3, 84–95, and passim. Jones arrived in July; see Vol. H, as at pp. 22–3.

[131] "Jurors Selected," WR, May 14, 1886.

addition, the number of cases featuring female jurors had shrunk: Four were heard by men alone. With the June term, 1885, women vanished on both grand and *petit* juries.[132] Why? Perhaps activists were unable to mobilize women; Olympia was less a women's-rights hotbed than Seattle or Tacoma. Perhaps the politically moderate John Hoyt disliked courtroom tumult. Or perhaps, as his passivity during the 1889 state constitutional convention suggests, he was changing his mind about the meaning of "housholder."

Incomplete payment records also suggest a shockingly small number of female jurors at the territorial capital. Not surprisingly, in 1883, throughout the Second District sittings, which included Thurston and part of Pierce County, jurors certified and paid for service were male. But women were largely absent from treasury-warrant listings after December 5, 1884, when activist Zerelda McCoy received payment for eight days' service in May as a grand juror from Pierce; no other woman received payment for more than four days for the rest of the territorial period, which is to say that the women who served as Olympian grand jurors did so for short periods. The vast majority of women were paid for one day and sent home (fifteen in May, 1885, for example). From that month through 1888–89, all women paid to wait or serve were from Pierce, not Thurston; by February, 1886, women received payment only for *petit*-jury service, in one case three at a time, usually only one or two. Women's names appeared for the last time in June, 1887, with payment for three female *petit* jurors in Pierce County.[133]

In Grays Harbor sessions of John Hoyt's Chehalis County district court, where paved roads and other urban luxuries were absent, two married women (Mrs. James B. Stewart and Mrs. C. A. Tompkins) served as grand jurors in September, 1886; others apparently were men, as were *petit* juries, criers, and bailiffs.[134] Jury lists are curiously missing throughout 1887, except in September, 1887, when Julius Seifert and "Mrs. Seifert" appeared. But neither was paid, and the clerk did not provide a list of jurors actually seated. Perhaps there were no indictments, although criminal cases went to trial. Did

---

[132] Thurston County, Clerk's Record, Second Judicial District Court, Olympia, Minute Book, 1878–85, WSA-O, pp. 211–14, 226–36, 255–72, 286–8. The book ends with calendar year 1886. Much depends here on interpretations of the clerk's style. If he did not change his notation style in 1885, the situation was as given; he uniformly listed women as "Mrs." or with a first name spelled out; men were listed with initials or with first names. But, if he changed his style and began to use two initials for women, women may have been present after December into 1886. In lists of witnesses, however, he continued to list women's names with "Mrs." or first names for the entire period. Refinement of these counts requires close research in census records; as earlier, errors are in the direction of undercounting.

[133] Second Judicial District, Thurston County [and others], Clerk's Office, Grand and Petit Juror Attendance Certificates, 1883–8[8], WSA-O, not paginated. Certificates apparently were presented to the treasurer for payment.

[134] Grays Harbor County originally was called Chehalis County; another book survives for Chehalis, the Clerk's Juror Check Book, covering only 1888–96; SWSA. Names are entirely male.

clerks not record the names of grand jurors for the first time in the court's history? Perhaps prosecutors had indicted by information. Lawyers and journalists occasionally evinced an interest in alternatives to grand-jury indictment, as with talk about a decision in Minneapolis to rely on prosecutorial discretion and eliminate "fossilized legal obstructions to justice."[135] In *Hurtado* v. *California* (1884), the nation's highest court had ruled that grand juries could be circumvented in state courts. But, as early litigation made clear, territorial courts' status was uncertain. Did Grays Harbor personnel resort to this alternative for one or two terms on the ground that territorial courts were not federal?[136] Interestingly, after an all-male grand jury adjourned in September, 1884, John Hoyt's court convened "at chambers" through November, 1885. In January, 1886, four women, all of them married or widowed, were empaneled as grand jurors; one of them, Mary Kelsey, was immediately excused. Three women actually sat as *petit* jurors – Mrs. Mary E. Holloway, Mrs. Julie Everett, and Mrs. Carrie Miles – each for two days. In fall, 1886, with Hoyt at the helm, women again appeared for grand-jury duty (Mrs. C. A. Tompkins, Mrs. Jane B. Stewart, and several more). Stewart was excused; others vanished from the record, such that only one woman served alongside eleven men. In February, 1887, Mary Newland and Etta Maker and twenty-three men received pay as petit jurors; thereafter, women officially entered the courthouse only as witnesses and, in one case, as a journal clerk. John Hoyt retired in early 1887 and George Turner weeks later. When Justice Frank Allyn – an obscure Democrat from Keokuk, Iowa – took on Hoyt's circuit in May, 1887, grand jurors included "twelve good and lawful men." Allyn adhered to law in two cases involving wives' separate property; in *Mary Walkins* v. *George Watkins* and *Magdeline Hickey* v. *Philip Hickey*, both

---

[135] "The Grand Jury System," *WR*, February 20, 1885. I did not find mention in any paper of the U.S. Supreme Court's ruling in *Hurtado* v. *California*, 110 U.S. 516 (1884), wherein indictment by information was ruled a lawful alternative to grand jury indictment in state courtrooms.

[136] The barebones record sheds no light. See Grays Harbor County Judicial Records, Territorial District Court, Day Book, 1884–90, pp. 12–13, 23, 29, 53, and passim, and Juror List, both Southwest Regional Archive, Grays Harbor. Perhaps grand juries did not convene in 1884–85. This clerk's style was erratic; it is possible, though unlikely (given name placements), that 1 or 2 more women appeared in 1886 with Stewart and Tompkins. In McCarty, the bench stood on *Reynolds* v. *U.S.*; see Carol Weisbrod and Pamela Sheingorn, "Reynolds v. United States: Nineteenth-Century Forms of Marriage and the Status of Women," *Connecticut Law Review* (1978), pp. 828–58 ("the territorial courts when trying an offense of this nature, under territorial laws, were not United States courts"). Hurtado was the first federal case to consider nationalization of the federal bill of rights (California prosecutors could follow a statute permitting indictment either by grand jury or by information without violating the Fourteenth Amendment). There is no sustained case biography of Hurtado. In 1890, the Washington State Supreme Court decided in *J. C. McCarty* v. *Washington*, 1 Wash Rpts 388 (1890), that citizens accused of felony during territorial years were "entitled to the guaranty of the United States constitution of presentment by a grand jury; and cannot be prosecuted therefor[e] by information."

decided in September, 1887, husbands had tried to pay debts with women's money. But juries were entirely male.[137]

In southerly Cowlitz County, part of Hoyt's arduous Second District Court circuit, women did not appear for jury duty until November, 1885, when at least three women, Mrs. William Davolt, Mrs. Benjamin [Susan] Holmes, and Annie P. Huntington, and possibly a fourth (Jesse Baker) responded to calls for service. Holmes sat on a *petit* jury for seven days, the others on a grand jury for three days each. Women reappeared on April 28, 1886, but as *petit* jurors (Mrs. N. R. Smith and Mrs. Florence [Walter] Crosby for two days each). George Turner's construction of women as non-householders ineligible for grand juries no doubt worried everyone; as we will see, additional test cases had been filed; and Hoyt was no firebrand. In October, 1886, Mrs. G. M. Lippery's husband reported for a four-day stint as a *petit* juror in her stead; Sarah Houghton and Jesse Hackett served three days each; Alice Martin, Emma Tippery, and Sue Micks two days each; and Mary Davidson one day. An unstable flurry of female grand jurors moved in and out of the courtroom: Caroline Reese and Eunice Olsen served for two days each, and Lucy Barnett, Mrs. E. J. Searles, and Antonia Klint earned four days' pay each. As with G. M. Lippery, E. J. Searles took his wife's place. Husbands' presence suggests an amount of stress at home or personal unease. In April, 1887, Mrs. James Huff appeared "as ordered by the court" to serve on a *petit* jury; she traveled twenty-two miles for the purpose, longer than anyone in the pool. Mary Bird and Elizabeth Ross served for one day each as *petit* jurors. Thereafter, only men were called or empaneled.[138]

By contrast, Roger Greene's behavior in an equally rural setting was unremittingly aggressive. In December, 1883, Greene adjourned the sitting, all-male grand jury in Whatcom County sessions of the Third District Court meeting at LaConner, far to the north of Seattle near the San Juan Islands, and summoned a new one, which included Lucy Alverson, Josephine Bradley, Jessy Corey, and nine men. Members of the bar accepted the result. On August 11, 1885, however, with Greene and prosecutor J. J. Calhoun in attendance, peaceable relations ended. The sheriff has returned an entirely male grand jury; Greene ordered the venire quashed, issued a new one, and adjourned for the day. The sheriff reappeared with four married women – Mrs. J. F. Dwelley, Mrs. Perry Polson, Mrs. F. S. Pool, and Mrs. H. McBride, named at the end of

---

[137] Lewis County, Clerk's Records, Jury Record [Book], 1886–1915, Vol. A (1886–89), WSA-O. This is a barebones record without case names or payment amounts. The clerk, however, segregated all women at the beginning of jury lists with "Mrs." or full first names. See also Grays Harbor [Chehalis] County Records, Clerks Records, Jury Record, Vol. I, WSA-O, for male names (1888–1903), and Clerks Records, Civil Journals, 1883–89, WSA-O, pp. 20, 62–5, 229 (women's appearance in 1886), 252–5, 320–1 (Allyn's appearance), 372–4 (Hickey), 388–90 (Watkins), and passim.

[138] Cowlitz County, Clerk's Records, Misc. Court Records, Cases and Jury Lists, 1887–1904, Court Journal Entries, Juror and Witness Affidavits, 1887–1915, WSA-GH. The 1885 journal pages are in two dated folders. The books have not survived.

the list as if in quarantine. Attorney G. M. Haller took exception to the group on the ground that the jury was "not all the regular panel" (a reference either to the absence of familiar men or to Greene's irregular adjournment of the old jury) and that a portion were not householders. Predictably, Greene overruled objections and granted exceptions. A Whatcom editor, disgusted with the mixed-sex drama, proposed that, in future, the chief justice select "two negroes, male and female; two Irishmen, male and female; two Frenchmen, male and female; two Germans, male and female ..., giving each county and people ... equal representation." He did not understand why an equal number of males and females was necessary. The same procedures and objections attended grand-jury empanelment in early 1886; by autumn, as Roger Greene's health began to fail, women quite suddenly disappeared.[139]

East of the Cascades and in counties near Oregon, equal suffrage had been more hotly contested than along the seaboard. Mrs. Margaret McKell of Kidd, Washington, exhibited a fairly typical ambivalence, confiding in 1886 that, while she cared little for the ballot itself, she did care that "men and women be equal" and therefore accepted political responsibilities.[140] But for others living in the counties surrounding Spokane Falls, perhaps with farms or families to tend, a trek to town and especially to remote courthouses required planning and sacrifice. In Spokane's sparsely documented First District, women likely did not appear at all as jurors; newspaper listings name only men for both grand and *petit* juries throughout the 1880s.[141] In Walla Walla, women were not paid for official work from 1869 until 1885, two years after the adoption of equal suffrage. In 1885, two women responded to grand jury summonses; in 1886, Mrs. Hoss Lee was called with a large number of men to form a grand-jury pool. But these women's names do not appear on final grand-jury payment lists. Into 1885, perhaps on the advice of the attending prosecutor, the clerk scratched out "men" and wrote "persons," or entered "persons" without correction. On one occasion in 1886, for the session following Mrs. Lee's appearance, White commanded the marshal to summon eighteen persons from the First Judicial District, whereupon men gathered. From 1878 through 1884, in the district's Columbia County sittings and for one 1884 term at Dayton, men filled all seats. In 1886, the clerk began to use the term "lawful citizens," as in Walla Walla, but, in payment records, women appear only as witnesses. After 1887, pre-1885 conventions returned ("men"), untouched by impartiality.[142]

---

139 "At LaConner court last week ...," WR, August 21, 1885, editorial page. See Skagit (Whatcom) County Government, County Clerk, Territorial District Court Final Record, Key 624, NW 329/ 3–3, pp. 45–6, 53–4, 381, and passim, WSA-Belle.

140 "Mrs. Margaret McKell, of Kidd, Spokane County ...," NN July 22, 1886.

141 E.g., "Commissioners' Report," The [Spokane] *Morning Review*, February 19, 1886, or "Jurors," SFR, February 24, 1887 (all-male lists for both grand and *petit* juries). Such reports appear periodically and reflect jurors actually seated. If women were summoned, they likely were not employed.

142 First Judicial District, Territory of Washington, Walla Walla County, Daily Court Dockets, 1880–81; Grand Jury Summons, 1884–87; Jury Lists and Excuses (1869–87); Grand Jury Roll

One major exception, however, makes clear that female bodies could be seen as unapproachable mysteries, to be scrutinized only by other women or kept at home. A Columbia County justice of the peace had arrested John Patrick for rape; a male grand jury had passed him on to trial. On January 7, 1885, Judge Lewis quashed the venire and summoned a new *petit* jury composed entirely of women (Alice Cavana, Helen Edminston, and others), complete with a female foreman. After one day, the women acquitted Patrick;[143] the jury was adjourned, and another, masculine grand jury summoned to consider other cases. In the absence of additional examples, it is hard to know whether this departure from unrelieved masculinity, the equivalent of a traditional matron's jury, happened elsewhere in Washington; scholarship indicates, however, that such juries sat in Oregon.[144]

Into 1886, women certainly noticed resistance and exclusion. Numerous citizens in Colfax submitted a remonstrance to the legislative Council, recorded on January 6, 1886, against "women not being allowed to serve as jurors."[145] Nor were they alone. But, as mixed-sex practices encountered heavy winds and as word percolated through the bench and bar about imminent reconsiderations of the entire bundle of political rights, court personnel either gave up in sheer exhaustion (as in Roger Greene's courtrooms and perhaps in Hoyt's) or seized upon shifts in women's fortunes to re-masculinize juries. One particularly tantalizing page survives in clerks' records for Cowlitz County, seemingly a draft of a non-surviving journal entry for April term, 1887. The scrawled document indicates that, in an unnamed case that probably originated a year earlier, a defense attorney moved the court to "quash the Indictment found by the Grand Jury in this Cause for the Reason that there were four Women acting as Grand Jurors." The Court denied the motion, reconstituted the panel, and recommitted the cause to jurors. Justice Frank Allyn probably anticipated an anti-suffrage conclusion in litigation then moving through the courts, notably the *Harland* v. *Territory* ruling. But the Supreme Court's decision in that case was still six months away.[146] Confirmation appeared elsewhere: The dispute involved timber-land fraud; the federal grand jury that indicted the crooks had been "partly composed of women." In light of decisions declaring that women were not legal voters, said Los Angeles journalists, the

---

(1880–89); for White's order, see Jury Lists and Excuses, 1886, n.p. See also Dayton, Civil Cases Journal (1883–85). All WSA-Cheney.

[143] First Judicial District, Territory of Washington, Columbia County Court Journal, 1878–85, *Washington* v. *John Patrick*, January 7, 1885, p. 339. WSA-C. Additional detail has not survived.

[144] See Inara K. Scott, "A Window for Change: Conflicting Ideologies and Legal Reforms in Late Nineteenth-Century Oregon," *Willamette Law Review*, Vol. 37 (2001) for a similar, all-female jury.

[145] "Council. Jan. 6," *TDL*, January 8, 1886.

[146] Cowlitz County, Clerk's Records, Misc. Court Records, Copies of Journal Entries, WSA-GH, numbered p. 220, dated from internal evidence. For litigation, esp. *Harland* v. *Territory*, see Ch. 5.

lumber men had been able to argue that such women were "not legal grand jurors"; Allyn had found the point well taken, assumed that the Jones Court would affirm the lower-court ruling in a few months, and quashed the indictment.[147]

****

On February 10, 1886, the *Daily Ledger's* beleaguered editor addressed "The Problem" at some length. Two days earlier, fifteen-hundred citizens of Seattle had risen "in their might" to remove the Chinese. In Pennsylvania, strikers had "fired upon unoffending men"; simultaneously, 10,000 starving laborers in London met to discuss their grievances and were set upon by police, turned into a "howling mob," and dispersed. "Does anyone imagine," he asked, "that the causes which led to these ominous disturbances in widely separated quarters of the globe were merely local? When the body is afflicted with numerous ulcerated sores a cure cannot be [a]ffected by the application of a healing salve." Symptoms spoke to an "inherent unsoundness" and "deeply seated social diseases."[148]

In many circles, evidence of creeping sickness included not only strikes and alien migrations, but women's unsettling presence in courthouses, vigorous female entry into the marketplace and party politics, and a rising tide of zealotry aimed at masculine preserves. As Abigail Duniway put it in July, 1886, "the poor women of Washington Territory are considered to blame by everybody for everything that now happens in every community in the Territory." Equal suffrage could be justified on the ground of womanly representations of home and property; given women's relative scarcity and civil contributions, social practice could expand far enough to include decorous, brief appearances. A woman in Walla Walla noted that female voters might "come straight from their home sanctities as representing them," without delay or ancillary burdens. To vote, one need not be a "Male Woman."[149]

But jury service posed insurmountable challenges to gender and other social practices: Women could not impersonate men. They brought children to court, nursed babies, and got "sick." When jurors spent the night in small anterooms, women slept on make-shift beds, disclosed privacies, and experienced bullying or harassment. Exaggerated efforts to remove spittoons, greet women courteously, or provide hymnals underscored the chaos that sustained male-female interaction had produced. In summer, 1886, a Whatcom writer registered an amount of sexual fright: In Missouri, women were being "called

---

[147] "A Novel Point. Indictments Void by Reason of Women Serving on the Grand Jury, Vancouver, April 7," *LAT*, April 8, 1887, p. 4. Allyn had been a law clerk for Justice Samuel Miller of the U.S. Supreme Court. In 1889, he resigned to practice law in Tacoma, where he also served on inferior state courts for some years. I have not found a case matching this description in appellate records.

[148] "The Problem," *TDL*, February 10, 1886. [149] "Why They Howl," *NN*, July 8, 1886.

away from their families to go to other towns to serve on grand and *petit*
juries .... Promiscuous juries of men and women are liable to be locked up
together over night."[150] Another critic spoke of "uncongenial arisings" in
courthouses: "The Male Women have shown themselves to be very fair
jurymen, pretty astute politicians and no doubt would make good soldiers
and road workers – all of which avocations are recognized as the
constitutional accompaniments of suffrage. ... We know ... many women
who believe that woman's kingdom is home" and therefore "shrink in dismay
from the duties and uncongenial arisings that accompany the right of suffrage."
Juries belonged to "man's rough sphere."[151]

Hence, by the time legislators had approved the Local Option Act, proposals
were well afoot to tighten election laws, partly to curb voter fraud, but also to
restore male control of courthouses and grease statehood petitions through
Congress. Delegate Voorhees's statehood bill was reported out of committee
in the nation's capital in mid-February, 1886, triggering fierce debate about the
extent to which acquiescence in Washington's case would effectively nationalize
equal suffrage and its accompaniments. At the same time, businessmen and
workaday men resented having to choose, as one man put it, between
"fanaticism or whiskey in the attempt to secure a little breathing room in
which to mind his own business, and thereby prepare a solid foundation for
future expansion and enterprise."[152]

Modified social hierarchies thus began to emerge from legal-cultural
instability. A fully sovereign member of the constituent power would be
manly and white (hence never Chinese); devoted to private property and
co-equal household agency (and therefore not Indian or Mormon); an
opponent of European ideologies that weakened male headship; and a critic
of political experimentation that diminished the state's power to maintain social
peace. In the workplace, women would occupy a buffer zone between white
men and lesser beings.[153] Spouses perhaps need not embody sovereignty
identically, undertake the same work, or claim property-based authority in
shared domains, to be co-sovereigns.

Dark undertows also appeared. On January 8, 1886, Representative
J. B. Kinnear of Seattle signaled the onset of incremental reconsiderations of
women's property rights, sometimes in the guise of progress, with the
introduction of a seemingly innocuous bill to simplify forms for deeds and
mortgages which made it unnecessary to take the "separate acknowledgement
of the wife, except as to mortgages of the homestead." The editor of the *Tacoma
Daily Ledger* hailed the bill as the final purging of a "vain and useless survival"

---

[150] "Somebody sent us ...," *WR*, July 30, 1886.
[151] "The Seattle Papers ...," *SFR*, correspondence page, February 10, 1887. Scholars often find an
abstract unsexing of women; these developments suggest a physical, hyper-sexualized threat.
[152] "The State of Washington," *SDPI*, February 14, 1886; "A Few Words from a Conservative,"
SDPI, February 5, 1886, p. 1.
[153] E.g., Cynthia Eagle Russett, *Sexual Science* (Cambridge, MA, 1989).

from former times when husbands could not be trusted. Republican J. R. Lewis of Seattle – a champion of equal suffrage – charged Kinnear with encroachments on the rights of women. Current law required an officer taking the acknowledgment to apprise the wife of her rights; by the new proposal, her property rights could be annulled. When Kinnear accused Lewis of character assassination, Lewis said that he meant only to defend a vulnerable class. The bill was tabled.[154]

This is not to say that legislators abandoned women: Session by session, they tinkered with the code. On January 9, 1886 – the same week that a local-option law increased social strain – legislators amended the criminal-procedure code. Originally, Section 392 provided only that husbands and wives could not be forced to testify against one another in civil actions without the consent of the affected partner. Now, in "all actions, civil and criminal, involving the chastity of the wife, in which the husband is a competent witness," the wife also could testify, which increased the odds that women might be heard in suits involving the use or abuse of their bodies.[155] Another law establishing uniform procedures in cases of election fraud declared that masculine nouns and pronouns would be construed to include women.[156] Lawmakers also amended the code, probably by accident, to include the possibility of marital rape. "If *any person* ravish or carnally know *any female* of the age of sixteen years or more," the law now read, "by force and against her will, or carnally know and abuse any female child," he would be punished by long imprisonment.[157]

Nevertheless, imputations of co-sovereignty and sex-blind legitimacy, always contingent and partial, had softened, and many of the territory's leading figures were looking elsewhere. In February, 1887, Grover Cleveland signed the Interstate Commerce Act; economic integration increasingly occupied center stage.[158] For Roger Greene, the future of the republic seemed to hinge on mixed-sex representations of sovereignty. Others fell back on a stabilizing, pre-political constitution of social practice, modified to take account of civil equality. Witness a speech delivered in mid-January, 1888, by Henry M. Knapp – a farmer, ex-Democratic legislator, and county assessor from Clarke County, just as Washingtonians commenced the final march to statehood. Much of Knapp's oration addressed the practical effects of equal suffrage for statehood; but, in his broader castigation of sex-blindness, he managed to detach, narrow, and resituate women's sovereignty. When late

---

[154] "Conveyancing Simplified," *TDL*, February 4, 1886, ed. page; "Territorial Legislature," ibid., January 9, 1886, p. 4.

[155] An Act to Amend Section 392 of the Code of Washington Territory, Washington Territory Acts, 1885–86, pp. 73–4.

[156] An Act to Amend Sections 3079 and 3084 of Chapter 242 of the Code of Washington Territory, Relating to Elections, Washington Territory Acts, 1885–86, pp. 128–9.

[157] An Act to Amend Section 812 of the Code of Washington Territory, Washington Territory Acts, 1885, p. 84. Emphasis added.

[158] For the Interstate Commerce Act, signed February 4, 1887, see 24 Stat. at Large 379 (1887).

nineteenth-century men trained as lawyers spoke of "realms" and "rule," they had in mind domains infused with and supported by law. Critics might say, Knapp began, that he sought to "deprive the woman of all right and make her practically a slave. Far from it. There is no right that I enjoy but that my wife has the same right – *she in her sphere[,] me in mine.*"[159]

Knapp then constitutionalized republican motherhood while rejecting Turner's wholesale masculinization of unitary headship. Women's sovereignty persisted, but law-making authority – rooted in private agency with property, including marital estates, not merely in social theory – barely extended beyond the front gate. Woman suffrage would be a matter of grant; even in 1883, as Greene noted repeatedly, when enthusiasm for equal suffrage waxed full, woman had not stood firmly enough on constitutional ground nor exercised obligations of citizenship beyond jury duty. "When I enter the house," Knapp said, "I am in my wife's domain. Her word is law there. When she comes into the fields she is in my domain. The property and the purse are common, to which one has the same right as the other. Some deeds are in her name, some are in mine.... This is what I call *equality according to nature's own law,* and any other system will miserably fail." Women would be civil and marital equals – that is, would exercise sovereign authority at home and with their own property – without adjacent, property-based claims to a political personality.[160]

Formalization of such constructs lay in the future. Even as disasters rocked Washington Territory, publicists still championed sex-neutrality in education and at work. One writer whose paper opposed equal suffrage nevertheless decried "the meanness, the despicability of men who begrudge a woman the right to work anywhere in any honorable calling."[161] But women's standing within the constituent power had been altered. At work, where contributions were welcome, they occupied a mid-zone between white men and the Chinese. At the polls, a female presence could be justified as representations of property or women's sovereign domain. Not so in courtrooms. There, Greene's attempts to connect private and public governments had failed. Women had seen and revealed more than men could bear; worse, they spoke as women, not as representatives of the community. It was time for Washingtonians to secure statehood, economic integration, and a reputation for political maturity. As delegate Charles Voorhees put it in May, 1886, membership in the nation "dwarfs ... all other objects."[162]

[159] "Mr. Knapp on the Suffrage Bill," *WS*, January 20, 1888, front page. Emphasis added.
[160] Ibid. These ideas mirror the "separate but equal" thinking apparent in Myra Bradwell's case and, a few years later, in *Plessy v. Ferguson*.
[161] See, as good examples, "Woman and Home" and "How Business for Women," *Northwest Enterprise*, February 2, 1884. For meanness, see "A Woman Has a Right to Do Anything She Can Do Well," ibid., July 11, 1885. This new print emphasized commerce.
[162] "Mr. Voorhees on Admission," *WS*, May 7, 1886.

5

"A double head in nature is a monstrosity"

Internecine warfare

... Congress tells the inhabitants of a Territory, 'If you choose to indulge in any isms; if you choose to indulge in any idiosyncrasies; if you choose to indulge in any cranky notions, so far as your municipal and domestic government is concerned, we will permit you to do it, and you may enjoy it as much as you please;' ... But when the people of a Territory come before Congress ..., then upon Congress rests the responsibility whether it will ... indorse whatever passing craze may affect that Territorial population.

– Senator James Biddle Eustis of Louisiana (1886)[1]

In October, 1877, two years before the passage of Washington's radical equal-rights statute, Governor Elisha Ferry had attributed Washington's near-miraculous exemption from the depression afoot since 1873 to its "isolated position" and workplace amity.[2] Into the next decade, exceptionalism retained its appeal. Migrants supposedly came to the New Northwest because "*a man counts for more than in the crowded communities of the East.*" In Lelia Robinson's words, capitalists had a "magnificent opportunity here to make money, and at the same time to make the country." But making the country required stability and maturity. "The substitution of a State government for that of a Territory," wrote a journalist in 1883, "imposes upon the citizens ... more solemn duties and graver responsibilities than those to which they have been accustomed." A scant five years later, citizens were urged to suppress radical differences of opinion.[3] Perhaps the west had to "build upon the eastern plan"

[1] Congressional Record, United States Senate, 49th Congress, 1st session, 1886, p. 3318.
[2] Governor Elisha P. Ferry to the Sixth Biennial Session of the Legislative Assembly, October 3, 1877, in Charles Gates, ed., *Messages of the Governors of the Territory of Washington to the Legislative Assembly, 1854–1889* (Seattle, WA, 1940), p. 193. The downturn commenced later and lasted longer than in the east.
[3] "Come to the New Northwest," WR, May 30, 1884; "The Attractions of Washington Territory," SDPI, April 17, 1885. Emphasis in the original. The author was "supposed to be Miss Lelia J. Robinson." See also "Mr. Caton's Memorial," November 23, 1883, WS; in the same vein, see

in education and commerce. A *sui-generis* past featuring rough-hewn cabins and men differently constituted than easterners yielded to continental uniformities. Said a poet in 1887, "They do not sit down by the tombs of the dead,/ They live in the world of today;/ For the Present is here and the Past has fled,/ and the Future is on the way."[4]

A bright line between past and future appeared first in eastern Washington, coincident with the arrival of Henry Villard's Northern Pacific in 1883. "For over a quarter of a century," wrote an overwrought Walla Wallan, "the ragged men and hardy women who, traveling with patient oxen and nervy horses, carrying their household goods ... suffering hunger and thirst, ... fighting savages, ... have been waiting for the time when they could enter a railway carriage, and ... revisit the scenes of their childhood." Railroads brought arid eastern counties into conversation with the "people and markets of the world." A Belleville householder welcomed sameness: Once, travel had taken half a year; but settlers' energy and good luck had "obliterated the 'out west,' robbed distance of its weariness and *carried Progress [on] ringing rails to where it has solved the last mystery of solitude and strangeness.*" Months of wagon travel had become "five or six days in a palace car."[5]

As statehood neared, an "imagined fraternity of white men" emerged in the public imagination.[6] As early as 1886, during discussions of statehood proposals in Washington, DC, Senator Orville Platt (a Connecticut Republican) praised the class of men destined to "maintain the institutions of a State." These men would "join hands with brothers elsewhere," the "bone of our bone and flesh of our flesh."[7] A Spokane writer noted that his city no longer met strangers with brass bands; the "emigrant is not confronted with a crowd of leading citizens armed with a ... series of resolutions. People out here hustle for a living." A visitor would be carried by streetcar to a hotel; the "grim walls of wealth-producing factories will stare at him ... along the river banks." Without undue ceremony, he would join a surging throng bent on trade and labor.[8]

---

unidentified clipping, "THE NEW GOVERNOR," Governor's Papers, Box 2-1-8 (1888?), WSA-O.

[4] "Olympia Schools," *TDL*, January 21, 1885. See also "Schooled but not Educated," *WWS*, April 14, 1883, laying out opportunities for "men" and "boys" that educational reform would open. See also "The West," from Northwest Magazine, repr. *SDPI*, January 2, 1887. The bygone past/ present/future trope was common enough; for another example in the same issue, "Wheel and Forge," ibid. (on the past, present, and future of Seattle industry).

[5] Editorial, "Realizing a Dream," *WWU*, September 22, 1883; "For Immigrants," *WR*, January 2, 1885, emphasis added. On strangeness, see Christopher Tomlins, *Freedom Bound: Law, Labor, and Civic Identity in Colonizing British America, 1580–1865* (New York, 2010), pp. 537–69 and passim.

[6] Dana Nelson, *National Manhood: Capitalist Citizenship and the Imagined Fraternity of White Men* (Durham, NC, 1998).

[7] *Congressional Record*, Senate, 49th Congress, 1st session, March 26–30, 1886, pp. 2910–13. See also "The Admission Bill," *TDL*, April 2, 1886. Every major paper carried reprints.

[8] "Spokane Falls," *SFR*, February 28, 1885.

Nasty confrontations appeared between George Turner's allies and a coalition of equal-rights advocates, legislators, and the new, Democratic governor Eugene Semple. The governor (said by his friends to be a "very genial gentleman" and by others a man of dull visage) had come to office promising as much support for equality and social purity as the badly split Republicans had mustered; as a short-timer, he pledged to honor the popular will.[9] But Democrats plainly expected Semple to fall in line. Much had gone awry; perfect equality had insulted women and destabilized public judgment. "If we concede the ... electoral franchise to woman," wrote an editor in 1887, "we must also concede ... all the burdens, duties, and labors pertaining to public matters; ... she must endure the hardships of road labor as well as jury service, and she must share the dangers in the army or navy .... What kind of an impression would a woman create, standing on the hustings delivering a political speech! How would she look with a pick and shovel .... What a comical figure she would cut ... climbing the rigging of a man-of-war as a sailor!" Statehood required respectability and maturity. As Tacoma's most progressive editor noted, "Modern methods have made new conditions. We have progressed so far in an unrestricted development that we are coming around again to the point where much more is required."[10]

Careful planning among anti-suffragists bore fruit. In 1887, Congress suddenly limited the topics that territorial lawmakers might address through emendation; one forbidden topic was the summoning and empaneling of grand or petit jurors.[11] Then, as debates about the terms of Washington's admission continued, an appeal appeared on the Territorial Supreme Court docket involving a rogue named Jeffrey Harland. When conservative jurists derailed mixed-sex suffrage and jury service on technical grounds, the assembly, governor, and pro-suffrage camp fought back and temporarily prevailed. But George Turner resigned the bench in 1888 to argue a feigned case involving an anti-suffragist named Nevada Bloomer, and then to serve as kingmaker in two statehood conventions. Meanwhile, Roger Greene experienced a breakdown: A friendly Seattle paper reported "extreme nervous prostration"; the workload had "overtaxed his strength until it completely failed him."[12] When he returned to court after a summer's rest at Vancouver, his half-realized, mixed-sex republic had been decimated.

---

[9] "Gov. Eugene Semple," *WJ*, February 4, 1888; "He Omitted Them," *ST*, September 20, 1889.

[10] Untitled article, editorial page, *WS*, December 16, 1887. For encounters between Robinson, Greene, and others, see Jill Norgren, *Rebels at the Bar* (New York, 2013), pp. 166–7. Struve later became mayor of Seattle. See also "Noblesse Oblige," *TDL*, December 6, 1889, p. 2.

[11] "Limitations of Territorial Legislatures," *LCB*, December 2, 1887. The measure had been adopted in June, 1886.

[12] On resignation, see, e.g., "Judge Turner Resigns," *TDL*, February 17, 1888; on Greene's health, see "We are glad ...," *True Tone*, June 5, 1886.

"I THOUGHT THERE COULD BE NO DIFFERENCE OF OPINION"

In January, 1887, as his tenure as chief justice drew to a close, Roger Greene mounted another defense of co-sovereignty. In *Ada Andrews* v. *Julius Andrews*, he challenged the inferior court's paternal regard for a divorced wife who had bought up her husband's share of the community at a forced sale and then sued to recover a separate estate and eliminate debts which, she claimed, her husband had incurred without consultation. Ada swore that she had handed over wages from teaching and butter-making to Julius and, trusting in his good nature, had not maintained separate accounts; years later, claiming to be "in rags and sick," she sought to recover separate property before debtors could seize it. Speaking as the community's administrator, Julius testified that he had submitted a list of partly fictitious debts in order to prevent Ada from realizing her interest in community lands.[13]

Greene ordered a re-hearing; Ada had a right to law, especially if separate property had been co-mingled. He was especially troubled by the very idea that counsel might argue to the contrary. "In these days of wisdom ...," he wrote, "this is a most important question, *and one on which I thought there could be no difference of opinion.*" But testimony also suggested a conspiracy to evade creditors. Ada's counsel had tried to use *Holyoke* v. *Jackson* against Julius's creditors, contending that the community was off-limits to liens if the wife had been tricked or not consulted. No, said Greene; a husband's creditor could, "regardless of the wife, pursue him to judgment, and take his property in execution, not excepting even the community personal property." Greene could re-affirm *Holyoke* while rejecting an expansion of its findings merely to shield women: The ruling had "determined nothing as to the power of the husband to bind the community real estate by a judgment recovered against himself for a community debt." Ada surely was entitled to her day in court to argue for or against the sale of lands. But when she entered a courtroom, the burden was on her to prove that the community contained separate property. She – perhaps they – had feigned a suit and lost. Greene thus confirmed civil equality, secured creditors' lawful claims, and discouraged judicial paternalism.[14]

Still, trouble appeared in unexpected places. Suffragists had assumed that the war for equality would be fought over the political rights and duties, not bedrock civil rights and domestic-relations law. They were wrong. The judicial arm of Washington's anti-suffrage juggernaut entered the fray quietly in May, 1886: News broke in Olympia of a curious appeal from William Langford's district in eastern Washington, where anti-suffragism steadily

---

[13] *Ada Andrews* v. *Julius Andrews, et al.*, 3 Wash Terr Rpts 286 (1887), 290–1.

[14] Ibid., emphasis added. Two years earlier, in *Lemon et al.* v. *Waterman et al.*, 3 Wash Rpts 485 (1885), Turner similarly conceded departures from the law of coverture. Noting that legislation offered "a wide door ... for fraud upon creditors," he suggested that laws be read stringently; p. 493. Greene and Wingard concurred.

gained strength, affecting laws enacted during the previous year. The case at hand, *Susenberg and Co. v. Bucher*, had to do with whether an attachment might commence before notice had been filed with the clerk. On appeal, the issue became whether the statute governing attachments had been properly titled; Langford said no and struck it down. Observers were appalled. If *Susenberg* stood, laws with only the number of the statute or law-code section in titles would be invalid; jury decisions and appellate rulings would have to be reversed or reargued. Losses in time and money would be staggering.[15]

Rumblings about lawmakers' ineptitude had been afoot for years. "The work of framing laws," wrote a concerned citizen in 1883, "should be entrusted to ... men learned in the science of the law, [and] familiar with the rules of construction." While a few laws were models of clarity, most were not; they would "return to plague the inventor."[16] A month later, Seattle journalists pointed to a new, sloppily titled omnibus act encompassing a dozen topics – e.g., civil actions, injunctions in nuisance cases, homestead selection, and justice-court jurisdiction. Greene supposedly said that the act conflicted with the organic act; in keeping with rules of statutory construction, Section 1924 provided that every law would "embrace but one subject," to be expressed in the title. Greene had condemned the amateurish "smuggling in of hurtful legislation ... under a title which does not indicate the object of the bill." John Hoyt had agreed, which was *"practically a decision of the matter."* Informally, justices had declared the law "unconstitutional," in the reporter's phrase, notwithstanding the organic act's statutory character.[17]

Abigail Duniway immediately announced that *Susenberg* had "wiped out the Woman Suffrage law," the title of which included only the number of the amended law-code section. Lawmakers perhaps had resolved problems with the 1886 election law's clear title.[18] But, with statehood campaigns afoot, legislative incompetence of any kind, much less on the suffrage question, was potentially disastrous. What if the laws of 1883 and 1886, as well as civil rights and community-property laws, bore invalid titles? Ominously, just before the ruling, in debate of statehood petitions and woman-suffrage in the nation's capital, Kentucky senator Joseph Blackburn noted inconsistencies in the territorial law codes' treatment of

---

[15] "An Important Decision," *SDPI*, May 7, 1886. Warnings were common; e.g., "Important Legislation, A dispatch from Walla Walla ...," *WR*, May 21, 1886 ("Every session of the legislature does hasty work .... This will give the lawyers something to employ their time").

[16] "Imperfect Statutes," *SDPI*, November 18, 1883. See also "Unconstitutional," *PSWA*, February 10, 1887.

[17] "Unconstitutional," *SDPI*, December 14, 1883. See also "An Act to Correct Errors and Supply Omissions in the Code of Washington," Acts of the Territory of Washington, November 28, 1883, pp. 44–5. Unfortunately, the writer did not specify where the discussion occurred. Emphasis added.

[18] "Woman Suffrage Safe," *NN*, May 20, 1886.

alien women. Was it "unsafe" to bring Washington into "the brotherhood of States"?[19]

In Seattle, rumors of a judicial *coup* multiplied. Democrats sought to commit their party to "anti-prohibition, anti-gross earnings law, and anti-woman suffrage"; Justices Turner and Langford openly supported all three positions. The plan was to "secure a Democratic Judge when Chief Judge Greene goes out; one who will hold that the law is not constitutional, and have it first upset by judicial procedure, and then attack it before the people." Few doubted that "a deep laid plan is on foot" to smash equal suffrage and mixed-sex juries.[20] Greene tried to put out fires. While Langford proposed invalidating many statutes, including the one extending suffrage to women, he had been wrong. First, the titles *did* express legislative intentions: "If you aim to amend a particular statute, you say so and name the statute." Second, the law in question had only one object. Third, the organic act mandated only a "fair expression" of contents. He conceded that the attachment-law amendment did not betray its contents, but titles of acts of undisputed validity were similarly vague, as with an amendment of the 1869 act incorporating Seattle. Citing relevant New York and California rulings, Greene pronounced the law valid. But he knew that a newspaper article had no legal weight.[21]

In May, 1886, the chief justice provided another stinging editorial in response to Langford's district-court decision against aberrant statutory titling in *Otto* v. *Hanford*, a dispute having nothing to do with women's rights. But Greene clearly perceived grave danger to democratic governance: Women, he began, had long been exercising rights at the polls and in courtrooms; even the Supreme Court has ruled that they might sit on juries. But now came a "flood of new light . . . , and if Judge Langford's late ruling is the law, we have been laboring under a delusion. From whence did our women derive these rights?" Women had served since 1883; nobody had criticized statutory titles, even as they criticized policies.

The organic act of the Territory declares that every law shall embrace but one subject, and that shall be embraced in the title. The Legislature at its late session enacted a law . . .which Judge Langford has decided is void. There are thirteen such statutes in the session laws of 1883, including the act conferring suffrage on [women] . . . . The only statutes of 1883 which were approved by Congress are . . . the Omnibus bill and a few other minor ones. If Justice Langford's decision be correct, our Judges . . . have mistaken the law in permitting women to act as jurors; our Supreme Court erred in holding that they are qualified . . . . Under such ruling, not only the act of 1883 . . . is void, but the act of 1886 . . . is also void; in addition, there are 19 acts of 1886 for like reasons void.

---

[19] "Woman Suffrage," *SDPI*, May 8, 1886 (two articles with the same title), and a third piece, "Woman Suffrage," ibid., May 9, 1886. Senate rules prohibited amendment of a statehood bill.
[20] Editorial, excerpting Port Townsend Argus, *SDPI*, July 22, 1886.
[21] Roger S. Greene, "Important Decision," *SDPI*, October 6, 1886. See also editorial, *SFR*, December 2, 1887 ("the slovenly manner in which many of the laws" had been written).

While it was improper to litigate legal problems in newspapers, said Greene, he wanted to "call to the attention of the voters and judges of the Territory" the seriousness and direction of Langford's rulings.[22]

While awaiting the *Hanford* appeal, Greene noted that, so far as legislative sentiment could be known, prevailing views had been entirely in favor of statutory validity.[23] But the chief justice's mind was elsewhere: In his Seattle district courtroom, he had confronted Langford's big gun – a case involving Jeffrey Harland and two other perpetrators of a "swindling game called bunko, or twenty-one."[24] Anti-suffragists had been waiting for a case originating in Greene's district to force his recusal from the four-member appellate bench, effectively silencing him. Amelia Parker, an aspiring lawyer, claimed that the case had been instigated by Harry Morgan, a "boss gambler of Tacoma"; Harland was one of his "henchmen."[25] As in *Rosencrantz*, Harland appealed, challenging the legitimacy of five married, female grand jurors. In February, 1887, a Seattle paper suggested on information provided by Tacomans that the bench had coerced lawyers: "Jeff J. Harland, a gambler, was convicted ... for fleecing a man named J. C. Livensburger out of $610 by loaded dice .... He fled to Portland ..., was arrested there, extradited, tried, convicted and sentenced to one year and a half in the penitentiary." On appeal, counsel argued that the assembly in expanding the suffrage had not intended to seat women on juries, but they had not cast doubt on the law's validity. Unnamed justices had "hinted that it would be desirable for him to do so."[26]

In the *Harland* appeal, with Greene on the sidelines, Turner and Langford had free rein. Counsel for Harland argued that wives were not householders; adhering to Turner's *Rosencrantz* dissent, they defined jury service, not as a right or privilege, but as a "burden on citizenship" requiring separate statutory enactment. Such burdens could not be found by implication in election laws. But, as promised in Turner's *Rosencrantz* dissent, the long-term target was the division of household headship: Lawmakers had presumed to "revolutionize those laws of marriage and household divinely instituted at the dawn of creation." Surely a husband was "the natural head of the family" and the wife a household dependent. Counsel termed the law purporting to confer the elective franchise on women unconstitutional as well as illegal, citing no

---

[22] R. S. Greene, "Are the Women of Washington Territory Entitled to Vote and Act as Jurors?" *SDPI*, May 14, 1886. He relied on Thomas Cooley, *Constitutional Limitations* (a decision against a law's validity had to be "placed in their judgment beyond a reasonable doubt").

[23] "Important Decision," *SDPI*, October 6, 1886. The appeal of *Otto v. Hanford* cannot be found.

[24] *Jeffrey Harland v. Territory of Washington*, 3 Wash Terr Rpts 131 (February 1887), 132. See also Jeffrey Harland v. Territory of Washington, 1887, Judicial Records, Territory of Washington, Case File No. 505, WSA-O. For lower-court opinion, see "Judge Langford's Opinion," *SDPI*, February 12, 1887.

[25] Adelia M. Parker, [untitled article, n.p., n.d., in clippings collection, sent to unknown recipient by "C.W.M.," probably Catherine Waugh McCulloch, ed. *Chicago Law Times* and NWSA official], Schlesinger Women's Studies Manuscripts, Reel 14, No. 0279.

[26] Untitled, repr. *TDL*, *PSWA*, February 10, 1887.

authority for the constitutional claim. On the other side, in a one-paragraph brief, White pointed to *Rosencrantz* and the 1881 code, noted that wives were householders as well as citizens, and deemed the indictment lawful.[27]

Turner easily brushed *Rosencrantz* aside;[28] a newly staffed bench had been "unable to agree" with John Hoyt's views. In *Jeffrey Harland v. Territory of Washington*, Turner eliminated female grand jurors on the ground of legislative sloppiness, read an edited version of his *Rosencrantz* dissent into the majority opinion, and excavated beneath it to cast doubt on election and community-property statutes, the underlayment of mixed-sex political and legal practices. As in his *Rosencrantz* dissent, he praised the common-law exclusion of the female class *propter defectum sexus* (by reason of a defect or deficiency of sex),[29] extolled the virtues of a legal system tied to the past, plagiarized sections of *Bradwell* and *In Re Lavinia Goodell* (a Wisconsin ruling against female bar admission, ultimately appended to *Harland*), and moved quickly to a "question not considered in Rosencrantz" and, as critics pointed out, not raised at any point in lower-court proceedings – the validity of woman suffrage.[30]

In his formal opinion, Turner wisely avoided the law of coverture: Women claimed co-tenancy of marital communities, equal civil rights, full membership in the constituent power, and the right to represent property at the polls. But Harland's attorneys had observed in passing that one chapter in the law code, contrary to what Hoyt had said in *Rosencrantz*, retained elements of coverture and contained only "statutory changes from the common law made relative to the rights of husband and wife." Indeed, the act's title, which was "bound to express its objects," indicated only that it regulated the property rights of marital partners. It said nothing about elections or jury-duty obligations, and neither could be found by implication. In the same chapter, the husband managed community property and selected a homestead; mothers controlled children only after men died. Statutes thus modified but did not "revolutionize these laws of marriage and household divinely instituted at the dawn of creation." Not only were election laws improperly titled, but Hoyt had based his defense of mixed-sex juries on a non-existent transformation.[31]

On the narrow question of titling, Turner entirely agreed with counsel, thus affirming old linkages between the right to vote and jury duty: If equal suffrage collapsed, jury duty also fell "to the ground a broken and shapeless mass." The

---

[27] *Harland* v. *Territory*, 132–3, 136–52. Langford concurred separately.

[28] Newspapers regularly got Greene's role wrong; e.g., "Woman Suffrage," ibid., February 4, 1887, or "The Woman Suffrage Decision," ibid., July 22, 1887 (in both, Justice Greene "dissenting").

[29] The best source is still Sir William Blackstone, *Commentaries on the Laws of England*, Book 3, Ch. 23, "Of the Trial by Jury," any modern edition; a better translation, suggested by Blackstone's text, might be "by reason of sexual inadequacy" (women as imperfect men). See Judy M. Cornett, "'Hoodwink'd by Custom': The Exclusion of Women from Juries in Eighteenth-Century English Law and Literature," *William and Mary Journal of Women and the Law*, Vol. 4, No. 1 (1997), pp. 1–89. My thanks to Elaine Clark.

[30] *Harland* v. *Territory*, 132–3.   [31] Ibid., 134–5.

election law of 1883 abrogated the organic-act rule by which every law embraced one object, to be expressed in the title.³² If legislators aimed to create female jurors, they had not said so, could not in any case include multiple subjects in a statute, and had referred to numbers in the 1881 code, not to woman suffrage or jury service. While courts preferred not to invalidate statutes, they also defended legal science and Congressional intentions, even if it meant declaring laws "unconstitutional." Again, in Turner's mind, the organic law had constitutional properties. Female jury service had been a "fruit of disobedience to the wise and salutary restraint of the Organic Act." If the public favored the practice, lawmakers could remake statutory titles. "A measure of such a character," he concluded, "involving changes in our social and political structures so momentous, and ... so disastrous ..., ought never to be urged or passed" under doubtful circumstances. Women were "not voters in this territory, and not being voters," were "not competent to sit on juries."³³

Unable to resist, Turner set out in dicta ("some additional thoughts") his vision of how stability might be restored. He also took revenge on his enemies: Both judges who adhered to *Rosencrantz*, after a "service of long duration, in which they have honorably illumined our judicial history by great learning ... and by the purity of their lives" were about to retire, and the bench would be further changed in the near future, without "such great detriment to the public interest." He ridiculed a "visionary enthusiast" who had found jury service in an election law. With Lelia Robinson in the gallery, he cited the ruling bearing her name in Massachusetts as evidence of women's unfitness in courtrooms. He quoted Greene's opinion in *Jackson* v. *Winn*, which promised that when "a man becomes a lawyer he does not have to lose his wits, nor does a judge have to be a fool." In a closing fillip, he revealed that a case like *Harland* had come before him several months earlier, but he had put off ruling until questions might be "authoritatively determined" – i.e., until a suitable case appeared in one of Greene's circuit courtrooms, leaving John Hoyt as the sole defender of egalitarianism. For detail, he encouraged lawyers to read his *Rosencrantz* dissent.³⁴

---

³² Suffragists ridiculed everyone: Attorneys and anti-suffrage justices had made use of an old edition of federal statutes, not the Revised Statutes; see "The Bloomer Decision," *SP*, August 15, 1888.

³³ *Harland* v. *Territory*, 152. Here, as elsewhere, Turner conflated organic acts with constitutions. Challenges to titles that embraced more than a single subject (or failed to describe topics) recurred, as in October, 1909, when opponents of primary elections sought to invalidate the statute authorizing them; see, e.g., "Yes, Any Qualified Voter May Vote," *TDL*, October 22, 1909. Harland's wife secured a divorce; see "From Olympia Transcript," *WR*, March 1, 1887, ed. page.

³⁴ *Harland* v. *Territory*, 131 Wash Terr Rpts (1887), 136–8, 140–1, 151. See esp. 137: "I shall not reiterate the arguments embraced in the dissenting opinion read by me in the first case." For Eustis and McCall, see below. Turner worried about appearances; see, e.g., George Turner to H. G. Struve, May 7, 1888 and May 12, 1888, asking Struve in his capacity as reporter to remove lines from a manuscript opinion (Territory v. Miller) which critics termed "harsh and intemperate"; H. G. Struve Papers, Box 79, George Turner File, UWSC.

Still, in scrawled notes sent to the clerk with his opinion, Turner betrayed some anxiety about the power and scope of the ruling – only in dicta had he closed doors on political and civil equality – and perhaps about his skid over the 1886 statute, which had been passed in part to address the titling problem.[35] The title and relevant sections of the 1883 law, he said again, "relating as they do to the mere minutia of elections, could not . . . be amended so as to confer the elective franchise on any one. Nor has any amendment of them been attempted." Turner added a final note about a recently discovered Arkansas case that cast doubt on his ability to invalidate a law unless the organic act expressly granted the power to courts. But there, he said, "no constitutional question was involved,"[36] as if such a question had arisen here. Later, in transmitting *Harland* to the reporter, Turner characterized it as weaponry. He could imagine improving the text, but it was too late; pages would have to be "fired off as they are."[37]

Langford's concurrence set out two astonishing claims. After interrogating the phrases "bunko and twenty-one, or top-and-bottom dice," he argued (after Turner in *Rosencrantz*) that legislators, in creating a community-property regime, had never intended to invest spouses equally with sovereignty, to create two householders, or to create mixed-sex juries. Such legislation had been adopted in "many other States" (as if Washington had become one), including Oregon, yet legislators had said "not a word about her being lord of the household, or juror, or the like." And how was she "disabled"? Was jury duty essential to personal adequacy? Was a postmaster unable to sit as a grand juror suffering under a disability? Most amazingly, he announced that the 1883 election law had not created new voters because legislators had amended an extra-legal document, the code of 1881. While lawmakers had commissioned the work and relied on it, they had never received it as a *legal* document. "We have a book," he wrote, "which is marked on the fly-leaf 'The Code of Washington.'" It did not claim to be an authenticated act of the assembly. It had been edited and compiled by a private party; it contained "no titles to acts, no enacting clause, no signature of president of the council . . . or governor." Was it this private book that the 1883 act had amended? Legislators could amend their own acts but not "the works of a private author."[38]

Eleven months later, the Court made clear that it objected, not just to married women on grand juries, but to all women. In *William M. White* v. *Territory of Washington* (1888), Chief Justice Richard Jones reversed White's homicide

[35] The statute also controlled fraud by requiring that voters reside in the precinct for six months before elections; "Vote at Home!," *SR*, October 13, 1886.

[36] Cover note with manuscript opinion, Harland v. Territory, signed G. T., Judicial Records, Territory of Washington, Case File No. 505, WSA-O.

[37] George Turner to Allen Struve, Supreme Court Reporter, Seattle, June 27, 1887, Allen Struve File, UWSC, Acc. No. 4200, Box No. 81.

[38] *Harland v. Territory*, 156–8. See also the transcription in "A Celebrated Case," *WS*, February 18, 1887, p. 1. One pro-suffrage editor called the code "a disgrace"; "The Legislature," *SP*, December 5, 1887.

indictment on the ground that one of the jurors, the unmarried Maggie Farr, had been empaneled illegally. In addition, justices remanded the 1885 conspiracy case of *Territory* v. *Cornelius Bradshaw* for a rehearing: The grand jury had included five women (Mrs. Switzer, Mrs. J. C. Davenport, Miss M. R. Bybee, Mrs. J. S. Mount, Mrs. J. W. Range), one of them single. Yet lawyers objected to all five (the panel had "no authority" to find a true bill).[39] Similarly, in *Rumsey* v. *Territory*, decided on January 7, 1888, justices agreed that A. E. Horton, J. D. DeMott, and Harriet E. Herndon were residing with husbands and therefore not householders; three others were "females" and thus ineligible. In July, 1887, the "delighted convict" gained freedom.[40]

Ailing and distraught, Greene tried to submit a document variously described as an amicus brief and a dissenting opinion. On July 19, 1887, he told the chief justice that he expected in "a day or two" to be able to submit his views in writing. Would the Court permit it? "I should have prepared & filed it, while still on the bench but for the intervention of other matters that to me seemed more pressing. A judge retired is qualified ... & while he can never be compelled to assign reasons for his judgment, he may be allowed, perhaps, to record his dissent even when no longer a member of the court."[41] After Greene missed a deadline, Jones published only this comment from his predecessor: "From all that is decisive, and from much that is not decisive, in the very able opinions just

---

[39] *William M. White* v. *Territory of Washington*, 3 Wash Terr Rpts 397 (1888). Immediately after statehood, the case reappeared as a suit for damages; *White* v. *Territory of Washington*, 1 Wash Rpts 279 (1890). See also "The White Case," *SP*, July 12, 1888, which claimed that exception had not been taken during the original hearing, but had arisen during the criminal trial when two women served on the *petit* jury. Details do not appear in case files. After Harland, the sheriff in Vancouver, "not having the fear of the Supreme Court before his eyes," may have "summoned three ladies on the Grand Jury venire for the April term." Jury rolls do not survive. See "Sheriff of Vancouver ...," *SP*, March 18, 1887, p. 1. On Maggie Farr, see Ch. 3 (she served with twenty men in Tacoma in October, 1886). See also *Cornelius G. Bradshaw* v. *Territory of Washington*, 3 Wash Terr Rpts 265 (1887) and Territory of Washington v. Cornelius Bradshaw, Case File No. 404, WSA-O.

[40] *Dewitt Rumsey* v. *Territory of Washington*, 3 Wash Terr Rpts 333 (1888), 332, and Rumsey v. Territory of Washington, Case File No. 484, pp. 5–6, WSA-O. Rumsey had been "one of a party who assaulted the Chinese in Squaw Valley" in 1886, killing three. Attempts to convict the group of murder had failed; they were indicted for riot and Rumsey was convicted. Los Angeles reporters later said that, after prosecutors had made opening statements, justices "unanimously held that no reply was needed, and declined to hear from the opposing counsel"; "Woman Suffrage. The Washington Territory Law Declared Unconstitutional," *LAT*, July 22, 1887, p. 4. See also Angus M. Claire v. Territory of Washington, Case File No. 572, 1887, WSA-O, an unsuccessful attempt to use *Harland* when women were not involved.

[41] Letter from Roger S. Greene to Honorable Richard A. Jones, July 19, 1887, in Harland v. Territory, Case File No. 505, WSA-O. Notations indicate that a clerk "answered" Greene's letter on July 20, 1887. See also "The Supreme Court," *WS*, July 22, 1887, conveying Harland and reporting that rumors were "floating about the bar" that Greene was "about to file a dissenting opinion in regard to the legality of the female suffrage laws." The language was identical; Greene likely had circulated his letter.

read I totally dissent." Greene promised "in due time" to submit a full opinion,[42] but if he did, it has been lost.

"THE WOMEN ARE POLITICALLY DECAPITATED"

In March, 1887, members of a Los Angeles woman-suffrage club met to consider the implications of *Harland*. They had invited a distinguished Washingtonian to the event. "If the decision against woman suffrage is correct," said the aging, widely revered Benjamin Dennison, "the Territory has had no legitimate legislation since 1883 .... The incoming legislature is not legally elected, and all cases tried before a jury, partially composed of women, are to be set aside." The justices themselves held court "without authority of law. All suits for the collection of debts before juries partly composed of women are usurpations, and all criminals convicted under such conditions are punished unlawfully, and may collect damages. The local option bill is ... a nullity, and all sheriffs, probate judges, and other county officers since 1883 should step down." Washingtonians had stumbled into "a labyrinth of perplexities."[43]

The Los Angeles speech was an abridgment of an earlier, blistering response to *Harland* – a text so long it had to be serialized. Few citizens carried such weight: Here was an ex-chief justice of the territorial Supreme Court (1866–67), university regent, codifier, and framer of the Walla Walla constitution. It was "actually painful," he wrote, "to notice how hard these able and astute Judges labored to overthrow a law, which had been fully considered by two Legislative Assemblies, approved by two Governors, and generally endorsed by the people." Assemblymen had been aided by debate in territorial newspapers. Dennison feared the erosion of other rights secured by statutes with vague titles. Justices had "adroitly ... hurled missiles from different positions"; they claimed, for instance, that only one opinion existed among the "great mass of the people," male and female, about jury duty. Why, after women had been sitting in jury boxes for years, did not this "great mass" demand the removal of such an "imposition"? They also called women "unsuitable and unfit" but offered no proof – and even if true, why should a "*court* ... undertake to deprive them of the elective franchise?" Women should "*prepare to bid farewell to the other rights of citizenship* .... All women who are made qualified *electors* by the act of 1883 are not qualified *grand jurors*."[44]

---

[42] *Harland* v. *Territory*, 162 (Greene's remarks). See also "Chief Justice Greene ...," *OR*, February 5, 1887, for reprint of his official statement. The decision appeared in papers throughout Washington and Oregon; e.g., *OR*, February 4, 1887. The phrases "I totally dissent" and "from all that is decisive" became rallying cries for suffragists.

[43] "Woman Suffrage Club. Opinions on the Washington Territory Decision," *LAT*, March 10, 1887, p. 3.

[44] B[enjamin] F. Dennison, "Those 'Opinions,'" and "Argument Against the 'Opinions,'" *NN*, February 17 and 24, 1887. Installments were reprinted widely.

Nor was it clear that territorial courts could sit lawfully or rely on judicial precedent or election returns. A regard for public policy, wrote *Standard* editors, should have restrained justices from radical extremes. Invalidation of the Code would be a "serious calamity." A San Francisco reporter thought that *Harland* compelled "the vacating of all verdicts of juries upon which women have acted." Local prints circulated lists of statutes with bad titles. William White reminded Turner and Langford that, in re-hearings of *Rosencrantz* and *Harland*, which might be required if courts had convened illegally, they would have to vacate rulings. Greene thought it might be "interesting to see how these same judges will accept the fruits of their former decision."[45]

The chief justice decided to consult broadly. On February 7, 1887, he opened an extraordinary Supreme Court session at Seattle. On cue, White objected to the chief justice's call to order until he could rule on the merits of Langford's opinion. Greene adjourned the Court until 2:00 PM and interrogated virtually the entire King County bar. Hours passed. Attorneys spoke at length as to whether *Harland* reached beyond suffrage (most thought it did not); whether the code was valid (most agreed that it was, if only because it was notorious); and whether justices could undo the productions of an entire government (two thought they could not). Greene offered thanks for courtesy and promptness: "I am very clear in my mind that the act is valid and that it will be upheld by any future Supreme Court of this Territory." The title was indeed defective: Within the "logic of the arguments advanced by the Judges ... in the case of Harlan[d] v. the Territory, this act would be void." A new statute was needed. But *Harland* likely would be narrowed over time; he judged the act to be valid for present purposes and opened the session.[46]

Lawyers generated reams of technical criticism. On February 10, an anonymous "distinguished lawyer" insisted that, while legislators had not passed the code "as a code, with its present numbering of sections," the document had gained "such notoriety that it is as easy to understand what the legislature means when it refers to a section ... by number." A Spokane critic suggested, first, that legislators pass a new election law in acceptable form without jury duty, and, second, that they petition Congress for an act

---

[45] "Legal Complications," *WS*, February 11, 1887, also quoting a Portland newspaper. See also *In Re Rafferty*, 1 Wash 382 (1890), a rape case, citing *Harland* as precedent on the question of titling (failure to mention "rape" in title). The territorial bench had ruled earlier that titles did not have to be perfect to be adequate; *Brown Bros. Co. v. Joe. Forest*, 1 Wash Terr Rpts 199 (1867), 200.

[46] "A Puzzled Court," *SDPI*, February 8, 1887, and, similarly, "A Celebrated Decision," *WS*, February 11, 1887, front page. Duniway concluded, too, that the Supreme Court's sessions might be unauthorized; "Woman Suffrage in W. T.," *NN*, February 10, 1887. Perhaps Delegate Voorhees had been elected illegally and the territory had had "no legitimate legislation since 1883"; "Mrs. Duniway's Letter," ibid. For Greene's letter of thanks to the bar for "courtesy and promptness," see [Greene], "The Decision," *SP*, February 8, 1887.

retroactively approving the law code and its emanations.[47] As of March, 1887, Senator Dolph and Delegate Voorhees were said to be rushing such a bill through Congress; it foundered when some lawmakers feared accidentally validating woman suffrage.[48] A local judge, John McGilvra, accused the justices of sophistry and worse: Every "manly man" who himself deserved to vote would "protest against that privilege being taken from women by judicial legislation or legal legerdemain. Courts as Courts are entitled to the greatest respect," but the "habitual disposal of causes on technical and captious grounds" was contemptible.[49] Attorney Charles F. Munday saw cabalism and arbitrary rule: Had the case emanated from his or Langford's district, the decision would have been the reverse. Legislators should submit the question to the "whole people, women and all, and let it be voted upon without resort to trickery."[50] The *Standard* opened a subscriber debate: "We have a Supreme Court composed of four Judges, any two of whom can on … mere technical grounds, annul laws made by the people …, even those which have been declared sound by the remaining two judges." What did readers think? Should lawmakers "quietly acquiesce in rulings which depend upon mere change [on the bench] for vitality? … Well may such an unfortunate exercise of power be … condemned by the people. The evil wrought is irreparable."[51]

William H. White was undone. Working women would lose a toehold in public life; social peace would be shattered with "endless litigation."

Titles … will be unsettled. As far as the criminal business of the United States is concerned, the decision is disastrous. It will result in setting aside all the indictments against the Chinese conspirators …. I believe in the uttermost enlargement of political

---

[47] Untitled editorial, *PSWA*, February 10, 1887; "A Plain Protest," *SFR*, February 18, 1887, front page. According to the same paper, the declaratory-act proposal failed because Delegate Voorhees offended anti-suffragists in Congressional committee by suggesting they include woman suffrage; "It is now charged …," *SFR*, March 6, 1887. For detail, see "Mr. Voorhees as an Obstructionist," *SFR*, March 17, 1887.

[48] See "A Manly Man," *SP*, March 14, 1887, and "The passage of the Dolph bill …," March 4, 1887, ibid., reporting passage of a bill by the Senate "yesterday." The fate of the bill is unclear.

[49] Hon. John J. McGilvra, "Equal Suffrage. The Elective Franchise and Jury Duty," *SP*, March 11, 1887, front page. In the same vein, see "Vindex," "Equal Suffrage, *SP*, February 15, 1887. On "excitation," see "A Dangerous Power," *TDL*, February 5, 1888. In the same vein (judges had "twice found it necessary during the last year to promulgate their views … in the place of … representatives"), see "Nullifying Laws," ibid., February 1, 1888.

[50] "Sharp Criticism," *PSWA*, February 17, 1887. For a defense, including a defense of the Turner-Langford decision, see editorial, "A [Rotten?] Insinuation," *SDPI*, February 5, 1887. On Munday, see H. James Boswell, *American Blue Book, Western Washington* (Seattle, 1922), p. 144. See also "The Woman Suffrage Issue," *WR*, March 30, 1888, revealing Munday's affiliation (Democrat), title (Deputy U.S. Prosecuting Attorney), and pro-suffrage stance. Orange Jacobs made virtually identical arguments; see Jacobs, "The Legal Status of the Equal Suffrage Question," *SDPI*, February 9, 1887.

[51] "Are They Above Criticism?" *WS*, February 25, 1887. This responded to a screed by Judge Charles H. Ayer, for whom criticism of judges was seditious; Ayer, "A Few Words for the Judges," *WS*, February 11, 1887. See also "Once More to the Breach," ibid., February 25, 1887.

rights. In this territory half-breed Indians and Kanakas can vote. The only class of persons excluded ... are Chinamen, full-blooded Indians and white, intelligent women. ... [L]ike the Tacoma Ledger, I say 'Shame!' ... [T]he plain, homely people of Washington ... are almost without an exception in favor of the law. Against it are the conservatives, who yet believe in the ... Apostle Paul's idea of womanhood, the dudes and dudines and the social people [who] believe that the highest object in life is progressive euchre .... Before the law was tried many of the laboring class were opposed to it, but it has been fully demonstrated in the recent election ... that the mothers, sisters and wives of the laboring men ... stand up for ... the rights of labor.[52]

Angry and saddened, women saw resurgent patriarchy and dishonesty. Activists Helen and Harriet DeVoe decided that Americans were "yet but semi-republican," governed by "a male aristocracy ..., the worst kind of an aristocracy, because it includes the ignorant and vile, ... and excludes talent ... if embodied in a woman's form."[53] Writing from a settlement north of Seattle, "A.M." railed against the suggestion that women had forced themselves into masculine spaces. Many women and men were "dissatisfied and grieved over the disgrace that has befallen our territory .... But we think the greater mistake is in alleging that the women of the Sound have *pushed themselves into the jury*. Surely no one has forgotten the consternation that prevailed among the women when it first became known that ... they could also be required to sit on juries." They "bravely took their places" – only to be sent home.[54]

The chorus included an array of voices. The Democratic, pro-suffrage *Daily Ledger* blasted the two justices' exclusion of contrary opinions. Professor O. S. Jones, the Democratic superintendent of Seattle schools, pronounced political equality "right in principle and policy. ... As for the women sitting as jurors, it is a necessary corollary of suffrage and is all right, though a judge ... can make it very unpleasant for the ladies." At a dinner for bar members, Roger Greene's wife said that she could imagine no reason for "giving men the right to the ballot and to sit on juries which will not equally apply to women." At the same event, Orange Jacobs noted that women paid taxes, and "taxation without representation is tyranny. So our fathers thought, and on this principle they fought the battles of the revolution"; equality was demanded "on the broad ground of right." The Liberal League of Seattle formally published resolutions condemning the "infamous outrage," demanding a special meeting of the Assembly, Congressional affirmation of all laws exactly as passed, and a dressing down of the Supreme Court ("two men dressed in authority, as against the wisdom ... of two other men equally high in authority,

---

[52] "Sharp Criticism," *PSWA*, February 17, 1887. The idea that "white women" ought to be able to vote if Indian men could do so was common; e.g., "Indian Voters," *WR*, November 23, 1888. The titling problem persisted for years. In a rape hearing, e.g., Harland appeared as precedent for a unlawful arrest claim, given the absence of "rape" in the statute's title; *In Re Rafferty*, 1 Wash 382 (1890).

[53] Harriet and Helen DeVoe, "The Suffrage Question," *SDPI*, February 13, 1887 (two letters).

[54] "A. M.," "Woman Suffrage in W. T., A Letter from a Woman on the Subject," *OR*, February 11, 1887. Emphasis added.

upon a mere technical pretense"). They mailed the text to newspaper offices and to President Cleveland. In February, 1887, in response to a Cheney editor's call for a hundred-gun salute to honor Turner and Langford, an *Oregonian* headline read, "This Man Would Seem to be an Ass."[55]

In March, 1887, Seattle suffragists mobilized behind closed doors to re-organize the WERA and adopt a new constitution. They forcibly ejected an anti-suffrage reporter.[56] Everywhere, women took to their pens. Abigail Duniway played into anti-suffragist hands: The "boomerang was thrown, and ... the women are politically decapitated in the recoil." She had warned them "not to make their fire too hot, lest they should cook the ballot yeast." Now, they could only hope to elect good men.[57] Others located blame where it belonged. On February 19, 1887, one activist noted that women, far from wanting to "push themselves into notoriety by sitting on juries," forcing themselves into courthouses or otherwise trespassing, had "simply responded to a call of duty and performed it conscientiously." May Sylvester called women's performance an insurmountable argument for continuance. She especially objected to the notion (set out by another correspondent) that equal suffrage had been an "insult to the manliness of men" and a suggestion that they were "not competent to wield the strong arm of government." Did he really mean to "correct all evils and manage everything"? Would he revise property or divorce laws? What about earlier days when women stood "co-equal with man"? Paternalism might do if all men were manly, but they were not. Women had to take care of themselves with ballots and unions.[58]

---

[55] Editor, "Judge Hoyt ...," *TDL*, January 4, 1888, editorial page; "Prof. O. [S]. Jones," *PSWA*, February 17, 1887, wrongly spelled O. F. Jones (Jones had been the victorious Democratic opponent of Florence Chick in 1884 school elections); and Frederick Bolton, "High Schools in Territorial Washington, Conclusions," *Washington Historical Quarterly*, Vol. 24, No. 4 (October 1933), p. 278. See also "Personal Opinions," *Woman Suffrage Facts and Opinions*, December 1887; "An 'Infamous Outrage,'" *PSWA*, February 10, 1887; "Sentinel," "This Man Would Seem to be an Ass," *OR*, February 6, 1887; reprinted a year later, "The Oregonian ...," *TDL*, January 18, 1888. Additionally, see untitled, *PSWA*, February 17, 1887 (the Court had committed "hari-kari").

[56] "Suffrage Meeting," *SP*, March 4, 1887. See also "Important Meeting," ibid., March 2, 1887 ("closed doors"). For earlier meetings and resolutions, see "Woman Suffrage ...," ibid., February 9, 1887.

[57] Abigail Scott Duniway, "Woman Suffrage in W. T.," *OR*, February 10, 1887; see, in the same vein, Duniway, "The Women May Blame Themselves, *NN*, February 10, 1887 (women had "spurned the counsels of this journal"). See also publication of batches of complaints from Bellingham women; "Disenfranchised," *WR*, February 18, 1887, and "Woman Suffrage," ibid., February 11, 1887, front page.

[58] "An Important Decision," *WS*, February 4, 1887; A Few Words for the Judges," ibid., February 11, 1887; "A Denial of the Soft Impeachment," ibid., February 18, 1887; May Sylvester, "Some Reasons Why Women Should Not Be Deprived of the Ballot," ibid., February 25, 1887. On election and statutory invalidation, see, e.g., "The Effects of the Decision" and "Legal Complications," ibid., February 11, 1887. See also "Women Organizing," repr. Woman's Journal, *WS*, September 16, 1887.

In contrast, anti-suffragists lavishly praised Turner's validation of tradition. In January, 1888, for instance, a Turner disciple argued that *petit* kingship prevented "a divided house, and *one cannot serve two masters.*" Others trusted that the unsavory mess would be swept away in time for statehood. Turner himself kept a trophy – a harsh critique from the *Evening Chronicle* pasted into his scrapbook beside articles about decorous and degenerate women; if the number of clippings is any measure, the latter kind fascinated him. "Some people," the reporter chided, "must be technical or nothing." Spokane journalists claimed to be suffused with a "deep satisfaction" and judged the original laws, "backed by a following of strong minded – to [use] a mild term – women who flocked to Olympia to wheedle the legislators into passing the bill," to be undesirable and unnecessary. "All praise to Judges Turner and Langford."[59] Meanness appeared: The territory, said another well-satisfied pundit, had not been reduced to "barbarism," as suffragists predicted. "Say, give us a rest, won't you? . . . What great reformation is female suffrage going to bring about anyhow? . . . Will their children love them any better for their masculine attainments? . . . If so, then by all means let us have it. If not, let us stop our whining."[60]

Responses to *Harland* left little doubt that mixed juries had been a step too far. As one suffragist put it, "'women on the jury' has been a weapon cunningly and dexterously used" to purge women from politics and sometimes from a living: "[P]oor women, who have been obliged to wash for a living or ply the sewing machine eighteen hours a day find it not only restful to mind and body to serve on the jury, but an honorable and easy avenue" to earn money. When Mrs. M. J. Hayden, an ex-grand juror from Vancouver, gave Turner and Langford a "regular scourging," an anti-suffragist ("Fair Play") charged womanly incompetence. Images of trespass recurred, as did tautologies: Charles Ayer accused women of "push[ing] themselves into notoriety by sitting on juries" as well as into politics. Government was "directly the agent of men." While it protected the "lives, liberty and property of all, the "duty of men in government is doing the work of men."[61] Activists struggled to save what they could. On February 1, 1887, the pro-suffrage *Lewis County Bee* announced that it still supported equal suffrage but did not want jury duty to be "imposed." A Walla Wallan suggested that women be enfranchised but "exempted from jury duty

---

[59] "Invalidated," *WS*, December 9, 1887, and "J.C. No. 9," pseud., "Letters from the People," *WS*, January 20, 1888; "The People," *SDPI*, February 15, 1887; "Technical or Nothing," *Evening Chronicle*, undated clipping, George Turner Collection, Scrapbooks, Vol. 1, p. 45, WSU-SC. Turner organized the scrapbooks and gave them to his wife. See also "The supreme court in session," *SFR*, February 10, 1887.

[60] "J. C. Co9," "The Other Side of the Question," *WS*, March 4, 1887.

[61] Editor quoting correspondent to the *OR* ("W. H. K."), in "A Denial of the Soft Impeachment," *WS*, February 18, 1887; Charles H. Ayer, "A Few Words for the Judges," ibid., February 11, 1887. See also Oregonian essay excerpted in "Fair Play," *WS*, March 18, 1888. For criticisms, see "Fair Play," "Law and Logic," *WS*, March 18, 1887. This writer was sure that Turner and Langford had acted as law required, and that Greene had gone rogue.

and not required to go to war or bear arms"; with statehood, exclusions could be revisited. Olympians vacillated: *Harland* had been a "lightning stroke," the end of an "experimental test"; women rejected citizens' duties. Initially, they had said that equality "had done much to break down the barriers of prejudice" while generating "evils"; later, they praised female voters *and* jurors.[62]

One particularly astute woman perceived that a resurgent, customary constitution had undermined manmade law. On January 7, 1887, as news of *Harland* reached the countryside, Mrs. Alma M. Beach read a composition "gleaned from humble observations" at the Whatcom Literary Union in Bellingham. She used the term enfranchisement in its "broadest, fullest meaning": The ballot was not "the only weapon to free women from servitude and bondage." The problem lay with "custom, society and education" which had "enthralled woman more than she is ready to admit." When a woman could assert "her own convictions of right and wrong . . . , then will her enfranchisement have commenced." Arguments against jury service had been "unanswerable" – not because they were right, but because of deeply embedded prejudices and associated "sophistry." The remedy began at home. Sons had yet to learn that "no labor the mother performs is too menial for their hands." Daughters fussed in mirrors while sons learned a trade. "Wouldn't it be well to so educate the rising young men of today" that "shame might not . . . effeminate their morale" when they worked at home, but rather "prove an index to the tenderness of their hearts and nobility of their souls?" There were "many steps to take, many things to learn, before we enjoy enfranchisement." Washingtonians, in short, would have to remake gender.[63]

"I AM SO INDIGNANT THAT I AM UNCOMFORTABLE"

In February, 1887, thirty-six suffragists met in Seattle to organize an "indignation meeting." One woman averred that, when "that meeting comes off, Judges Turner and Langford had better stand from under, for something is going to drop." Another urged women to storm the polls, to "do as I am going to. When election day comes I'll get my ticket in my hands and march up to the polls and demand the reasons why my vote is refused. These men have stirred up a hornets' nest." Feeling both furious and unladylike, another one said, "I am so indignant that I am uncomfortable." Laura Hall agreed: "I am indignant, and I want a chance to express my indignation. Let us get up a big meeting . . . , and we'll show them how indignant we are. I tell you I am indignant, and I want a big meeting down stairs."[64] Even as the anti-suffrage press pounced on divisions

[62] "Laws Mixed," *LCB*, February 11, 1887; "An Important Decision," *WS*, February 4, 1887, and editorial, ibid., February 25, 1887. For ruling reprint, see "A Celebrated Case," ibid., February 11, 1887, p. 1.

[63] Mrs. Alma M. Beach, "Enfranchisement of Woman," *WR*, January 7, 1887.

[64] "The Woman's Meeting," *SDPI*, February 10, 1887. Instigators included "Mrs. Nettie Wood, Mrs. Kenworthy, Laura Hall, Mrs. W. P. Smith," Florence Chick, and others.

between the WERA and WCTU, a "bigger meeting" convened at the opera house on February 21, 1887, with at least a half-dozen male speakers and a respectable, mixed-sex audience. Charles Munday presided. An irate Orange Jacobs pulled a treatise out of his pocket that examined the woman question from the "time of Eve down to the present," which he handed over to others for reading. "So here, I say, sink or swim, survive or perish. I am ... forever in favor of equal suffrage, because I believe it is right." Other speakers focused on the *Harland* disaster and the curious fact that mixed-sex juries had apparently unhinged George Turner.[65] Bravery appeared in unexpected places. The Seattle board of registration decided in July, 1887, to enroll "800 women, who were registered before the law was declared unconstitutional, and also the names of eight women who had not previously registered" – as the *Post-Intelligencer* put it, in "open and flagrant violation of the law."[66] The clerk then refused to register suffragist Juliet Dawson so that her lawyer might file a writ of mandamus demanding that courts show cause why registration had been refused. On July 1, 1887, Chief Justice Jones ruled that women were not lawful electors and not entitled to register; the clerk removed the names, which inspired additional civil disobedience.[67]

Over time, legislators and even William H. White made the situation worse. In January, 1888, assemblymen entertained a bill (ultimately softened, perhaps to comport with Semple's views)[68] forever prohibiting women from serving on juries – a measure sponsored by White. In the House, he predicted that the bill would "stir the suffragists up lively," but it embodied his most recent views. Among the petitions presented in the House and Council were requests to be relieved of both the suffrage *and* jury service, as with a remonstrance from "thirty-one citizens of Waukiskum County against the granting or imposing on women any further duty than now"; they were "burdened with the care of their households."[69] The WERA had formally protested exclusion from jury duty, insisting that access to juries was protected by the federal constitution. But, in newspaper canvasses, support was tepid at best: "It's all right for women to sit

---

[65] "The Suffragists. Meeting at Frye's Opera House Last Evening," *SDPI*, February 22, 1887.

[66] "In Defiance of Law," *SDPI*, July 10, 1887. For "trickery," see "They Will Not Vote," ibid. As it turned out, the clerk's office had been ordered to purge the women's names, did so, and decided independently to restore them; e.g., "The city clerk of Seattle ...," *WJ*, July 21, 1888, front page.

[67] "Woman Suffrage," *SDPI*, July 2, 1887; "A Change of Program," *SP*, July 5, 1887. See also "The Suffrage Plank," ibid., July 3, 1887.

[68] Semple's opposition to mixed-sex juries coincided with concern about jury corruption. See, e.g., speech, c. 1888, Eugene Semple Papers, Box 14, folder 3, UWSC: "Those who are called respectable people ... persistently neglect their ... duties ... [T]he discrepancy is made up for by bystanders, who are often bad men ... In this way corruption has crept into our courts"; p. 11. Or, at p. 14, "Honorable people will sacrifice convenience, to duty, and cheerfully serve on juries, to the exclusion of these professionals who hang around the Lobbies." He did not see women as a remedy.

[69] "Legislative Schemes," *SDPI*, January 4, 1888, front page. An anti-suffragist from Walla Walla termed this the "only bill" worth supporting if equal suffrage had to be re-enacted; "Some Good Bills," *WWU*, January [4?], 1888. "The Council," *TDL*, January 4, 1888.

on juries," if they want to, but I don't like such politicians' experiments"; "I believe women should vote on school matters, because they pay more attention ... than men, but not sit on juries and fool with politics"; " ... the women who work and who have responsibilities are willing and anxious to make laws and select officers," but not to sit on juries; or, "I am opposed to such things, and do not at all desire to vote or serve as a juror." Both sides knew that, without a mixed-sex public forum, legislation would be "more based upon the same general principles as those of the States of the Union."[70]

More and more, then, sentiments diverged, tugging citizens who had been sitting on fences toward standards of practice elsewhere – if not on suffrage, then surely on jury duty. As early as February, 1887, a few social democrats took White's eventual position, skidding over historic relationships between voting and ancillary rights. At a WERA event, a Republican member of the House in 1885–86 insisted that the Court had not said that women could not vote – only that grand jurors had to be householders. Voting and jury duty were "separate and independent sections" of the code; women should settle for ballots. Others held fast to Greene's views. District Attorney J. T. Ronald praised women's jury service and the elimination of spittoons and wood chips; he also condemned allusions to a "crinoline line," with women on one side and men on the other. Women should "keep cool."[71]

Much depended upon Eugene Semple – a businessman who had accepted Grover Cleveland's offer of a governorship in 1887. Semple was the first Democrat to occupy the statehouse since 1866–67 and would be the last until the fusionist Democrat John Rogers sat briefly in 1897.[72] Turmoil lay ahead: No sooner had he assumed office than anti-Chinese rioting broke out; he then struggled to prevent confrontations between miners and mercenaries at Roslyn and elsewhere.[73] In response to Turner's ruling, the governor unhesitatingly

---

[70] "Territorial Assembly," *SDPI*, January 25, 1888, front page. Presumably the WERA had in mind the 14th amendment. See also "Woman Suffrage," ibid., February 4, 1887 (for the canvass). On "regretted ...," see "Woman Suffrage Act," ibid., February 4, 1888. For letters from men which refer to jury duty as incumbent on suffrage, see "The Suffrage Question," ibid., February 3, 1887.

[71] "The Suffragists. Meeting at Frye's Opera House Last Evening," *SDPI*, February 22, 1887. For much of the same, see "Equal Suffrage. Its Friends Turn Out in Great Numbers," *SP*, February 22, 1887. Organizers are listed in "A Citizens' Suffrage Meeting," ibid., February 17, 1887; all were married, some to prominent lawyers.

[72] On Semple, see Alan Hynding, *The Public Life of Eugene Semple, Promoter and Politician of the Pacific Northwest* (Seattle, WA, 1973), which devotes only a few pages to suffrage and wrongly casts Semple as an anti-suffragist motivated solely by respect for legislators.

[73] On labor unrest, see, e.g., Eugene Semple Papers, Box I, folders 11–18, 1888, UWSC. For a typical account of unrest as the suffrage crisis crested, see "The Labor Question," *SP*, February 9, 1887. On Roslyn, see "The Roslyn Troubles," *SP*, September 7, 1888; or "The Roslyn Outrage," ibid., August 31, 1888. See also "Something about Semple," *SDT*, September 21, 1889, criticizing his response to unrest at Roslyn, and, generally, John Putnam, *Class and Gender Politics in Progressive-Era Seattle* (Reno, NV, 2008). Eugene Semple to Secretary of the Interior, August 31, 1887, Eugene Semple Papers, Acc. No. 174532, Box I-6, UWSC.

rose to women's defense. When a new election law with a proper title finally came up for a vote in mid-January, 1888, Semple, the territorial secretary, and Justices Jones, Turner, Allyn, and Langford visited the Council; during their closed meeting, "a couple of dozen ladies" and "half a hundred men" occupied the lobby. Representative Lewis and allies saved the bill from last-minute hitches (e.g., an attempt to include exemption from jury service in the title).[74] When a Seattle lawmaker suggested a bill to permit any qualified elector of the territory to hold elective or appointive office with "no discrimination ... on account of sex," he lost; but, when WERA representatives formally protested H. R. 189 exempting women from jury duty, they also lost.[75]

Onlookers were said to be almost as numerous as lawmakers; notwithstanding keen interest in railroads, the great contest of the session was said to be woman suffrage. The final bill, introduced by Councilman O. G. White of Columbia County, conferred "the right of suffrage equally upon the sexes, except that it exempts women from jury duty." Opponents (led by Haines of King County whose law firm had led the battle in *Rosencrantz* against mixed-sex grand jurors) used "all obstructive tactics known to parliamentary science." But suffragists had a majority of five; thus, the re-enactment of the woman suffrage law depended only on Semple's signature. Reporters noticed almost at once that the political-rights bundle had unraveled: "Woman suffrage passed the House today [Jan. 16] by a vote of [14?] to 9. It exempts women from jury service."[76] The proposed statute, which carried a precise title, refined alien-voter qualifications, reaffirmed universal suffrage, and warned that no part of the act should be construed as to "make it lawful for women to serve as jurors." In one writer's view, it did not contain a "single feature to which justices can take reasonable exception."[77] Henry Browne Blackwell thought the move comported with women's views. In January, 1888, he noted inaccurately that women in Washington could volunteer to serve on juries, but that he expected most would not; the exemption had been a "concession to the prejudices and interests of many respectable men and

---

[74] E.g., "Law Givers at Olympia," *SDPI*, December 18, 1887; "The Legislature," ibid., December 9, 1887; "Assembly at Olympia," ibid., January 13, 1888; "Disrespectful Methods," January 14, 1888; or "Territorial Assembly," ibid., January 17, 1888, announcing House passage and predicting a veto. For imminent passage, see "From Olympia," *SFR*, January 12, 1888. The Spokane press noted Congressional unwillingness to admit a state with equal suffrage; e.g., "We earnestly believe ...," ibid., January 19, 1888.

[75] "Olympia Notes" and "Laws at Olympia," *TDL*, January 25, 1888.

[76] Untitled, *PSWA*, January 19, 1888, front page. See also "Wednesday, January 11. Council," *WS*, January 13, 1888. For Council, see also "Their Work Is Over," *TDL*, February 3, 1888. See also notice of jury-duty purge, "In the Washington Territory Legislature ...," *WJ*, January 7, 1888, front page; and "By the new law ...," ibid., January 21, 1888, front page ("The women themselves had not asked to be exempted from the duty").

[77] An Act Prescribing the Qualifications of Electors in the Territory of Washington, Acts of the Territory of Washington, January 18, 1888, pp. 93–4; "Woman Suffrage," *CC*, January 21, 1888, editorial page; An Act Prescribing the Qualifications of Electors in the Territory of Washington, Laws of Washington Territory, 1887–88, Ch. 51, p. 94. The act's text was widely reprinted; e.g., "The Woman Suffrage Act," ibid., January 24, 1888.

women." In a new land, "great family inconvenience might attend compulsory jury service by women."[78] Other observers sensed a "very general feeling of willingness to let this law stand," if supported by voters; anti-suffragists had pressed the idea, "used as sheet-iron to terrify timid ones," that sex equality threatened statehood.[79]

Further legislative action was swift. On February 2, 1888, the House and Council adopted an act imposing jury duty on male citizens of the United States above the age of twenty-one years, and all other male inhabitants of the same age, who satisfied residency and loyalty requirements; householders would serve as grand jurors. There followed an overwhelmingly masculine list of exemptions (e.g., "civil and judicial officers ..., attorneys at law, ministers of the gospel or priests, school teachers, practicing physicians, locomotive engineers, active members of the fire department ..., all persons who have served twice as a juror within two years, and all persons over sixty years"). Jury composition could not be challenged after the usual, initial rounds had ended. Separate legislation provided for men on justice-court juries, although "persons" still could vote for justices of the peace.[80] Separately, lawmakers expanded jury pools and the discretionary powers of county boards. Now, commissioners would select from a county's adult population the names of 100 persons to serve as petit jurors and another hundred qualified to serve as grand jurors, conveying the names on separate lists to the clerk. If a board could not locate the requisite number, they could agree to choose a lesser number. Remarkably, a failure on the part of any officer to perform any of the duties required by the act within the stated time would not invalidate the jury pool as drawn. Commissioners therefore could omit undesirables; if anyone demanded a new list, officials could procrastinate until the next term.[81]

Anti-suffragists perceived a serious blow to women's co-sovereignty. The organic act, after all, even as it empowered legislators to govern elections, was not a constitution, as Roger Greene had noted repeatedly. Opponents of sex equality sometimes admitted that, in political affairs, associations between ballots and property had been decisive. But law-making authority perhaps could be re-distributed by social role. "It does not follow," wrote an out-of-state lawyer, "because men and women are equal that they should engage in the

[78] H. B. B., "Women and Jury Duty," *WJ*, January 28, 1888, editorial page. The new bill did not make provision for women to volunteer.

[79] "Editorial Correspondence, Olympia," *PSWA*, January 26, 1888. The lobby crowd was "supremely happy"; "Woman Suffrage," *TDL*, January 12, 1888.

[80] An Act in Relation to Grand and Petit Jurors, Acts of the Territory of Washington, 1887–88, p. 117; An Act to Amend Sections 1770, 1771, 1772, and 1773 ... of the Code ... relating to Trial by Jury of Actions Before Justices of the Peace, and An Act Relating to the Election of Justices of the Peace, Acts of the Territory of Washington, 1887–88, pp. 188–220.

[81] An Act to Amend Section 2080 of Chapter CLH of the Code of Washington Territory ... [and also] Section 2082 ... relating to Grand and Petit Jurors, Acts of the Territory of Washington, 1887–88, pp. 115–16. Emphasis added. For another report with texts, see "The New Jury Laws," *CC*, March 3, 1888.

same pursuit any more than it does that they should therefore adopt the same costume. Of the two . . . one argument is that women holding property in their own name, and taxed for that property, have a natural right to a vote in the legislation which . . . applies that tax. This argument seems to me unanswerable, as far as it goes. Taxpayers surely have a right to their vote." But they could be divided by "function." The *Ledger's* editor was perplexed: How had "natural rights" vested differently in women than in men? Were rights really specific to occupations? If so, was sovereignty somehow differently situated in women than in men?[82] But sentiment varied: Those who denied the fact of investitures in property typically characterized women's political rights as a kind of retractable leasehold; the same New England lawyer viewed suffrage, not as an incident of sovereignty tied to property, but as a grant: "The re-enactment of the woman suffrage law . . . vitally affects the interests of the citizen. Again the women have been given a probationary test of the ballot. If they . . . exercise the right conferred without prejudice, passion, or sectarian dictation," they could retain it; if not, "the *authority conferred* will be of brief nature."[83] Thirty-one unidentified, female tax-payers entirely understood relations between property and sovereignty. In January, 1888, demanded in a petition to the Assembly that, if suffrage was not restored, "one-half of the community property of married persons, all separate property of married women and property owned by unmarried women be exempted from taxation" – a logical outgrowth of the doctrine of "no taxation without representation."[84]

The woman-suffrage bill landed on Eugene Semple's desk on January 20, within a few hours of adoption. Groundwork had been laid. On January 12, 1888, as if to counter the recurring charge of feminine disinterest, Semple had released census figures with commentary: In 1886, 76 percent of qualified men had exercised the privilege and 61 percent of eligible women. Tacomans called the numbers remarkable, given the social practices ("prejudices and habit") that kept many women from the polls.[85] The governor's clerks logged in hundreds, perhaps thousands, of letters and telegrams; legislators similarly were pelted with petitions.[86] For the most part, correspondents did not address obligations. Rather, supporters (including WCTU leaders, members of the WERA, and out-of-state suffrage organizations) warned Semple of fraud at county meetings and rallied around principles of republican constitutionalism.[87] More important,

---

[82] Ibid.

[83] Ibid., and "All's Well That Ends Well," *WS*, February 3, 1888. Emphasis added.

[84] "A petition has been sent . . . ," *TDL*, January 11, 1888, ed. page; see another petition, attributed to Zerelda McCoy and others, making the same constitutional point (" . . . exempt from taxation so long as they are deprived of their right to vote"); "Prefaced with Petitions," ibid., August 16, 1888.

[85] "What the Census Shows," *TDL*, January 12, 1888. See also "More than 13,000 women . . . ," ibid., January 18, 1888.

[86] E. L. Smith to Eugene Semple, January 19, 1888, Semple Papers, file I-18. On passage, see "Woman Suffrage," *TDL*, January 17, 1888, and "The Suffrage Bill Passed [on January 16]," ibid. On hundreds of petitions, see "Olympia Statesmen," *TDL*, January 13, 1888.

[87] E.g., "Woman Suffrage," *WWU*, February 18, 1888; telegram, Mary Tucker, President, and Laura Moore, Secretary, Vermont Woman Suffrage Association, to Eugene Semple, January 18,

the great bulk of Semple's mail urged him to reject the measure as an impediment to statehood and economic development. Bankers and industrialists led the assault – as with Pacific National Bank cashier T. B. Wallace's contention (to offer one example among dozens) that, if the bill became law, it would "retard the growth and prosperity of this territory more than any other one thing."[88] The president of the Tacoma Foundry and Machine Company termed it a "matter of grave concern" that legislators had defied courts. The act expressed the sentiment of a small minority of citizens; a veto would prevent calamity. Gender equality worked serious injury by postponing statehood and deterring capital investment "by men in states where such a measure has never even been agitated." A stationer protested the bill as a Democrat and recent investor in a business; the law unsettled trade and made the territory a "rendezvous for cranks, and all the different isms known to the ... frail of mind."[89]

To be sure, hackneyed strains appeared: One woman warned that, when mothers were associated with "force" and "control," they destroyed boys younger than thirteen, and one banker contended that only undesirable women clamored to be "felt and heard in Politics." Citizens of the anti-suffrage Idaho panhandle referred to jury duty indirectly; grim "duties" would befall wives if every person could "grasp the sword."[90] But the vast majority urged Semple to reject a bill that would retard statehood and "material development." Henry Knapp spoke plainly: Washington needed statehood in order to "enjoy and exercise the full rights and privileges of American citizenship; that capital shall be invited here to build our railroads, to develop our vast resources." Many Congressmen otherwise inclined to support admission would use the law to justify rejection. A veto would secure statehood and satisfy "a large majority" of Clark County women.[91] Objectors also included the Spokane Falls Board of Trade, the *Spokane Falls Review*, the mayor and council of Cheney, and James Odell, chair of the Democratic Central Committee; only one complained that women had not been asked "to share the burdens of citizenship."[92] William Bowman of Alderton observed that partisan

---

1888, Semple Papers, file no. II-12. See also President of the Waitsburg WCTU and 11 other citizens [at least five men], telegram of [January 1888], ibid., file II-10.

[88] Examples are legion; e.g., T. B. Wallace to Eugene Semple, January 18, 1888, file II-12. See also James Sprague, President, Tacoma National Bank, to Eugene Semple, January 18, 1888, file I-19; or Robert Wingate, Tacoma National Bank, marked "Private and Confidential," to Eugene Semple, January 18, 1888, file I-17; all Eugene Semple Papers, WSU-SC.

[89] S. A. Wheelwright to Eugene Semple, January 19, 1888, Semple Papers, file I-18; L. H. Wheeler to Eugene Semple, January 18, 1888, ibid.

[90] "Woman Suffrage," WWU, July 28, 1888; S. B. Pettengill, "The Tacoma," January 18, 1888, Semple Papers, file I-18. See also "They Favor a Vote," TDL, January 19, 1888; "Indignation Unabated," SDPI, January 21, 1888; "Non-Combatants, Not Voters," WWU, June 30, 1888.

[91] "Mr. Knapp on the Suffrage Bill," WS, January 20, 1888. He described himself as "a farmer," when in fact he was an influential force in the Democratic Party.

[92] "Spokane is Angry," SDPI, January 17, 1888; Spokane Falls Board of Trade to D. M. Drumheller, January 18, 1885, Semple Papers, file II-10, including memo from councilman

FIGURE 5.1. Washington's penultimate territorial governor, Eugene Semple (1840–1908), heroically defended legislators' right to shape the electorate; n.d. From the collections of the Washington State Historical Society, Tacoma, WA. Used by permission.

pledges did not go on forever and that jury duty had spoiled the pudding; Washington's "bright, intelligent and virtuous women are not in a condition to discharge the duties devolving upon electors .... *The right of suffrage of necessity carries with it the duty to perform service as jurors*, and no gentleman will ... say

Stine of Spokane Falls; "From Olympia," *SFR*, December 20, 1887 as well as "Friends and advocates ...," ibid., December 31, 1887; and F. A. Pomeroy, Mayor, D. F. Percival, and J. H. Hughes, Cheney, January 19, 1888, Semple Papers, file I-18. See also "Woman Suffrage," *SFR*, January 17, 1888. For burdens, see "The opponents of woman suffrage ...," *SFR*, January 20, 1888, ed. page.

that our wives and daughters are benefited" by courthouse experiences. This was a serious obstacle to statehood: "We have seen that this is no idle fear."[93]

Occasionally, prominent citizens approved, as when a banker praised Semple for resisting hate mail; he had never been a "pronounced woman suffrage man" but saw no reason to oppose the practice. Lawyer Junius Rochester objected, as Greene had done, to changing the "fundamental political structure" without constitutional amendment; suffrage was not a "rightful subject of Legislation," though he did not expressly oppose equality. A few pastors lent support. Rev. G. E. Wilcox of Endicott, quoting Abraham Lincoln, trusted that Semple would rise "in behalf of God and Home" and "make that *Act a law*!" Later, the pastor of Seattle's First Baptist Church advised Semple to plan on attending "several *first class* funerals of ... false prophets" and resist urgent petitions from Spokane. More often, though, entrepreneurs threw darts: As one put it, why not emulate the laws of "old and established states" where elections were no longer an "experiment?"[94]

Chicanery likely was afoot. Denying that they were "agitators & active supporters of woman suffrage," twenty-eight Spokane Falls men rejected assertions that Spokane was overwhelmingly opposed to the measure or that suffrage would prevent annexation of the panhandle.[95] Mrs. E. T. Trimble, wife of the president of Colfax College, warned that efforts were afoot to persuade citizens that a popular majority opposed the law. She had been circulating petitions in eastern Washington and learned that a large majority favored it; a *"very much larger* number of names could have been secured" on a petition circulated at a mass meeting, had there been room. "As women," she said, "we ask this law first, as a matter of justice and secondly, because [legislators] were elected by women as by men with the distinct understanding that ... they would support it." Passions cut across gender lines: Walla Wallans submitted a "petition as long as a rail fence"; in Seattle, a deluge originated with "certain male woman suffragists."[96]

[93] W. J. Bowman, Alderton, W. T., to the Honorable J. Stewart, House of Representatives, January 2, 1888, Semple Papers, file II-13. Emphasis added.

[94] J. C. Weatherred to Eugene Semple, January 26, 1888, file II-13; L. W. [illegible] to J. P. Stewart, House of Representatives, January 4, 1888, file II-13; telegram, Junius Rochester to Eugene Semple, January 16, 188[8], file I-18; Rev. G. E. Wilcox to Eugene Semple, January 20, 1888, file I-18; D. J. Pierce, Pastor, First Baptist Church of Seattle to Governor Semple, January 19, 1888, file I-18; all Semple Papers. References recur in public prints to the practices of other states and Washington's incompatibility; see, e.g., editorial, *SDPI*, February 2, 1887, p. 2 (" ... it exists here alone and is foreign to the institutions of every State in the Union"). For denunciations of his decision as a threat to business and statehood, see "Council and House," SDPI, January 20, 1888. Democrats accused Semple of betrayal; see, e.g., "Territorial Assembly," January 31, 1888.

[95] Telegram from W. D. Turner et al., Spokane Falls, to Eugene Semple, January 17, 1888, Semple Papers, file II-18. Spokane journalists insisted that signatories had been flattered into signing; e.g., "A strong effort will be made ...," SFR, December 2, 1887.

[96] Mrs. E. T. Trimble, Colfax College, Colfax, January 19, 1888, to Governor Semple, Semple Papers, file No. II-12. Emphasis in original. See also "Woman Suffrage," *SDPI*, December 20, 1887 (on Walla Walla); "Woman Suffrage," ibid., January 6, 1888.

Despite Spokane-area suggestions that approval would compromise his "manliness," Semple signed the equal-suffrage bill within days of transmission.[97] While Duniway rightly said that he had been a moderate suffragist from the beginning, he also believed that a short-timer should defer to legislators.[98] Later, he was "fiercely abused" and threatened. The *Woman's Journal* staff urged readers to reward his selflessness.[99] Accolades poured in. The *Lewis County Bee* printed the names of those responsible for victory – four Democrats, four Republicans, and assorted others; a "strange feature" of the bill was that "the most active lobbyist against the bill were Republicans, while the most active lobbyists for the bill are Democrats." Seattle's L. W. Redmond credited Semple with helping to "break the backbone" of Republicanism; he would be "enshrined" on a *"roll of honor"* with others who had made America "the Home of the Free."[100] But Semple's fate was sealed: Benjamin Harrison appointed a placeholder, Walla Walla merchant Miles Conway Moore, until the state's first elected governor could be installed.[101] Democrats grudgingly put

[97] "All honor to Councilman Lewis . . . ," *SFR*, January 18, 1888. A Whatcom newspaper wrongly thought that Semple opposed all aspects of political equality; "Let the Women Rejoice," *WR*, January 13, 1888. For the title ploy, see "From Olympia," *SFR*, January 17, 1888.

[98] "Ill Founded Fears," *TDL*, January 20, 1888. See also Duniway, "More News from Washington Territory," *WJ*, February 4, 1888. For signing, see "The Bill Signed," ibid., January 19, 1888, or "Latest from Olympia," *WR*, January 20, 1888. For denunciations of his decision as a threat to business and statehood, and also suggestions of bribery or undue influence, see "Council and House," SDPI, January 20, 1888. For additional accusations of partisan betrayal, see "Territorial Assembly," January 31, 1888. For Council approval, see "The Suffrage Bill," ibid., January 12, 1888. The Whatcom newspaper wrongly thought that Semple opposed all aspects of political equality; "Let the Women Rejoice," *WR*, January 13, 1888. For the title ploy, see "From Olympia," *SFR*, January 17, 1888.

[99] "Washington Territory Notes," *WJ*, February 11, 1888. In the same vein, see Abigail Duniway, "Latest News from Washington Territory," ibid. For publication of the act, see "The following is the text . . . ," ibid., February 18, 1888.

[100] "Special to the Bee, January 18, 1888," *LCB*, January 20, 1888. Republicans opposed to the bill included Stewart, T. Clark, Hume, and Reed; Democrats in favor, Elder, Stevenson, Baker and Keane. See also L. W. Redmond to Governor Eugene Semple, January 19, 1888, Semple Papers, file I-18. On struggles with mining companies and mercenaries, see, e.g., Eugene Semple to U.S. Attorney, Washington, DC, and H. W. McNeill, Oregon Improvement Company, January 24 and February 11, 1889, Semple Papers, files I-17 and I-18, UWSC.

[101] Semple had tried to make good on his promise to be "a servant of the sovereign people"; clipping, Inauguration of Governor Semple, in *Papers of Grover Cleveland*, with letter of April 30, 1887, Microfilm Edition, Series 2, Reel 48. For one printing, see "The New Governor," *SFR*, April 24, 1887. For criticism, see "Gov. Semple," *SFR*, July 20, 1889 ("As governor he wrote reports . . . clothed in correct English, but containing nothing new or startling. His first official act of importance was the hasty approval of the bill to confer the ballot on women, an act performed in spite of the united protests of the Democracy and the earnest protest of many Republicans.") Before leaving office, Semple thanked dozens of people in Spokane Falls, Vancouver, Indiana, Pennsylvania, New York, and other locations for support during the suffrage crisis; Semple Papers, files I-6, I-9, I-10, I-14, I-16, UWSC, all dated March and April, 1888. For praise of Semple for doing the "right thing," see "The Suffrage Act," *WS*, editorial page, January 20, 1888.

Semple on the ticket again in 1888; when Elisha Ferry won the race, Semple returned to business, where he experienced unremitting disappointment.

"WE WILL TAKE YOU BY THE THROAT": THE CASE OF NEVADA BLOOMER

Washingtonians and members of the United States Senate had been watching one another closely since at least 1884. As statehood campaigning intensified, scrutiny increased: Washington would be the first territory to apply for statehood with an experienced, mixed-sex polity, as well as the first territory to permit men and women to vote in statehood-related elections. The standoff over jury duty and suffrage, combined with labor and anti-Asian violence, introduced additional complications. But all else was in order: The territory had more than fulfilled population and resource requirements.[102] Given the common-law rule by which uncontested usage implied consent and investiture, Congress's failure to challenge electoral practices aided women's cause, as did Democrats' traditional regard for "home rule." The question, then, was how to surmount a reputation for radicalism, instability, and violence. Warnings abounded. At Christmas, 1885, for instance, a Californian advised the people of Washington and Dakota not to give ammunition to enemies; on the eve of an 1886 local option election, a Seattle writer begged neighbors to "not attempt too many things at a time," lest reformism collapse in a heap.[103]

In early 1886, alarm and confusion increased. The boost that Republicans expected from women after admission did not comport with the election of a Democratic governor, with Democratic' (and fusionist) support for suffrage when stripped of jury duty, or with Congressional delegate Voorhees' ongoing, heroic defense of women's equality.[104] Voorhees' statehood petitions also collided with Sixteenth-Amendment efforts. As Susan B. Anthony told Elizabeth Boynton Harbert, "Our friends in the U.S. Senate think it best to let our 16th am't resolution wait – until after the House has acted on the Washington Territory Bill ... lest the full discussion and vote might wake up the enemy to combine against the admission of Washington into the Union!! because of its *women's* holding the ballot!! – There may be force in the plan – but I see no ... better way than to let our champions on whom we must depend

---

[102] Population figures were widely publicized; e.g., "Washington Territory," *WS*, October 9, 1885, when requirements had been surpassed.

[103] "The State of Washington," rep. San Francisco Chronicle, *SDPI*, December 24, 1885. See also "W," "Prohibition in Seattle," *SDPI*, May 29, 1886.

[104] On assumptions and confusion, see, e.g., "The Movement for Admission," *SDPI*, December 2, 1887 ("The attitude of the Democratic Party" could prevent admission); or "Admission of the Territories," ibid., November 14, 1888. A well-publicized letter from Alexander Montgomery, a member of the King County Democratic central committee, to Senator Daniel Voorhees of Indiana, accused the latter of betrayal: In his anxiety to advance the interests of his son, Charles, he had harmed Democrats; see Montgomery, "Treachery to the People," *SR*, April 22, 1886. This letter has been cited to prove that partisanship alone guided statehood decisions.

for action – work in their own way & time."[105] Washingtonians complained incessantly of tyranny and emasculation. Surely the founders had not instructed Congress to govern "populous and wealthy communities in so crude and degrading a manner." Territorial governments had been created for "wild and unsettled districts" but had come to serve the interests of tyrants – among them, railroad magnates. Olympians railed against weak-minded men whose capacity for good judgment had been compromised: "Are the people not supreme? Is not their will law? In theory the proposition is admitted; in practice rejected. . . . Free government can only be assured when the condition exists."[106]

In the Senate, old associations between, on one hand, Democrats and state rights, and on the other hand, Republicans and federal energy, gradually reversed. Following exhaustive debate of possible admission-bill combinations, Louisiana's Democratic Senator James Biddle Eustis proposed amending the third section of Washington's draft constitution with the word "male" to ensure qualified electors in the ratification canvass. He also warned the "woman-suffrage Senators" that he intended to make admission hinge on a convention composed entirely of male delegates. Massachusetts Senator George Hoar accused Eustis of attacking the principle of self-government and state's rights. Eustis did not disagree: He intended to prevent Congress from sanctioning woman suffrage. Senator Dolph, after all, had said that, with Washington's entry, Americans would "witness the spectacle of a State government founded in accordance with the principles of equality, and have a State at last with a truly republican form of government." Dolph, in turn, wondered why Eustis had abandoned home rule in Washington's case: Surely every community could be entrusted with shaping the electorate. True enough, said Eustis. But there had been no instance in American history where Congress, simply by accepting local criteria for the electorate, had embraced sex equality. Why not hold the line?[107]

A remarkable tennis match ensued. Hoar insisted that the right to vote formed an "essential and fundamental principle of State rights"; he was shocked that a southerner would think otherwise. How could any senator reject a measure if a state or territory freely and fairly chose to recognize "the power of women to vote on equal terms with men?" Congress had not contested Washington's decision in 1883 or thereafter; political rights now were vested. Eustis asked Hoar to say why he found it "harsh" that Washington should "conform to the constitution of every State" and the "theory of the Federal Government." Hoar replied that he merely recognized a community's right to

[105] Susan B. Anthony to Elizabeth Boynton Harbert, June 3, 1886, in Ann D. Gordon, ed., *Selected Papers of Elizabeth Cady Stanton and Susan B. Anthony*, Vol. IV (New Brunswick, NJ, 2006), pp. 506–7. Incorrect syntax in the original.

[106] "The Struggle for Admission," *SDPI*, January 22, 1886; "Public Service and Private Labor," *WS*, August 27, 1886.

[107] Congressional Record, Senate, 49th Congress, 1st session, April 8, 1886, p. 3259. Eustis noted that this would be the "first time in the history of this Government that the Congress . . . has ever been called upon to give its legislative sanction to woman suffrage"; he aimed to "call the attention of the Senate to the importance of this question."

determine voter qualifications for themselves; if states added a property qualification or "a qualification of sex or ... no distinction of sex, it is their affair." Eustis raised the specter of a female senator; Dolph characterized the exchange as a contest between liberty and oppression. Race entered the conversation. Democratic Senator James Beck of Kentucky averred that, while he supported economic equality, he was not prepared in Washington or anywhere else to confer equal suffrage. Given the Fifteenth Amendment, sex neutrality would enfranchise the most intelligent woman in America alongside "the most ignorant colored woman." Best to entrust public affairs to men schooled in public affairs and not invite corruption or destabilization. In response to Eustis' proposals, Senator Platt argued that senators had to defend "the idea of civil liberty" unless a territory did something inconsistent with principles of republican government; he therefore could not object to woman suffrage. Vermont's George Edmunds, author of anti-polygamy legislation, argued that black women were beside the point; southerners aimed to destroy the bill for partisan reasons. When Eustis denied such a purpose, Edmunds asked, "Now what is the point?" Washingtonians had chosen, under the authority of the organic act, to enfranchise both sexes. Women formed part of the sovereignty, yet were not permitted to speak on the substance of a constitution. This was a simple case of a well-regulated territory where "everybody is free," and where people had decided lawfully that women should vote; he was "glad they have it if they like, because it is their affair."[108]

The question of vested rights triggered bedlam: Constitutional principle militated against the confiscation of rights long exercised without challenge. On April 9, Senator Butler announced that he was going to vote against Eustis' amendment even though he was opposed to woman suffrage: "The right of the women of Washington Territory to vote has been in existence for about three years. Congress has certainly acquiesced in the exercise of the right. ... [T]he people of that Territory have the power to regulate those matters for themselves, I shall vote against the amendment. It is their affair and not mine." James Beck hurled insults: Congress had a duty to supervise backwoodsmen. Great care should be exercised in framing a constitution for a new state about to be inhabited by people from every state in the union. He did not think that "the people who first happen to go to a Territory ... should be regarded absolutely as the only persons who are entitled to frame the fundamental law ... for all time to come." As evidence of ineptitude, he recited the election law of 1883, which seemed to permit "a squad of Chinamen" to vote. Citizens had a right to the best available government.[109]

Debate narrowed, as before the Civil War, to the question of whether the organic act of 1853 was merely a statute by which Congress granted authority

---

[108] Congressional Record, Senate, 49th Congress, 1st session, 1886, pp. 3261–2, 3315–16.
[109] Ibid., pp. 3314–16.

to a territorial assembly to establish a government and regulate local elections, reserving all other decisions for Congress, or whether the act had constitutional properties, vesting lawmakers with power to depart from Congress' intentions, call a convention, and ratify whatever eventuated. Colorado Republican Henry Teller announced that no-one in Washington, male or female, had a legal or constitutional right to vote for delegates to a convention; his colleagues could not disfranchise territorial women because they had no legal right in the first place. Said John T. Morgan of Alabama, "A voter is an office-holder. He is a man who, in virtue of the fact of his being a person qualified ... to vote, holds in trust the power to choose persons to office." Only one householder governed. Some men "may desire to abandon their manhood and take up the functions of the female sex. Let them do it .... When God made me a man, he ... made it my duty ... to take care of those who might be dependent upon me." It was unnatural to place "the instrument of man's power" in women's hands: "Think of a stump-speaking woman!"[110]

For days, senators beat dead horses. South Carolina's Matthew Butler took issue with Eustis' empowerment of Congress at the expense of states and territories. While the people of Washington were in their "state of Territorial pupilage ...., it was quite innocent for them to indulge in cranky notions, in isms, as to mere municipal regulations ... yet when you come to the exercise of the highest right of sovereignty, ... then Congress is to come in and say, 'We will discipline you.'" It was unseemly to say, "Although we have acquiesced in these cranky notions and isms ... for three years, now that you are going to prepare ..'. for Statehood ... we will take you by the throat and say you shall only do it upon certain conditions." Butler opposed woman suffrage but thought that he could imagine a "greater calamity to social order" than conferring of the right of suffrage on American mothers. Eustis replied that the institutions of the country had been entrusted to male voters. Said Butler, a state could impose "just such qualifications as she pleases upon her voters, provided she does not discriminate on account of race or color." Washington boasted an immense acreage and a population sufficient for a member of Congress. Why interfere with people newly emerging from a "condition of dependence" and hamper them in the exercise of "sovereign rights"?[111]

Daniel Voorhees, no doubt in support of son Charles' efforts as Washington's House delegate, also pointed to an unseemly dependence. Washington was "laying off her pupilage ... and putting on her garb as a State .... [T]o raise such an issue at this time is sticking in the bark."[112] Wilkinson Call of Florida agreed: Congress had nothing to do with local suffrage practices, any more than they had established polygamy in Utah. Morgan tried a scare tactic. "It is hasty and unwise legislation," he said, to

---

[110] Ibid., pp. 3317, 3325. [111] Ibid., p. 3320.
[112] Ibid. The idea of "probation" had been internalized, as when Abigail Duniway reminded women to heed their "probation" and not squander it with foolish associations (the WCTU); "Mrs. Duniway's Letter," *NN*, February 10, 1887.

bring Washington into the "brotherhood of States until Congress shall have had an opportunity of passing upon the Constitution. ... Lay your precedent down here and wait perhaps twenty or thirty years .... Let polygamy run riot in Utah Territory." One day, Mormon patriarchs would approach the Senate with a mixed-sex electorate and demand the same concession that Washington Territory enjoyed.[113]

Democrats had been torn between a defense of home rule and aversions to woman suffrage (and the consequent enfranchisement of black women), which required a defense of Congressional power. In May, 1886, senators finally declared an impasse, tabling statehood petitions as well as the Sixteenth Amendment. But, in the end, Eustis emerged as the architect of Turner's legal strategy. In response to Edmund's persistent questioning (did not women have the right in Washington to vote "for anything that a male has?") and relying on some of Butler's language, Eustis laid out constitutional objections: Women indeed enjoyed perfect legal equality with men in most transactions. He contended instead that neither men nor women in Washington had "to-day the legal or constitutional right to vote at all for the purposes of this bill." They claimed only the rights that Congress had conferred in the organic act decades earlier, which had not included the right to frame a constitution. It came to "the source of power, which is Congress": That body had to ratify the act before it had the "slightest legal or constitutional validity." Because there was no vested right in any citizen, male or female, to vote on statehood, a vote against what came to be called the Eustis Amendment was a vote to directly confer woman suffrage; the people of Washington could not confer it upon themselves.[114]

An exchange ensued between Butler and Eustis, the former contending that women already had a vested right to vote, the latter that manhood suffrage alone passed constitutional muster and that experimentation necessarily ceased when a territory petitioned for statehood. In Eustis's view, the masculinity of the bodies called to create and ratify state constitutions had been fixed in 1853: When Congress approved the organization of a territory, it had "limited the right of suffrage to male citizens, as it provided that 'every male citizen above the age of twenty-one,' &c., shall have the right to vote for members of the Legislature at the first election. Why should my proposition be so monstrous and outrageous when the Congress ... has declared by a law which stands unrepealed and applies to every Territory, that when that Territory shall be organized it shall be organized only by male citizens?"[115] After further

---

[113] Congressional Record, Senate, 49th Congress, 1st session, 1886, pp. 3321–23.

[114] Ibid., pp. 3325–6. Rebecca Mead briefly attributes southern Democratic opposition to fear of black women's enfranchisement. But it is possible that Eustis meant what he said: He deplored the weakening of male headship. See Rebecca Mead, *How the Vote Was Won: Woman Suffrage in the Western United States* (New York, 2004), pp. 47–9. "No Free Coinage," *TDL*, April 9, 1886; "During the discussion ...," *SR*, March 15, 1886. Newspapers charted the amendment's progress; e.g., "Woman Suffrage" and "The Woman Suffrage Question," *TDL*, May 7, 1886, p. 1; "Admission of Washington Territory," ibid., January 26, 1886.

[115] Congressional Record, Senate, 49th Congress, 1st session, 1886, pp. 3317–18.

contestation, Eustis lost patience: When a territory became a state, it indeed had the power to confer the right of suffrage on whoever it pleased. A state might "confer it upon men; it may confer it upon women, and … if it chooses, upon Chinese, upon Indians."

Now, what is the theory of the law? It is that so far as any exertion of power by Congress is concerned, even at the time of the organization of a Territory, the right of suffrage shall be limited to Male citizens alone. But Congress tells the inhabitants of a Territory, 'If you choose to indulge in any isms; if you choose to indulge in any idiosyncrasies; if you choose to indulge in any cranky notions, so far as your municipal and domestic government is concerned, we will permit you to do it, and you may enjoy it as much as you please'; … Congress has no interest whatsoever in interfering with any of the cranky notions which may find room and spread in any Territory …. But when the people of a Territory come before Congress to exercise its legislative power, then upon Congress rests the responsibility whether it will approve … whatever passing craze may affect that Territorial population …. [It] is because I believe that true Democracy means manhood suffrage in this country that I am opposed to woman suffrage. … [T]hose who framed this system of government never contemplated … that the secure foundations upon which they have rested for a hundred years of manhood suffrage should be changed to the shifting foundations of … mixed suffrage …. That view finds support … as late as the fourteenth amendment.[116]

On April 9, Eustis warned that, to preserve social relations and public order, his influence would be exerted to retain the institutions of government "such as they are." It was "wise and prudent and statesmanlike" to protect the original constitutional design, fending off "any dangerous experiment."[117]

A day later, the bill authorizing Washington to apply for statehood passed without amendments. But the absence of a clear Senate majority for admission with equal suffrage suggested that, to avoid delay or rejection, Washingtonians would have to consider the odds and choose accordingly.[118] On February 21, 1887, Dolph informed the governor of Senate developments; he was sure that the report of the majority of the Committee on Territories, which supported woman suffrage, would neutralize objections.[119] At the same time, Dolph was lobbying for the Sixteenth Amendment. Local journalists published debates in full, including a February 3 discussion of jury duty and lactation. Significantly, Dolph had moved Washington's application forward partly by distinguishing, in the case of sex, between rights and obligations. Jury duty loomed large. "The stage of ridicule of the movement," he began hopefully, "was past"; women

---

[116] Ibid., p. 3318.
[117] Ibid., p. 3319. James Biddle Eustis (1834–99) graduated from Harvard Law School in 1854. He served as judge-advocate during the Civil War in the Confederate Army and as a Louisiana legislator in both houses until 1873, when he filled a vacancy in the U.S. Senate occasioned by that body's refusal to seat secessionists. He was a professor of civil law at University of Louisiana until 1884, when he returned to the Senate.
[118] Congressional Record, Senate, 49th Congress, 1st session, 1886, pp. 3351–2.
[119] Senator J. Dolph to Governor Watson Squire, February 21, 1887, Watson Squire Papers, file I-1, UWSC.

would secure an equal voice in government with or without a federal amendment. Eustis asked Dolph whether he believed "if woman had the right of suffrage, she also ought to be required to serve on juries"; Dolph thought that jury duty need not follow. But in Washington, female voters also "served on juries and to the great satisfaction of the judges and lawyers." Was jury duty detachable? Turner had not thought so, nor did Eustis, who insisted that "under all the state laws those duties were considered correlative." He also condemned undue familiarity with women. Was it a "decent spectacle to take mother from her nursing infant and keep her up all night sitting on a jury?" Dolph was certain that such a woman could be excused. The motion to permit equal suffrage failed, 16 to 34.[120]

Political agendas in Congress and in Washington Territory, then, were not identical, but they were bound together. In the nation's capital, the main bone of contention had been suffrage itself and Congress' power to limit territorial governments; in the territory, unease over women's political obligations, combined with social distress in many forms, had inspired efforts to get at the taproots. As one anti-suffragist put it, co-sovereign women tended to "disturb ... public sentiment, engender animosities and create needless strife."[121] George Turner agreed. To eliminate threats to statehood and to masculine command, Turner needed to placate members of Congress who perceived radicalism, a swarm of white and black women at the polls, and an assault on reliable juries. Turner also had to deal with women's claims to civil equality and agency with property, upon which bedrock equality had been erected, and legislative and gubernatorial responses to *Harland* – although the decision to eliminate jury duty probably played into Turner's hand by seeming to concede ineligibility and severability. Hence, Turner shifted his focus to a broad reading of Congress' authority and a historicist reading of the organic act. Here was an Alabaman, in league with a Louisiana Democrat, planning to argue that the Congress, having decided against electoral democratization in 1852–53, had imposed permanent limits on legislators' ability to deviate from a government of men as it moved toward statehood.

In Washington, rumors circulated about a new plot to unhinge equality on the ground that "a woman is not a citizen within the meaning of the organic act." The prospect gave pause: "If a woman is not a citizen, what is she?"[122] As it turned out, an appeal was moving toward Olympia from the newly appointed, anti-suffrage Justice Lucius B. Nash's Fourth District in eastern Washington – George Turner's old district – with the purpose of razing the foundations of mixed-sex jury service.[123] If co-sovereignty and its emanations

---

[120] For local circulation, see, e.g., *Port Townsend Weekly Argus*, "In the U.S. Senate," February 3, 1887. For broader circulation, see "Woman Suffrage," *LAT*, January 26, 1887, p. 4.

[121] "Still Harping," *WS*, December 30, 1887.   [122] "Not Becoming," *TDL*, January 21, 1888.

[123] For biographical information, see "Associate Justice Nash," *SDPI*, February 29, 1888, front page. A judge advocate during the war, Nash had been associated with Vice President Garland in an Arkansas law firm before moving to Washington in about 1873 to establish law practices

triggered unrest in courtrooms, jeopardized social peace, and blocked statehood, judges would put an end to it.

During city elections of April, 1888, Nevada Bloomer, a Spokane Falls woman married to a dance-hall owner, had persuaded election judges to reject her ballot in order to force a test of re-titled election laws. Witnesses (among them, Henry Browne Blackwell) claimed that other women at the same poll voted without impediment. Bloomer charged Todd with "fraudulently, maliciously, and without sufficient cause, and with intent to injure her, refusing to receive her ballot" and claimed 5,000 dollars in damages. As a female citizen of the United States of sufficient age, a resident, and a qualified elector, she had been barred from the polls unlawfully.[124]

Nash played along, foregoing a written opinion while implying some knowledge of the Butler-Eustis positions: "[A]s the decision will probably be reviewed by a higher court, I will only say ... that the federal congress, in legislation on the question of the Territories, and in granting the right to them in the organic act to confer suffrage, had all the time in view males only, and has at all times ... excluded females from occupying and holding office." This was the "all controlling point in the case." In a stunning display of illogic, he examined Lelia Robinson's case and Roger Taney's decision in *Dred Scott*:

A similar principle has been decided in Massachusetts ... on the question of the admission of women to practice law. They are ... citizens, but not contemplated as such by the law when made conferring the right upon citizens to practice law. So, also, in the Dread Scott decision. Scott was a native-born American, but the Supreme Court ... held that he was not a man within the meaning of the constitution of the United States. ... All the legislation of congress on the subject of suffrage refers to males only, and excludes females. ... [T]he most fanatical advocate of woman suffrage ... is forced to admit that congress now and always has been opposed to woman suffrage.[125]

Anti-suffragists waited impatiently. Surely the Supreme Court would affirm Nash's decision, and if they did not, an appeal to the U.S. Supreme Court would ensure the result. Women's defenders were outraged. At stake was a community's right to its own law as well as women's right to ballots and jury

in Walla Walla, Seattle, and Spokane Falls, where George Turner also practiced. On his resignation, see "Judge Nash Resigns," *BBR*, April 12, 1889.

[124] "The Women Again in Tribulation," *WS*, May 25, 1888.

[125] Ibid., "Women Cannot Vote," *TDL*, May 24, 1888; or "Woman Suffrage, Judge Nash's Weak Decision ...," *WR*, June 1, 1888. See also "Public Opinion," ibid., June 1, 1888, characterizing Nash as "more of an old fogy than Langford" and registering disgust at Dred Scott references in decisions about citizens. Women apparently could not be disfranchised because a black man once was viewed "as a horse or a bale of cotton." See also "Women Disfranchised," ibid., May 25, 1888 ("This is the second time that the courts ... have set aside the wishes of our people.") Henry Blackwell blasted the analogy; "Woman Suffrage Constitutional," *SP*, July 20, 1888 ("Judge Taney did not decide that women were not citizens," only that blacks could not be; he trusted that Nash did not mean to enslave women). See also "Emerson and Hunter vs. Nash," ibid., July 18, 1888. For *Dred Scott v. Sandford*, 60 U.S. 393 (1857). See also "The Last Infamous Decision," *TDL*, May 26, 1888, or "Opinions about Nash," ibid., May 29, 1888.

duty; Nash and his allies intended to "limit and narrow the construction placed upon the organic act by the people of the territory through their representatives." When anti-suffragists again alluded to women's absence in militias, suffragists cried foul. Woman had "from time immemorial rendered substantial aid in the enforcement of law." They had carried swords and muskets, commanded armies, and "contributed service quite as essential to the successful prosecution of war as marching and fighting." As a Tacoman put it, paraphrasing an argument made in Virginia and Francis Minor's brief in *Minor* v. *Happersett*, "Voting is not simply putting a piece of paper in a box. Nor is it merely the privilege of standing up to be counted when a choice of sheriff or county clerk is to be made. The suffrage is the right to a voice in the making of the laws under which we live ... *The ballot is but one means through which that voice finds expression.*" Dayton journalists hoped that the appeal might move slowly. As it stood, women were disfranchised only in the Fourth District; if Bloomer succeeded, all territorial women would be barred from November elections, particularly if a federal appeal was docketed and then postponed.[126] Benjamin Dennison called the ruling a "fine specimen of judicial imbecility and nonsense." Alice Blackwell assailed the Dred Scott comparison: In what sense were women like slaves? Taney's ruling was kindred only in the sense that it was "so flagrantly contrary to justice and common sense as to have passed into a by-word." Did Nash really want to be compared to Roger Taney?[127]

Dozens of women registered to vote in municipal and school elections in mid-1888; in Tacoma, a large number of women came to the polls "without escorts, depositing their ballots and going away as quietly as if returning from church."[128] Some years later, Alice Stone Blackwell showed that, in the aftermath of Semple's generous and selfless act, as many as five-sixths of eligible female voters in western Washington turned out to vote in local elections. Some of them likely had been inspired by *Bloomer*'s probable effect on a school-election law of 1877. If *Harland* had "clogged the business of the courts and annulled a large number of laws," said one angry

---

[126] "Judge Nash's Reasons," *TDL*, May 25, 1888, editorial page; "They Do Their Share," ibid., June 23, 1888; "Suffrage a Natural Right," ibid., June 17, 1888; "Judge Nash," and "Several exchanges have published ...," *CC*, June 9, 1888, editorial page. See also "Woman Suffrage," *SR*, June 28, 1888. An "early hearing," he hoped, would "settle the whole question." Emphasis added.

[127] A. S. B., "The Case in Washington Territory," *WJ*, June 9, 1888, p. 182, reprinting the Nash non-opinion. See also "Judge Nash's unlikely comparison ...," ibid., June 16, 1888, front page, and Abigail Scott Duniway, "About Washington Territory," ibid., June 23, 1888.

[128] "Last Day of Registration," *TDL*, April 20, 1888. Ordinances had not been changed to purge women; e.g., "Voters Registering," ibid., April 11, 1888. Journalists thought that women held the balance of power in Tacoma; e.g., "Organized to Protect Their Rights," ibid. The same paper noted that eight women registered with "proud satisfaction," "Registration of Voters," ibid., March 28, 1888. See also, e.g., "City Election," *CC*, July 14, 1888; "Seven Republicans," *TDL*, May 2, 1888, p. 4.

citizen, *Bloomer* weakened schools merely to satisfy a desire to defeat equal suffrage at any cost.[129]

Roger Greene was distraught: Nash's half-baked opinion was an "erroneous ... assertion of Salic law." Anglo-American history belied the "false idea that the exercise of sovereign power by females is a new thing to the people who rule America." But suffragists complained most bitterly about the fact of a cabal. "All parties to the case are strongly opposed to the law," wrote a Daytonian, "and have conspired for the sole purpose of defeating it, by fair means or foul; there is no danger of any objection being interposed to a hearing in July. Indeed, that is part of the program." The matter had been "so planned as to shut out all friends of equal rights." For Benjamin Brown, judges and Senators alike exhibited an appalling ignorance of law; property in rights could be protected and regulated but not created by legislation. National figures said much the same thing. The error originated with "half-fledged jurists" who thought that regulating the polls was tantamount to creating rights in the first instance. Nash admitted that women were property-bearing citizens, yet denied their sovereignty.[130]

On August 14, 1888, the Supreme Court finally confronted the *Bloomer* appeal, which had been docketed with preternatural speed.[131] Ex-judge George Turner, with two other lawyers, represented several election officials including John A. Todd, a Spokane Falls IRS agent involved in campaigns to annex the anti-suffrage Idaho panhandle before statehood.[132] In 1910, after woman suffrage finally had been restored, the *Seattle Star*'s editor revealed that Turner had resigned from the bench expressly to eliminate the practice.[133] In *Bloomer* v. *Todd* (1888), William Murray – Bloomer's attorney and a

[129] See Alice Stone Blackwell's account of women's territorial experiences in a leaflet distributed by the Woman's Journal in c. 1909; "The Case of Washington," Equal Suffrage Leaflet, Emma Smith DeVoe Papers, Box 4, Folder 54, WSHS. She also touted women's excellence as jurors. See also editorial, *SP*, August 30, 1888. For more criticism of Nash, see, e.g., editorial, "The Woman Suffrage Decision," *TDL*, June 1, 1888; "A," "The Woman Suffrage Decision," ibid., June 1, 1888; and editorial, "The Woman Suffrage Decision," ibid.

[130] "Two Opinions," *TDL*, June 16, 1888, repr. Seattle Press.; "Judge Nash's Decision," *TDL*, June 5, 1888, repr. Columbia Chronicle. This writer blamed Roger Greene for supporting men who ultimately betrayed female citizens. See also Benjamin F. Brown, "Woman's Right to the Ballot," *WS*, June 8, 1888, and Brown, "Women's Right to the Ballot," ibid., August 3, 1888, reminding readers that the 14th Amendment had been held to enfranchise both women and black men in the federal district.

[131] Nevada Bloomer v. Todd, Statement, Case File No. 573, WSA-O. Newspapers gave early and then fuller notices; e.g., "As the Chronicle predicted ...," CC, August 18, 1888.

[132] See "Col. Turner Takes the Stump," *SR*, January 19, 1888, noting that two attendees, James N. Glover and John A. Todd, one of them a "grandfather of the town," opposed woman suffrage; both feared that equality sabotaged annexation. They apparently knew Turner. Todd also directed an agricultural fair association as of 1890; see Rev. Jonathan Edwards, *An Illustrated History of Spokane County* (Spokane, WA, 1900), pp. 66, 258. My thanks to Charles Hansen for this source.

[133] "Editorial," *SS*, July 2, 1910, home edition, p. 5. Corroboration has not been found. It is also possible that he resigned to avoid removal; he was Republican. In the same vein, see "Justice

woman-suffrage advocate – relied mainly on the assembly's authority to alter election laws. But he also pressed the authority of uncontested usage. As in Wyoming, where Congress's long-term failure to stop woman suffrage had tacitly validated it, so federal lawmakers had validated Washington's practices. The statute of 1883, though in force only for three years, and the present law, which had never been challenged, had been "impliedly confirmed"; at the least, the "right of the territories to legislate on the subject is recognized." He discounted biological ethics – the idea, advanced by Greene and others, that society benefited when lawmakers actively used male and female attributes. What mattered was woman's equal right to law and to social harmony: "She is equally interested with men in the good order and morality of society, in the prosperity of the state ... [and] in the welfare of the family."[134]

Because Turner's allies still could not deny women's economic agency or sovereignty, they did not rely primarily on the law of coverture. Instead, they turned to legislative history. Were women, whether married or not, qualified electors under the laws of Washington? The answer was no: Local elections laws violated the organic act. The framers of that act, in turn, had defined "citizen" to mean "male citizen." Oddly enough, given criticisms of Greene and others for imaginative readings of texts, he decided to ignore the wording of relevant texts: "Those who insist on the interpretation of statutes according to the literal reading, refuse to understand the philosophy of the law." It was "wisely left to the courts to extend statutes" – including the organic act – "by construction when the words are not broad enough to effectuate the legislative intent" or to "limit by interpretation where they are too broad."[135]

He then turned his attention to civil-rights and community-property laws. In 1853, Congress had followed the "common-law principle, founded in nature, and as vitally true to-day as it ever was, that married women are under the influence and control of their husbands." Impartial suffrage did not comport with the "government of men." Citing *Minor* v. *Happersett* (where federal justices refused to find federal citizenship rights for women in Reconstruction amendments), the *Bradwell* ruling, and recent state decisions hostile to women's rights, Turner invalidated statutes that permitted woman suffrage and, by extension, mixed jury service. With Senator Morgan, he noted as well that *men* had been denied their constitutional right to execute a public "trust" as electors, jurors, and magistrates.[136]

Turner," *SDPI*, February 18, 1888. An anti-suffrage print reported that Turner's reasons for resignation were "purely personal"; "Turner Resigned," *WWU*, February 25, 1888.

[134] *Nevada Bloomer* v. *John Todd, J.E. Gandy, and H.A. Clarke*, 3 Wash Terr Rpts 599 (August 1888), 600, 602. As earlier, where the case file and printed opinion differ, I follow the latter. For the fullest statement of women's capacity for civic contribution because of genetic differences, see Florence Kelley, *Some Ethical Gains Through Legislation* (New York, 1905).

[135] *Bloomer* v. *Todd*, 603–8.

[136] *Bloomer* v. *Todd*, 603–9, 612–23. See also "A Day in the Supreme Court," *WS*, July 27, 1888. *SDPI* writers happily dubbed woman suffrage "a practical failure" that ended with Bloomer; "Woman Suffrage Rejected," August 15, 1888. See the original opinion at "Unconstitutional,"

According to observers, the scene in Olympia had been "much more than an ordinary day in the history of American jurisprudence." Todd's advocates simply repeated the contents of Turner's brief: Bloomer was a woman and therefore not entitled to vote. Journalists quickly identified the main question: When Congress passed the organic act in 1853 authorizing the territorial legislature to proscribe voter qualifications, had members contemplated or approved the enfranchisement of women? Turner said no. On Bloomer's side, Murray held that the election law's language was explicit, with no room for interpretation; woman suffrage was consistent with the "spirit of our institutions as expressed from time to time in Congress" – which body, after all, had referred to equal suffrage in Utah as an "existing fact and legal."[137] Turner's presentation lasted about ninety minutes; many of his authorities were state and federal rulings against female bar admission. Turner argued, too, that, while legislators were authorized to confer suffrage on all citizens, Congress had not intended by that term to include citizens not yet enfranchised. "Citizen" had to mean what Congress intended, "the same as if Congress should pass an act authorizing the drafting of all 'citizens' into the army." Surely no one would say that such an act included women.[138]

Chief Justice Jones basically converted Turner's brief into the majority opinion. He distinguished between the construction and interpretation of legal texts, claiming the former duty for courts so that the populace might not "carry the state out upon a sea of revolution, with only passion for a guide." He explored rules of statutory construction and the composition of the electorate in the 1850s. In a case having nothing to do facially with juries, he addressed them at length: In the 1850s as in the 1780s, jurors were "officers"; the entire structure of the Constitution had been based on the idea that officers would be male. The very idea of a woman holding office was "as foreign to the mind as that a woman might be president." He cited the rule of non-superfluity: "Words have different significations at different times and in changed circumstances, but in a fundamental law they must always be of the same meaning." Since colonial times, when persons accused of crime were tried by a jury of twelve men, the word "jury" had meant the same thing. Hence, it could have only one meaning until competent authority declared otherwise. When the organic act was passed, the word "citizen" appeared as a qualification for voting and holding office; it then meant "male citizenship, and must be so construed." He had not been asked to say whether mixed-sex practices might be better public policy;

SDPI, April 17, 1888; and "The Territory. Woman Suffrage Decided Unconstitutional," ibid., August 15, 1888.

[137] "A Day in the Supreme Court," *WS*, July 27, 1888. One scholar described Bloomer as a dance-hall girl; see Hynding, *Public Life of Eugene Semple*, p. 81. Newspapers printed the ruling with commentary; e.g., "Woman Suffrage. Full Text of the Supreme Court Decision," *TDL*, August 17, 1888.

[138] "A Day in the Supreme Court," *WS*, July 27, 1888. For the Bloomer text, see also "The Suffrage Case," ibid., August 17, 1888.

Washingtonians could decide after statehood. It should be noted that neither Jones nor Turner distinguished, as Eustis had done, between ordinary juries and elections, which territories lawfully regulated, and statehood-related convocations or elections, which only Congress could organize.[139]

Bloomer thus declared that expansion of the electorate had been illegal and unnatural; citizens did not have to live with "the drafting of all citizens," female lawyers, or mixed-sex juries. Certainly women could not participate in statehood elections. Jones and Turner assumed as well that ballots and ancillary duties still inhered in citizens as a bundle; to have one element was to have them all. References to military service seemed to one reporter to be particularly outrageous; the case had to do with Bloomer's right to vote well after jury duty had been eliminated. Nor had Congress *created* a military service obligation for either sex, any more than it had created jury duty. But onlookers sensed Eustis' presence in the courtroom: As one writer explained, the Court had acted on the supposition that the Senate's views were relevant to the "discussion of the validity of the law."[140] Jones apparently had invited Roger Greene, Benjamin Dennison, and J. C. Haines to present their views. Haines had taken Turner's position; the others had not appeared. One journalist speculated that, "under the invitation of the court," Greene and Dennison would have been compelled to speak as lawyers, not as individuals, and so stayed away. In any case, Jones' opinion controlled the mixed-sex suffrage and jury question unless Bloomer appealed to the nation's highest court; the decision did rest on a federal statute.[141]

Roger Greene told a different story. On July 19, with the territorial Supreme Court in adjournment and after Turner and Nash had filed the appeal, Jones had invited Greene, Dennison, and Haines to submit *amicus* briefs by August 13 – a date well past oral arguments. Greene later said that he had "made none," but not by choice. On July 20, he had written to Jones, Langford, and Allyn, not about the invitation, but about an item in the *Post-Intelligencer* and the possibility of addressing the court directly. He had passed along four circulars, unaware that judges had perceived the circulars to be "annoying and even threatening"; they had been attributed to a "prominent woman-suffrage attorney of Seattle." Greene admitted the deed but insisted that he had acted "in the integrity of my heart, as an act of thoughtful friendship." Physically weak, he had declined an offer to represent Bloomer and was glad to be asked to write as a friend. But he needed time: "I really want to be heard,

---

[139] Bloomer v. Todd, pp. 620–3.
[140] "A Day in the Supreme Court," *WS*, July 27, 1888; "The Woman Suffrage Case," *TDL*, July 18, 1888.
[141] "A Day in the Supreme Court," *WS*, July 27, 1888. *Oregonian* printed the opinion without comment; "The Suffrage Act Invalid," *OR*, August 16, 1888. See also "The Woman Suffrage Law of Washington Territory Invalid," 20 *Chicago Legal News* 431 (1887–88); Myra Bradwell was "satisfied that the court places a false construction upon the Organic Act" and thus upon the statute.

being very deeply impressed with the exceeding ... magnitude of the questions involved & I sincerely hope your honors will see the way clear to extend the hearing or defer decision with leave to me either to speak orally or by type-written or printed argument."[142] Jones extended two days to a week, then proceeded without him.

To make matters worse, Greene was under attack by Republicans, supposedly because of his drift toward the Prohibitionist Party. Extreme venom prompted the conservative *Spokane Falls Review* to warn Greene's critics not to mistake "abuse of Judge Greene for argument and party policy."[143] Greene himself blasted friends for presuming to speak on his behalf: "I will fight my own battles .... The most I ask in any event, is to be absented from ... untruthful reports."[144] On August 27, 1888, the judge addressed a *Woman's Journal* request for a copy of his opinion in *Bloomer*. Illness, he said measuredly, and the Court's refusal to grant him the time required for preparation prevented him from filing a brief. The bench was "cramped" and so could not accommodate a "mere friend of the court." But, for the record, he offered an equal-protection argument. In *Bloomer*, the court had ruled that Washingtonians were "not as free to regulate ... the purely local matter of the qualifications of voters as are the people of the States." An American citizen did not possess as much freedom in the territory as in a state and, indeed, a settler likely renounced part of her freedom. This would deter female migrants. Worse, Nevada Bloomer was "so well satisfied" that she refused to appeal. He saw no prospect of reversal. Only Congress or new litigation could alter the situation; since the territory soon would cease to exist, a new appeal could not be brought in time. The decision to feign a case, he decided, sprang from the "unwillingness of the old political leaders to accommodate themselves kindly ... to the revolution in political conditions which the enfranchisement of women involves." Perhaps *Bloomer* would "solidify" pro-suffrage "sentiment and forces" so that representative government might prevail.[145]

---

[142] "Is It a Trap?" *TDL*, July 25, 1888, editorial page. See especially Roger Greene to the Honorable Richard Jones, and William Langford and Frank Allyn, July 20, 1888, in Nevada Bloomer v. John Todd, Case File No. 573, WSA-O. On the two-day limit, see, e.g., "The Suffrage Case," *SP*, July 20, 1888. See a slightly different text, "Letter from Ex-Chief Justice Greene, dated August 27, 1888, *WJ*, September 15, 1888. Meanwhile, courts were thrown into turmoil because the language of venires kept changing; e.g., "A Defective Venire," *TDL*, July 3, 1888.

[143] "Some of our republican journalistic friends ...," *SFR*, July 26, 1888. Editors made clear that they did not support woman suffrage.

[144] "Ex-Chief Justice Greene Speaks a Word," *SP*, September 4, 1888.

[145] "Woman Suffrage in Washington Territory, Ex-Chief Justice Greene in answering a commu-nication ...," 21 *Chicago Legal News* 17 (1886), p. 17, repr. from *WJ*. Nor does the Supreme Court case file contain amicus briefs from Dennison and Haines. A Dayton print confirmed that the bench had "appointed Chief Justice Greene, ex-Chief Justice Dennison and Col. J. C. Haines as amicus curiae to present any law or argument either way ..."; "Supreme Court," *CC*, July 20, 1888. On the short time granted to Greene, see "The Woman Suffrage Case," *TDL*, July 27,

Contemplative observers did not miss a fundamental shift in courtrooms. "It is unfortunate . . . ," wrote an editor as the thuggish William M. White left prison, "that the entire supreme bench is composed of judges opposed to woman suffrage." The "first essential of a court is that it should be fair and impartial"; these judges were "anxious to see the statute books freed from the law."[146] On August 16, the *New York Times* parsed *Bloomer* on the front page, with emphasis on the meaning of "citizens" in 1853. Reporters also concluded that *Bloomer* excluded women from political office: The organic act provided that a territory send one delegate to Congress, with the proviso that the delegate would be a "citizen."[147] After January, 1888, liberal assemblymen had been inundated with letters from entities like the *Woman's Journal* and the AWSA offering leaflets, delegations, and aid with petitions. Lucy Stone, Henry Blackwell, and others – even as they labored to mend fences between NWSA and AWSA – wondered aloud whether interference would help or hinder. In April, 1889, legislator Walter Thompson dejectedly wired Blackwell from Tacoma: "Unwise now to force issue with agitation before election."[148]

Had public offices been masculinized as well? Relying on the 1881 code, which explicitly granted office-holding rights to citizens, Zerelda McCoy – by 1889, the new president of WERA – had applied for a notary-public position in March, 1888, well before *Bloomer*. Attorney General James Metcalfe saw nothing untoward in McCoy's application; he warned only that, should the law be invalidated, unprocessed documents would be turned back to McCoy and others, occasioning "inconvenience if not disastrous consequences." After *Bloomer*, McCoy petitioned Semple for advice; he in turn asked Metcalfe to say whether "the recent division of the Supreme Court on the question of Woman

1888, indicating that the Court had extended Greene's time to slightly more than a week; Dennison swiftly "withdrew."

[146] Editorial, "The Woman Suffrage Laws in the Courts," *TDL*, July 12, 1888. "The Suffrage Decision," *TDL*, August 15, 1888, ed. page. See also "Woman Suffrage in Washington Territory," August 11, 1888, *WJ*, p. 254, and the commentary by Henry Blackwell on August 18, 1888 ("Adverse Decision in Washington Territory," ibid., p. 262), contending that the ruling imperiled the rights of women in all territories. Historicism ruled the day: See *Hiram Thomas* v. *R. D. Hilton*, 3 Wash Terr Rpts 365 (1888), appealing a jury decision in an insolvency case (the provision in the law code permitting trial by "six or more men" was unconstitutional because in the past, the word "jury" once had meant "twelve"). Langford dissented; the court had "defeat[ed] the jury trial intended by the legislature" and, by imposing rules expressly rejected, dishonored "the constitutional will" underlying legislation.

[147] E.g., "A Bold Position," February 16, 1883, as well as "The Vote for 1884" and "A Woman's Party," August 22, 1884, all *WS*. See also the jubilant report, "Against the Women," *WWU*, August 18, 1888. See "Woman Cannot Vote," *NYT*, August 16, 1888, p. 1, and "Women Can't Vote There," ibid., May 26, 1888, p. 5, describing Bloomer as a "test case."

[148] Henry Blackwell for *WJ* to Walter Thompson, April 1, 1889, Women's Suffrage Collection, File No. 5, WSHS. The same collection (e.g., Files 1–5) contains exchanges between Thompson and other nationally known suffrage figures as well as correspondence from local activists, all offering assistance. Intervention continued. See, e.g., Anna Shaw, "The Important Topic [a letter written for "Male Voters of this State"], *TDL*, July 2, 1889.

Suffrage" disqualified McCoy. Interestingly, Semple referred to a bench "division," as if the case had not been settled. On August 18, Metcalfe pointed to the organic act, which he now said had limited the right of holding office to male citizens. Territorial laws to the contrary were irrelevant; women could not serve as notary publics. The ruling also stripped offices from several women who sat as notaries, or who had been elected or appointed to other offices since 1886.[149]

Washingtonians had not seen the end of it. In late summer, 1888, Arthur S. Austin, a renegade lawyer who had sat through the *Bloomer* proceedings, suddenly filed paperwork for an appeal to the nation's highest court. Austin claimed to have filed "elaborate briefs" in *Bloomer*, although they do not appear in case files.[150] Austin may have met with Abigail Duniway in Washington, DC, and offered to file an appeal. A reporter described a meeting between Justice Allyn in Tacoma and Austin; in a transaction described as "the first attempt made to take the appeal," Austin sought approval of a $500 bond, signed by "Mrs. McCoy, Mrs. Pratt and John Murray." Allyn reportedly signed it.[151] By late summer of 1888, Austin was claiming to be Bloomer's attorney. In August, 1888, William Murray asked clerk of court Francis Henry why Austin had been given the file and permission to appeal, when, earlier, the court had merely allowed him to submit his views. Anything done since the ruling was "wholly without authority"; Austin's name had been "entered upon the appearance Docket at his special request" as *amicus curiae* for "citizens of Tacoma." Murray knew that the majority opposed an appeal but did not think they intended irregularity. Henry had promised to file the letter with case papers and send a copy to Allyn, to whom application for an appeal bond would be made, "*if at all.*" In October, Henry sent copies of relevant papers to Murray, with the

[149] For a brief treatment of McCoy and others, see Rebecca Mead, "Votes for Women!" *Columbia* (Winter 2010–11), pp. 5–11. See also James Metcalfe to Governor Eugene Semple, March 27, 1888; Eugene Semple to James Metcalfe, August 15, 1888; James Metcalfe to Eugene Semple, August 18, 1888; Governor's Papers, Box 1N-1-1, Attorney General file, WSA-O; and the draft of Semple's note to Metcalf, March 22, 1888, in Papers of Eugene Semple, UWSC, Box I-16. Finally, see "A recent application of a woman . . . ," *WS*, August 24, 1888; and "The Women Must Go," *TDL*, August 25, 1888.

[150] See Bloomer v. Todd, Case File No. 573, National Archive, DC. But see especially Francis Henry, Clerk, Supreme Court W. T., to William M. Murray, August 23, 1888, Letter Book, Supreme Court of the Territory of Washington, op cit., pp. 16–17. The court reporter noted Austin's presence during arguments; *Nevada Bloomer v. John Todd et al.*, 3 Wash Terr Rpts 599 (1888), 603 ("Mr. A. S. Austin, as amicus curiae, filed a brief, and argued for the Plaintiff in Error"). For confirmation, see the same language in Supreme Court Letter Book, Henry to Murray, op cit. See also "Supreme Court," *CC*, July 21, 1888. If the briefs existed, and two papers reported as much, then they were either purged from case files or sent to parties organizing an appeal. CC referred to "A. S. Austin of Tacoma."

[151] "From Tacoma," *OR*, August 25, 1888, p. 2. See also "For Woman Suffrage," *TDL*, August 22, 1888, describing a meeting at Alpha Hall on August 21; Zerelda McCoy offered a resolution, unanimously adopted, "deeply deplor[ing]" the Bloomer ruling.

further news that Austin had forwarded materials to Washington, DC.[152] On August 28, 1888, Austin himself declared that he had appealed the cause to the U.S. Supreme Court and retained Robert G. Ingersoll for the purpose. He asked for donations to allay expense, remitted to himself at Tacoma or to Mrs. Johnie Flanigan of Olympia.[153] California lawyer-activist Laura DeForce Gordon also arranged for the file's delivery to Sacramento; she and others hoped to overturn *Bloomer* and invalidate the ratification election. Certainly Senators Hoar and Platt thought that an appeal had been lodged; Platt hoped the case would be advanced on the calendar with dispatch.[154]

Did Austin abscond with the file? On September 23, 1888, Duniway cast Austin as an ally in what she called the reassertion of women's rights.[155] No direct evidence survives of Austin's agency in delivering the file to suffragists – only the report that papers in "Nevada Bloomer against Todd and others, being the woman suffrage test case," had been forwarded to the Supreme Court at Washington, where it indeed was received. "If the case is decided ... previous to Nov. 6, in favor of the women," wrote a tongue-in-cheek Duniway, "it will cause a sensation ..., as the women will insist on voting."[156] There was reason to think that the appeal might lie, given the Supreme Court's May, 1886, ruling in several polygamy cases. As the Court explained in *Lorenzo Snow* v. *U.S.*, which explored Washington and Utah organic acts, writs could lie when

---

[152] On the "curious Vermonter," Arthur Austin, see John Fahey, "The Nevada Bloomer Case: An Obedient Wife Played a Key Role ...," *Columbia: The Magazine of Northwest History* (Summer 1988), 45. See Francis Henry, Clerk, Supreme Court W. T., to William M. Murray, Esq., August 23, 1888, Letter Book, Supreme Court of the Territory of Washington, 1888–92, WSA-O, pp. 16–17. See also Francis Henry to Zerelda McCoy, President of Washington Chapter, NWSA, Tacoma, September 21, 1888, Letterbook, ibid., p. 32, in which McCoy learned that the appeal had been filed. Since Austin had signed on as amicus for "citizens of Tacoma," McCoy likely was involved. See also Henry to D. A. Clements, Olympia, September 11, 1888, ibid., p. 29 (appeal taken but no "cost bill" in hand) and Francis Henry to William M. Murray, October 1, 1888, ibid., p. 35.

[153] "The Woman Suffrage Case," WR, September 7, 1888, front page. Henry Blackwell thought that Bloomer had "accomplished what she wanted" and so refused to allow an appeal, forcing Austin to carry it forward; "The Case in Washington Territory, WJ, August 24, 1889, p. 268. Blackwell also said that politicians "wild for Statehood" had cooked up a case; ibid.

[154] Nevada Bloomer v. John Todd, U.S. Supreme Court Record Group, File No. 573, National Archives, DC; and "Concerning Washington Territory ... U.S. Senate," WJ, March 9, 1889.

[155] "Woman Suffrage," TDL, August 21, 1888 (for "jugglery"); "The recent decision," TDL, August 25, 1888, repr. *Philadelphia Record* of August 18, 1888. See also "The Supreme Court Decision," SP, August 17, 1888 ("The case will be carried to the United States Supreme Court, where ... a decision may be had on the law in the matter, i.e., whether a Territorial Legislature is or is not a constitutional law-making body").

[156] "Woman Suffrage Test Case. From the Portland Oregonian, Olympia, Washington, September 12," NYT, September 23, 1888, p. 16. In September, 1889, before Abigail Duniway spoke at a Spokane Falls rally, Mrs. Bessie Isaacs read some resolutions, among them: "Resolved, We have appealed from that adverse decision, and it is now before the supreme court of the United States, where there is no reasonable doubt but that it will be reversed"; "Equal Suffrage," SFR, September 14, 1889.

territorial decisions involved the federal constitution, a treaty, acts of Congress, or citizens' loss of "personal freedom."[157]

"THE GOVERNMENT IS SOVEREIGN, THE INHABITANTS ARE SUBJECTS"

Bloomer v. *Todd* enjoyed an extended career: Anti-suffrage members of the constitutional convention in Wyoming used *Bloomer* to strengthen their case against equal suffrage, and lawyers endlessly re-litigated the case. The local, pro-suffrage press also lambasted the ruling as unlawful and retrograde; Utah, Wyoming, and England allowed women to represent property at the polls, a qualification that attached to almost every woman in Washington. In the fall of 1888, the *Albany Times* and Myra Bradwell's *Chicago Legal News* featured critiques by two Massachusetts luminaries. Suffragist Hamilton Willcox, with Henry Blackwell's ringing endorsement, offered a scathing indictment of the "strange mixture of ignorance and hypocrisy" masquerading as legal analysis; the renowned abolitionist William Ingersoll Bowditch charged Nash with unconstitutional takings of vested rights.[158]

 Predicting that "freedom's friends" would boycott Nash in future contests for judicial posts, Willcox posed a myriad of questions: How could territories be akin to states ("a state legislature may enact any law for the welfare of the people") and unlike states (the organic act furnished "a constitutional limitation" beyond which legislators dared not go)? Did legislators really create the right to vote and serve as jurors? How could governments create and then destroy fundamental rights? Either suffrage formed part of a citizen's right to freedom and self-government, or America was a despotism. If the right to vote was merely a grant, who authorized it? If the sovereign, then "the law gets its authority to confer power from the very persons on whom it confers power!" Surely the Court's desperate resort to Congressional intentions disregarded the fact of unbroken acquiescence and investiture. Most of all, Willcox despised partisan attempts to use courts against the pro-Sixteenth Amendment majority report in the Senate: Washington justices had wisely concealed their intentions until they had secured seats on the bench. Grover Cleveland, a "just man," would have withheld appointments, had he known that they meant to "pervert law to rob

---

[157] The Bloomer case file suggests that arguments were continued into the late 1890s without a hearing. See also *Lorenzo Snow* v. *U.S.*, 118 U.S. 346 (1886), reprinted in 18 Chicago Legal News 320 (1885–86), involving three polygamy cases.

[158] See www.uwyo.edu/RobertsHistory/wyoming_constitutional.htm. Woman suffrage almost scuttled Wyoming's statehood bid; Section 6 of its constitution permitted it with amendatory legislation. See also "Woman Suffrage in Washington Territory. Judge Nash's Opinion," 20 *Chicago Legal News* 369 (1887–88), continued at 788. For the original, see William Bowditch, "Washington Territory, Judge Nash's Decision," *WJ*, June 30, 1888, p. 210. See also "Emerson and Hunter vs. Nash," *CC*, August 11, 1888; excerpted with commentary, "Judge Nash's Decision," *SP*, July 16, 1888.

half the people of their liberties." Willcox urged non-compliance: Until the appeal was resolved, women should vote where election judges had "the manhood to do their duty."[159]

Remarkably, the anti-suffrage *Spokane Falls Review* concluded that Jones had deprived the territory of home rule; the doctrine that citizens could not shape the electorate was "antagonistic to every principle upon which the free institutions of this government are supposed to be founded." Prohibitions in an organic act had to be unambiguous to justify curtailments of local self-government, to say nothing of sweeping away the rights exercised by thousands of people by judicial construction.[160] An amount of sleaze also appeared: Journalists revealed that, in Olympia the previous winter, some of the justices had lobbied against the passage of the woman-suffrage act and made "stump speeches" in the hotel rooms of a notorious lobbyist. Until there could be "a change of venue" to Washington, DC, they deemed it the duty of every woman to continue voting.[161]

Still, legal analysts remote from the scene made clear that James Eustis and Judges Nash and Jones were not wrong so much as crabbed and underhanded; by eighteenth-century design, territories *were* quasi-colonial dependencies. Tempers had flared so hotly (and Turner's shenanigans were so patently devious) that compromise had been forestalled.[162] Seattle lawyer John Arthur, a self-described Republican suffragist, noted that, when stringently applied, rules of statutory construction did mandate the result in *Bloomer*. Partisanship had not played a role. Turner was Republican, Semple a Democrat, the U.S. attorney a pro-suffrage Democrat, and Voorhees a Democrat. The Council had been equally divided, and women tended to align with minor parties. Congress had merely enforced standards set out in 1789. More controversially, he insisted that Turner had been activated less by spite than by his "convictions as a lawyer."[163] Similarly, Chicago scholar James DeWitt Andrews laid out the "unreversible," medieval character of territorial apprenticeships: Perhaps Washington's sad experience would inspire Americans to move territories to statehood more rapidly. He had been

---

[159] Hamilton Willcox, "Woman Suffrage in Washington Territory," from the *Albany Times*, September 2, 1888, reprinted in 21 *Chicago Legal Times* 7 (1888–89), 11–12. The Times misspelled his name as Wilcox.

[160] "The Suffrage Question," *SFR*, August 15, 1888.

[161] "Supreme Court Prejudices," *WR*, Bellingham Bay, June 8, 1888, front page. Voorhees continued to press the pro-suffrage case; e.g., Congressional Record, 50th Congress, U.S. Senate, 1888, 1st session, p. 6998 and passim, into the 2nd session. Decades later, critics still gnawed on Bloomer; e.g., editorial, *SS*, July 2, 1910, p. 5 (women had been "tricked and cheated" out of their suffrage).

[162] On Turner's illiberal reputation, see, e.g., "Men of Mark," *TDL*, July 4, 1888.

[163] John Arthur (Seattle), letter dated September 5, 1888, "Woman Suffrage in Washington Territory," *The American – Journal of Literature, Science, the Arts, and Public Affairs*, Philadelphia, Vol. 16, No. 921 (September 15, 1888), p. 347.

annoyed by willful blinking at standard legal reasoning, as with critics' use of state decisions, when territories lacked key attributes of states.[164]

Nor did popular sovereignty exist in territories. Andrews (and then the *Albany Law Journal*) underscored two difficult facts. First, a territory's people were not sovereign and had no civil or political rights; their assemblies had only the powers and rights expressly granted by Congress. Second, a law had to be construed in light of the surrounding circumstances at the date of passage. It had been understood since the 1780s that the federal Constitution did not extend to territories, which literally were wholly owned colonies of the nation: "The government is sovereign, the inhabitants are subjects, the cause of power is the reverse from that between the States and the United States, the source of it is in Congress, not in the Territory," and surely not in the people. In light of these facts, he said again, Americans should convey self-government as quickly as possible; territorial citizens could not claim that they had "no *pater familias*, no liege lord" to virtually represent "vassals."[165]

In Washington, women were dazed. Suddenly, equality and perhaps co-sovereignty depended on federal rules of practice in 1853, and then on federal approval of atypical suffrage practices, all of which smacked of re-impositions of legal incapacity in a community that had valorized mutuality. Reformers from often-warring associations found common cause. Seattle residents, for instance, again mounted an "enthusiastic meeting" in Frye's Opera House that treated suffrage, women's wages, child abuse, and temperance in a well-attended event. Elizabeth Saxon, a former WCTU leader, issued a strong plea for aid from a broad array of societies. She deplored the way that legislators had treated some petitions; long lists of names were "merely glanced at and then thrown on the floor and kicked into the waste basket, with the remark: 'What does all this amount to? It is only women's work.'"[166] Activists sometimes sought advice from the lame-duck governor – as when the secretary for the Cheney WCTU chapter asked Semple whether, given judicial division, he would advise women to defy *Bloomer* and storm the polls. In the wings lurked Roger

---

[164] For an example of the kind of criticism that nettled Andrews, see letter from Mr. W. S. Bush (Seattle lawyer), dated August 17, 1888, to Catherine Waite's *Chicago Law Times*, which argued that the court had ignored long lines of state decisions; "Suffrage in Washington Territory," 2 *Chicago Law Times* 384 (1888), at 384. See W. S. Bush, "The Bloomer Decision," *WJ*, October 6, 1888 (case had advanced to the Supreme Court "by agreement" and had been an "outrage on justice").

[165] Charles DeWitt Andrews, "Woman Suffrage in Washington Territory," 21 *Chicago Legal News* 431 (1888–89), at 431. See also "Current Topics. The case of Bloomer v. Todd ...," *Albany Law Journal*, Vol. 38, No. 285 (1888–89), at 285, dated October 13, 1888 ("We suspect that Chief Justice Jones will find himself the target for a great deal of feminine objurgation, but poor man! It is not his fault. He can no more alter the Constitution ... than he can change that of the present aspirants to the right of suffrage. Probably this case will be taken to the Federal Supreme Court as a test"). The journal was a pro-suffrage outlet for material from *Chicago Legal News* and *Chicago Law Times*. Bradwell published lower-court rulings in Bloomer; 20 *Chicago Legal News* 369 (1887–88), 370.

[166] "A Plea for Justice," *SP*, August 27, 1888.

Greene. Did the ruling debar women from voting while awaiting an appellate decision, or did the right continue until federal justices delivered bad news? Greene advised the latter: "I quote his own words. 'In my opinion every woman in the Territory is entitled to vote .... Her right to suffrage is not conclusively denied, until denied by decision of the court of last resort, or by paramount legislation.' But of course the only weight attaching [to this] ... is that it comes from a man well versed in law, of great experience, and standing high in his profession. It carries no authority, and it seems to us that an opinion from a source which will carry authority is greatly needed .... Can you render ... one?" A staffer filed the letter; it would "not be proper to give an opinion."[167]

An aura of danger surrounded the polls; the *Post-Intelligencer* flatly warned those who planned to vote that it was "not safe."[168] Even as legislators acted against *Harland*, newspapers reported scattered attempts in Tacoma and elsewhere to turn women away rather brusquely from school elections, which had been uncontested ground, because of *Bloomer*. In one district, three unnamed women were challenged, then allowed to vote only because they had had no official notice of the decision.[169] In November, 1888, Bessie Isaacs of Walla Walla reported that poll keepers had courteously declined the ballots of six well-deported ladies. In one case, an inspector said, "'Mrs. ___, are you a citizen of the United States?' 'Yes, I am,' was the reply. 'But the Supreme Court, I'm sorry to say, says you are not.'"[170] In a later school contest, twenty-six women's ballots were scrutinized and finally accepted, at which election the pro-suffrage Mrs. Hawthorne was re-elected overwhelmingly as school clerk, even though she probably had no legal right to occupy the position.[171] In January, 1888, suffragists brave enough to circulate petitions in favor of re-enactment were accused of unladylike force. In response to a suggestion that women in Yelm, Washington, had forced men to sign petitions, Lou Jackson Longmire responded on behalf of her comrades that no such thing had occurred in Yelm or anywhere else: Potential signers had been "asked"; those who refused had been "polite and kind." This was a vicious attack.[172]

In advance of general elections in November, 1888, Zerelda McCoy took to the barricades as an officer of NWSA. With the equality principle at the forefront, she urged organized disobedience and close attention to the evidence required in future lawsuits: "Every woman who is a citizen has an equal right with every man to the ballot. Only force, fraud and intimidation can prevent her ballot from being ... counted. If the judges ... refuse the vote of even

[167] H. A. Range, Corresponding Secretary of WCTU, Cheney, WA [November 1887?], Governors Papers, Box 1N-1-5, Governor Semple Administration, WSA-O.
[168] "Not Safe," *SDPI*, July 9, 1887.   [169] "Invalidated," *WS*, December 9, 1887.
[170] Bessie Isaacs, "Letter from Washington Territory," dated November 10, 1888, *WJ*, November 24, 1888.
[171] "School Election," *SDPI*, November 4, 1888. The vote for Hawthorne was 435 to 113 (her opponent was male).
[172] Lou Jackson Longmire, "Letters from the People. An Accompaniment to 'The Harper'," *WS*, January 6, 1888, a response to "Still Harping," ibid., December 30, 1887.

one woman, and this appeal is decided in our favor, the returns from that precinct can be thrown out. In behalf of the National Woman Suffrage association I call upon the women of Tacoma to come out today and vote."[173]

McCoy then attended the polls with talking points in hand; suffragists, too, could set up test cases. When she offered a ballot in Tacoma, "the inspector and one judge ... claimed to be willing to accept it but for the printed instructions received from the republican central committee." Mr. F. Fleming, a "friend of equal suffrage," took her oath. McCoy then claimed a "title to the ballot vested in her" from past, uncontested usage; property rights could not be divested by any court without cause; she also called *Bloomer* a "usurpation of the power of congress"; even if it was valid, her "right and title to the possession and use of the ballot" continued until the appeal had been resolved. Her ballot was rejected decisively, then endorsed: "This ballot was offered by Mrs. Zerelda N. McCoy and rejected by the election board of Artondale precinct for the reason that the supreme court ... has decided that male voters only are entitled to vote at a general election." One judge dissented. After discussion, officials finally deposited the ballot in the box, to be "preserved and returned according to law." Many women reportedly would have come to the polls, had McCoy succeeded, but were "intimidated." A dozen women voted successfully at Gig Harbor. In Tacoma's Fourth Ward, Mrs. Elizabeth Lister, Mrs. Dudley, Mrs. Frances Barlow and Mrs. Annie Stephens – the same WERA members who had braved jury boxes – went to the polls *en masse*. When Lister and Barlow were rebuffed, they offered to take an oath. The exchange elicited "derision and voices, presumably those of the judges were heard from the region of the ballot box, calling out, 'You can't vote! You can't vote!'" The crowd complained that "they were taking up too much time! 'Rats! Rats!' And these American citizens, being afraid of rude treatment, withdrew." When anti-suffragists declared equal suffrage dead, one woman shot back, "Not so fast, brother, woman suffrage is not dead .... Take in your coffin."[174]

As the pre-statehood crackdown advanced, women's political personalities were not the only casualties. In February, 1888, in an article thanking public officials for making an end to the suffrage controversy, the editor of Olympia's newspaper of record further suggested that proposed changes in licensing laws to prohibit or otherwise restrain the liquor trade might not pass constitutional muster. Would the WCTU's gains go up in flames? Territorial judges were giving serious thought to constitutional limitations on legislative interference with entrepreneurial choices. The idea that either legislators or municipalities might be mobilized to limit social hazards – or, for that matter, consumer

---

[173] Zerelda N. McCoy, "To the Citizens of Tacoma," *TDL*, November 6, 1888.
[174] "Intimidating Voters," *TDL*, November 8, 1888; "Further Intimidation of Legal Voters," ibid., November 9, 1888; "One of the Disfranchised" and "Woman Suffrage. The Cause Refuses Burial," *SP*, November 30, 1887. For ongoing WERA activism and the Listers, see "The Equal Rights Association, *TDL*, January 22, 1888. The full extent of resistance is unknown.

choices – was a "disputed proposition."[175] On these questions, Justice Langford found backhanded ways to contribute to theories of unitary command sharply at odds with Greene's "kings" and "queens." On the last day of 1888, Langford ruled in the case of *C. C. Thornton* v. *Territory of Washington* – an appeal of a rehearing of a conviction for selling intoxicating liquors in violation of the 1886 local option law that George Turner (supposedly Langford's comrade-in-arms) had declared constitutional. Now, Langford decided, with Justices Jones and Allyn concurring and Turner dissenting without opinion, that the law violated the organic act and federal constitution. Langford did not name the Fourteenth Amendment; rather, he referred only to unlawful delegations of police powers to municipalities. "Towns and cities," he wrote, relying on state authorities, "are governments within the government; adding something to, but not taking anything from, the state government; not acting as the delegate of the state," but acting by virtue of power granted by the state. Towns and cities could not "enact, or reap, or affect state laws."[176]

More important, Langford addressed the doctrine of sovereign indivisibility, in effect rolling up the sidewalk on democratic experimentation. Citing Blackstone's *Commentaries*, he insisted that sovereignty in republics resided, not in "kings" or "queens," and not even in the people, but within branches of a newly masculinized government, to protect its indivisible character. All "ancient governments, and most modern ones, have been constructed upon the theory that sovereignty cannot be divided, but that executive, judicial, administrative, and legislative functions are all united in one body." In America, different entities performed different functions in order to protect private rights, which could be limited only when three departments agreed. Legislators wrongly imagined an "absolute democracy"; republicans could not be subjected to the "hasty impulses of local majorities."[177]

In all of this, it was hard to miss perceptions of gender-led social derangement: Women had invaded seats of power, violated binding rules of male–female deportment and responsibility, and threatened statehood. The polls were the least of it. One anti-suffragist rather tellingly implied, as Alma Beach had done more overtly in her Whatcom Literary Society oration, that women's losses resulted from affronts to customary practices. Legal rules did not operate or have meaning in a vacuum. Political equality had never been wholly naturalized or, for that matter, fully defined: Did it impose a fictitious sex-neutrality? Or would women contribute as women? Surely it had not garnered the necessary "degree ... of respect due to a legislative enactment,"

<hr/>

[175] "All's Well That Ends Well," *WS*, February 3, 1888.
[176] *C. C. Thornton* v. *Territory of Washington*, 3 Wash Terr Rpts 482 (1888), 482–3, 490–3.
[177] Ibid. For Blackstone on sovereign command, see 486, 492–93. See also report of an unnamed U.S. Supreme Court opinion on state regulation of the liquor trade in Kansas, which did not comport entirely with Langston's; "The Supreme Court has decided ...," *WS*, December 9, 1887. Editors likely had in mind *Mugler* v. *Kansas*, 123 U.S. 623 (1887), validating statutes banning spirits and "nuisances."

and so had "not, by any means, become a part of the *fundamental law of the territory.*"[178] In June, 1889, a Tacoman rose to speak ("This is the first time I have ever spoken in public, and I hope it will be the last") in a suffrage meeting to say that she objected less to the ballot *per se* than to its accompaniments, which disrupted her sense of self: "If it stopped at the ballot it would not be so bad, but it will not stop there." Women, "if they wish the ballot, must run for office, filling the seats of our city council and other offices"; they would never be "quite the same."[179]

****

On August 4, 1888, a few days before *Bloomer*, George Turner had been given a hero's welcome at a Republican gathering in Spokane. He predicted victory in the upcoming elections, which would mean to westerners "just coming on the stage of industrial activity and who are in the condition now that our brothers in the east were when the system was first adopted, the difference between poverty and disorder and wealth and prosperity." He urged an end to citizens' detachment from national politics; it was time to restore "manhood suffrage," to "quit talking about barren idealities," and to "grapple with the questions which our brothers are grappling with elsewhere."[180] Turner had repudiated the Republicans' 1886 suffrage plank ("We affirm our unswerving devotion ... to the personal rights and liberties of citizens in all the States and Territories" and the "sovereign right of every lawful citizen ... to cast one free ballot in popular elections"); by 1888, the plank had vanished.[181]

For his part, Roger Greene practiced law, pursued reform, and occasionally ran for office as a Prohibitionist. In October, 1888, as part of his ongoing re-argument of *Bloomer*, he mailed another essay to a newspaper office. The 1888 suffrage law was valid; he expected the federal judiciary to say so if it got an opportunity. Although the immediate question had been, "Can women vote in Washington Territory?", the better question was, "Have the people of Washington territory the power to make a law which will secure to woman a voice?" The former had to do with women's particular freedom and the latter the general freedom of all people. Each touched the "liberties of the citizen, *both in his or her rights as subject and prerogatives as sovereign,*" but Bloomer had threatened two aspects of the latter – home rule and a people's right to a "potent representation"

---

[178] "An Unusual Obstacle," *SDPI*, January 20, 1888. Emphasis added.
[179] "A Woman's View," *WWU*, June 8, 1889.
[180] "Solid Doctrine. Judge Turner's Speech before the Lincoln Club," *SFR*, August 16, 1888. See also "Republican Rally," *TDL*, October 28, 1888, for further elaboration. Republican platforms in 1888 had nothing to say about woman suffrage; e.g., "The Convention. The Pierce County Republican Nominations," ibid., October 3, 1888, and "John B. Allen," ibid., September 12, 1888. On high tariffs, see also "Spokane County," ibid., September 15, 1888.
[181] Ibid., and Editorial, "Bolting Their Party," *SP*, August 18, 1888.

in government. It is unclear whether Greene, who intended to help, ever saw the extent of his complicity in women's catastrophic loss of ground.[182]

Meanwhile, statehood boosters tuned out "whiners" and launched themselves into the 1890s. The *Spokane Falls Review* tacitly applauded *Bloomer* with essays about "Woman's Kingdom," which portrayed women as domestic monarchs. A Republican electoral sweep in November, 1888, did not revive interest in women's rights; campaigners emphasized internal improvements and wealth production.[183] In March, 1889, attendees at a public meeting in Olympia, after memorializing forefathers, lauded the "young men who were now doing so much towards developing the country." Government, wrote an Olympian, was never subject to greater danger than when lawmakers forgot about the "the special fitness of men" for the job. Suffrage, the method used to ensure peace and stability, became the means for its undoing. The jury fiasco had shown that relational beings were not a "safe element to be admitted to a franchise which is to guard the rights of individuality," much less to juries. Women had a limited conception of the duties of citizens. Until statehood, advised a journalist, no new laws should appear; best to "give up entirely the juvenile system and devote all our energies to the assertion of our manhood and local independence."[184]

Strong voices reminded anti-suffragists that women's interests and property were subject to laws made by others. Who would convey her instructions to legislators and judges? Suffragists argued, too, that only an amalgam of civil and political equality would secure intelligent female labor.[185] But reactionary voices grew louder. Even the *Whatcom Reveille*, a fiercely pro-suffrage print,

---

[182] "Washington Prohibitionists," *WR*, May 25, 1888, and "Judge Greene …," *TDL*, May 18, 1888, or "And now Judge Roger S. Greene …," ibid., May 16, 1888. He lost. See also "Prohibition and the Solid South," *TDL*, June 3, 1888. "The Bench, the Bar, and the Press," *TDL*, October 15, 1884; "Judge Greene on Woman Suffrage," *PSWA*, October 18, 1888, emphasis added; "Judge Greene Speaks," *SPI*, October 7, 1888; also "Judge Greene on Woman Suffrage," *WJ*, November 10, 1888, p. 356. See also "The Prohibitionists," ibid., May 18, 1888. In 1894, he served as justice pro tem; e.g., "Warrant Should Be Warranted," *ST*, November 21, 1894 (City of Seattle liable for damages associated with warrants served on innocent parties); or "Our Awful Bugbear," ibid., November 19, 1894 (forcing City to pay for road grading where Council had exceeded lawful powers).

[183] E.g., "Woman's Kingdom," *SR*, November 15, 1888, p. 2. Republican John B. Allen replaced Charles Voorhees as the territorial delegate to Congress; for a typical notice of election returns, see "Allen Elected Delegate …," *WR*, November 9, 1888. For talk about "home" as an amalgam of finance, commerce, and manufactures, see "Fight for Home," ibid., November 2, 1888.

[184] "The Suffrage Question," *WS*, May 17, 1889; "Woman Suffrage," ibid., May 10, 1889; "The Duty of Citizenship," ibid., November 2, 1888; "The Spirit of Progress," ibid., March 15, 1889; editor, "Admission of the State," *TDL*, September 26, 1888; "Scarcity of Labor," *SDPI*, July 14, 1887.

[185] "Woman Suffrage. Why Woman Should Cast the Ballot in Elections," *WR*, October 12, 1888, inside page; even here, the editor used patronizing verbs ("women should be permitted … "). See also "The Future of the Girl-Graduates," *SDPI*, January 14, 1887 ("The higher education is not to unsex women … "); see also "In Feminine Fields," ibid., November 11, 1888, and "The

began to depict women in stereotypic ways, as with a saccharine poem about "The Little Wife at Home." Women were "not all talented or witty or beautiful," wrote an editor. "The trouble often is that women want to look too far afield."[186] Walla Wallans complained that girls objected to housework if they could find other work, which led to maid shortages. As sheep specialized in "meat and wool," so women did domestic labor while serving as "equal" managers of money. Parents were advised to train sons for business, wealth, and distinction; women should cultivate "the outer woman" and employ corsets.[187] As social hierarchies continued to mutate in response to shifting legal boundaries, native-born, working-class, white women retained social status in part because the Chinese still occupied lower rungs, and because marriageable women still were scarce.[188] Perhaps foreign-born white women could further displace Asians and relieve less muscular, native-born women of drudgery. Unlike women who eschewed domestic work beyond home, Jews and Russians had been "inured by the custom of ages" to hard labor; they could replace "John Chinaman" in kitchens.[189]

Participants understood these developments to be part of an intensifying flirtation with varieties of paternalism. In 1893, the historian Matilda Gage associated *Bloomer* with "the protective tendency" and with married women's tendency to petition government for "protection against freedom for themselves, and all others of their sex." In her view, the "protective theory reached its lowest depths for women by an attack upon her already vested rights of the ballot" in Washington, where a wife had conspired to eliminate equality.[190] State-sponsored protectionism had many faces. In May, 1888, an editor suggested that a protective tariff was merely "the application to the

Lot of Women," WR, May 20, 1887 (on the need to prepare for earning a living, even if married).

[186] "The Little Wife At Home," WR, March 25, 1887. In the same vein, see, e.g., "A Word to Mothers," ibid., March 4, 1887 (on "home influences" to socialize girls) and "For Woman's Bread," SPI, December 12, 1888, p. 6.

[187] "A Domestic Problem," WWU, November 17, 1888; "The True Sphere of Christian Women," ibid., May 5, 1888 (for sheep); "The Wife's Allowance," ibid., October 13, 1888 (the limited "allowance" was abolished). See also the letter from San Francisco, "Women and Chinamen," WJ, August 18, 1888 (with expulsion of the Chinese, there was "an opening for the labor of women"). See also E. E. Martin, "Train Boys for Business," SFR, September 19, 1887; "Blame the Corset," ibid., December 23, 1888, front page; and "The Perfect Woman," WWU, March 10, 1888.

[188] "A Craving for Girls," SP, March 17, 1887. Such advertising persisted. See as well the essay urging women to move west where they would find a mate in less than a week; "Go West, Girls," TDL, September 24, 1885. At least one journalist urged women to come to Washington in order to supplant the Chinese; "Chinese Labor v. White Labor," ibid., October 8, 1885.

[189] "Immigration Investigation," TDL, August 9, 1888; "A 'Long Felt Want,'" WS, May 31, 1889, editorial page.

[190] Matilda Gage, *Woman, Church and State: A Historical Account of the Status of Woman through the Christian Ages* ... (New York, 1893, repr. 1985), p. 537. See also Alice Stone Blackwell's "Woman Suffrage Leaflet," DeVoe Papers, WSHS; it was "imperative to deprive the women of their votes before the members of the convention were chosen."

whole country of the policy we adopt as ... communities. We are all protectionists in local affairs and should be liberal enough to be all protectionists in national affairs."[191] Later, Republican women affirmed that they "had always been the party of protection; protection of the citizen; protection to the negro; protection to the ballot-box; protection to the wage-earner; protection to the wage-payer, and ... protection for the home."[192] Such policies included a defense of the individual "in his life, limbs, possessions .... Civil laws define his rights, and courts protect him in them. Criminal laws are enacted to shield society from the ... wicked; police and courts are there to enforce the protection." Workplace protection was a natural step toward social advancement. The Republican *Walla Walla Union* lauded its party's support for national and domestic protection: "What is true of the individual is equally true of the Nation." It was a small step to public superintendence of classes taken to be vulnerable, impaired, and semi-sovereign.[193]

---

[191] "All Protectionists," *TDL*, May 24, 1888, ed. page. See also critique of Republican tariff policies and excessive "protection" across the nation; "Free Trade or Protection?" *SP*, July 2, 1888.

[192] "Address of Republican Women," *WJ*, August 25, 1888, p. 274.

[193] "The Logic of Protection," *WR*, June 1, 1888, ed. page; "Free Trade Protection," *WWU*, September 15, 1888, front page.

6

"Fraternalism permeates the atmosphere"

Remaking gender and public power

> The situation of the State of Washington is like that of a young man entering upon the serious business of life . . . . Behind him are incomplete and unsatisfactory experiences which are totally inadequate to . . . furnish rules for future conduct. The commonwealth of Washington has arrived at manhood. Its childhood, its youth, are passed.
>
> – Governor Elisha Ferry, 1889[1]

With statehood at hand and equal suffrage temporarily stymied, Washington's leadership turned to constitution making, economic development, and labor unrest. Devastating urban fires in 1889 did not temper shameless self-promotion. Tacomans claimed to have erected a thousand houses in a single year, creating the nation's greatest metropolis.[2] Publicists in Seattle anticipated a state with "wide fields of industrial activity" and vast resources; citizens' dauntless spirit surmounted even the loss of the business district.[3] The Northern Pacific's arrival west of the mountains in October, 1889, was another step "onward and upward" – notwithstanding labor walkouts, ongoing women's-rights agitation, and a growing army of social reformers.[4] In 1883,

---

[1] "Gov[ernor] Ferry's Message," *WS*, November 29, 1889, p. 1; see also "Governor's Message," *TDL*, November 23, 1889, p. 10. See also "Washington Leads," ibid., September 12, 1889, p. 4.

[2] "A Thousand Houses," *TDL*, January 1, 1889, front page. This was a *TDL* survey. R. F. Radebaugh sold the Ledger in 1898, then returned in 1907 with the *TDT*, which ran for five years. By 1918, titles merged (News Tribune and Ledger).

[3] E.g., "Full of Hope," *SPI*, June 8, 1889, front page; "A Mighty State," ibid., January 1, 1890; "Ellensburg Fire," ibid., July 6, 1889; or (on Seattle) the entire issue, ibid., June 10, 1889. For Spokane, see "Spokane's Calamity," *TDL*, August 6, 1889, front page.

[4] "At Last," *ST*, October 14, 1889. "The Greatest Need," *SPT*, March 18, 1892. See also "The Carpenters' Strike," *TDL*, August 30, 1888; "A Carpenters' Strike," ibid., August 29, 1888 (for a nine-hour workday; not successful). See also an earlier, unsuccessful drive for state-wide eight-hour workdays for industrial workers of both sexes; "The Eight Hour Bill," *SP*, December 17, 1887. Newspapers publicized the parallel U.S. Senate drive for eight-hour limits for federal contractors, "The Eight Hour Law," ibid., July 18, 1888; and the AFL's eight-hour movement,

Governor Newell had lauded Washington's "extensive competition and improvement of lands, building of towns, increase in manufacturing, commerce and navigation, and railroads." By 1889, statehood had joined the list: Immigrants to Washington would find a Pacific coast entirely lined with "free and powerful states," not a line broken by a territory's "unnatural ... dependency" on Congress.[5]

Elisha Ferry's young men eagerly set about dealing with problems attendant on rapid economic expansion. Virtually everyone championed "civilizers" – manufactories, roads, rail lines – and increases in public spending.[6] Might government serve as a parental curb on industrial excesses? As one journalist put it, "The tendency of the times is toward ideas of government ... similar to that called paternal." The term had "an ugly sound at first." When kings governed and subjects lived to serve them, personal liberty was limited; a struggle ensued to "raise the point of personal liberty and lower that of governmental power." Now that personal liberty has been expanded and guaranteed, paternalism would be "as different from that of the past as the twentieth century [is] from the tenth."[7]

Within this implicitly Progressive rubric, bracketed on one side by legislative energy and on the other by constitutional limitations of such energy, Washingtonians ratified a state constitution, mounted a pavilion at the nation's centennial, elected state officers, and funded improvement programs. Equal suffrage and prohibition had been "snowed under," as one wag put it; "manified" women could choose between the dependency prescribed by nature's God and unnatural competition, devoid of public sympathy or assistance.[8] Fraternities, worker's associations, and women's clubs flourished; YMCAs promised to transform rough lads into "strong men, morally and physically," ready for business. At least before the downturn of 1892–93, Socialists seemed less fearsome, if only because they had not smashed capitalism after all. Urban squalor seeped westward. Only natural disasters could postpone social purification and economic growth: After the 1889 fires, citizens were urged to "give the labor question, and woman's suffrage and prohibition, and the tariff, and the uselessness of the democratic party, and

"The Eight Hour Movement," ibid., December 19, 1888. On "waste," see "Labor's Weakness and Needs," ibid., February 18, 1889.

[5] "Governor's Message," *SDPI*, October 4, 1883. Women do not appear. On migrants, see "Thousands Coming," *TDL*, March 27, 1889. See also "A Progressive Year," *SPI*, January 1, 1889.

[6] E.g., "The Great Need," *TDL*, February 16, 1888; "The Westward Migration," ibid., February 22, 1888; "Big Mass Meeting for Progress, Enterprise, and Improvements," ibid., May 1, 1888; "Celebrating the Tunnel," ibid., May 6, 1888; "Roads as Civilizers," ibid., May 9, 1888; "How Tacoma Grows" and "Tacoma's Manufacturing Status," ibid., September 16, 1888.

[7] "Paternal Government," *SDPI*, July 19, 1885.

[8] Governor's Papers, Centennial Celebration file, 1889, Box 1N-1-1, WSA-O. For paternal institutions, see, e.g., "One of the First Duties," *SPI*, May 5, 1889; "Our School System," *TDL*, January 1, 1890; "State Notes," *PH*, October 5, 1889; "Woman's Rights," *ST*, October 2, 1889.

the hoggishness of the republican party a few days' rest, and organize fire companies."[9]

Paeans to male founders celebrated the "best type of Western American manhood," the many thousands who "by the work of their hands built up an empire." By 1890, however, brains had overtaken brawn. To be sure, Washington still needed "men to work our mines, plough our fields, cut our timber, build our railroads, and engage in all enterprises" that underlay wealth production. But fabrication and high finance had supplanted an extractive past. Rail and telegraph lines had tamed mountains and forests; Indians, the embodiment of "freedom and power," no longer roamed the continent. Washington was as close to New York City as a "man in that city had been to western New York" only a few years earlier.[10]

Not surprisingly, gender and other social practices absorbed and expressed these changes. Well-deported, white women could expect public or quasi-public respect and tending, whether wanted or not, especially if poor or wage-earning.[11] Hierarchies apparent by 1887–88 reflected increased attention to motherhood, women's work, and the sex's supposedly ineradicable shortcomings – even as women continued to deal in property. They also reflected the valorization of white men and the identification of dangerous races and classes – chief among them, Asians. When Laura De Force Gordon addressed suffragists in April, 1889, she thanked men on behalf of all women for "not ranking them with Chinese." On that score at least, well-meaning, protection-minded legislators had been "quick to see the point."[12]

Woman suffrage did not re-emerge as a viable possibility until after 1900 (an 1898 campaign failed miserably). In 1883, Abigail Duniway had rallied troops around the idea that enfranchised westerners would be pointing the way for eastern sisters;[13] by 1889, counter-narratives suggested that full equality had been a philosopher's conceit. Hustlers guided the state. George Turner speculated in silver and other local commodities; Roger Greene did not. Women's slim reed continued to be the state's formal recognition of civil and marital equality. But the reed weakened. Even as Washingtonians affirmed

[9] E.g., Rev. M. S. Hartwell, "Young Men's Work," *TDL*, November 17, 1889, on the YMCA's annual day of prayer for Tacoma's boys. Seventy percent were unchurched. The Masons and other fraternities spawned women's auxiliaries; e.g., Order of the Eastern Star (Masons). See also "Socialism," *ST*, July 22, 1895 (socialism not synonymous with anarchism), and "Many New Companies," *TDL*, November 13, 1889 (claiming 114 new companies in Tacoma in eight months). For an exception, see "Drift toward Socialism," *TDL*, January 25, 1890 ("paternalism" was Bellamy's socialism). See also "Sociological Reform," *ST*, August 27, 1895; "Pullman's Friends," *PH*, July 12, 1890.

[10] "Consistency," *SFR*, October 7, 1886; "The Men We Need," *WWU*, May 11, 1889; "Argonaut," "March of Civilization in the United States," *WR*, February 27, 1885.

[11] Seattle police conducted a major raid on brothels in 1889; "Seattle's Bad People," *TDL*, April 16, 1889; they arrested a dozen madams and filled others with "trepidation."

[12] "For Woman Suffrage, Mrs. Laura De Force Gordon in the Lists," *TDL*, April 22, 1889, p. 6.

[13] "Editorial Correspondence," *NN*, November 29, 1883, on ratification of equal suffrage bill.

equal chances in the marketplace, they introduced new forms of public and private headship, drawing common-law and continental rules of practice into closer communion. Once, sovereignty had been a birthright that both sexes claimed; as with marital estates, men and women had occupied the constituent power jointly and severally. Now, sovereignty came to be partitioned by sex and gender – i.e., according to biological differences and social function. As co-sovereignty mutated, a new generation waged a decorous campaign for the home vote. A few intellectuals championed strict equality. Others held that experimentation had been "too broad"; women had compelled "the people to swallow the bait, hook, line and pole all at a gulp, or avoid it altogether."[14]

"THE WOMEN THINK THERE IS A SCREW LOOSE SOMEWHERE"

As Washingtonians made the difficult passage to statehood, equal-rights activists occupied soft ground. In December, 1888, a worried but undaunted Zerelda McCoy asked lame-duck governor Eugene Semple, on behalf of the local NWSA chapter, "Will you not write personal letters to members of Congress urging them to incorporate in the enabling act a clause allowing women to vote for delegates to the State Constitutional Convention and at the election for the adoption of the Constitution in every territory" where legislation had not been repealed? "Please give us the help of your official position in every way possible."[15] When he demurred, WERA members fanned out over the territory, singly and in groups, to educate the citizenry; in the spring of 1889, they also organized a ten-meeting lecture series to be held in Tacoma's opera house.[16]

A consequence of Washington's extended crisis had been the appearance, as during the Civil War, of sustained talk about the nature of republican citizenship, and especially the relationship between rights, duties, and sovereignty. After *Bloomer*, journalists contributed to the discussion as never before. Chief among them was Randolph F. Radebaugh, the erudite owner-editor of Tacoma's pro-suffrage *Daily Ledger* (by 1909 the *Daily Tribune*), who preferred categories of exclusion bounded by intelligence and social contribution rather than by sex, race, or class.[17] Radebaugh's daily seminar in constitutional theory emphasized popular sovereignty – a concept that referred,

[14] "The voters of Whatcom County ...," *BBR*, September 13, 1889, ed. page. The reunification of AWSA and NWSA to form NAWSA is widely remarked.

[15] Zerelda McCoy to Eugene Semple, December 21, 1888, and Eugene Semple to Zerelda N. McCoy, Tacoma, December 26, 1888, Papers of Eugene Semple, Box I-16, UWSC. On the suffrage-petition campaigns, see "The Women at Work," *TDL*, April 18, 1889. McCoy's group composed and published circulars; e.g., "Suffrage in the Constitution," ibid., April 15, 1889.

[16] "Let the Women Vote ... Yesterday's Enthusiastic Meeting," *TDL*, April 29, 1889. This was the second of ten meetings. Seattle activists hosted similar events. For the lecture circuit, see, e.g., "A Suffrage Meeting [at Wallachet Bay]," *TDL*, April 18, 1889.

[17] Editorial, *TDL*, June 1, 1889, editorial page. See also Roger I. Sherman, "Looking Backward," ibid., June 6, 1889. On intellect, see "Qualifications of Voters," ibid., April 15, 1889.

he said, not to "distinct individuals," but to the political capacity of collectivities. America's extra-governmental monarch was indivisible and "indefeasible"; as George Turner had asserted in *Harland* to different ends, sovereignty was either whole or absent, incapable "by any juggle ... of being defeated or abrogated." To be sovereign was to animate and legitimate exercises of political power, to command property, and to expect state protection and support in lawful pursuits. The lesson of the late war, he argued, had been that governments were not free to demote human beings for scant cause; he admired Coleridge's allusion to the "free fermentive life and energy of the state acting through its original forces."[18]

The *Ledger*'s stable of writers exhibited uncommon sensitivity to the constitutive power of formal law, social practice, and language. In May, 1889, the editor himself noted that accomplished men *and* women were construed to be manly. "The poverty of a language is often as expressive as its wealth"; the fact that the "sterner virtue" had not been recognized in women showed "in how little honor they have been held."[19] The unrelieved "nanization" of women (the word described "the art of dwarfing large trees") spoke to the brute force of custom, yet Americans made "no allowance for the enormous effect of laws and customs and of social opinion" as constraints on women's "free development."[20] A female correspondent noted that the long-standing worship of womanly virtue and beauty, and woman's aversion to publicity and risk, originated in "subjugation." Women had been taught to "love their bonds"; the enlightened view in play for fifty years could not undo the work of countless generations. Timidity and anti-intellectualism were "Christianity materializing."[21]

In June, 1889, lawyer-businessmen W. W. Hartley addressed the problem of how societies made gender from sex difference: "The laws of nature govern male and female alike; if woman violates them she suffers the same penalties [as] man, and she enjoys the same rights and privileges, life, ... free air .... Not so with laws of man, by these she is held to a stricter accountability yet denied the rights ... man has selfishly arrogated to himself." Women were shut out of professions and, if forced to earn a living, accepted menial work, prostitution, or starvation. He, too, thought that physical and mental weakness flowed from social practice: "Her lesson books ..., the pulpit, the courts, the rostrum, the stage, all treat her as an effeminate something to be ... seen not heard, ... useful but submissive, a companion but not an equal." Her spirit of independence dashed, she became effeminate. If a strong-willed sister contended for equality, she met the ridicule of those who had

---

[18] "The Question of Sovereignty," *TDL*, June 14, 1889, p. 2. See also a letter from Tennessee's governor, affirming that members of the sovereignty were equal; "Woman Suffrage, How the Question is Discussed in Southern States," ibid., May 9, 1889.
[19] "Appreciation of Women," *TDL*, May 27, 1889, editorial page.
[20] Editor, "The 'Nanization' of Women," *TDL*, June 24, 1889, ed. page.
[21] Anonymous, "A Lady Contributor," *TDL*, May 19, 1889, p. 6.

"folded their hands in helpless resignation." This was intolerable. Women were an important constituent of the state, dealt in property, and claimed sovereignty equal to man's, whether they wanted it or not.[22]

Tempers flared in response to anti-suffragist Mary R. Keith's screed against a female presence in government. In her estimation, electoral qualification was a matter "not of abstract justice but of expediency." Could women "back up their choices with force"? Men performed the world's heavy labor, including combat; without willing performance of duties identical to men's, women depended on "gallantry." Radebaugh adopted Keith's categories: Was it not expedient to mobilize women against ignorance and filth? How did this objective conflict with "abstract right"? When had republican principle become irrelevant? Elsewhere, too, the suggestion that women shirked obligations triggered outrage. While not providing exactly what men provided, said one woman, her sisters served the nation "in their own way, not less than men. They suffer as much as men from the horrible effects of war," yet were excluded from policy making. Quoting Roger Greene's 1884 Port Townsend jury charge, suffragist Maria Hidden asked if unfit soldiers would be run out of polls and jury boxes alongside good women.[23]

Anti-suffragists' tethering of ballots and temperance in the ratification election made matters worse. In Iowa, Washington, and elsewhere, women attended polls, whether voting or not, "praying, button-holing, beseeching, demanding, persuading," and "confronting the men ... responsible for much human degradation." Zealotry found its way into print, as when the WCTU's Lucy Washington of New York advised Mrs. Mackey ("No True Woman in Tacoma Wants the Right to Vote") that the ballot needed women more than women needed the ballot. Mrs. Annie Harper of Port Townsend had threatened in a WCTU address that, when the territory finally shed "garments of childhood," there would be *"no uncertain justice."*[24] A decade later, interviewees admitted, when asked whether they opposed saloons, that women generally took the "business view of the matter" and were "no more inclined to be fanatical" than men.[25] But apocalyptic imagery set teeth on edge.

---

[22] W. W. Hartley, "From a New Comer," *TDL*, June 23, 1889.

[23] Mary R. Keith, "The Affirmative," *TDL*, May 30, 1889, p. 4; editorial, "Is Woman Suffrage Expedient?" ibid., May 2, 1889, p. 2; editorial, "The Bullet and the Ballot," ibid., June 4, 1889; Maria Hidden, "More Suffrage Talk," ibid., June 4, 1889.

[24] "Women at the Polls," *OR*, October 28, 1883; Lucy H. Washington, "Reply to Mrs. [Mildred] Mackey," *TDL*, May 23, 1889 and "The Annual Session," ibid., June 17, 1889, p. 6 (for Harper), emphasis added; and "The Work of Women, Why Mrs. Lucy H. Washington Preaches Temperance," ibid., May 4, 1889. See also Lucy Washington's brief letter, "The Mire of Politics," ibid., May 24, 1889, contending that woman suffrage fulfilled the law of the "universe" and of the founders, and the WCTU's fierce resolutions, "The Last Day of the WCTU Convention ...," ibid., June 18, 1889.

[25] "How Women Voted in Washington," *WS*, December 17, 1909. The assumption that all women opposed saloons persisted; e.g., W. W. Hartley puzzling over the fact that anti-saloon men still refused to give women the vote; "Mr. Hartley's Answer," *TDL*, June 29, 1889. See also "Are the

In January, 1888, a journalist ordered suffragists to stand down: "The one great, paramount object ... is admission to statehood .... Anything that would tend to weaken or divide counsels is directly against our best interests. ... Let us get statehood, and settle these matters afterward."[26]

Still, disenfranchised Washingtonians were not inclined to stand down or abandon constitutional abstractions. Mary A. Macready, in response to Mary Keith's multiple essays, grounded women's-rights claims in sovereignty and the equality principle. Man had "taken care to see that his rights have been secured; why should woman not do the same? Her rights are as sacred as his." Miranda Hardy agreed. But, Hardy, with others, had come to see that American constitutions had not yet sanctified women's freedom alongside men's; as Greene had warned, sovereignty was more fundamental than rights and more jealously guarded by powerful men. Hardy offered a poem: "If you admit she can rule o'er a nation/, Then just tell us why, in the name of creation,/ She can't rule herself in a free land – which means/ That all men are kings, and the women all queens!"[27] Lawyer Paul Weston reminded Mary Keith (who posited a nation of contented wives) that a "very large percentage of the women of the world are unmarried," or married unhappily; only they could represent themselves. Men who thought that women were content with civil equality and economic agency were "ignorant"; a man who would tax women "without giving them a voice in law-making is ... a selfish craven." Nebraska's Clara Colby, speaking at a Tacoma rally alongside Addie Barlow (now president of the WERA in Tacoma) and the well-known Matilda Hindman, noted that demands comported with basic republican principles, including the right to be free of unconstitutional takings: While politicians might look to "the 'people,' the 'citizens,' the 'inhabitants,' the 'residents,' and even 'persons'" without including women, the latter could not be excluded from the "governed and ... taxed." Taxation without representation was akin to "highway robbery.'" Anti-suffragists, in contrast, stonewalled equality: Citing Blackstone and St. Paul, Emma Barrett held that it made "no difference whether women are property holders or not, they are as a class represented in the government by men."[28]

Many social democrats, however, had lost their footing, in some cases in response to new talk about women's physical and mental vulnerabilities. In Tacoma, Miles B. Hunt argued a bit too strenuously that, if delegates could not write an equal-suffrage constitution, voters should reject it. The republic was "supposed to be of the people – women are people – by the people – that is women – and for the people. They are certainly people!" Nor did women agree

Women Natural Prohibitionists?" *Seattle Republican*, February 26, 1909, p. 1 (no more "fanatical" than men).
[26] Editorial, "Woman Suffragists ...," *PSWA*, January 10, 1888, inside page.
[27] A. Macready, "To Mrs. Keith Again," *TDL*, June 1, 1889; Mrs. Miranda A. Hardy, "Resolved, That Women Should Vote," ibid., May 30, 1889, p. 6.
[28] Paul Weston, "More of the Same," *TDL*, June 7, 1889; Emma M. Barrett, "An Olympian on Woman Suffrage," ibid., September 16, 1889.

on the merits of mixed access to offices, a term that variously denoted officers of the court (lawyers, bailiffs, jurors) and elective or nominative posts. Some women applauded mixed-sex office holding; in 1889, one "woman-on-the-street" hoped to vote for another woman because men "had been at the top just long enough." But another generally pro-suffrage interviewee feared that women's "constitution would not stand the strain of public life"; when they got excited, they were "good for nothing." Mildred Mackey, an anti-suffragist roundly denounced for a speech in which she declared that no true woman would vote, said this: "If it went no further than the ballot we might consider it. ... But it will not stop there. Woman suffragists to be consistent must run on our tickets, filling ... city offices from mayor to chief of police." Critics reminded her that good men voted but did not rush to fill public offices. But more than one citizen quailed at the prospect of women in law-related posts. Witness W. W. Hartley's disclaimer after a defense of mixed suffrage: "'How would I like my wife to run for sheriff?' I would not .... But this does not deter me, for I know her to be too sensible a lady to ever think of such a thing."[29]

As journalists worked overtime, activists fanned out over the countryside and invited out-of-state speakers to obscure towns. In early May, distinguished citizens (among them, Zerelda McCoy) hosted California's Laura De Force Gordon in remote Puyallup, complete with a "double quartette."[30] Suffrage organizers generally waged a more disciplined war than their opponents, who were disorganized, chary of constitutional arguments, and given to repeating passages from Blackstone or the Bible. Still, the burden was on suffragists to persuade statehood boosters of American devotion to the equality principle – a task that became more difficult with rumors that pragmatists from both camps intended to shuffle the question off to the ratification election in the form, yet again, of joined-at-the-hip prohibition and suffrage amendments.[31] During her summer lecture tour, Hindman condemned the idea, driving home republican doctrine (especially the equality principle) and the travesty of *Bloomer*. It was the duty of the framers of the state constitution to embrace "the principle of equal protection to all citizens"; she asked no less protection for women than was granted to men. Republics rested on consent of the governed; Americans rejected taxation without representation. States that resisted these doctrines

---

[29] Miles B. Hunt, "The Suffrage Debate," *TDL*, May 31, 1889; "Mrs. Colby Speaks," ibid., May 13, 1889. See also "When Women Vote ... Women's Rule," ibid., May 25, 1889; Mildred F. Mackey, "Mrs. Mackey Answers," ibid., May 25, 1889. See also "Can She Be Mistaken," ibid., May 26, 1889, p. 4, containing shocked and angry responses to Mackey's remarks. Many writers thought that possession of ballots would lead more women than men into office. See also "Woman Suffrage and Natural Law," *TDL*, May 29, 1889; W. W. Hartley, "Mr. Hartley's Answer," ibid., June 29, 1889.

[30] "Affairs at Puyallup," *TDL*, May 4, 1889, p. 6. McCoy had a long-standing association with the Puyallup Indian reservation.

[31] But see as well the suggestion, lodged anonymously, that men should "keep their mouths shut and let the women settle the question themselves" in a women's election; Fair Play, "Let the Men Stand Aside," *TDL*, June 27, 1889.

were "not truly democratic." Takings again appeared: It was criminal to steal, yet "men ignobly stooped to the baseness of robbing women of their civil and political rights." Perhaps in emulation of Matilda Gage, she argued that no more unrighteous act ever had been perpetrated in a courtroom than the reading of *Bloomer* v. *Todd*.[32]

Suffragists knew that a mixed-sex polity would be lost without powerful help at the convention. Hence, on July 3, a day before the event opened, Benjamin Dennison, Zerelda McCoy, and other members of WERA and NWSA gathered in Olympia's Good Templar Hall to adopt resolutions and lay plans. Participants asserted, to give a few examples, that three successive legislatures had enfranchised women with gubernatorial, popular, and partisan approval; that equal suffrage must be embedded in the constitution; that judges dared not defy the popular will and the organic act, as determined in the U.S. Supreme Court in *Pratt* v. *Ramsey*; that the rights of sovereign citizens were off-limits to voters, especially when the electorate included "patrons of the prize ring, wife-beaters, tramps, swindlers and drunkards"; that because lawmakers derived all lawful power from the consent of the governed, any constitution to the contrary was void; and that the promise of new federal amendments would not be realized until each citizen "entered into the inheritance of equal liberty, equal justice and equal rights." The final resolution betrayed considerable alarm: Activists demanded "that the existing law regulating the property rights of husband and wife ... remain upon the statutes of the territory, where it has been since 1869, until ... repealed or amended by the [state] legislature."[33]

Rhetorical violence and silencing escalated. In the midst of a debate at Tacoma's Optimists Club, a suffragist accused men of "burglarizing" women's rights ("Woman has already the right to vote"), adding for good measure that "the strong-minded suffragist is after you" and would "shunt you and your bad politics to the side track." An indignant man from Artondale had learned that "for a male voter to believe that women should be allowed to vote would disfranchise him also." M. H. Hunt had been named inspector of elections but then removed when leaders in Tacoma learned that he was a suffragist. A woman styling herself 'Liberty' had dared to say that "harm was lurking" in the constitution and that it was no answer to say that "we are a disfranchised people because we are not a state." Friends urged her to "desist"

[32] Matilda Hindman, "Woman Suffrage," *SFR*, May [30?], 1889. Her comments about Bloomer are virtually identical to those of Matilda Gage; see above. In the same vein, see Matilda Hindman, "From Miss Hindman," *TDL*, May 12, 1889. The Ledger interviewed Hindman in early May; see "Miss Hindman's Work," ibid., May 6, 1889 (a biographical piece). She stayed until October, 1889.

[33] "Going to Olympia," *SPI*, July 3, 1889, front page; "Chairman Hoyt," ibid., July 4, 1889, front page, or "The Suffrage Convention," *WS*, July 5, 1889. *Pratt* v. *Ramsey*, said to be in 1884 but delivered in 1885, was part of a cluster of Utah cases; Pratt was distinguished from other parties because she had not been a bigamist and so, with the Edmunds Act, plausibly had been deprived of her ballot unlawfully. But the Court did not strike down the Act on those grounds.

and "not abuse . . . freedom of speech," whereupon she decided to speak to male voters under a pseudonym: "Every man who holds the ballot wields the power of a king, and may you use that privilege in a thoughtful way" to protect the rights of others. Gratuitous insults yielded surprises – as when an anti-suffrage woman from Pullman disputed the idea that suffragists neglected home duties; in fact, she said, "more – yes, more – remain in their duties" than not.[34]

Even former allies discouraged fulsome debate. The NWSA's Elizabeth Lyle Saxon, who had traveled along a railroad line in eastern counties to discuss women's rights, found good audiences in Colfax. But when a Republican rally began, "an undefined something began to be felt, and the conviction would arise – that can only be felt not told – that there was some hidden influence at work adverse to these meetings." Prohibitionists silently shunned her, and the "women who advocated the ballot, don't know what to do, are afraid to try to vote, even for the amendment article, to show that women do desire to vote." She would go to Walla Walla, but "if the republican rallies are as vigorous as I have found them elsewhere," she would be helpless. Once a voter, she was now an "old crowing hen."[35]

Notwithstanding heroic campaigning, then, anti-suffragists had the upper hand. Long years of strife over ancillary rights and gender destabilization had taken a toll. Too many opponents held, with a self-described Republican woman in May, 1889, that they did not like the spectacle of women in masculine settings. She chose to express opinions by electioneering for Harrison and "keeping up with the times." In her view, each household merited one vote; only if the man died should his widow vote.[36] During opening ceremonies on July 5, 1889, a speaker crowned future sovereigns and praised their helpmeets: "Boys, a prince of England may become a king, but some one of you may be a greater monarch than he if you possess the qualities that make monarchs . . . . Girls, you can help the boys to be men and monarchs . . . . Be content, I pray you, with the great responsibilities and privileges nature has apportioned you."[37]

---

[34] On the dire effects of fires in Seattle's business district, see, e.g., "Stricken Seattle," *TDL*, June 7, 1889, p. 4. See also A. Macready, "Glad It Has Started," *TDL*, May 24, 1889. Finally, see "M. B. Hunt, "Disfranchises the Men, Too," *TDL*, September 26, 1889; Liberty, "A Slap at the Constitution," *TDL*, September 20, 1889; "X," "Communicated," *PH*, August 10, 1889. Ferocity was apparent early in eastern counties; e.g., "[From] Vancouver Independent," ibid., December 15, 1888, warning men not to "raise the ghost" of suffrage if they wanted public office.

[35] Elizabeth Lyle Saxon, "Discouraging," *TDL*, September 22, 1889, p. 6. Saxon promoted suffrage, prohibitionism, and spiritualism. Republicans completed the state ticket in secret and in place of woman suffrage endorsed the idea of separate amendments; "Convention Closed," *TDL*, September 6, 1889, p. 8. In May, a public meeting in Colfax tabled a resolution favoring separate amendments; "At Colfax," *PH*, May 4, 1889.

[36] "When Women Vote . . . Some Who Wouldn't," *TDL*, May 25, 1889.

[37] "Olympia Celebration," *TDL*, July 5, 1889; "The Rights of Citizenship," *TDL*, July 6, 1889.

"WOMAN SUFFRAGE IS NO LONGER CONSIDERED A LIVE QUESTION"

Two convocations provided the nationalizing opportunity to which Chief Justice Richard Jones had referred in *Bloomer* v. *Todd* – a preliminary gathering at Ellensburg in spring of 1889 to establish guidelines for a territory-wide election of delegates, and the constitutional convention at Olympia on July 4, 1889. Regionalism marred the first event. During a Christmas Eve meeting in 1888, eastern and western factions of both major parties locked horns over the proportion of delegates; in the end, they left the matter with the mayor, who would appoint delegates after conversations with businessmen.[38] Seattle Democrats, including union leaders, met to identify men who would frame a constitution "for the whole people and not for a party"; they also declared opposition to any provisions related to woman suffrage or prohibition. When delegates met at Ellensburg, senior members of the Seattle bar (John Hoyt, Watson Squires, J. C. Haines, and Orange Jacobs) led the western bloc; only Hoyt and Jacobs sympathized with equal suffrage.[39]

Castigated by opponents for undue ambition,[40] George Turner of Spokane Falls entered the two convocations with both railroaders and unruly women in the crosshairs. Turner opposed the lines' appetite for the tidelands and knew that suffragists would disrupt statehood deliberations.[41] Women's aggression probably reinforced Turner's paternalism. In September, 1888, John L. Wilson (a Spokane Falls ally) had used the term "protection" a half-dozen times in a speech nominating the pro-tariff Republican as a delegate to the Ellensburg convocation; among them were not only the protection of markets, factories, and laborers, but also protection of American homes and impartial suffrage, the latter to purge single-issue "cranks." The "manly" Turner, who supposedly resisted "wild impulses," supported "combat for an impartial suffrage and the equality of all men before the law." He epitomized what Judy Hilkey calls the "sexualization of success, the celebration of willpower, and the presentation of self-mastery as a precondition for mastery in the world." When Turner gave his

---

[38] "Statehood," *SP*, December 24, 1888.

[39] "Voters Attention," *SP*, May 10, 1889. Voter turnout for Ellensburg delegates was light; see, e.g., surprise at the "lightness of the vote all over the territory," *SPI*, May 15, 1889. See also "The Election," *SFR*, May 15, 1889, front page. Finally, see "Statehood Meeting," *TDL*, January 3, 1889, p. 8.

[40] E.g., "There are some folks ...," *TDL*, May 10, 1889, editorial page, alleging that Turner had "become so accustomed to office-holding that he does not feel at home as a common, every day citizen." But see "Judge Turner," ibid., October 2, 1889, noting Turner's popularity in eastern Washington.

[41] Journalists typically assumed a male statehood electorate; "Local Brevities [stating candidate positions]," and "Declaration of Rights [by Emery McGinnis] ... ," *BBR*, May 10, 1889. See the essay about ballot reform which describes voters as "he," ignores women's disfranchisement, and lists (as likely exclusions) vagrants, criminals, foreigners, and "ignoramuses"; [A. P. Thornton?], "The Question of the Hour," *BBR*, April 26, 1889. On reform, see also "Electoral Reform," ibid., March 15, 1889.

two-volume scrapbook to his wife in 1935, he wrote, "Trees, like men, that stand in high places have many blasts to shake them."[42]

Turner had twice sought the help of former governor Elisha Ferry, a Republican known to be a frontrunner in state gubernatorial elections. "What I want to suggest," Turner wrote privately soon after the enabling act's adoption, "is that there will be little satisfaction in being Governor or any thing else ... if we let the cranks capture the Constitutional Convention and reproduce the Constitution made some years ago, or perhaps worse." Surely Ferry could secure a seat for himself and then "reach an understanding with all elements ... like minded with ourselves whereby none but liberal broad minded men shall be sent to the Convention?" Stubborn delegates could be treated to a "little active interference."[43] The last election had not "eliminated the long haired element from the body politic on Puget Sound," as it had to the east. "Woman suffrage is no longer considered a live question in this locality – and I do not think we will feel required to make any pledges. And I can hardly believe from your past experience that any such are needful ... in King County. ... Certainly the plan proposed by you" – i.e., turning the question over to male voters – "is the least harmful plan that could be adopted. My only fear is that it may make the cranks cry foul again." He invited Ferry to his home for a private meeting.[44]

---

[42] "A Talk for Turner," *SFR*, September 15, 1888. Turner pasted the "manly" comment in his scrapbook. See Judy Hilkey, *Character is Capital: Success Manuals and Manhood in Gilded-Age America* (Chapel Hill, NC, 1997), pp. 150–1. Turner's meticulously maintained scrapbooks, which fairly bulge with stores or pictures of women, permit a glimpse of his polarized views; women were either virtuous or dangerous; George Turner Papers, Scrapbooks, Vols. 1 and 2, Vol. 1, pp. 4–5, WSU-SC; testimonials at pp. 16, 17, and passim. For examples of deranged women, see "The Doll Question" (on Willard), p. 3; "Another Prodigious Sham" (women and false charity), p. 3; "Two Jolly Ugly Women" (beauty through artifice), p. 5; "Miss Varina Davis ...," (sweet but dangerous); "Is Marriage a Failure?" from the New York World (marriage's disadvantages for women), p. 6; "The Surface Croppings of the Painted Ball Room Wife ...," (a woman "all frizzed up and rigged out"), p. 7; "A Study in Flirting" (the wanderlust of women who danced well), p. 8; "A Late Religious Novel" (man led astray by a woman's lies), p. 10; "Dreaming of Our Summer Wanderer" (a flirtatious woman), p. 11; "A Patchwork Character" (poem about a dutiful wife), p. 11; "Mrs. Lofty and I" (a woman putting on airs), p. 16; "She Haunted Him" (a woman haunts a man for life, eventually killing him), p. 19. For "blasts," see Vol. 2, p. 65.

[43] George Turner to Elisha Ferry, February 25, 1889, Elisha Ferry Papers, UWSC, Box I-49. Cf. Robert Ficken, *Washington Territory* (Pullman, WA, 2002), pp. 209–12, contending that "no major voice of influence called for rejection" of the constitution; suffragism does not figure in his account, though he rightly notes preoccupations with railroads and the economy (see, e.g., "The Vital Question," *WS*, August 2, 1889). Railroaders probably tried to bribe Turner to get him out of the constitutional convention.

[44] George Turner to Elisha Ferry, March 4, 1889, Ferry Papers, Box I-49. No further evidence of the meeting at Turner's home could be found. Pro-statehood mobilization had been particularly fierce in eastern Washington, including Turner's home town; e.g., "Washington News. Spokane Falls Agitating for Admission ...," *SPI*, December 12, 1888, p. 8.

When the convention finally convened on July 4, 1889, delegates turned first to government's role in demographic and economic growth, granting legislators and executive officers vast discretion with finances and transportation. The mild-mannered John Philo Hoyt accepted the post of convention president. Turner, in contrast, seemed to epitomize what one reporter called "the young energies, brawn and brains" of a modern state. His supporters were said to include many "laborers and mechanics, merchants and capitalists, sporting men and moralists, lawyers and doctors, and men of various shades of opinion."[45] Once it became clear that Seattle delegates controlled the floor, Turner had risen to nominate Hoyt, who had never been called a 'crank' and wanted a seat on the state's appellate bench. When friends tried to draft Turner as president, he reportedly was "very very angry."[46]

The Hoyt-Turner alliance, while awkward, symbolized the range of credible, partisan opinion on sex-blind equality and perhaps on the efficacy of a politics rooted in republican idealism; having weathered a firestorm, they now asked practical men to set aside differences in aid of a higher cause. In 1889, the two men did not anticipate a speedy Fuller-Court hearing of the *Bloomer* appeal. As the same reporter put it, while Turner had gone "further than was thought proper by many in his decisions against the validity of the woman suffrage law," he now proposed submitting the question to voters as a "separate ordinance."[47] Neither Hoyt nor Turner addressed ancillary rights. And, while Hoyt presided, Turner led the judiciary committee, where he could remind delegates, whenever they strayed, of *Bloomer* v. *Todd* and suffragism's toxicity in Congress. In April, an anti-suffrage Walla Walla editor warned that equal suffrage in the body of the constitution would "endanger the adoption of that instrument and, very probably, prevent the admission of Washington .... Who besides the woman suffragists wish to do that?" Better to offer it to electors as a stand-alone proposition, not "sugar-coated until it becomes admission with woman suffrage or stay in a Territorial condition indefinitely."[48]

At Olympia, procedural and staffing decisions also shaped outcomes. Delegates had decided to use the state constitution of California as a model, in part because it was a new western state with seaport cities, but also because it had embraced community property. Inconveniently, Section II of that document

---

[45] Unidentified clipping ("Sentinel"), Turner Papers, Scrapbooks, Vol. 1, p. 21.

[46] "The Convention," *SPI*, July 5, 1889, front page; "very very" in original. See also "Hoyt Made President," ibid., July 6, 1889, p. 4, and "Constitutional Convention," *WWU*, July 13, 1889. Proceedings were printed widely.

[47] Ibid. This had long been a favored anti-suffrage strategy; e.g., "Note and Comment," *WWU*, January 14, 1888, altered and repr. later as "Judge Turner and the Public," *SFR*, May 19, 1889, p. 4. Many examples appear. See also "Little Deal Legislation," ibid., January 14, 1888, proposing as a fallback measure that voters choose a delegate devoted to the elimination of equal suffrage.

[48] "Current Notes," *WWU*, April 27, 1889, ed. page. At the outset, minor political associations (e.g., the Prohibition Party) were squeezed out in favor of Democrats and Republicans. See also "How Do You Answer?" *WWU*, May 18, 1889.

left the electorate's gender to legislators.[49] Delegates chose one of Turner's anti-suffrage friends, Potter Charles (P. C.) Sullivan – the eccentric Pierce County Republican boss – as chair of the Committee for Elections, which, in turn, blocked attempts by Edward Eldridge's pro-suffrage minority to exploit Section II and eliminate both a masculine ratification electorate and separate articles.[50] As early as May, 1889, the widely revered Eldridge had announced support for equality. In his words, he had been the first man to "publicly advocate it" in Washington and would be "the last to abandon it." Setting justice aside, he believed that the future of the American system depended on delivery of the "right of self-protection" to women; so long as they involuntarily "tied themselves to men, where no love exists," and became mothers merely to survive, America would languish. Eldridge thus pledged to stand or fall for equality – for the sake of society and for the "honor of our manhood."[51]

Delegates had been warned about "an attack of woman suffragists," and tables indeed groaned with petitions. One bore the signatures of fourteen Yakima women demanding a constitution with a genuinely representative form of government. They did not seek to interject new ideas, only to call attention to the "burlesque we as a nation are playing before the world, pretending to teach that taxation without representation is tyranny, while we continue to tax and legislate for an unrepresented class." Petitions arrived daily into mid-August. Among the pro-suffrage signatories were John Hoyt; P. G. Hendricks, with 394 other men and 414 women; Francis Minor of St. Louis, the husband of Virginia Minor (of *Minor v. Happersett*);[52] and McCoy ("a taxpaying woman"). Minor reminded delegates that Supreme Court Justice Samuel Miller had invited Congress to invalidate anti-republican election laws in *Ex Parte Yarbrough* (1884).[53] Henry Blackwell, Orange Jacobs, and Bessie Isaacs of Walla Walla addressed the committee on elections in late July, where

---

[49] "A Sample Constitution," *TDL*, July 3, 1889, p. 2. The California document said only that "all citizens entitled to vote after six months' residence" would attend elections.

[50] Eldridge had withdrawn his name for convention president on the promise that he would chair the elections committee; "The First Nail," *TDL*, July 10, 1889, p. 4. ("He is not only not chairman but he is not a member of that committee. He is a member of two unimportant committees" and "aggrieved.")

[51] "Edward Eldridge, "To the Voters of the 16th Constitutional District," *BBR*, May 10, 1889, ed. page. A slightly altered version appeared during the convention; "Woman Suffrage," ibid., September 27, 1889. There, he spoke of independence as the quintessential trait of citizens, without which they would not realize "liberty and equality."

[52] *Minor v. Happersett*, 88 U.S. 162 (1874) (the right to an occupation not an incident of federal citizenship under the Fourteenth Amendment). Minor also urged John Hoyt to lend support to a state woman-suffrage amendment; "The Day's Session," *SPI*, July 16, 1889 (letter printed with petitions logged in the convention). For yet more petitions, see "The Convention," ibid., July 19, 1889, front page.

[53] See, e.g., "Federal Suffrage," *TDL*, July 22, 1889, p. 6. See also *Ex parte Yarbrough*, 110 U.S. 651 (1884), defending federal intervention where whites had deprived a black man in Georgia of the right to vote through intimidation.

they were grilled on women's preparedness for militia duty; Isaacs replied that "some men were exempted on account of age ... [or] physical inability, yet they voted all the same."[54] When Blackwell offered to address the body, Turner's allies argued that it was improper for outsiders to address the convention. Blackwell finally spoke to delegates and others (mostly the latter) at Tacoma Hall. On July 23, when suffragists met again, they decided to "lie low."[55]

Meanwhile, Washington's main parties continued to retreat. When Republicans were asked to honor promises made in past platforms, legislators said that, because promises had not been made recently, they did "not consider themselves bound by them." In June, 1889, delegate Francis Henry, the Supreme Court's Democratic clerk, responded to Zerelda McCoy's open letter to his party. McCoy had asserted that equal suffrage underlay any theory of government predicated on "equal protection of the ballot," a principle which Democrats had once claimed to support. Henry tried to bury the question: Surely it could have "no importance whatever" before the convention, nor could they properly arise when delegates derived power from citizens qualified to vote on May 15, 1889. Still, the barrage was so intense that a pro-suffrage reporter predicted in July, 1889, that the "burning question" of suffrage would delay the completion of work. On July 11, Henry finally allowed that delegates had the authority to enfranchise women, but he doubted the policy of doing so.[56]

From his Senate office at the nation's capital, George Hoar pelted newspaper offices and public officials with advice. One letter, aired in both the Boston *Transcript* and the New York *Times*, reminded delegates that nearly a majority of Senators favored equality, many urged state's rights, and Benjamin Harrison had voted while a Senator to "submit a woman-suffrage amendment to the States."[57] But, in Olympia, suffragists steadily lost. On August 8, the elections

---

[54] "Hearings in Washington Territory," *WJ*, August 3, 1889, p. 244. See also "The Law Framers," *SPI*, 24, 1889. For the initial suggestion of a presentation, see "The Woman Suffragists are disposed ...," ibid., July 22, 1889, front page. Exchanges about combat may have been related to parallel discussions about whether the militia ought to be subject to civilian supervision; "God and the Military," ibid., July 30, 1889, p. 8. See also "A Plea for Equal Suffrage," ibid., p. 8, noting that Hoyt attended the Tacoma Hall event with ten delegates, and (for "lie low"), "The Statemakers," ibid., July 23, 1889, front page.

[55] Ibid., and "The New States," *WJ*, August 10, 1883, p. 252. Blackwell asked subscribers to send help, financial and otherwise; "Help Washington Territory," ibid., March 23, 1889. See also solicitations of money, to be sent variously to Zerelda McCoy and Roger S. Greene; e.g., "Aid Washington Territory," ibid., June 22, 1889, or "Latest from Washington Territory," ibid., September 7, 1889. See also "Argument for Suffrage," *TDL*, July 30, 1889, p. 8, and "Woman Suffrage in Washington," *WS*, August 2, 1889 (on Blackwell).

[56] "The Convention," *SPI*, July 10, 1889, front page; "At the Capital," *TDL*, July 3, 1889. See also [McCoy challenge to Democrats and letter from Henry], "A Delegate's Views, Hon. Francis Henry Writes an Open Letter," *TDL*, June 14, 1889, and "The Elective Franchise," ibid., June 15, 1889, p. 2 (continuing the discussion).

[57] "The President a Woman Suffragist," *NYT*, August 11, 1889, p. 8.

committee received a final, desperate petition from a myriad of activists: Why not submit the constitution to voters with a chapter mandating an early referendum after statehood? Women then might stand a chance.[58] Eldridge tried to amend an unfriendly provision ("and all females possessing qualification of electors shall vote on this question") but lost. On August 12, he tried to strike the word "male" from Article VI, failing by the decisive margin of fifty to eight ("All male persons of the age of twenty-one years ... shall be entitled to vote at all elections. ... [A]ll male persons who at the time of the adoption of this Constitution are qualified electors of the territory, shall be electors.") During an all-male ratification election, voters would confront suffrage and prohibition articles, as in the 1870s. When Eldridge tried to further amend the suffrage article to give lawmakers power to resubmit the question to the voters in the future, he lost again, forty-three to twenty-eight. On August 15, after multiple ballots that suffragists managed to spread over the record, delegates engrossed the new election articles. Only five out of seventy-two opposed the plan. The *Post-Intelligencer*, noting blandly that conditions had changed since equal suffrage had been "in vogue," predicted a masculine sweep at the polls.[59] McCoy astutely sensed a *coup*; until the *Bloomer* appeal had been concluded, she said hopefully, women retained the right to vote, the "title to which has been granted and confirmed to them by three acts of three successive legislatures."[60] But, with statehood a *fait accompli*, brave assertions rang hollow.

Members did not altogether forsake women. The constitution included mixed-sex school suffrage and office-holding – though, even there, delegates forestalled future expansions.[61] On August 12, Delegate Eshelman moved to allow women to vote for "school officers and measures, and to hold school offices." Delegate Ralph Dunbar swiftly closed a possible loophole in the draft's language ("The Legislature may provide that there shall be no denial of the

---

[58] Rosenow, Journal, pp. 634, 636–7. For text of articles, see ibid., p. 878. Manuscript journals are housed at WSA-O. The final text appeared in local prints; e.g., "The Constitution," *SPI*, August 23, 1889. The suggested chapter to force a referendum read: "At the time of the election of county officers ... in November in the year 1890, a proposition to amend this Constitution by striking out the word 'male' from the article on elections ... shall be submitted to the electors of the state." On separate articles, see "To Decide at Olympia," *TDL*, July 25, 1889, p. 4. On efforts to mount a separate election for women only on the amendments, see, e.g., C. P. Culver, "Suffrage and Liquor. To Enable Women to Settle the Suffrage Question," ibid., July 23, 1889. See also Fair Play, "'Fair Play' Again," ibid., July 6, 1889. For the odds against defeating the separate-article idea, see Flynn, "Monday at Olympia," ibid., July 16, 1889, p. 4.

[59] Ibid., and editorial, "Trying Again," *SPI*, August 18, 1889.

[60] "No Representation," *TDL*, August 13, 1889, p. 4. For debates and drafts, "Committee Meetings," ibid., July 31, 1889, p. 8; "Elective Franchise," ibid., August 9, 1889, p. 8; Zerelda N. McCoy, "Woman Suffrage. A Communication from the President of the Woman Suffrage Association," *TDL*, August 19, 1889.

[61] For adoption of school suffrage, see "On Corporations, The Convention Finally Disposes ...," *SPI*, August 7, 1889, front page, where the new, general election chapter also appeared ("male").

elective franchise *at any school election on account of sex"*), fearing that it would allow the legislature to grant woman suffrage. In the end, the word 'any' vanished ("... at school elections"). Delegates also chose a construction so jaw-dropping that editors printed it in full ("The next section, excluding, in addition to women, all idiots, insane persons, and persons convicted of infamous crimes, unless restored to civil rights, from the elective franchise, was adopted"). Several delegates rose on August 12 to mount last-ditch pleas. Eldridge argued that, if the question were left to future legislatures, it would be endlessly disruptive. But, in the end, even an amendment permitting women to serve as school superintendents lost narrowly (thirty-one to thirty).[62]

Sometimes, the problem of woman's political personality tied delegates in knots. On July 25, for instance, in a discussion of Section 19, Article I, which addressed freedom of elections and read, "All elections shall be free and equal ...," Delegate Cosgrove nervously inquired after the meaning of "equal." Delegate Moore "said it meant the same as 'free.'" Not satisfied, Delegate Dyer moved to substitute "open" for "equal." T. M. Reed supplied the word "impartial." Another member suggested striking the section altogether. In the end, they fastened on "the free exercise of the right of suffrage," thus eliminating what might have been an opening for equal ancillary rights.[63] By August 19, as the convention wound down, political equality had become the butt of jokes. Cosgrove offered a resolution providing that "after 1895 only married people, ... each of them to have half a vote and an additional one-half vote for each ten children; the issue of their marriage, but no widow or widower or divorced person to have the rights of elector." The resolution was referred to the "Tide Lands Committee, although Mr. Dunbar preferred that it should go to the Committee on Insane."[64]

Elsewhere, members acted less to prevent female invasions of courtrooms than to forestall grand-jury overreach in the future. Reformers had been seeking alterations of (or alternatives to) the grand jury for years; as John La Farge explained in an 1890 issue of *Century Magazine* about frames of government in Washington and Montana, "little by little, the constitutions have introduced provisions by which causes may be brought to trial without the intervention of a jury, before the court, or before an office qualified to preside in the case." Uncertainties attendant on the jury system were "slowly relegating trial by jury into a choice of methods, or into a respectable place in judicial history."

[62] Rosenow, Journal, pp. 633–4, 636–8, and "Our Law Framers," WS, August 16, 1889, p. 2. For Eldridge's long speech and reactions, see "State Elections," SPI, August 13, 1889, front page. See also "Carried at Last," TDL, August 13, 1889, p. 8.

[63] Rosenow, Journal, pp. 508–9.

[64] "Our Law Framers," WS, August 23, 1889. Debate in the House of Representatives, unlike debates in the Senate, involved the shape and range of the bill, whether to treat territories separately or in an omnibus bill, why New Mexico was being omitted, with Democrats (excepting Delegate Voorhees) stalling and Republicans in support. Woman suffrage does not figure in the House; Congressional Record, House, 50th Congress, 2nd Session, 1889, pp. 500–2179.

Law-minded Washingtonians knew of these developments; pre-*Bloomer* experiences perhaps encouraged them. In July, a journalist noted a general feeling that grand juries should be abolished or stripped of power. The press sometimes defended the "palladium of our liberties" if juries could be kept pure; surely most men could divest themselves of opinions gathered from newspapers or from courtroom evidence, as women allegedly could not do. But, for many, the system had been damaged seriously, if not fatally.[65]

Delegates finally compromised: The right of trial by jury remained inviolate, but, to hedge the state against dangerous grand juries, they allowed indictment by prosecutors or by grand juries at judges' discretion. A Seattle writer noted that the grand jury had been "deprived of very much of its importance."[66] On July 11, members adopted Article 1, Section 26, which provided for grand juries composed of fifteen qualified electors to be summoned annually and used at judges' discretion. Non-voting women thus entered courtrooms as plaintiffs, defendants, clerks, witnesses, and perhaps as lawyers (chapters related to counsel were sex-neutral, although Judge Nash had refused to admit Mrs. Samuel Thompson of Kittitas County to the bar in 1888), but not as neighborhood exemplars. Some part of these efforts also smacked of attempts to empower judges and disempower citizens: Turner and Hoyt, for example, defeated an amendment that would have transformed judges into figureheads in relation to jurors' fact-finding role. Both held that judges had to be able to intervene to "prevent error."[67]

Ratification of the new document, while probable, was not inevitable. As the convention wound down and in advance of the election, debate continued. On August 7, 1889, for instance, just as delegates struggled with equal suffrage, two aspirants to the Pierce County bar, Albert E. Joab and D. J. Griffiths, squared off in public. On the pro-equality side, Joab emphasized republican constitutionalism and women's capacity for sound judgment. Women were

---

[65] John La Farge, "Washington and Montana," *Century Illustrated Monthly Magazine*, Vol. XXXIX, No. 4 (February 1890), p. 505; "Editorial, *BBR*, July 6, 1889, ed. page; "The Cron[i?]n Case," *ST*, October 16, 1889; "The Jury System," *ST*, September 17, 1889.

[66] Rosenow, Journal, p. 510; "The Convention," *SPI*, July 26, 1889, front page.

[67] "A Woman Refused Admission," *TDL*, October 9, 1888. She had been "reading law for a good while," had "passed a very creditable examination," was of "good moral character," yet was refused. See also Rosenow, Journal, p. 513. On juries, see "The Convention," *SPI*, July 12, 1889, front page, describing progress toward a bill of rights, and "One Clause Finished," *TDL*, July 21, 1889, p. 4. Turner's interest in securing appropriately masculine courtrooms (and preventing another Roger Greene from mesmerizing women) extended to the procurement of state justices. As chair of the judiciary committee, he supported non-partisan, at-large election of justices. At the same time, he opposed short terms; if judges were to "truckle to public opinion," better to have them do so infrequently. Nobody mentioned sex. But, given the purging of women at Turner's hand, the prospect of women eventually voting in general elections probably lent urgency to his unsuccessful arguments for long terms and non-partisan ballots. Rosenow, Journal, pp. 600–1, 608 (the latter on July 19). Cf. Charles K. Wiggins, "George Turner and the Judiciary Article," www.appeal-law.com/constitution.turner.html, which barely touches on the woman problem.

obviously as intelligent as men: He had toured public schools, interviewed teachers, and learned that the vast majority favored equality. Without representation in government, women were in a state "worse than were the slaves in the south," deprived unlawfully of human rights. Inasmuch as lawyers, doctors, and ministers were excused from jury service, he added, it was little more than common courtesy to excuse women – not in response to lack of capacity, but as a "social necessity." Why burden women with home *and* state? On the other side, Griffiths pointed to mental incapacity and Blackstone; he found none of the "wisdom necessary to govern, or stand at the helm of the ship of state."[68] Home-bound women often agreed, if for other reasons. "We do not want suffrage," said "One Woman" in May, 1889, "because to grant it would be not only not to remedy but to double existing difficulties." Why should they bear responsibility for domestic *and* public peace?[69]

Regional and local journalists closely followed events in Olympia; Californians predicted that eastern counties would reject the document on the ground of "too many judges and legislative officers," and that supporters of equal suffrage had labored to defeat it.[70] Citizens were admonished to remember that "everything evil in it can be corrected by amendment"; rejection meant that Washington would "continue in the condition of territorial servitude." In Seattle and elsewhere, women handed out tickets and were "very free in their advocacy" for the suffrage amendment as well as for pro-suffrage legislators.[71] Benjamin Brown, while conceding in September, 1889, that the *Bloomer* appeal was moot, urged women to attend polls beside their husbands "on terms of perfect equality" and cast votes against the constitution. Why walk meekly behind men "like the women of China"?[72]

Meekness certainly did not characterize Duniway, McCoy, and others as they again urged women to storm the polls and deposit ballots in main or separate boxes; rumors multiplied of fraudulent tickets that lacked the "against" choice. McCoy's faith in the sanctity of constitutions and rights persisted well beyond ratification. Time and again, she vilified those who would deprive republican citizens of their franchise. Did not the enabling act

[68] "Shall Women Vote?" *TDL*, August 8, 1889. For an earlier discussion of educators' pro-suffrage views, see "The Talk of the Time," ibid., May 28, 1889. Not all teachers agreed. In July, members of the Teachers' Institute adopted resolutions proposing a literary test and adoption of equal suffrage only for educated people; "What the Teachers Say," CC, Dayton, W. T., July 6, 1889, ed. page.

[69] "One Woman," "They Do Not Want Suffrage," *TDL*, May 23, 1889.

[70] "It Must Not Be," *LAT*, October 1, 1889, p. 4. Duniway's letters urging both non-compliance and "yes" votes were widely published; e.g., "From Mrs. Duniway," *TDL*, September 27, 1889, and "Mrs. Duniway Again," ibid., September 29, 1889, p. 6. See also a report of Duniway's arguments at a meeting in Walla Walla, "They Want to Vote," *ST*, September 7, 1889, front page.

[71] E.g., "Vote for It," *ST*, September 27, 1889, ed. page, or "Non-Partisan Issues," ibid., September 28, 1889; and "Election Day," ibid., October 1, 1889.

[72] Benjamin F. Brown, "The New Constitution," *WS*, September 27, 1889, front page.

guarantee a state "republican in form" that comported with the principles of the Declaration of Independence? Surely citizens had an "inherent right to give consent to government and to protect their individual rights." The conspiracy by which courts had tried to rob women of their "*title to the ballot* and reduce them to slavery" delegitimized the convention as well as members of the state's first assembly.[73] McCoy urged women to go to the polls and demand that their ballots be accepted; with Hindman, she characterized the separate-amendment scheme as an insult to those who had demanded "constitutional security" for woman suffrage. She urged women to take two witnesses (at least one a friend of suffrage) to the polls and take the oath given to a challenged voter. If rejected, women should insist that the cause be written on the ballot and signed by an official. Voter and witness then would seek out a notary and send the result to her for use when suffragists filed suit. "We have no soft words to spare for men who pretend to be our friends and are not willing to ... be counted on our side." One of them, in fact, challenged his peers to no longer "creep around like servile cowards" and to reject a document "half slave and half free."[74]

Into September, 1889, the *Woman's Journal* reported that Washingtonians would "do what they must." When ballots were refused, they would carry their cause to the nation's highest court. They did not know how extensive their movement might be or whether they could elect a liberal assembly. One anxious anti-suffragist said that, if women tried to "bulldoze" poll personnel, they would be "humiliated by the refusal of the judges" and endanger the territory itself. Duniway, who was largely absent, advised women to ignore *Bloomer*: "Push a full vote. If men refuse to accept your ballots, have polls and poll books of your own." In Walla Walla, activists planned a federal suit based on statutes that permitted illegally disfranchised citizens to pursue damages.[75]

Real confusion attended elections. At Walla Walla school elections on November 2, in one woman's words, "forty-one women tax-payers voted, and, strange to say, no objection was made. Strange, because óne year

---

[73] Zerelda N. McCoy, "Rights are Inherent," *TDL*, September 9, 1889, p. 6. Emphasis added. McCoy's fluency in law suggests significant legal study or advice; she had not been admitted to the bar and her husband, James, was an army surgeon.

[74] Zerelda N. McCoy, "From the People," *TDL*, September 12, 1889. She also named Matilda Hindman and Elizabeth Lyle Saxon official representatives of the local association. On Hindman's tour, see Albert Cushman, "Woman Suffrage in the Campaign," ibid., September 8, 1889. See also J. E. Goodin, "Governed without Consent," ibid., September 17, 1889.

[75] "Editorial Notes," *WJ*, September 14, 1889, front page; "Suffragists Have Been Badly Advised," *WWU*, September 14, 1889, and Abigail Scott Duniway, "Women Moving in Washington Territory," dated September 3, 1889, *WJ*, September 21, 1889. See also women's determination to "take steps" to participate in ratification; "The women of Washington Territory ...," *WJ*, September 21, 1889. See also Abigail Duniway's account of the filings, "The Situation in Washington," ibid., September 6, 1890, p. 288, "now pending before the Washington courts." Women wanted to learn "whether a territorial Legislature had really any rights which judges were bound to respect"; the answer may well have been no. NAWSA's Carrie Chapman Catt later condemned Duniway as "unbalanced"; Catt to Mrs. [Catherine Waugh] McCulloch, April 24, 1900, Schlesinger Women's Studies Mss., Reel 30, No. 0013–15.

previous … women's votes were refused" in light of *Bloomer*. "That decision, if ever in force, must be in force now; and the constitution expressly states that 'the Legislature may extend school suffrage without distinction on account of sex.' The women think there is a screw loose somewhere." In Pierce County, a married woman announced that she intended to vote despite the re-imposition of "disabilities."[76] When "quite a number" of women voted in Walla Walla on October 1, 1889, ballots were deposited in a separate box and the names listed in separate books. Poll judges rejected at least fifty names. In December, Walla Walla's indefatigable Bessie Isaacs reported that about 250 women had voted; later, six complaints were filed from "as many precincts against officers of election." Some votes were accepted but not counted; others were rudely rebuffed. Some of the women bringing law suits "voted full tickets; others only on the constitution and separate articles." Filings with the most promise would "take the lead" on the long road to Washington, DC.[77] Laura DeForce Gordon personally took Isaacs' grievance to federal district court on the fond hope that a successful *Bloomer* appeal would force a new election. But, on November 10, 1890, the bench ruled otherwise. Since *Bloomer* had not been reversed or overruled, "it must have controlled the defendants … in giving their decision as to the plaintiff's right to vote …. If the decision be erroneous, the supreme court is responsible for the error; and as the law shields the judges of that court from an attack of this nature," election judges were protected "by the same shield."[78]

In the end, voters approved the constitution; elected an overwhelmingly Republican government, including the entire Republican judicial slate; and rejected the suffrage and prohibition amendments by a margin of almost three to one.[79] Even the suffrage warhorse, Edward Eldridge, who had made a study of electoral systems in advance of the Olympia convention, had fallen silent on key elements of the political-rights bundle. To be sure, manhood suffrage meant that laws were made by a minority of the people, instead of by a majority; it also narrowed the minds of legislators and drove "the ablest and purest minds in the land" from government. But he had not demanded full access for citizens to

---

[76] Bessie J. Isaacs, Sec'y, Wash. W. S. Association, "Hopeful Facts from Washington," *WJ*, December 21, 1889, p. 402; Mrs. S. C. Stannus, "One Who Will Vote," *TDL*, September 30, 1889. In the same issue, see Zerelda McCoy, "Warning to Women."

[77] See Executive Committee, E. S. L., Walla Walla County, "Washington Women Claim Damages," *WJ*, October 19, 1889, p. 330. In 1888, this had been Bessie Isaacs' committee.

[78] *Isaacs v. M'Neil*, 44 Federal Reporter 32 (1890), 33.

[79] Rosenow, Journal, pp. 646–8. On the outcome, see August Mires, "Remarks on the Constitution of the State of Washington," *Washington Historical Quarterly*, Vol. XXII (October 1931), pp. 282–3, which reports 16,521 voters in support of woman suffrage and 35,913 opposed. See also "Northwestern Elections," *NYT*, October 4, 1889, p. 2 (Republicans won by 8,000 votes). On the Republican sweep, see, e.g., "Victory. Democracy Routed at the Polls …," *ST*, October 2, 1889, front page; and "Republican Ticket," ibid., September 24, 1889. John Hoyt had been attacked for supporting women's rights; e.g., "Fearless and Upright," ibid., September 26, 1889. For praise of the results, see "Have Chosen Wisely," *ST*, October 2, 1889, ed. page; "Elections To-Day," ibid., October 1, 1889.

public offices or the return of mixed-sex juries; he simply urged representations of property at the polls.[80] Given vexed associations between political equality and temperance, the result perhaps was most remarkable for the large number of men prepared to treat women as equals in public life – and then to sweep unpleasantness under rugs. When a respected citizen printed a summary of the steps leading to statehood, the fact of pitched warfare over suffrage had vanished. As early as August 30, 1889, the pro-suffrage *Standard*, with no hint of irony, praised the convention for establishing rules of action and moral guidance that would "mould the character of the people." In the U.S. Senate, the only discussion (or so New Yorkers said) surrounded efforts to censure a committee for rejecting equal suffrage in Washington; Congress then approved the statehood bill. After delay, the President signed the proclamation on November 11, 1889, with a pen of native gold.[81] There ensued the usual array of parades, dinners, and cannonades. In 1890, as if to pay homage to an ancestor, Governor Ferry sent a delegation to New York to celebrate the inauguration of George Washington;[82] at virtually the same moment, Wisconsinites secured statehood with equal suffrage after a male-only ratification election.[83]

What about the *Bloomer* appeal? In 1891, judicial action was said to be imminent. Although the Jones Court had generally ruled against woman suffrage and female office holding, wrote a journalist, the case would be called for a hearing in the U.S. Supreme Court at the coming October term. Arthur Austin, attorney for the Bloomers, would contend that the suit had been collusive and that the statute conferring suffrage on women was entirely constitutional. In Austin's view, a reversal would mean that women had been legal voters at the election held to select convention delegates, forcing Washingtonians to "set aside the Constitution."[84] Suffrage leaders also pressed hard. Writing on

---

[80] Edward Eldridge, "Our Elective System," *SPI*, April 17, 1889.
[81] Elwood Evans, "Territory vs. State. A Brief Resume of the Steps Leading to the Admission ...," *TDL*, November 11, 1889, p. 3. Since the 1850s, Evans had served as legislator, commissioner, judge, and mayor of Olympia; he was an historian of the Northwest. See also "The End Is Near," *WS*, August 30, 1889, and "The Bill ... [untitled editorial]," *NYT*, February 21, 1889, p. 4. For the pen, see "Washington a State," *SPI*, November 12, 1889, front page. See also 26 Statutes at Large, Proclamations, November 11, 1889, p. 10. Forwarding the certificate of elections to President Harrison caused delay; "The politicians of Washington ...," November 23, 1889, *WJ*, p. 1, and "Will Have to Wait," *SPI*, November 6, 1889, front page.
[82] E.g., "Garb of Statehood," *SPI*, November 19, 1889, front page. For the new governor's speech, see "Gov. Ferry's Message," ibid., November 23, 1889, front page. See also "Washington A State," *TDL*, November 12, 1889. On Washington's birthday, see Governors Papers, Box 1N-1-1, "Centennial Celebration" file [1890], WSA-O.
[83] "Suffrage for Women," *WP*, June 27, 1890, p. 7.
[84] "The Bloomer Woman's Suffrage Suit. Olympia, Washington, July 9," *NYT*, July 10, 1891, p. 3. On Austin, see also "Woman Suffrage. Decision of the Supreme Court ...," *TDL*, August 15, 1888 ("Immediately after the opinion was filed, Mr. Austin, on behalf of the plaintiff, took an appeal to the supreme court of the United States.")

NWSA letterhead, Laura DeForce Gordon besieged the clerk of court with requests for the date of hearings. The Court's decision as to whether to accept the appeal rested on the validity of Austin's claim to be attorney of record. Nevada Bloomer signed an affidavit swearing that she had never met him, that Murray was her lawyer, and that she had not appealed; Murray averred that Austin was an imposter. In July, 1891, Austin boasted that if either of his arguments prevailed, the ruling would have "a greater political effect throughout the Union than the most ardent woman suffragist has yet dreamed of." But, on December 16, 1891, the Fuller Court dismissed the appeal as improperly brought. Costs were assigned to Austin; DeForce Gordon may have paid the bill, but a Pullman reporter disclosed that Austin had incurred "great expense."[85]

Perhaps the justices did not want to unsettle a ratification election. But Washington's own bench exacted revenge only nine days before the *Bloomer* dismissal in the otherwise forgettable case of *Marston v. Humes*. There, John Hoyt decimated Turner's *Harland* decision and the hack lawyering in *Bloomer*. In October, 1891, Arthur Austin filed an appeal from King County on behalf of a debtor contending that Judge Thomas Humes had relied on a civil-action statute with an imprecise title. Hoyt seized the occasion to review *Harland*. Many of Turner's authorities, he wrote, setting aside his characteristic mildness, "could not have been examined" or they would "never have been cited" in support of the result claimed. In some instances, Turner had upended judges' actual findings; Hoyt could not find "more than one or two cases" that fully supported *Harland*, and even those admitted to several interpretations; the court had construed rulings "so narrowly as to invalidate titles like the one at bar." Turner had been "wide of the mark." He also had ignored Thomas Cooley's advice, to the effect that the "generality of a title is no objection to it, so long as it is not made a cover to legislation incongruous in itself." Finally, he lambasted Turner and Langston for exploiting the fact that one justice always recused. Had the same case arisen in other districts, a contrary decision would have followed. Hoyt would "hardly be justified in blindly following and accepting as the law of this state" a suspect precedent, and so he turned back the appeal. But, in losing, Austin had won. While Hoyt limited his ruling to Marston's case, he had laid bare Turner's charade, exonerated Roger Greene, and honored Zerelda McCoy's phalanx of women.[86]

[85] Ibid. See also "Woman Suffrage, Olympia, July 7," *PH*, July 10, 1891, and Bloomer v. Todd, Case File No. 573, WSA-O. In July, 1910, journalists sometimes retold the *Bloomer v. Todd* story as a cautionary tale; e.g., "How Washington Women Were Given Suffrage by Pioneers ...," *SS*, July 2, 1910.

[86] *H. L. Marston v. T. J. Humes, Judge*, 3 Wash. 267 (1891), 274–8, and Marston v. Humes, Case File No. 366, Appellant's Brief, WSA-E. See also untitled, *SPT*, January 28, 1892, ed. page (reporting that suffrage forces wanted Robert Ingersoll to argue *Bloomer* in the nation's capital).

"DO TRY AND FORGET YOURSELF!"

In the new state, economic citizenship jostled for attention with its political counterpart. Had economy eclipsed polity? In June, 1895, while apologizing to farmers, loggers, and other extractive laborers for dislocations caused by internal improvement, a journalist noted the arrival of a "new doctrine of American citizenship – to secure good wages is the chief object at which a voter ought to aim." At the same time, Washington's laboring classes steadily diversified, further altering the hierarchies that had emerged in the tumultuous mid-1880s. Northern-European migrants won praise and status; Germans were said to vote with a "formed deliberate judgment." Modest increases in black populations elicited concern among white men, particularly when industrialists and miners hired black men as strike-breakers;[87] in some public prints, black men also embodied unnamed, sexualized dangers. But black men and women also worked for wages, opened a myriad of small businesses, and organized political clubs.[88]

The Chinese and a growing number of Japanese, by contrast, still elicited hatred for alleged plans to defeat Americans in a commercial war; and, as earlier, Chinese men's laundry skills, queues, and raiment triggered assault and insult.[89] A dockside observer witnessed a man "on his knees" begging a tormenter not to cut off his braid: It was a great disgrace, he said, to walk in public without it – a violation akin to walking in public "in the garb of a woman," as Chinese men did regularly and as Occidentals would never do. What could be said about Asians crossing the Canadian border disguised as "French country women"?[90] Here, as nowhere else, Washingtonians resisted engagement and assimilation. When writers in Victoria warned that taxation of the Chinese and

---

[87] "May Employ Negroes, Black Diamond Coal Company ...," *SPT*, June 5, 1891. On blacks in labor camps as scabs or as competition, see, e.g., "Trouble Expected," ibid., June 30, 1891 (a violent strike at Franklin); "Down in the Mines," ibid., May 22, 1891, front page (about 300 "colored men" and discontent among whites, plus an account of a white woman who "thought the darkies would attack her"); "Colored Men for Newcastle," ibid., June 20, 1891 (angry mine owner promising to "get out the coal" and "fill all our orders, ... blacks or no blacks," and promising to hire black workers if whites do not work). Blacks at polls attracted attention; e.g., "Colored Voters in Line," *SPT*, September 21, 1892.

[88] "An Effect of Bondage," *TDL*, December 13, 1889, p. 2. But see also "Injustice against the Negro," ibid., January 27, 1890, condemning violence against blacks. Vague sexual threats also appeared; e.g., "Driven to Her Death," *TDL*, February 4, 1890 (woman committed suicide rather than marry a mulatto); "A Ravisher at Large," *SPT*, June 27, 1891 (black or "Indian" ravisher in hiding); "Girl Held in Bondage," ibid., July 1, 1892 (black man charged with abducting a white girl from Canada).

[89] E.g., one cartoon shows a ram labeled "National Laundrymen" about to butt a queued Chinese man with a big laundry basket into the Pacific; "Something Coming His Way," *TDL*, August 24, 1909.

[90] "Chinatown is Crazy," *ST*, August 17, 1895; "Cut Off the Queues," ibid., August 15, 1895; "No Deluge ...," ibid., July 2, 1895; "Chinese Traffic in the East," *SPT*, October 8, 1892, p. 1. Suspicions of moral or gender transgressions abounded. See, e.g., "Mongolian Mormons," ibid., April 1, 1892 (Chinese men had multiple wives in "direct violation of the civilized doctrine of

admission of their children to local schools might necessitate enfranchisement, even suffragists took alarm.[91] To pre-empt homesteading, communities began to ban Chinese laborers. In 1909, Tacomans reported a "powerful movement" to evict all Asians; the Nelson-Johansen Company, for instance, fired forty "Japs" who were "cheaper than white men" but "not as desirable." Again as earlier, white female laborers were implicated: When Asians at Pacific American Fisheries rejected night work because of cut fingers and owners moved them to days, white women shunted to the night shift were scandalized.[92]

American Indians' fate was only slightly better. Resistance to removal plans elicited impatience and anger,[93] and viciousness was not hard to find, as with this cartoon: "Killed any elk today?" "No. It's agin the law. Besides it's more fun to shoot Indians." Philanthropists sometimes doubted Indians' willingness to 'civilize' beyond the "thinnest of veneering." But praise also appeared for persuasive performances of white manhood. Indians produced wealth in cities and exhibited loyalty. When a former policeman and Quiniault elder died on a reservation, he was said to be part of a generation of redeemable Indians. The number of Indians enrolled in schools increased geometrically.[94] Certainly indigenous people, notwithstanding an association with federal custody and hence with dependence, garnered more praise than Asians. As a Seattle writer explained in 1892, "The Indian is an American. The Chinaman never can be, and a system of political practice that tolerates him in the face of Indian oppression is, to say the least, 'damnably out of kilter.'"[95] In 1902, the

monogamy"), or "White Women Marrying Chinese," *Seattle Republican*, July 2, 1909, p. 1 (warnings about degenerate unions).

[91] "Chinese in the Schools," *TDL*, May 3, 1889.

[92] "Must not Employ Coolie laborers," *TDT*, April 16, 1909; "Powerful Movement . . . Force Japs to Quit Coast," ibid., April 30, 1909; "Japanese Workmen Prove Failure," ibid., February 2, 1909. Asiatic features could trigger venom, as with an attack on Russians; "The Tartar Horde," *SPT*, September 9, 1892, described as "barbarians." See also laundry owners' claim that an eight-hour law would put them out of business unless they hired "Japs"; "Senators Hold Up Labor Bill," *BH*, February 26, 1909, p. 6. On scandal, see untitled editorial, *BH*, March 6, 1909. See also one of many warnings about the replacement of white laundresses with Asians; "White Laundry Circular," *SPT*, April 28, 1891.

[93] "Our Indian Reservations," *TDL*, July 30, 1889, p. 2 (reservation land too valuable to leave much longer with Indians who had not adopted white habits); or "The Payallups' Land," ibid., July 12, 1889, condemning Indians as hopelessly dependent. Complaints abound. But see also "The Poor Indian," *ST*, December 24, 1894 (Indians without allotments were idle and starving) and "The Indian Problem," *TDL*, November 14, 1889, p. 6 (impatience with Indians' slow adaptation).

[94] Cartoon, "Sport Among the Rockies," *ST*, August 22, 1895; "After a Generation," *TDL*, July 19, 1908; "Indian Dies at the Age of 100 Years," ibid., July 22, 1908; "Indian School to Open September 8," ibid., August 13, 1908 (enrollment increased at the Payallup School by 40 percent in one year). See also praise for a Seneca chief in Connecticut who was "loyal as steel" to the federal government; "Was a Good Indian," *ST*, August 31, 1895. See also "Quileute Indians Print Paper," *TDT*, February 18, 1909.

[95] "Sram," untitled letter to the editor, *SPT*, April 19, 1892. See also Congressional Record, House of Representatives, 48th Session, 1st Session, January 30, 1884, pp. 752–3 (rewarding Indians

attorney general ruled that state law authorized all men older than twenty-one years to vote; hence, Indian men who had lived in the state the requisite period and naturalized could vote, hold office, and (if heads of household by American standards) sit on juries.[96]

What about girls and women? Child labor was commonplace. But white girls were especially compelling candidates for public and quasi-public supervision. After 1900, Washington boasted a well-articulated system of juvenile courts and reform bureaus, some of them staffed by women's clubs and other voluntary associations.[97] Among child-savers, pluck *per se* was not seen as transgressive. As an example, in 1908, a sixteen-year-old named Goldie Wheeler had volunteered for detective work. "I don't want to play the part of a stool pigeon," she reportedly told police. "I want to some day get on the regular force and demonstrate that a woman can cover herself with glory as a detective the same as a man can." Even when she failed to solve the case, officers praised her diligence.[98]

But Goldie was unpaid and had living parents. More often, girls' bodies were sexualized and "bad mothers" condemned for failing to prevent daughters' ruination. As early as 1889, reformers warned girls to beware of Chinese brothels. In 1892, a "female fiend" in her 80s was said to be enslaving girls; a "sad" girl searched for her lost mother in bawdy houses.[99] In Tacoma, delinquent girls allied with toughs had been caught with stolen money. Maude, another bad girl, had run away from home; girls who taught boys to steal, drank in public parks, and picked pockets were said to "lack experience in

    for performances of white manhood; whites would gain access to Indian landholdings, which would be opened to settlement, once Indian men began to wear citizen's dress, functioned as "heads of families," and competed for land).

[96] Papers of the Attorney General, W. B. Stratton, Report of the Attorney General of the State of Washington, 1902–03, Box 2D-1-1, p. 303, WSA-O.

[97] See, e.g., "Consider Need of Juvenile Court in Tacoma," *TDT*, February 3, 1909; "Problem of the Children Solved by Judge Lindsey," ibid., February 3, 1909, describing attempts to merge "love" with "justice"; or "Court will Help Juveniles," ibid., February 4, 1909 (volunteers serving as "probational officers"; twenty-five of forty-six were married women; a half-dozen were ministers). For opening, see "First Case . . . ," ibid., February 5, 1909. Similar campaigns existed in Seattle and Spokane.

[98] "Goldie Wheeler, Girl Detective," *TDL*, July 13, 1908.

[99] "In Vile Dens," *ST*, October 17, 1889; "A Female Fiend," *SPT*, February 18, 1892. See also "Loved a White Girl," *ST*, September 13, 1894. See also "Brutal Negroes," ibid., September 13, 1894 (a white woman assaulted by "three Negroes" in her kitchen, setting the house afire "in the heart of the city") or "Girl Kidnaped as Means of Rescue," *TDT*, March 6, 1909 (daughter of a white woman married to a black man kidnapped to improve her surroundings). Girls were warned about other girls in big cities; e.g., "A Tale of Crime" and "Can Such Things Be?" ibid., October 17, 1889 (bands of girls in New York beating other girls to death); "A Home Made Desolate" and "A Child's Sad Story," *SPT*, May 28, 1892. On bad girls, examples are legion. But see, e.g., "Maude Is missing," *SPT*, April 7, 1892; "Bad Girls Sent Home," ibid., October 13, 1892; cartoon ("Could you kindly oblige me with a light?"), *ST*, August 16, 1895; "Boys Taught to Steal by Girls," *TDL*, August 9, 1908; "Girls Get Drunk in Wright Park," ibid., July 4, 1908; editorial, ibid., July 5, 1908 (on brazen pickpockets).

home life." As a Seattle editor put it, a "heavy responsibility rests with those who have the early care of girls ... when the very influences which should strengthen, build up and morally entrench, are lost."[100]

Self-supporting girls challenged governments as never before; boys, while often complicit in varieties of seduction, were supposedly less apt to be lured into wrongdoing. In 1901–02, for instance, the newly formed state labor bureau confronted a practice that had gone unnoticed in the years before urban congestion – the use of girls as messengers. At the instigation of Seattle-Tacoma women's clubs, telegraph companies were summoned to hearings. The question was whether girls could deliver messages without risk of personal degradation. Telegraphers contended that they used young women only for deliveries to respectable addresses. A Seattle messenger, Margarette (Rita) Garnett, testified that her physician had urged a restorative move from the Bon Marche department store to outdoor work.[101] A labor-bureau panel, however, seized on Rita's irregular circumstances (she was an orphan whose guardian had arranged housing). When she described wholesome domestic and work encounters, interrogators pushed harder. "Before you start out," asked one, "you don't know who the party is you are going to see?" "No sir," she replied. "You don't know whether it is a lawyer or doctor or who?" "I can tell by the name on the door," she said, "what he is." "But you don't know when you start out?" "No sir." When panelists learned that boys and girls actually conversed at the dispatch counter, they closed ranks. The idea that Bon Marche might be far worse for a girl's health – as Rita put it, there was "such a crowd up there, and they have got steam heat and it makes me too hot" – mattered little. Nor did they care about loss of wages: Girls were said to "hamper the service." The bureau recommended banning the use of all boys under fourteen and all girls. Legislators temporized. But, in 1905, they abolished child labor except in hardship cases as part of an act establishing compulsory schooling for children younger than 15.[102]

Adult white women also bore the weight not only of changes in political and economic prospects, but also of alterations in prevailing views of gender (femininity and masculinity). The loss of political autonomy surely increased associations between women and dependency. But it also made independent women more susceptible to yellow-journalistic suggestions of incapacity, Eve-like sensuality, and weak judgment. In July, 1889, to give an especially ripe example, police arrested Mrs. Minerva Allen in Tacoma for burglary; her young son had accompanied her as decoy and lookout. Readers were treated to a

---

[100] "A Sad Example," *ST*, December 19, 1891.
[101] State of Washington, Bureau of Labor Report, 1902, "Recommendations for Legislative Action" and "Investigation into the Employment of Girl Messengers," pp. 237–9, 317, and passim.
[102] Ibid. See also Act Relating to the Compulsory Attendance of Children between ... 8 and 15 in Public Schools, Session Laws, State of Washington, 1905, Ch. 162, p. 316; Sect. 2 provided for certificates of exemption (school superintendents at their discretion could issue work permits).

serialized morality tale as the "notorious red-haired woman" and "Baby Allen" moved from trial to prison and foster home. One writer concluded that the best men "as boys had the best mothers." Seattle's seedy Whitechapel district also was said to attract dozens of "fallen women of the lowest types," some with children in hotel rooms.[103]

Sophisticates labored to distinguish between fallen women and the New Woman: While nobody liked a "cigarette-smoking, loud-talking, home-ignoring, unsexed creature," the New Woman was "intelligent, educated and self-reliant" and did not "forget her sex" or shirk its special responsibilities. In 1895, she aspired to *home-centered* independence and virtue: "The real new woman is the self-reliant, self-respecting, well-balanced girl, who in time will, of choice ..., ripen into intelligent motherhood, or may ... live an honorable, independent life of spinsterhood, earning her own livelihood and maintaining her self-respect. The new woman will drive out the 'old maid.'" She would "raise a family, not under protest, but because of her God-given instinct of maternity." Where would Washingtonians draw lines between naughtiness and degeneracy? Boiler-plate tales delivered up Zola-like inevitabilities, as with the 1889 transmutation of an "innocent, confiding, loving" girl into a complicit rape victim.[104]

To the extent that both sexes internalized public information, this deepening pool of suspicion about women's innate incapacity and weakness greatly complicated individuals' sense of self as well as efforts to stem erosions of women's agency. Renewed concern emerged with particular force in vice-ridden Tacoma – although energy was expended less to combat insinuations of inadequacy than to shelter or educate presumably endangered women. Club women renewed their support for the Woman's Exchange (a "boon to bachelors") and a training school for young women threatened with servility or worse; at the same time, journalists warned girls and their parents about wily sex traders. In July, 1889, importers of non-Asian domestics collided with city purifiers determined to beat back young women of dubious character.[105] Temperance workers pummeled the governor with letters demanding

---

[103] "Mother's Responsibilities," *TDL*, October 15, 1889. See also "Women Held Up Stages," *ST*, April 4, 1892; "Whitechapel Visited," ibid., February 16, 1891 ("haunts of vice" beckoned); "Which Is Correct?" ibid., January 23, 1891 (on estimates of the number of "fallen women" ranging from 250 to 2,500). See also "Everything Closed," ibid., February 23, 1891. Alleys teemed with "hardened men and still more hardened and depraved women," but club women and police had driven them out. As elsewhere, rising divorce rates contributed to a sense of danger; e.g., "Many Divorce Suits," *ST*, June 29, 1891; "Federal Government Issues Report on Divorce ...," *TDT*, January 2, 1909. See also Mike Jordan and Lynn Jordan, "The Invisible Sex: The Approach of Statehood Heightened Awareness of Women's Roles," *Columbia*, Vol. 2, No. 4 (Winter 1988–89), pp. 1–2.

[104] "The New Woman," September 10, 1895, *ST*, p. 2; or "A Bad Case," *WS*, July 19, 1889, about the Wickersham–Brantner seduction scandal. Here, a young woman supposedly lacked the character and will to either resist overtures or tell the truth.

[105] *TDL* exhibited a growing taste for salaciousness. See "The Woman's Exchange," *TDL*, August 30, 1889; "Exchange for Woman's Work," ibid., September 9, 1889; "Boon for Bachelors,"

enforcement of anti-saloon ordinances and the arrest of drunks. So effective were women's clubs as agents of social ordering and public alarm that men complained about exclusion.[106]

State agencies recognized women's groups as informal arms of government, establishing and enforcing best practices; put differently, private maternalism and state paternalism advanced together. In 1892, the Washington Bureau of Associated Charities announced that it would not relieve the Ladies' Relief Society of its work; the women's club was a "general investigating bureau" that picked up where they stopped. In 1908–09, a business called the Sanitary Market complained that club women were harassing them ("you do not have to cudgel us with laws and threats").[107] The Women's Pure Food Committee forced city councilmen to require all firms supplying food to keep the premises neat and sanitary and all foodstuffs away from dirt, flies, and other contaminants.[108] The WCTU expanded activities to include the abolition of tobacco, support for women's exchanges, and scientific cooking.[109] In 1909, the Tacoma Police Department announced that it would hire three female helpers to assist "the Christian association, the Humane society, and the police department to care for unattended girls who visit Tacoma during the

ibid., September 24, 1889; "The Woman's Exchange," ibid., October 24, 1889; "The Tacoma Woman's Exchange," ibid., December 22, 1889. See also "Work for Our Girls," ibid., September 6, 1889; "Help for Our Girls," ibid., August 10, 1889; "School of Home Economy," ibid., November 11, 1889; "A Note of Warning," ibid., October 28, 1889. A father from Shelton found his daughter in an opium den; "A Girl's Downfall," ibid., November 8, 1889. In the same vein, see "A Word of Encouragement," ibid., October 30, 1889. The thread continued; e.g., "Women Denounce Disregard of the Law," ibid., March 20, 1909. On Canadians, see "Imported Domestics," ibid., July 1, 1889.

[106] E.g., Officers of Ellensburg Lodge No. 53 to Governor, Governors Papers, Box 2D-2-2, Ellensburg Temperance File, 1903 (on "saloon-cursed city" and requests for help), WSA-O. See also Letters from WCTU officers, ibid., January, 1903. These materials crossed the governor's desk continually. Workers could secure only local option and Sunday closing laws. On men, see "Woman's Club," *WS*, January 25, 1884; "Features of Women's Clubs," *TDL*, August 14, 1908.

[107] "Labor of Charity," *SPT*, April 6, 1892; "Club Women," *TDT*, March 4, 1909. See also Karen Blair, *The Clubwoman as Feminist: True Womanhood Redefined, 1868–1914* (Boulder, CO, 1980).

[108] "Pure Food Law Is Now In Force," *TDT*, March 5, 1909. See also "Pure Food People Urging Their Cause," ibid., February 8, 1909.

[109] "The Ways of Women ...," *SPT*, February 2, 1892. On temperance and Greene's presidency, see "State Temperance Alliance," ibid., January 20, 1892. On the WCTU, see "Report of the Central WCTU," ibid., June 20, 1891. See also "It was Flower Day," ibid., June 10, 1891 (WCTU visits to prisoners with flowers); "Central WCTU," *TDL*, December 18, 1889 (support for the woman's exchange and artisanship). On temperance workers, see, e.g., "Work of Temperance," *SPT*, November 16, 1891. For anti-cigarette campaigns and admonishments to enforce existing laws, see correspondence with statehouse, as with Margaret Peatt, President, and Mrs. Margaret Munns, Western Washington WCTU, to Attorney General W. P. Bell, September 15, 1910, with response, Papers of the Attorney General, Correspondence, 2DW-9, Box 21, WSA-O.

summer." The WCTU nominated many of the helpers responsible for meeting trains and boats, as well as a woman detective specializing in pick-pockets.[110]

Volunteers worried especially about the morals of girls and women, encouraging owners of night schools to waive tuition and pursuing surrogate homes for working or visiting women.[111] In Tacoma and Seattle, women raised money to provide respites for youngsters struggling to support themselves or to help their parents. The Sarah Yesler Home for Working Girls served visiting ladies as well as working girls; another house, run by a minister and his wife, featured "unsectarian Christian influences" and parenting for girls away from home. In 1891 and 1892, relief-society members organized a children's home and poor house as well as a Women's Protective and Benefit Association for working women. As with non-voting office holders in the recent past, many of these women did not see themselves as political actors. In April 1892, a founder of a Seattle working-girls home said that she did "not believe in women voting." But she did believe in "equal rights in the home," where women's sovereign authority (including bedrock rights to deal in property) remained more or less intact, if corralled at the front door.[112]

"WHETHER THE WIFE SHALL TAKE HER SHARE OF THE RISK"

As gender ascriptions mutated, social scientists worried aloud about an "imperfect reform" – a reference to women's low wages, their exclusion from higher education, unequal managerial powers within marital estates, and (notwithstanding laws to the contrary) sex-based rejection in labor markets.[113] White women's elevated status and co-sovereignty had been sustained in large part by associations with property, within and beyond marriage. With the loss of political rights, the legalities supporting women's economic agency came under fresh scrutiny. What if community-property rules of practice and economic equality worked a disservice to men and women, to commerce, to families, and hence to the public? In anti-suffrage circles, it went without saying that, with property-based claims to shared sovereignty weakened or quashed, it would be difficult indeed for suffragists to demand ballots and ancillary rights. As if to test the waters, influential Washingtonians

---

[110] "Tacoma to Have Women Police," *TDT*, April 3, 1909; "Woman Police Officer Is Chosen," ibid., April 23, 1909.

[111] E.g., "Night School Growing," *SPT*, October 5, 1892 (ten girls enrolled). But see also "The Night School," ibid., February 27, 1892 (all examples are boys and men drifting into "evil channels").

[112] "Women's Home," *SPT*, September 2, 1892; "Woman's Home Open," ibid., September 29, 1892. The home was not well funded; "The Women's Home," ibid., March 24, 1892. See also "Among the Toilers," ibid., May 13, 1892; "Good Work of a Year," ibid., April 5, 1892; "Home for Children, ibid., January 20, 1891; "A Good Move," ibid., March 25, 1892; "A Home for Women," ibid., April 4, 1892. See also "Doing Noble Work," ibid., January 18, 1892 (on the Ryther Home, an "asylum for fallen women").

[113] "An Imperfect Reform," *TDL*, August 20, 1889, p. 2.

began to reconsider elements of the law of coverture, some of them lurking in the law code, buttressed by authorities recognized in other states.[114]

In December, 1888, with the prospect of statehood at hand, members of the legislature's new law-code commission sent a letter to members of the bar. The *Ledger*'s liberal editor printed the text and invited Tacoma suffragist Addie Barlow to respond. Commissioners declared that the most important topic to be considered would be community property. During a recent Supreme Court session, an unnamed justice had remarked, off the record, that when he was "obliged to render a decision under the law, he hardly knew whether he was male or female." The comment supposedly showed the judge's "state of embarrassment." If the present laws continued, wrote the commission chair, suggesting some doubt, no man of means would be safe unless he had "in his vault a will signed by his wife, evading almost every provision of the law, and ... three fourths of this class in Washington territory are now evading the law in this way." Evasion was necessary: "In case of the death of the wife one-half of their entire property is swept out of their reach" by the law. Questions followed: "[W]hat changes would you suggest ... ? If ... it should not be retained ..., what would you suggest in lieu of it? What state or territory has a law relating to the property rights of married persons that most nearly reaches perfection ... ? What is the state of public opinion in your community?" Allusions to Roger Greene's legacy were hard to miss: Did the bar favor a rule by which a person with title would be deemed the owner, capable of passing title without "joining the other member of the 'compound creature of the statute called a community'?" Questions were not posed as a "courtesy, but in the interest of the whole people."[115]

Barlow perceived an assault on marital and civil equality. The men who had framed territorial law, she wrote, had been fair to both sexes, who now should protest "a few men wresting from us the privileges granted us. Our property laws ... are the best in the United States." Women should be "free to her half, to her children, her aged parents or any one she chooses shall profit by her economy." Once, Barlow had believed that "would-be-woman-voters wore short hair, were masculinely inclined, and anything but lady-like," but no longer. Citizenship entailed "equality before the law .... *The women of this territory feel secure in their property rights. Let them beware.*"[116]

By April, 1889, activists had mobilized in defense of economic agency. In Zerelda McCoy's words, women were "practically disfranchised"; the "enemies of human rights propose to provide in the constitution that only male citizens can vote or hold office. If this provision is adopted, no woman

---

[114] Compare this section to Alvin E. Evans, "Community Obligations," *California Law Review*, Vol. 10, No. 2 (May, 1922), pp. 120–44, arguing that, until 1920, when judges supposedly fell prey to galloping paternalism, lawmakers labored to protect wives' property. Evans emphasized tort cases.

[115] Editor and Addie G. Barlow, "The Code Commission," *TDL*, June 29, 1889.

[116] Ibid., emphasis added.

can vote at any school election, or have any voice in making or enforcing laws. *The liberal legislation of the past with regard to personal and property rights of women will be abrogated*, and the subjection of women be completed." The constitution should adhere to the principle that that political rights inhered in "every man and woman ... *capable of making contracts.*" On August 7, the *Ledger* took sides. "It seems strange," said Radebaugh, "that under a democratic government ... there should be an obstinate prejudice against admitting to representation a class which constitutes one-half the community." Critics claimed that women were "virtually represented by their husbands, if they happen to have one. This is essentially the same argument ... used so long in England against the representation of the working classes."[117] In his view and for many subscribers, few doubts remained that retrenchment formed part of paternalism – the doctrine that "the individual cannot develop in isolation, independently of social helps." Those helps would be undertaken by "manly" lawmakers, in government as in families. In the workplace, the unrepresented woman was peculiarly susceptible to the vagaries of employers. This was a "kind of paternalism," wrote an annoyed Tacoman. "But no one seems to object to it on that point."[118]

In 1889, John Hoyt and other social democrats had demanded that the "existing law regulating the property rights of husband and wife commonly known as the Community law" remain upon the law books until properly amended by legislators.[119] Community property had been under heavy fire for at least eighteen months: In January, 1888, after *Harland*, as legislators reconsidered election laws, King County Democrat Thomas Humes announced opposition both to woman suffrage and to "the law allowing them a voice in the disposition of community property." He was interested especially in widows' ability to fend off ruinous creditors' claims and otherwise control a man's estate. On January 17–18, he offered "a batch of bills" to rein in wives' property rights. Among them were two law-code amendments – one that divided estates upon the death of a husband and then subjected the entire estate to community debts, and a second that deprived women of family allowances and testamentary capacity when partners died intestate. On February 2, Humes presented four bills outside of regular channels. A reporter was irate: Humes cravenly aimed to deprive women of "the most valuable rights they possess with respect to community property." Men would be able to dispose absolutely of all the community

---

[117] Zerelda N. McCoy, "To the People of Washington Territory," CC, April 27, 1889, front page, emphasis in original, and "Virtual Representation," *TDL*, August 7, 1889, p. 2.

[118] "Men Wanted and Why," WS, September 6, 1889, ed. page; "The Forgotten Woman," *TDL*, August 15, 1889, p. 2.

[119] "Chairman Hoyt," *SPI*, July 4, 1889, front page; "The Suffrage Convention," WS, July 5, 1889. On the final resolution, see discussion below.

property by will or otherwise, robbing a wife of "what she may have worked a life time to acquire."[120]

One point of weakness in the community-property regime always had been husbands' vague role as manager of estates beyond real or inherited property – a discordant element of the law code that lawmakers had retained for administrative efficiency. On February 2, 1888, the assembly had passed one of Humes' bills – a property act regulating the conveyance of real or personal property between marital partners. It provided, among other possibilities, that a man might "give, grant, sell or convey directly to his wife, and a wife may give, grant, sell or convey directly to her husband his or her community right, title, interest or estate in all of any portion of their community [estate]," which would "divest the real estate therein from any or every claim or demand as community property," vesting it in the grantee as separate property. Partners were warned never to use conveyances to defraud creditors. But husbands could dismantle community property and either sell or make a gift of portions of it, as if it were entirely his. In addition, the managing partner could make and execute letters of attorney, acting for both. The law blurred the line between real and personal property; perhaps to expedite commerce, it also did not anticipate coercion or provide ways for women to safely blow the whistle on aggrandizing men.[121]

Another Humes proposal succeeded in March, 1891: Now, a spouse with an interest in real estate by virtue of marriage, the legal title to which was (or would be) held by the other spouse, could protect his or her interest from sale by filing an affidavit in the auditor's office confirming that the person recording the document was indeed married to the person with legal title. If either spouse neglected to file, whether by mistake or from ignorance, within ninety days from the moment the title was recorded, a *bona fide* purchaser became the owner, free and clear of the other spouse's claims, as at common law. Once filed, the document formed a cloud on real-estate titles which could be removed only by permission of the complaining party or by a court, should the land prove to be the separate property of the person holding title. Spouses who had acquired land previously had three months to comply. In January, 1892, a Seattle writer cut to the heart: A seller needed only "the signature of the one in whose name the property stands," not both spouses; with land held in severalty, conveyance could occur if either spouse had failed to submit the required paperwork.[122]

---

[120] "Watch Mr. Humes," *TDL*, January 18, 1888, ed. page. The batch was not described. Thomas J. Humes became a judge and mayor of Seattle. See also "Among the bills . . . ," ibid., February 2, 1888.

[121] An Act relating to the Conveyance or Other Disposition of the Property of Married Persons. Community Property, Acts of Washington Territory, February 2, 1888, pp. 52–4.

[122] Act to Protect Innocent Purchasers of Community Real Property, February 25, 1891, Ch. CLI, Laws of the State of Washington, 1891, pp. 368–9. See also explanation of Sect. 1 of the 1891 statute: It "assumes that the purchaser is an actual bona fide purchaser"; if the person "knows that the grantor is married . . . , then it is necessary for husband or wife . . . to join in the conveyance, otherwise no title at all passes." The common-law rule was that a purchaser "takes a conveyance free from all claims not of record and of which he has no notice." The

In 1891, moreover, a revision of the 1881 code's probate chapter protected widows but not widowers with lifetime use of personal property and a stay of public debts – a dramatic example of re-introductions of gender privilege within marriage.[123]

Why not let women take care of themselves? In July, 1889, WERA leaders reminded convention delegates of the anti-republican character of manhood suffrage and the illegality of confiscations of rights.[124] But they also demanded that delegates preserve the existing "community-property law" until altered by duly elected state legislators.[125] The *Ledger* worried publically about economic agency, as when Radebaugh condemned the depiction of women as "minors." Correspondence pages included (to give one example) letters from Bessie Isaacs warning that Hume had in mind requiring a filing of an inventory of community property, and where there was no filing, that "either spouse, without consent of the other, may give a good, perfect, and indefeasible title to said property." Other bills aimed to repeal community property and installed English rules, as with the law of descent. She pointed as well to an unnamed judicial finding that community property could not be attached for more than half its value in debt settlement; the legislature's Judiciary Committee had opined that "the man makes all the money and ought to have all the say about the property." Another writer attributed these insults to disenfranchisement: "While the women voted, it would have been impossible to pass such a law."[126]

To what extent did the state's new Republican judiciary (John Philo Hoyt, Ralph E. Dunbar, Theodore L. Stiles, Elmon Scott, and Chief Justice Thomas Anders) deviate from the equality principle? Between 1890 and 1910, appellate decisions uniformly disallowed physical abuse or flagrant examples of male strong-arming of wives. In an 1891 decision, justices unanimously (and, given confusion on the procedural point, generously) decided that a battered woman named Nellie Lee need not prove every material fact with corroborative testimony; she was a competent witness on her own behalf.[127] In 1897, Justice

---

act's main result was to "bring the community estate under this rule and make it subject to the law of notice." So unnamed women had no remedy; "Community Property," *SPT*, February 22, 1892. See also "Conveying Real Property," ibid., January 26, 1892.

[123] An Act in Relation to Proceedings in Probate, amending ... the Code of 1881, March 9, 1891, Ch. CLV, Laws of the State of Washington, 1891, pp. 380, 385–6. See also May Sylvester to Gentlemen of the Supreme Court, State of Washington, c.1895, Struve Collection, Box 8, Incoming Letters Folder, Washington Supreme Court, 1892–96, UWSC. She included a copy of *McDonough* v. *Craig*, which she said "might help, 6 Wm. 499" (when women's claims seemed to threaten innocent male purchasers, courts were failing to protect wives). In defense of "innocent men," see "Lattine Captured," *SFR*, July 25, 1889.

[124] "Equal Suffragists," *TDL*, July 4, 1889 (opening day of convention), p. 4.

[125] "Chairman Hoyt," *SPI*, July 4, 1889; "Washington Territory ...," *WJ*, July 20, 1889, p. 228.

[126] "A Free Country," *TDL*, August 21, 1889; "Retrogression in Washington," *WJ*, March 15, 1890; editorial, "The women of the new State of Washington ...," ibid., March 29, 1890, ed. page.

[127] *Nellie Lee* v. *Theodore M. Lee*, 3 Wash Rpts 236 (December 1891). Also *State of Washington* v. *Bert S. Frye*, 45 Wash Rpts 645 (1907)(women could be trusted to testify about their own status; lawyers in a lower court had demanded that a woman prove, solely because of her sex,

Ralph Dunbar found for a wife whose land had been attached by powerful men for community debts; she had leased, managed, and personally worked a farmstead for years and "had a right to prosecute the business of farming as her separate business, entitling her to the products and increase of the business as her separate property."[128] A year later, the same justices halted a husband's circumvention of established rules in cases of spousal death; he had argued that, because he had owned part of the estate before marriage, the entire community was his.[129] In 1907, they decided, despite common-law rules about domicile, that a "frail educated and refined girl" forced to work for her husband's abusive family to pay off his debts was free to live with her sister.[130] In divorce and debt cases that did not involve community property, justices defended women from the ravages of inveterate drunks; they even affirmed a divorce awarded to an actress of dubious character on the ground that her mate was even more disreputable.[131] Even when disputes involved commercial exchange, justices sometimes rose to women's defense when disputes involved obvious fraud or force. In 1895, they were outraged by a husband's attempt to encroach upon title to a woman's separate property simply by putting up a fence at his own expense. Some years later, in *Ida Harvey* v. *Sparks Brothers* (1907), a real-estate firm challenged Harvey's right to deal in property at all, much less miss a payment; justices easily condemned a crass attempt to steal a married woman's land. In 1911, they also rejected creditors' attempts to define earnings from separate estates as "trusts" so that interest might redound to the community.[132]

More and more, however, paternalistic justices shielded women, not just from attempts to misuse territorial law, but from ordinary entrepreneurial risk,

that she had been married to the man). All of the justices except Anders had served in the constitutional convention.

[128] *John U. Brookman* v. *State Insurance Company of Oregon*, 18 Wash Rpts 308 (1897), 308.

[129] *Stanton Warburton* v. *Matilda B. White*, 18 Wash Rpts 511 (1898), 511.

[130] *V. M. Bond* v. *J. M. Bond* (1907), 45 Wash Rpts 511 (1907). Absent physical abuse, however, outcomes were mixed. In a 1911 inheritance case, Justice Gose made another exception to received doctrine in the case of a man who had abandoned his wife and taken in a "widow"; but he made clear that Washington's civil-rights legislation "was not intended to authorize a wife to establish a domicile for herself, irrespective of her husband's domicile," during marriage; *Frederick W. Buchholz* v. *Orlin W. Buchholz*, 63 Wash Rpts 213 (1911), 213. See also *Potter* v. *Potter*, 45 Wash Rpts 401 (1907), permitting a woman to divorce her husband on the ground of cruelty, even though she still had a husband in Pennsylvania; her new partner had signed documents as a husband and tried to evade performance on the ground that he had never married, even though he knew of bigamy. See also *Robert Patterson* v. *Elizabeth Patterson* (1907), 45 Wash Rpts (1907), 297 (a man not obliged to make earnest effort to secure wife's return; he has a right to determine domicile, even when the family quarreled).

[131] *Swain* v. *Swain*, 45 Wash Rpts 184 (1907), 186; *Querin* v. *Querin*, 45 Wash Rpts 487 (1907).

[132] *David H. Webster* v. *Mary E. Thorndyke et al.*, 11 Wash Rpts 390 (1895), 390–1; *Ida Harvey* v. *Sparks Brothers*, 45 Wash Rpts 578 (1907), 581; *Eliza Guye* v. *John W. Guye*, 63 Wash Rpts 340 (1911), 341–2 ("The natural enhancement in value ... of the separate property ... is not property acquired during marriage, within the spirit of the community property statutes ... "; separate estate not a "trust")

even when commerce was disrupted. These tendencies, in turn, revealed schism on the bench and impatience with property and domestic-relations law. To some extent, these shifts reflected the depression of 1892–93 and a tidal wave of litigation, which increased calls for speed and protection of the weak. However explained, justices permitted women to evade responsibility and modified the all-important concept of "jointly and severally" to better comport with the common-law notion of division by half.

On February 5, 1890, the Supreme Court considered *Brotton* v. *Langert*, an appeal of the Pierce County District Court's conviction of Ina Brotton's constable husband, Mina Brotton,[133] for wrongly handing over property in which Ina had a special interest to Charles Langert and other holders of a lien against the community. The property in question was a thousand-dollar portion of Ina's separate estate, which Langert insisted had been merged by consent. A municipal judge had restrained the sale, holding the constable and not the community responsible. The Brottons did not dispute the merger. Rather, Ina claimed that the lien settlement reduced her *portion* of the estate – as if it were divisible by half – merely to pay damages for a debt to which she had not been privy.[134]

On February 5, 1890, Dunbar, speaking for everyone but Theodore Stiles, dismissed the appeal, ending all possibility of collection (the constable had no separate property). As Elwood Evans pointed out in 1922, the Brottons probably had portrayed Ina as Mina's victim in order to avoid a forced sale. But Dunbar had in mind protecting women from men's bad choices; the constable was alone responsible for a debt "not incurred for the benefit of the community."[135] Pointing to Roger Greene's opinion in *Holyoke* v. *Jackson* – the community interest, Greene had said, was "blended in one, and is held as a unity by the husband and wife" – and ignoring legislation after 1879, Dunbar decided that a tort committed by a husband could not become a burden on the community. He could reach her *portion* of blended property only if the same claim could be lodged against her separate estate. The insinuation of common-law preferences for men clearly annoyed him: The community, he chided, was "purely a statutory creation; and to the statute alone must we look for its powers, its liabilities and its exemptions." While he might look to the common law for help in statutory construction, legislators plainly intended to "depart from the common law and breathe into legal existence a distinct and original creation ... termed a 'community.'" The statute determined who the members of the community might be, how they might acquire property, and who might deal in property; it also protected estates from unlawful acquisition by others. Langert argued that stringency would result in hardship to creditors;

---

[133] Case papers identify him only as "M. Brotton." In 1888, the pair lived in Tacoma; he was a "policeman." He died in 1925, she in 1930. Thanks to Jean Fisher, Northwest Room, Tacoma Public Library, for undertaking research.

[134] *Brotton* v. *Langert*, 1 Wash Rpts 73 (1890). The ruling was widely reprinted with discussion; e.g., "Community Property Law," *TDL*, February 10, 1890.

[135] Evans, "Community Obligations," op cit., pp. 126–8.

Dunbar replied that it was not the court's job to speculate on the practicality of laws. Ida's portion had to be protected. Stiles dissented, and not only because the Brottons had manipulated law. Rather, he objected to paternal meddling with risk: "A good or a bad bargain cannot make the difference between right and wrong, and the community of husband and wife has not yet become so helpless a thing that we need presume in its favor as though it were a minor or an imbecile.... Here the question is simply whether the wife shall, while she is fully protected in the possession of her separate property ..., take her share of the risk ... and whether the husband himself shall be allowed to hide behind the ample skirts of his wife, in case of his torts," to the ruin of his creditors.[136]

A sharp turn away from continental rules of practice also appeared in divorce cases. In 1890, Sarah and David Webster of King County had been granted a divorce. They had amassed a valuable estate, starting in 1869 with the purchase of Seattle town lots. Over time, the couple improved the Seattle properties with David's earnings and money from a second mortgage. When the final payment was made on a lot valued at about $25,000, title was recorded in Sarah's name only, but had not been deeded to her or given as a gift. The pair also had bought land with rental income.[137] To Sarah's surprise, lower-court judges ruled that the wall between community and separate estates was permeable. Suddenly, all real estate was to be "divided equally, share and share alike, subject to the debts, which should be paid in the same way," with any residual debt paid out of Sarah's own property. She appealed. Conceding the court's decision to ignore her name on one of the deeds, largely because the land had not been inherited, she insisted that her separate real property lay beyond the reach of community creditors.[138]

In turning back the appeal, Dunbar looked not to community-property legislation of the 1870s, but to the common law, perhaps justifiably: Part of the couple's accumulated property, though not most of it, antedated 1879. In 1863, before adoption of community-property rules, legislators had granted courts the power to dispose of the property of married people justly and equitably. Wrote Dunbar, the law did not say that judges would "make such disposition 'of their joint property,'" but rather that it should dispose of "the property of the parties." The language was "comprehensive; it is an equitable division of the property rights of the parties that the court is authorized to make." Other statutes defined separate property, who controlled it, and who managed real property, but those statutes referred to property rights "during coverture." Before 1879 at least, the status of a wife's estate was "*simply a circumstance for the court to take into consideration in making the division.*" Courts could ignore the wall between separate and community estates. In a later appeal brought to resolve procedural problems, Dunbar again claimed

---

[136] *Brotton* v. *Langert*, 74–8. See also *James F. Bolster* v. *C. H. Stocks*, 13 Wash Rpts 460 (1896), asserting that men could sell property without wives' knowledge when buyers of property had no reason to doubt what the men said. For the Holyoke case, see Ch. 2.
[137] *Sarah Webster* v. *David Webster*, 2 Wash Rpts 417 (1891), 420–1.   [138] Ibid.

discretion to make "such divisions of the joint *and separate* property" as might be equitable.[139]

Then, in an 1891 appeal of another divorce settlement, Dunbar imposed the *Webster* doctrine on a situation that did not involve pre-1879 transactions. Sarah Fields (an "aging woman") had been at odds with her drunken ex-husband, Fletcher Fields, and his brother, to whom Fletcher had conveyed all of his land in a clumsy attempt to evade property distribution. Dunbar noted, as had the lower court, that the estate indeed was Fletcher's separate estate. But he also affirmed the lower-court decision to award custody to Sarah and to view Fletcher's fraudulently conveyed property as community wealth for the benefit of children. The case turned, said Dunbar, on the "*status* of the property with relation to the community property laws." Fletcher claimed that much of the property was his own; Sarah contended that it was community property. The court's ruling in *Webster* v. *Webster* offered a path forward: Judges could divide the property of both parties, whether community or separate, and could view the source of the property "*as a circumstance to aid it in making an equitable division.*"[140]

The idea that post-1879 separate-estate status was merely a "circumstance" to be considered during property divisions infiltrated adjacent legal headings. In May, 1892, for example, arguments were heard in four consolidated cases appealed from Whatcom County that pitted a married woman, Mary Hayden, against the Board of Trade of the City of Seattle and others. In the early 1890s, J. P. Hayden had established a mercantile firm in a building erected on Mary's land, managed as separate property. They went to Seattle to buy dry-goods. On one occasion, he was asked who constituted the firm. He said, "My wife is the only partner I have." She sat nearby. A sales agent asked the man a similar question, and he repeated the claim, again with Mary close at hand.[141] After a failure in 1891, creditors sued for access to all assets, including Mary's; she was a partner "holding out." The 1879 statute provided that every spouse had "the same right and liberty to acquire, hold, enjoy and dispose of every species of property, and to sue and be sued, as if he or she were unmarried." Attorneys for creditors insisted that the statute meant what it said about co-agency; nothing precluded a business partnership, particularly when the firm

[139] Ibid. Much of the opinion summarized rulings in older, common-law jurisdictions. There had been warning of the fusion of separate and community estates: In March, 1891, relying largely on Texas and California decisions, the court made community property available for the payment of debts incurred by separate estates when a widower died intestate; community property was said to be a "primary" fund and separate property "secondary," no matter where the debts originated. The majority noted a slippery slope: While they had not ruled that "the interest in the community property of a contracting spouse may not be reached during the lifetime of the community for a separate debt," exemption might follow; *Columbia National Bank* v. *Allen Embree, Executor*, 2 Wash Rpts 331 (1891), 331, 336. See also *Sarah Webster* v. *David Webster*, 2 Wash Rpts 480 (1892), 483, emphasis added.

[140] *Fletcher R. Fields et al.* v. *Sarah J. Fields*, 2 Wash Rpts 441 (1891), 442–3. Emphasis added.

[141] *Board of Trade of City of Seattle, et al.* v. *Mary Hayden*, 4 Wash Rpts 263 (1892), 270.

operated on her land. That she should lose in the bargain was little more than bad luck. The lower court, finding evidence of a partnership and the use of Mary's assets in business, had ruled that, if separate funds could be used as backing, they ought to be made available to creditors.[142]

Not so, said Stiles. The law code need not be read literally if such a reading harmed members of a protected class. He offered dozens of citations from common-law jurisdictions in which a man contracting with his wife had made a contract with himself. Could lawmakers have intended a "change so radical" as to permit business partnerships between spouses? What was to prevent bad men from stealing wives' property? It was the purpose of the statutes, wrote Stiles, borrowing lavishly from a Michigan case, "to secure to a married woman the right to acquire and hold property separate from her husband, and free from his influence ..., and if she might enter into a business partnership with her husband it would subject her property to his control." Stiles conceded that spousal relationship in relation to common property was like a partnership, but such a resemblance did not mean that women shared risk equally. "Why so much solemnity with regard to her interest in community property," he asked, "and such ... absolute want of protection with regard to her separate property, which ... it was the first purpose of this act to secure?" Here was an example of the "evil effects" of strict equality: "The wife held certain real estate which she claims is her separate property – it is all she has." Sustaining the judgment would render every wife's estate wholly unsafe and defeat the law's "beneficial purpose."[143]

Dunbar, a strict constructionist and *laissez-faire* champion, fairly exploded. Why not accept the law as written – as a simple statement of sex-blind equality? Business entailed risk. Did business women require supervision? On what ground did a court find a limitation that legislators did not include, negating the law as passed? Courts should not "wander off in hazy theories" about legislative intentions and policy. His colleagues, sidetracked by chivalry, decided that lawmakers did not mean what they said – that they had removed "all civil disabilities" in the exercise of property rights, in derogation of common law. The statute assumed competence; it was not a court's duty to "stand in *loci parentis* or to sally forth in Quixotic zeal to relieve women from conjugal oppressors, or from burdens real or imaginary."[144]

In 1891, ironically to empower women and speed up business transactions, John Hoyt further eroded the concept of title in severalty – this time with a wife transacting business alone. In *Castor* v. *Peterson*, he declared that a women by herself could endorse commercial paper; she was fully competent to make a personal contract under local law; indeed, her endorsee stood "in a much stronger position than under the common law." The majority had not forgotten that all property acquired after marriage belonged to the estate; but the recipient had to know swiftly that the negotiable paper was valid. Any other

[142] Ibid.   [143] Ibid.   [144] Ibid., pp. 280–2.

rule would complicate commerce.[145] A year later, in *Littell and Smythe* v. *Miller*, Justice Scott permitted special circumstances to trump general principles. A firm sought to foreclose Littell's interest in the community to settle a lien judgment without making the wife a party. Adopting the creditor's view that a small portion of the estate was "less than an estate in fee simple" and thus susceptible to the husband's management, the court ruled that general provisions of the civil-rights act yielded to special ones; in this case, managerial rights trumped co-tenancy of an estate, which included real property.[146] In 1894, Hoyt converted another woman's separate estate into community property; Stiles and Dunbar, while not ready to say that considerations of convenience were bad, still found it remarkable that Hoyt would "set aside all the hitherto well-understood principles of law and practice" with the sole object of "bringing in the wife," and for the purpose to "convert a presumption into a certainty." In their view, no more "curious proceeding was ever taken in a court of justice."[147]

What's more, by 1891–92, after the adoption of Humes's revised notification requirements, women could be eliminated more expeditiously from property settlements. When John Ryan died in 1891, for instance, Lucy Ryan sued to regain her half of community land when a mortgager filed an action of ejectment against her. On appeal, justices found that a sale could proceed; notice to the widow was unnecessary, unless required by statute, which was not the case. Remarkably, the court referred to the "community property of John Ryan," ignoring Lucy's presence. Justice Mark Fullerton willfully misread Roger Greene: If a community was "unified," it could fall entirely to a creditor. Ralph Dunbar was incensed. The law could not have been plainer; the court was not free to rule as it thought the law ought to be, but rather as it was. But he stood alone.[148] Justices also decided that a woman living far away, asserting "none of her rights as his wife, and unknown to the community where he dwelt," could not set aside a deed if the buyer had made a reasonable effort to

---

[145] *Castor* v. *Peterson*, 2 Wash Rpts 204 (1890), 208. Four years later, a Seattle reporter told of four unnamed cases filed in city courts. In each, a husband had claimed power of attorney from his wife, though he had no such power, and signed for her. In "many instances," the wife did not "join with the husband" as to the amount at issue – all of which indicates an amount of disregard of the code in daily practice; "Very Grave Defects," *ST*, February 5, 1895. An 1891 revision of bar exams probably encouraged slippage toward common-law rules of practice; "A Higher Standard," *SPT*, November 13, 1891 (examinees would master "the constitution and code of Washington/Code pleading and practice/Equity Jurisprudence, Story/Evidence, Greenleaf/Blackstone's and Kent's commentaries/Contracts, Bishop/Real property/Boone/Constitutional Limitations, Cooley").

[146] *Littell & Smythe Manufacturing Co.* v. *P.V.M. Miller*, 3 Wash Rpts 480 (1892), 483. See also *Little & Smythe* v. *Miller*, Case File No. 296, Petitioner's Brief, WSA-O. See also *W. S. Conrad* v. *Carrie M. Mertz*, 45 Wash Rpts 119 (1906), where the majority rejected claims that a wife's separate transactions did not attach to the community.

[147] *Thomas McDonough* v. *Charles Craig and Annie Craig*, 10 Wash Rpts 239 (1894), 246. See also *E. Main* v. *John D. Scholl*, 20 Wash Rpts 201 (1898) (woman could not establish a separate estate after marriage simply on the ground that she had earned and invested money herself).

[148] *Lucy A. Ryan* v. *David Fergusson*, 3 Wash Rpts 356 (1891), 356–7, 360, 369–70.

determine the seller's marital status. This was more than Hoyt could bear. Surely a spouse could not dispose of an estate without the other person joining, whether or not they lived together. Only if separation continued for years, such that persons of reasonable prudence might believe the union had ended, could they pronounce the community ended.[149]

Finally, in the mid-1890s, before the depression had lifted, Justice Elmon Scott dramatically expanded husbands' administrative powers so that they comported with rules of practice elsewhere. One telling moment involved a public sale of a grocer's stock to satisfy creditors; the debt involved the husband's separate estate and originated before marriage. Dora Powell had sued to prevent sale of the groceries, which were community property. Said Scott, the husband served as estate manager; his power to manage implied absolute power to sell. To no avail, Justice Merritt Gordon assailed Scott for relying on the laws of other states. Local law plainly made the husband an agent for community business; he was not free to subject everything to his own debts, especially when debts arose before marriage.[150]

State courts, then, seemed to be further hybridizing the legal system, reaching back in time and across the nation for rules that better comported with a nationalizing economy and with skepticism about women's capacity for self-rule. In Washington, as elsewhere in America, policy makers modernized policy most eagerly in support of entrepreneurship and political union, and women predictably lost place. In Robert McCloskey's now-classic words, "Nineteenth-century conservatism ... consisted not of '*laissez faire*,' nor of 'free enterprise,' nor even of 'rugged individualism,' but rather of an attempt to define good and right as that which the economic man does to achieve success."[151] Difficulties persisted. In 1920, Sophie Clark, president of the Women's Legislative Council, perceived that lawmakers still viewed

---

[149] *Sylvania N. Sadler, et al. v. U.R. Niesz and Ada Niesz,* 5 Wash Rpts 182 (1892). Here, as elsewhere, it is hard to distinguish between a conservative defense of marriage and a desire to expedite economic exchange; both interests were served. See also *Commercial Bank of Vancouver v. Eli Scott and Martha Scott,* 6 Wash Rpts 499 (1893) (a wife need not be notified or listed as a party). In disputes over public works, the Court was even more aggressive; e.g., *Town of Elma v. John Carney and Lestina Carney,* 4 Wash Rpts 418 (1892), 419, ruling that an assessment against the community for street grading could issue in the name of the husband only; the wife's name was required only if contested. In *Schwabacher Bros. v. H. G. VanReypen and Carmi Dibble,* 6 Wash Rpts 154 (1893), justices ruled that a bona-fide purchaser of land could not be expected to investigate a dishonest man's marital status. See also *A. Harker v. James Woolery,* 10 Wash Rpts 484 (1895) (affidavit of good faith made by the husband alone was sufficient); *Nellie Douthitt v. A. E. MacCulsky,* 11 Wash Rpts 601 (1895); and *James F. Bolster v. C. H. Stocks,* 13 Wash Rpts 460 (1896). See also *Rasmus Konnerup v. J. C. Frandsen and Elizabeth Frandsen,* 8 Wash Rpts (1894), 551 (wife could consent to sale of marital estate in his name only). See also *Davidson v. Mantor,* 45 Wash Rpts 660 (1907) (the court blinked at husband's failure to disclose details of a deal undertaken by a trustee).

[150] *Dora Powell v. F. M. Pugh, Sheriff,* 13 Wash Rpts 577 (1896).

[151] Robert Green McCloskey, *American Conservatism in the Age of Enterprise, 1865–1910* (New York, 1951), pp. 173-4.

community-property rules as inimical to commerce; the council had crafted a bill that would "not in any way hinder legitimate business, yet shall give a wife and mother partnership rights in the control of personal community property." In March, 1920, she told attorney-editor Catherine Waugh McColloch in a scrawled note that, since the control of community property was in the hands of husbands, it could not be said that "their rights in community states are eminently equal. Personal com[munity] prop[erty] is absolutely under husbands control – This has been a fruitful cause of divorce – Separate property comes under distinct laws. Either spouse can make a will over … separate property, entirely excluding husband or wife." She had lobbied for "equal control" of community property, real and personal, to no avail.[152]

"A WOMAN IS A LAW UNTO HERSELF": THE CASE OF HATTIE SOMERVILLE

As wage earners or entrepreneurs, white women entered the statehood era without political protection or assurances that the community-property regime would survive. To be sure, they could never descend to the level of Asians, and indeed had been constructed from an early moment as the primary victims of Chinese laborers. But, when the new state legislature finally convened, women had reason to worry about displacement across many fronts. The assembly's task was daunting. Many territorial statutes as well as the old code had been tainted with illegitimacy; regulation had not kept pace with the economy; utilities and transportation systems (especially roads and port facilities) were woefully inadequate. Into 1891, many statutes carried "emergency" designation, to be revisited when time permitted, as with school laws in desperate need of funding emendation. In keeping with the constitution's sex-specific suffrage, jury, and office-holding chapters, enabling legislation contained masculine pronouns ("he" and "his") amidst sex-neutral nouns ("householders," "voters," "persons").[153]

---

[152] Sophie L. W. Clark to Mrs. Catherine Waugh McColloch, March 13, 1920, Schlesinger Women's Studies Mss., Series I-E, Reel 25, Doc. No. 0246; Clark to National Chm. of Uniform Laws Commission, National League of Women Voters [McColloch], May 11, 1921, ibid., Series I-C, Reel 25, Doc. No. 0278; Clark to Mrs. Catherine W. McCulloch, September 16, 1920, ibid., Series I-E, Reel 25, Doc. No. 0265. But women sometimes resisted equal responsibility for debts: See attorney Lady Willie Forbus, Seattle, to McCulloch, May 10, 1921, ibid., Series I-E, Reel 25, Doc. No. 0276, arguing that "each partner should be equally liable for its just debts. It is a far way to go, and it is not surprising that women, who have suffered so long under the oppressive yoke of the common law, cannot now go the whole … breadth of vision and be willing to accept the burdens with the benefits."

[153] An Act to Amend Sections … of an Act Entitled "An act to establish a general uniform system of common schools," and Declaring an Emergency, Laws of the State of Washington, 1891, Ch. CXXVII, February 25, 1891, p. 237. See also Act to provide Grand Jurors for the Superior Courts …, Laws of the State of Washington, February 11, 1890, p. 331; Act to Authorize and Regulate Primary Elections …, ibid., December 23, 1889, p. 419; all Laws of the State of Washington, 1890.

When it finally appeared, however, civil-rights legislation fairly bristled with egalitarianism, which offered some hope. On March 27, 1890, assemblymen adopted a remarkable law, far in excess of federal standards, that protected "all citizens in their civil and legal rights" by prohibiting racial and ethnic discrimination in both public and private establishments ("inns, public conveyances ..., theatres and other places of public amusement and restaurants").[154] They also seemed to promise equal employment opportunity for men and women: "[E]very avenue of employment shall be open to women; and any business, vocation, profession and calling followed ... by men may be followed and pursued by women, and no person shall be disqualified from engaging in or pursuing any business, vocation, profession, calling or employment on account of sex." Taxation statutes spoke of persons and did not distinguish between spouses on the question of assessments against personal or marital property. At the same time, though, legislators undermined women's prospects, as in the otherwise path-breaking equal-opportunity law which warned that it could "not be construed ... to permit women to hold public office." Economic parity would not support mixed-sex office holding.[155] Lawmakers also moved quickly to make the workplace more comfortable for women employed in stores, offices, or schools; employers failing to allot each woman a seat to facilitate rest when duties permitted would be charged with a misdemeanor and, if convicted, fined. Men could be uncomfortable and unrested.[156]

Reformers' and legislators' increasingly custodial posture toward poor and wage-earning women expressed two seemingly contradictory facts: Women contributed increasingly to the state's economy but were not represented in government. A large number had operated profitable farms since the 1850s, initially as a consequence of the Donation Land Claim Act of 1850. Indeed, the Supreme Court of Washington fiercely defended women's original title to lands secured in their own names under federal homestead acts, particularly when conniving men tried to divest them of it.[157] Success stories were commonplace.

---

[154] An Act to Protect All Citizens in their Civil and Legal Rights, Laws of the State of Washington, 1889–90, March 27, 1890, p. 524. Blacks entered citizenship discourses in a visible way after 1889–90; e.g., "Want Their Rights," *ST*, September 17, 1889; or "For Shame," ibid. September 19, 1889, accusing Democrats of political pandering and hypocrisy in pursuit of black Washingtonians.

[155] An Act to Secure Equal Privileges and Rights to Residents of the State of Washington, Irrespective and Regardless of Sex, Laws of the State of Washington, 1889–90, March 28, 1890, p. 519; Revenue and Taxation, Ch. XVIII, Laws of the State of Washington, February 14, 1890.

[156] An Act to Better Protect the Health of Female Employees, Laws of the State of Washington, 1889–90, March 26, 1890, p. 104. The governor initially objected on the ground that fines were imposed without due process, whereupon the bill was altered to require a bench trial; "Acts of the Solons," *SPI*, November 30, 1889, front page, and "He Will Not Sign," ibid., January 19, 1890.

[157] E.g., *Lizzie H. Forker* v. *Samuel Henry*, 21 Wash Rpts 235 (1899) (an attempt to defraud Forker). But see also two decisions against women's claims to portions of estates originating in

In December, 1908, while advising women to enter stock herding because they were good at detail, Indiana's Virginia Meredith offered another incentive: Female farmers could sell goods "on merit, with never a suggestion that the price be discounted because the product comes from a farm managed by a woman." The federal Census of 1900 revealed increases in women's farm ownership, including a surge when Indian lands were opened. "Economic conditions have changed since 1900," wrote an editor, "and so has the status of women .... Nowadays women are seeking independence and nowhere is more independence to be found than on a farm. As to marriage, the ownership of good broad acres ... will doubtlessly increase the number of opportunities, so ... settle down and obtain title."[158]

Into the 1890s, however, enthusiasm shared space, as we have seen, with a groundswell of concern about women's minds and bodies, and particularly their lack of readiness for (or interest in) domestic and reproductive work. Observers of the fractured social scene wondered (as an 1895 writer put it) whether superior learning might be "a dangerous thing after all." While a girl should be self-reliant, she should be able to cook, mend, "be gentle," and avoid gossip – that is, be "a womanly woman." In 1897, an out-of-state educator advised girls to sell fancy work and embroidery; women could teach "cooking and sewing and swimming," work in banks, and make matches or violins. Small wonder that women learned to guard against undue ambition, if only because of jarring adjacencies on newly segregated women's pages. In 1908, a Tacoman lauded the brilliant Miss Laura Lenhart's completion of a degree at Smith College, immediately alongside fashion news and advice on how to keep a man.[159]

Washington's self-providing women had cause to be confused and alarmed. No sooner had the state assembly convened than members adopted both a factory-safety law and a labor-statistics act providing for a commission to collect and report information across all industries, including wages, hours, sex, marital status of works, and sanitary conditions. The *Ledger* called these statistical compilations "a fund of amusement." But hours legislation posed difficulties. The notion of a mandatory eight-hour day had long attracted strange bedfellows – for example, women's groups and clubs determined to protect girls and women from abuse in traditionally masculine workplaces; unions like the Knights of Labor who contended for reduced hours without loss of income; and, sometimes, municipalities or firms offering hazardous work. In early 1891, however, legislators killed an eight-hour bill for city

federal homesteading laws on the ground that federal law, not state, controlled land division; *R. Cunningham* v. *Harry Krutz*, 41 Wash Rpts 190 (1905) (husband controls entire homestead); and *Anna M. Hall* v. *Estella B. Hall*, 41 Wash Rpts 186 (1905) (in divorce, federal law controls disposition of woman's share of a federal homestead).

[158] "Women as Stock Farmers," *WS*, December 11, 1908; "Many Women are Farmers," *TDT*, August 29, 1909.

[159] "Lacking One Charm," *TDL*, October 4, 1891; "A Girl Should Learn," *TDL*, September 20, 1891; "A Question of Profit," *ST*, July 6, 1895; "Completes Course at College," "Society," and "Lovers Should Not Ignore Every One Else," *TDL*, July 5, 1908.

workers when an unfriendly amendment extended it indiscriminately to all individuals and companies.[160]

A revised measure passed in 1899, however, and again with further emendation in 1903. The Washington Supreme Court ruled in two appeals – *In Re Broad* (1904), involving James Broad, a Spokane laborer thrown into jail for exceeding the hours limit, and *Normile* v. *Thompson* (1905), which pitted a contractor against a Seattle city official who had cancelled a street-paving contract for hours-law violations – that both statutes were constitutional. A state or city had a right to "do its work in any manner it sees fit, and no violation of private rights is involved." A year later, justices re-validated the statutes in *State* v. *W. H. Davis* (1906).[161] At the same time, men in Washington and elsewhere sued to escape regulation on the ground that it imposed undue burdens or deprived them of liberty of contract. One example suffices: Plumbers sought to invalidate a statute that required them to prove, as a condition of licensing, familiarity with rules of sanitation. In *State ex rel. Richey* v. *Smith* (1906), the state supreme court ruled that lawmakers might provide for a sanitary inspection of plumbing work in aid of "system" and public health. But, in their view, it was unreasonable to expect plumbers to have scientific knowledge apart from plumbing; such a burden deprived them of property rights in their occupation.[162]

Well into the new century, municipal workers sought to retain an eight-hour day: In 1908, a reporter noted the determination of workers at a Central Union Council meeting to resist anyone "monkeying" with the rule. But entrepreneurs and some unions urged men to "acquaint themselves more intimately with movements of national importance – political social industrial and economic – and act in all things with discretion." As with plumbers and scientific knowledge, eight-hour limitations seemed to constrain men who might choose workplace risk or longer days.[163] Witness, for instance, the muscular arguments mounted in Tacoma against interference with men's choices by unions or anyone else, with pro-union, pro-protectionist leaders close at hand. At issue was manliness as well as the due-process language of

---

[160] "They Grind Slowly," *TDL*, November 20, 1889, p. 8; "Eight-Hour Bill Knifed," *ST*, January 29, 1891.

[161] *In Re Broad*, 36 Wash Rpts 449 (1904), *Normile* v. *Thompson*, 37 Wash Rpts 465 (1905), 465–6; and *State* v. *W. H. Davis*, 43 Wash Rpts 116 (1906). In 1906, Broad was back in court contending that a minimum-wage law for public workers violated the 14th Amendment; the Court disagreed; *George Gies* v. *James C. Broad*, 41 Wash Rpts 448 (1906). Coal miners, with other men in dangerous trades, sought and eventually secured an eight-hour workday alongside better wages and a closed shop; "Coal Miners Ask Increased Wages," *TDL*, July 25, 1908. Dentists tried without success to evade regulation; e.g., *State* v. *E. J. Brown*, 137 Wash Rpts 97 (1905) or *In Re E. G. Thompson*, 36 Wash Rpts 377 (1904). Horse-shoers evaded regulation: See *In Re Ronald Aubrey*, 36 Wash Rpts 308 (1904) (statute requiring horse-shoers to purchase licenses or pay a penalty was unconstitutional).

[162] *State ex rel Richey* v. *L.C. Smith, Sheriff of King Co.*, 42 Wash Rpts 237 (1906), 243–4.

[163] "Oppose Change in Eight-Hour Law," *TDL*, July 23, 1908.

state and federal constitutions: "This eight-hour business ... is a bad move. Who wants to be forced to remain idle sixteen hours out of twenty-four? ... Every free American citizen ought to have the privilege of working one hour or twenty-four as he chooses." There was "no freedom where men join some labor organization that will beat out their brains if they don't follow the dictation of the leaders."[164]

While resistance to state limitations of men's workdays had grown, sentiment was drifting, as one writer put it, toward "lighter work for women."[165] Principled resistance also grew. As early as 1889, amidst the tooth-and-nail struggle to secure equal suffrage in the state constitution, Ida Wright warned her comrades that limitations of economic agency might be next: British men in their attempt to protect women from hardship in coal mines had banned women from labor "unfit" for them. While done with the best intentions, she said, she did not always "thank men for acting upon their good intentions." The right to limit women's labor implied the power to say whether they should labor at all.[166]

Still, legislators adopted a ten-hour day for women in 1901 – a decision that probably reflected not only a growing sense of women's susceptibility to exogenous forces, but also the influence of Republican fascination with protectionism of all kinds. As the Republican Central Committee explained in September, 1889, the new state would "speak with no uncertain voice in favor of protection to American Industries and American Labor."[167] Three years later, an influential Seattle protectionist reminded his neighbors that benevolence and shepherding began at home: While it was right to have "full sympathy for the down-trodden laborer in the east," it was "better for you and for him to help along first the struggling laborer in Seattle," perhaps with higher wages for men and shorter workdays for women.[168]

The state's new Supreme Court agreed. In *State v. A. G. Buchanan* (1902), justices validated the 1901 hours statute which forbade the employment in "any mechanical or mercantile establishment, laundry, hotel, and restaurant" of female operatives for more than ten hours a day, only in part because of actual or prospective motherhood. Buchanan operated Bon Marche, the Seattle department store where Rita the messenger and others toiled in dark,

---

[164] On the eight-hour day, see "Eight Hours Only" (for eight-hour days, with or without the same pay), April 30, 1886, and "The Eight-Hour Plan," April 27, 1886 (on employers' suggestions of eight-hour days with reduced pay); both *TDL*. For the opposing view, see "Eight Hour Stupidity," ibid., May 23, 1886.

[165] "The Women Workers of France," from NY World, *WS*, October 6, 1909.

[166] Ida Wright, "Reply to Mary Keith," *TDL*, May 25, 1889. See also *Los Angeles Herald*, September 28, 1890, p. 5; "Miss Ida Wright" went to Tacoma and "never returned." In 1889, Wright was secretary of the Tacoma Woman Suffrage Association. See also Ida Wright, "Men Made Laws for Women," *TDL*, May 10, 1888, p. 6, pointing to the Czar of Russia's supposed representation of women.

[167] Circular letter, September 25, 1889, Struve Allen Hughes and McMicken Papers, UWSC.

[168] "'Protection is a local question,'" *SPT*, February 1, 1892.

hot rooms.[169] Validation of the statute, however, had not been certain. In 1902, well before the High Court ruling in *Muller* v. *Oregon*, Justice Dunbar had to find his way through a thicket of inconsistent state and federal rulings. State courts had disallowed sex-specific hours legislation on many occasions, as with *Ritchie* v. *Illinois*, which attorneys on both sides explored in detail. The department-store owner argued that the law arbitrarily permitted women to work ten hours in one mercantile firm and then in a similar firm for yet more hours, all in the same day; it also allowed them to take other jobs for limitless hours (e.g., farm laborers, government-office staff, or domestic servants). At the same time, male municipal workers were limited to eight hours each day. In *Holden* v. *Hardy*, they noted, federal justices had approved limitations when men undertook obviously dangerous work. But Bon Marche did not operate a mine or lumbering camp. They also pointed to Fourteenth-Amendment doctrines that required compelling proof of a public interest in regulation. Dunbar should rely on *Ritchie*. Why? In Washington, "females who are of legal age are *sui juris*, and every such female is free to enter into any lawful contract. They are placed by our laws upon the same plane as males in that respect."[170]

Prosecutors disclaimed any intention of disputing the general idea that hours-limitation statutes were unconstitutional. Nor did they quibble with women's economic agency. They argued instead that the "trend in modern authorities" was to protect all vulnerable classes from harm. Justices had not been asked to judge the efficacy of the law, only to say whether it exceeded legislators' police powers. After a recitation of authorities that permitted a decision either way, Dunbar simply ducked. Excepting one reference to legislative protection of the "mothers of succeeding generations," he ignored the law's sex-specific language. The assembly was protecting vulnerable *classes*; it was enough that the law fell within the scope of the state's police powers.[171]

Nor did women always disagree. Well into 1909, as women's groups patrolled towns and cities, anti-protection lobbyists protested the introduction of a "women's eight-hour bill, the miners' eight-hour bill and other measures of particular interest to the labor unions." They also attended legislative committee meetings to speak for classes who sought income but were taken to be imperiled by long shifts.[172] In the end, however, the 1901 ten-hour statute was revised and elaborated with significant help from women. The left-leaning Women's Label League, for instance, held public meetings to explore ways to defend American labor against outsiders and advance the cause of

---

[169] Washington (State), *Annual Report of the Labor Department* (Olympia, WA, 1913), p. 22. See also Act to Regulate and Limit the Hours of the Employment of Females ..., Session Laws, State of Washington, Ch. LXVIII, 1901, p. 118. Women could work ten hours in every twenty-four; the same act mandated "suitable seats" for women.

[170] State of Washington v. Buchanan, Case File No. 4235, Respondents Brief, pp. 7–9, Appellants' Brief, pp. 3–5, WSA-O. See also *State of Washington* v. *Buchanan*, 29 Wash Rpts 602 (1902).

[171] Ibid.   [172] "Eight-Hour Bills in Danger," *TDT*, February 11, 1909 (formerly TDL).

women in the workplace. In 1909, the League mounted public events featuring two female speakers "prominent in the movement for the amelioration of conditions that obtain in the employment of women." Leaguers anticipated a large attendance of workers, heated debate of the question of an eight-hour law for women, and representatives of the business community in Tacoma. Women would also learn "how to manage it," since many would experience a loss of income.[173]

When a sex-specific, eight-hour bill finally appeared in the Assembly on February 17, 1909, a fracas ensued over the proposed exemption of cannery workers. How could it be constitutional to impose limits on women at all manufactories except one? When another member argued that "some girls get into trouble by having too much leisure," Representative Bell contended that "the Japs would be working in the laundries" and soon "would own them"; perhaps hours legislation would encourage white women to wash clothes. The law "did not attempt to give all women an eight-hour law, but merely favors classes not touching domestics." He also threw a few darts at Lincoln County's delegate, who wondered whether the measure might hurt "girls working in country hotels and restaurants by interfering with their right of contract." An opponent tried to clog the works with an amendment to exempt both domestic and cannery workers, but a compromise emerged. The bill passed fifty-one to thirty-six.[174] Washington's amended statute required mechanized firms not engaged in seasonal occupations (i.e., canneries) to send women and children home after eight hours of work each day. Only men were free literally to work themselves to death.[175]

In late summer, 1911, local authorities cited Henrietta (Hattie) Somerville for encouraging Mattie Garse and other female operatives to work nine or more hours per day. The case was almost certainly feigned by Somerville and her employees. As of September 9, 1911, when a complaint was filed, Hattie and her husband, R. S. Somerville, were partners in the Washington Paper Box Company in Seattle, where they employed a female work force. When Judge John F. King of the King County Superior Court convicted and fined Somerville in a bench trial, she appealed to the Supreme Court. There, her lawyers argued

---

[173] "Needs of Working Women Topic," *TDT*, February 19, 1909, and "Women to Discuss 8-Hour Law, Label League to Hold Open Meeting ...," ibid., February 6, 1909. On union support, see, e.g., "What Labor Delegates Will Do in Convention," *SP*, January 2, 1910, p. 8 (unions to push hard for sex-specific labor laws). See also "Women Are Busy in Progressive Work," *TDT*, March 3, 1909 ("Better Conditions and Closer Organizations for that Purpose" the subject of open meeting of Tacoma Woman's Label league).

[174] "Women Toilers' Measure Is Passed," *BH*, February 17, 1909, p. 6. See also "Labor Bill Killed on Final Vote," ibid., p. 1. For additional detail, see John C. Putnam, *Class and Gender Politics in Progressive-Era Seattle* (Reno, NV, 2008), which does not emphasize women's industrial protection.

[175] Act to Regulate the Hours of Work in Canneries and Other Mechanical Firms ..., Session Laws, State of Washington, Ch. 37, 1911, p. 131. It may be that cannery women had organized petition drives in pursuit of longer hours; "That Eight-Hour Law," *TT*, January 27, 1911, p. 3.

that the eight-hour law unconstitutionally deprived her self-supporting employees of their right as fully constituted citizens to strike up their own bargains in the workplace.[176]

During the King County proceedings, moreover, Hattie and three self-supporting employees (June Olander, Tessie Gleason, and Hazel Kirk Somerville, another self-described "partner," probably a daughter-in-law) made clear that legal fictions obscured social and economic reality: Short days would render them less safe, less healthy, and less able to support themselves or their families. Two workers testified that they wished to work nine hours rather than eight; Somerville swore that employees had spoken to her "as to their voluntary desire to work nine hours." Why? "Most of the girls work piece work," she explained, "and they can make more money in nine hours than they can in eight hours; and if they work nine hours they have Saturday afternoons; if they had the one hour rest during the week they would not be able to do anything or go anywhere, whereas having Saturday afternoons off they can go out in the open air." The prosecuting attorney was astonished: "If they had the eight hour law they would have to work Saturday afternoon?" "Yes sir," Hattie replied.[177]

In lower court, the district attorney explored the health of the workers, the cleanliness of the facilities, Hattie's experiences as a mother, her family's health, whether machines and box making were "simple," workers' stools, the likelihood of speed-ups, whether male supervisors oversaw women, and other fruitless lines of inquiry. Somerville's lawyers, however, had turned *Muller* v. *Oregon*'s best-known innovation (the so-called Brandeis Brief, submitted in support of Oregon's ten-hour law) to different advantage. Extra-legal evidence proved the arbitrariness of legislative decisions – the eight-hour number, generalizations about "all" factories and "all" industries, women's supposed weakness, and damage to working-women's children (a number of offspring were exhibited in court). Nor did Somerville, an expert box-maker, require male supervision. The company occupied a new facility with transoms, lunchrooms, huge windows and sky-lights, electricity, and Puget Sound breezes. State inspectors had testified to the facts after a surprise visit; they even swore to

[176] In the case file and newspapers, Hattie Somerville is described as "Superintendent," but the company formed part of the marital estate. When Somerville sued, she was probably in her late 40s. The 13th Federal Census lists her as household head in 1910, though not widowed, and forty-eight; Population Schedule, Sheet 9-A, King County/Seattle, Washington, line 36. She may have been older; official records show burial in 1947 at age eighty-five; Washington Death Records, Image 896, Doc. No. 42, Ref. ID 386. Thanks to Charles Hansen of Spokane and Jean Fisher of Tacoma.

[177] *State* v. *Somerville*, 67 Wash Rpts 638 (1912), and for briefs, transcripts of lower-court testimony, and photographs, State of Washington v. Henrietta Somerville (1912), Case File No. 9898, WSA-O. For words quoted, see Q and A, Defendant's Case, ibid., pp. 20–2, 42–4, and passim. See *Lochner* v. *New York*, 198 U.S. 45 (1905). In *Somerville*, Justice Crow mentioned "private" (that is, union- or company-led) decisions to limit workdays in order to justify state intervention generally.

FIGURE 6.1. One of the workers at the progressive Washington Paper Box Factory, Seattle, WA; her supervisor, Henrietta Somerville, was plaintiff and then the appellant in *Somerville v. State of Washington* (1912). From Exhibits, Case File No. 9898, now housed at Washington State Archive, Central Branch, Olympia, WA (formerly WSA-E).

the accuracy of photographs submitted by the defense to prove healthfulness. Well-fed, smiling women sat proudly at machines in a dust-free room, sporting hair bows and clean frocks, as if to say, "We need no help from anyone."[178]

As in *Buchanan*, the district attorney ultimately retreated into questions of law enforcement and constitutional limitation. He would not seek to justify the statute as a health law, he said, but would argue "simply the constitutionality of it, the fact they are employed; the legislature saw fit to enact it, and the testimony does not tend to controvert it at all; that they simply worked nine

[178] State v. Somerville (1912), Case File No. 9898, Exhibits, WSA-O.

hours, and upon that alone." He conceded the fact of pleasant conditions "for the purpose of making the record." Somerville's attorney pounced. In the stand was a physician who had said that women required no help from legislators: "Every woman is a law unto herself?" "Yes sir," replied the doctor. "As a matter of fact, Doctor, since a woman is a law unto herself, there could be no reason, from a medical standpoint, from enumerating any facts, why a certain number of hours would be deleterious, unless such a number would exhaust any one physically or mentally?" "I know of none," said the practitioner.[179]

Judge Main chose the path of least resistance, declaring the eight-hour law a reasonable exercise of state police powers, compatible with "common knowledge" about working women, and, given Somerville's superficial resemblance to the 1908 *Muller* v. *Oregon* ruling, constitutional. He ignored as "irrelevant" the information assembled by Hattie Somerville's young lawyers, David Trefethen and Loren Grinstead, founders in 1910 of a new firm in Seattle known for pursuing progressive causes. It was enough that the statute fell within the bounds of state police powers and comported with federal decisions on the same topic.[180]

An appeal was lodged; within days, the bench published an opinion. Justice Herman Crow ignored compilations of fact and accepted legislators' (and Judge Main's) readings of "common knowledge," validating the statute as a reasonable exception to the due-process requirements of the Fourteenth Amendment and two sections of the state constitution. Legislators were free to meddle in bargains struck up between women and employers in mechanized firms. The facts and legal issues in *Muller* and *Somerville* were virtually identical, said Crow; but, unlike the Court's less-than-solid footing in Buchanan, Crow now had *Muller* in hand. He therefore copied out long sections of Justice David Brewer's opinion in *Muller*, explaining that he did so because the arguments were "convincing and unanswerable." Women were "not upon an equality"; as "minors, though not to the same extent" as children, they required "especial care." Crow acknowledged that the general right to contract formed part of the "liberty of the individual," but this liberty was "not absolute." States could intervene as fictive parents. Repeatedly citing "common knowledge," Crow held that Washington's interests in promoting actual or prospective motherhood and defending vulnerable classes from exploitation justified intervention. In a concurrence, Justice Stephen Chadwick noted ample evidence of "clean and wholesome" conditions – a circumstance that ordinarily might have led him to question the law's sweeping terms. But, here, he thought, federal authority imposed limits; he therefore asked why the court had not struck down the cannery exception. If legislators worried about brutal workdays, harvest-related labor more than qualified. He approved of this example of class legislation if it bettered the

---

[179] State v. Somerville, Case File No. 9898, Defendant's Case, p. 22.
[180] Ibid., passim. While Main's opinion has not survived, its contents can be partly surmised.

"condition of *human beings*"; if the exception benefited canners and hurt women, it was irrational.[181]

Plainly outraged, Trefethen and Grinstead demanded a re-hearing *en banc* of a case that was not only important to clients but "absolutely unique as a precedent" in Washington legal history. They did not intend to present new evidence; piles of relevant, uncontested information had been presented at trial. Instead, they reminded the Supreme Court that, while Judge King had focused on one factory, evidence had been arrayed to show the "general conditions in the paper box manufacturing industry" throughout the state. The court would not find, as implied in the ruling, dire conditions in other paper-box factories. They had searched the records of every box maker in the state; they challenged the court's right to "pass upon the constitutionality of this question" until prosecutors presented and discussed the evidence. Without facts, there could be no lawful determination of individual rights or public power. Apparently, the state could not offer "any scientific, economic, physical and other pertinent facts"; they merely contended, as if by rote, that the statute must be a "proper exercise of the police power" because legislators had said so. To be sure, courts resolved doubts in favor of statutes. But in *Somerville*, facts had been called irrelevant. The ten-hour law in *Muller* was perhaps rightly sustained; facts had been gathered by statisticians from across the world showing ten hours to be a reasonable limitation for laundresses. But if eight hours was rational for miners, how was it also reasonable for healthy, adult women in a well-ventilated box factory?[182]

Finally, Trefethen and Grinstead addressed the central issue, in the process pointing to a road not taken: Hattie Somerville, her daughter-in-law, and all of her female operatives were enfranchised, propertied adult women, almost all of them self-supporting. The women in *Muller* v. *Oregon* would not be enfranchised until 1912. The two cases were not analogous after all; indeed, federal justices had implied, in *Muller* and elsewhere, that disenfranchisement affected outcomes.[183] This was not a question of the "'propriety,' advisability or 'wisdom' of this statute," wrote the pair, quoting sardonically from Crow's

[181] *State v. Somerville*, 67 Wash Rpts 638 (1912), pp. 642–5, 650–1, 655. A year earlier, the same court had ruled that a "workingmen's compensation" law did not violate liberty of contract; *State of Washington v. C. W. Clausen*, 65 Wash Rpts 156 (1911), 156–7. When California courts validated a ten-hour law in 1910, observers predicted that Washington's courts would do the same; "Washington Law Good," *TT*, June 10, 1911, p. 1.

[182] Somerville v. State, "Petition for a Re-Hearing En Banc," Case File No. 9898, pp. 2–4. See also "The supreme court . . . ," *LE*, July 19, 1912, p. 4 (Supreme Court refused to grant a rehearing; the only way to proceed would be an appeal to federal courts). Washington had passed its own eight-hour law for miners. But the court ignored it, citing *Holden v. Hardy*, 169 U.S. Rpts 366 (1898), which validated a Utah statute limiting miners to eight hours and barring women from mines. A miner had worked ten hours; the law was a reasonable exercise of state police powers (work was unhealthy and unsafe).

[183] See also *Adkins v. Children's Hospital*, 261 U.S. Rpts 525 (1923), in which the Supreme Court also pointed to the 19th Amendment as ground for universalizing *laissez-faire*.

opinion. It was a question of *"absolute right on the part of an elector of this State to preserve to herself the constitutional right of contract."* If legislators could pass "any law that it may desire as to women, because of her sex and dependent relations," what limits could be placed on legislation? If the court meant to resolve the general question of constitutionality "without any regard to any fact presented before it," and further chose not to address the question of co-sovereignty, then it should at least pass judgment on the particular exceptions carved out for seasonal or domestic workers. As Chadwick had noted, the health, welfare and safety of those workers had been ignored arbitrarily. Lawmakers could not have passed the law without the cannery exception. If that provision fell, it tainted the entire statute; rules of statutory construction required that, if part of an act violated law, the whole must fall.[184]

****

Nothing happened – at least not in Somerville's case. But the 1910 hours law represented one example among many of state interventions in workplace and market relations; in that sense, male exemption from paternal constraint formed an exception to a general rule of expanding public oversight of private transactions, including those that implicated women's bodies. As we have seen, intervention was most likely when non-Asian laborers were taken to be unrepresented in government, capable of disrupting the exercise of property rights, susceptible to workplace abuse, or potentially pregnant. In Washington, judicial and legislative majorities fulsomely embraced industrial limitation across a broad range of topics; into the new century, statute books bristled with factory laws and other impositions on employers, especially public-interest exceptions. Washington, for instance, was one of eight western states to adopt bank-deposit guarantees before 1910.[185] In 1913, after months of agitation by clubs and unions, the assembly adopted a minimum-wage law for women and minors, which reinforced sex segregation of workers and established a commission to oversee women's wages and surroundings. Unionists who had opposed the eight-hour law unless it applied to everyone castigated lobbyists for their ignorance of basic principles of capitalism. Associations strengthened between women's legal standing as propertied, fictive minors and the state's power to intervene on their behalf in the workplace.

Courts repeatedly signaled their willingness to defer to the letter of legislation. A well-publicized example appeared in 1913, when the Pacific American Fisheries – a cannery generally exempted from the eight-hour rule – found itself convicted in a King County courtroom of violating the eight-hour law with female can-lacquerers. On appeal to the state's highest court, newly

[184] Ibid., emphasis added. See also "If You Were a Girl Worker," *LJ*, November 4, 1910, p. 1 (If all citizens had to bear such burdens, they would "enthusiastically endorse suffrage").

[185] See Morton Keller, *Regulating a New Economy: Public Policy and Economic Change in America, 1900–1933* (Cambridge, MA, 1990), p. 201.

appointed Associate Justice John F. Main concluded for the majority that the mere lacquering of cans was "not a part of the work of canning fish if the lacquering" was not "immediately necessary" to preserve fish; it could be done in the usual course of business by eight-hour, female workers.[186] In the same year, justices decided in *State of Washington* v. *Mountain Timber Company* (a ruling subsequently appealed to the U.S. Supreme Court, which affirmed the state's ruling) that the workmen's compensation law expressed "such standards of morality and expediency as have by gradual process and accepted reason" come to be synonymous with "the will of the people," as articulated by legislators. Still smarting from the *Somerville* fiasco, Main's colleagues also praised legislators for tending to the needs of "laborers, especially female laborers."[187] Deference continued, in part because the law code expressly required it unless a statute was flagrantly improper. In 1936, for instance, just as the federal judiciary came under fire for its opposition to Franklin Roosevelt's economic interventions, the state bench again characterized the right to legislate in the public interest as "an attribute of sovereignty ... and a function that cannot be surrendered."[188]

Officials thus ignored and eventually discredited radical invocations of the equality principle in the case of women; the idea that women had rights as electors (or, in an allusion to sovereignty, that each woman "was a law unto herself") yielded to the "common knowledge" of female inadequacy and dependence, alongside "common knowledge" of the unfitness (albeit for different reasons) of other classes beyond white men and women. Even when women's constitutional standing varied from case to case, as with *Somerville* and *Muller*, courts inscribed them with sameness, revealing the immense power of customary constitutions and the extent to which women's claim to co-sovereignty had been compromised since 1888–89. None of this should have been surprising. As early as 1882, when a Walla Walla editor learned of a Chicago drive among male workers to secure an eight-hour workday, he inveighed against it on the ground that the demand for fewer hours was most loudly demanded "by those whose avocations are followed for only a part of the year, or whose employment is uncertain" – that is to say, by those who worked dependently or temporarily. "Selfishness and not principle" governed men unwilling to work long hours to enrich families and society. Small labor prints condemned *Somerville* v. *State* as a "blow at personal liberty," given medical

---

[186] *State of Washington* v. *Pacific American Fisheries*, 73 Wash Rpts 37 (1913), 452.

[187] *State of Washington* v. *Mountain Timber Company*, 75 Wash Rpts 581 (1913), 588–9, emphasis added. The U.S. Supreme Court affirmed the decision in *Mountain Timber Co.* v. *Washington*, 243 U.S. 219 (1917). For Chadwick, see *State* v. *Somerville*, 651. States generally objected far less to regulation of workplaces than many historians have reported, at least by the turn of the century; see Katz, "Protective Labor Legislation in the Courts," op cit. Two years earlier, the supreme court also affirmed the legality of the compensation law's requirement that high-risk company owners create a fund for payment of damages in cases of injury; *State of Washington* v. *C. W. Clausen*, 65 Wash Rpts 156 (1911).

[188] *Shea* v. *Olson*, 185 Wash Rpts 143 (1936), 153–4.

testimony showing that work up to ten hours per day did not injure female workers.[189] But employers mostly ignored it; they could "work the girls overtime" with impunity and pay a small fine, especially when funding ran out for enforcement agencies. In Spokane, where 3,000 women were affected, businesses following the rules; in nearby Tacoma, the law took effect in mid-1911 "without a hitch."[190]

Two stories capture Washington's embrace of a remodeled gender hierarchy. On July 4, 1895, Seattle residents converged on the center city to view a parade. One journalist expected to see "every veteran of any war and every citizen, from the ragged urchin ... to the dignified man of affairs"; the procession included "the state's citizen soldiery," "the national guard," and "men and horses." He described a chorus of male voices; Indians sent a grandson of the old Chief Seattle. No women appeared – not even, as earlier, to read the Declaration of Independence.[191] Thirteen years later, at a Fourth of July gathering of the National Union, 200 men enjoyed a banquet. Governor Albert Mead celebrated a rising tide of fraternalism that tethered a community of men to government. The "feeling of fraternalism," he said, permeated the "atmosphere of every state and the government of a nation." No other influence had advanced Washington's growth more than fraternalism; every fraternal organization was "an agency of the state in building up the spirit of patriotism." The movement "commands, urges, inspires and illustrates a spirit of human brotherhood, *uniting with one's fellows in government, in philanthropy, in industry, in order to promote the common welfare.*" Here was a quasi-public, interstate academy wherein men came to be "of the same mind one toward another." What about women? In 1894, a Seattle wag offered consolation: "If a woman cannot be a Mason she can be the next best thing – almost a Mason – by joining the Order of the Eastern Star ... [O]nly mothers, sister, wives, or daughters of Masons are eligible."[192] Women occupied the same building, but not the same floor.

[189] "Eight Hours," *WWS*, December 2, 1882, ed. page; "State News Items," *LE*, September 15, 1911, p. 6. In the same vein, see "Eight-Hour Law Is Upheld," *SJI*, September 15, 1911, p. 2.

[190] E.g., "Worked Women Eleven Hours," *TT*, January 19, 1912, p. 8 (hotel fined twenty-five dollars for each of two violations); "Investigate Violations of the Eight-Hour Law, Department is Handicapped for Funds," *LJ*, August 15, 1913. See also "Shorter Hours for Women ... in Harvest Field," *SJI*, August 15, 1913, p. 1 (recommending amendment of eight-hour law to include harvesters);"Eight Hours for Women," *LJ*, January 26, 1912, p. 1 (eight-hour law "bitterly assailed" by manufacturers and attributing the cannery exemption to them); "Preparing for Eight-Hour Workday for Women," *SJI*, March 31, 1911, p. 1; "How it Works in Tacoma," ibid., June 16, 1911, p. 2. The same may have been true in Olympia; "Labor Laws Well Observed," ibid., August 4, 1911, p. 3.

[191] "We Will Celebrate," *ST*, June 29, 1895, p. 1; in the same vein, "Basis of Civilization," ibid., June 22, 1895, p. 1.

[192] "Mead Talks on Fraternalism," *TDL*, July 3, 1908. Emphasis added. For Eastern Star, see "Gossip for Women," *SPT*, April 21, 1894, p. 2.

7

"We contemplate no sweeping reforms"

Constitutionalizing the home vote

> The notion seems to be, "If you can't work woman suffrage off upon such communities as these half-wild Territories, who ever will take it?" Hence woman suffrage must be in a very bad way indeed.
>
> – *Woman's Journal*, 1889[1]

In August, 1885, amidst unprecedented social unrest and violence, the *Washington Standard* circulated a parable about the restoration of a rooster's headship in a local chicken coop. A contributor reported that, at dusk, when "all well-disposed chickens seek their roosts," the distraught bird had come "trotting up to our kitchen door" and "started on a trot toward the hen house, looking back to see if anyone was following him." When the farmer complied, the rooster led him "into the henhouse," where he found "all the chickens sitting on the floor," nervous and disoriented. "The pole on which my chickens roosted had fallen to the ground," he explained, "and they had no place to get a satisfactory night's rest. That rooster made up his mind to have the accommodations of the henhouse made as good as ever. . . . I put the pole up in its place. The hens flew to the perch, and then the rooster took his place on it. He gave one rousing crow, and . . . settled down with his family for the night."[2]

After 1879, a good many territorial "roosters" had been displaced and dismayed by the workings of democracy. Hence, the experiment had been short-lived. Within a decade, conservatives and self-styled patriots had regained their footing, driven women from jury boxes as well as from the polls, and weathered a ratification election, securing approval of a male-centric constitution. Only in 1910 did Washington's adult women regain access to ballot boxes in all elections, but without automatic service on juries and without much hope of partisan office holding. Women could enter jury boxes by personally waiving a general exemption from service by reason of sex.

---

[1] "Not from the West, but from the East," *WJ*, August 24, 1889, repr. from Boston Transcript.
[2] "A Rooster That Reasoned," *WS*, August 14, 1885.

But, once in the waiting room, they would be marked as interlopers in masculine spaces. Brief forays into polling places to cast the "home vote" were less transgressive and certainly less traumatic. Until social practice mutated, women could hope (in the words of a Chicago suffragist) that, while they were "not yet in the jury-box," they might be "getting more and more into the hearts of jurymen" who still presumed to speak for them.[3]

The re-enfranchisement of women occurred within a radically altered society. Few suffragists doubted that sex-blind assumptions of obligations had been a step too far. Moreover, the decades-long remapping of gender, political economy, and law eventuated in strategies and goals strikingly at odds with Zerelda McCoy's. This shift of gears amounted in part to a retreat into what suffrage scholars call "expediency"; reformers chose strategies that might win the day, to some extent occupying the enemy's own turf by characterizing women as civic housekeepers and neighborhood mothers. In so doing, though, Washington's new wave of suffragists faithfully expressed the gender discourses produced in the cauldron of economic and political modernization well afoot by about 1886. To be modern or progressive was to protect "minors" in the workplace and then to secure women's right to speak for home on election day; if the constituent power had been partitioned, women still were situated more securely on propertied foundations than their nineteenth-century sisters had been. The supposedly pre-modern, sex-blind conception of a pervasive equality and sovereignty, with attendant burdens and social penalties, had been relegated to a wild past, where settlers had been forced to live against nature and in privation. For Americans elsewhere, the message was clear: Naïve political experimentation in developing regions had mostly failed; Washingtonians had proved unwittingly that customary constitutions resurged when citizens perceived illegitimacy within the constituent power, injustice, or threats to individual self-construction. In the years before 1910, neither positive law nor property-based, constitutional co-sovereignty had been powerful enough to defeat perceived violations of gender and other social practices, particularly when the boundaries of practice had been altered abruptly with destabilizing or humiliating consequences.

"WE CONTEMPLATE NO SWEEPING REFORMS": THE HOME VOTE

In the wake of crushing legal-political losses and amidst galloping paternalism, women's clubs and reform societies doggedly pursued women's re-enfranchisement. Women complained loudly about the need to vote by proxy: In 1892, for instance, Clara Crawford of Seattle favored a new ship canal and wrote a letter to the editor asking all men to "vote for the best interests of the home," as she could no longer do, on behalf of the women of Seattle. Meanwhile women struggled to retain school suffrage, their remaining

[3] "Woman's Column," *SP*, November 17, 1887.

electoral toehold. In 1892, anti-suffragists tried to eliminate women in Pierce County school elections on the ground that they were not registered to vote in state elections. Eighty women alongside a few others who lived in other precincts had been thrown out of the polling place. Justices basically threw the trouble-makers out of court: The women were entitled to vote and, in school elections, were not required to register.[4] In the same year, as local newspapers continued to give front-page space to campaigns for a Sixteenth Amendment, Dr. Sarah Kendall ran for school superintendent in King County. When anti-suffragists contested her modest ambitions, the Superior Court decided in her favor – as did women who had declared their intention of voting for her.[5]

In 1896, another quandary appeared. The Holmes and Bull Furniture Company had accused the county treasurer of overreach in a school election. In cities with more than 10,000 inhabitants, women could vote in school elections – but could they vote on financial matters as well as board membership, as they had done in several counties? The company contended that the measure itself was class legislation, and that financial matters exceeded the scope of school elections. A unanimous Supreme Court tossed out both claims. But the bench reserved special ire for the second, probably because of the company's transparent attempt to evade taxes. Statutes required only that school elections did not discriminate against women and that every person should be a legal voter; nothing limited the topics that voters might consider if they fell within school boards' purview.[6]

As the 1890s advanced, organized suffragism had experienced a changing of the guard. In 1898, however, with explicit support from temperance groups (especially the WCTU), women's clubs, Populists, and left-leaning laborites, suffragists held out some hope that a referendum would prevail in 1898. Idahoans apparently thought so; the *Boise Statesman* (and then the *New York Times*) reported in 1897 that Washington might join Idaho in extending the suffrage to women. Legislators had gone so far as to refer the question to voters at the next general election. In January, 1897, NAWSA dropped other initiatives to devote energy to Western States; the new battlegrounds were Washington, Oregon, California, and Nevada. As in the past, local and national organizers campaigned on the time-honored ground of equal and fair representations of property. Not surprisingly, suffragists lost again, in part

---

[4] Clara M. Crawford, "Lake Washington Ship Canal," *SPT*, November 1, 1892, p. 2; *Luzader et al. v. Sargeant et al.*, 4 Wash Rpts 299 (1892), 304.

[5] E.g., "For Woman Suffrage," *New York Daily Tribune*, February 9, 1890, p. 3, or "A Plea for Woman Suffrage," *SPT*, January 18, 1892. See also "A School Election," ibid., November 3, 1892. The outcome is unknown.

[6] *Holmes and Bull Furniture Co.* v. *John Hedges, County Treasurer*, 13 Wash Rpts 697 (1896), 706–7.

because the referendum had been paired with another poison pill, a controversial single-tax proposal.[7]

The news, though, was not entirely bad: Even with an all-male electorate, women lost by only 10,000 votes, a much narrower margin in relative terms than in earlier canvasses. In organizational terms, moreover, suffragists and minor parties owned the result. They had received precious little support from Republicans or Democrats – though the Republicans at least gave lip service to the idea of a "free and honest popular ballot," the "just and equal representation of all the people," and their "just and equal protection under the law."[8] Time and again, suffrage leaders observed that every political party, including Populists, permitted anti-suffrage figures to speak at their gatherings, omitted the issue in party platforms, and failed to respond to pro-suffrage requests for floor time. In 1890, the Farmers' Alliance's Declaration of Principles was less than courageous.[9] Partly because Roger Greene appeared again in 1892 as the Prohibition Party's candidate for governor, that party offered a platform demanding a constitutional amendment giving to women "the privilege of suffrage equal with men." But the old guard held firm: In 1902, when NAWSA's Susan B. Anthony sought support from George Turner, who had moved steadily away from the Republican Party, he sent her packing with a terse "I regret on your account to say no."[10]

What more could be done? One possibility was a lawsuit demanding restoration of vested rights unlawfully confiscated in 1887–88. Bellingham activist Dora Cyderman consulted a lawyer who examined local law as well as analogous situations in other jurisdictions and concluded that there was no hope – not "one chance in a thousand." Nor would an attorney of any reputation take on the cause.[11] Given ongoing Congressional deadlock on the

---

[7] "From the Boise Statesman, Woman Suffrage," *NYT*, March 21, 1897, p. 16; "Woman Suffrage Policy," ibid., January 31, 1897, p. 5; "Woman Suffrage Defeated in Washington," *LAT*, November 18, 1898, p. 8. The second proposal was for a single tax.

[8] T. A. Larson, "The Woman Suffrage Movement in Washington," *Pacific Northwest Quarterly* (April 1976), p. 55. Larson confirms widespread support for mixed suffrage before the late 1880s. Anti-suffragists called the margin "monumental." See also "Hunting a Mare's Nest," *SPT*, August 18, 1892.

[9] E.g., Susan B. Anthony to Ella Smith DeVoe, August 25, 1894, in Elizabeth Cady Stanton and Susan B. Anthony Papers, microfilm edition, Reel 32, pp. 1027–8, and passim; "Declaration of Principles," *WS*, August 15, 1890 ("That we demand equal rights to all, and special favors to none.")

[10] For Greene and the prohibitionists in 1892 alone, see "Prohibition State Ticket," *SPT*, October 4, 1892; "The State Prohibitionists," ibid., June 2, 1892; "Political Pointers, The Prohibitionist Party . . .," ibid., February 6, 1892 (Greene in attendance); or "The Prohibitionists' Ticket," ibid., August 27, 1892. In September, 1886, George Turner had embraced all but the first part of the Republican platform, which praised the law conferring suffrage on women and opposed its repeal or modification; "Republican Platform," Special Supplement, *LCB*, September 14, 1886; see also "Republican Platform," *SFR*, September 11, 1886. In the same issue, a Spokane writer called Republican support for women "chivalrous"; "Fall In Boy," ibid. See Turner to Susan B. Anthony [card], November 6, 1902, Stanton/Anthony Papers, Microfilm Ed., Reel 42, Frames 876–7.

[11] Dora Cyderman to ESD, August 16, 1907, Emma Smith DeVoe Papers, Box 1, Folder 9, WSHS.

Sixteenth Amendment, suffragists could hope only to secure a state constitutional amendment – an uphill climb, to be sure, but a course of action that offered some possibility of success.

By 1905–06, suffrage associations had built a formidable political machine under new leadership and forged new alliances with NAWSA.[12] The state's leadership carefully distanced itself from English-style radicalism and the appearance of zealotry within the WCTU. It mattered little whether observers were right: Common knowledge had it, particularly among out-of-state reformers, that temperance had derailed suffragism across the nation; in one lecturer's words, "had not the effort been made to mix politics and religion, it is probable that a more lenient view would have been taken." Washingtonians still feared that cities would be "menaced by a form of Blue Laws" akin to those found in New England.[13]

Within prestigious suffrage associations, good manners won praise. Emma Smith DeVoe embodied the social graces, facility with language, and political finesse of the ever-changing WERA. DeVoe was not dissembling. She was an adroit politician but also, within the bounds of political and gender discourses, a truth-telling realist who knew that her every move would be scrutinized. She preferred polite conversation, performances of femininity, and genteel public events and spectacles. WERA members sold postcards and womanly cookbooks emblazoned with suffrage slogans. Designed by Mrs. D. C. Coates of Spokane, the cards carried a red and green banner ("Votes for Women") and the words of "Forward Sister Women"; they also lauded the arrival of woman as "a refining, sympathetic, and justice-loving influence" in politics.[14]

As early as 1890, DeVoe had urged pro-suffrage forces, in Susan B. Anthony's presence, to "flatter" men into submission, praising their farming skills or telling them "how much they had improved since the Mayflower landed."[15] Humor and suasion supplanted weighty arguments

---

[12] The reunification of NWSA and AWSA after the civil war-era schism is widely noted; but, for local notice, see untitled article, *WS*, February 21, 1890, naming NAWSA officers.

[13] On English methods, see "Suffragists are Met by Police," *TDL*, June 1, 1908; or editorial, ibid., July 5, 1908 (English women interested in "buns and bombs"); "The Woman Suffrage Club," *WS*, December 17, 1909 (speaker a visiting lecturer). The WCTU and other groups in Tacoma continued to battle vice, in 1909 assailing the mayor for his failure to make good on promises; e.g., "Fifteen Hundred Women Will Know the Facts," February 19, 1909; "Women Demand Resignation of Mayor, An Open Letter to the City Council," and "Linck Confesses His Unfitness," February 20, 1909, p. 1; "Jamieson Statement Twisted in Argument for Indecency," February 23, 1909; "Mayor is Arraigned by Women," February 24, 1909; all *TDT*.

[14] "Suffrage Post Cards," *WS*, March 11, 1910. The song used the score of "Onward Christian Soldiers"; see ("Forward sister women!/Onward ever more,/ Bondage is behind you,/Freedom is before … "); under the title "The Women's Battle Song" at www.thesuffragettes.org. On cookbooks, see "Recipes May Win Votes for Women," *TDT*, February 26, 1909 ("a slim oilcloth covered volume." By "enabling [men] to eat the best of fare" they would "win his gratitude and votes for the amendment").

[15] "Notes from Dakota Letters," in *Woman's Tribune*, January 11, 1890, Stanton/Anthony Papers, microfilm edition, Reel 27, Frame 1027.

FIGURE 7.1. Emma Smith DeVoe (1848–1927) led suffragists to victory in 1910, particularly west of the Cascades; n.d. From the collections of the Washington State Historical Society, Tacoma, WA. Used by permission.

about constitutional equality; public confrontation was anathema. The western association held essay contests on household subjects and offered programs on pure food and model menus; a monthly paper, *Votes for Women*, emerged during the campaign's final year, with ads "written in suffrage terms."[16] The

---

[16] For this and other information, see Ida Husted Harper, ed., *History of Woman Suffrage*, Vol. 6 (New York, 1922, repr. 1985), pp. 673–86.

new suffragist, in other words, was a principled but decorous New Woman. Campaigners waved handkerchiefs, not canes. In June, 1910, Mrs. P. P. Stalford of Spokane earned special mention not only for "running down the police [and] advocating woman suffrage" but also for her graham bread. She had proved that women could excel in both "public reforms and housekeeping." Stalford agreed: A woman's first duties were at home; the balance of her time might go elsewhere.[17]

Spokane's colorful May Arkwright Hutton, initially president of the state's eastern chapter of WERA and then, after infighting in 1909, head of the separate Political Equality League, adopted a less ladylike tone inflected with socialism and unionism; she claimed to speak for "the laundry worker, the shop girl, the stenographer, the teacher, the working woman of every type, whose home and fireside and bread are earned by their own efforts." In the Coeur d'Alene mining district of Idaho, May Arkwright and Levi Hutton had invested in a mine and become immensely wealthy. May had supported IWW strikers, run a "restaurant" of uncertain reputation, and helped Idaho women win suffrage in 1896; for his union work, Levi had been jailed. In 1909, however, from her new home in Spokane, even the outlandish Hutton (who used rough language, sometimes wore men's suits, and drove a gaudy red automobile) urged accommodation. Women, she said, did not want to "usurp the reins of government," but rather to take their places in well-paid jobs and solve social problems at the polls. Americans were in serious trouble; women could "help make conditions better." In 1910, she explained further that success in both Idaho and Washington had to do with granting men their intelligence and relying on local talent. She had little time for NAWSA. Hutton preferred (in her phrase and Duniway's) a "still hunt," not the parades, fancy teas, and array of famous visitors that DeVoe's NAWSA-affiliated organization favored.[18]

Increasingly, however, three problems influenced suffragists' choices. First, more than one activist concluded that men were more amenable to change than were women, in part because of the multiplication of duties associated with political equality. In November, 1908, an officer of WERA (possibly DeVoe) opined that, while many men supported suffrage, women were retarding the movement: If not for the "narrow prejudice in the minds of so many wives, mothers, etc., to influence the voters against their own liberal judgment, we could secure our political freedom tomorrow." How could suffragists address this problem? DeVoe decided to hew a path between Duniway and Hutton on

---

[17] "Mrs. Stalford Proves that Women Can Win in Both Public Reforms and Housekeeping," *SP*, June 13, 1910.

[18] May Arkwright Hutton, quoted in Rebecca Mead, *How the Vote Was Won: Woman Suffrage in the Western United States, 1868–1914* (New York, 2004), p. 108; Hutton, Letter to Editor, *SR*, October 25, 1909; "Mrs. Hutton tells Why Woman Suffrage Won at Polls," *SP*, November 9, 1910, p. 1. She also wrote a Spokane newspaper column. On still hunting, see May Hutton to Dr. Cara Smith Eaton, Seattle, November 5, 1908, May Arkwright Hutton Collection, Northwest Museum of Arts and Culture, Spokane.

FIGURE 7.2. Spokane's feisty suffragist and laborite, May Arkwright Hutton (1860–1915), was an extraordinarily effective organizer and publicist; 1912. Harris & Ewing Collection: Harris & Ewing, photographer. Courtesy of American Memory Collection, Library of Congress. LC-H261- 1516 [P&P].

one side (the "still hunt"), and NAWSA, which championed a public, "all-speaking campaign."[19]

Second, suffragists needed to address wage-earning women's plight. Such women no longer formed an exception to a general rule of unpaid homework. A California suffragist noted that Washington, which once claimed more women farmers and housekeepers than office-workers and saleswomen, had shifted gears. Now, the majority of female workers were "teachers, book-keepers and stenographers." Industrialization brought advantages for suffragism: Factory and mill hands and "those engaged in other higher forms of labor" wanted suffrage to demand fair reward for their work, and many laboring men were willing to help; in one writer's words, "a labor woman without a vote is a millstone about their necks." As John Putnam's scholarship shows, unions indeed lent support, particularly in Seattle-Tacoma, where laborites in January, 1910, praised DeVoe's victories and promised an education program to persuade members of the merits of suffragism.[20]

---

[19] Emma Smith DeVoe to Carrie Chapman Catt, DeVoe Papers, Box 4, Folder 54, November 23, 1909; unknown to Mrs. LaReine Baker, ibid., November, 1908, Box 1, folder 2. On paraphernalia, see Shanna Stevenson, *Women's Votes, Women's Voice: The Campaign for Equal Rights in Washington* (Tacoma, WA, 2009), pp. 60–2.

[20] Hutton brought financial support; Elsie Wallace Moore, "The Suffrage Question in the Far West," *The Arena: A Twentieth-Century Review of Opinion*, Vol. 41, No. 232 (July 1909), pp. 417–18. See also "Woman's Suffrage," *LJ*, January 21, 1910, p. 1.

Certainly Hutton's guerilla tactics and union alliances meshed more completely with working-class interests than did DeVoe's white-shirted marchers. As San Francisco's Maude Younger explained in 1910, "Male wage-earners have two methods of improving their condition, by unionizing and by the ballot. Women wage-earners have but the one means – by forming unions."[21] A syndicalist editor in the free-thinking town of Home, Washington, noted the extent to which ballots alone were toothless: "The women are, of course, entitled to it. They are entitled to all they can get. But there are many things we are entitled to which are not worth the effort, and the ballot is one of them. While men control the means by which women live they will control their votes. ... Property makes the laws of the world, have always done so; and the great mass of propertyless voting men have been unable to remedy the evil. So they are forsaking the ballot for more effective means." The taproot of inequality was the "lack of economic opportunity."[22] The Farmers and Laborers' Union and the 15,000-member Grange agreed as early as 1889 to support suffragism, again citing women's economic concerns; in 1909, a print addressed mainly to agriculturalists predicted that equal rights would empower women "all over the country and especially ... on the farms," if only because they could speak their minds as self-interested citizens. Laborites argued that ladies with "poodledogs in their laps" posed a "direct threat to the women of the working class"; a Tacoman forthrightly urged "proper legislation for the woman who works."[23]

Finally, Washington's suffrage organizations needed to find a way to ease tense relations with NAWSA. In 1897, Iowa suffragists allied with NAWSA had declared western states – among them, Washington, Oregon, California, and Nevada – an arena for immediate attention. Reformers were urged to devote all of their attention to states where suffrage campaigns were losing ground.[24] National organizers tried to tailor their message to Washington's rank-and-file women, as with a handbill carrying a union bug: America needed "the working power of ALL its citizens."[25] In mid-1909, Tacoma organizers held a meeting to plan for the arrival in July of twelve cars full of national suffrage leaders.[26] But it was nowhere clear that most suffragists, most of the time, welcomed intrusions by national-movement figures, except as financial supporters. Hutton certainly preferred to go it alone. Well into 1910, both Hutton's organization and WERA engaged in separate lobbying and mass-

---

[21] "Woman Wins Labor Men," *NYT*, November 16, 1910, p. 10.

[22] Fred Moe, "Women and the Ballot," *Agitator*, December 1, 1910. Home, WA, was founded in 1901 as a haven for non-conformists.

[23] "Joining Issues," *TDL*, December 7, 1889. "Equal Rights," *The Ranch* (Seattle), May 15, 1909, p. 11, and "15,000 Men In Line with Suffragists," *ST*, February 27, 1910. Also as a clipping in Emma Smith DeVoe Scrapbooks, Vol. H, WSHS. See also Everett Suffrage Club, "Woman Suffrage," *LJ*, October 28, 1910; "Suffrage," *TT*, April 30, 1910, p. 8.

[24] "Woman Suffrage Policy, Des Moines Iowa, Jan. 30," *NYT*, January 31, 1897.

[25] "About Voting," NAWSA Collection (1910?), WSHS.

[26] "Tacoma to Receive Suffragettes," *TDT*, April 9, 1909.

marketing with printed posters, newspapers, leaflets, and colorful buttons – all "manly" ways to win adherents.[27]

In late June, 1909, tensions between DeVoe and Hutton finally exploded, as did relations between WSEA and NAWSA. Hutton's supporters stormed the NAWSA convention in Seattle intending to "oust" their rivals as the official state delegation. A ruckus ensued, described by anti-suffrage forces as a "riot." When a "squad of bluecoats" arrived, they supposedly found "weeping and ... hissing" and a walk-out by Hutton's contingent. Enraged NAWSA officials seated both delegations, but without a vote.[28] In her 1922 account, Ida Husted Harper alluded as well to a withdrawal of NAWSA financing on the eve of the 1910 victory, though support had always been sparse; indeed, within WERA, one bone of contention had been DeVoe's stipend from NAWSA for work as a suffrage organizer in South Dakota and Illinois – a tie that NAWSA terminated in 1909. In the same year, Seattle insiders challenged DeVoe's leadership, not because of ineffectiveness, but because of arrogance. In Harper's telling of the final campaign, for which DeVoe had provided most of the information, Hutton appeared as a minor helper. In reality, Hutton labored heroically and at great personal expense; in 1909, she also bore the brunt of vicious attacks on her character when WERA officers produced "evidence" of Hutton's alleged work as a prostitute in Idaho. Accusations were never proved, nor were the rifts mended. By contrast, Spokane writers insisted that victory had to do with Hutton's work in the Spokane area.[29]

As earlier, oppositionists insisted that equal suffrage damaged families and unsexed women, exemplified in April, 1910, when a long poem appeared in Olympia: "Woman's rights," wrote "Temple Bar," "What do these words convey?/ ... The right to minister to those that need;/ ... Forgetting self, to labor to the end/ To be a gracious influence for good./ To be the ladies of creation's lords,/As mother, daughters, sisters, or as wives;/To be the best that Earth to them affords.../ Right to be perfect, right to be pure, ... / Those are the rights of the true womanhood." But suffragists now occupied the enemy's turf: Mixed balloting supposedly helped families by "stimulating interest and study,

---

[27] Emma Smith DeVoe to Carrie Chapman Catt, DeVoe Papers, Box 4, Folder 54, November 23, 1909. For paraphernalia, see Stevenson, *Women's Votes*, op cit., pp. 60–2. On these political tangles, see Mead, *How the West Was Won*, Ch. 6.

[28] "Like Men, Good Sized Riot at Suffragette Meeting, Seattle," *LAT*, July 1, 1909, p. I-1. On the convention disaster, see, e.g., "Suffragists Listen to Leaders of Movement," *BBR*, July 4, 1909 ("Certainly no one can ever again accuse Washington women of not being interested in the ballot. Between three and four hundred people were here ... for the state convention"); "Women's Rights There in Politics," *BBR*, July 1, 1909, p. 1 (delegates engaging in "hysterics"); "Good Sized Riot at Suffragette Meeting," *LAT*, AP Night Report, July1, 1909, reprinting early reports. For appeals to NAWSA and responses, see Mary Jane Cogeshall, [draft of article], Schlesinger Women's Studies Mss., Reel 10, No. 0502, Seattle 1909; and "Suffragists of the State are Jolted," *BBR*, July 4, 1909. Hutton correspondence is available on-line at Eastern Washington Historical Society, Spokane. See DeVoe's complaints about Hutton; WERA to Carrie Chapman Catt, DeVoe Papers, Box 4, Folder 54, WSHS.

[29] "Mrs. Hutton," *SP*, November 9, 1910, p. 2.

on the part of women, in public affairs"; it gave "great dynamic force to a fresh
... interest in the state." To the charge that reform smashed the home, activists
pointed to states where spousal "comrades" stood together in support of the
commonweal. Who could charge suffragists with male impersonation when
ladies with teapots offered cakes and an "interesting program of recitations,
readings, and poems, also stories"?[30]

In January, 1909, suffragists learned that a majority of legislators had
approved a constitutional amendment and referendum to restore suffrage, this
time without divisive companion proposals, but also without jury duty or the
right to hold public office. The suffrage bill had been stymied briefly in the
Senate after a "healthy majority" passed it in the House. A number of serious
and jocular changes had been proposed and rejected – among them, a proposal
to "limit the franchise to married women who have become mothers." DeVoe
countered that she would introduce a bill making it illegal for men to vote if they
had no children.[31] After the House victory, Hutton reported that "words of
encouragement from almost everywhere" poured in. There had been "perfect
harmony in our work," she said. "A few years ago this could not have been
possible. When the suffragists first came to Olympia few of the legislators
believed that we were in earnest. We have neither importuned nor bothered
the legislators but we have simply ... laid the question before them. We are not
asking them to give us votes, what we want ... is to give the people an
opportunity to say if we shall have the right of ballot." The verdict of voters
was "a matter wholly outside of the present issue."[32]

In November, 1910, a male electorate approved mixed-sex balloting, though
not any other part of a woman's political personality, by a margin of roughly two
to one.[33] WERA volunteers had checked the form of ballots across the state,

---

[30] "Temple Bar," "Woman's Rights," *WS*, April 1, 1910; "Equal Suffrage Benefits the Family,"
Seattle Republican, November 4, 1910, p. 5. See also Esther Frances Boland, "Woman's Suffrage
for Washington," ibid., September 18, 1908 (reform would "cement" relations with men). On
story-telling, see, e.g., "Women Must Vote," *TDT*, February 15, 1909, and, similarly,
"Anspacher on Suffrage," *NYT*, January 28, 1910. But see also Mrs. Julian Heath, "Would it
Help Wage Earners," *NYT*, March 7, 1909; the National League for the Civic Education of
Woman held that ballots had nothing to do with wages; the question of equal pay had "no place
in a discussion of the merits of the demand for equal suffrage."

[31] "Big majority Favors Vote for Women" and "Champions of Female Suffrage Score Decisive Victory
in First Battle – Vote Stands 70 to 18," *TDT*, January 29, 1909, front page. See also "Senate Bumps
Suffrage Bill," *BH*, February 2, 1909, and "Senators Solid for Women Votes," ibid., February 23,
1909, p. 1 (only nine senators voted against it, passed to governor and then to the electorate). On
House passage, see "Suffrage Measure Passes House," *TDT*, January 29, 1909, p. 1, and for
positive votes in both houses, "Woman Suffrage," *Seattle Republican*, March 5, 1909, p. 4. On
"mothers and children" bill, see "Freak Suffrage Measure May Block Lobby," *BH*, January 23,
1909; DeVoe confirmed the story, "Mrs. DeVoe ...," *TDT*, January 23, 1909, p. 1. See also
"Women with One Child May Be Allowed to Vote," *Seattle Star*, January 23, 1909, p. 1.

[32] "Is Reasonable Bill, Say Women, So-Called Woman Suffrage Measure Doesn't Give Women Vote,
Senate Expected to Pass Law Submitting Amendment to People of State," *TDT*, January 30, 1909.

[33] "Woman Suffrage Carries by Nearly Two to One," *TDT*, November 9, 1910, p. 1; "Looks
Good," *SP*, November 8, 1910, p. 1.

watched polls, and electioneered. Decorum reigned: "There was no militancy about it. . . . Not a man had been dragged by unwilling ear to the polling-places: there was scarcely a woman about the election booths . . . . All was as orderly as a pink tea." On the seaboard, DeVoe earned praise for a becoming modesty. When asked what women would do with ballots, she fulsomely embraced the idea of a "separate but equal" law-making realm: "For the present, we are going to rest and think. We are not going to engage in spectacular political methods, nor in spectacular demands, nor in spectacular legislation."

We realize that we are under the scrutiny not only of this State, but of all other States . . . . We have no intention of attempting to overthrow the laws that have been made by men. We contemplate no sweeping reforms . . . . Most of us have the belief that in many matters pertaining to business affairs and legislation, men are superior. But we believe that we can be of assistance along certain lines, as . . . in the making and enforcement of pure-food laws, in sanitation, in legislation pertaining particularly to women and children, in civic beautification, and, to a certain extent, in the management of the schools.[34]

The new amendment added perhaps 230,000 voters to the state's roster.[35] When Carrie Chapman Catt received a telegram at 7:00 AM announcing the victory, she supposedly said, "I can stand defeat . . . but victory is almost too much for me. This is the first one we have had in fifteen years." Catt later presided over WERA's victory celebration, in part to fete DeVoe, with whom she had worked since the 1890s.[36]

As it turned out, the problem lay not with the election, but with implementation. In December, 1910, would-be voters still did not know whether the amendment was self-executing. "Many regarded it simply as an enabling act," wrote a flummoxed journalist, "as most constitutional amendments are, authorizing the lawmaking power to provide for the concession made; others jump at the conclusion, under the assertion that the constitution is the supreme law of the land, that it over-rides all details . . . , and that simply a proclamation of the Governor . . . wipes out all impediments to the ballot." As a result, women voted in some counties and, in others, waited until pathways had been clarified. In Spokane, the objection of non-registration had been averted by allowing women to register out of season. There, Hutton was the first woman to register; others took the oath in groups. Four clerks were required to complete the task. Mrs. Bertha Fife was the first woman to vote; thereafter, women "fairly besieged the ballot-box." In Olympia, the retiring City Attorney advised women to wait until all possible impediments had been removed. The advice was generally respected. When two women from the

---

34 "Woman's Victory in Washington," *Collier's*, Vol. 46 (January 7, 1911), pp. 25–6.
35 "Woman Suffrage Carries in State . . . ," *Colville Examiner*, November 12, 1910.
36 For Catt's reaction, see "Jubilee for Suffragists," *NYT*, November 10, 1910, p. 4. See also "Women Win in Washington," ibid., p. 1. On Catt's participation, see Jacqueline VanVoris, *Carrie Chapman Catt: A Public Life* (New York, 1987), p. 81.

Second Ward were told that judges were not empowered to accept ballots from unregistered voters, they left quietly.[37]

Elsewhere, women were less obedient. In late November, 1910, a newspaper editor in Edmonds asked Attorney General Bell to forestall civil disobedience. An unnamed suffragist leader had made a "semi-public declaration to the effect that she is going to vote at the city election, whether or no. It is understood that the judges of election have ... discretion in the matter and they may allow her to swear in her vote." She had "managed to get her name on the registration books in spite of the clerk's protestations that he did not believe that she was entitled to register." If this woman or any other succeeded in casting a vote, he asked, would the vote in that ward or city be thrown out? Would there be criminal action? Suffragists apparently intended, given a division of opinion about legality, to force the issue. Bell confusedly hedged his bets: No woman had a "right to register to vote before the registration books closed on the night of November 15th," and therefore no right to vote in the city election. But, "if with her vote a person is elected to office, and without her vote there would be a tie," then the situation would be treated as if it were a tie. On the other hand, "if with her vote there is a tie, then it should not be so counted ... and the party against whom she voted would be elected."[38] Public officials jockeyed for position: The governor issued a proclamation in November, 1910, authorizing women to vote at once without further legislative action. There was "no warrant in the constitution," wrote a disgusted Olympian, "for the governor to act without the legislature. He was not particularly keen on woman suffrage until it happened"; now, he was ready to "seize upon a plank when he finds one afloat." Chicken-coop imagery reappeared: The "rooster on the top rail" should be less precipitous in declaring the job done. Haste would "destroy that harmony that may make the change ... effective."[39]

"WOMEN WILL NOT BE BARRED, BUT WILL NOT BE INVITED": ANCILLARY RIGHTS

As of December, 1910, women claimed a constitutionalized, separate-but-equal home vote. What about obligations? In 1909, Tacoma's Randolph Radebaugh had pointed to ample work that the "good women of the city" might do to fulfill citizens' duties. Wives could not be expected to "shoulder muskets and go out on the firing line, but like the pioneer women of America they may load muskets while husband, father and sons fire them to drive off the enemy of decency." Women could defend "right and decency" on vice-

---

[37] "Still Unsettled," *WS*, December 9, 1910.

[38] Editor, *Tribune Review*, Edmonds, WA, to Attorney General Bell, November 23, 1910, Papers of the Attorney General, General Correspondence, Box 28, 2dw-9, WSA-O. Her name is unknown.

[39] "Equal Suffrage Amendment," *WS*, November 18, 1910; "Women as Voters, ibid., December 2, 1910.

infested urban streets.[40] In 1910, activist Lilla Spurlock Billings of Olympia waxed eloquent about the woman voter's vital contributions to the education and well-being of boys and men; as with their revolutionary forebears, Washington's women taught children "wholesome ideals of citizenship." Billings gently upbraided those who accused women of shirking duties. Juries and militias were men's way to serve. Home-centered, sovereign women had "borne more than their half of the nation's burdens, both in time of peace or war"; now, women justifiably claimed a voice "by franchise, instead of by proxy, because we have proved worthy of that place of equality ... which was a right inherited from Heaven and one which we are yet deprived in exercising because of ... unfounded prejudice." She had predicted accurately that fair-minded men would "march to the polls and free us."[41]

To say the least, the problem of women's access to public offices and to spaces in which partisan work occurred had not been resolved, though office holding continued to be less problematic than service in jury boxes. The occasional woman disputed her sex's readiness for office – as in April, 1892, when an anonymous women announced simultaneously that, were she not "a slave," she would vote for Cleveland, and that women would not be ready for public offices "until the female mind has been warmed in the civic furnace for a generation or two." The office-holding problem also appeared when citizens proposed charitable exceptions to a general ban on female notoriety; in August, 1892, for instance, residents of tiny Ballard petitioned the governor to appoint Mrs. Ida Ralston, a needy widow and mother of five children, to the position of postmaster of Fremont.[42]

Legislators had muddied the waters early on by excluding mixed office holding from their equal-employment statute. In 1896, the Supreme Court offered a ray of hope. Ella Guptill had been lawfully elected to the office of county superintendent of schools in Clallam County, a coastal area west of Seattle. Her opponent, Charles Russell, contended that the Code of 1881 expressly precluded women from holding any office whatever ("All American male citizens ..."); the state constitution indicated only that legislators might confer the right to hold such an office upon any citizen. To be sure, said Justice Anders, the legislature had used the pronoun "he" in the statutes of 1889–90; but the code also said that "he" or "his" should be read to include feminine pronouns. "If the legislature ... did not contemplate that women might be elected to the office," the language was "entirely without force or meaning. It was idle and senseless for them to say, in another section about school officials, 'she shall take an oath of office'" if they did not mean that women might hold the office described. Since justices' job was to give effect to "every word of a

---

[40] Editorial, "Work for Women," *TDT*, February 23, 1909, p. 1.
[41] Lilla Spurlock Billings, Olympia, "Suffrage II," *WS*, February 11, 1910.
[42] "A Woman Votes for Cleveland," *SPT*, April 13, 1892; "She Should Have the Place," *SPT*, August 12, 1892. The result is unknown.

statute, rather than to attribute to the legislature either folly or ignorance of the words they employ," they found no reason to deny Guptill her post.[43] In autumn of 1911, moreover, women joined Pullman election boards without incident: For the first time in the city's history, woman had been eligible to act as inspectors or judges on such boards, except in school elections.[44]

On other occasions, however, women were advised to wait their turn or stand aside. In 1894, for instance, the editor of the *Seattle Times* noted that "ladies" were "entitled to vote at the school election, and they will, it is to be hoped, join with the male voters in united support of a good candidate" for school offices. At the next election, two directors would retire; he hoped to be able to "support a lady to fill one of the vacancies." But it was a "mistake to put forward a lady candidate at this time, and we appeal to the fair voters not to split the vote ..., but throw their entire strength in favor of the man they consider best qualified among those offering."[45] The attorney general, moreover, drew the line at female notary-publics. In March, 1901, attorney-general W. B. Stratton advised Governor Henry McBride that in 1900, his office had decided that women could not hold office in Washington. He saw no reason to revisit the question; the constitution named men. Ironically, in November 1903, Stratton ruled that, when a notary candidate was a "married man, in order to secure a bond," he had to offer "separate property, or the signature of the wife to the bond" would be needed.[46] Five years later, the attorney general again ruled that a woman could not hold appointive office. In acts passed by territorial and state assemblies about the appointment of commissioners of deeds, the masculine pronoun appeared. Because legislators had "deemed it necessary in order that a woman may hold any public office such as an office provided for by the Code of Public Instruction ..., or the office of notary public, to expressly provide that women shall be eligible for such offices," he concluded that they were ineligible.[47]

Even disputes over poll taxes proved at their core to be about citizens' obligations. In 1906, the winning argument in *Thurston County* v. *Tenino Stone Quarries, Inc.*, contributed powerfully to an emerging picture of woman as a fragile being capable of little more than dropping slips of paper into boxes. Thurston County had assessed Tenino Stone Quarries for its male

---

[43] *Charles E. Russell* v. *Ella Guptill*, 13 Wash Rpts 360 (1896), 361–4. By 1909 in Oregon, a woman could be a "deputy governor"; the governor said he had "no hesitancy" leaving his secretary in the governor's seat while he was away; "A Woman for Governor," *WS*, February 19, 1909.

[44] "Election Board," *PH*, October 27, 1911, p. 1. Given modest electoral participation in eastern counties in the 1880s, this may have been true for most women.

[45] "A Word to the Ladies," *ST*, October 13, 1894.

[46] W. S. Stratton to J. Howard Watson, Secretary to Governor, November 13, 1903, and Stratton to Henry McBride, May 11, 1903, Governor's Papers, Attorney General File, Box 2D-1-1, WSA-O.

[47] "Women Not Eligible for Appointment," *TDL*, July 12, 1908. Journalists followed parallel developments elsewhere; e.g., Miss Florence Davidson, "Women's Civil Status," *SPT*, June 14, 1893 (Tennessee woman deprived of office already held; law did not support appointment).

employees' poll taxes, as provided by law. The quarry sued on the ground that only certain citizens were subject to tax – a violation of state and federal constitutions, since privileges and immunities had been extended only to women. They argued, too, that a male-only tax law ran afoul of prohibitions against class legislation.[48]

In the high court's unanimous judgment, legislators' reluctance to impose poll taxes on women, who voted in school elections and were about to benefit from the 1910 amendment, reflected a laudable desire to shelter women. Partial suffrage had been a chivalric reward for public service; immunity to taxation attached to women in part because they lacked male musculature. The "nature and purpose of a poll tax is such that its application should not be universal, but by means of appropriate classifications." Such taxes had been imposed on men alone for all of American history; it was also common practice for citizens subject to poll taxes to "work out" the tax on public highways. The inappropriateness of women with pick-axes was "readily apparent"; the law deferred to women because of the "physical limitations imposed by nature." The most telling point came last: Tax exemptions were essentially reimbursements for the denial of "various privileges held and exercised by males."[49]

In the world of party politics, women encountered resistance where events had been customarily masculine. One example makes the point: Pro-suffrage Governor Ernest Lister, who wrote many letters to Americans elsewhere explaining that anti-suffragists had been converted to the suffrage cause, registered annoyance when, on April 7, 1913, Mrs. Mary Jackman complained about the exclusion of women from a Democratic Party banquet celebrating Thomas Jefferson ("women will not be barred, but will not be invited and are not expected because there will be wine and cigars served, and 'Rocky Stories' told"). Why should an event honoring the author of the Declaration of Independence be masculine, and why not refrain from "Rocky Stories"? The Governor's secretary marked it "File."[50] The potential for emasculation when men were denied access to political spaces or offices was driven home in 1892 when journalists defended a clergyman said to be ineligible for public office. Did a minister "cease to be a man," they asked, "when he settles over a church?" Why should he not run for office? "We will go further and say ... that we do not believe a clergyman ceases to be a man and a citizen, or to enjoy the rights of either, or to share the responsibilities and duties of either, by becoming a clergyman. The pulpit is the most popular, powerful, direct ... of public teachers and can teach pure politics ... as well as pure

---

[48] *Thurston County v. Tenino Stone Quarries, Inc.*, 44 Wash Rpts 351 (1906), 352–4.
[49] Ibid. The court did not say that the reason women had paid no poll taxes at the "foundation" of government was because they could not vote.
[50] See entire Woman Suffrage File, Governors Papers, Box 2H-2-94, WSA-O, esp. Mary G. Jackman to Dr. D. C. Newman, President of the Thomas Jefferson Society of Spokane, with copy to the governor and "Mrs. Lister."

principles in social and business relations." If he decided to make deals, they would reconsider, but, as it was, to be deprived of the right to run for office was an attack on an enfranchised citizen's manhood.[51]

As in the 1880s, however, the jury-service obligation generated seemingly unending contestation and confusion, in Washington and elsewhere. After 1889, the fate of women seated on juries in Wyoming, South Dakota, and Washington forced a nation-wide conversation about the efficacy and legality of mixed-sex or same-sex juries. Equally important, women's ejection from jury boxes (or, in some jurisdictions, the denial of admission in the first place) proved their inadequacy. In 1893, the *Washington Post*'s stable of writers seemed to agree that nearly all western women voted, but "beyond this do little." Mixed-sex juries were said to work best in "sparsely settled" regions; where small populations made it difficult to staff juries, they were then an "unqualified good." Elsewhere, they were not so clearly a boon.[52]

Almost everywhere, women expressed ambivalence or hostility. In October, 1909, after California had adopted universal suffrage, Santa Monica resident Johanna Engleman ("a good natured German woman") registered surprise at a jury summons. She thought it was all right for women to be active in school matters and serve on juries," but she averred that a woman "generally is too tender-hearted to make a good juror," wanted nothing to do with placing "a rope about a man's neck," and was not certain she should go. "The place for woman is at home," she added. "Men should do all the voting, conduct the campaign and fill the offices." She was "not inclined to favor the filling of man's place by woman as the bread-winner" and "deprecate[d] the movement of the suffragettes." Engleman got her wish: Those who "wanted to get rid of her" succeeded after a series of peremptory challenges.[53]

Where, if anywhere, would women jurors be most effective? And what could be done about the sex's competing obligations? In 1895, the *Washington Post* speculated at length about the "fairness" of Kentucky's experiment with all-female juries in trials of women. In 1906, two women were apparently summoned to serve on a jury in a Denver district court; their names appeared on the tax rolls as property owners, which officially qualified them for jury service. Instead, a middle-aged man appeared: "I came to represent my wife," he said. "She couldn't leave the children, so if you need a juror I will take her place." Another woman, Mrs. Fidella Newman, "could not bear the thought of serving on a jury with eleven men." The presiding judge ordered the volunteer to return to his wife, and told the traumatized juror to go home as well. When

[51] "Politics and the Pulpit," *SPT*, August 2, 1892 (vicar seeking the lieutenant governorship).
[52] "How Woman Suffrage Works," *WP*, May 24, 1893, p. 4.
[53] "Woman Summoned for Jury Service in Los Angeles. Santa Monica, Oct. 13," *LAT*, October 14, 1909, Part II, p. 10; "Woman Juror Costly Error," *LAT*, November 30, 1909, Part I, p. 12. See also the long article, "First Woman Juror Drawn Says She Wants to Serve," *LAT*, October 20, 1909, Part I, p. 13.

Colorado women formally petitioned for access to jury boxes in 1911, one judge thought that jury service was "no more than fair"; he believed that women "should be permitted to serve as jurors." But he found it most appropriate in cases involving the interests of women and children, as with service in the juvenile courts. A district judge, though, noted that the statutes "expressly preclude female inhabitants" from service; a new law would be required to empanel them.[54]

For these citizens, as for others, the equality doctrine violated both social practice and visible evidence of sex distinctions. Anti-suffragists, moreover, occasionally contended, with the widely read Sydney Ford, that balloting without commensurate performances of the same obligations undertaken by men was simply unfair. It was male impersonation or nothing; the "separate but equal" idea nowhere appeared. "If the vote means simply dropping a ballot into a box to register an opinion once or twice a year, that is one thing," she wrote, "and if a vote means the bearing of a responsible part in the government, that is quite another." Men had not fought and died to put a "piece of paper, with one's opinion on it, into a square box." Democracy involved a fixed list of rights and duties. Men provided "personal jury service, personal service in case of riot, personal service in case of war." Women inexplicably retreated. "To grasp at the vote without any intention of rendering the necessary service seems … unfair …. The ballot box, the jury box, the cartridge box, the sentry box go together."[55]

In the new state of Washington, talk about juries – the quality of panelists, the selection procedures, a lack of objectivity, or seemingly intractable corruption – continued unabated, sometimes eclipsing talk about the purity of elections.[56] Observers agreed that legislators should repair the *petit* jury's "manifest defects" and provide alternatives to grand juries, the discrediting of which had accelerated during women's brief invasion of courtrooms. Hence, the state convention had formalized indictment by information as an alternative to traditional presentment; judges could decide not to empanel grand juries, as might have been the case earlier at Grays Harbor; and, overall, *petit*-jury size had been reduced. Legislators had re-enacted the 1888 statute that prohibited jurors from asking for or otherwise procuring a seat on a jury for unethical purposes; sheriffs and other officials would be

---

[54] "Women for Jurors," WP, October 19, 1895, p. 6; "Women Drawn for Jury," *LAT*, January 17, 1906, Part I, p. 1; "Women Seek Jury Service. Denver, Aug. 25," ibid., August 26, 1911, Part I, p. 16.

[55] "Facts, Features and Fancies for Women, by Miss Sydney Ford," *LAT*, May 1, 1909. Part I, page 17, emphasis added.

[56] For ongoing talk about Australian ballots and similar reforms, see, e.g., "The Australian System," WS, July 26, 1889, or "Primary Elections," ST, October 12, 1889. On ways to guard against fraudulent voting, see also "Ballot Reform," TDL, May 15, 1889. Ballot reforms (including Australian ballots) were implemented without incident.

charged with a misdemeanor as well if they participated in such plans or complied with an irregular request.[57]

Washingtonians, however, were loath to abolish or radically refashion juries. As early as 1889, a Seattle journalist opined that the right of trial by jury, while not an absolute right, would "hardly be given up by any people having the inheritance of freedom, and the jealous love of equality which distinguish the American citizens."[58] The jury system, said another, had long been tied to the advancement of the human race; society "ought not lightly to contemplate the abolition of such a system, but should rather endeavor to see that it is reformed and made more in keeping with modern social conditions than it is." Still, notwithstanding talk everywhere about women as agents of social purification and uplift, the possibility rarely appeared of women serving on juries with the express goal of perfecting or moralizing them. At the polls, women responded to choices laid out largely by men; courtroom decisions, in contrast, had no such built-in safeguard beyond the capacity of bench and bar to instruct and lead. Hence, Washingtonians sought ways to reshape and redirect masculine panels. Perhaps jury duty should be mandatory for all voters with no occupational exemptions so that it fell equally upon the "capitalist and the day laborer"; business and professional men would have to make good. As early as 1891, local judges registered annoyance at endemic shirking of jury duty; too often, the empaneling of "professional jurors" led to "soft" verdicts in capital cases. "Today's jury trial is a farce when it is not made a tragedy," Charles Lugrin concluded, "for the 'good men, and true' seek by every possible means to avoid jury duty, and the lawyers resort to every ... quibble to exclude such from the jury box. The admission of a man that ... he does not possess intelligence enough to form an opinion – ... that he is an ignorant imbecile, is the surest open-sesame to the jury box." He proposed schooling and exams for prospective jurors.[59]

To eliminate hangers-on, legislators in 1895 expanded the pool in each county to 500 and reduced the number of men actually summoned to 18 and 36. The bone of contention seemed to be whether one must be a "freeholder, a householder or a taxpayer" to qualify. Even as re-enfranchisement neared, opinion makers stonewalled the possibility of empaneling allegedly virtuous

[57] Editorial, "The State Constitution, *SPI*, June 5, 1889; An Act Making It a Misdemeanor for Any Person to Ask or Request for Himself or Another to be Placed Upon Any Jury ..., Laws of Washington, Ch. LXIV, 1888, p. 114.

[58] "Trial by Jury," *TDT*, January 2, 1909.

[59] "The Jury System," *ST*, August 12, 1895; "The Ellensburg Lynching," ibid., August 14, 1895. See also "The Jury Law Dead," ibid., May 28, 1895, front page. "Better Juries Needed," ibid., July 23, 1895, and "There are Many Defects [in the jury system]," ibid., February 6, 1895; "The New Jury Law," ibid., April 26, 1895; The Jury System," ibid., May 14, 1895. See also "Excuses of Jurors," ibid., December 8, 1891, and Charles H. Lugrin, "Defects of the Jury System," ibid., April 29, 1891. On schools, see G. R. Reynolds, "A School of Judiciary," ibid., April 29, 1891.

mothers and wives; lawmakers settled again on the "voter and householder" standard for grand-jury service, a high bar that only propertied widows or single women could hope to meet, and then only as voters. Weakened community-property practices, combined with *Harland* and *Bloomer*, carried the bar even higher. Other changes dramatically decreased the chances of a summons for male householders; finding 500 men with the qualification of householder (the "head of a family") was no mean trick.[60] That difficulty may well have animated Justice Gordon's finding in the 1896 case of *Oliver Redford v. Spokane Street Railway Company;* when pushed to say why it was constitutional to require grand jurors to be householders and at the same time to fill empty slots with truants in the lobby, the majority said lamely that, under the state constitution, privileges available to one citizen had to be available to all.[61]

Before all else, qualified jurors were supposed to embody objectivity, an ideal the daughters of Eve could never realize. The supposed fact of sex-based disability often arose indirectly. In 1895, Judge Ballinger of Jefferson County had made "strong remarks about the duties of jurors"; a Seattle editor called the speech timely, perhaps because agitation for the ultimately unsuccessful 1898 suffrage referendum was well afoot. Jurors, he had said, sometimes had been "inclined to constitute themselves 'courts of sentiment.'" The judge had reminded jurors that they were not responsible for moral judgments, but rather for weighing evidence and determining what it proved. He belabored the point: Considerations of mercy should never "find any other expression than in a formal recommendation." A juror violated his oath if he permitted sympathy to sway him from duty; the reasonable man determined facts in the "every day fashion in which we weigh the statements of those with whom we come in contact."[62] To ensure competence, Judge Thomas Humes – the ex-legislator responsible in 1888 for assaults on community-property law – had quashed the venire in an 1895 murder case: Trials conducted according to rules of practice set out in the territorial code were nullities. In response to questions about proper jury-selection rules, he allowed that lawmakers had moved "in the right direction" with the elimination of women; it remained for them to purge other, kindred pollutants such as jurors with "no visible means of support."[63]

These developments did not bode well for women, if only because they stood on a substantially smaller and more contingent zone of sovereign authority; equally important, they apparently had withdrawn consent to laws that seemed to impose unequal burdens in the name of equality. Nevertheless, many supporters of equal suffrage still conceived of political freedom as a bundle of

---

[60] "New Jury System. Blow at Professional Jurors," *ST*, May 29, 1895.
[61] *Oliver Redford v. Spokane Street Railway Company*, 15 Wash Rpts 419 (1896), 421.
[62] "The Duty of Jurors," *ST*, June 19, 1895.
[63] "The Jury Muddle," *ST*, May 29, 1895.

rights and obligations undifferentiated by sex, or believed that the elimination of women from juries had been irrational and counterproductive. Said one Pullman writer, women to be consistent must "run for office, filling the seats of our city council and other offices," including the office of juror.[64] As early as 1889, a few suffragists in Washington had tried to engage opponents in a debate about the possibility that women might improve juries. One observer reminded opponents of mixed juries that men were excused from juries for the flimsiest of reasons. Why not excuse women when they could not handle double burdens instead of tossing all of them in dust bins? But newspaper subscribers did not rise to the challenge.[65] In 1896, two years before the referendum, Mrs. Frank Immler put jury duty and other ancillary privileges center stage: Originally, suffragists had been told that women were incapable of voting; then they said that voting had to be linked to military service; now, we hear "the jury argument. A mother who has the care of an infant cannot serve on a jury, therefore women should not vote, though men need not be excluded from that privilege because physicians, teachers, policemen, firemen, and others are exempt from serving as jurors. They will tell us occasionally that women cannot serve on juries in the trial of promiscuous cases .... If men can serve, why not women? Is not an unclean story just as disgusting to a refined man as to a refined woman? ... An ideal jury is not composed of filthy-minded or pitiless men."[66]

But, for the most part, suffrage leaders in Washington maintained a deafening silence. Only May Arkwright Hutton contended for women's value and fitness as jurors, adding only partly in jest that "women who stand behind counters, or in factories, at the cook stove, wash tub, ironing table, dish sink, and baby crib, would be mighty glad to sit on almost anything for a rest."[67] Elsewhere, supporters of mixed-sex service were scattered at best. Based on reportage twice removed, for instance, the *Washington Post* asserted that, in South Dakota, contestations between the sexes disrupted courtrooms: If women were to "do the job at all, the juries would have to be composed "entirely of women. Such juries might never agree," but it would be "better to get along without agreement than to demoralize communities."[68] In 1895, an *American Magazine of Civics* reprint identified a main engine of resistance: "When the state summons a man to the courts it says to him, 'Drop your business and serve me; your highest duty is your civic duty.' To the woman – after having excluded

---

[64] Optimus, "A Woman's View," *PH*, June 8, 1889.

[65] "Statistics and Woman Suffrage," *TDL*, August 26, 1889 ("As for jury service, the number of men now excused from it ... is so great that it would hardly need to be greater in the case of women").

[66] Mrs. Frank O. Immler, "Woman's Natural Debarments from Political Service," A Reply [to December, 1895, article by Florence Percy Matheson], *American Magazine of Civics* (March, 1896), API online, p. 271.

[67] May Arkwright Hutton, quoted in Mead, *How the Vote Was Won*, p. 108.

[68] "Disagreements Are Frequent, Results in South Dakota of Having Women on Juries, From the Chicago Chronicle," in *WP*, May 17, 1896, p. 24.

the long list of 'excused' – it would be obliged to say: 'Leave your domestic affairs and attend to me; the state has the right to summon you peremptorily from your home.' This right, by fixing arbitrarily, for uncertain periods of time, the woman's absence from home, would establish the principle that personal duties may ... become secondary in a woman's life, and ... would clog many a wheel in domestic machinery." Hence, jury duty metamorphosed from a "practical into a social and ethical question."[69]

On the eve of re-enfranchisement, Washingtonians again amended jury legislation; Tacomans and others complained, not about women's exclusion, but about legislators' indifference to professional jurymen – the "loafers who infest almost every court house of a class easily 'reached' by crooked litigants." As of July 1, 1909, only qualified men would be summoned. Such a man had to be an elector and taxpayer of the state, a resident of the county for more than one year before service, more than twenty-one years of age, in "full possession of his faculties," and literate in English. Classes still exempt from service included officers of the state and nation, lawyers, teachers, doctors, firemen and policemen, and all persons older than sixty. Their names "if known" would be omitted from the jury list. Labor leaders immediately complained that the new law excluded laborers: Said the *Labor Journal*, most workers were not tax payers; a "corporate hand" kept a "majority of electors from jury duty."[70]

Even after Washingtonians had restored woman suffrage in 1910, it was unclear whether jury duty followed automatically. Suffragists within and beyond the legislature, after all, had ceded mixed jury service in 1888 to salvage the ballot. In 1911, Governor Marion E. Hay said that he wholeheartedly supported the suffrage amendment, the eight-hour law for women and municipal workers, and the excusing of women from jury duty.[71] As state legislators debated the state's position, women trickled back into courtrooms and a few journalists affirmed relationships between rights and obligations. "With woman suffrage," said a Seattle publisher, "comes all of the duties incumbent on those enjoying the pleasure even to jury duty and whether women do or do not like it they must take their medicine. To sit on a jury when called upon to do so is a duty every person enjoying the rights of suffrage should be ready and willing to perform. Of the twenty-three women drawn on the jury in Seattle, not one of them should seek to dodge the duty."[72]

In late December, 1911, as legislators dawdled, writers in mountainous Leavenworth sensed a "slight probability of women serving upon juries in the

---

[69] "In Woman's Field. Woman and Jury Service," *American Magazine of Civics*, December 1895, p. 666, repr. New York Commercial Advertiser.

[70] "New Jury Law," *TDT*, April 28, 1909; "Severe Blow for Labor," *LJ*, May 20, 1910, p. 1. From time to time, journalists suggested that unions feminized men; see, e.g., "Will Not Let Gompers Do Their Voting," *TDL*, July 19, 1908 (discussion of whether weak-minded miners would be led by unions).

[71] "Governor Hays Tells of State Affairs," *PH*, July 7, 1911.

[72] "With woman suffrage ...," *Seattle Republican*, August 18, 1911, p. 5.

superior court of Chelan county for some time," or so "county court officials and attorneys" believed. "Much discussion has been indulged in as to whether women will be eligible to serve as jurors in the superior courts." Prevailing law required that jurors "must be not only of age and taxpayers," but also have "voted at least once before their names can be drawn as jurors." Would legislators forestall mandatory service? What about women who wanted to serve? The legislature soon would be forced to "define the status of women as regards jury service."

> Some of the leading lawyers favor the exemption of women from jury service. Others believe jury service by women should be optional, as in the case of some men, such as ministers. Some women have no objections to the service, and it is argued they should be allowed to do so when they become eligible. At present there is no provision in the laws of this state denying women the right to serve as jurors if they are voters and taxpayers.[73]

Reporters tracked the career of a new jury statute: Lawmakers would either reinstitute the late territorial statute eliminating jury duty for women or, as a Yakima correspondent speculated, choose "the wisest course" and adopt the proposed plan of the lower house, making jury duty optional. Why? Jury boxes would not be congenial; violations of social practices scandalized good women. "Court houses are not equipped for mixed juries ... and service on a jury will be extremely traumatic to perhaps a large majority of the feminine sex." Worse, the most virtuous women would be penalized: A women who took "delight in that sort of thing, will soon become known to the legal profession and she will have no opportunity to qualify. The duty will therefore fall almost altogether on those women to whom such a burden will be obnoxious in the extreme." In early February, a Pierce County legislative delegation apparently suggested that women might serve as jurors "to try all women" and men to try men; otherwise, the sexes might not deal equitably with one another or with testimony.[74]

Everyone contributed to ambivalence and paternalism. In 1895, in a swipe at home-bodies, anti-suffragists pointed to "the cheapening of patriotism" whenever classes voted without the ability to leave home or "place their lives at the disposal of their country."[75] WERA minimized women's responsibilities beyond periodic trips to the polls. On the eve of the 1910 elections, Seattle's pro-suffrage *Votes for Women* laid out duties for those who feared unequal or humiliating burdens. "What, then, are the political duties?" the editor asked. "What are the higher duties? How far does the one kind obstruct or assist the other? The political duties are informing one's self on ... politics at issue, on candidates for office, and then going to the polls and depositing a ballot.

---

[73] "Jury Duty for Women," *LE*, December 23, 1910, front page.

[74] "Jury Duty Optional," *Yakima Herald*, February 1, 1911, p. 4; "Want Women to Try Women," *TT*, February 2, 1911.

[75] "The Cheapening of Patriotism," *ST*, May 23, 1895. This issue contained a number of essays about the obligations of citizenship to make the general point.

The so-called higher duties are the bearing and rearing of children. .... How much time must a woman spend on her political duties? ... If she does her own housework, she can take ten minutes on her way to market for voting .... She can talk with her family and friends. This she does now; she will then do it more intelligently." Women's duties, more or less synonymous with voting on behalf of home and property, excluded obligations incumbent on men.[76]

"TO BRAVE THE HOSTILITY OF THE PUBLIC"

In the end, legislators permitted women after a summon had issued to opt out of jury service without providing an excuse – that is, "by reason of sex," without reference to parenting, salaried occupation, "sickness," or any other nameable impediment.[77] In 1911, Chicago's Catherine Waugh McCulloch wrote to Seattle lawyer Charles Shepard seeking clarification of women's status. He replied accurately that women were qualified to vote and therefore were liable to jury duty; "Chapter 57 of the Session Laws of 1911 was passed to provide for that new state of things." Women could be empaneled "under the same circumstances and within the same classes as men," except that they might claim exemption "by giving notice to the Sheriff before the date for appearance, when summoned."[78] East of the Cascades, women usually were excused in advance of actual venires, which was not precisely what legislators had intended. In western Washington, the situation was more complex. In Bellingham, Seattle, and Tacoma, women sat with some frequency – in the case of women's-rights activists, perhaps to defy expectations. As early as 1909, clerks compiled lists of potential jurors from election lists and then identified "tax-payers" with an X. King County women re-appeared on county-payment rolls in autumn, 1911. On September 6 and 7, for instance, Mary Ewing, Margaret Brass, and Jennie Gordon received payment for *petit*-jury service in King County Superior Court; a month later, five other women appeared on a list of three dozen. The first mixed-sex jury to sit in the State of Washington may well have been empaneled in Whatcom County's Superior Court in September, 1911; six women served with six men. Among them was Laura Higgerson, whose husband had returned the summons for her, claiming exemption; when she found out, she told the judge that she had "every intention of serving." In Tacoma's Pierce County, as of December 5, 1910, juries were masculine; on January 3, 1910, the clerk indicated cryptically, "Woman; did not appear." In September, 1911, however, the doors opened. Clerks listed 120

---

76 Editor, "Woman's Political and "Higher' Duties," *Votes for Women*, Vol. 1, No. 8 (1910), p. 5, WSHS digital publications.

77 Chapter 57, section 2, Acts of the Legislature of Washington, 1911. Jury provisions had been part of the procedural code; by 1911, they were separate enactments.

78 Charles Shepard to Mrs. Catherine Waugh McCulloch, June 10, 1911, Schlesinger Women's Studies Manuscripts, Series I-E, Reel 20, No. 0572. In practice, most clerks of court assumed exemption until women notified them to the contrary.

potential petit jurors, 37 of them female. But twenty-four women either claimed or were automatically granted "exemption on account of sex"; eleven actually served. A jury list dated October 2, 1911, includes seventy-one names, ten of which were obviously female, but names of excused women are missing. A month later, on a list of sixty-five, another ten were women, and from another list of thirty, eight women appeared; on both lists, every woman's name was marked "ex sex." Thereafter, exclusion was usual. On December 4, 1911, on a list of forty-six, seven women claimed "exemption on a/c sex"; again, it is unclear whether they appeared in person to claim exemption or whether relief was *pro forma* without action to the contrary. Into 1912, the number of women formally called increased to about half of the total, but one or two at most actually served.[79]

In a 1913 magazine article, Seattle's G. M. Farley got the numbers slightly wrong, but his account of the atmosphere in the Superior Court of King County makes clear that, sometimes, women still had to walk through a wall of hostility. Nor had the pay increased. In the twenty months of "practical working of the women's suffrage amendment, in Seattle, Washington, as it applies to jury duty, the number of women jurors on duty ... has arisen from one, the first month, to forty during the month of April, 1913." He noted, too, that "prejudice against the innovation has been dissipated, and the woman juror is now accepted as a distinct success." Farley's observations eerily resemble earlier reports. In September, 1911, twelve women were summoned for jury duty "under the provisions of the suffrage amendment."

Of the twelve who came in fear and trembling, braving a local hostile public sentiment, eleven took advantage of the alternative sex exemption, and were excused .... One alone, an aged woman, remained to brave the hostility of the public, courts and attorneys alike, and drew her $3 per diem without participating in a single case. This aged woman submitted to a silent boycott that was both embarrassing and irritating, but she clung to her public duty, and her tenacity 'broke the ice' and made the way easier for three women to accept the same duty during the following month .... Gradually, the woman juror worked into the harness, brought down tradition, shattered precedent, and brought in verdicts that were ... as just and equitable as any the all-male juries had rendered.[80]

Other witnesses were decidedly less upbeat. On September 10, 1911, Mrs. Jennie Gordon of Seattle, an activist and allegedly "the first woman juror to qualify in Seattle since the adoption of the suffrage amendment," was peremptorily rejected by counsel in a civil proceeding; in the reporter's

---

[79] King County Judicial Records, County Clerk, Record of Jury and Witness Certificates, 1911–14, and Jury Roll, 1909–11, WSA-Belle. See also Pierce County Judicial Records, County Clerk, Jury Lists, 1909–10; Jury Time Books, 1902–14. Poll registers are also available for Seattle, 2nd Ward, 1884–1932; clerks placed checks beside the names of women eligible for jury duty. After 1888, the clerk lined out women's names. The use of abbreviations uniformly applied (as with "ex sex") beside names in the same ink and hand suggests that clerks assumed exclusion until told otherwise; WSA-Belle.

[80] G. M. Farley, Seattle, "Women on Washington Juries," *The Independent Weekly* [New York], Vol. 75, No. 3370 (July 3, 1913), pp. 50–1.

FIGURE 7.3. Mixed-Sex Petit Jury, Whatcom County Superior Court, September, 1911. Photographer: J. W. Sandison. This was the first mixed-sex jury (six men, six women) empaneled in Belleville and probably in the state after women's re-enfranchisement in 1910. Laura Higgerson (second from the right, front row) contested her husband's decision to return her summons on the ground of sex; her name was restored and she served. From the collections of the Whatcom County Historical Museum, Belleville, WA, No. X3219.002413. Used by permission.

estimation, she was rejected "because of her sex ... no other reason was given." Payment records suggest that she had offered to serve again after the initial September 6–7 payment. The non-scandalous case at hand involved the city's attempt to exercise eminent domain. Two other women called to service two weeks earlier in the Superior Court, perhaps Mary Ewing and Margaret Brass, had appeared but had claimed the sex exemption. Gordon sought and was "qualified for the job, but the corporation counsel, after she had been passed ... , peremptorily challenged her and she was forced to vacate her place in the jury box. She was highly indignant." As in 1885–87, courtroom denizens exhibited heightened awareness of women's bodies, sometimes characterizing them as an expensive nuisance. When confronted with the problem of "what to do with these women overnight," a Seattle judge ordered a "small hall rented, installed cots, had a heavy curtain hung across the center of the room, and had the men jurors tucked away in one end of the room, and the women jurors at the other," guarded by bailiffs, one of each sex.[81] In *John G. Lybarger v. Washington*, Justice Dunbar ended lawyerly machinations on the point: An appeal did not lie for judges' failure to separate jurors by sex during deliberations; lawyers were responsible for making proper arrangements.[82]

Throughout these years, moreover, women's presence in jury boxes continued to be newsworthy, whether because of novelty or surpassing strangeness, both in and beyond Washington. Readers in Washington, DC, learned of Colorado's decision in 1893 to seat a woman on a jury for the first time, and, several years later, of a Chicago criminal-court empanelment of two women, described erroneously as the "first instance of the kind in the history of this country." In mid-December, 1910, reporters in Colfax, Washington, noticed that six "prominent Olympia women" had been seated on a jury to try a minor justice-court case. This, they thought, was the first female jury drawn in the state of Washington. Well past 1910, sex-conscious clerks still segregated women's names at the start or end of venire listings with status markers (Mrs., Miss, or, for widows and young or familiar women, a given name, "Mary"), listing men in the usual way with two initials and surname.[83] In December, 1911, journalists in Leavenworth reported the first "big trial" – a Seattle conspiracy case – in which two women had qualified for *petit*-jury service. At Yakima, it was newsworthy a year later that one woman and several men sat on a coroner's jury to view the body of a murder victim. Even women's absence was notable: In August, 1911, puzzled Tacomans reported no female jurors in Lewis County for the entire September term, as did residents of Chehalis County, who had expected that women would serve on juries in every county. Trials became notorious when numbers of women appeared as jurors

---

[81] "Woman Barred from Jury," *LAT*, September 7, 1911, Part I, p. 3. Ewing and Brass would have been paid for their appearance, even if they left at once; cf. Farley's account. Into the 1920s, opponents of mixed-sex jury service insisted that women were in jeopardy. See Burnita Shelton Matthews' remarks: "Another problem ... is the keeping of the jurors together while a long trial is in progress and during the jury's deliberations. However, it has been found practicable to place a woman bailiff over the women jurors, a man bailiff in charge of the men, and to provide separate rooms for sleeping quarters, or else arrange partitions between the two sexes in the same room .... [F]or years men and women on trains have occupied the same Pullman car with only curtains to separate the sleeping quarters of one person from those of another, and yet there has been no cry of impropriety, or that ... women were contaminated." See *Women Lawyer's Journal*, Vol. 15, No. 2 (January 1927).

[82] *John G. Lybarger v. Washington*, 2 Wash Rpts 552 (1891).

[83] "Colorado Woman Accepted as a Juror," *WP*, April 23, 1896, p. 1; "Women Accepted as Jurors," ibid., August 4, 1896, p. 3; untitled, *Colfax Gazette*, December 16, 1910, p. 1. See also "First Mixed Jury," *SJI*, September 8, 1911 ("first mixed jury in Bellingham") and illustration above. King County clerks were the first to begin merge notation styles on registration as well as jury lists, beginning in about 1885. Eastern counties did not merge systems before 1910.

with female lawyers – as in October, 1912, when Leona Browne argued a "womanly" case before a jury with seven women.[84]

Still, to be novel or brave was not to be credible. No sooner had the law changed than critics began to assail women's character and credibility; however motivated, absences indicated unfitness, laziness, or disinterest. In January, 1911, women in Anacortes were said to be "begging off from jury service" and proving to be both pliable and ineffective on the liquor question. Lower-court judges began to resist jury-pool expansion. Superior Judge Ben Sheek in remote Hoquiam said in December, 1910, "I hope that the legislature of the state of Washington will pass a law exempting women from jury duty in this state . . . . I hardly believe that women are anxious to serve on juries and this will keep them away from their homes . . . . The jury work can be well cared for by the men of the state." A Walla Walla judge with limited skill in arithmetic flatly refused to seat female jurors. "I do not believe that a woman is strong enough to stand the strain of jury service, where there is possibility of days and nights of disagreement," he declared. "I do not think attorneys would care to risk women jurors. There are two classes of men who want to see women on juries. One class believes that when granted suffrage[,] women obligated themselves to take up jury work and like duties; another class, against equal suffrage, want to see it out of spite" – for some, in other words, it was a punishment – "and a third class out of curiosity." At least one Tacoma journalist regretted interference: "With 4,000 women eligible for jury duty, Seattle ought to get a few crumbs of substantial justice – if judges don't interfere."[85]

To some extent and only in some counties, commissioners' discretion in selecting juror's names helps explain the absence of women in pools: In

---

[84] "Two Women on Blethen Jury," *LE*, December 8, 1911; "Self Defense the Verdict," *Yakima Herald*, January 18, 1911, p. 7; "State News," *TDT*, August 17, 1911; untitled editorial, ibid., August 23, 1911, p. 3; "Womanly Case," ibid., October 22, 1912. On the related suggestion that women might gang up on men in court ("seven women" and a "woman lawyer" secured a huge award from a man for breach of promise to marry), see "With a woman lawyer . . . ," ibid., October 22, 1912, p. 8. For a few examples of notice, see "Before a courtroom," ibid., September 12, 1912, p. 1; "Whitman Jury," *PH*, September 15, 1911, noting one married woman from Pullman on a jury list; "Women Hear City Suit," *TDT*, September 8, 1911, p. 3 ("jury of women" in Superior Court to hear a condemnation suit); "Women May Try Nude Bathers," ibid., August 11, 1911, p. 3; "To Have Women on This Jury," ibid., January 20, 1911, p. 3 (six women in an assault case); "Panel Drawn for the January Term Will Have the Names of Several Women On It," *Yakima Herald*, November 15, 1911, p. 1; "Northwest News," *SJI*, August 18, 1911 (eight Whatcom County women drawn for jury duty in September); "A Short Term," ibid., May 10, 1912 (justice court trial, *State v. William Chappell*, where a third of the jurors were women who might sit again); notice of eight women drawn for service in Ellensburg, untitled, *TDT*, September 11, 1912, p. 8; "Many Women Jurors," ibid., May 13, 1912 ("Twenty-nine female jurors have been summoned for jury work next month, breaking the previous record of 22").

[85] "Ice Cream Buys Women's Votes . . . ," *LAT*, January 19, 1911, Part I, p. 1; "Exempt Women From Jury Duty, Says Judge," *Seattle Star*, December 30, 1910; "No Women Jurors for This Judge: Says They are Not Strong Enough," *TT*, February 2, 1911; "A Dream of Fair Women," ibid., August 16, 1911.

1902, for example, well before re-enfranchisement, attorneys in the case of *State v. A. P. Vance* revealed that commissioners in Pierce County routinely chose as few as 960 men out of 5,000 qualified electors; discretion permitted them to select "none but persons whom they believe to be of good repute for intelligence and honesty," but surely "none that they had been requested to select."[86] But naming practices probably mattered as much or more than malicious tampering with lists. Clerks in San Juan County, for instance, claimed to be unable to compile mixed-sex jury lists because they could not find the proper names of the women eligible for jury duty; too many women appeared in public records as, for instance, "Mrs. Jones."[87] In the case of *State v. Rholeder*, decided just after legislative decisions against mandatory, mixed-sex jury service, Justice George Morris admitted, in the face of complaints about the veracity of poll books, that even a close inspection of tax rolls and poll books would not determine the whole number of qualified jurors resident in any county. Community property was now assessed "in the name of the husband. The wife might not care to exercise her right of suffrage, so that her name would appear neither on the tax rolls nor poll books. Such absence would not of itself determine her qualifications as a juror: Many tax payers and electors ... are by statute exempt from jury service, yet their names might appear on the ... books." A woman could volunteer her name if she appeared nowhere; the statute was "one of exemption and not of qualification."[88]

Predictably, in Washington's more conservative eastern counties, women served much less often than in coastal areas. In Columbia and Kittitas Counties, women never sat on juries through 1912.[89] In Spokane County from 1889 onward, women appeared regularly as witnesses but not as jurors. For most of 1911, *petit* jurors were entirely male. In August, the superior court for Spokane County summoned 100 *petit* jurors, of whom twenty-two

---

[86] *State of Washington v. A. P. Vance*, 29 Wash Rpts 435 (1902), 436–37. Prosecutors disagreed.

[87] "Women's Rights as Jurors," *SJI*, August 18, 1911. The San Juan County clerk thought that the jury law of 1911 required him to include women on venires; women then might "claim exemption by signing a written or printed notice thereof and returning same to the sheriff before the date for appearance, and if exception is claimed by reason of sex no fee shall be allowed for her appearance."

[88] *State v. Rholeder*, 82 Wash Rpts 618 (1914), 620. The particulars of the complaint are not given in the case reports or file.

[89] Kittitas County Government, Superior Court Clerk, State District Court, Jury Rolls, 1889, 1899–1912, WSA-E; Columbia County, Jury Record, 1909–11, Columbia County Superior Court, WSA-E. These poorly kept records are very nearly intractable. Women might have been lost in regime shifts. In 1914, Governor Ernest Lister explained that it would be impossible to say how many women had registered to vote because only initials were used (E. F. Smith) in registration logs. This was a change of methods: The "constitutional amendment giving women in this State the ballot, places them on a par with male voters," necessitating uniform notation. Governor Ernest Lister to Mr. Alexander Baillie, Tacoma, January 31, 1914, Governor's Papers, Woman Suffrage File, 2H-2-94, WSA-O. In eastern jury records before 1912, as in some western counties, juror names typically carried two initials for men and "Miss" or "Mrs." for women, as in territorial records.

were women; seven actually were called to service (Mrs. James A. Goodwin, Mrs. C. E. Longee, Mrs. L. Newton, Mrs. E. Richards, Mrs. Eliza Riggs, Mrs. Eliz[abeth] Rudd, and Henrietta West). The word "exemption" accompanied all other female names. As months passed, such notations obviously were being supplied at one sitting. In September, another thirty-nine names appeared, all male. In October, the clerk entered 132 names, 33 of them female, and a separate list of 21 male names. Three women were said to be "missing"; twenty-four claimed exemption. Language reminiscent of coverture soon became formulaic: On October 9, five women claimed exemption "on account of being a woman," two of them listed as "Mrs." Two days later, nine women claimed exemption for the same reason.[90]

Women tried to ameliorate hostile or unsavory conditions in courthouses. In October, 1911, as in the 1880s, the Women Voters' Council of Seattle asked the county commissioners to prohibit smoking in mixed-sex jury rooms; they asked as well for better facilities, particularly but not only when "all night sessions were required." Also as earlier, a strong whiff of sexual threat or personal embarrassment permeated even second-hand stories about female jurors, particularly when forced to stay overnight. Wrote a rather cynical editor, "Washington women have the ballot. And they seem to like it. Now they are being put on juries. How do they like that? And how will the men like it? . . . One woman says she would not ask the legislature to exempt women from jury duty; it is women's responsibility as voters. She said, 'Possibly there might be situation that would be embarrassing to some, but personally I should not be afraid to be locked up in a jury room with men jurors if I were the only woman. I feel that men are honorable.'" Whereas women offered "all shades of opinion" about jury service, husbands were "stumped as regards their wives remaining out all night in the jury room." Meanwhile, in Bellingham, staff laid elaborate plans to accommodate and "lock up" mixed-sex juries in anterooms and other spaces.[91]

Sometimes, the news was good. A formerly anti-suffrage print in Tacoma, apparently in a contest with journalists in Colfax and Seattle, insisted in December, 1910, that a trial "just concluded at Olympia" was the "first in this country where a female juror drawn from a venire of jurists has rendered a verdict." But, here, reportage coincidentally revealed something of the jury's class bias. "Judge Gilles . . . says that this jury of women was superior in every way to any other that ever sat in his court. Now, we think this matter of very high importance." The case involved a milkman's suit against a contractor for damages. Six women had been called to the jury; one was excused "on account

[90] Records of Spokane County, Witnesses Time Books, Spokane County, 1889–1903, WSA-Ch; Spokane County, Jury Journal, Superior Court, Spokane County, 1909–12, WSA-Ch. Jury records for these counties are sparse; it is possible, though not likely, given anti-suffrage and anti-jury sentiment in these locations and newspaper jury lists, that non-surviving records might have shown more women on juries (grand jury records are nowhere to be found, for example).

[91] "Women Jurors Want Smoking Stopped," *TT*, October 24, 1911, p. 3; "If wives are held nights in jury room," ibid., January 12, 1911, p. 1; "State News Items," *LE*, September 15, 1911, p. 6.

of her sickness. . . . Well, you interject, the others swore they were too busy or made false excuses for not doing their duty, just like male perjurors? No sir! The jury finally sworn in consisted of Mrs. McReed, governor's stenographer; Miss Sapp, supreme court stenographer; Mrs. McDowell, physicians' wife; Mrs. [blank], wife of a prominent democratic politician; and Rev. Genevese Ratke, one of the few ordained female ministers of the state." Jurors heard evidence, "did their duty conscientiously, and left without further ado." In Colfax, with two men on each side of the question, a debate ensued in early 1911 at "the Literary" as to whether women ought to serve on juries, and the affirmative won. Also in 1911, women in Tacoma foiled lawyers, who had tried to empanel as many as possible to elicit sympathy; instead, they were said to be "fairminded and balanced" in judgment. And, while others disagreed, one woman in Tacoma who was forced to leave five children at home thought that duty lay with answering a jury summons. In October, 1911, prospective male jurors allegedly came up with flimsy excuses ("I can't read very well"), while only two women out of ten asked to be excused ("I'd like to serve, but my baby is sick").[92]

In August, 1912, as federal courts began to summon women, Mrs. Kat Connors of Tacoma, a homemaker, spoke with a reporter about her devotion to ballots and ambivalence about juries. She was a "big, healthy, kindly-faced woman, with ideas of her own. Yet she is distinguished from the rest in that she is the first woman to be drawn on a federal court jury . . . during the fall term of the United States district court of Western Washington." She opposed capital punishment and life imprisonment. She would serve "if everything seems all right," but preferred that another woman serve; she was not "sufficiently familiar with court house business to go through without a blunder. In spite of all that, she will serve, perhaps. There is just a bit of a doubt in Mrs. Connor's mind. 'I have reason enough to give the judge,' she said, 'if I want to be excused. I have baby to care for and my husband's meals to get.' 'But if they should tell you they would provide a nursery – then what?' she was asked. 'Oh that would be all right and I would have to serve, I suppose,' she replied. 'Why wouldn't a nursery be a good idea for all courts, now that women vote and sit on juries?' 'Do you vote?' 'You bet I'm a voter,' she said emphatically . . . . 'Yes, sir, I think every woman should vote.'"[93]

Well beyond 1912, women who asked to serve as jurors periodically encountered the kind of scrutiny reserved for nuisances or fools. In 1918, to give an example, a man convicted of robbery in Spokane County fruitlessly

[92] "What the Women Showed," *TT*, December 19, 1910, p. 4; "Correspondents," *Colfax Gazette*, February 17, 1911, p. 3; editorial, *Yakima Herald*, September 20, 1911, p. 4; "Left Babies to Send Five Men to Pen,' . . . Says Woman Juror," *TT*, October 4, 1911. See also "Only Two Women Out Of Ten Dodge Jury Duty," ibid., October 2, 1911.

[93] "First Woman Federal Jurors Says She Will Serve If?" *TT*, August 28, 1912, p. 1. The question mark is in the original title. See also "Voters or Not, No Jurywomen for Uncle Sam," *LAT*, January 12, 1912, p. I-16; Federal District Judge Wellhorn ruled in California that, under state as well as federal law, "women could not legally act as jurors, whether "voters or not." Verdicts could be set aside.

· LIFE ·

"LADIES OF THE JURY—"

FIGURE 7.4. Well into the twentieth century, satirists still portrayed female jurors as deranged, incompetent, or 'manified' threats to defenseless men; "Ladies of the Jury –!" cartoon from *Life Magazine*, Vol. 74, No. 1931, October 30, 1919.

appealed his conviction on the ground that one female juror sequestered with eleven men had been "permitted to retire to the judge's chambers," violating the requirement of non-separation of jurors. Said Chief Justice Overton Ellis, the law making women eligible for jury service "necessitated, and was of itself, a change in the existing system relating to the separation of juries." But "the rules of society, propriety, and common decency require that mixed juries be allowed to separate according to sexes at stated intervals."[94] The same year, in an appeal of a Snohomish County decision in favor of a claim of compensation for labor, the defendant seized on whispers between two female jurors – they "just hated that lawyer with a moustache" – as evidence of misconduct. The "woman jurors," wrote Ellis, merely referred to the mustache "as a mark of identification, or were only innocently voicing the age old prejudice against the hirsute adornment of the face which some of the sex have nursed ever since the days of Delilah. Then, again," he added unnecessarily, "we can almost take judicial notice of the fact that the present generation is extravagant of speech. Terms in young ladies' seminaries, and even college careers, have sometimes netted no more in the way of a vocabulary ... than 'I just hate,' 'I just love,' ... terms applied without reference to ... things animate and inanimate, from marshmallows to men and from breakfast foods to works of art." Having

[94] *State* v. *Harris*, 99 Wash Rpts 475 (1918).

established that women might be expected to behave like foolish schoolgirls, he affirmed the lower court's ruling.[95]

****

Americans exhibited an insatiable appetite for jury-related stories. In 1911, after the adoption of equal suffrage, Californians reported that women were "not only willing but in some cases anxious to serve on juries as an adjunct of their newly-acquired citizenship." When a panel of thirty-six names in Watts came up entirely female, nobody protested. A constable had been impressed that "most of them seemed genuinely anxious to do their duty ... [and] did not appear to ... be inspired by curiosity or for the distinction of serving on the first jury. They asked no questions except as to when they should appear .... [F]ew of the women drawn are suffragists," he added, "but inquiry showed that practically everyone ha[d] registered." Americans variously depicted mixed-sex juries as progressive, promiscuous, unnatural, or dangerous. In Chicago, a state attorney who had failed to secure the conviction of a woman charged with killing her husband concluded that, in such cases, courts perhaps should empanel women. "Men will not do it," he insisted. " ... This view may be radical, but it is the only way to stop this emotional injustice, this giving back of life and liberty to women who have ruthlessly taken human life. If a jury of women had sat in judgment on Florence Bernstein they would have sent her to the gallows ... in five minutes." A Seattle Republican castigated a New Yorker's suggestion that an all-male jury unwilling to convict a woman of her husband's murder might have benefitted from the presence of women. Not true, he said, quoting Roger Greene's testimony about women's good sense. In 1910, a judge in San Francisco, in a case involving child custody, drafted twelve of the women in the courtroom and moved to judgment in a state that did not yet permit women in jury boxes.[96]

Indeed, after 1911, chaos reigned in California for some years, with higher courts said to be the least amenable to mixed-sex panels.[97] While Colorado

---

[95] *Hansen v. Lemley*, 100 Wash Rpts 444 (1918), 448.

[96] "Women Jurors to Try Women," *LAT*, August 22, 1912, Part I, p. 3; "The Trial Jury," *Seattle Republican*, June 2, 1911, p. 2; "Case in California," *TT*, December 19, 1910; "Women Jurors," *SJI*, December 1, 1911 (women not eligible for jury service anywhere in California).

[97] Percy Edwards argued that, in California, there arose "more or less opposition to calling women as jurors in the higher courts"; Percy L. Edwards, "Constitutional Obligations and Woman's Citizenship," 75 Central Law Journal 244 (1912), p. 245. On chaos, see, e.g., "No Woman Jurors," *TT*, May 27, 1912, p. 1 (no women in Chico, CA, despite enfranchisement); for confusion as to whether women could sit at all, "Women's Status Doubted" and "Women Cannot be Juror," *SJI*, December 1, 1911, p. 2 (Judge Edger asserting that women cannot be grand jurors until legislature passes separate law). See also "Women Jury Row," *LAT*, September 12, 1911, p. 13 (statute providing for jury service declared unconstitutional and case remanded for retrial with male jury); "No Jurymen For Uncle Sam," ibid., January 12, 1912 (Judge Wellborn of U.S. District Court in Los Angeles says that juries have to be male; decision reversed on that account); "First Woman Juror Drawn Says She Wants to Serve," ibid., October 20, 1909, Part I, p. 13 (woman eager to

statutes did not permit mixtures, women and a few judges described the right at least to serve on juries in juvenile court as a "duty and privilege." In path-breaking Wyoming, opposition to a female presence in courthouses continued. Ex-legislator George Wilson told the *Washington Post* in 1911 that woman suffrage would not survive "an investigation of its workings. Where it is coupled with liability to jury duty it will give us the spectacle of mixed juries of men and women locked up together for twenty-four hours or more, whiling away the long hours of night discussing . . . the details of some very delicate case. Where it carries exemption from jury duty it would give the man-haters a chance to pass laws relating to the use of brute force as in keeping the peace or carrying on war, in whose enforcement nature forbids one class of the voters-to-be to take part."[98]

Nor did controversy cease in Washington. Where women served on juries, they sat without the acquiescence of the whole people, notwithstanding their formal, constitutionally established "equality" as voters and, more problematically, as members of the constituent power. Judge Chapman of the Pierce County Superior Court denied a request in a 1911 felony trial to reverse the conviction on the ground that the jury had been "illegally impaneled" – though, in this instance, counsel argued, not that sex disqualified women, but that the 1911 jury law had made a special case of them, violating principles of equity.[99] As late as 1943, lawyers still disputed women's presence. *W. E. Roche Fruit Co. v. Northern Pacific Railway* turned on the question of whether women lawfully volunteered for jury service. A clerk supposedly had erred in taking out an advertisement inviting women to volunteer for juries; women were never dispassionate; the law authorized women to opt out, not to volunteer. In ruling that female volunteers sat lawfully, justices finally affirmed women's capacity to render sensible judgments alongside men, if not women's obligation to do so. But the majority broadened the lens to accommodate, not merely volunteers, but sex-blind performances of obligations in the future. "It is the right of every citizen," wrote the majority, ". . . to fully participate in the administration of the laws by which he or she may be governed, and to deny it is to take away one of the valuable prerogatives of citizenship. It is a right as well as a duty which cannot be taken from any class of person who . . . possesses the necessary qualifications. It is the right also of every person . . . charged with a violation of the laws to have such charge made and tried by grand and petit juries of his peers." Legislation ensured "the protection of the innocent as well as the terror of the guilty."[100]

---

serve); "Jury Service Awes Them Not," ibid., October 13, 1911 (thirty-six women "not only willing but in some cases anxious to serve on juries as an adjunct of their newly acquired citizenship"). For confusion in Idaho, "Over at Wallace," *PH*, January 21, 1899, p. 1.

[98] "Women Seek Jury Service," *LAT*, August 26, 1911, Part I, p. 16; further detail at "Woman Juror Costly Error," ibid., November 30, 1909, Part I, p. 12; George Wilson, "Female Suffrage in Practice," *WP*, April 3, 1911, p. 6.

[99] "Women Jury Row, Tacoma, Sept. 11," *LAT*, September 12, 1911, p. 13.

[100] *W. E. Roche Fruit Co. v. Northern Pacific Railway*, 18 Wash Rpts 484 (1943), 488.

8

"Every woman is a law unto herself"

Rights, obligations, and legitimacy

> The dignity and dry bones of the courts have no use for progressiveness .... They are founded on the common law principle which gives to the male citizen the right to command and be obeyed.
>
> – Percy Edwards (1912)

Gender Remade began with two interrelated puzzles – the swift, poorly explained rise and demise of political equality before statehood, and the Washington State Supreme Court's curious failure to distinguish the enfranchised women in *Somerville* v. *State* from their non-voting sisters in *Muller* v. *Oregon*. When Hattie Somerville's young, enterprising lawyers filed suit in 1911, they could not have known that the ensuing courtroom drama would encapsulate, as if in a snapshot, the tangled relationships between formal law, social practice, and political economy that had shaped and given meaning to citizens' daily encounters since at least 1879. But discursive entanglements should surprise no-one, least of all historians of law. As Victoria Saker Woeste once declared, "Law is about" – that is, takes as its subject – "complexity, ambiguity, and the sheer messiness of social life."[1]

The two contestants in *Somerville* represented two distinct, if temporally correlated, strands of development. Justice Herman Crow's majority opinion spoke to the triumph of law over politics, especially in economic life, since at least the 1870s. It turned on *Muller*, emergent due-process jurisprudence, and still-current common law doctrines that barred divisions of sovereign authority and valorized masculine control of sites of public judgment. Crow also wielded "common knowledge" – an amalgam of social and gender practices and findings, some derived from cutting-edge social science – to support constructions of women as a vulnerable class of citizens incapable of self-government beyond

---

[1] Victoria Saker Woeste, in Robert Gordon and Morton Horwitz, eds., *Law, Society, and History: Themes in the Legal History of Lawrence M. Friedman* (New York, 2011), p. 45. Emphasis added.

marital estates or polling places. In contrast, the young lawyers on Somerville's side mobilized a small mountain of systematically gathered facts about box makers in Washington State, the testimony of physicians, and legal texts explaining relations between property rights, the ballot, and self-determination. They heaped scorn on the antediluvian law of coverture and relied on a second line of constitutional argument, epitomized by *Lochner* v. *New York*, affirming the capacity of individual men to assume risk and strike up their own workplace bargains without state interference. Women, they argued, similarly were self-governing individuals, a "law unto themselves," co-sovereigns and law givers alongside husbands and fathers. But, as it turned out, the box maker could only lose, less because *Muller* controlled the case than because the two sexes no longer occupied sovereign ground jointly and severally.

"THE RIGHT TO COMMAND AND BE OBEYED"

In Washington Territory, as we have seen, women had approached co-sovereignty as well as legal-political equality and agency by 1883. Without more, the territory's renovations of civil and domestic-relations legalities – excepting perhaps the division of unitary "*petit* kings," which Americans had long refused to undertake[2] – might have been absorbed without triggering social and gender chaos or full-throated retribution. Many states and territories had adopted married-women's property acts, if only to liberate scarce capital for investment, and several (e.g., California, Oregon, Texas, New Mexico) had embraced community-property regimes. But Washington lawmakers went further: They enfranchised women on the ground that republican constitutionalism required it, admitted women to public office, and opened juries to both sexes because, in American experiences of electoral diversification, the incidents of political freedom always had been bundled. In some respects, territorial status aided women's cause: Washingtonians were constrained mainly by the under-explicated terms of a federal statute and not by a state constitution; while a comparative vacuum rendered legislative extensions of freedom less secure, they also opened a free space for experimentation.[3] Physical and cultural isolation encouraged innovation, fluency in prevailing legalities, and courage. By 1880–83, territorial men and women had begun to naturalize the radically egalitarian idea, not only that women could vote and deal in property alongside men, within and beyond marriage, but also that the two sexes stood, jointly and severally, in the polity *as in marriage*, on the sex-blind ground of property-based sovereignty. Zerelda McCoy, Roger Sherman Greene, Benjamin

[2] Linda K. Kerber, "The Paradox of Women's Citizenship in the Early Republic: The Case of *Martin* v. *Massachusetts, 1805*," *American Historical Review*, Vol. 97 (April 1992), pp. 349–78, revised and reprinted in Kerber, *No Constitutional Right to Be Ladies*, op cit.

[3] On spaces open to democratic conversation and experimentation, see Sara Evans and Harry Boyte, *Free Spaces: The Sources of Democratic Change in America* (Chicago, IL, 1992), Chs. 5–6.

Dennison, the *Tacoma Ledger*'s Randolph Radebaugh, Matilda Hindman, and many other social democrats carried the equality banner into the mid-1880s; into the new century, Populists, laborites, Loyal League activists, the old guard in NAWSA, and civil-rights lawyers continued to say that government should emancipate rather than constrain self-governing citizens. These ideas finally landed in Herman Crow's courtroom, where Somerville resoundingly lost. It was difficult, if not impossible, to contend that women resembled New York City's male bakers, less because of the work *per se* – the court even conceded that box makers enjoyed better conditions than miners or lumberjacks limited to the same eight hours – than because, at their core and ineradicably, women were not men.

The second, ultimately dominant thread in *Somerville*'s fabric originated perhaps with opponents of Susan B. Anthony and the men who had heckled Mary Olney Brown's husband for failing to govern his wife. It persisted into the 1880s, visible initially as an undertow rooted less in constitutional theory than in theology, social and gender practices, and resurgent elements of the law of coverture. By 1885–86, it emerged as a serious threat to egalitarianism. Courtrooms effectively shut down as lawyers rose in court to dispute the presence of women claiming to be household heads in severalty with their husbands, and in some cases to vilify all "females" presuming to sit in men's places. At the same time, in the press and elsewhere, Washingtonians were remaking social and gender hierarchies in response to economic modernization, workplace violence, and women's apparent complicity in social disarray and gender confusion. Internecine warfare broke out between departments of the territorial government; eventually, allies of George Turner and other social conservatives purged women from polling places, offices, and jury boxes, and, with the aid of sympathetic federal sponsors, pushed a masculinized state constitution through a ratification election. Elements of the law of coverture also resurged to weaken central elements of the new state's community-property system. By 1912, Justice Crow could say without hesitation that "common knowledge" about the female class – notwithstanding the 1911 restoration by constitutional amendment of women's right to vote – mandated reliance on *Muller* v. *Oregon*. At issue was women's sovereignty, not their right to drop ballots in boxes as representatives of home. Without a requirement of jury service and access to other sites of public judgment – that is, without the sex's co-sovereignty and co-headship – Crow could not easily find agency or autonomy; at hand was a class of citizens rendered vulnerable before and during the passage to statehood who now claimed little more than a constitutionalized right to vote, access to property, and, perhaps, "separate but equal" sovereignty at home.

Why exactly did Washingtonians decide to remake gender and their nascent democracy? Surely the comparatively swift closure of democratic spaces – the elimination of mixed-sex political practice and the related decision to install an entrepreneurial fraternity at the public table – had to do in part with the speed with which industrial capitalism and statehood fever overtook unstable, developing communities. As chaos deepened, novel legalities seemed naïve at best, and at worst anti-modern and opposed to the self-evident blessings of national integration. As early as 1885, with violence expanding geometrically, citizens began to generate social hierarchies capable of securing social peace and forging productive as well as harmonious relations between workers, entrepreneurs, and agencies of government.

Equally, however, women's sudden loss of standing after the jury-duty crisis reflected the power of gender and other social practices, especially as communities confronted public responsibilities to which citizens had not yet consented. By 1885, Washingtonians knew that ancillary rights, and especially mixed-sex jury duty, would be a good deal more problematic than balloting. A rising tide of seemingly anti-masculine temperance zealotry made a bad situation much worse. With more decades, Washingtonians might have found ways to exempt mothers, midwives, and home-bound cheese makers from jury duty or perhaps to remodel the concept of obligations to include women-friendly contributions to the commonweal. As it was, women were forced to choose between a forced march in men's shoes or no march at all; many exercised agency as self-governors – bolstered by systems of belief as disparate as Christianity, the common law, and the lore passed from woman to woman about how to serve family and community – and simply refused to participate.

It mattered, too, that Roger Sherman Greene – his powerful personality, his conception of republican government, and his essentialism – came to embody arguments for both legal equality and socio-biological differences. Greene made no secret of his view that, in the 1880s, as in earlier chapters of Anglo-American history, juries functioned as a stabilizing rudder and repository of social wisdom; with panels expanded to include exemplars of "woman" and "man," and with the wall razed between home and government, the republic would be perfected and preserved. Surely if the whole people were permitted to speak through legislation and "judicial ballots," momentary fright would ease. "What is right in regard to possessory rights in property, the enforcement of contracts, the obligations of citizenship?" wrote a champion of broad representation. "Manifestly what the people declare is right, by means of a statute, which is the only way in which the people can make such a declaration." Voting mattered: Electors responded to choices made by others and determined who would speak for the constituent power in the assembly; female voters thus advanced the great work of resolving policy disputes and building consensus. As direct representatives of neighborhoods, however, grand jurors enforced legislative commands, deciding at the front line whose behavior offended the citizenry sufficient to warrant accusation and trial; only householders were vested sufficiently in the community to undertake such work. Petit jurors, by contrast, weighed evidence for and against conviction for wrong-doing, and, under the watchful eye of judges, deprived citizens of freedom or life.[4]

Hence, grand juries in particular lay at the heart of republican governance. But customary constitutions rejected sudden, disruptive violations of gender and other social constructs. Community property had required adaptation, as did representation of home at the polls. But juries had been a step too far, for men and women alike. Women vanished from citadels of public power less for their associations with "law and order" and temperance agitation – though connections were made soon enough – than for repeated, often involuntary introductions of women's bodies in masculine spaces, and women's own reticence (interpreted sometimes as laziness or, less nastily, the withdrawal of consent), given domestic duties, apprehensions of double burden or inequality, and the public's seeming inability to modify categories of exemption to include women's domestic responsibilities and traditional ways of contributing to the commonweal. As women registered distress, and as juries came to be associated both with legal-political zealotry and anti-vice campaigns, a significant crisis grew much worse. On one side, women wanted no part of public humiliation; on the other side, the suspicion grew that they were incompetent, lazy, or incapable of performing obligations dispassionately or objectively. As we have seen, statehood fever and economy-related disorder augmented social tensions. But it was women's disastrous entry into courthouses that crystallized doubt about the wisdom and adequacy, not only of women, but of the broader egalitarian project. Washington required incontrovertible jury verdicts and leaders infused with "kingly" reason, not sentimentality, moral pontification, or erratic subjectivity. Jury duty, not suffrage *per se*, triggered feigned cases, which in turn led George Turner and others to interrogate the subtext – i.e., the territory's "radical" civil rights and domestic relations regime – well into the twentieth century. Herman Crow inherited a legal culture riddled with doubts about women's legitimacy as custodians of the republic in sites of public judgment beyond the polls. Equal-suffrage advocates had established, to their own satisfaction, the *power* of lawmakers to expand the polity and women's *power* as propertied citizens to cast ballots and determine the fate of other citizens. But they had not persuaded skeptics of legislative *authority* to divide and redistribute sovereignty or of women's *authority* to make rules and impose judgments.

"WILLIAMS AND MARYS, FERDINANDS AND ISABELLAS"

Popular sovereignty is a homogenizing fiction dependent for its force, in 1889 as in 1789, on its sacro-ideological properties; a law or jury verdict cannot

---

[4] "The Law's Obligation," *ST*, August 22, 1895. For a contemporary argument against stuffing juries (or judicial benches) with "woman" and "man" with the fond hope of realizing justice, see Sally Kenney, *Gender and Justice: Why Women in the Judiciary Really Matter* (New York, 2013), as at 161–5 (what matters is diversity of experience and wisdom, not diversity of sex).

contribute significantly to self- or social constitution if citizens doubt its legitimacy or withdraw consent. Unlike forward-leaning rights discourses, sovereignty points backward to original compacts and uninterrupted usage. Republicans' sprawling, unstable, constantly interrogated substitute for a traditional Crown lacked the coherence and personalization, not to mention the historicity, of its antecedents. Particularly after 1860, Americans agreed less and less about the merits of unitary, patriarchal, white headship and multiple forms of legal dependency; disagreement and heterogeneity, in turn, continually jeopardized stability. In Edmund Morgan's considered judgment, the new-fangled doctrine of popular sovereignty always had been a "way to consolidate the power of a few over the multitude," such that the latter imagined themselves against fact to be the more powerful. It also required "a means by which some body or bodies capable of doing so could speak decisively and authentically for the people," thereby containing government "within the framework and the limits which that speaking body prescribed for it." Problems, however, inhered in the new fiction; chief among them was the difficulty of reconciling "the wishes and needs and rights of actual people" with the overriding will of a monolithic, artificially homogenized popular sovereign.[5]

In the mid- and late nineteenth century, the constituent power remained susceptible to admixtures and "disenchantment," as with the archetypal, pre-modern shift from Puritan to Yankee or Americans' calamitous loss of faith in the sovereign will after 1850.[6] But modernity and continentalism at least held out the promise of prosperity, technological mastery, and a broader citizenship. In Washington, liberal reformers not only had abandoned the common law – a body of rules and prejudices long since mystified and naturalized – but had discounted its deep historical roots and primary role in the ongoing construction of gender. The loss of familiar legalities left women and men without a framework or foundation – not a state constitution, not even a unifying body of experiences older than the 1850s. The community's own social and gender practices were not consulted; instead, women were shoehorned into practices as ancient and masculine as the law of coverture. In Nancy Hirschmann's words, women were "forced to be free"; the sheriff's knock at the door disregarded their own interests and self-constructions. In a sense, women's rejection of an oppressive, sex-blind "freedom" affirmed a sovereign right to resist tyranny, even as it offended and angered would-be

[5] Edmund S. Morgan, *Inventing the People: The Rise of Popular Sovereignty in England and America* (New York, 1989), p. 82.
[6] E.g., Christopher Childers, *The Failure of Popular Sovereignty: Slavery, Manifest Destiny, and the Radicalization of Southern Politics* (Lawrence, KS, 2012). On Weberian disenchantment (the collapse of mysticism in the face of the modern), see Lawrence Scaff, *Fleeing the Iron Case: Culture, Politics, and Modernization in the Thought of Max Weber* (Berkeley, CA, 1991).

emancipators; among anti-suffragists, resistance provided ammunition for charges of unearned privilege, lassitude, and disinterest.[7]

Certainly George Turner's shrill denunciations of hermaphroditic household heads detached from historical practice, and women's supposed inability to speak as sex-neutral citizens, betrayed anxiety about the capacity of an emasculated sovereign to bear the weight of citizens' obligations. But they also pointed to a sharp disjuncture between inherited legalities, including the binding force of gender ascriptions, and democratic practice. To remake gender without the extended conversations and near-consensus that successful shifts in social process typically require – indeed, to remake the notion of masculine headship at home and in government, declaring divisible (and shareable) that which had long been regarded as unitary – was to court a powerful resurgence of the citizenry's informal "fundamental law," as more than one citizen put it. It was perhaps unsurprising that such a resurgence led to sharp interrogations of the legitimacy of the constituent power as amended and legalized. Within a few short years, statutes and codes were revealed to be little more than stately proposals dependent on Congress, friendly legislators, and social practices for longevity and force.

Where did authority reside? Washingtonians turned first to the organic act. Jurists disagreed about its nature. Was it a quasi-constitution, as George Turner contended, second only in authority to the federal constitution? Or, as Roger Greene believed, was it merely a federal statute dependent entirely on Congress for its authority and on legislators for implementation and interpretation? Wide-open spaces permitted not only liberation but also the transmutation of legal-cultural disagreements into social and constitutional fright. Who had authorized a discontinuous revolution in law and gender? Juries were especially problematic: Could women and judicial "cranks" ensure social peace and supplies of good beer? In the absence of authoritative public judgments, liquor licenses could be confiscated without due process; the Chinese could be murdered with impunity, jeopardizing federal treaties. A sheriff might decide to summon only men or to suspend juries altogether; a judge might retreat to chambers rather than issue a mixed-sex venire; women might fall prey to charismatic lawyers. What prevented riots and lynching, children running wild in Tacoma, the locking of mothers and wives in anterooms with strange men, or judicial trashing of legislative decisions?

In 1883, suffragists typically assumed that, with enfranchisement, a bundle of ancillary rights vested automatically in women, excepting only obligations requiring brute force – in which case, substitutes could be deployed. Activists and pro-suffrage lawyers did not consider immediately whether those obligations might be performed in various ways, as when poor men fixed roads in place of taxes. Perhaps a new class of voter might require avenues to

---

[7] Nancy J. Hirschmann, *The Subject of Liberty: Toward a Feminist Theory of Freedom* (New Haven, CT, 2003), pp. 235–6.

fulfillment not yet contemplated. Women, after all, had not been shirkers. They had served as spies and soldiers in every war; they had defended the home front, made bandages, raised future soldiers, and blown up bridges. Why not create woman-friendly categories of gainful employment – say, motherhood or 16-hour-a-day midwifery – and exempt individuals rather than an entire class? Obligations were mandatory: As Linda Kerber reminds us, the "primary meaning of obligation is to be under compulsion."[8] To perform obligations was to affirm equal membership in and commitment to the popular sovereign and the governments emanating from it.

Much depended, in other words, on citizens' ability to claim that men and women together authorized, made, and enforced law for the community, and that women might be able to perform obligations without extraordinary hardship or trauma. Greene sought a theoretical framework that would mobilize the entire sovereign body and permit women to fulfill a traditional obligation *as women* rather than as male impersonators; if he could show that diversity (and particularly the presence of virtuous women) strengthened the whole, he could sidestep offense to social practice and skepticism about the reliability of women's preparation and judgments. But he made scant provision for women's sense of violation or the ferocity of backlash from all sides; in the end, he contributed to a countervailing sense of social disintegration. By rejecting Congressional views of organic acts, moreover, he likely invited Turner's characterization of the act as an immutable quasi-constitution opposed to unprecedented, grotesque changes in unitary headship and in the composition of juries.

In the end, though, women fell prey not to individuals but to fatal compromises of constitutional sovereignty. Claims of unmediated relationships with property had long been the marker and reward of sovereignty. But, having proposed the bifurcation of unitary headship and infused both partners with economic agency, territorial lawmakers had not eliminated the common law root and branch. Instead, they established a hybridized regime, surrounding their amalgam of sex-blind civil and marital equalities with many of the common-law practices that had constructed men, in both law and culture, as householders and woman as helpmeets – notably, but not only, the old rule by which men ordinarily managed the non-landed marital estate with women's acquiescence. Worse, legislators had declared before and after 1889 that in the absence of rules to the contrary, Washingtonians would adhere to the common law, which invited backward glances. Justice George Turner in *Harland* and *Bloomer* therefore pursued the restoration not only of male electors and jurors but also of critical elements of the law of coverture. Others followed suit. By 1910, even community-property rules of practice, once a point of pride, no longer figured prominently in official depictions of the state.

---

[8] Linda K. Kerber, "The Meanings of Citizenship," *Journal of American History*, Vol. 84, No. 3 (December 1997), p. 835.

In summer of 1910, a woman in San Diego wrote the attorney general of Washington asking about the "age of majority for women"; he told her that it was eighteen. He then laid out state practice in detail, including the fact that a "married woman may hold property in her own name when acquired with her own separate funds. The mother and father have equal control of children." Nowhere did he mention joint tenancy of estates, which had been drawn into closer communion with their common-law cousins.[9]

Did Washington's women suffer primarily from unequal rights? Scholarship amply shows that women (especially married women) gathered a hefty bundle of economic and marital rights as the nineteenth century advanced. By the end of the century, in fact, most married women could not only deal in their own property but also retain earnings – the latter a stunning blow to the notion of unitary male headship in households. In 1883, the women of Washington enjoyed, if not every right in men's quiver, a longer, fuller allocation than did most women. But, as modern campaigns for equality amply show by repeatedly gathering in rights and coming up short, grants of right – even a full quiver's allotment – did not ensure immunity from special, sex-based legislation or intimidation. Nor, as Washingtonians learned the hard way, did multiplications of rights deliver up political and social equality. Additional factors – seen clearly in struggles over the jury-duty obligation and right to hold public office – together guaranteed authoritative, enforceable grants of right. Without co-sovereignty, for example, women were voters by permission and wards of a paternal state.

Sovereignty, however, was not the whole of it. In Washington, an untidy collection of social facts – the distance to courthouses, the absence of decent sanitation, the extractive nature of the territorial economy – and deeply embedded gender practices contributed powerfully to the defeat of radical democratization. Women charged with educating children, or making butter for market, did not welcome and rarely could manage thirty-mile treks to courthouses. Anti-suffragist backlash and the retreat of many women (some of them pro-suffrage) from the burden of yet more duties had been couched not only as crimes against Biblical and other inherited bodies of learning, but also as expressions of outrage over insults hurled at women struggling to perform democratic rituals, often at great sacrifice. The prospect of three-dollar days aside, these were visceral concerns, not in the least abstract, and major threats to women's emotional and personal well-being. At issue were not only the inconvenience of travel, filthy latrines, and day-care emergencies, but also a woman's identity and what Elizabeth Cady Stanton called self-sovereignty. Men and women alike were repulsed when wives had to tell strangers about morning sickness or menstruation, suspend long-held beliefs about divisions of labor, or spend the night without proper clothing. Mothers typically nursed

---

[9] Assistant Attorney General to Charlotte J. Baker, M.D., San Diego, CA, August 5, 1910, Papers of the Attorney General, Box 2, General Correspondence, WSA-O.

babies privately, not in crowded anterooms. The presence of children in courtrooms exacerbated a sense of social derangement. In the absence of meaningful democratization of households and apt categories of exemption, charges of injustice were well-founded; women's agency found expression not only in pre-statehood invasions of polls, but also in rejections of harassment and unsolicited notoriety in courthouses.

In sum, and as Crow's brethren unwittingly made clear, the fundamental causes of persistent, seemingly ineradicable dependence for women in the workplace and in public spaces beyond the polls were social practices, including gender, and the incremental degradation of the propertied core of women's co-sovereignty. The view took hold, supported additionally by cutting-edge biological and social science (not to mention yellow-journalistic exploitation of stereotype), that women might readily "attend to the duties which will devolve upon her as a voter," but ought never to assume "the duties of an important public functionary of any kind" – legislator, juror, judge – "with the prospect of doing either herself or the office credit."[10] Turner's allies had eliminated not only the ballot but also the sex-neutral, *encompassing* foundations from which political equality had sprung. Only within marital estates did women still claim substantial, if compromised, legitimacy as members of the constituent power and wielders of a constitutionalized home vote. Consider the fictitious John and Mabel, who were deeply in debt until Mabel of the "lily white hands" announced that, as ruler of the home, she would control family finances, fire the servants, undertake housework herself, and bank the savings. Over John's objections, Mabel did just that at the cost of her hands; at home, Mabel laid down the law. Soon, they were debt free with healthy children and a "handsomer home" than their parents had enjoyed. "It would be well," said the author about Mabel, "if more *heads of families* could come to a similar conclusion."[11] Well into the 1920s, lobbyists (including the Woman's Legislative Council) pushed not only for widow's and mother's pensions, but also for state recognition of the "occupation" of housekeeper, to use their term, as work of "equal value to that of the other spouse," on the ground that unpaid labor depressed salaries elsewhere and degraded women.[12] But, with few exceptions, efforts came to nothing for another fifty years.

---

[10] Florence Percy Matheson, "Woman's Natural Debarments from Political Service," *American Magazine of Civics* (December 1895), p. 593. The reply, written by Mrs. A. L. Cornwall, had nothing to say about equality or sovereignty, emphasizing woman's capacity for social purification. By omission, it conceded Matheson's main argument; see *American Magazine of Civics* (July 1896), 77–82.

[11] [Aubertine] Woodward Moore, "On a Cash Basis," *ST*, September 20, 1889. Emphasis added.

[12] Sophie L. W. Clark to Mrs. Catherine Waugh McColloch, March 13, 1920, Schlesinger Women's Studies Manuscripts, Series I-E, Reel 25, Doc. No. 0246; Clark to National Chairman of Uniform Laws Commission, National League of Women Voters [McColloch], May 11, 1921, ibid., Series I-C, Reel 25, Doc. No. 0278; Clark to Mrs. Catherine W. McCulloch, September 16, 1920, ibid., Series I-E, Reel 25, Doc. No. 0265.

Should we blame the social-feminist members of WERA for expediency or myopia in accepting stereotypes as well as sex- and status-based exemptions from obligations – or, for that matter, for refusing to serve on juries? Certainly equality-minded contemporaries did, and candidates for public office live still with the legacy of Blackstone, George Turner, Emma Smith DeVoe, and the 'separate-but-equal' republican, Roger Greene. Only by the 1960s could jury-movement activists, aided by altered social practices and renewed interest in sex-blind equality, persuade oppositionists of the merits of mixed-sex juries, female office-holding, or (much less certainly) economic autonomy. In 1908, however, DeVoe and Hutton inhabited a modernizing society bent on escaping territorial 'bondage' and a myriad of humiliations borne of gender. George Turner aimed to discredit and patronize public women; social feminists certainly did not. By 1905–06, DeVoe and to a lesser extent Hutton spoke a language, in "still hunts" and elsewhere, that citizens of good will might use to elevate, honor, and protect neighborhood girls and women, beginning with a legitimizing association with home and the propertied marital estate.

These were matters of justified belief; contemporary affirmation of the right to make choices unlike our own in defense of self surely represented what Hirschmann calls "the practice of liberty," if not the elimination or interrogation of essentialism.[13] The fact that women struggled to escape wardship and dependency for another century reflects, not the failure of suffragists, but the power and resilience of gender discourses. For many women and men, the emanations of legal equality – among them, the prospect of unwanted intimacy in anterooms or the certainty that, with office holding, a woman would be altered beyond recognition – represented a step too far, a nightmare rather than the republican dream.

Well before *Harland* and *Bloomer*, mixed-sex democracy had emerged in the public imagination as a source of increasing social violence rather than as an avenue to social peace; small wonder that, by 1910, women had been remade as domestic 'queens' (not 'kings'), a non-hyperbolic term that differed substantially from its early American antecedent, the republican mother. White women, unlike the Chinese and other discounted or purged classes of men, had not been denied membership in the constituent power; nor, for civil purposes, did they lack formal rights. Instead, the sovereign domain (notwithstanding the supposed theoretical impossibility of division) likely had been partitioned. Certainly the prevailing socio-legal notion of 'separate but equal' (Myra Bradwell and Homer Plessy spring to mind) replaced sex-blindness, to the extent that such a condition ever had been realized, within the constituent power. It was impossible to deny propertied citizens agency and authority, but entirely possible to cordon off public offices, jury boxes, and professions, on the ground that women's peculiar constitution fitted her for the "home vote," domestic governance and reproduction, community

---

[13] Hirschmann, *Subject of Liberty*, p. 238.

improvement, wealth production, and (within new limits) co-management of community property. In short, Harriet Somerville's employees could be patronized and subjected to "common knowledge" in the place of fact, not because they had been denied or lacked "rights," but because sovereignty had been fatally compromised and, in ways that remained unstable and murky, divided between male and female realms, "kings" and "queens."

"AN EMPIRE OF LIBERTY FOR WOMEN"

What about the notion of the west as a seedbed of women's emancipation? Into the new century, western exceptionalism was anything but self-evident, though the myth (as Frederick Jackson Turner's shelf-life demonstrates) has enjoyed a long career in suffrage studies and elsewhere. On one side, Washingtonians in 1883 had taken "pride in knowing that this territory, so young in years," might be credited "in history with taking the lead of century-old states in performing an act of such transcendent wisdom and justice."[14] Oregon's Helen M. Gougar argued similarly that westerners were "far in advance of the East. Legislators listen to the demands of Western women with respect and consideration, and Eastern men snub their women as if they belonged to a separate race or class. The matter of suffrage is far more fairly dealt with in the West than the East, and the empire of liberty for woman will first take its place in the West. In society ... [and] laws relating to property rights and suffrage, the Eastern men could learn some valuable lessons by going West and becoming imbued with the spirit of respect for woman that is a part of Western civilization."[15] Or, as suffragist Elsie Wallace Moore put it in 1909, "Our four *free* states are populated by the most broad-minded, energetic, ambitious and generous men and women from all the Eastern states and particularly the Middle-Western states. This same sort of men forms the population of the Pacific coast states and those states immediately adjacent on the east. Here, where there are better schools ... than in any eastern section, ... one feels reassured in saying that public sentiment will very soon become a dominant force in our favor. The great grain belt ... will be the next section procuring suffrage for its women; and eastern bound the wave of liberty will sweep, crossing the Middle West and the Great lakes until it strikes the eastern and southern coasts where people are still provincial and men are most selfish and autocratic. Even here women shall soon be free."[16]

DeVoe and Catt also advanced the notion of a liberty-seeking, woman-friendly west, albeit with only a half-loaf in hand. "Freedom," wrote DeVoe in 1910, "has always come out of the West," a region populated by "free souls

[14] "An Important Event," *SFC*, November 22, 1883.
[15] Helen M. Gougar, "Western vs. Eastern Men," *NN*, December 20, 1883. The paper circulated widely in Washington.
[16] Elsie Wallace Moore, "The Suffrage Question in the Far West," *The Arena: A Twentieth-Century Review of Opinion*, Vol. 41, No. 232 (July 1909), p. 424.

who gladly gave up the luxuries of the east in order to escape its slavery. Each generation, the west has been further on; . . . it has reached the Pacific Ocean . . . . What charters of liberty will be fashioned here, and washed back over the East with the returning tides of humanity? . . . The Rocky Mountain States, Idaho, Utah, Colorado and Wyoming have equal suffrage." If it prevailed in Oregon and Washington, and notwithstanding the southwest, Americans would boast a "free people from the crest of the Rocky Mountains to the Pacific Ocean." As if to say that first-generation suffragists had got it wrong, she added that the laws regarding women and children in Washington were "next best to those in the four suffrage states probably because we did have equal suffrage here in territorial days. . . . We want to lay the Corner Stone for the True Temple of Human Liberty – Equal Opportunity for all people to work out their own salvation."[17]

Sometimes, westerners looked to Washington for inspiration. In March, 1897, for instance, the *New York Times* circulated Idahoans' celebration of the fact that Washington seemed to be "in a fair way to join Idaho in extending the right of suffrage to women." Legislators had passed a bill to submit the question to the people at the next election; whatever influence Idaho could exert it would gladly provide. "We have come out into the light here, and are ready to assist our neighbors to emerge from the darkness." The *Los Angeles Times* attributed a "wave of interest" in equal suffrage to Washington's grant of "full citizenship on equal terms with men," as if ballots alone sufficed.[18] In rapid fire, California, Colorado, and Wyoming universalized suffrage. So compelling was the wave that one journalist wondered whether women would introduce "serious economic problems into politics," especially in industrial cities. But, in the process, territorial experiences sometimes vanished. Annie Ramsey of *Lippincott's* offered a brief account of the states and territories instituting woman suffrage "after the civil war," omitting Washington Territory. "By economic exigencies, by the introduction of luxury, by the invention of labor saving machines, women have been forced forward and thus made more . . . free to enter public life. Therefore the army of suffragists has largely been recruited in the last fifteen years from the most . . . reflective part of the community. When such a stage is reached in any movement founded on a plea whose abstract justice is admitted, it is certain that the end will soon be attained."[19]

At the same time, a counter-narrative emerged, organized around the supposed failure of mixed-sex suffrage and the related and more telling problem of obligations. The extent and force of this anti-mythic discourse

[17] "Spirit of the West," February 25, 1910, *Mount Vernon Argus*, in Emma Smith DeVoe Scrapbooks, Vol. H, WSHS. In the same mythic vein, see also "The Republic of Women," *TT*, November 2, 1911, p. 3.

[18] "From the Boise (Idaho) Statesman, Woman Suffrage," *NYT*, March 21, 1897; "Wave of Interest in Woman Suffrage Sweeps Country," *LAT*, November 13, 1910, p. 1.

[19] "The Seventh Suffrage State [Ohio]," *NYT*, May 23, 1912; "Woman's Views on Woman's Suffrage," *TT*, July 18, 1908.

awaits further investigation. Clearly, though, it had as least as much to do with sovereignty and citizens' obligations as with ballots. At an early moment, New England's Henry Goodwin supplied a template, in the process associating women with a domestic realm, envisioned not as an anti-political sphere of influence, but as a sovereign domain bounded and empowered by social practice. Western lawmakers had placed an "intolerable burden" upon women, he began, by imposing "political questions and duties in addition to those already borne." Women's claim to legitimacy lay, not with the "constitutive idea" of the polity, but with pre-political family governments, where "true sovereignty" lay. Much of Goodwin's argument had been heard before: Woman had sacred domestic and social duties upon which society depended; the power of the ballot had been "exaggerated." But his reliance on constitutional tropes, albeit for illiberal purposes, was telling. What did sovereignty entail, he asked? "Moral sentiment" antedated constitutions, and it was primarily the "work and privilege of woman." Here, said Goodwin, lay "her true sovereignty." This was not hyperbole: Whereas anti-suffragists sometimes referred to women's sphere as an anti-political, anti-legal realm, Goodwin and others understood that propertied women inhabited a separate-but-equal zone of real authority. This was not to say that women enjoyed an equality with men, any more than Homer Plessy enjoyed equality in segregated rail cars. It was to say instead that access to property set Washington's women sharply apart from their dependent forebears. To say that a "false theory of . . . individual rights" could not demolish the foundations of civil government – indeed, that the family came "before civil government" – was to grant binding force to the customary constitution that had resurged to smash mixed-sex juries, and that had proved, for better or worse, to be capable of trumping formal instruments. Liberal Washingtonians surely believed that laws and constitutions comported with popular aspirations; as Hendrik Hartog explains, Americans generally "reject any delegation of interpretive responsibility to a distant legal priesthood," such as the benches occupied by George Turner and William Langford. Such illegitimacy impedes democratization. But perceptions of illegitimacy from within the citizenry can function in the same way, even when supported by black-letter law. An anti-liberal outcome becomes more certain when the aspirational class seems to be sabotaging an objective like statehood, especially when suffused (as in Washington) with fraternalism and transcendent nationalism.[20]

After the 1898 loss of another woman suffrage proposal, New York anti-suffragists attributed its defeat to a western anti-suffrage alliance that opposed not the ballot itself or even the possibility that women might be tainted in polling places – though such concerns emerged – but the fact that suffrage

[20] Rev. Prof. H[enry] M. Goodwin, "Women's Suffrage," *New Englander* (March 1884), p. 7. Emphasis added. See Hendrik Hartog, "The Constitution of Aspiration and the 'Rights That Belong to Us All,'" *Journal of American History*, Vol. 74, No. 3 (December 1987), p. 3 and passim.

"brings responsibilities which woman are, and ever will be, unable to meet."[21] Sometimes, ballots appeared alone, as when Rhode Islanders opined that the defeat was "rather more than an ordinary one for the women and their allies since Washington, when a Territory, used to allow ballot privileges to the gentler sex. Evidently the experience was not satisfactory, for not only was woman suffrage left out of the Constitution ... but the people out there still adhere to a conviction that it is undesirable after having had experience both with and without it." Elsewhere, and well into the new century, critics pointed to obligations. In 1890, a Wyoming representative deplored the very idea of "women in public offices, women to do military duty, women to work on the roads; and men to wash the dishes, nurse the babies, and stay at home while the women were making stump speeches." In reporting a 1911 anti-suffrage rally in Sacramento, a writer heard one woman say that, in Washington, the newly enfranchised women "already were begging off from jury service." Another commentator lambasted Washington women for claiming the right to vote while clinging to a "right to be excused from jury service."[22]

To say the least, into the 1910s, Americans did not lack information about women's loss of ground, the jury-duty disaster, the extent to which women participated in general elections,[23] and the lessons gleaned as westerners conducted democratic experiments. Attentive citizens in New York or Chicago could not have imagined an unbroken saga of progress for women in the west. Abigail Duniway and Roger Greene alone generated hundreds of letters and editorials expressly for republication in eastern prints describing each success and failure. In 1908, Mrs. Humphrey Ward of London, England, could tell a New York audience that, after sixty years' agitation and the "forcing of a constitutional amendment in favor of the woman's vote in four of the sparsely peopled States of the West," suffrage was "in process of defeat and extinction – and that not at the hands of men, but at the hands of women themselves." Women's-rights activists "from this side of the water" had attempted to revive it, with little success.[24]

[21] "Against Woman Suffrage, The Fourth Annual Report of the Chairman ...," *LAT*, May 24, 1899, Part I, p. 3. A New York agent – perhaps the same one – named Mrs. W. Winslow Crannell of the Albany Anti-Suffrage Association, had appeared in California a few months earlier; "Anti-Suffrage Meeting," ibid., December 10, 1898, Part I, p. 6.

[22] "Equal Suffrage, From the Providence Journal," *WP*, November 27, 1898, p. 6; "[Mr. Reagan on] Admission of Wyoming," ibid., June 29, 1890, p. 7. See also "Women as Jurors [and] ... the Wyoming Cattlemen," *NYT*, January 4, 1893, p. 5, and "Ice Cream Buys Women's Votes ...," *LAT*, January 19, 1911, Part I, p. 1. In their 1923 account of the politics of suffragism, Carrie Chapman Catt and Netti Rogers Shuler observed that Wyoming anti-suffragists assumed that jury service would be "so obnoxious to the public" that citizens would reject suffrage; Catt and Shuler, *Woman Suffrage and Politics* (Seattle, WA, 1969, repr.), as at pp. 80–1, 153, 174.

[23] Inquiries to newspapers abounded as to which states had equal suffrage; see, e.g., "Where Women Can Vote," *LAT*, October 8, 1897, citing only Colorado and Wyoming as universal suffrage states, Arizona and Oklahoma with limited suffrage, and twenty-one states with partial suffrage.

[24] Mrs. Humphrey Ward, London, "Woman's Suffrage Not Inevitable," *NYT*, July 12, 1908.

Sometimes, journalists seized on western failures to prove the wisdom of easterly caution. In August, 1889, for instance, the *Woman's Journal* reprinted an essay originating in Boston that associated the entire spectacle with barbarism: "The notion seems to be, 'If you can't work woman suffrage off upon such communities as these half-wild Territories, who ever will take it?' Hence woman suffrage must be in a very bad way indeed." It was "not from the West, but from the East, that women take their fashions."[25] A year later, Samuel Williams Cooper noted a retreat in fourteen locations, including Washington Territory, where "until lately" women could vote "and hold office, serve on juries, and act in other manly capacities." But there, "as well as in Montana and North and South Dakota, the experiment has not proved satisfactory to the electoral majority"; by a "large vote, the woman suffrage amendments were rejected from the constitutions of the applicants for Statehood." This showed "a distinct retrograde movement"; losses provided "unpalatable food" for "hungry innovators."[26] The student-run *Albany Law Journal* faithfully documented events in Washington, publishing pro-suffrage commentary as well as texts of *Bloomer* and other rulings. When Californians applauded the fact that the 1889 attempt in Washington to amend the male-only constitution had been defeated handily, they reprinted voluminous comments from the Portland *Oregonian*, which claimed that "political suffrage for woman" was "without excuse for further existence." Like socialism, it was a "barren ideality."[27]

Elsewhere, journalists offered cautionary tales. The *Washington Post* reprinted a Missouri article chiding critics of universal suffrage for false predictions of radical social derangement in places like Wyoming or Colorado, but also reporting the defeat of a competent female legislative candidate in 1896 because many women voted against her.[28] As late as 1908, the *New York Times* reprinted a communiqué originating in London, written by anti-suffragist Mary Ward, who predicted ongoing defeat for woman suffrage in the emergent West. In her view, suffragism had not only failed, but also had "checked the legitimate development of woman's influence in the spheres which most truly belong to them." In Oregon, she noted, a suffrage amendment had been rejected "within the last two years by a 10,000 majority." Women had protested the burdens that outside agitators sought to impose. Washington, she added, where woman suffrage existed before 1889, refused to grant it when it became a state.[29]

---

[25] "Not from the West, but from the East," *WJ*, August 24, 1889, repr. Boston Transcript.

[26] Samuel Williams Cooper, "The Present Legal Rights of Women," *The American*, October 25, 1890, in Angela Howard et al., eds., *Anti-Feminism in America*, Vol. I: *Opposition to the Women's Movement in the United States, 1848–1929* (New York, 1997), pp. 229–30.

[27] E.g., 38 *Albany Law Journal* 288 (1888–89), reprinting *Bloomer v. Todd*; "Woman Suffrage Defeated in Washington," *LAT*, November 18, 1898, p. 8.

[28] "The Woman Vote, From the St. Louis Globe Democrat," *WP*, November 19, 1900, p. 9

[29] Mary Ward, "Woman's Suffrage Not Inevitable, London," *NYT*, July 12, 1908, p. C-3.

These experiences raise important questions about how other *fin-de-siecle* westerners managed the passage to statehood. The northwest quadrant of the United States entered the union in or around 1889–90; analogous public conversations occurred in Dakota, Idaho, Montana, and Wyoming.[30] Even in much-touted Wyoming, where woman suffrage first appeared in 1869, the record was fraught. For every letter by Governor Hoyt singing women's praises, counterpoints appeared. As early as 1883, Washington, DC, citizens learned that, in Wyoming, exercise of the right to sit on juries had not been a "congenial" duty, and so the "custom" died out. There followed a tasteless but telling story about a drunken husband whose wife, a local constable, had dared to fine him for intemperance – whereupon he punished her with sex, such that she was "unable to get out of bed for two weeks." In 1887, Judge Cary of Wisconsin swore that woman suffrage had been a boon and advanced the notion that woman suffrage "will begin in the Territories and newer States and gradually spread." But in less-noted parts of the speech, he made clear that suffrage was voted out two years after adoption, that jury service also vanished, and that suffragists struggled mightily (with the governor's help) to get the ballot reinstated.[31]

Washingtonians typically did not aim to provide either civics lessons or a developmental template for the rest of modernizing America. But, as they made their way from political adolescence to equality within the union, from linear economic growth to three-dimensional development, and from physical detachment to integration, they modernized and remade citizenship and gender. In particular, Washingtonians and other westerners created and exported important justifications for severing the right to vote from a female citizen's obligation to sit on juries. In the process, the domestic realm absorbed and re-expressed what remained of women's legitimacy and sovereignty; partial but still substantial authority sustained women's agency with private property and access to the ballot, but not the more equivocal and controversial claim to citizens' obligations, now off-limits except on request. Erosions of authority and legitimacy, in turn, permitted the result in *Somerville* v. *State*. Women could hardly be blamed for equivocations. But, in the wrong hands, and given prevailing social and medical theory, women's absence from power-laden sites 'proved' incapacity and unsuitability. As early as 1883, the *New York Times* trumpeted the "failure" of mixed suffrage in Wyoming; "facts" showed that women "can not or will not do away with corruption at the polls" and had refused to fulfill their obligations.[32]

---

[30] New Mexico entered the union roughly at the same moment, but histories, social fissures, and strategies differed substantially.

[31] "Where Women Vote," WP, July 22, 1883. See also "The Women in Politics," ibid., December 23, 1883, assuring readers that woman suffrage had failed in Wyoming, and "Woman Suffrage in Wyoming," WS, April 22, 1887.

[32] "Women as Politicians, The Failure of Woman Suffrage in Wyoming" and untitled editorial, *NYT*, December 9, 1883, pp. 8, 14. See longer discussion of Wyoming's "experiment" and

As information about western reassessments and retreats moved eastward, opponents of electoral reform readily gathered evidence against radical experimentation. Westerners supposedly had learned that equality invited political and social instability – that the burden of republican judgment could be borne safely only by sensible, fully constituted men; women's realm lay in the home, in social service, and (within important limits) in the marketplace. Politically engaged Americans probably did not envision a uniformly progressive west, a beacon of liberalism, a Brave New World to be held at bay until World War I, when politicians capitulated to what had become a state-by-state fait accompli. Rather, Americans in Chicago, Los Angeles, Washington, DC, New York and elsewhere learned from newspapers, journals, and telegraphs that western experiments had gone up in smoke, and made of the fact whatever their political proclivities dictated – a tragedy, an omen, a gift from nature's God. Without the discursive failure of fundamental law (including and especially powerful social conventions) to absorb innovation, Justice Herman Crow might have had a harder time shoe-horning Harriet Somerville's independent women into the categories established in *Muller* v. *Oregon*. But failures and conundrums were more than evident, at home and abroad. In the 1880s, Elizabeth Cady Stanton saw the severity of the rips in social fabric that radical constitutional equality entailed, and probably the power of likely backlashes when gender practices were violated without conversation and education. But the remedy eluded her: She imagined a sex-blind, contract-based civil society where promises were made and broken for cause, not an organic equality mindful of differences.[33]

In Washington, it should be noted, the passage to statehood involved not only a retreat from political equality and the all-important notion of co-equality within the sovereign power but also the discrediting for several generations of liberty-rich alternatives to private and public paternalism. High on the list of losses was the severing of traditional links between the suffrage and the right to be responsible alongside men for decisions about who would be indicted, convicted, and punished for harming the community, although modern Americans have managed to expand jury-duty exemptions, and the sexes occupy increasingly egalitarian ground when they enter courtrooms. But in the 1880s, the decision to detach suffrage (and then a relatively limited "home vote") from ancillary rights in the case of sex bore great symbolic weight: The jury has long been taken to be one of the ways in which neighbors 'spoke' justice. To be present was to be part of the body, to be possessed of legitimacy in the inner sanctum. To the extent that modern Americans no longer value the jury as an expression of community sentiment and associate citizenship more or less with balloting and wealth production, we barely comprehend the

failure, "The Wyoming Experiment," *NYT*, November 19, 1883, p. 4. A rejoinder appeared in *Cheyenne Leader;* see *Washington Post*, November 22, 1883.

[33] For the now-classic discussion of an equality rooted in difference, see Joan Wallach Scott, *Gender and the Politics of History* (New York, 1999, rev. ed.), Chs. 2, 10.

importance to past generations of these practices, losses, and insults. The situation confronting women as they set about distributing cookbooks (or negotiating a longer work day) vividly illustrates the necessity, not of ever-longer lists of rights, but of a watchful, consenting, diverse sovereign. We see, too, the power of customary constitutions, as with disastrous collisions between jury-duty legislation and gender practices. Seattle's Percy Edwards said this in 1912: "The dignity and dry bones of the courts have no use for progressiveness .... Courts are formal, fixed, unresponsive. They are founded on the common law principles which give to the male citizen the right to command and be obeyed. There, it is not surprising that opposition is found in the courts to allowing women to be summoned as jurors."[34]

The discrediting of Washington's close brush with egalitarianism and the consequent remaking of gender entailed an amount of amnesia. As in Hawaii, where 'official' narratives and approved facts came to supplant the experiences and memories of indigenous people,[35] so territorial romance was eclipsed by narratives of timely escapes from unnatural pathways and relationships. In Olympia, editor Miller Murphy offered a detailed enumeration of the many American jurisdictions and foreign lands in which woman suffrage had been adopted over the past eighty years, in response to those who claimed that suffragism had made little progress. Amazingly, he omitted Washington's own experience with democracy. In its place was the claim, in very few words, that suffrage no longer seemed to be as unpopular as in the past. In much the same way, Lilla Spurlock Billings announced that Washington State's women would "lead the way," as if *de novo*. No longer were they "women of the nineteenth century."[36]

✱✱✱✱✱✱✱✱✱✱✱✱✱✱✱✱✱✱✱✱

Many decades later, observers of American constitutional politics typically proceed on the assumption that a mass electoral democracy eclipsed virtually every other instrument of self-rule, to include not only the periodic courthouse gatherings of old, but also and especially juries – in effect repatriating them to a conceptually distinct criminal-justice system. The severance of old associations between sovereign command and representation – epitomized perhaps by the loss of the old right of instruction – probably contributed to the juries' loss of place in the public imagination into the twenty-first century, even as the panels

---

[34] Percy L. Edwards, "Constitutional Obligations and Woman's Citizenship," *Central Law Journal*, Vol. 75, No. 244 (1912), pp. 247–8.

[35] Rona Tamiko Halualani, *In the Name of Hawaiians: Native Identities and Cultural Politics* (Minneapolis, MN, 2002), esp. Ch. 5.

[36] "Progress of Equal Suffrage," *WS*, May 14, 1909, p. 2. See also editorial, "Progress of Impartial Suffrage," ibid., April 30, 1909, p. 2, about the politics of suffragism in Europe and "our own country," with no mention of the territorial experience. For Billings's statement, see "Suffrage," ibid., February 18, 1910; women were "leaving the 19th century behind." But see also "How Washington Women Were Tricked Out of Their Right to Vote," *SP*, July 8, 1910, p. 5.

have become more diverse. In the 1880s, however, and for better or worse, old ideas persisted, particularly in isolated communities, where woman suffrage or equal suffrage called to mind a bundle of rights and duties which together comprised republican citizenship. In the words of a Pennsylvania lawyer a few decades earlier, indictment and trial by one's peers spoke not only to procedural due process, but also to individual and communal self-rule. "Take from [an American] the right of trial by jury," he warned, "and you dispossess him of the most valuable of his political privileges. You remove the corner stone of ... the institutions of his country, and ... involve the whole in a common ruin."[37] In 1881, a writer for the *Daily Oregonian* said much the same thing in an otherwise scathing review of old English practices: "Among the list of those cast-off garments which we have outgrown we cannot find the trial by jury. ... [T]he people hug the trial by jury to the heart .... They regard it as a precious and peculiar right; and perhaps there is no other constitutional privilege they enjoy of which they are more proud and for which they would more quickly fight. And why? The ... right of trial by jury brings the people in their own proper persons upon the carpet of authority and power. *It is a civil institute that brings the sovereign into action at first hand.*" Into the twentieth century, access to an unbundled right to vote increasingly came to be synonymous with democratization, in academic circles and elsewhere. But, in 1886, Washington Territory's Eugene Semple still could say this about the republic's main bulwarks against tyranny: "The Ballot. The Jury. The writ of habeas corpus. These constitute the Trinity of Liberty."[38]

[37] Professor B. Tucker of Pennsylvania, 1834, quoted in Stacy Pratt McDermott, *The Jury in Lincoln's America* (Athens, GA, 2012), p. 10.
[38] Editorial, *OR*, October 20, 1881, emphasis added; speech draft [Vancouver], March 8, 1886, Papers of Eugene Semple, Box 14, Folder 12, UWSC.

Afterword: A bibliographic commentary

Gender Remade emerged in the company of scholars working in vineyards with indistinct, often overlapping borders. This essay does not include a number of works cited in footnotes, and, with some exceptions, it omits the voluminous article literature. Nor should it be read as an exhaustive compilation of potentially relevant work. Rather, it suggests entry points for readers seeking information or fresh vantage points. The essay is organized roughly by topic; its order says nothing about relative importance.

The book has been enriched by cross-disciplinary talk about the many ways that Americans forge communities. Feminist theory and gender studies provided scaffolding; for central works, see below. But anthropologists also contributed fundamentally to the book's interpretive apparatus. Chief among them is Clifford Geertz – notably, but not only, the essays collected in *Available Light: Anthropological Reflections on Philosophical Topics* (Princeton, NJ, 2000). See also Victor Turner's evocation of civic dramas, as in courtrooms or ritualized passages from one civil state to another, in *Dramas, Fields, and Metaphors: Symbolic Action in Human Society* (Ithaca, NY, 1974). From an adjacent realm, Pierre Bourdieu's *Outline of a Theory of Practice* (New York, 1977) and other works offer ways to connect formal structures to daily life. Valuable as well are the essays collected in Austin Sarat et al., eds., *Law in Everyday Life* (Ann Arbor, MI, 1995). And, while Benedict Anderson's ideas are well known, the idea of calling into existence one's own community apart from state action still has great force; see *Imagined Communities* (New York, 1991, Verso repr.).

While constitutions and statutes purport to create, re-create, and order public spaces, they operate in tandem with other instrumentalities. Notwithstanding apt criticism from feminists, Jürgen Habermas made it possible to appreciate the role of public prints in forging new, if persistently gendered and racialized (and therefore hierarchical), political communities; see *The Structural Transformation of the Public Sphere* (Cambridge, MA, 1991), and *Theory of Communicative Action, Volume 1: Reason and the Rationalization of Society* (Boston, MA, 1983). See also Habermas and William Rehg, *Between Facts and Norms: Contributions to a Discourse Theory of Law and Democracy* (Cambridge, MA, 1998); Michael Warner, *The Letters of the Republic: Publication and the Public Sphere in Eighteenth-Century America* (Cambridge, MA, 1992), and *Publics and Counterpublics* (Cambridge, MA, 2005). On western newspapers, see Patricia Nelson Limerick, "Making the Most of Words," in William Cronon et al., eds., *Under an Open Sky: Rethinking America's Western Past* (New York, 1992), and Edmond Meany, *Newspapers of Washington Territory,* http://journals.lib.washington.edu/index.php.WHQ. On relations between stories and civic identity, see Priscilla Wale, *Constituting Americans: Cultural Anxiety and Narrative Form* (Winston-Salem, NC, 1995).

This book will not resolve decades of disagreement about law's instrumentalism, constitutive powers, or autonomy – or, for that matter, what legal and constitutional historians ought to take as their subjects. But, on law's necessarily social character, see Christopher Tomlins, "How Autonomous Is Law?" *Annual Reviews in Law and Social Science,* Vol. 3 (2007), pp. 45–68. See also George Steinmetz, ed., *State/Culture: State-Formation After the Cultural Turn* (Ithaca, NY, 1999). On the power of informal constitutions, see Hendrick Hartog's landmark essay, "A Constitution of Aspiration and the 'Rights That Belong to Us All,'" *Journal of American History,* Vol. 74, No. 3 (1987), pp. 1013–34. Robert Gordon's vintage and therefore little remarked "Introduction: J. Willard Hurst and the Common Law Tradition in American Legal Historiography," *Law and Society Review,* Vol. 10, No. 1 (1975), pp. 9–55, forced me and many others to rethink the subject of legal history. See as well Christopher Tomlins and Bruce Mann, eds., *The Many Legalities of Early America* (Chapel Hill, NC, 2001), which refashions the concept of legalities. And, for a provocative study of public memory and forgetting, see Thomas J. Brown, ed., *Reconstructions: New Perspectives on the Postbellum United States* (New York, 2008), esp. Ch. 8, "Civil War Remembrance as Reconstruction."

Accounts of popular constitutionalism have proliferated since the 1990s, as part of a defense of judicial review and popular authorization of government. For substantial evidence of the centrality and force of popular sovereignty and, to some extent, binding customs, see, as leading examples, Bruce Ackerman, *We the People,* Vol. I, Foundations (Cambridge, MA, 1993); Akhil Reed Amar, *America's Unwritten Constitution* (New York, 2012); and especially Larry Kramer, *The People Themselves: Popular Constitutionalism and Judicial Review* (New York, 2005).

HOW THE WEST BECAME LESS STRANGE

Isolated places afford a degree of freedom from cultural inheritances; particularly in capitalist societies, they also generate reconsiderations and retreat. For the broader western story, see Clyde Milner et al., *Oxford History of the American West* (New York, 1996); for a sweeping account of America's retreat from strangeness, see Christopher Tomlins, *Freedom Bound: Law, Labor, and Civic Identity in Colonizing English America, 1580–1865* (New York, 2010). Elsewhere, whether explicitly or implicitly, scholars labor in the shadow of Frederick Jackson Turner's seminal essay, *The Significance of the Frontier in American History*, available in a myriad of editions. See, e.g., Henry Nash Smith's still-controversial *Virgin Land* (Cambridge, MA, 2007, repr.), and John Mack Faragher, *Re-reading Frederick Jackson Turner* (New Haven, CT, 1999). Increasingly, western, environmental, and intellectual history meet on the ground of culture formation – as with Steven Aron's *How the West Was Lost* (Baltimore, MD, 1999) and *American Confluence* (Bloomington, IN, 2009), which speak to the incremental loss of cultural distinctiveness; Jon Gjerde, *The Minds of the West: Ethnocultural Evolution in the Rural Middle West, 1830–1917* (Chapel Hill, NC, 1997); and David Wrobel's *Promised Lands: Promotion, Memory, and the Creation of the American West* (Lawrence, KS, 2002), which explores the consequences of boosterism for cultural distinctiveness and memory.

Since at least the late 1880s, imaginative scholarship has disrupted regional and national master narratives. See Patricia Nelson Limerick's foundation work, *Legacy of Conquest: The Unbroken Past of the American West* (New York, 1987), and Limerick et al., eds., *Trails: Toward a New Western History* (Lawrence, KS, 1991). Others carried the ball – e.g., William Cronon et al., eds., *Under an Open Sky: Rethinking America's Western Past* (New York, 1992); Richard White, *"It's Your Misfortune and None of My Own": A New History of the American West* (Norman, OK, 1993); Valerie J. Matsumoto et al., eds., *Over the Edge: Remapping the American West* (Berkeley, CA, 1999); and Frieda Knobloch, *The Culture of Wilderness: Agriculture as Colonization in the American West* (Chapel Hill, NC, 1996). For uncommon sensitivity to biological differences, see Marian Perales, *Writing the Range: Race, Class and Culture in the Women's West* (Norman, OK, 1997). Nature comes to the fore in Donald Worster, *Under Western Skies: Nature and History in the American West* (New York, 1994). Robert Slotkin's trilogy, including *Regeneration through Violence* (Tulsa, OK, 2000), *The Fatal Environment* (Tulsa, OK, 1998), and *Gunfighter Nation* (Tulsa, OK, 1998), encompasses western developments from 1600 to the present. But see also Robert Hine, *The American West: A New Interpretive History* (New Haven, CT, 2000); and, for background, Anne F. Hyde, *Empire, Nations, and Families: A New History of the North American West, 1800–1860* (Ecco reprint, 2012). On continental rail lines as darkly modernizing forces, see Richard White, *Railroaded: The Transcontinentals and the Making of Modern America* (New York, 2012).

Post–Civil War legal developments in the west often diverged from easterly practices. On the west generally, see Gordon M. Bakken's contributions – among them, *The Development of Law on the Rocky Mountain Frontier: Civil*

Law and Society, 1850–1912 (Westport, CT, 1983); *Hers, His, and Theirs: Community Property Law in Spain and Texas* (Lubbock, TX, 2010); *Law in the Western U.S.* (Norman, OK, 2001); *Rocky Mountain Constitution Making, 1850–1912* (Westport, CT, 1987); *The Development of Law on the Rocky Mountain Frontier, 1850–1912* (Westport, CT, 1983); *The Development of Law in Frontier California* (Westport, CT, 1985); and *The American West*, Vol. 3, The Gendered West (New York, 2001). See also analyses of new legalities in the accident-prone west: John Fabian Witt, *The Accidental Republic* (Cambridge, MA, 2006), on workers' compensation and industrial accidents; Barbara Welke, *Recasting American Liberty: Gender, Race, Law and the Railroad Revolution, 1865–1920* (New York, 2001); and Jonathan Levy, *Freaks of Fortune: The Emerging World of Capitalism and Risk in America* (Cambridge, MA, 2012). Still valuable on law's migration are Robert Dykstra, *The Cattle Towns* (Lincoln, NE, 1983); John P. Reid's *Law of the Elephant: Property and Social Behavior on the Overland Trail* (San Marino, CA, 1997); and John McLaren et al., *Law for the Elephant, Law for the Beaver: Essays in the Legal History of the North American West* (Regina, 1992).

The New Northwest has attracted its own historians. Carlos Arnaldo Schwantes provides a particularly fine regional account, *The Pacific Northwest: An Interpretive History*, rev. ed. (Lincoln, NE, 1996). Additional information, much of it specific to Washington, can be found in Robert E. Ficken's *Washington Territory* (Pullman, WA, 2002); Mary W. Avery's classic, *Washington: A History of the Evergreen State* (Seattle, WA, 1965); and an array of specialized or thematic works – e.g., D. W. Meinig, *The Great Columbia Plain* (Seattle, WA, 1968); Edwin Bingham and Glen Love, eds., *Northwest Perspectives: Essays on the Culture of the Pacific Northwest* (Seattle, WA, 1979); Dorothy Johansen and Charles Gates, *Empire of the Columbia* (New York, 1967); and a valuable older collection, David Brewster and David Buerge, eds., *Washingtonians: A Biographical Portrait of the State* (Seattle, WA, 1879). Charles H. Sheldon provides information about territorial and state judges in *The Washington High Bench: A Biographical History of the State Supreme Court, 1889–1991* (Pullman, WA, 1992), and *A Century of Judging: A Political History of the Washington Supreme Court* (Seattle, WA, 1988). See also Brad Asher, *Beyond the Reservation: Indians, Settlers, and the Law in Washington Territory, 1857–1889* (Norman, OK, 1999), which includes much more than its title suggests.

For parallel developments in Dakota, begin with Norman K. Risjord, *Dakota: The Story of the Northern Plains* (Lincoln, NE, 2013) and John K. Lauck et al., eds., *The Plains Political Tradition: Essays on South Dakota Political Traditions* (Pierre, SD, 2011). Historians of other territories that entered the union in the 1880s–90s often treat the statehood era, but comparative scholarship has yet to appear. New Mexico, for instance, lost its contemporaneous statehood campaign; see Robert W. Larson, *New Mexico's*

Quest for Statehood, 1846–1912 (Albuquerque, NM, 1968) and a reprint of L. Bradford Prince's contemporary *New Mexico's Struggle for Statehood* (Santa Fe, NM, 2010). For early public-policy decisions on the Northwestern border, see Tony Freyer and Lyndsay Campbell, eds., *Freedom's Conditions in the U.S. Canadian Borderlands in the Age of Emancipation* (Durham, NC, 2011).

GENDER AND RACE

Feminist practices radically alter scholarship. What follows is the tip of the proverbial iceberg. On gender as a category of analysis, see Joan Wallach Scott's transformative *Gender and the Politics of History* (New York, 1999), esp. Chs. 2, 3, and 10. See also Carol Pateman, *The Sexual Contract* (Stanford, CA, 1988), her less well known *Participation and Democratic Theory* (New York, 1970), and *The Disorder of Women* (Stanford, CA, 1989). For one particularly effective use of the concept of gender chaos, see Lori Ginsburg, "Pernicious Heresies ...," in Alison Parker and Stephanie Cole, *Women and the Unstable State in Nineteenth-Century America* (College Station, TX, 2000), pp. 139–61.

Washington women's loss of place after 1888 was anything but novel. For early decisions against sex equality, see Linda Kerber, *No Constitutional Right to Be Ladies* (New York, 1998), especially the chapter on *Martin v. Massachusetts*, and Kerber, *Women of the Republic: Intellect and Ideology in Revolutionary America* (Chapel Hill, NC, 1997); Mary Beth Norton, *Liberty's Daughters: The Revolutionary Experience of American Women, 1750–1800* (Boston, MA, 1980); and Ronald Hoffman et al., eds., *Women in the Age of the American Revolution* (Charlottesville, VA, 1989). On the American Civil War's valorization of male citizenship, see Faye Dudden, *Fighting Chance: The Struggle over Woman Suffrage and Black Suffrage in Reconstruction America* (New York, 2011); Laura F. Edwards, *Gendered Strife and Confusion: The Political Culture of Reconstruction* (Chicago, IL, 1997); Catherine Clinton, *Divided Houses: Gender and the Civil War* (New York, 1992) and *Battle Scars* (New York, 2006); and Ellen DuBois, *Woman Suffrage and Women's Rights* (New York, 1998). On the French Revolution, see Olwen Hufton, *Women and the Limits of Citizenship in the French Revolution* (Toronto, 1999); Joan Landes, *Women and the Public Sphere in the Age of the French Revolution* (Ithaca, NY, 1988); Dominique Dogineau and Katherine Streip, eds., *The Women of Paris and the French Revolution* (Berkeley, CA, 1998); and Sara Elson Melzer and Leslie W. Rabine, *Rebel Daughters: Women and the French Revolution* (Berkeley, CA, 1992).

In modernizing America, medical and social sciences provided seemingly indisputable ways to distinguish between and characterize sexes and races. See, for openers, Mike Hawkins, *Social Darwinism in European and American Thought, 1860–1945* (New York, 1997) and Carroll Smith-Rosenberg's now-classic *Disorderly Conduct: Visions of Gender in Victorian America* (New York, 1985), which lays bare the consequences of medicalized social theory. See also Thomas Haskell, *The Emergence of Professional Social Science* (Baltimore, MD, 2000); Dorothy Ross, *The Origins of American Social Science* (New York, 1992, repr. ed.); Charles Rosenberg, *No Other Gods: On Science and American Social Thought* (Baltimore, MD, 1997); and W. F. Bynum, *Science and the Practice of Medicine in the Nineteenth Century* (New York, 1994). For medical science in the case of a western woman accused of murder, see Carole Haber, *The Trials of Laura Fair: Sex, Murder and Insanity in the Victorian West* (Chapel Hill, NC, 2013). On women's bodies and sensationalism in public culture, see Alison Piepmeier, *Out in Public: Configurations of Women's Bodies in Nineteenth-Century America* (Chapel Hill, NC, 2004).

Shifting views of manhood form an essential part of the American and western story. Most generally, see E. Anthony Rotundo, *American Manhood: Transformations in Masculinity from the Revolution to the Modern Era* (New York, 1994); Michael Kimmel, *Manhood in America: A Cultural History* (New York, 2011); and R. W. Connell's classic, *Masculinities* (Berkeley, CA, 2005, repr.). On late Victorian manhood and race, see Gail Bederman, *Manliness and Civilization: A Cultural History of Gender and Race in the United States, 1880–1917* (Chicago, IL, 1995); Dana D. Nelson, *National Manhood: Capitalist Citizenship and the Imagined Fraternity of White Men* (Durham, NC, 1998); and Mathhew G. Hannah, *Governmentality and the Mastery of Territory in Nineteenth-Century America* (New York, 2000). For late-Victorian masculinity, see as well David T. Beito, *From Mutual Aid to the Welfare State: Fraternal Societies and Social Services, 1890–1967* (Chapel Hill, NC, 1999); Kevin Murphy, *Political Manhood: Red Bloods, Mollycoddles, and the Politics of Progressive Era Reform* (New York, 2010); Marc C. Carnes, *Secret Ritual and Manhood in Victorian America* (New Haven, CT, 1991). Judy Hikey, *Character Is Capital: Success Manuals and Manhood in Gilded Age America* (Chapel Hill, NC, 1967), addresses male uncertainties in the late nineteenth century.

In Washington, "race" denoted Asians and indigenous people first, then African Americans. The long history of encounters between whites and Indians cannot be addressed here. But shifting conceptions of race have occupied center stage in new western and environmental histories, cited earlier. For additional, innovative writing about discourses of race, paternalism, and colonialism in constructions of native peoples, see Cathleen D. Cahill, *Federal Fathers and Mothers: A Social History of the United States Indian Service, 1869–1933* (Chapel Hill, NC, 2011) as well as Jane E. Simonsen, *Making Home Work: Domesticity and Native American Assimilation in the American West, 1860–1919* (Chapel Hill, NC, 2006). Simonson includes a spectacular bibliography. On marriage and Indians, see Catherine J. Denial, *Making Marriage: Husbands, Wives and the American State in Dakota and Ojibwe Country* (St. Paul, MN, 2013). For blacks in Washington's main city, see Quintard Taylor, *The Forging of a Black*

Community: Seattle's Central District from 1870 Through the Civil Rights Era (Seattle, WA, 1994). On white-Chinese conflict, see generally Doris Chan, *The Chinese in America: A Narrative History* (New York, 2004). But see also Erika Lee, *At America's Gate: Chinese Immigration During the Exclusion Era, 1882–1943* (Chapel Hill, NC, 2007), and Andrew Gyory, *Closing the Gate: Race, Politics and the Chinese Exclusion Act* (Chapel Hill, NC, 1998), contending that labor did not contribute mightily to adoption of the act. On the Chinese and American law, see Lucy Salyer, *Laws Harsh as Tigers: Chinese Immigrants and the Shaping of Modern Immigration Law* (Chapel Hill, NC, 1995). On attempts to model Asian 'concubines' into virtuous women, see Peggy Pascoe, "Gender Systems in Conflict: The Marriages of Mission-Educated Chinese American Women, 1874–1939," in Ellen Carol DuBois and Vicki Ruiz, eds., *Unequal Sisters: A Multi-Cultural Reader in U.S. Women's History* (New York, 1990), and *Relations of Rescue: The Search for Female Moral Authority in the American West, 1874–1939* (New York, 1990). For a brilliant analysis of the multiple (e.g., Asian, Filipino, black) racial constructs at the heart of miscegenation law, see Pascoe, *What Comes Naturally: Miscegenation Law and the Making of Race in America* (New York, 2010). On legal-spatial strategies in a mixed-race culture, see Renisa Mawani, *Colonial Proximities: Crossracial Encounters and Juridical Truths in British Columbia, 1871–1921* (Vancouver, BC, 2009). For trans-national debasement of South Asian populations, in part because they destabilized gender ascriptions, see Nayan Shah, *Stranger Intimacy: Contesting Race, Sexuality, and the Law in the North American West* (Berkeley, CA, 2011). Finally, and most generally, see Mark Stuart Weiner, *Americans Without Law: The Racial Boundaries of Citizenship* (New York, 2006).

WORKERS AND THE WORKPLACE

Scholars have shown that isolation breeds innovation, struggle, and, with capitalist advances, predictable retreats, in the workplace and elsewhere. The most sweeping account of discursive shifts into the nineteenth century is Tomlins, *Freedom Bound*. For other explorations of declension, see, e.g., Cornelia Hughes Dayton, *Women at the Bar: Gender, Law, and Society in Connecticut, 1639–1789* (Chapel Hill, NC, 1995), tracing women's disappearance from early courtrooms, and Laura Edwards, *The People and Their Peace: Legal Culture and the Transformation of Inequality in the Post-Revolutionary South* (Chapel Hill, NC, 2009). For organized labor's victories and failures, see David Montgomery's *The Fall of the House of Labor: The Workplace, the State, and American Labor Activism, 1865–1925* (New York, 1980). Compare this paradigm with Melvyn Dubofsky, *Industrialism and the American Worker, 1865–1920* (New York, 1996); Victoria C. Hattam, *Labor Visions and State Power: The Origins of Business Unionism in the United States*

(Princeton, NJ, 1993); and Philip Dray, *There Is Power in a Union: The Epic Story of Labor in America* (New York, 2011).

Legal discourses structured union formation and reformation; they also shaped decisions to valorize and empower white men. On English and American labor law, see Christopher Tomlins, *Law, Labor, and Ideology in the Early American Republic* (New York, 1993), esp. Part 3; Robert Steinfeld, *The Invention of Free Labor: The Employment Relation in England and American Law, 1350–1870* (Chapel Hill, NC, 2002); Tomlins, *The State and the Unions* (New York, 1985); William Forbath, *Law and the Shaping of the American Labor Movement* (Cambridge, MA, 1991). For unions and suffragism in Seattle, see John C. Putman, *Class and Gender Politics in Progressive-Era Seattle* (Reno, NV, 2008).

Throughout the south and west, agrarian societies and general-membership unions organized communities as well as workplaces. On the Knights of Labor, see Leon Fink, *Workingmen's Democracy: The Knights of Labor and American Politics* (Urbana, IL, 1983) and Robert Weir's culturally sensitive *Beyond Labor's Veil: The Culture of the Knights of Labor* (University Park, PA, 1996). Treatments of Populism move from rejections of modernity through radical anti-capitalism to forward-looking reform; see Richard Hofstadter's dismissive treatment in *The American Political Tradition and the Men Who Made It*, rev. ed. (New York, 1989), then Michael Kazin, *The Populist Persuasion*, rev. ed. (Ithaca, 1998) and Lawrence Goodwyn's abridgment, *The Populist Moment* (New York, 1978); and finally Charles Postel, *The Populist Vision* (New York, 2009). Thomas W. Riddle analyzes territorial and state Populism, *The Old Radicalism: John R. Rogers and the Populist Movement in Washington* (New York, 1991). On the role of women in Populism and modern politics, see Michael Lewis Goldberg, *An Army of Women: Gender and Politics in Gilded Age Kansas* (Baltimore, MD, 1997). Agrarian reformers succeeded most fully as policy shapers rather than as bureaucrats; see Elizabeth Sanders, *Roots of Reform: Farmers, Workers, and the American State, 1877–1917* (Chicago, IL, 1999).

Progressive constitutionalism framed discussions of workplace regulation and agency. Michael Les Benedict, "Laissez-Faire and Liberty," *Law and History Review*, Vol. 3 (Fall 1983), pp. 295–331 rejects the idea that *laissez-faireism* was merely reactionary. On liberty of contract, see Paul Kens, *Judicial Power and Reform Politics: The Anatomy of Lochner v. New York* (Lawrence, KS, 1990), abridged as *Lochner v. New York: Economic Regulation on Trial* (Lawrence, KS, 1998). For reconsideration, see Howard Gillman, *The Constitution Besieged: The Rise and Demise of Lochner Era Police Powers Jurisprudence* (Durham, NC, 1992), and David E. Bernstein, *Rehabilitating Lochner* (Chicago, IL, 2011). For a recasting of relations between early and later protectionism, see Claudio J. Katz, "Protective Labor Legislation in the Courts: Substantive Due Process and Fairness in the Progressive Era," *Law and History Review*, Vol. 31, No. 2 (May 2013), pp. 275–324. On women and

Muller, see the introduction to Nancy Woloch, *Muller* v. *Oregon: A Brief History with Documents* (New York, 1996). For paternalism, maternalism, and economic citizenship generally, see (for a few examples) Noralee Frankel and Nancy Dye, eds., *Gender, Class, Race and Reform in the Progressive Era* (Lexington, KY, 1991); Alice Kessler-Harris, *In Pursuit of Equity: Women, Men, and the Quest for Economic Citizenship in 20th Century America* (New York, 2003); Molly Ladd-Taylor, *Mother-Work: Women, Child Welfare, and the State, 1890–1930* (Chicago, IL, 1995) and Seth Koyen and Sonja Michel, eds., *Mothers of a New World: Maternalist Politics and the Origins of Welfare States* (New York, 1995). For the global picture, see Ulla Wikander et al., eds., *Protecting Women: Labor Legislation in Europe, the United States, and Australia, 1880–1920* (Chicago, IL, 1995). For the aftermath, see, e.g., Robyn Muncy, *Creating a Female Dominion in American Reform, 1890–1935* (New York, 1994); Julie Novkov, *Constituting Workers, Protecting Women: Gender, Law, and Labor in the Progressive Era and New Deal Years* (Ann Arbor, MI, 2001), and Gwendolyn Mink, *The Wages of Motherhood: Inequality in the Welfare State, 1917–1942* (Ithaca, NY, 1996). For the eight-hour movement, see Montgomery, *Fall of the House of Labor*, and Montgomery, *Citizen Worker* (New York, 1995). William Mirola, *Redeeming Time: Protestantism and Chicago's Eight-Hour Movement, 1866–1912* (Chicago, IL, 2014), ties shorter days to health; a kindred study is Roy Rosenzweig, *Eight Hours for What We Will: Workers and Leisure in an Industrial City, 1870–1920* (New York, 1983).

FEMINISM AND RIGHTS

The question of whether rights have to be identical to be "equal" – indeed, whether rights regimes will ever generate sex equality – has yet to be resolved. But see Carol Smart, *Feminism and the Power of Law* (New York, 1989), esp. Ch. 7, and Elizabeth Kingdom, *What's Wrong with Rights?* (Edinburgh, Scotland, 1992). On needs-based justice, Martha Minow essential work is *Making All the Difference: Inclusion, Exclusion, and American Law* (Ithaca, NY, 1991). For legal separatism and the presumed impossibility of justice otherwise, see Catharine MacKinnon, *Toward a Feminist Jurisprudence* (Cambridge, MA, 1991). Sally J. Kenney argues for male–female collaboration as a way to end discriminatory practices gradually in *Gender and Justice: Why Women in the Judiciary Really Matter* (New York, 2013); Iris Marion Young, *Justice and the Politics of Difference* (Princeton, NJ, 2011) offers ways to think about the failure of distributive justice and re-impositions of homogeneity in democracies.

Accounts of American suffragism fill bookshelves. For the movement in general, see Ellen DuBois, *Feminism and Suffrage* (Ithaca, NY, 1999) and DuBois, *Woman Suffrage and Women's Rights* (New York, 1998); Suzanne Marilley, *Woman Suffrage and the Origins of Liberal Feminism in the United States, 1820–1920* (Cambridge, MA, 1996); Aileen Kraditor, *Means and Ends in American Abolitionism* (Chicago, IL, 1976), Ch. 3, "The Woman Question"; Kraditor, *Ideas of the Woman Suffrage Movement* (New York, 1981); Marjorie Spruill Wheeler, *One Woman, One Vote: Rediscovering the Women's Suffrage Movement* (Troutdale, OR, 1995); Steven Buechler, *The Transformation of the Woman Suffrage Movement: The Case of Illinois, 1850–1920* (New Brunswick, NJ, 1986); Sara Hunter Graham, *Woman Suffrage and the New Democracy* (New Haven, CT, 1996); Jean Baker, ed., *Votes for Women: The Struggle for Suffrage Revisited* (New York, 2002); and Lee Ann Banaszak, *Why Movements Succeed or Fail* (Princeton, NJ, 1996). On women's relationship to the state generally, see Sara M. Evans, "Women's History and Political Theory: Toward a Feminist Approach to Public Life," in Nancy Hewitt and Suzanne Lebsock, eds., *Visible Women: New Essays on American Activism* (Champaign-Urbana, IL, 1993), pp. 119–39. On shifting relations between home and public life, see Paula Baker, "The Domestication of Politics: Women and American Political Society, 1780–1920," *American Historical Review*, Vol. 89, No. 3 (1984), pp. 620–47. On anti-suffragists' introduction of social theory, see Suzanne Lebsock, "Woman Suffrage and White Supremacy ...," in Nancy Hewitt and Suzanne Lebsock, eds., *Visible Women: New Essays on American Activism* (Champaign-Urbana, IL, 1993).

Western suffragism sometimes merges seamlessly with the history of western borderlands. For example, see Cathy Luchetti, *Women of the West* (New York, 2001); Paula Petrik, *No Step Backward* (Boise, MT, 1987); Julie Jeffrey, *Frontier Women*, rev. ed. (New York, 1998); Genevieve McBride, *On Wisconsin Women* (Madison, 1993); and Rebecca Mead, *How the Vote Was Won in the Western United States, 1868–1914* (New York, 2006). See also diaries and travel accounts; e.g., Ruth Barnes Moynihan et al., *So Much to Be Done: Women Settlers on the Mining and Ranching Frontier* (Lincoln, NE, 1998); Joanna Statton, *Pioneer Women: Voices from the Kansas Frontier* (New York, 1982); Linda Peavy and Ursula Smith, *Pioneer Women: Lives of Women on the Frontier* (Norman, OK, 1998); Sandra Myers, *Westering Women and the Frontier Experience, 1800–1915* (Albuquerque, NM, 1982); Lillian Schlissel, *Women's Diaries of the Westward Journey* (New York, 2004); and Susan Armitage and Elizabeth Jameson, *The Women's West* (Norman, OK, 1987). See also Marian Perales et al., eds., *Writing the Range: Race, Class and Culture in the Women's West* (Norman, OK, 1997).

On suffragism in the west, see Rebecca Mead, *How the Vote Was Won: Woman Suffrage in the Western United States, 1868–1914* (New York, 2004). For purposes of comparison with other regions, see Beverly Beeton, *Women Vote in the West: The Woman Suffrage Movement, 1869–1896* (New York, 1980); McBride, *On Wisconsin Women*, op cit.; Ruth Barnes Moynihan, *Rebel for Rights: Abigail Scott Duniway* (New Haven, CT, 1983); Marjorie Spruill Wheeler, *Votes for Women: The Woman Suffrage Movement in Tennessee, the South, and the Nation* (Knoxville, TN, 1995); and Wheeler, *New Women of the New South* (New York, 1993). On blacks, see Ann Gordon et al., eds., *African American Women and the Vote, 1837–1965* (Amherst, MA, 1997) and Rosalyn Terborg-Penn, *African-American Women in the Struggle for the Vote, 1850–1920* (Bloomington, IN, 1998). On anti-suffragism, see Angela Howard et al., eds., *Antifeminism in America: A Collection of Readings from the Literature of the Opponents to U.S. Feminism, 1848 to the Present* (New York, 1997), in three volumes; and Susan Marshall, *Splintered Sisterhood: Gender and Class in the Campaign Against Woman Suffrage* (Madison, WI, 1997). Modern constitutional amendments are beyond the scope of this study, but see, as entry points, Eleanor Clift, *Founding Sisters and the Nineteenth Amendment* (New York, 2003) and relevant chapters in David Kyvig, *Explicit and Authentic Acts: Amending the U.S. Constitution, 1776–1995* (Lawrence, KS, 1996). On ERA, see Susan Becker, *Origins of the Equal Rights Amendment: American Feminism Between the Wars* (Westport, CT, 1981).

Washington's women followed their own path. See, e.g., Shanna Stevenson's illustrated *Women's Votes, Women's Voice: The Campaign for Equal Rights in Washington* (Tacoma, WA, 2009), and Karen J. Blair's valuable anthology, *Women in Pacific Northwest History*, rev. ed. (Seattle, 2001), which includes essays about women of color and a promising study by Maureen Weiner Greenwald, "Working-Class Feminism and the Family-Wage Ideal," which picks up the story at World War I. On Abigail Duniway's career, see Ruth Barnes Moynihan, *Rebel for Rights: Abigail Scott Duniway* (New Haven, CT, 1983), or Duniway's self-aggrandizing autobiography, *Path Breaking ...* (Portland, OR, 1914). In late life, Duniway wrote a formulaic novel, *From the West to the West* (Chicago, IL, 1905, repr. Bibliolife), in which characters embody critiques of common-law marriage and the treatment of Indian women ("squaw wives"). On Emma Smith DeVoe, see Jennifer M. Ross-Nazzal, *Winning the West for Women: The Life of Suffragist Emma Smith DeVoe* (Seattle, WA, 2011). See also Mary Barmeyer O'Brien's undocumented *May: The Hard-Rock Life of Pioneer May Arkwright Hutton* (Guilford, CT, and Helena, MT, 2013) and James W. Montgomery's *Liberated Woman: A Life of May Arkwright Hutton* (Fairfield, WA, 1985). The best account of the club movement is Karen Blair, *The Clubwoman as Feminist: True Womanhood Redefined, 1868–1914* (New York, 1980). See also Nelson A. Ault, "The Earnest Ladies: The Walla Walla Woman's Club and the Equal Suffrage League of 1886–1889," *Pacific Northwest Quarterly*, Vol. 42, No. 2 (April 1951), pp. 123–37 and Sandra Haarsager, *Organized Womanhood: Cultural Politics in the Pacific Northwest, 1840–1920* (Norman, OK, 1997), which emphasizes the statehood era. See also Blair's dated but still useful *Northwest Women: An Annotated Bibliography of Oregon and Washington Women, 1787–1970* (Pullman, WA, 1997). Finally, see Clarence Bagley, "The Mercer Immigration: Two Cargoes of Maidens for the Sound Country," *Quarterly of the Oregon Historical Society* (March 1904). For women and bar admission, see Mary Jane Mossman, *The First Women Lawyers* (Portland, OR, 2006) and

Jill Norgren, *Rebels at the Bar* (New York, 2013), which includes information about Washington's women.

Access to and agency with property as well as with adequate wages dramatically improved women's situation. On economic citizenship and the "family wage," see Alice Kessler Harris, *In Pursuit of Equity,* op cit.; *Out to Work* (New York, expanded ed., 2003); and *A Woman's Wage* (Lexington, KY, 1991). See also Leslie Woodcock Tentler, *Wage-Earning Women: Industrial Work and Family Life in the U.S., 1900–1930* (New York, 1982). The classic studies of early American improvements in married women's situation include Marylynn Salmon, *Women and the Law of Property in Early America* (Chapel Hill, NC, 1986); Peggy Rabkin, *Fathers to Daughters: The Legal Foundations of Female Emancipation* (Westport, CT, 1980); Norma Basch, *In the Eyes of the Law: Married Women's Property in Nineteenth-Century New York* (Ithaca, NY, 1982), and an older article, "Invisible Women: The Legal Fiction of Marital Unity in 19th-century America," *Feminist Studies,* Vol. 5 (Summer 1979), pp. 346–66. Kathleen Sullivan interrogates the idea that the common law of marriage was women's sole enemy or that grants of right would equalize the sexes in *Women's Rights Discourse in Nineteenth Century America* (Baltimore, MD, 2007). On earnings, contractualism, and self-construction, see Amy Dru Stanley, *From Bondage to Contract: Wage Labor, Marriage, and the Market in the Age of Slave Emancipation* (New York, 1998). On the abolition of dower and curtesy, see Michael Grossberg, *Governing the Hearth: Law and the Family in Nineteenth-Century America* (Chapel Hill, NC, 1988). On wives' right to a nationality and separate domicile, see, e.g., Candice Bredbenner, *A Nationality of Her Own: Women, Marriage, and the Law of Citizenship* (Berkeley, CA, 1998). See also the bibliographic essay in Sandra VanBurkleo, *"Belonging to the World": Women's Rights and American Constitutional Culture* (New York, 2001).

CITIZENS' OBLIGATIONS AND JURY DUTY

On the all-important question of citizens' (and women's) obligations, see Kerber, *No Constitutional Right to Be Ladies,* which threw down the gauntlet on gender's operation as women struggle to experience citizenship. For women's obligation to home and republican motherhood, see Kerber, "The Republican Mother: Women and the Enlightenment – An American Perspective," *American Quarterly,* Vol. 28, No. 2 (Summer 1976), pp. 187–205, and, for a fuller account, Kerber, *Women of the Republic.* On obligations in general, see Cara Wong, *Boundaries of Obligation in American Politics: Geographic, National, and Racial Communities* (New York, 2010). For scattered but useful information, see also James Kettner, *Development of American Citizenship, 1608–1870* (Chapel Hill, NC, 2005), and Rogers M. Smith, *Civic Ideals: Conflicting Visions of Citizenship* (New Haven, CT, 1997). Finally, see Bill Novak's important account of pre-modern views of civic membership in Meg Jacobs, et al., eds., *The Democratic Experiment* (Princeton, NJ, 2003).

Juries and jury reform have engaged Americans into modern times. Alexander Keyssar's *The Right to Vote: The Contested History of Democracy in the United States* (New York, 2000), gives short shrift to ancillary rights or obligations. Others treat juries variously as an aspect of representative government or as an element of civil procedure. See, for background, J. R. Pole, *Contract and Consent: Representation and the Jury in Anglo-American Legal History* (Charlotte, VA, 2010); William Forsyth, *History of Trial by Jury* (1852) (New York, 1996, repr.); John Langbein, *The Origins of Adversary Criminal Trial* (New York, 2005); Shannon Stimson, *The American Revolution in the Law: Anglo-American Jurisprudence Before John Marshall* (Princeton, NJ, 1990); William Nelson, *Americanization of the Common Law* (Athens, GA, 1994); Leonard Levy, *Palladium of Justice: Origins of the Trial by Jury* (New York, 2000); and Steven Wilf, *Law's Imagined Republic* (New York, 2010). Christopher Waldrep, *Jury Discrimination: The Supreme Court, Public Opinion, and a Grassroots Fight for Racial Equality in Mississippi* (Atlanta, GA, 2010), also explores the jury's origins. For a Midwestern study, see Stacy Pratt McDermott, *The Jury in Lincoln's America* (Athens, GA, 2012). And, on early Americans' expansions of old associations between juries and civic identity, see Lois G. Schwoerer, "Law, Liberty, and 'Jury Ideology': English Transatlantic Revolutionary Traditions," in Michael Morrison et al., eds., *Revolutionary Currents: Nation Building in the Transatlantic World* (Lanham, MD, 2004), pp. 35–64.

For women and juries, in Washington and elsewhere, see Johanna Grossman, "Women's Jury Service: Right of Citizenship or Privilege of Difference?" *Stanford Law Review*, Vol. 46 (1993–94), pp. 1115–60; Gretchen Ritter, "Jury Service and Women's Citizenship before and after the Nineteenth Amendment," *Law and History Review*, Vol. 20, No. 3 (Autumn 2002), pp. 479–515, locating jury duty within the tradition of representative government. See also Aaron H. Caplan, "The History of Women's Jury Service in Washington," *Washington State Bar News*, No. 59 (March 2005), which tells part of the story. Matilda Fenberg, "Women Jurors and Jury Service in Illinois," Chicago 1940, Pamphlets in American History, No. W062; Cristina M. Rodriguez, "Clearing the Smoke-Filled Room: Women Jurors and the Disruption of an Old-Boys' Network in Nineteenth-Century America," *Yale Law Journal*, Vol. 108 (May 1999), pp. 1805–44; Barbara Babcock, "A Place in the Palladium: Women's Rights and Jury Service," *University of Cincinnati Law Review*, Vol. 61 (1993), p. 1139; Babcock, "Women Defenders in the West," *Nevada Law Journal*, Vol. 1 (Spring 2001), pp. 1–18; Albert W. Alschuler and Andrew G. Deiss, "A Brief History of the Criminal Jury in the United States," *University of Chicago Law Review*, Vol. 61 (1994), pp. 867–928; and attorney Lelia Robinson's account of juries in Washington, "Women Jurors," *Chicago Law Times*, Vol. I (1887), p. 22. For denial of Anthony's right to a trial by peers when charged with the crime of voting in a federal election, see N. E. H. Hull, *The Woman Who Dared to Vote: The Trial of Susan B. Anthony*

(Lawrence, KS, 2012). On modern attempts to secure mixed-sex jury service, see Richard F. Hamm, "Mobilizing Legal Talent for a Cause: The National Woman's Party and the Campaign to Make Jury Service for Women a Federal Right," *Journal of Gender, Social Policy and the Law*, Vol. 9, No. 1 (2001), pp. 97–117.

FAMILIES AND THE LAW OF DOMESTIC RELATIONS

Washington's peculiar mix of common-law and continental rules of practice in domestic-relations and property law belie the larger fact that a good many communities had done much the same thing, particularly in the new west, but also in mid-American and southern jurisdictions. Indeed, to some extent, every American jurisdiction had absorbed continental rules to some extent. On civilian legalities, see John Merryman, *The Civil Law Tradition*, 3rd ed. (Stanford, CA, 2007) and M. H. Hoeflich, *Roman and Civil Law 'and the Development of Anglo-American Jurisprudence in the Nineteenth Century* (Atlanta, GA, 1997), which shows the extent to which all American jurisdictions are hybridized. For early examples of regime shifts, see Morris Arnold, *Unequal Laws upon a Savage Race: European Legal Traditions in Arkansas, 1686–1836* (Fayetteville, AK, 1985), and George Dargo, *Jefferson's Louisiana: Politics and the Clash of Legal Traditions*, rev. ed. (Clark, NJ, 2009, repr.). Many of the titles listed earlier as part of western legal practices also apply here.

Americans' decision to lodge responsibility for domestic relations in states and territories had lasting repercussions; see especially Hendrik Hartog, *Man and Wife in America: A History* (Cambridge, MA, 2002). On varieties of paternalism, see Grossberg, *Governing the Hearth* (Chapel Hill, NC, 1988); Mary Ann Mason, *From Father's Property to Children's Rights* (New York, 1996); and Peter Bardaglio, *Reconstructing the Household: Families, Sex, and the Law in the Nineteenth-Century South* (Chapel Hill, NC, 1995). For connections to women's history generally, see Nancy Cott, *Public Vows: A History of Marriage and the Nation* (Cambridge, MA, 2002). See also Elizabeth Bowles Warbasse, *The Changing Legal Rights of Married Women, 1800–1861* (New York, 1987); Richard Chused, "Late Nineteenth Century Married Women's Property Law: Reception of the Early Married Women's Property Acts by Courts and Legislatures," *American Journal of Legal History*, Vol. 29 (January 1985), pp. 3–35, and Chused, "Married Women's Property Law: 1800–1850," *Georgetown Law Journal*, Vol. 71 (1983), pp. 1359–425. See also Karen Maschke, ed., *Women and the American Legal Order* (New York, 1997) and Norma Basch, "Marriage and Domestic Relations," in Michael Grossberg et al., eds., *The Cambridge History of Law in America*, Vol. 2 (New York, 2008), pp. 245–79. Reva Siegel's work is indispensable; e.g., "The Modernization of Marital Status Law: Adjudicating Wives' Rights to Earnings, 1860–1930," *Georgetown Law Journal* (1995), pp. 2127–211; "She the People: The Nineteenth Amendment, Sex Equality, Federalism, and the Family," *Harvard*

Law Review (2002), pp. 947–1046; "The Rule of Love: Wife Beating as Prerogative and Privacy," *Yale Law Journal* (1996), pp. 2117–206; and "Home as Work: The First Woman's Rights Claims Concerning Wives' Household Labor, 1850–1880," *Yale Law Journal* (1994), pp. 1073–217. The pioneering Seattle attorney, Lelia Robinson, published the best-selling *Law of Husband and Wife: Compiled for Popular Use* (Seattle, WA, 1889).

For examples of localized studies, see Reva Siegel, "The Oregon Donation Act of 1850 and Nineteenth Century Federal Married Women's Property Law," *Law and History Review*, Vol. 2 (1984), pp. 44–78. On Texas, see Jean Stuntz, *Hers, His, and Theirs; Community Property Law in Spain and Early Texas* (Lubbock, TX, 2010) and Kathleen Elizabeth Lazarou, "Concealed under Petticoats: Married Women's Property and the Law of Texas, 1840–1913," Ph.D. Dissertation, Rice University, 1980. On Wisconsin, see Catherine Cleary, "Married Women's Property Rights in Wisconsin, 1846–1872," *Wisconsin Magazine of History* (Winter 1994–95), pp. 125–34. Last, but certainly not least, see Julie Cooper Davis, *Neglected Stories: The Constitution and Family Values* (New York, 1997).

POLITICAL ECONOMY, LAW, AND SOCIAL PURIFICATION

Several works provide foundations for the modernization of government and the economy after Reconstruction; see, e.g., Morton Keller, *Affairs of State: Public Life in Late Nineteenth-Century America* (Cambridge, MA, 1977); Robert Wiebe's still useful, *The Search for Order, 1877–1920* (New York, 1966); and Thomas McGraw, ed., *Regulation in Perspective* (Cambridge, MA, 1997). Leon Fink's splendid *The Long Gilded Age: American Capitalism and the Lessons of a New World Order* (Philadelphia, 2014) describes structural changes in American labor, business, and governance as global engagement expanded. For brief overviews of domestic developments from various vantage points, see Robert Cherny, *American Politics in the Gilded Age, 1868–1900* (New York, 1997); Vincent de Santis, *The Shaping of Modern America, 1877–1920* (Hoboken, NJ, 2000); Sean Cashman, *Americans in the Gilded Age*, 3rd ed. (New York, 1993); and Glenn Porter, *The Rise of Big Business* (New York, 2005). Innovative writing abounds. See Jonathan Levy, *Freaks of Fortune: The Emerging World of Capitalism and Risk in America* (Cambridge, MA, 2012); Maury Klein, *The Genesis of Industrial America, 1870–1920* (New York, 2007); Richard F. Bensel, *Yankee Leviathan: The Origins of Central State Authority in America, 1859–77* (New York, 1991); Olivier Zunz, *Making American Corporate, 1870–1920* (Chicago, IL, 1992); and, for cultural change, Alan Trachtenberg, *The Incorporation of America* (New York, 2007), and Jackson Lears, *The Making of Modern America, 1877–1920* (New York, 2010). For a brilliant analysis of intellectual developments after the Civil War, see Nancy Cohen, *Reconstruction of American Liberalism, 1865–1914* (Chapel Hill, NC, 2001). For post-1877 economic and corporate development, see Michael Zakim and Gary Kornblith, eds., *Capitalism Takes Command: The Social Transformation of Nineteenth-Century America* (Chicago, IL, 2012); Martin Sklar, *The Corporate Reconstruction of American Capitalism, 1890–1916: The Market, the Law, and Politics* (New York, 1988); and Sklar, *The United States as a Developing Country: Studies in U.S. History in the Progressive Era and the 1920s* (New York, 1992). Western economies experienced slowdowns later understood to be harbingers of the depression of 1892–93; see Douglas Steeples and David Whitter, *Democracy in Desperation: The Depression of 1893* (New York, 1998), but also Frank Brown Latham, *The Panic of 1893* (New York, 1971).

For Gilded-Age legal and constitutional development, see William Wiecek, *The Lost World of Classical Legal Thought: Law and Ideology in America, 1886–1937* (New York, 2001); Stephen Skowronek, *Building a New American State: The Expansion of National Administrative Capacities, 1877–1920* (New York, 1982); Morton J. Horwitz, *The Transformation of American Law, 1870–1960: The Crisis of Legal Orthodoxy* (New York, 1992), especially for treatise writers; Loren Beth, *Development of the American Constitution, 1877–1917* (New York, 1972); and Morton White's classic account of paradigmatic shifts, *Social Thought in America: The Revolt Against Formalism* (New York, 1957). The best account of Radical Republicans' "adequacy of the constitution" idea and its context is still William Wiecek and Harold Hyman, *Equal Justice Under Law: Constitutional Development, 1835–1875* (New York, 1982). On property rights and substantive due process, see, e.g., James Ely, Jrs., *The Guardian of Every Other Right: A Constitutional History of Property Rights* (New York, 1992); Michael Phillips, *The Lochner Court, Myth and Reality: Substantive Due Process from the 1890s to the 1930s* (Westport, CT, 2000); and John Semonche, *Charting the Future: The Supreme Court Responds to a Changing Society* (Westport, CT, 1978). See also Gillman, *Constitution Besieged.* On the Fourteenth Amendment, typically with an eye trained on nationalization of the Bill of Rights, see William Nelson, *The Fourteenth Amendment: From Political Principle to Judicial Doctrine* (Cambridge MA, 1988); Michael Kent Curtis, *No State Shall Abridge: The Fourteenth Amendment and the Bill of Rights* (Raleigh-Durham, NC, 1990); Kurt Lash, *The Fourteenth Amendment and the Privileges and Immunities of American Citizenship* (New York, 2014) and Garrett Epps, *Democracy Reborn: The Fourteenth Amendment and the Fight for Equal Rights* (New York, 1007). Finally, see Laura Edwards, *A Legal History of the Civil War and Reconstruction: A Nation of Rights* (New York, 2015), which argues persuasively for a remapping of citizenship and federalism during the war.

On post-bellum law practice and legal scholarship, see especially David Rabban, *Law's History: American Legal Thought and the Transatlantic Turn to History* (New York, 2012). But see also Horwitz, *Transformation*; N. E. H. Hull, *Roscoe Pound and Karl Llewellyn: Searching for an American Jurisprudence* (Chicago, IL, 1998); Arnold Paul, *The Conservative Crisis and the Rule of Law* (New York, 1969); and Clyde Jacobs still valuable *Law Writers and the Courts: The Influence of Thomas M. Cooley, Christopher J. Tiedeman, and John F. Dillon upon American Constitutional Law* (Berkeley, CA, 1954).

Temperance agitation antedated the Gilded Age; see, e.g., William Rorabaugh, *The Alcoholic Republic: An American Tradition* (New York, 1979) and Holly Berkley Fletcher, *Gender and the American Temperance Movement of the Nineteenth Century* (New York, 2007). Prohibitionism and the woman-centric WCTU appeared later in the century. See, e.g., Ian Tyrrell, *Woman's World, Woman's Empire: The Woman's Christian Temperance Union in International Perspective, 1880–1930* (Chapel Hill, NC, 1991); Ruth Bordin, *Women and Temperance: The Quest for Power and Liberty, 1873–1900* (New Brunswick, NJ, 1990); Barbara Leslie Epstein, *The Politics of Domesticity: Women, Evangelism, and Temperance in Nineteenth Century America* (Middletown, CT, 1986); Daniel Okrent, *Last Call: The Rise and Fall of Prohibition* (New York, 2011); and, on the prohibition amendment, Norman Clark, *Deliver Us from Evil* (New York, 1976), as well as Richard Hamm, *Shaping the Eighteenth Amendment, 1880–1920* (Chapel Hill, NC, 1995). On domestic violence and manhood, see Elaine Frantz Parsons, *Manhood Lost: Fallen Drunkards and Redeeming Women in the Nineteenth-Century United States* (Baltimore, MD, 2003), and Scott C. Martin, *The Devil of the Domestic Sphere* (Chicago, IL, 2010).

The purification impulse extended to brothels and white slavery, revealing anxiety about women's character and the unleashing of female sexuality in crowded cities. See Mark Thomas Connelly, *The Response to Prostitution in the Progressive Era* (Chapel Hill, NC, 1980); Mary Oden, *Delinquent Daughters: Protecting and Policing Adolescent Female Sexuality in the United States, 1885–1920* (Chapel Hill, NC, 1995); Michael Rutter, *Upstairs Girls: Prostitution in the American West* (Helena, MT, 2005); Ruth Rosen, *The Lost Sisterhood: Prostitution in America, 1900–1918* (Baltimore, MD, 1983); Anne Butler, *Daughters of Joy, Sisters of Misery: Prostitutes in the American West, 1865–90* (Champagne-Urbana, IL, 1987); and, on white slavery, David Langum, *Crossing over the Line: Legislating Morality and the Mann Act* (Chicago, IL, 1994).

The so-called Progressive Era, with its juxtapositions of democratization and classism, localism and centralization, emancipation and restraint, defies summation. For classic accounts, see Arthur Link and Richard McCormick, *Progressivism* (New York, 1983); John Chambers, *Tyranny of Change: America in the Progressive Era* (New Brunswick, NJ, 2000); and Noralee Frankel et al., eds., *Gender, Class, Race and Reform in the Progressive Era* (Lexington, KY, 1994). For broad readings, see Daniel Rodgers, *Atlantic Crossings: Social Politics in a Progressive Age* (Cambridge, MA, 1998); James Kloppenberg, *Uncertain Victory: Social Democracy and Progressivism in European and American Thought, 1870–1920* (New York, 1988). See also Maureen Flanagan, *America Reformed: Progressives and Progressivism,*

1890s-1920s (New York, 2006); Steven J. Diner, *A Very Different Age: Americans of the Progressive Era* (New York, 1998); and Michael McGerr, *A Fierce Discontent: The Rise and Fall of the Progressive Movement in America, 1870–1920* (New York, 2005). For a shift in vantage point, see Nell Irvin Painter, *Standing at Armageddon: A Grassroots History of the Progressive Era* (New York, 2008). And, for skepticism about Progressivism's integrity, see Paul Moreno, *The American State from the Civil War to the New Deal: The Twilight of Constitutionalism and the Triumph of Progressivism* (New York, 2013). Relevant as well is Robert Johnston, *The Radical Middle Class: Populist Democracy and the Question of Capitalism in Progressive Era Portland* (Princeton, NJ, 2006).

Index

[Author's note: Individual names appear below – as with jurors or activists – only when they occur more than once or when public contributions were sustained.]